Principles of Comparative Politics

GREGORY S. **MAHLER**

Earlham College

PEARSON

Boston Columbus Indianapolis New York San Francisco Upper Saddle River
Amsterdam Cape Town Dubai London Madrid Milan Munich Paris Montreal Toronto
Delhi Mexico City São Paulo Sydney Hong Kong Seoul Singapore Taipei Tokyo

Senior Acquisition Editor: Vik Mukhija
Editorial Assistants: Isabel Schwab, Beverly Fong
Executive Marketing Manager: Wendy Gordon
Production Manager: Meghan DeMaio
Creative Director: Jayne Conte
Cover Design: Bruce Kenselaar
Project Coordination, Text Design, and Electronic Page Makeup: Kiruthiga Anand,
    Integra Software Services Pvt. Ltd.
Printer/Binder/Cover Printer: Courier Companies

Library of Congress Cataloging-in-Publication Data

Mahler, Gregory S.,
  Principles of comparative politics / Gregory S. Mahler.—1st ed.
    p. cm.
  ISBN-13: 978-0-205-85252-9 (alk. paper)
  ISBN-10: 0-205-85252-1 (alk. paper)
  1. Comparative government. I. Title.
  JF51.M425 2012
  320.3—dc23   2011043726

10 9 8 7 6 5 4 3 2 1—CRW—15 14 13 12 10

ISBN 10: 0-205-85252-1
ISBN 13: 978-0-205-85252-9

For Marjorie, Alden, Darcy, and now Miriam

BRIEF CONTENTS

DETAILED CONTENTS

LIST OF FIGURES

LIST OF TABLES

PREFACE

For the first part of the year 2011, the world watched as the political face of the Middle East was dramatically changing. Governments that had been stable as a result of authoritarian rule and ruthless suppression of public opposition were suddenly appearing vulnerable. Despots were being overthrown, often in a nearly-peaceful way, or at least in a manner that involved a minimum of violence. The Arab Spring, as it was called, was a function of a number of different factors, and might be referred to by historians as the first social media revolution. The ability of large number of individuals to communicate with each other was a force that the authoritarian governments were simply not able to reckon with.

We do not yet know the final outcome of the events of the Arab Spring. Tunisia has changed its leader. Egypt has changed its leader, although at the time of this writing the nation is being led by a group of generals and it is not at all clear that the forces of democracy will actually triumph there. Morocco has changed its constitution to move much political power away from the king and to the elected government. Jordan has started down the same road. The government of Libyan strong-man Muammar Gaddafi has been overthrown, and Gaddafi himself has been killed. The government of Syrian despot Bashar al-Assad, the son of despot Hafez al-Assad, is ruthlessly trying to suppress Syrian forces working for openness and democracy. The final chapter of the story has yet to be written. Why have these events happened? How did they come about? Why are they developing as they are?

Elsewhere in the region, as the final manuscript of this book was being submitted to Longman, the new nation of South Sudan came into existence. South Sudan, which is Africa's fifty-fourth state, almost instantly found itself at the bottom of just about every ranking used by social scientists today: weakest domestic economy, lowest levels of education, least natural resources, shortest life expectancy, and on and on. This, along with the Arab Spring that swept the Middle East over the preceding six months, reminds us, yet again, of the ever-changing nature of the political world.

The world is changing, and continues to change. We must be able to observe the world and observe that change. We must be able to observe that change and *understand* that change. The purpose of a textbook such as this volume, and the purpose of courses in colleges and universities that use this book, is to help prepare citizens of the world to *understand* the setting in which they live, and to be able to *respond to the world* in an understanding and enlightened way. We cannot do that if we do not know and understand how political systems are structured and how they operate.

This book offers both a *cross-national* perspective of comparative politics (in the first eight chapters) and a *country-focused* perspective of comparative politics (in the second eight chapters). It includes individual chapters on

Britain, France, Germany, Russia, and Mexico, as well as chapters on Canada, China, and Kenya. Canada was, actually, included in the Fourth Edition of my *Comparative Politics* book (2003), but was cut from the Fifth Edition because of space limitations. I am delighted that Editor Vik Mukhija agreed that it should be re-included here. Kenya has been included in this edition in place of Nigeria in earlier editions, because Nigeria's instability has made our ability to generalize from its case very difficult, indeed. China has been added to this edition because it is simply not possible to talk about the contemporary political world without including China. Even though China's political institutions are more unique, and offer less in the way of generalizability than many other nations, it has become clear that including China was something that past readers of this text wanted.

The inclusion of "area" chapters from the African (Kenya), East Asian (China), and Latin American (Mexico) contexts is an example of an effort to include substantial discussion of *all* types of political systems; space and time limited the number of individual political systems that could receive detailed description in the text, however. As was indicated in the last several editions, a good deal of what has happened in Kenya, China, and Mexico in recent years is characteristic of other African (and Asian, and Latin American) nations, so these case studies are of some value to us and to our students in our comparative undertaking.

FEATURES

This text has a number of features that students and faculty alike will find helpful.

- *Approach*: This volume places an emphasis on political institutions—as indicated by the title—because of their *ease of comparison*, their *facility of identification and classification*, and the extent to which they *lend themselves to analysis*. This emphasis on political institutions, combined with the cross-national perspective of this volume, gives students both the tools and the perspective to undertake a meaningful cross-national introduction to the political world in which they must operate.
- *Organization*: This text is divided into two sections. The first half of the book is explicitly *cross-national* and *comparative*. In any of the eight chapters in the first half of the book we are likely to discuss well over a dozen different nations, sometimes many more than that. The goal of these chapters is to get as *broad* coverage as possible and to expose the student to as great a diversity of institutions and behaviors as possible.

In the second half of the book, we explicitly focus on an *area studies* or *country-studies* approach. Although we may make some comparative observations as we discuss a particular nation's political institutions, the focus is on *that nation*, and on some in-depth understanding of the way politics operates in that setting. Our country chapters are similar (if not identical) in organization, and the intention is to follow the organizational plan of the first half of the book.

Thus the first half of the book emphasizes breadth, not depth. The second half of the book emphasizes depth, not breadth.

- *Pedagogy*: In all chapters we try to provide students with both *theoretical* information and *empirical* data to support the observations we are trying to make. Maps, tables, figures, graphs, and text boxes are all included to provide students with *data* to support the general observations and principles that they are reading about. Each chapter opens with a box titled "Learning Outcomes" that indicates the goals for the chapter. In a similar manner, each chapter ends with a box of "Discussion Questions" and a list of key terms that have been set in bold type in the chapter. A glossary can be found at the end of the book, providing students with definitions for some of the most difficult terms in the text.
- *Coverage*: The text includes material through the 2011 national elections in many of the nations that are included here. The most recently available data from international sources—including the United Nations, the U.S. Government, the Inter-Parliamentary Union, and so on—are included, as appropriate. The most timely and pressing topics in the study of politics, such as *globalization*, and *public policy*, and *development economics*, can be found in the text.
- *National coverage*: National cases are provided on Britain, France, Germany, Canada, Russia, Mexico, China, and Kenya.

Chapter One, "Comparative Political Analysis: An Introduction," is designed to provide the student with a rationale for what we are doing in the text. We discuss what *politics* is and why we study politics. We talk about *comparative politics* as distinct from other subfields of the discipline, and introduce the student to key concepts such as *the political system*, *political culture*, and *globalization*. We also explain to the student why we have chosen to follow the *institutional approach* in this book, with examples of why the study of institutions seems to make more sense for an introductory textbook than alternative approaches.

In the second chapter, "Constitutions and Ideologies," we explain to the student some of the most basic theoretical underpinnings of the state. The nature and purpose of *constitutions*, and constitution-like structures is explained, as is the importance of constitutions generally. This chapter also includes discussion of *political ideology*, and the student is introduced to many of the major "isms" of the contemporary world.

In Chapter Three, "Legislative Institutions," we introduce the student to the first of three chapters that focus on the political structures that John Locke indicated were key to the survival of a political regime. Here we discuss *legislative structures*, whether legislatures are unicameral or bicameral, and the role of *political parties* in legislatures. We also talk about different ways of electing legislators to office. Finally, we include some discussion of key legislative *functions* and *structures*, including how legislative *committees* work and how the *legislative process* works in most nations. The chapter ends with a discussion of the relationship(s) between legislatures and executives.

Locke's second key institution was the political executive, and that is discussed in Chapter Four, "Executive Institutions." Here we discuss the *presidential* and *parliamentary* models of *political executive* comparatively, then spend more time on the parliamentary model and how it developed. We also discuss *coalition governments*. The chapter includes discussion of two other executive functions, the *military*, and the *bureaucracy*.

The third of the "Lockean" chapters is Chapter Five, "Judicial Institutions," which focuses upon *courts* and *legal systems*. We discuss the *idea* of *law*, and the notion of a *legal culture*. This leads to a discussion of sources of law. This is followed by presentation of key *structures* in legal systems, and the *functions* performed by judicial institutions. The chapter ends with a comparative conversation about the role of courts in political arenas, including the idea of *judicial review*.

In Chapter Six, "Political Behavior and the Political Environment," we discuss the context within which politics operates. This chapter includes a presentation of the concepts of political *socialization* and political *recruitment*, and specifically discusses the impact of social *class* and *gender* upon the socialization/recruitment process. The role of the political *elite* is also presented, so the student can reflect on different conceptions of the idea of democracy and democratic government. Finally, a less-common dimension of political behavior—political *violence*—is the subject of study, and the student is presented with a framework for discussing this kind of action.

Chapter Seven, "Pluralism, Parties, Interest Groups, and Social Movements," discusses how *groups* of individuals might be organized in politics. We start by discussing *pluralism* and *corporatism*, the idea of "*collective action*," and the differences of political behavior in nominally democratic and nominally nondemocratic systems. We specifically examine how *interest groups, political parties,* and *social movements* are organized, how they operate within *civil society,* and consider both similarities and differences among these entities.

The final chapter in the first half of the book examines the "output" of the political process. Chapter Eight, "Public Policy," starts with a discussion of *kinds* of public policy, and describes several *stages* in the policy-making process. *Domestic* policy is discussed, as are *international* and *foreign* policy, and the student is invited to try to draw links between the policy-making process and the public policy output itself.

Chapters Nine through Sixteen make up the second half of the book, and these chapters—as we suggested above—are intended to be as focused as the first eight chapters are intended to be broad. Each of these chapters focuses upon a single nation—Britain, France, Germany, Canada, Russia, China, Mexico, and Kenya—and the goal of the chapter is to show how the many political structures that were introduced in the first eight chapters *fit together* in one political system in the nation being examined. Although there are some individual (national) variations (for example, the chapter on Canada has a section on how French Canada and Québec influence the operation of Canadian politics; the chapter on Kenya has a section on ethnic and tribal tensions), the organization of the chapters runs parallel to the first eight chapters, including a discussion of *the constitutional context* of the nation, its *federal* or *unitary* nature, its *executive structures*, its *legislative structures*, other key institutions *(e.g., courts, local government, bureaucracy)*, and its *political parties* and *elections*.

SUPPLEMENTS

Pearson is pleased to offer several resources to qualified adopters of *Principles of Comparative Politics* and their students that will make teaching and learning from this book even more effective and enjoyable. Several of the supplements for this book are available at the Instructor Resource Center (IRC), an online hub that allows instructors to quickly download book-specific supplements. Please visit the IRC welcome page at www.pearsonhighered.com/irc to register for access.

MySearchLab For over 10 years, instructors and students have reported achieving better results and better grades when a Pearson MyLab has been integrated into the course. MySearchLab provides engaging experiences that personalize learning, and comes from a trusted partner with educational expertise and a deep commitment to helping students and instructors achieve their goals. A wide range of writing, grammar and research tools and access to a variety of academic journals, census data, Associated Press newsfeeds, and discipline-specific readings help you hone your writing and research skills. To order MySearchLab with the print text, use ISBN 0-205-23158-6.

Passport Choose the resources you want from MyPoliSciLab and put links to them into your course management system. If there is assessment associated with those resources, it also can be uploaded, allowing the results to feed directly into your course management system's gradebook. With MyPoliSciLab assets like videos, mapping exercises, *Financial Times* newsfeeds, current events quizzes, politics blog, and much more, Passport is available for any Pearson political science book. To order Passport with the print text, use ISBN 0-205-23157-8.

Pearson MyTest This powerful assessment generation program includes multiple-choice questions, true/false questions, and essay questions for each chapter. Questions and tests can be easily created, customized, saved online, and then printed, allowing flexibility to manage assessments anytime and anywhere. Available exclusively on the IRC.

Longman Atlas of World Issues (0-205-78020-2) From population and political systems to energy use and women's rights, the *Longman Atlas of World Issues* features full-color thematic maps that examine the forces shaping the world. Featuring maps from the latest edition of *The Penguin State of the World Atlas*, this excerpt includes critical thinking exercises to promote a deeper understanding of how geography affects many global issues.

Goode's World Atlas (0-321-65200-2)   First published by Rand McNally in 1923, *Goode's World Atlas* has set the standard for college reference atlases. It features hundreds of physical, political, and thematic maps as well as graphs, tables, and a pronouncing index.

ACKNOWLEDGMENTS

I would like to again acknowledge the assistance and encouragement of the outstanding professionals at Pearson who have been associated with this undertaking. Vik Mukhija was extremely enthusiastic about the idea of doing this book, and he provided more emotional and imaginative energy than I think I have ever received from an editor. I very much appreciated his encouragement and his pressing me to think about what would make this a *better* book, not just an *updated* book. Thank you to everyone involved with the production process at Pearson.

I also want to thank the scholars who have been contacted over the years by Longman, and before that by Prentice-Hall, to review the several editions of the book and make suggestions for changes. These scholars have made a number of very helpful suggestions for improvements. Much of the book's improved comprehensiveness is because of these individuals' advice, which was much appreciated.

Finally, I want to once again acknowledge the role of my students in the production of this book. It was comments of my students that initially convinced me to try my hand at writing a better introductory-level text in comparative politics than existed in the marketplace at the time, and their subsequent comments over the years—at the University of Vermont, the University of Mississippi, Kalamazoo College, and here at Earlham College— have helped me a great deal in deciding what should be included in this type of work and the best way of presenting the material. For this edition I was very fortunate to have some truly outstanding students here at Earlham College who helped me by providing fresh eyes for critically reading the manuscript, and who helped to gather information for updating bibliographic materials. Key in this edition were Molly Mitchell-Olds, Molly Slothower, Ben Self, and Stephanie Gossett. I greatly appreciate their assistance.

As I have done so frequently in the past, I want to dedicate this book to my wife Marjorie, who has been so tolerant as I have spent evening hours, weekend hours, and vacation hours working on this project rather than being involved in other activities. I have also enjoyed being able to dedicate past books to my two daughters, Alden (now married to Scott) and Darcy (now married to Chris); I am delighted to add (Darcy and Chris's daughter) granddaughter Miriam Grace to the list: welcome to the world of books, Miriam!

Comparative Political Analysis: An Introduction

The "Arab Spring" brought a level of political participation and activism to many nations of the Middle East and North Africa. Here a child participates in Cairo's Tahrir Square demon-

LEARNING OBJECTIVES

- Explain why we study politics.
- Describe the different approaches to how we study politics, and explain the relative value of each of the different approaches.
- Understand the nature of comparative political analysis, and be able to explain the difference between comparative politics and area studies.
- Describe the concept of a political system, and give examples of different kinds of systems and subsystems.
- Appreciate the importance of the idea of a political culture, and explain why an understanding of a political culture is crucial to understanding how politics operates in a context.
- Offer illustrations for why an institutional approach to the study of comparative politics is important, and show how an institutional approach differs from other approaches to this study.

WHY DO WE STUDY POLITICS?

Politics. The word conjures up visions of political campaigns, voting, military action, subtle political influence by lobbyists, or a long and painfully drawn out process of policy decision-making. For the student who is more politically experienced, the word may also suggest other images—images such as legislatures, courts, and interest groups. The more advanced student may also associate concepts such as power, influence, socialization, or recruitment with the concept of politics.

One point that is clear to all students is that the term *politics* is an extremely broad one. It means all of the things indicated above, and more.[1] Political science as a discipline can be traced back to the time of Plato (c. 427–c. 347 B.C.) and Aristotle (384–322 B.C.). Aristotle is often referred to as the first "real" political scientist—and we could add first "comparativist" as well—because of his study of the many political systems that he found in the political world of his time. His comparisons of constitutions and power structures contributed many words to our political vocabulary today—words such as "politics," "democracy," "oligarchy," and "aristocracy."[2]

The study of **politics** can be characterized as the study of patterns of systematic interactions between and among individuals and groups in a community or society.[3] This study does not involve random interactions, but rather focuses upon those interactions that involve power or authority. Aristotle saw many different types of relationships involved in this "political" association, but central to the concept was the idea of *rule*, or *authority*. In fact, one of the central criteria by which Aristotle classified constitutions in his study involved *where* power or authority to rule was located in the *polis*, the political system.[4] The seventeenth-century philosopher Thomas Hobbes felt that power had to do with the general capacity to attain goals in society.[5] Harold Lasswell put the question succinctly in the title of his classic book, *Politics: Who Gets What, When, How?*[6] Much more recently, David Easton referred to politics as dealing with the "authoritative allocation of values for a society."[7] Thus, the study of politics may involve the study of legislatures, the study of voting, the study of political parties, the study of the role of a minority group in a political system, more generally the study of how public policy is made, or all of these—and more.

Why do we study politics? It could be argued that political scientists since the time of Aristotle have been studying the same things—constitutions, rulers, the ruled, the behavior of political actors, and so on—and have not yet managed to come up with a formula for the establishment of a perfect society. Why do we continue to study politics, then? If we have not found what we are looking for by now, are we ever likely to? What *are* we looking for? These are all good questions, and they are hard questions to answer, too.

What are we looking for? The subjects of inquiry are many. Some political scientists are trying to learn about justice. Others are concerned with how social policy is made; they may study political structures that are involved in the policy-making process. Others seek to understand why a given election is won by one political party rather than another. Still others study politics simply because political relationships seem to be important to our daily lives.

More than this, there is a remarkable range in *how* we study politics, something to which we shall return several times in this volume. Some studies approach politics from a philosophical perspective, perhaps asking questions related to whether political institutions or behavior are *good* or *bad*. Others approach politics from a more *measurement-oriented* perspective, seeking to quantify different dimensions of politics. These different approaches contribute to the wide range of political perspectives in the literature.

In short, there are as many different reasons for studying political behavior as there are different aspects of political behavior to study. One thing, however, is clear: Political science is only one of the social sciences concerned with helping us to understand the complex world around us. The others, including (but not limited to) economics, sociology, and anthropology, also study the same general types of social phenomena that we study.

The same type of questions can also be asked in relation to comparative politics: Why should we study comparative politics? What can we hope to learn? Before we can answer these questions, we have to decide what "comparative politics" is, and how it can be said to differ from the more generic "politics." Many American political scientists tend to label as comparative politics anything that does not fit into one of the subdisciplines of international relations, methodology, political theory, or American politics. For them, the subdiscipline of comparative politics would include "politics in England," "politics in Zimbabwe," and so on, with the general formula being "politics in X" where any nation other than the United States could be substituted for the "X."

It should be added that American political scientists are not the only ones to have this perspective. If one were to travel to France, the study of American politics would be found within the subdiscipline of comparative politics; there, any area studies other than French politics would fall into the comparative basket. The same could be said for anything other than German politics in Germany, or anything other than Canadian politics in Canada.

But comparative politics should be more than that. Studying "politics in X" more properly can be referred to as "area studies." **Area studies,** involving a detailed examination of politics within a specific geographical setting, is a legitimate kind of inquiry, but not one that necessarily involves any explicit *comparison.* In fact, Macridis and Brown many years ago criticized comparative politics at the time for not being *truly* comparative, for being almost completely concerned with single cases (e.g., "Politics in Egypt") and area studies (e.g., "Politics in the Middle East").[8] Comparative politics is—or should be—*more* than "area studies." This is an area of debate in the discipline that continues to receive a great deal of attention and continues to cause a great deal of discussion.[9]

When we speak of **comparative politics** in this book, we are including the idea of the *actual act of comparison.* We all know what comparison is, it involves terms of relativity, terms such as *bigger, stronger, more stable, less democratic,* and so on. Comparative politics, then, involves no more and no less than *a comparative study of politics*—a search for similarities and differences between and among political phenomena, including political institutions (such as legislatures, or political interest groups), political behavior (such as voting), or political ideas (such as liberalism, or Marxism). Everything that politics studies, comparative politics studies as well; it just undertakes the study with an explicitly comparative *methodology* in mind.

We could make the argument, in fact, that all of political science is comparative. The study of international relations compares diplomatic relations and strategies over time and between nations. The study of political behavior compares types of activity in different political contexts. The study of political philosophy compares perspectives of what ought to be and what is. Even the study of American politics is implicitly comparative: We study the power of the president as compared to the power of the Congress, or why one interest group is more powerful than another, and so on.

To return to the question of why we should study comparative politics, then, an answer now may be suggested. As Dogan and Pelassy observed,

> Nothing is more natural than to study people, ideas, or institutions in relation to other people, ideas, or institutions. We gain knowledge through reference....We compare to evaluate more objectively our situation as individuals, a community, or a nation.[10]

The study of comparative politics is useful because it gives us a broader perspective of political phenomena and behavior, and this broader perspective can contribute a great deal to both our understanding and our appreciation of the phenomena we are studying. We compare to escape from our ethnocentrism, our assumptions that everyone behaves the same way we do; we seek to broaden our field of perspective. We compare to discover broader rules of behavior than we might find in more narrow studies.

For example, the simplicity and brevity of the Constitution of the United States is even more impressive when it is examined alongside longer constitutions of other nations.[11] We can better understand the significance of presidential government when we know about *alternatives* to presidential government. We can learn about those factors contributing to political stability by studying a country that is regarded as being politically stable. We can learn even more by including a country *not* regarded as stable in our study, and looking for similarities and differences between the two countries.

HOW DO WE STUDY POLITICS?

Broadly speaking, there are two paths on the road of inquiry; one is called the *normative* approach, and the other is called the *empirical* approach. The **normative** approach focuses upon philosophies, or "shoulds." The **empirical** approach relies on measurement and observation. Normativists might investigate exactly the same questions as empiricists, but they go about their investigations differently. Normativists might study justice, equality, the "good society," and so on, and so might empiricists. The difference between the two groups is simply in how these questions would be approached.

Let us take an example to highlight differences in approach, studying the concept of "justice." The normative approach might focus on the concept of justice itself: What is justice? What is a just society? How do we decide what is just and what is unjust? Does the concept of justice ever change or vary? *Should* it do so? *Should* all citizens in a society have equal resources? *Should* there be free education? What policy would principles of justice demand?

The empirical approach would not ask many of these questions. The job of the empiricist is not to ask what *should* be, but simply to ask what *is*. The empirical approach might involve interviewing policymakers and ascertaining what *they* feel justice is. It might involve studying laws and their enforcement. It might involve examining economic distribution in order to observe patterns of material distribution. *Do* all people in a society have roughly equivalent resources? *Do* all people in a society have equal access to education? In brief, although both approaches would study the same general subject, the approaches would be different.

In fact, the empirical approach does not utilize only one method of gathering information.[12] Arend Lijphart has suggested that there are four basic methods of discovering and establishing general empirical propositions. One of these methods is experimental, while the other three are nonexperimental. The nonexperimental methods are the case study method, the statistical method, and the comparative method.[13]

The **case study method**[14] involves "the intensive study of individual cases. Case studies run the gamut from the most microcosmic to the most macrocosmic-levels of political phenomena."[15] Micro-level work might focus on individuals; macro-level work might focus on political interest groups, regional groups, or institutional groups. An area study, as described earlier, might be a case study (such as voting behavior in Lesotho), but clearly not all case studies involve area studies. In this method, the investigator picks one case—whether that case be a single nation, a single voter, or a single political structure—and studies it. Through the case study method one develops a certain amount of expertise in whatever one is studying, but the scope of one's study may be quite limited.[16]

The **statistical method** involves more sophisticated forms of measurement and observation. Public opinion polls, survey research,[17] and various other forms of quantitative measurement are used to help make the measurement and observation that is characteristic of the empirical approach even more accurate.[18]

The **comparative method** may be likened to two or more case studies put together. We focus upon a particular political structure or behavior, and examine it in a comparative perspective. We look for similarities and differences. We may do our comparison in one setting, but compare across time—this is called "diachronic comparison." For example, we may compare a given legislature in 2011 with the same legislature in 1911 and 1961, in order to observe differences in the relative power and structures of that legislature. Or we may compare institutions or behavior at one point in time—"synchronic comparison"—but compare across national borders—for example, examining the role of the legislature in Great Britain with the role of the legislature in Thailand or Jordan.[19]

These three nonexperimental methods are based exclusively upon observation and measurement. The **experimental** approach involves manipulation of variables. That is, whereas in the case study method one simply *observes* something, in the experimental method, one *manipulates* one variable in order to observe its effect upon another variable. This is difficult to do in political research, because we are asking questions of extremely broad scope and usually cannot control the environment within which we are operating. We cannot, for example, set up two identical presidential elections at the same time in the same place—one with two candidates, and one with three candidates—in order to see the relationship between the number of candidates and voting turnout. Society is too complex to enable us to manipulate and experiment with many political structures and institutions.

Each of the methods in the empirical approach has its own advantages and disadvantages for the researcher. The chief advantage of the comparative approach is the broad perspective that was mentioned earlier. For example, studying the British Parliament in 2011 may tell us a great deal about that institution. We will learn more about the significance of what we are observing, however, if we *compare* our observations—either compare the observations with observations of the British Parliament of 1811 and 1911, or compare our observations of the British Parliament of 2011 with observations of the Indian Lok Sabha, the Japanese Diet, or the Israeli Knesset in the same year.

The study of comparative politics—or more properly, the comparative approach to the study of politics—is more and more common in the discipline of political science today. We find comparative studies of legislatures,[20] political elites,[21] ideologies,[22] women in politics,[23] constitutions,[24] legal cultures,[25] revolutionary movements,[26] political executives,[27] and political parties.[28] We also find comparative studies of the role of the military in government,[29] of democracies,[30] of *new* democracies,[31] of political development,[32] of political culture,[33] and of political behavior.[34]

THE NATURE OF COMPARATIVE POLITICAL ANALYSIS

How do we go about using the comparative method? If we start indiscriminately comparing every object on the political landscape with every other object, in a very short time we will find ourselves inundated with measurements of similarities and differences, most of which will turn out to be trivial distinctions either in scope or in significance. Suppose, for example, that we examine legislatures. One of the first things that we will note is that legislatures are not physically the same. One legislature may have 100 seats, another may have 75 seats, and a third may have 500 seats. One building may be five stories high, another only two. One legislature may have its seats arranged in straight rows, while another may have its seats arranged in semicircles; indeed, one legislature may give its members individual desks, while another may only have long benches upon which many legislators must crowd.[35]

So what? Before we get bogged down in inconsequential detail (and of course detail *need not* be inconsequential), we need to plot a course of inquiry. We need to decide what questions we are interested in investigating, and why, and we need to understand the relationships between and among the objects of our scrutiny.

Here we are interested in presenting an introduction to the comparative study of politics. What does this mean? It means that we want to show how comparative analysis is undertaken, and why it is undertaken, and we want to provide examples of the types of things that one might look at while engaging in this kind of study.

In one very useful analysis of the values of comparative inquiry many years ago, Adam Przeworski and Henry Teune discussed two general approaches to the comparative method that they called the "**most similar systems**" design and the "**most different systems**" design. They argued that most comparativists use the "most similar systems" design: Investigators take two systems that are essentially similar, and subsequently study differences that exist between the two basically similar systems. They may, then, observe the impact of these differences on some other social or political phenomenon. These studies are based on the belief that "systems as similar as possible with respect to as many features as possible constitute the optimal samples for comparative inquiry."[36] If some important differences are found between two essentially similar countries, "then the number of factors attributable to these differences will be sufficiently small to warrant explanation in terms of those differences alone."[37]

An example may help to make this clear. We could study two essentially similar nations, say Canada and Australia. These two nations have similar political histories, political structures, and substantially similar political cultures. If we notice that in Australia public policy appears to be made easily and efficiently, while in Canada it appears to be very difficult to enact public policy, we can conclude that the cause of this difficulty is probably *not* the substantial number of political institutions, historical factors, and cultural characteristics that they share. It must be *something else* that accounts for the difference, and we will be able to look at a relatively small list of possible factors for explanation.

There is, however, a different approach to comparative inquiry, one that Przeworski and Teune call the "**most different systems**" approach. This approach directs us to select two or more systems to compare that are not essentially similar. Instead of looking for *differences* between two or more essentially *similar* nations, focusing upon nation-states, for example, we look for *similarities* between two or more essentially *different* nations.[38]

Let us take as an example of this approach the cases of Britain and the United Arab Emirates, two very different nations in terms of their political structures and behavior. If we find a political behavior that is similar in the two systems and we are interested in knowing why that behavior is the way that it is, we know that the explanation *cannot* lie in the many political structures and patterns of behavior that differ in the two nations; we must look elsewhere.

The point of all of this is to indicate that a number of different approaches are possible within the broad framework that we call the "comparative method." The important consideration in all cases is a *theoretical rationale*: *Why* are we undertaking the comparison that we are undertaking? *What kind* of objects do we want to study? The subjects of comparative political inquiry are as disparate and varied as one might imagine. Generally, it can be suggested that there are three broad categories of subjects of examination in the comparative study of politics: public policy, political behavior, and governmental structures.

In studies of comparative public policy,[39] the focus of attention is upon *what governments do*. Comparisons may be made between governments of different nations, governments in various stages of development (for example, "developed" nations versus "underdeveloped" nations) or governments and policy over time (e.g., the government of Poland in 1961 and the government of Poland in 2011). Although the focus is upon what governments do, these studies will invariably pay some attention to the related questions of how and why governments act, as well as what the stimuli are that help governments to decide to act in the direction that they do at the time that they do.

A second general thrust of study is oriented to *political behavior*. Studies of this type may focus upon voting behavior, leaders in politics, and so on.[40] The central ideas of this approach involve the assumption that if one understands how people behave in a political system—and this includes all people, both the leaders and the led—then one will develop an understanding about the political systems within which that behavior takes place. This approach will include discussion of comparative public policy, primarily as an example of the behavior that is the focus of study, and also may include some study of the governmental institutions within which the behavior takes place.

The third general approach focuses upon the *governmental institutions* themselves. This type of study may focus upon legislatures, executives, courts, constitutions, legal systems, bureaucracies, and perhaps even political parties.[41] By studying the institutions of a regime, we are in a better position to understand how the regime operates than we would be with either the behavioral approach alone or the policy approach alone. This approach may well include some secondary subjects of scrutiny. It is possible that a study of governmental institutions might include a subject of policy output as an example of what it is that governmental institutions produce. In addition, a study of governmental institutions might include discussion of political behavior—both behavior of governmental officials as well as behavior of the public that may influence the government to act.

Often, in comparative analysis we focus our attention on countries. Countries are important to study for a number of reasons, not the least of which is that they happen to be the units into which the contemporary world is divided. That is, it would be difficult to engage in comparative research without touching upon the political structure that we call the *nation-state*. Beyond this, however, nation-states often are useful bases for analysis because of what they represent.

A "nation," a "state," and a "nation-state" are not, strictly speaking, the same thing.[42] The concept of "**nation**" has been used in an anthropological way to denote a group of people with shared characteristics, perhaps a shared language, history, or culture. A "**state**," on the other hand, is an explicitly political entity, created and alterable by men and women, based upon accepted boundaries. It implies the notion of "sovereignty," having the ability to make final decisions regarding policy, as well as the concept of "legitimacy," the idea that the citizens of the state owe allegiance to the government, and that other states diplomatically recognize the state and consider that the government in question has a right to exist. (When citizens of a state do not consider the state to be legitimate, we often find a situation of rebellion, revolution, or civil war; when other states do not consider the state to be legitimate, we often find a situation of international warfare.) A "**nation-state**" involves an instance in which the "nation" and the "state" overlap, where the unit that is found on the map corresponds to a meaningful use of the term *nation*.

Political borders can (and do) change, either as a result of war, as a result of agreement between parties involved, or, perhaps, as a result of both. For example, the United States and Mexico have reached agreement over a method of having periodic meetings between the two countries to "correct" the mapping of their border because of the gradual movement of the river that serves as a part of their common border, the Rio Grande![43]

It is possible to find self-proclaimed "nations" that are not "states" as the term was used earlier. For example, many Canadian citizens today who are living in the Province of Québec argue that there is a French "nation" in Canada that should be recognized as a state and given independence. They are not content with being a self-perceived nation within a state (Canada), having an identifiably different language, culture, and heritage, and with the powers that the Canadian federal balance gives to Québec alone; many citizens of Québec want to formalize their perceived differences with the rest of Canada and become an independent nation-state.[44] Similarly, the notion of Zionism at the turn of the twentieth century was based upon the idea that there was a "nation" of Jewish people who were "stateless" although living in a number of nation-states around the world, and that a Jewish state was needed for them to call their home. This Zionist concept subsequently gave birth to the State of Israel.[45] It is indeed ironic that in a very similar manner today Palestinians are claiming the need for a state of their own, independent of Israel, Jordan, Egypt, Saudi Arabia, and other Middle Eastern states.[46]

In any type of comparative political inquiry there are certain analytical problems of which we should be aware that might make our work more difficult than it otherwise might be. The first of these problems involves what we call the *levels of analysis* and relates to the types of observations and measurements we are using and the types of conclusions that we can draw from those observations and measurements.[47] Generally, we can speak of two levels of data, or observation: an **individual** level, and an *aggregate* or **ecological** level. As the names suggest, the former focuses on individuals, the latter on groups.

We have all met what can be called problems of "overgeneralization" in our lives. This is the case when an individual takes an observation made at the general level, and assumes that it can be validly applied to *every* individual within that population. For example, to take a nonpolitical case, let us imagine an individual has had negative experiences with fast-food restaurants in the past and does not like the food served in these establishments. One day she finds herself traveling, looking for a place to have lunch; the only places available are fast-food restaurants. She enters, expecting to hate the food, and finds to her surprise that the food in *this* establishment is better than her past experiences would have led her to expect. What we have here is an instance in which she has made a general observation (i.e., food in fast-food restaurants is not very good), and she has encountered an individual case for which her general rule simply is not valid, or correct.

In political science we refer to this type of error as an "ecological fallacy." That is, we take data, a measurement or an observation from the broad, "ecological" level and apply it *incorrectly* to an individual case. The observation may be quite correct over a large population, on the general level as a generalization (e.g., as a general rule food in fast-food restaurants is not very good), but that does not mean that it will be correct in *every* individual case within that population, and we need to be aware that when we make generalizations of this kind we may be making an error of this type.

More broadly, we have here a problem of two different levels of analysis—the individual level and the ecological, or aggregate, level. To take a political example, if we find on a national (aggregate) level that Republicans tend to vote more frequently than Democrats, that does not guarantee that *every* individual Republican who we might meet is going to vote and *every* individual Democrat who we might meet is not going to vote. It means that, on the whole, over the large population, Republicans *as a group* are more likely to vote than Democrats *as a group*.

To take another example, if we find in our cross-national research that the population of the Ivory Coast has overall a lower level of education than does the population of the United States (two aggregate-level observations), that does not mean that *every* citizen of the Ivory Coast is less educated than *every* citizen of the United States. It might in fact be the case that if we took a random sample from each nation, we might select an American with a sixth grade education and a citizen of the Ivory Coast with a Ph.D. from Duke University. In short, an "ecological fallacy" involves (incorrectly) taking what may be a perfectly valid observation or generalization on the aggregate level and assuming that it will always apply to every case on the individual level. It may apply in *most* cases (which may be why it is a general observation), but we may be leaving ourselves in a vulnerable position—and we may be drawing incorrect conclusions from our data—if we assume that it will *always* apply in *every* case.

We must also be aware of the reverse of the ecological fallacy that is called the "individualistic fallacy." This occurs when we make an individual-level observation and incorrectly generalize from it to the aggregate level. For example, to stay with the example we just introduced, it would clearly be incorrect to conclude from meeting one Duke-educated Ph.D. from the Ivory Coast that all citizens of the Ivory Coast have Ph.D. degrees from Duke, or that all Ph.D. recipients from Duke come from the Ivory Coast. To be sure, there may be several individuals in this category, but we would be incorrect to generalize from this individual case to the entire population.

The importance of the "levels of analysis" problem can be summed up, then, by stating that observations made on one level of analysis, either the individual level or the aggregate (or ecological) level, are safely used only on that level. It does regularly happen, of course, that we will undertake a study in a situation in which we are forced to use data from one level to learn about another level. We may not be able to afford to question every individual in the Ivory Coast about his or her level of education, and we may have to rely on ecological or aggregate data. If all we have available to us is aggregate-level data about education (e.g., average number of years of education), or health care (e.g., number of hospital beds per population unit), or some similar characteristic, then we have to do our best with the data that we have. We simply must keep reminding ourselves that conclusions we draw from one level of data must be used *carefully* on another level.

Another major pitfall in comparative analysis that we want to avoid involves making assumptions about the functions performed by political structures. It is possible that we will find in our research two institutions, or patterns of behavior, that look alike in two different settings, but which perform entirely different functions in their respective settings. We might study, for example, the House of Commons in Britain, and see that the legislature in that setting is most important in the process of selecting government leaders and in establishing governmental legitimacy. In another setting, however, a similarly structured legislature may not be at all significant in the creation of a government or in the establishment of legitimacy, and to assume that because the British House of Commons is significant in this regard that *all* legislatures are significant in this regard would be an example of an individualistic fallacy: incorrectly generalizing from the individual (i.e., "It works that way in Britain") level to the aggregate (i.e., "It works that way everywhere") level.

Although the major role of the American legislature may be that of passing laws, the major function legislatures such as those that existed in East Germany prior to German unification in 1989–1990 was *not* passing laws; in the East German case, the legislature met for only about two days a year, and simply "rubber stamped" everything suggested to it by the Communist party organization there. The primary function of the legislature in East Germany was that of being a showcase, to demonstrate that East Germany had a "democratically elected" legislature.

The converse of this is true, too. Whereas we might find one structure (e.g., a legislature) that performs two entirely different functions in two different nations, we might also find two entirely different structures in two different nations that perform similar or identical functions. Although the Congress performs the legislative function in the United States, the real designing of legislation in East Germany was done by the Central Committee of the Communist Party, not the legislature (although the legislature did subsequently give its approval to the measure prior to its becoming "official").

This type of error of "over-assuming" can be especially troubling when students from stable, established Western democracies turn their attentions to non-Western systems. The problem of **political ethnocentrism**—of assuming that because political institutions or relationships work one way in stable Western democracies they must work the same way in all political systems—is a real one, and we must be continuously on guard against making these types of assumptions, or falling victim to cultural bias. This is especially true when we turn our attention to political systems that are not stable, not "developed," or not Western.[48] Indeed, this paragraph would represent an example of Western ethnocentrism in its own right if we did not observe that in many settings the very institutions or patterns of behavior that we take for granted in the West—such as legislatures or elections—may simply be irrelevant to other political cultures. Many critics of American foreign policy dealing with Iraq in the recent past have noted that articulated American goal of "exporting democracy" to Iraq was too simplistic: Democracy is very complex, and cannot be exported like commercial goods, or transplanted like a plant from one pot to another. Iraq does not have a history of stable Western democracy, and because democratic institutions work in the United States does not necessarily mean that they will work in Iraq.

When we undertake comparative political analysis, then, we need to keep our eyes open for errors that we can make by simply assuming too much. We must take the political environment into consideration before drawing conclusions or making broad generalizations; we must make sure to "scout out the landscape" to make sure that we have included in our analysis all of the factors that may be of significance *in that particular political system*. In some systems the list of significant factors may be very long; in others it might be very short.

THE POLITICAL SYSTEM

We have been discussing comparative political analysis, and problems that may ensue in the research process, but we have not as yet laid out any framework for establishing the ground upon which we will base our research. The central concept in discussions of political analysis is that of the *political system*. Generally speaking, not confining ourselves only to the political, there are two types of systems that we can discuss: analytic systems and concrete systems.

We are all familiar with the concept of a system. Such terms as *nervous system*, *electrical system*, or even *solar system* are all examples of instances in which we use the term *system* in our daily lives. When we speak of a system such as one of these, we are speaking of a *set of related objects*. With a **concrete**, or **real system** we can actually see (or touch, or feel, or measure) the system itself. For example, we could actually touch the components of a skeletal system if we wanted to. In an electrical system we can touch wires involved and follow them along from one object to another. The solar system is a bit more difficult, since we cannot directly *touch* the force connecting the member units, but it can be measured with sophisticated instruments and observations. These, then, are "concrete," or "real" systems.

Much more interesting for us as political scientists, however, are "*analytic*" systems. We can define **analytic systems** as groups of objects that are connected with one another in an analytic way. That is, it is our theories and perceptions that provide the links between the objects in question. The political system that we refer to as American government is not "real" or "concrete" in the same manner than the plumbing system of a house is. We cannot actually touch or feel the links between and among the House of Representatives and the Senate and the Supreme Court and the White House. (Literally, of course, we probably could make the argument that one could touch a telephone wire and trace it to a central switchboard where all Washington telephones are connected, and thereby claim that these institutions are, in fact, physically connected, but that would be stretching the point.) The important and meaningful connection among these institutions is *power*, and the power relationship that is to be found in the Constitution of the United States and in American political tradition.[49]

When we talk about "developing nations" or "the political left" or "legislatures" or "interest groups," or "the Middle East," we are using analytic concepts to bring together groups of objects—in many cases individuals, in other cases regions, nations, or institutions—that we perceive to have something in common. These are *political systems*, sets of political objects or political concepts that are theoretically related to each other in some analytic way. These systems of objects—analytic systems—are the basis of comparative political research.

We cannot stop at the level of the system, however. Systems can be broken down into *subsystems*. A subsystem is an analytical component of a political system that is a system in its own right. The American political system has many subsystems, each of which could be studied on its own. To begin, of course, are fifty subsystems that we call states. If we wanted to, we could study the political system of one state on its own; if our focus is on the United States, however, the state would be perceived as a subsystem, not a system. Other subsystems of the American political system might be "the bureaucracy," "the legislature," "political parties," and so on. We can also talk about sub-subsystems, sub-sub-subsystems, and on and on.

Similarly, we can use the term *supersystem* to refer to that collection of objects of which our focus is only a part. If our focus is (still) on the American political system, then a supersystem might be "Western governments," or "democracies," or "presidential systems"—all groups of objects of which our focus is simply an example. Table 1.1 provides an illustration of the way in which we can use these terms.

We can shift our point of focus, too. If our focus is the American political system, then the Congress is a subsystem, and the House of Representatives is a sub-subsystem, and the Foreign Affairs Committee of the House of Representatives is a sub-sub-subsystem, and Republicans on the Foreign Affairs Committee are a sub-sub-sub-subsystem. If our focus were the House of Representatives, the Congress would be a supersystem, the American political system would be a super-supersystem, and the Foreign Affairs Committee would be a subsystem. And so on.

Although these terms may seem confusing at first, they can be extremely valuable in our analysis of politics. Unlike chemists or physicists, who may use sophisticated physical instruments to help them in their measurement and analysis, we political scientists have to rely on concepts and theoretical frameworks to help us with our measurement, observation, and analysis. Terminology, then, is important for us.

Just as with many of the other terms we have introduced in this chapter, the concept of a "system" is not as simple as it first appears. There have been

---

TABLE 1.1

Using Systems as Frames of Reference

Level	Set 1	Set 2
Super-supersystem	World governments	Constitutional systems
Supersystem	Democracies	Presidencies
System	**The American Political System** (focus)	
Subsystem	A state	The Congress
Sub-subsystem	A county	The Senate

many different approaches to political systems over the years, each developing its own vocabulary and literature. Probably the two biggest contributions to "systems theories," in terms of their subsequent generation of literature in the discipline, have been made by David Easton and Gabriel Almond.

Easton's variation on the political system first introduced in the mid-1960's has been referred to as **"Input-Output" analysis.**[50] Although many political scientists today feel that Easton's variation never realized its potential as a framework capable of explaining the operation of the political system, it did give rise to a great deal of literature on **"systems theory,"** and it can still be cited as one way of looking at the political system, even if it does not provide all of the answers that earlier theorists had hoped it might.

Easton's analytic framework viewed the political system as a continuously operating mechanism, with "demands" and "supports" going in ("inputs"), and authoritative decisions and actions coming out ("outputs"). Demands are defined as "an expression of opinion that an authoritative allocation with regard to a particular subject matter should or should not be made by those responsible for doing so."[51] Supports are those inputs between the political system and its environment that remain after demands have been subtracted.[52] The framework includes very elaborate regulatory mechanisms for preventing demand overloads and for maintaining the smooth operation of the system.

One of the major criticisms of Easton's framework involved its ethnocentrism, a concept we introduced earlier. Many of the assumptions of Easton's model suggest that there will inevitably be the types of political structures and behaviors found in stable Western democracies (such as legislatures, bureaucracies, and so on), assumptions that are clearly not always valid. Further, the model was criticized by many because of what they suggested was an implied goal of "system maintenance" that put too much emphasis on political stability and that was inherently conservative.

The other major variation on systems theory was suggested by Gabriel Almond, and is referred to as **"structural-functional" analysis.**[53] This analysis focuses upon what Almond refers to as political "structures," by which he means either political institutions or behavior, and political "functions," by which he means the consequences of the institutions or the behavior. This kind of analysis asks the basic question, "What structures perform what functions and under what conditions in a political system?" While "function" may be interpreted to mean "consequence," the framework introduced a new term as well, "dysfunction." Simply put, a function (or "eufunction") is a *good* consequence, and a dysfunction is a *bad* consequence.

Both of these approaches, it should be explicitly noted, are quite sophisticated and quite substantial—far beyond our ability to discuss them adequately in this context. In addition, they are not the only variations on what is referred to as "systems theory." They are, however, significant, and the test of time has indicated their impact on the discipline of political science. The concept of the political system, whether we use Easton's input-output framework, or Almond's structure-function framework, or any of a number of other variations on the theme, is another tool we have at our disposal to help in our cross-national comparison.

It is important that we observe that a political system need not be the same thing as a nation or a state. It may be convenient to use a nation or state as a point of departure in comparative analysis, but a "system" may be something else, as well. We may want to study a "legislative system"—that is, a collection of objects that are in some analytic way related and whose relationship is based upon legislation or the legislature. We may want to study the O.E.C.S.—the Organization of Eastern Caribbean States. We may want to study electoral systems. In short, although nation-states are convenient to study because we can find them on a map and their borders are (relatively) clearly defined, many of the subjects of comparative political analysis do not lie clearly within one set of national borders.

POLITICAL CULTURE

The concept of "political culture" is terribly important in the study of comparative politics. As Gabriel Almond has noted, "something like a notion of political culture has been around as long as men have spoken and written about politics,"[54] and related concepts—such as "subculture," "elite political culture," "political socialization," and "cultural change"—have also been used in a variety of settings since time immemorial. Indeed, Almond argues that the concept of political culture played a very important role in Plato's *Republic* when Plato observed:

> that governments vary as the dispositions of men vary, and that there must be as many of the one as there are of the other. For we cannot suppose that States are made of "oak and rock" and not out of the human natures which are in them.[55]

The concept of a political culture can be traced from Plato through Aristotle, Machiavelli, Montesquieu, Rousseau, Tocqueville, and up to modern times.[56]

Political culture, Almond tells us, "is not a theory; it refers to a set of variables that may be used in the construction of theories."[57] It consists of "the system of empirical beliefs, expressive symbols, and values which defines the situation in which political action takes place."[58] It "is concerned with psychological orientation toward social objects ... the political system as internalized in the cognitions, feelings, and evaluations of citizens."[59] Among the major dimensions of political culture are included a sense of national identity, attitudes one holds toward one's fellow citizens, attitudes about governmental performance, and knowledge and attitudes about the political decision-making processes.

In fact, scholars tell us, we can refer to three different directions in which political culture runs a "system" culture, a "process" culture, and a "policy" culture.[60] The system dimension of political culture is made up of attitudes toward the nation, the regime, and the authorities who control power at any given time. This includes values related to national identity, regime legitimacy, institutional legitimacy, and the effectiveness of individuals who hold significant political positions. The process dimension of political culture is made up of attitudes toward the role that the individual him- or herself plays in the political arena, and attitudes about other political actors. The policy dimension of political culture focuses upon the results of politics, the "outputs" of the political system.

As we suggested earlier, the importance of the political culture is that it refers to a number of political variables that we may use in our analysis of the political world and in our construction of political theories. Political culture has been argued to be significant in the process of political development, in the development of regime legitimacy, in economic and industrial development, and in social integration and regime stability. It is a concept that we shall use on a number of occasions in this study, especially in the second half of this text when we turn our attention to some area studies to illustrate the importance of the political institutions and political behaviors that we shall examine in the first part of this book.

When we consider political culture we must be aware of the danger of an *ethnocentric* approach to our study. We should not make the assumption that the way social relationships and institutions exist in our culture and society is necessarily the same way that they exist in all other societies, or is the standard for institutions and behavior that other cultures strive to develop. There are many characteristics of what can be called "Western culture" that are definitely not sought by non-Western societies. Indeed, there are many characteristics of contemporary Western society that we do not like ourselves, such as contemporary crime rates, drug problems, the weakening of the nuclear family unit, and so on. We must keep in mind that Western capitalist democracies are not always the model chosen by others in the world, and whether we agree with this or not, we must be careful not to assume that *our* way is the *only* way.

GLOBALIZATION

While the term *culture* refers to the way people or groups of people interact and the values that they may hold, there is another broad-ranging term that we should meet at this point in our study that also deals with ways that people or groups of people intereact, and that is the term *globalization*. This term is increasingly used today as shorthand for a huge range of impressive and important issues. The World Bank has noted that globalization "is one of the most charged issues of the day," although it notes that "there does not appear to be any precise, widely-agreed definition" of the term.[61] While there are clear supporters and opponents of the process—the former seeing globalization as the key to the future for the developing nations and the latter seeing it as a sure-thing destroyer of the environment and economic oppressor of citizens of have-not nations—there is no consensus on its meaning or on exactly how it should be measured.

Students of the process believe that the "core sense" of the concept of **economic globalization** "surely refers to the observation that in recent years a quickly rising share of economic activity in the world seems to be taking place between people who live in different countries (rather than in the same country)." This includes such topics as international trade, foreign direct investment, environmental policy, human rights, and a variety of other issues. The position of the World Bank in this debate is that

- it is necessary to distinguish between globalization's different forms, including trade, investment, market behavior, regulation, and so on;
- It is necessary to recognize that globalization does not affect all nations in the same way or to the same extent; participation in globalization varies widely;
- globalization is not new, only the *extent* to which it seems to be expanding appears to be new;
- we must be careful to distinguish between the times that we use "globalization" in its economic sense and the times that we use it in other ways.[62]

The fact is that nation-states in today's environment are interrelated in ways that could only have been dreamed about in years past. Not only are nations connected by internet and e-mail in a way that wasn't imaginable, but their economies are integrated and interdependent in a way similarly unimaginable even a decade ago. In his book *The World Is Flat*, Thomas Freedman shows how buying a computer in the United States directly affects the economies of a half-dozen nations—all in ways that may be invisible to the American consumer![63]

There are several different dimensions of what we can refer to as "globalization" today. These include (a) the movement of money around the world, (b) multinational corporations, and (c) international trade. Each of these merits brief discussion here.

Capital moves around the world today as if there were no such thing as the nation-state. The Chinese government, about which we shall write considerably more later in this book, owns a considerable share of the American national debt, and this worries many American policymakers in terms of the potential problems this might lead to in future years. People in one nation, whether that nation be the United States, Japan, China, or India, have the ability to invest in industry and business in other nations. While this is a good thing for those businesses and industries that are seeking outside investment, it may have the consequence of making it more difficult for national governments to plan—and control—their own economies.

Multinational corporations (MNCs) may have the same effect. The behavior of most MNCs is focused on increasing their "bottom line," the profits that they earn for their shareholders. This means that in most situations the MNC has very little or no loyalty to the community or nation in which it is operating. If it can make more money by paying lower wages, it will do so. If that requires the MNC to move, so be it. For many years this behavior was relatively invisible to most Americans in an international context, although they were often aware of mills and factories in the North closing in order to move to Southern states where labor was cheaper and labor unions were less powerful or nonexistent. Today, of course, even those Southern factories have closed and the jobs have moved to Mexico, or Asia, or Ireland, or other settings around the world where the MNC involved can pay lower wages, with lower benefits (such as health insurance), and increase its profits.

And, at the end of the day, the balance sheet of globalization can be summarized by international trade figures. Today's "de-industrialization" in the United States and in the wealthier nations of the world (as industry moves to the poorer nations of the world where wages are lower) means that significant consuming funds are flowing outward, to nations where goods are produced. Increasingly, of course, this means China.

So, while "globalization" in the abstract may have many different definitions, its net effects can be seen in terms of jobs and trade, which in the final analysis pits all governments against other governments, and states against states, to attract business and capital to their settings.

THE INSTITUTIONAL APPROACH

There are several different approaches that an introductory textbook of comparative politics might take to its subject matter. Some books focus on political individuals, emphasizing the importance of national leaders in the political operation of a political system. At one point in time, one of the leading texts in Comparative Politics had a chapter on the leader of Britain, one on the leader of France, one on the leader of Germany, and one on the leader of the Soviet Union, one on the leader of India, and one on the leader of Mexico. There is no doubt that the student using this book would have learned a good deal about politics in these six nations, but when the mantle of leadership changed, how much would still apply?

Another approach is to focus on public policy, looking at the nature of politics and conflict in the public arena and the products of that conflict: public policy. The problem with this approach is that it leaves too much undiscussed. We can begin to understand *what* policy is without any exposure at all to *how* policy is made. If we want to understand how politics operates, and be able to look broadly at political institutions around the world, we cannot focus our attention only on policy outputs.

The approach to comparative politics that is used in this volume is an institutional one. Although there is no doubt that either an emphasis on public policy or political behavior would be a vehicle that would "work" in an introduction to comparative politics, the institutional approach has been selected here for several reasons. First, it *lends itself to generalization* more readily than do the other approaches. When we learn how a "Westminster model" parliamentary system works in Britain, and we subsequently learn that Grenada, Tuvalu, and India have essentially Westminster-model parliamentary systems, we can relatively easily, and relatively accurately, transfer a good deal of what we learned about one system to another. An emphasis on public policy (e.g., British housing policy) or political behavior (e.g., British voting patterns) would not permit this transferability.

Second, the institutional approach *is more enduring*. Although it is true that individual nation-states do change their basic political institutions on occasion, it is much more often the case that political institutions do not change either as radically or frequently as either individual policies or aggregate behavior. The French electoral system was changed in 1985, and subsequently changed again shortly thereafter, but this was a true deviation from the French norm and from the norm we shall see in other settings. On the other hand, housing policy, health policy, foreign policy, or environmental policy are subject to political change as the corresponding political climate changes.

Third, the institutional approach *lends itself to observation and measurement* more readily than do other approaches. Although polities such as Britain, France, or Germany have been the subject of a great deal of policy analysis and examination of political behavior, there are many polities in the world in which sophisticated policy analysis is simply not done, nor is detailed analysis of political behavior undertaken. We can, on the other hand, undertake an examination of their political institutions.

To be sure, the institutional approach does not work all of the time; thus we will not restrict ourselves to only its use here. We shall discuss aspects of public policy and political behavior in our analysis here, but the *primary* vehicle for analysis will be that of political institutions. In the case of our description of Russia, for example, we shall begin by observing that it is a polity in which an institutional approach has not appeared to work very well in recent history, and there we shall focus our efforts in alternative directions. However, on balance, we believe that the institutional approach is the best vehicle for an introduction to comparative politics.

THE COMPARATIVE METHOD IN PERSPECTIVE

Throughout the remainder of this text we shall endeavor to follow the guidelines that we have set down thus far as to the comparative method of inquiry. The value of the comparative method is in the broad perspective that it offers the student of political science; we will focus upon this broad perspective as we continue.

In the next several chapters, we will develop a base for further inquiry. We will present a number of different political structures and behaviors comparatively, looking first at the existence of a structure in one setting and then at the same structure elsewhere. We will also search for similarities and differences in the structures under examination, to try to understand how the political environments within which they exist have influenced them. Subsequently, we will turn our attention to a number of brief area studies "portraits," which will give us the opportunity to better understand the political contexts within which the various political structures operate.

DISCUSSION QUESTIONS

1. Can you explain why we study politics? How does the study of politics compare with other social sciences?
2. Describe the different approaches to how we study politics, and explain the relative value of each of the different approaches.
3. What are the principle characteristics of comparative political analysis? How does a comparative approach differ from an area studies approach?
4. Can you describe the concept of a political system? What is the relationship between a political system, a political subsystem, and a political supersystem? In what way can these concepts be of analytic value?
5. What is a political culture? Why is the political culture of a polity an important thing to study and to understand?
6. What does the author suggest are the major advantages of an institutional approach to the study of comparative politics? What are the strengths of the institutional approach? What are its weaknesses?

KEY TERMS

Analytic systems   13
Area studies   4
Case study method of inquiry   5
Comparative method of inquiry   6
Comparative politics   4
Concrete systems   13
Ecological level of analysis   10
Economic globalization   18
Empirical   5
Experimental method of inquiry   6
Individual level of analysis   10
Input-output analysis   15
"Most Different Systems"   8
"Most Similar Systems"   7
Multinational corporations   18
Nation   9
Nation-state   9
Normative inquiry   5
Political culture   16
Political ethnocentrism   12
Politics   2
Real systems   13
State   9
Statistical method of inquiry   6
Structural-functional analysis   15
Systems theory   15

SUGGESTED READINGS

Gabriel Almond and Sidney Verba, eds., *The Civic Culture Revisited* (Boston: Little, Brown, 1980). This is a very good introduction for the beginning student to the idea of a civic culture, and to the study of the role of a civic culture in the political system.

Mattei Dogan and Dominique Pélassy, *How to Compare Nations: Strategies in Comparative Politics* (Chatham, NJ: Chatham House, 1990). This is a wonderful introduction to strategies of research design, showing the student how to design and explain research projects, while being careful about keeping cross-cultural and cross-national structural differences in consideration.

David Easton, *A Systems Analysis of Political Life* (New York: Wiley, 1965). This is one of the classics of political science theory. David Easton described in this volume a way of looking at political institutions and political behavior that has dominated political analysis for over a half-century, and that has provided a good deal of the most important vocabulary for political analysis.

Thomas Friedman, *The World Is Flat: A Brief History of the Twenty-First Century* (New York: Farrar, Strauss and Giroux, 2005). Although Freedman's book is not a "scholarly" volume, this is an absolutely captivating study of the issues involved in the study of globalization, intellectual property, and international trade.

Lois Duke Whitaker, *Women in Politics: Outsiders or Insiders?* (Upper Saddle River, NJ: Prentice Hall, 2006). We know that there are gender differences in political participation around the world. This book does two things: it shows what those differences are, and it discusses why those differences exist.

NOTES

1. Two very good recent general texts that show the range of concepts related to the term *politics* are Marcus Ethridge and Howard Handelman, *Politics in a Changing World: A ComparativeIntroduction to Political Science* (Belmont, CA: Thompson/ Wadsworth, 2008), and M. Janine Brodie and Sandra Rein, *Critical Concepts: An Introduction to Politics* (Toronto, ON: Pearson Prentice Hall, 2008).

2. See Ernest Barker, ed. and trans., *The Politics of Aristotle* (New York: Oxford University Press, 1970), pp. xi-xix

3. See Joel S. Migdal, *State in Society: Studying How States and Societies Transform and Constitute One Another* (New York: Cambridge University Press, 2001).

4. Ibid., p. 111

5. See the classic essay by Talcott Parsons, "On the Concept of Political Power," *Proceedings of the American Philosophical Society* 107:3 (June, 1963): 232.

6. Harold Lasswell, *Politics: Who Gets What, When, How?* (New York: McGraw Hill, 1936). See also Michael Saward, *Democracy: Critical Concepts in Political Science* (London, UK: Routledge, 2007).

7. David Easton, *A Framework for Political Analysis* (Englewood Cliffs, NJ: Prentice Hall, 1965), p. 50. See also Peter Bachrach and Morton Baratz, "Two Faces of Power," *The American Political Science Review* 56:4 (December, 1962): 947–52.

8. See Roy C. Macridis and Bernard E. Brown, eds. *Comparative Politics: Notes and Readings* (Homewood, IL: Dorsey Press, 1977), pp. 2–4. This criticism is still the focus of debate.

9. The January 10, 1997, issue of *The Chronicle of Higher Education* introduced a new version of a long-running debate over the value of area studies as distinct from comparative politics. See Christopher Shea, "Political Scientists Clash Over Value of Area Studies," p. A 13. Harvard University's Robert Bates suggests in this essay that a focus on individual regions leads to work that is "mushy and merely descriptive." See also several of the essays in Margaret Levi, *Designing Democratic Government: Making Institutions Work* (New York: Russell Sage Foundation, 2008).

10. Mattei Dogan and Dominique Pélassy, *How to Compare Nations: Strategies in Comparative Politics* (Chatham, NJ: Chatham House, 1990), p. 3. See also Todd Landman, *Issues and Methods in Comparative Politics: An Introduction* (New York: Routledge, 2008).

11. See, for example, the historical work by George Billias, *American Constitutionalism Abroad: Selected Essays in Comparative Constitutional History* (New York: Greenwood Press, 1990); or Emilios Christodoulidis and Stephen Tierney, *Public Law and Politics: The Scope and Limits of Constitutionalism* (Burlington, VT: Ashgate, 2008).

12. See Jarol B. Manheim, Richard C. Rich, and Lars Wilnat, *Empirical Analysis: Research Methods in Political Science* (New York: Longman, 2008); or Janet

Johnson and H.T. Reynolds, *Political Science Research Methods* (Washington, D.C.: CQ Press, 2005).

13. Arend Lijphart, "The Comparable Cases Strategy in Comparative Research," *Comparative Political Studies* 8 (1975): 159. See also Theodore Meckstroth, "'Most Different Systems' and 'Most Similar Systems': A Study in the Logic of Comparative Inquiry," *Comparative Political Studies* 8 (1975): 132. Mattei Dogan's 1990 book *How to Compare Nations: Strategies in Comparative Politics* (Chatham, NJ: Chatham House, 1990), does a very good job of discussing these issues at greater length.

14. See James B. Christoph and Bernard F. Brown, *Cases in Comparative Politics* (Boston, MA: Little, Brown, 1976), for a good example of this approach.

15. See Harry Eckstein, "Case Study and Theory in Political Science," in Fred Greenstein and Nelson Polsby, eds., *Handbook of Political Science: Strategies of Inquiry* (Reading, MA: Addison-Wesley, 1975), p. 79.

16. Examples of this kind of work can be found in Stella Theodoulou, *Policy and Politics in Six Nations: A Comparative Perspective on Policy Making* (Upper Saddle River, NJ: Prentice Hall, 2001); or Matt Smith, *Negotiating Boundaries and Borders: Qualitative Methodology and Development Research* (London, UK: Elsevier, 2007).

17. A very good essay on this can be found in the essay by Richard Boyd and Herbert Hyman, "Survey Research," in Greenstein and Polsby, eds., *Handbook of Political Science: Strategies of Inquiry*, pp. 265–350. See also Willem Saris and Irmtraud Gallhofer, *Design, Evaluation, and Analysis of Questionnaires for Survey Research* (Hoboken, NJ: Wiley Interscience, 2007).

18. For a good introductory-level example of this approach, see Dvora Yanow and Peregrine Schwartz-Shea, *Interpretation and Method: Empirical Research Methods and the Interpretive Turn* (Armonk, NY: M.E. Sharpe, 2006); or Charles Ragin and Claude Rubinson, "The Distinctiveness of Comparative Research," in Todd Landman and Neil Robinson, eds., *The SAGE Handbook of Comparative Politics* (Thousand Oaks, CA: SAGE, 2009), pp. 13–33.

19. A good essay on the comparative method may be found in Todd Landman, *Issues and Methods in Comparative Politics: An Introduction* (New York: Routledge, 2008).

20. For example, Scott Morgenstern and Benito Nacif, *Legislative Politics in Latin America* (New York: Cambridge University Press, 2002); or David Arter, *Comparing and Classifying Legislatures* (New York: Routledge, 2007).

21. For example, Mattei Dogan, *Elite Configurations at the Apex of Power* (Boston: Brill, 2003); or Fredrik Engelstad and Trygve Gulbrandsen, *Comparative Studies of Social and Political Elites* (Oxford, UK: Elsevier, 2006).

22. For example, Terence Ball and Richard Dagger, *Political Ideologies and the Democratic Ideals* (New York: Pearson Longman, 2009); or Leon Baradat, *Political Ideologies: Their Origins and Impacts* (Upper Saddle River, NJ: Prentice Hall, 2009).

23. For example, Julie Dolan, Melissa Deckman, and Michele Swers, *Women and Politics: Paths to Power and Political Influence* (Upper Saddle River, NJ: Pearson/Prentice Hall, 2007); Lois Duke Whitaker, *Women in Politics: Outsiders or Insiders?* (Upper Saddle River, NJ: Prentice Hall, 2006); or Kathryn Gleadle, *Borderline Citizens: Women, Gender and Political Culture in Britain, 1815–1867* (Oxford, UK: Oxford University Press, 2009).

24. For example, Ivo Duchacek, *Power Maps: Comparative Politics of Constitutions* (Santa Barbara, CA: Clio Press, 1973); Robert Maddex, *Constitutions of the World* (Washington, D.C.: CQ Press, 2008); or Donald S. Lutz, *Principles of Constitutional Design* (New York: Cambridge University Press, 2006).

25. For example, Lawrence Friedman, *Legal Culture in the Age of Globalization* (Stanford, CA: Stanford University Press, 2003); or William MacNeil, *Lex Populi: The Jurisprudence of Popular Culture* (Stanford, CA: Stanford University Press, 2007).

26. See, for example, James DeFronzo, *Revolutions and Revolutionary Movements* (Boulder, CO: Westview Press, 2007); Kalowatie Deonandan and David Close, *Contemporary Revolutionary Movements: Revolutionaries to Politicians* (New York: Palgrave-Macmillan, 2008).

27. For example, Ludger Helms, *Presidents, Prime Ministers, and Chancellors: Executive Leadership in Western Democracies* (New York: Palgrave, 2005); Nicholas Baldwin, *Executive Leadership and Legislative Assemblies* (New York: Routledge, 2006); or Robert Elgie and Sophia Moestrupl, *Semi-Presidentialism Outside Europe: A Comparative Study* (New York: Routledge, 2007).

28. See Kurt Luther and Ferdinand Muller-Rommel, *Political Parties in the New Europe* (New York: Oxford University Press, 2005); Russell Dalton and Ian McAllister, *Political Parties and Political Development: A New Perspective* (London, UK: SAGE, 2007).

29. For example, Eric Nordlinger, *Soldiers in Politics: Military Coups and Governments* (Englewood Cliffs, NJ: Prentice Hall, 1977); Rebecca Schiff, *The Military and Domestic Politics: A Concordance Theory of Civil-Military Relations* (London, UK: Routledge, 2008).

30. Arend Lijphart, *Electoral Systems and Party Systems: A Study of Twenty-Seven Democracies, 1945–1990* (New York: Oxford University Press, 1994); or Kenneth Benoit and Michael Laver, *Party Policy in Modern Democracies* (New York: Routledge, 2007).

31. Goran Hyden, Julius Court, and Kenneth Mease, *Making Sense of Governance: Empirical Evidence from Sixteen Developing Countries* (Boulder, CO: Lynne Rienner, 2004); or Paul Webb and Stephen White, *Party Politics in New Democracies* (New York: Oxford University Press, 2007).

32. For example, Ole Elgström and Göran Hydén, *Development and Democracy: What Have We Learned?* (New York: Routledge, 2002); or Bruce Scott, *Capitalism, Democracy, and Development* (New York: Springer, 2008).

33. For example, the classic in this area is Gabriel Almond and Sidney Verba, eds., *The Civic Culture Revisited* (Boston, MA: Little, Brown, 1980). See also Craig Carr, *Polity: Political Culture and the Nature of Politics* (Lanham, MD: Rowman and Littlefield, 2007); or Larissa Adler de Lomnitz and Elena Salazar, eds., *Symbolism and Ritual in a One-Party Regime: Unveiling Mexico's Political Culture* (Tucson, AZ: University of Arizona Press, 2010).

34. For example, Pippa Norris, *Electoral Engineering: Voting Rules and Political Behavior* (New York: Cambridge University Press, 2004); Oliver Woshinsky, *Explaining Politics: Culture, Institutions, and Political Behavior* (New York: Routledge, 2008), or Joey Power, *Political Culture and Nationalism in Malawi: Building Kwacha* (Rochester, NY: University of Rochester Press, 2010).

35. For an incredible collection of comparative data dealing with legislatures, see Valerie Herman, ed., *Parliaments of the World* (London, UK: Macmillan, 1976). There is an entire section of this 985-page book dealing with seating arrangements in legislatures, and make sure to note Table 21 on seating arrangements that is itself seven pages long!

36. Adam Przeworski and Henry Teune, *The Logic of Comparative Social Inquiry* (New York: Wiley, 1970), p. 32. See also Frank Lechner and John Boli, *The Globalization Reader* (Malden, MA: Blackwell, 2008).

37. *Ibid.* See also Dogan and Pelassy, *How to Compare Nations*, chap. 16, "Comparing Similar Countries," pp. 117–126.

38. See Dogan and Pelassy, *How to Compare Nations*, chap.17, "Comparing Contrasting Nations," pp. 127–132.

39. For example, see Stuart Nagel, ed., *Global Policy Studies: International Interaction Toward Improving Public Policy* (New York: St. Martin's Press, 1991); or Frank Baumgartner and Christoffer Green-Pedersen, *Comparative Studies of Policy Agendas* (New York: Routledge, 2007).

40. For example, see Norris, *Electoral Engineering, supra.*

41. There are few integrated and structural comparative studies. One is left to rely on more specific comparative studies, such as comparative studies of legislatures (see note 15), or comparative studies of executives (see note 22) for example.

42. See, for example, Walter Opello and Stephen Rosow, *The Nation State and Global Order: A Historical Introduction to Contemporary Politics* (Boulder, CO: Lynne Rienner, 2004); or D.L. Hanley, *Beyond the Nation-State: Parties in the Era of European Integration* (New York: Palgrave-Macmillan, 2007).

43. See the article by Douglas Littlefield, "The Rio Grande Compact of 1929: A Truce in an Interstate River War," *Pacific Historical Review* 60:4 (November, 1991): 497–516.

44. A very good discussion is provided by Wayne Reilly, "The Québec Sovereignty Referendum of 1995: What Now?" *American Review of Canadian Studies* 25:4 (1995): 477–496. See also my essay "Canadian Federalism and the 1995 Referendum: A Perspective From Outside of Québec," *American Review of Canadian Studies* 25:4 (1995): 449–476.

45. A very good discussion of the concept of Zionism as a nationalist movement can be found in the study by Shlomo Avineri, *The Making of Modern Zionism* (New York: Basic Books, 1981).

46. For discussion of the Palestinian case see my recent volume *Constitutionalism and Palestinian Constitutional Development* (Jerusalem: Palestinian Academic Society for the Study of International Affairs, 1996). See also Amaney Jamal, *Barriers to Democracy: The Other Side of Social Capital in Palestine and the Arab World* (Princeton, NJ: Princeton University Press, 2007).

47. Good discussions of problems of levels of analysis and other methodological difficulties can be found in Paul Pennings and Hans Keman, *Doing Research in Political Science* (London, UK: SAGE, 2005); or W. Phillips Shively, *The Craft of Political Research* (Englewood Cliffs, NJ: Prentice Hall, 2004).

48. Two very good—but different—illustrations of this concept can be found in Johanna Bimir, *Ethnicity and Electoral Politics* (New York: Cambridge University Press, 2007); and Mitchell Young and Eric Zuelow, *Nationalism in a Global Era: The Persistence of Nations* (New York: Routledge, 2007).

49. See Scott Frickel and Kelly Moore, *The New Political Sociology of Science: Institutions, Networks, and Power* (Madison, WI: University of Wisconsin Press, 2006).

50. David Easton, *A Systems Analysis of Political Life* (New York: Wiley, 1965).

51. Ibid. , p. 38

52. Ibid., p. 159.

53. Gabriel Almond, "Introduction," in Gabriel Almond and James Coleman, eds., *The Politics of the Developing Areas* (Princeton, NJ: Princeton University Press, 1960).

54. Gabriel Almond, "The Intellectual History of the Civic Culture Concept," in Gabriel Almond and Sidney Verba, *The Civic Culture Revisited* (Boston, MA: Little, Brown, 1980), p. 1.

55. Ibid., p. 2.
56. Ibid. See also Jan-Erik Lane and Svante O. Ersson, *Politics, Culture and Globalization: A Comparative Introduction* (London, Sage, 2001); and Irene Thomson, *Culture Wars and Enduring American Dilemmas* (Ann Arbor, MI: University of Michigan Press, 2010).
57. Almond, "Intellectual History," p. 26.
58. Sidney Verba, "Comparative Political Culture," in Lucian Pye and Sidney Verba, eds., *Political Culture and Political Development* (Princeton, NJ: Princeton University Press, 1965), p. 513.
59. Carole Pateman, "The Civic Culture: A Philosophic Critique," in Almond and Verba, *The Civic Culture Revisited*, p. 66.
60. This is a summation of a much more detailed discussion in Almond, "Intellectual History," pp. 27–29.
61. PREM Economic Policy Group and Development Economics Group, "Assessing Globalization, Part I: What is Globalization?" *Briefing Papers: What is Globalization* on World Bank web page: www.worldbank.org/html/extdr/pb/globalization/paper1.htm/. See, as illustrative of a growing literature in this area, Alfred Pfaller and Marika Lerch, *Challenges of Globalization: New Trends in International Politics and Society* (New Brunswick, NJ: Transaction, 2005); or Sarah Radcliffe, *Culture and Development in a Globalizing World: Geographies, Actors, and Paradigms* (New York: Routledge, 2006).
62. *Briefing Papers: What is Globalization? Op. cit.*
63. Thomas Freedman, *The World Is Flat: A Brief History of the Twenty-First Century* (New York: Farrar, Strauss and Giroux, 2005). For a very good, more "academic" study, see Donald Boudreaux, *Globalization* (Westport, CT: Greenwood, 2008).

Constitutions and Ideologies

As we study the principles behind political institutions and political behavior, one of the sets of relationships that we need to understand involves the *sources* of political power. What is political power, and where does it come from? Why do individuals *want* political power? We saw in Chapter 1 that the study of politics includes many subjects, and that there are many different ways of undertaking such a study. In this chapter we shall seek to understand how the concept of power operates in politics, both through political institutions and constitutional structures and through political ideology.

CONSTITUTIONS AS POLITICAL STRUCTURES

One of the first things that an interested student of comparative politics will find, while perusing the literature in the discipline, is the emphasis placed on the *state* or the *nation* as the unit of analysis. While not all research takes place on this level—certainly a good deal of research has focused upon individuals, or policy, or developing societies, and so on—the *state* is a common subject of study.

Many characteristics of the state can be the focus for a basis of power in a comparative study—we will examine a number of them in this book—including *structural* characteristics (such as constitutions or legislatures), and *behavioral* characteristics (such as ideology or political participation). The initial area of our study should focus upon the structures that describe the system, the boundaries of the component structures found within the political system. In this way we turn our attention first to a brief examination of constitutions, and, subsequently, to a brief discussion of ideology and its place in political regimes.

It may be useful to think of **constitutions** as "power maps"[1] for political systems. It is often constitutions that tell us about the environment within which governments operate, and describe how power is distributed among the actors in the political environment. We look to constitutions for an explanation of who has power, and what limitations are on power. While these may change over time for a specific individual in a position of authority, or may change over time as *different* individuals occupy positions of authority, they are significant "markers" for the political regime. Although it is true that in some systems the constitution is not of much help in understanding how the regime operates on a day-to-day basis, in most of today's nation-states the constitution provides us with information that will help understanding of the operation of politics. The idea of a constitution as a fundamental expression of the power relationships in a political regime dates back to the Greek and Roman republics; constitutions were the focus for comparison in Aristotle's major studies of political systems.

WRITTEN AND UNWRITTEN CONSTITUTIONS

Studies of constitutional governments often rely on the written documents that we call constitutions. Yet, government with a written constitution is not the same thing as a constitutional government. A **written constitution** is an expression of the ideas and organization of a government that is formally presented in one document. Some constitutions are quite short—the U.S. Constitution, for example—while others are much longer, such as the constitution of India, the (now nonexistent) constitution of the former Soviet Union, or the constitution of Switzerland.[2]

On the other hand, **constitutional government** can best be described as limited government, specifically a limitation on governmental power. There are certain things that the government may not do, whether it wants to or not. The First Amendment to the American Constitution is a clear example of this principle, stating in part that "Congress shall *make no law* … abridging the freedom of speech …" (emphasis added). This is an explicit limitation upon the powers of government to act. Here we see a linkage between political institutions (in this case a constitution) and political power: The constitution controls the right, the ability, of the government to act.

We can find governments without written constitutions that can properly be called constitutional regimes, and conversely we can find governments that have written constitutions that do *not* properly fit the parameters we have set for a regime to be called a constitutional government. Several examples may help to make this clear.

The British government does not possess a document titled "The Royal Constitution." British political history points to many different documents that are part of what is referred to as British constitutional law. These documents include the Magna Carta (1215), the Bill of Rights (1689), the Act of Settlement (1701), and other special acts of the British Parliament. On the other hand, scholars agree that Britain *practices* constitutional government: There are limits beyond which the government may not go. Yet Britain does not have a single, written document that can be called a written constitution.

We may refer to Britain as a system with an **unwritten constitution**, a collection of constitutional principles that are widely accepted in the regime that are not formally approved as law.

The same thing can be said for Israel. Although there was no single document called a constitution when the state of Israel came into existence in 1949, Israel has been writing a constitution one chapter at a time over more than sixty years. Israel's constitution is now almost complete, but Israelis have been living without a formally written constitution and an entrenched bill of rights until this time.[3]

To take another example from the Middle East, the entity referred to today as the Palestinian Authority, the transitional power that seeks to become the recognized government of a yet-to-be-sanctioned Palestinian state, is devoting much time to the creation of a Constitution. A special committee of the Palestinian Legislative Assembly meets regularly to discuss what should be in a Constitution.

Although the Soviet Union had until its demise in 1991 a relatively new (1977) constitution that was highly specific,[4] many argued that the Soviet regime was not a "constitutional government," because there were no effective limitations on governmental power. Rights were conditional: for example, Article 39 of the Constitution stated that "the exercise of rights and liberties of citizens must not injure the interests of society and the state';[5] Article 47 stated that "USSR citizens, in accordance with the goals of communist construction, are guaranteed freedom of scientific, technical, and artistic creation...";[6] Article 51 stated that "in accordance with the goals of communist construction, USSR citizens have the right to unite in public organizations...."[7] These examples show that expressions of rights did exist; however, they were *conditional*, with the implication that if the government believed that the "goals of communist construction" were not being served, the rights in question might be lost.

There is one other, more subtle, distinction between these regimes that should be made explicit. One type of constitution *gives* rights, and the other *recognizes* rights. This is not merely a semantic difference. The Soviet Constitution, in stating that the government *gave* citizens certain rights, implied that the government also had the power to *take away* these rights; after all, if rights come from the state, the state can certainly take them away. In the (unwritten) British Constitution, or the (written) U.S. Constitution, rights are *not* given, they are *recognized*. The Constitution of the United States does not state that "citizens are given the right to free speech," although some people assume that it does. What is written in the Constitution is that "Congress shall make no law...abridging freedom of speech, or of the press..."; these rights and freedoms appear to *already* exist and belong to the people, and the Constitution recognizes this fact by forbidding the Congress to limit them. This is quite different from what was the case in the Soviet Union.

Even the existence of a written constitution in a constitutional culture of limited governmental power ("constitutional government") does not absolutely guarantee either limited or unlimited individual rights. Freedom of speech is not absolute in either the United States or Britain, to take two examples; in both systems there is substantial judicial precedent documenting instances in which government can, in fact, restrict individuals' speech.[8]

Even when we examine a polity with a history of constitutional protection of individual rights, short-term forces may occasionally motivate a polity to abrogate those rights: Japanese Americans who lived in California shortly after Japan attacked Pearl Harbor in World War II were denied "due process," lost their homes and possessions, and were sent to "relocation camps" for the duration of the war. The U.S. Supreme Court ruled at that time that this action on the part of the U.S. Government was permissible because of the emergency situation posed by the war.[9]

When we discuss constitutional governments, then, we are really not talking about whether there exists a single document; rather, we are interested in a kind of political behavior, culture, or tradition. The British Constitution is really a collection of documents and traditions, bound together in an abstract way. The U.S. Constitution is a single document, with subsequent judicial interpretation and expansion. The forms may vary, but the behavioral results are the same: Limits are imposed upon what governments may do.[10]

WHAT DO CONSTITUTIONS DO?

"Constitutions are codes of rules which aspire to regulate the allocation of functions, powers, and duties among the various agencies and officers of government, and define the relationship between these and the public."[11] Do constitutions make a difference? We have argued that having a written constitution may not guarantee the behavior of a regime; does having *any* constitution matter? Today, more and more political scientists are putting less emphasis on a constitution as a significant structure in politics. They argue that too often constitutions—whether written or unwritten—are not true reflections of the manner in which a political system operates, and therefore the constitution is of little use or value.[12]

Furthermore, constitutions may omit discussion of key political structures. For example, political parties are nowhere mentioned in the (written) U.S. Constitution, yet it is difficult to conceive of government operating in the United States without parties. To take another example, the (written) Canadian Constitution fails to mention the prime minister as a significant actor in the political system at all,[13] yet there is no doubt that this is the single most important office in the Canadian political arena. The (written) constitution of the former Soviet Union guaranteed certain rights, but practice indicated that these guarantees were hollow. Given all of this, why is it that constitutions seem to be universally accepted as necessary to a political system?

Several functions can be attributed to those political structures that we call constitutions, whether written or unwritten, followed or not, wherever they may be found. First, they serve as an expression of ideology, a subject to which we shall return. Very often ideological expression is found in a preamble to the constitution. For example, the preamble to Canada's Constitution Act of 1867 indicated that Canada would have a constitution "similar in principle" to that of Britain. This "similar in principle" clause has been seen by scholars as incorporating—all by itself—all of the hundreds of years of British constitutional tradition into the Canadian political realm, and accordingly has been regarded as being quite significant.[14]

Second, constitutions serve as an expression of basic laws of the regime. These laws play a central role in the regime and are often so special that they can be modified only through extraordinary procedures. Sometimes they cannot be amended at all, for example the clause in the German constitution guaranteeing human rights. Whereas an ordinary law can usually be passed with a "simple majority" approval of the legislature—a majority of those present and voting at the time—basic laws of the regime expressed in the constitution usually require special majorities of the legislature (two-thirds or three-quarters, for example) for approval.

Third, constitutions provide governmental organizational frameworks. These are often explained in the text of the document. It is common for constitutions to contain several sections, and to devote a section each to the legislative branch, the executive branch, the judicial branch, and so on. Constitutions discuss power relationships among actors in the political system, covering the legislative process, the role of the executive in policy formation, and checks and balances among actors. They may include discussion of impeachment of the executive and dissolution of the legislature, and perhaps discussion of succession as well.

Fourth, constitutions usually outline the levels of government of the political system. They discuss how many levels of government there will be, and whether nations will be unitary, confederal, or federal. They often describe what powers fall within the jurisdiction of the national government, and what powers it does not have.

Finally, constitutions usually have an amendment clause. No matter how insightful the authors of a constitution try to be, they cannot foretell the future. Constitutions invariably need to be amended at some point down the road, and must contain directions for modifications; failure to do so might mean that when change becomes necessary, the entire system could collapse for want of a mechanism of change.

Constitutions play an important role in regimes. Some constitutions will be more important in one of the functions described above than in others. For example, the constitution of the Islamic Republic of Iran may be more important as an expression of ideology (and theology) than as a real organizational diagram of the government there.[15] Similarly, the American Constitution is more important as an expression of governmental organization and as a guideline for regime power relationships than as an expression of regime philosophy; the latter is usually said to be better expressed in the *Declaration of Independence* and the *Federalist Papers* than in the Constitution.

CONSTITUTIONALISM AND FEDERAL GOVERNMENTAL POWER

Another dimension of our study of politics and political power involves how systems and power are organized. We can identify several major possible frameworks, including unitary, confederal, and federal political systems. It is important to understand the distinctions among these organizational forms so as to appreciate fully some of the differences between governmental systems.

A *unitary* system has only one level of government above the local level. Great Britain, until the relatively recent past, was the model for unitary government: although there were city governments and county governments in Britain, true **sovereignty**—the real power to make political decisions—resided with the national Parliament; it had the right to control whatever powers the cities or counties might exercise. Parliament had the power to grant the cities and counties more influence, or to take away policy jurisdiction they might already control.

The chief advantage of these systems is their simplicity—there is only one responsible government. Unitary governments, however, are less effective for large nations than for small nations, and do not allow for ethnic and regional groups to exercise some degree of autonomy. Britain's unitary government was the subject of tension because some in Wales, Scotland, and Northern Ireland argued that it did not give regional and ethnic groups as much power as they deserved. Ultimately, as we will see later in this volume, some political power of the national government "devolved" to the regional government level. France, Italy, and Japan are other contemporary examples of unitary nations.

A **confederal** system— sometimes called a confederation—is a union of sovereign states that each retain their powers, but agree to coordinate their activities in certain respects. A group of sovereign states may agree to coordinate trade barriers, or fishing activities, or oil production. The degree to which the units coordinate their behavior can vary greatly, as can the range of areas in which this coordination takes place.

The major advantage of confederations is their loose structure, which leaves much flexibility and autonomy to member units. This allows units to retain individual characteristics and, to varying degrees, their own sovereignty to chart the policy directions they want. This same characteristic can be seen as the main drawback of confederations as well: the inability to reconcile the varied interests of various member units. A confederation's citizens tend to identify most strongly with the member units, not the "confederal" unit, and priorities tend to be sectional, not broad. Often, action is taken only when all member units agree, which may mean that often no action is taken at all because unanimity is notoriously hard to achieve among large political units. Notable experiments in confederation that failed—the United States (1781–1787),

Germany (1815–1866), and Switzerland (1815–1874)—were all reorganized as federations after it became clear that the confederal system would not further necessary common objectives.[16]

The European Community (EC)—often referred to today simply as "Europe"—began as an organization regulating tariffs among a small number of European nations. It has grown in power over the last several decades and has become a real political entity in the region with a common currency. European nations not only elect their own national legislators, but they also elect Members of the European Parliament (MEPs) to represent their region and nation in the European Parliament.[17]

In a **federal** system there are two levels of government above the local level, *both* enjoying sovereignty in certain areas. The central government may have the sole authority to coin money, raise an army, or declare war; the intermediate level of government (such as the states, or provinces) may have sole authority to regulate education, criminal law, or civil law; citizens deal with both levels of government.

Federal governments have been shown to have numerous advantages over other types of governments.[18] Federalism allows for both the expression of regional goals *and* a coordinated expression of national goals. One of the advantages of a federal system for member states is that the national level of government can absorb, through economic redistribution among member units, some of the costs of new technology or programs that would have to be absorbed completely by member units in a unitary or confederal system.[19]

The concept of federalism can be seen to have its roots early in political history—as far back as the historic Greek city-states, in fact. These early federations, for the most part, were not very stable or long-lived.[20] Modern federalism is usually dated from the American Constitutional Convention in Philadelphia in 1787.[21]

There are relatively few federal states in the contemporary world. Of the approximately 192[22] nation-states today, only twenty-one claim to be federal.[23] These twenty-one nations, however, cover more than half of the land surface of the globe, and include almost half of the world's population.[24] Federalism is a significant element "in situations in which sheer size, involving the separation and divergence of communities, has been the dominating feature."[25]

Some authors argue that there is a direct correlation between large size and the advisability of federalism, and they quote Thomas Jefferson in support of their argument: "Our country is too large to have all its affairs directed by a single government."[26]

Of the six largest nations in the world, only China is unitary, and even China has some characteristics of federal government.[27] (The five other largest nations are Russia, Canada, the United States, Brazil, and Australia.)

There are many smaller federations, as well, including Venezuela, and Argentina in Latin America; Switzerland in Europe; and India in Asia. Many of these nations opted for federalism not because of their large land area, but because of regional, ethnic, or linguistic characteristics of component groups that made a federal type of organization necessary. In general, federalism allows countries involved to maximize economic growth and political strength, while at the same time allowing for the expression of regional characteristics.[28]

Switzerland, for example, chose the federal system because it was best suited to the needs of that country's three language groups, German, French, and Italian. The Swiss Constitution, in fact, recognizes three official languages. Of the twenty-two Swiss cantons, there are eighteen unilingual cantons, three bilingual cantons, and one trilingual canton; the Constitution guarantees citizens the right to communicate with the central government in any of the three languages.[29]

The federal system has been adapted in Germany. Rather than establishing clear divisions between areas of jurisdiction of the Bund (the central parliament) and the Länder (the member units), the German Constitution allows for a broad area of concurrent jurisdiction. The upper house of the national legislature, the Bundesrat, is chosen by the Länder governments, and it has an absolute veto over matters affecting the Länder, but only a "suspensory" veto over matters of "national" concern.[30]

There does not appear to be a universally accepted theory of federalism, nor, for that matter, a clear definition of precisely what behavioral attributes are characteristic of federal government.[31] The most common characterization of a federal government is that it is organized on two levels above the local level, one national unit and a number of intermediate units. Both levels of government rule over the same constituents, and both levels of government have the power to make certain decisions independently of the other.[32]

William Riker has suggested a useful framework within which the many federal governments of the world may be measured. He has suggested that federations can be measured along a "centralized-decentralized" dimension. This dimension may be defined by the following minimum and maximum, illustrated in Figure 2.1:

> *Minimum:* The ruler(s) of the federation can make decisions in only one narrowly restricted category of action without obtaining the approval of the rulers of the constituent units.
>
> *Maximum:* The ruler(s) of the federation can make decisions without consulting the rulers of the member governments in all but one narrowly restricted category of action.[33]

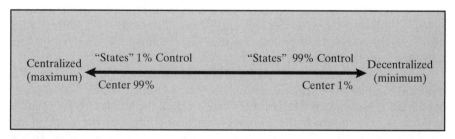

FIGURE 2.1
A Scale of Federalisms

The closer to the "minimum" end of the scale a federal government is, the more it can be described as a **peripheral federation**. The closer to the "maximum" end of the scale a federal government is, the more it can be described as a **centralized federation**.

Not all experiments with federation since the eighteenth century have been successes. The more decentralized or peripheral a federation is, the weaker the center is, the greater the centrifugal forces acting on the system, and the greater the likelihood that the federation will not endure. Cases such as the United Arab Republic, the Federation of the West Indies, or the Federation of Malaysia[34] are all illustrations of "premature federations"—unifications that took place before sufficient national integration was attained—and are examples of unifications that did not last.

Federalism is significant as a political variable because the federal balance in a polity often influences public policymaking.[35] For example, it is often difficult for the Canadian federal (national) government to set policy because many issues—such as health, education, and much resource policy—fall within the jurisdiction of the provinces. Accordingly, if the federal government wants to enact a new health policy or a new job training program, it must convene a meeting of the federal prime minister and the provincial premiers, or the federal education minister and the provincial education ministers (or comparable officials depending upon the policy area involved) to "negotiate" a policy that will be acceptable to the respective governments. The provincial representatives will then return to their respective capitals and introduce the policy in their provincial legislatures.[36]

THE SEPARATION OF POWERS

The notion that centralized power is dangerous—that power must be a check on power—reached maturity in the eighteenth century, and its first full-scale application was to be found in the Constitutional Convention in Philadelphia in 1787. Delegates to the convention regularly cited "the celebrated Montesquieu," John Locke, Thomas Hobbes, and others,[37] in support of the idea that political power, in order to be safe, had to be divided; the principle of the **separation of powers** was important to government. The legislature needed to have a check on the executive, and the executive on the legislature. Many of the ideas of John Locke were adopted in *The Federalist* (especially Number 47), among other places, and expressed the philosophy that the executive force had to be kept separate from the legislative force.[38]

Constitutions express the power relationships among the many actors in political regimes. The American Constitution is explicit about the degree to which the president can take control of the work of the legislature (he cannot), and the degree to which the Congress can take control of the work of the president (it cannot). The situation is one that can devolve into a stalemate: The President can veto work of Congress, and Congress can refuse to pass legislative requests of the president, but neither can force the other to *do* anything. Much American political unhappiness in the third year of Barack Obama's presidency is precisely the result of this stalemate: (liberal) President Obama can block the (conservative) House of Representatives, and the (conservative) House of Representatives can fail to pass legislative suggestions of the President. In other regimes the lines are less clearly drawn. For example, in France the president can, under circumstances that we shall examine later in this volume, issue decrees that have the force of legislation.

Hindsight tells us, as we will see in a number of instances throughout this text, that the explicit lines that were drawn by the Founding Fathers to separate the executive and legislative branches of government were not absolutely necessary to ensure democratic government. There are other power relationships, which we will discuss in later chapters, that are used elsewhere that have proven to be just as democratic and just as stable.

THE IMPORTANCE OF CONSTITUTIONS

Constitutions can be examined on two levels. On one hand, we can look at constitutions on a "piece" level, and examine them section by section to see what structures and behaviors they prescribe for a given political system. On the other hand, we can look at constitutions from the level of the political system, and ask: What do constitutions do? David Easton's framework of analysis is useful in examining this type of question.

In Chapter 1 we examined the concept of the political system, and we noted that Easton offered a variation of the general systems approach referred to as "input-output analysis."[39] Demands and supports are fed into the political system as *inputs*. They are "processed" by the system; the system is a giant conversion mechanism that takes demands and supports from the environment, digests them, and issues "authoritative allocations of values" in the forms of decisions and actions—*outputs*. These outputs filter through the environment as "feedback" and are subsequently reintroduced as new inputs, either demands or supports, and the cycle continues. The "digesting" and the "processing" phase of the system, what Easton labels "The Political System," is what government is all about: responding to demands and supports, making decisions, providing information, establishing legitimacy, and so on.

Instead of looking at constitutions from the perspective of what they say about the separation of powers, about the federal or unitary natures of systems, about checks and balances, and basic laws, we could ask the question of how constitutions help political systems to survive. To use Gabriel Almond's terms introduced in Chapter 1, what are the functions (consequences) of the structures that we refer to as "constitutions"?

Ivo Duchacek has performed just such an analysis; his work offers answers to the question "What do constitutions do?" Constitutions help political systems in the function of "system maintenance," by helping them respond to demands and supports that are directed to them in the form of inputs. The constitutional framework of powers helps to process demands and supports and to convert them into outputs, which are reintroduced as inputs. Demands and supports are processed more smoothly because of (1) commitment to responsiveness; (2) specific institutions for rule-making, enforcement, and adjudicating; and (3) commitment to goals, all of which are found in a constitution.[40]

CONSTITUTIONS IN A COMPARATIVE PERSPECTIVE

The political structure that we call a constitution is a good place for us to begin cross-national comparison, because it presents examples of some of the problems first discussed in Chapter 1. We cannot be rigid when examining constitutional frameworks in comparative perspective. Sometimes we will find a piece of paper entitled "The Constitution," and sometimes we will not. The mere existence of a piece of paper is no guarantee that a political system is constitutional, as we defined the term at the beginning of this chapter.

We have, then, the structures-and-functions problem that we mentioned in Chapter l: The structure of a written constitution may perform different functions (have different consequences) in different political systems. Furthermore, different structures (in some places a written constitution, elsewhere tradition and custom) may perform the same function in different political systems. This is a scenario that we will see repeated in the next several chapters.

IDEOLOGIES

One of the functions that we ascribed to constitutions was that they serve as an expression of ideology. The term **ideology** is often emotionally charged, and the term *ideologue* is often used as a description for an individual no longer having a rational perspective. Originally, *ideologue* referred to a student of how ideas were formed, and ideology was "a study of the process of forming ideas, a 'science of ideas.'"[41] The purpose behind the introduction of the concept of ideology was "to provide the new secular educators with a systematic educational theory. The unashamed view of the ideologues ... was that the minds of the young should be bent to new, more healthy purposes."[42]

Actually, the term *ideology* has a number of meanings and connotations:

1. One meaning is that of "deception," "distortion," or "falseness." It conveys the notion of *subjectivity* as opposed to objectivity.
2. Ideology also conveys the notion of a *dream*, an impossible or unrealizable quest.
3. Ideology means also what may be called the *consciousness* of a society at any given moment, the values and beliefs and attitudes that hold it together.
4. Ideologies often correspond to *social criticism*, confronting existing beliefs and attempting through argument and persuasion to challenge and change them.
5. Ideology also provides a *set of concepts* through which people view the world and learn about it.

6. Ideologies can be a call for *committed action*.
7. Ideologies often become, under certain circumstances, a powerful *instrument of manipulation*.[43]

Ideologies, then, involve ideas that relate to the social/political world, and that provide a general guideline for action. One scholar has indicated that "an ideology represents a practical attitude to the world";[44] another has suggested that "ideologies are actually attempts to develop political accommodations to the economic and social conditions created by the Industrial Revolution."[45] Ideologies can unite groups, help to articulate philosophies, or serve as tools of political manipulation. In each of these, we can see the same two critical components: a relation to political ideas and a relation to political behavior.[46]

Ideologies give the regime its *raison d'être*, its sense of purpose, and serve as a point of reference for political behavior and the exercise of power in the political system. Political theorist Michael Curtis has suggested that ideologies are amalgams of "facts, values, and mythology that provide some understanding of history and the supreme significance of or necessary leadership by a particular individual, group, class, or nation."[47]

Many different ideologies have existed in the modern political world. Some have come and gone in a brief period of time; others have long been in existence. Some have had much influence on world events; others have not. What we could call "classical liberalism" was a significant ideology at about the time of the American Revolution, and continues to be significant today. Certainly Marxism is an example of an ideology that has had a very broad and profound influence in society, one that has lasted for many years. Other "isms," including socialism, fascism, conservatism, and so on, have also become part of our vocabulary over the years.

Ideologies are often related to attitudes toward political change and the exercise of power, often conceived as fitting along a "left-right" spectrum, as illustrated in Figure 2.2. The "left-right" metaphor dates back to 1791, at which time the French legislative Council of 500 was arranged in a semicircular hall of representatives according to their self-determined place in the political spectrum.[48] Those generally supporting the monarch's policies sat on his right, while those who proposed changes in his policies sat on his left; hence,

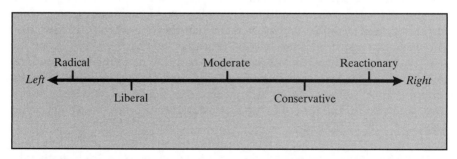

FIGURE 2.2
The Liberal-Conservative Spectrum

"leftists" favored change and "rightists" preferred the *status quo*. These same general labels are used today. It should be kept in mind that the positions in Figure 2.2 and the descriptions that follow relate to *classical* political values: Those who consider themselves conservative in the United States at the beginning of the twenty-first century do not hold the same values as would a "classical" conservative in the 1790s.

The **radical** position is often associated with violence, although that *need not* be the case.[49] Generally, radicals are extremely dissatisfied with the way society (and politics) is organized and are impatient to undertake fundamental changes in society. Of course, not all radicals are alike, and we could certainly distinguish among more or less "radical" radicals, depending upon the intensity of their beliefs, strategies they might wish to employ (including more or less violence), the immediacy with which they want changes undertaken, and so on.

The classical **liberal** position is more content with society than is the radical, but still believes that reform is possible, perhaps necessary. Among differences between liberals and radicals are their views toward the law. "Radicals find it hard to respect the law. Liberals, on the other hand, generally respect the concept of the law, and although they may want to change certain specifics of the law, they usually will not violate it. Instead they try to change the law through legal procedures."[50] Liberalism includes a belief in human potential, in the ability of individuals to change institutions for the better, in human rationality, and in human equality.

The **moderate** position is one that is basically satisfied with the way society is operating, and one that insists that changes that might be made in social rules and social values should be made slowly, gradually, and in a way that will not be disruptive.

The classical **conservative** position is the position that can be described as being most satisfied with the way society is operating, satisfied with the *status quo*. The major difference between conservatives and liberals is that "conservatives support the *status quo* not so much because they like it but because they believe that it is the best that can be achieved at the moment."[51] Classical conservatives do not share the optimism of liberals that individuals can improve society. They are more skeptical of human nature, and believe that human nature may be selfish. They place more emphasis on respecting institutions and traditions and are not sure that they (or others) are capable of devising a better system. They believe in elitism.

Finally, the classical **reactionary** position corresponds to that of the radical, only on the right end of the spectrum. The reactionary position proposes radical change backwards, that is, "retrogressive change," favoring "a policy that would return the society to a previous condition or even a former value system."[52]

It is important to note before we leave our discussion of the left-right spectrum that it is very much a relative scale. Someone who is a "radical-liberal" may view a "moderate-liberal" as an "ultraconservative." Description may be to a large degree a matter of perspective. Indeed, in a classic study Louis Hartz

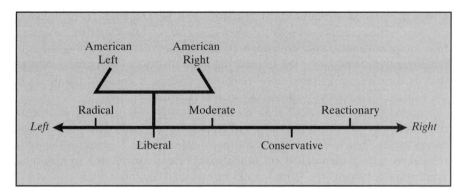

FIGURE 2.3
American Ideology on the Liberal-Conservative Spectrum

essentially suggested that *all* American politics is "liberal" politics: "There has never been a 'liberal movement' or a real 'liberal party' in America: we have only had the American Way of Life, a nationalist articulation of Locke which usually does not know that Locke himself is involved."[53]

Thus, while the American "left" is part of the "classical liberal" tradition, so too is the American "right," which Hartz suggests "exemplifies the tradition of big propertied liberalism in Europe."[54] America's entire "left-right" scale may be seen as existing within a very small range of the "traditional left-right" scale, as illustrated in Figure 2.3.

What is a radical policy today may be a moderate policy tomorrow; what is radical in one society may not be radical in another. To take one example, it was not long ago—relatively speaking—that talk of a Social Security system in the United States in which government became involved in retirement pensions was perceived as a *radical* socialist proposal, completely unthinkable. Yet, in 2011 few in American society seriously advocate doing away with Social Security; individuals may propose changing the way the system works, but most would not do away with the system completely. Another example could be found in proposals for socialized medical care. Completely socialized medicine may be seen today as a radical policy proposal in the United States—although clearly less so than it was thirty years ago—but such may not always be the case. Socialized medicine is not seen as radical in virtually all industrialized countries outside of the United States and has often been incorporated as part of the public sector.

CLASSIFICATION OF REGIMES

Care should be taken to avoid confusing ideologies—philosophies or values of political regimes—with the constitutional bases of regimes. The former concept asks the question "What does the regime stand for, what does it want to accomplish?" The latter asks the question "Who governs, how is power distributed in the political system?" As a general rule, "isms" refer to ideology—the principles of what regimes stand for—while the suffix "-ocracy" refers to governance, how governments operate or behave.[55] Calling the contemporary government of the Islamic Republic of Iran a "theocracy" tells us that its constitution is based upon religious precepts; it does not tell us about the values of the regime (other than those of Islam).

Apart from the "isms" that we have already met that are related to the "classical liberal-conservative spectrum," (i.e., radicalism, liberalism, conservatism, reactionism), there are many other "isms." Some of them are related to purely ideological considerations; others are related to economic arguments. Among these "isms" could be included the following:

Anarchism. A belief that all forms of government interfere with individual rights and freedoms and should, therefore, be abolished.[56]

Capitalism. A belief in an economic system in which the major means of production are owned by individuals, not by the government of the state. The economic philosophy emphasizes *private ownership* and a *market economy*, that is, nonregulation of the marketplace by the government.[57]

Communism. As a theory evolved from *Marxism* (see below) with modifications from Lenin in the early twentieth century. A belief in government ownership of the major means of production, and of the general "primacy of politics over economics,"[58] the government should actively regulate and control all sectors of the economy with little or no private property.[59]

Corporatism. A belief that advocates a close degree of cooperation and coordination between the government and labor and business groups in the formation of economic policy.[60]

Fascism. A belief that includes *National Socialism*, which usually is said to include seven components: "irrationalism, Social Darwinism, Nationalism, glorification of the state, the leadership principle, racism (more important in national socialism than in fascism), and anticommunism."[61]

Feminism. A system of beliefs that has emerged primarily in the West in opposition to oppression of women, and opposition to sexism in general. Different schools have developed, including Liberal or Reform Feminism, Marxist Feminism, Socialist Feminism, and Radical Feminism.[62]

Marxism. A complex framework describing the economic system and the inevitable conflict between the working class and the owners of the means of production. It suggested the inevitability of class conflict, and was adopted and modified by Lenin to create Soviet Communism.[63]

Nationalism. Includes identification with a national group and support for actions that will support and benefit the national group. This may or may not correspond to borders of a particular state as we defined the term in Chapter 1.[64]

Socialism. An ideology that developed out of the Industrial Revolution advocating governmental concern with individuals' quality of life, including education, medical care, and standard of living. It may be found in democratic versions—as in Sweden—or in authoritarian versions—as in Nazi ("Nazi" was short for National Socialist") Germany or Fascist Italy.[65]

Totalitarianism. A system in which the government controls individual political behavior and political thought. This is distinguished from *authoritarianism* by its degree: The focus of authoritarian rule is individual behavior that affects the stability of the regime; the focus of totalitarian rule is virtually total.[66]

This brief introduction to some ideological frameworks is intended to demonstrate the range of approaches to politics and ideas that are available to the student. We shall see applied versions of many of these issues later in this volume as we examine specific problem areas or specific political systems.

CONSTITUTIONS, IDEOLOGIES, AND CLASSIFICATION

Aristotle provided us with terms that are still used today to discuss both "good" government and "bad" government. Good government included the polity (rule by many in the general interest), the aristocracy (rule by a few in the general interest), and kingship (rule by one in the general interest). Bad government included tyranny (self-interest, rule by one), the oligarchy (self-interest, rule by a few), and (interestingly) the democracy (self-interest, rule by many). Aristotle provided what has come to be regarded as the "classical" division of systems of government, based upon two dimensions: the number of rulers in a system, and in whose interest the rulers rule. This framework is summarized in Table 2.1.

While knowledge of the constitutional structure of a regime and its ideology does not tell us everything that is important to know about that system, it tells us a great deal. It gives us an indication of the type of public policy that we can expect to see in that setting, and how that public policy is likely to be enacted. It also indicates the range and amount of political behavior that we are likely to encounter. It is a good beginning. Before we

TABLE 2.1

The Aristotelian Classification of Regimes

Number of Rulers	Rule in General Interest ("Right" Type)	Selfish Rule ("Wrong" Type)
One	Kingship	Tyranny
Few	Aristocracy	Oligarchy
Many	Polity	Democracy

turn our attention to more of the constitutional/political structures of the regime, however, it is important to examine the *environment* within which the institutions of the regime operate. It is to that task that we turn our attention in the next chapter.

DISCUSSION QUESTIONS

1. What is a constitution? How do constitutions differ from other important political documents?
2. What are the key differences between "written" and "unwritten" constitutions? Give an example of each, and show what the effect of having a written or an unwritten constitution is in the political behavior of that system.
3. What functions do constitutions perform for the political systems in which they are found?
4. What does the concept of "separation of powers" mean? What is separated? How do we know if true separation of powers exists? Give examples.
5. What are the differences between federal, confederal, and unitary governments? Can you give a contemporary example of each? What are the strengths of each? The weaknesses?
6. What do we mean by an ideology? Give several examples of significant ideologies, and explain how they differ from each other. Why are they important?
7. What was Aristotle's classification of political regimes? How does his framework compare with political categories today?

KEY TERMS

Anarchism 42	Corporatism 42	Radical 40
Capitalism 42	Fascism 42	Reactionary 40
Centralized	Federal 34	Separation of Powers 36
federalism 36	Feminism 42	Socialism 43
Communism 42	Ideology 38	Sovereignty 33
Confederal 33	Liberal 40	Totalitarianism 43
Conservative 40	Moderate 40	Unitary 33
Constitutional	Marxism 42	Unwritten
government 29	Nationalism 42	constitution 30
Constitutions 29	Peripheral federation 36	Written constitution 29

SUGGESTED READINGS

Leon Baradat, *Political Ideologies: Their Origins and Impact* (Englewood Cliffs, NJ: Prentice Hall, 2009). This is a very good introductory survey volume, presenting a wide range of political ideological positions and describing what each ideology stands for and the issues that are most important to it.

Ivo Duchacek, *Power Maps: Comparative Politics of Constitutions* (Santa Barbara, CA: Clio Press, 1973). This has been an extremely influential book in the area of the study of constitutions, cross-nationally. Duchacek discusses the importance of constitutions and the way their roles in their respective political systems vary.

William Ebenstein, *Today's ISM's: Socialism, Capitalism, Fascism, Communism, Libertarianism* (Upper Saddle River, NJ: Prentice Hall, 2000). This is a very comprehensive analysis of a comprehensive range of ideologies—the "isms" of the title—what they stand for, how they evolved, and what they advocate.

Louis Hartz, *The Liberal Tradition in America: An Interpretation of American Political Thought Since the Revolution* (New York: Harcourt, Brace and Company, 1955). This book focuses on American political thought, and is old, but it is a very valuable analysis of how political ideology has evolved in the United States, and how (Hartz argues) *all* American politics is "liberal".

Richard Simeon, *Federal-Provincial Diplomacy: The Making of Recent Policy in Canada* (Toronto, ON: University of Toronto Press, 2006). Although this book focuses on Canadian federalism, it is one of the best studies of federal politics in existence. Simeon shows how the Canadian federal system makes the passage of effective policy more difficult, because negotiations have to take place between levels of government.

NOTES

1. Ivo Duchacek, *Power Maps: Comparative Politics of Constitutions* (Santa Barbara, CA: Clio Press, 1973). See also the recent work by Larry Alexander, *Constitutionalism: Philosophical Foundations* (Cambridge, UK: Cambridge University Press, 2001).
2. "The Swiss Constitution of 1848, as amended in 1874 and in subsequent years, is a written document like that of the U.S.A., although it is double in size to that of the American Constitution." See Vishnoo Bhagwan and Vidya Bhushan, *World Constitutions* (New Delhi: Sterling Publishers, 1984), p. 321.
3. This is discussed in a very good book by Daphna Sharfman, *Living Without a Constitution: Civil Rights in Israel* (Armonk, NY: M. E. Sharpe, 1993). See also Steven Mazie, *Israel's Higher Law: Religion and Liberal Democracy in the Jewish State* (Lanham, MD: Lexington Books, 2006).
4. See Robert Sharlet, *The New Soviet Constitution of 1977* (Brunswick, OH: King's Court Communications, 1978).
5. Ibid., p. 89.
6. Ibid., p. 92.
7. Ibid., p. 93.
8. This is a very important issue. A 1999 volume by Karen Alonso, *Schenck v. United States: Restrictions on Free Speech* (Springfield, NJ: Enslow Publishing, 1999), reviews these issues in the United States.
9. For discussion of this episode of American history, see Roger Daniels, *Prisoners Without Trial: Japanese Americans in World War II* (New York: Hill and Wang, 1993); or Kermit Hall and John Patrick, *Equal Justice Under Law: Supreme Court Cases That Shaped America* (New York: Oxford University Press, 2006).
10. Two good examples of recent comparative study of constitutions are Jeffrey Goldsworthy, *Interpreting Constitutions: A Comparative Study* (Oxford: Oxford University Press, 2007); or Donald S. Lutz, *Principles of Constitutional Design* (New York: Cambridge University Press, 2006). See also Petra Dobner, *The Twilight of Constitutionalism* (New York: Oxford University Press, 2010).
11. S. E. Finer, ed., *Five Constitutions* (Sussex, UK: Harvester Press, 1979), p. 15.
12. Ibid.
13. The position of Prime Minister is mentioned in the Prime Minister's Residence Act—establishing an Official Residence for the Prime Minister—and the Prime Minister's

Salary Act—that authorizes the Prime Minister to receive a higher salary than other cabinet members—but the precise method of selection, powers, and similar important descriptions of the position are not included in constitutional documents. See Robert J. Jackson and Doreen Jackson, *Politics in Canada: Culture, Institutions, Behavior and Public Policy* (Toronto, ON: Prentice Hall Canada, 2001).

14. Richard Van Loon and Michael Whittington, *The Canadian Political System* (Toronto, ON: McGraw-Hill Ryerson, 1976), pp. 169–170. See also Stephen Tierney, *Multiculturalism and the Canadian Constitution* (Vancouver, BC: University of British Columbia Press, 2007).

15. See John L. Esposito and R. K. Ramazani, *Iran at the Crossroads* (Boston: Macmillan, 2001); Arshin Adib Moghaddam, *Iran in World Politics: The Question of the Islamic Republic* (New York: Columbia University Press, 2008); or Andrew Arato, *Constitution Making under Occupation: The Politics of Imposed Revolution in Iraq* (New York: Columbia University Press, 2009).

16. Thomas D. McGee, *Notes on Federal Governments: Past and Present* (Montreal, QC: Dawson Brothers, 1865).

17. Literature on the European Parliament is increasing in size. A good book on unification is by Stephen Wood and Wolfgang Quaisser, *The New European Union: Confronting the Challenges of Integration* (Boulder, CO: Lynne Rienner, 2008). See also Jo Shaw, *The Transformation of Citizenship in the European Union: Electoral Rights and the Restructuring of Political Space* (Cambridge, UK: Cambridge University Press, 2007).

18. A very good study is that by Erwin Chemerinsky, *Enhancing Government: Federalism for the 21st Century* (Stanford, CA: Stanford University Press, 2008). See also Michael Burgess, *Comparative Federalism: Theory and Practice* (New York: Routledge, 2006).

19. See Bruce Kobayashi and Larry Ribstein, *Economics of Federalism* (Cheltenham, UK: Edward Elgar, 2007); or Michael Burgess and Hans Vollaard, *State Territoriality and European Integration* (New York: Routledge, 2006).

20. See S. Rufus Davis, *The Federal Principle* (Los Angeles: University of California Press, 1978), p. 11; and William Riker, *Federalism: Origin, Operation, Significance* (Boston, MA: Little, Brown, 1964), p. 5. See also Nicholas Aroney, *The Constitution of a Federal Commonwealth: The Making and Meaning of the Australian Constitution* (New York: Cambridge University Press, 2009).

21. See Sobei Mogi, *The Problem of Federalism* (London, UK: Allen and Unwin, 1931). See also Max Edling, *A Revolution in Favor of Government: Origins of the U.S. Constitution and the Making of the American state* (New York: Oxford University Press, 2003).

22. One indicator of the number of nations is the number of members of the United Nations. While there were 51 member states in 1945, there were 99 by 1960, 127 in 1970, 154 in 1980, 159 in 1990, 189 in 2000, and as of July, 2006, the United Nations indicated that there were 192 members of the United Nations. See the U.N. web page: *www.un.org/Overview/unmember.html* (last consulted July, 2010).

23. Duchacek, *Power Maps*, p. 111.

24. Riker, *Federalism*, p. 1.

25. Arthur R. M. Lower, "Theories of Canadian Federalism—Yesterday and Today," in A.R.M. Lower, ed., *Evolving Canadian Federalism* (Durham, NC: Duke University Press, 1958), p. 3.

26. Ivo Duchacek, *Comparative Federalism: The Territorial Dimension of Politics* (New York: Holt, Rinehart, and Winston, 1970), p. 198.

27. Ibid.

28. Ronald Watts, *New Federations: Experiments in the Commonwealth* (Oxford: Clarendon Press, 1966).

29. See Ursula K. Hicks, *Federalism: Failure and Success* (New York: Oxford University Press, 1978), pp. 144-171.

30. Ibid.

31. Duchacek, *Comparative Federalism*, p. 189.

32. Ibid., p. 191. See also Michael Pagano and Robert Leonardi, *The Dynamics of Federalism in National and Supranational Political Systems* (New York: Palgrave Macmillan, 2007).

33. Riker, *Federalism*, p. 6.

34. See Amitai Etzioni, *Political Unification* (New York: Holt, Rinehart & Winston, 1965), pp. 97–183, or William Livingston, ed., *Federalism in the Commonwealth* (London, UK: Cassell, 1963).

35. Two recent studies of this problem are by Ian Peach, *Constructing Tomorrow's Federalism: New Perspectives on Canadian Governance* (Winnipeg, MA: University of Manitoba Press, 2007); and Garth Stevenson, *Unfulfilled Union: Canadian Federalism and National Unity* (Montreal, QC: McGill-Queen's University Press, 2004). See also Gregory Mahler, *New Dimensions of Canadian Federalism: Canada in a Comparative Perspective* (Rutherford, NJ: Fairleigh Dickinson University Press, 1987).

36. One of the best studies of this is by Richard Simeon, *Federal-Provincial Diplomacy: The Making of Recent Policy in Canada* (Toronto, ON: University of Toronto Press, 2006). Simeon discusses pensions, financial reform, and constitutional amendment as three case studies. See also Donald Doernberg and Keith Wingate, *Federal Courts, Federalism, and Separation of Powers: Cases and Materials* (St. Paul, MN: Thomson/West, 2008).

37. See especially Paul Spurlin, *Montesquieu in America: 1760–1801* (Baton Rouge: Louisiana State University Press, 1940); and Clinton Rossiter, *1787: The Grand Convention* (New York: Macmillan, 1966). A good study of Britain is by Roger Masterman, *The Separation of Powers in the Contemporary Constitution: Judicial Competence and Independence in the United Kingdom* (New York: Cambridge University Press, 2010).

38. See John Locke, *Second Treatise on Civil Government* (especially chap. 13, "Of the Subordination of the Powers of the Commonwealth," pp. 87–94) in Ernest Barker, ed., *Social Contract: Essays by Locke, Hume & Rousseau* (New York: Oxford University Press, 1970). See also Eoin Carolan, *The New Separation of Powers: A Theory for the Modern State* (New York: Oxford University Press, 2009).

39. See David Easton, *A Systems Analysis of Political Life* (New York: Wiley, 1965), p. 32.

40. Duchacek, *Power Maps*, p. 236.

41. Leon Baradat, *Political Ideologies: Their Origins and Impact* (Englewood Cliffs, NJ: Prentice Hall, 2009), p. 6. See also J. J. Schwarzmantel, *Ideology and Politics* (Thousand Oaks, CA: SAGE, 2008).

42. Howard Williams, *Concepts of Ideology* (New York: St. Martin's Press, 1987), p. xi.

43. Roy C. Macridis, *Contemporary Political Ideologies* (Cambridge: Winthrop, 1980), pp. 3–4.

44. Williams, *Concepts of Ideology*, p. 122.

45. Baradat, *Political Ideologies*, p. 20.

46. Very good studies of comparative political ideology are: István Mészáros, *The Power of Ideology* (New York: Palgrave Macmillan, 2005); and Terence Ball and Richard Dagger, *Political Ideologies and the Democratic Ideal* (New York: Pearson, 2009).

47. Michael Curtis, *Comparative Government and Politics* (New York: Harper and Row, 1978), p. 41. See also William Connolly, *Political Science and Ideology* (New Brunswick, NJ: Transaction Publishers, 2006).

48. Curtis, *Comparative Government and Politics*, p. 158. See also Robert Leach, *Political Ideology in Britain* (New York: Palgrave Macmillan, 2009).

49. This discussion of the left-right spectrum and the five general attitudes to be found on it is based upon much more extensive discussion in Baradat, *Political Ideologies*, pp. 27–40.

50. Ibid., p. 30.

51. Ibid., p. 35.

52. Ibid., p. 39.

53. Louis Hartz, *The Liberal Tradition in America: An Interpretation of American Political Thought Since the Revolution* (New York: Harcourt, Brace and Company, 1955), p. 11.

54. Ibid., p. 15.

55. See William Ebenstein, *Today's ISM's: Socialism, Capitalism, Fascism, Communism, Libertarianism* (Upper Saddle River, NJ: Prentice Hall, 2000); or Arthur Goldwag, *Isms and Ologies: All the Movements, Ideologies, and Doctrines That Have Shaped Our World* (New York: Vintage, 2007).

56. See Paul McLaughlin, *Anarchism and Authority: A Philosophical Introduction to Classical Anarchism* (Burlington, VT: Ashgate, 2007); or Irwin Morris, and Joe Oppenheimer, *Politics from Anarchy to Democracy: Rational Choice in Political Science* (Stanford: Stanford University Press, 2004).

57. See Richard Harvey Brown, *Culture, Capitalism, and Democracy in the New America* (New Haven: Yale University Press, 2005); or Nelson Lichtenstein, *American Capitalism: Social Thought and Political Economy in the Twentieth Century* (Philadelphia: University of Pennsylvania Press, 2006).

58. William Ebenstein, *Today's ISMs: Communism, Fascism, Capitalism, Socialism* (Englewood Cliffs, NJ: Prentice Hall, 1970), p. 31.

59. See Robert Service, *Comrades! A History of World Communism* (Cambridge: Harvard University Press, 2007); or Mark Sandle, *Communism* (New York: Pearson-Longman, 2006), for a recent discussion of modern communism.

60. See Jeffrey Anderson, *The Territorial Imperative: Pluralism, Corporatism, and Economic Crisis* (Cambridge: Cambridge University Press, 2007).

61. Lyman Tower Sargent, *Contemporary Political Ideologies: A Comparative Analysis* (Chicago: Dorsey, 1987), p. 162. See also Roger Griffin and Matthew Feldman, *Fascism: Critical Concepts in Political Science* (New York: Routledge, 2004).

62. See Shamillah Wilson and Anasuya Sengupta, *Defending Our Dreams: Global Feminist Voices for a New Generation* (New York: Palgrave Macmillan, 2005); or June Hannam, *Feminism* (New York: Pearson/Longman, 2007).

63. See Daryl Glaser and David Walker, *Twentieth-Century Marxism: A Global Introduction* (New York: Routledge, 2007); or Jolyon Agar, *Rethinking Marxism: From Kant and Hegel to Marx and Engels* (New York: Routledge, 2007), for examples of this literature.

64. See Philip Roeder, *Where Nation-States Come From: Institutional Change in the Age of Nationalism* (Princeton: Princeton University Press, 2007); or Michael Hunt, *Ideology and U.S. Foreign Policy* (New Haven: Yale University Press, 2009).

65. See William Pelz, *Against Capitalism: The European Left on the March* (New York: P. Lang, 2007).

66. The "classic" in this area is by Carl Friedrich, *Totalitarianism in Perspective* (New York: Praeger, 1969). See also Hannah Arendt, *The Origins of Totalitarianism* (New York: Schocken Books, 2004).

Legislative
Institutions

Legislatures are not only the source of legislation, but in many political systems they are also the source of a prime minister's power. Here Turkish Prime Minister Recep Tayyip Erdogan (center) and other Members of Parliament raise their hands to approve the platform of his new government in the parliament in Ankara on July 8, 2011.

ADEM ALTAN/AFP/Getty Images

- See legislatures as one of the three key branches of government as described by John Locke.
- Understand the importance of legislatures to their political systems.
- Distinguish between unicameral and bicameral variations of legislatures, and why they are that way.
- Appreciate the power relationship between two houses in a bicameral system.
- Explain the relationship of federalism to bicameralism.
- Perceive the functions of political parties in legislatures.
- Articulate how legislators are selected—the single-member district model and the proportional representation model, as well as some less common variations.
- See what legislatures do, the functions they perform for their political systems.
- Explain the accuracy of representation in legislatures for minority groups.
- Depict the role of legislative committees.
- Highlight the legislative process.
- Evaluate many of the issues related to legislative-executive relations.

INTRODUCTION

In this chapter we turn our attention to the legislature, one of the three governmental structures that were identified in the late seventeenth century by John Locke as key to the creation of a stable political system. We will turn to a discussion of executives and courts and judicial structures in the next two chapters. We examine legislatures and executives before courts because they are—to varying extents, in different nations—interrelated. Indeed, in the parliamentary model of government the executive actually *comes from* the legislature. In the presidential model of government, although the two branches are nominally separate, they typically interact in very important ways that require an understanding of both sets of functions if one is to understand the operation of politics.

In 1690 John Locke published his *Second Treatise on Government*, in which he discussed the "true original, extent, and end of civil government." In his discussion of why individuals would leave the "state of nature" and join society, Locke suggested that the prime motivation for people doing such a thing was the preservation of "their lives, liberty, and estates, which I call by the general name, property."[1] (This phrase was subsequently amended by Thomas Jefferson in the Declaration of Independence to read "life, liberty, and the pursuit of happiness.")

There are "many things wanting" in the state of nature, Locke suggested, and it was these missing structures that would prompt individuals to join society:

[Section 124:] First, there wants an established, settled, known law....

[Section 125:] Secondly, In the state of nature there wants a known and indifferent judge, with authority to determine all differences according to the established law....

[Section 126:] Thirdly, In the state of nature there often wants power to back and support the sentence when right....

[Section 127:] Thus mankind notwithstanding all the privileges of the state of nature, being but in an ill condition while they remain in it, are quickly driven into society.... And in this we have the original right and rise of both the legislature and executive power as well as of the governments and societies themselves.[2]

Legislatures are popular subjects of analysis by political scientists.[3] Among other reasons for this phenomenon is the fact that legislatures are usually important structures in their respective governmental systems.[4] In addition, legislatures are among the oldest political institutions known to society. Although the functions and powers of legislatures within their respective political systems have varied, and continue to vary today on a country-by-country basis,[5] they continue to be almost universally regarded as significant institutions.[6]

It has been suggested that legislatures may be more important in some contexts than in others, much as we suggested at the end of the second chapter might be the case in relation to constitutions. One example of this can be seen in the central role parliaments play in promoting regime stability,[7] or their effectiveness—or lack of it—in developing nations or in the process of modernization.[8] Although legislatures may have more direct impact upon some subjects or processes (such as regularizing group interaction in society)[9] than others (such as land reform), it is not difficult to imagine ways in which legislatures can affect wide areas of human concern.

ONE HOUSE OR TWO?

One of the initial characteristics of the legislative institution that we note when we look at a given legislature is whether it is **unicameral** or **bicameral**—whether it has one house or two houses.[10] The number of unicameral and bicameral legislatures around the world is about even,[11] but the distribution of unicameral and bicameral legislatures around the world is not random: Bicameral legislatures are much more prevalent in some areas than in others, as Table 3.1 indicates.

TABLE 3.1

Systems and Houses

Region (number)	Unicameral		Bicameral	
	Number	Percent (%)	Number	Percent (%)
Africa (50)	37	74	13	26
Americas (35)	15	43	20	57
Asia (33)	22	67	11	33
Europe (46)	28	28	18	39
Pacific (14)	11	79	3	21
Total (178)	113	63	65	37

Source: Inter-Parliamentary Union Web page (March, 2002): http://www.ipu.org/parline-e/parli-nesearch.asp/.

If we want to explain why some nations have bicameral legislatures while others have unicameral legislatures, we must be very careful about making broad generalizations. Why are some legislatures bicameral while others are unicameral? What do the second chambers do, where they exist? Before we can answer these questions, we must introduce a very important distinction in conceptual terms. This is the distinction between that which exists by legal establishment, *by law*, and that which exists *by actual fact*, although perhaps not by legal establishment. We refer to the former situation—establishment by law—as a *de jure* case, and to the latter situation—establishment in fact—as a *de facto* case.

In a number of instances we will see political structures that simply are not the same *in fact* as they are *in law*. We will see, for example, that *de jure* (in law), an upper house of a given national legislature may have the power to delay or veto a bill passed by the lower house. However, although the power may exist *de jure*, it may not exist *de facto*; that upper house may not have used its power of veto in over 200 years, and in the "real world," *de facto*, no matter what the law says it *may* do, custom and tradition may prohibit the upper house from exercising what may be its legitimate legal power. In many cases, the *de facto* rule of custom and tradition is stronger than any *de jure* rule.

Countries that are small in size are more likely to have one chamber than two, because "the problem of the balance of political power is less difficult to solve in them than it is in big countries."[12] Bicameral systems are often regarded in socialist countries as leading to complications and delays, and as contributing few advantages to offset these costs. With the exception of Norway, all of the Scandinavian countries have, in the twentieth century, replaced bicameral systems with unicameral ones.

According to a study undertaken by the Inter-Parliamentary Union, the earliest example of a bicameral system occurred in England toward the end of the thirteenth century:

It began with the institution of a Chamber for the high aristocracy and brought together the feudal magnates, the Lords Spiritual and Temporal.

This arrangement has been maintained to the present day, although the aristocratic characteristic of the House of Lords has been reduced by the appointment to it of Life Peers. [Appointments good only for the life of the holder that cannot be passed from one generation to another, as could traditional peerages.] Furthermore, the power of the House of Lords has been greatly restricted in favour of the popular House, the House of Commons.[13]

Bicameral systems are justified primarily by two arguments. First, in federal states (as we shall develop shortly) bicameralism reflects the split-government nature of the state. Second, in unitary states, bicameralism provides a "revising" chamber for legislation.[14]

The American "Great Compromise" in Philadelphia in 1787 is one example of the development of a bicameral legislature. The large states wanted representation based upon population, while the small states wanted representation based upon "equal representation" for the member units (i.e., an equal number of representatives per state). The Great Compromise meant that there would be a bicameral legislature, with one house based on population and the other based on an equal number of representatives for each state.[15]

To take another example, what today is the Province of Québec in Canada refused to join the Canadian confederation in 1867 without a guarantee that the future Dominion would be federal; Québec wanted assurances that it would continue to control certain areas of policy jurisdiction as only a federation would permit. Once this was decided, it was inevitable that the new national legislature would be bicameral, with one house (the House of Commons) based upon population and the other house (the Senate) not based upon population but instead based upon equal representation for the regional units of Canada.

Where we find federal states we will almost always find a bicameral legislature in which the "lower" house represents the national, popular jurisdiction, while the "upper" house represents the intermediate political structures or territories.[16] The United States, Canada, Mexico and Germany are all examples of federal states with bicameral legislatures in which the lower houses are "national" and the upper houses are "regional."[17]

Although federal regimes are typically bicameral, not all bicameral systems are federal. There are other reasons for bicameral structure besides federal status. A new nation might adopt a bicameral legislative structure because that is the structure that its colonial "parent" had, and that structure simply seemed the most normal alternative after independence was achieved (see Table 3.2).

The fact that virtually all federal systems are bicameral, but not all bicameral systems are federal, is illustrated in Table 3.3. We can see in this table that (1) federal systems are in a clear minority, and (2) unicameral and bicameral systems are just about evenly divided.

Where upper houses exist, the representational bases of the chambers vary. They may represent territorial units. (In Canada the Provinces of Ontario and Québec each receive twenty-four senators, while all four of the Western Provinces together receive twenty-four senators, and all of the Maritime Provinces together receive twenty-four senators, excluding Newfoundland, which joined the Confederation last and therefore received six senators of its own.

TABLE 3.2

Some Bicameral Systems

Nation	Lower House	Represents	Upper House	Represents
United States	House of Representatives	Districts (people)	Senate	States
Canada	House of Commons	Districts (people)	Senate	Regions
India	Lok Sabha	Districts (people)	Rajya Sabha	States
Australia	House of Representatives	Districts (people)	Senate	States
Bahamas	House of Commons	Districts (people)	Senate	Appointed
Britain	House of Commons	Districts (people)	House of Lords	Appointed

TABLE 3.3

Systems and Houses

Area	Unicameral	Bicameral
Unitary		
Atlantic area	7	9
East Europe and North Asia	10	—
Middle East and North Africa	6	4
South and East Asia	8	7
Sub-Saharan Africa	16	8
Latin America	7	10
Total	54	38
Federal		
Atlantic area	—	6
East Europe and North Asia	—	3
Middle East and North Africa	—	—
South and East Asia	—	2
Sub-Saharan Africa	1	—
Latin America	—	3
Total	1	14
Total	55	52

Source: Data from Jean Blondel, *Comparative Legislatures* (Englewood Cliffs, NJ: Prentice Hall, 1973), pp. 144–153.

The three Northern territories each have an additional senator.) Upper houses may provide equal representation for member units of a federation (e.g., two senators each for American states), or weighted representation for member units of a federation (e.g., in Germany, some Länder have three deputies in the Bundesrat, some have four, some have five, and some have six, depending upon their size.) Upper houses may simply provide an extra house in the legislature for a "sober second thought" on legislation, a house that is elected in the same manner as the lower house. Finally, they may provide several jurisdictions at once; the upper house in Japan represents both local and national units, and the British House of Lords represents hereditary positions, new political positions, judicial positions, and ecclesiastical positions.[18]

The terms *upper* and *lower* as adjectives for legislative houses are strictly a product of convention. The terms date from early British parliamentary history, when the House of Lords was felt to be superior to the House of Commons, even though (perhaps because) it was not elected by the people. It was felt that the aristocratic nature of the House of Lords, the fact that it was *not* chosen by the public, made it the superior, or "upper" house. Today, we use the term **lower house** to describe that house in a bicameral system (most) directly elected by the people, and **upper house** to describe that house farther from direct public control, although today many upper houses are elected directly by the public as well.

Where we find a unicameral legislature whatever power may reside in the legislature in that particular system resides in the single house. In bicameral settings the situation is not so simple. We may find instances in which the two houses act as equal partners in a cooperative venture; or the two houses have equal powers but are constantly feuding so that little is ever accomplished; or power is not balanced, and one house dominates the other.

When we speak of a power relationship between any two actors (we can call them A and B), three possibilities appear. A can have more power than B, A can have the same power as B, or A can have less power than B. The same options can be said to exist if A and B are two houses of a national legislative body. Let us briefly examine each of these possibilities, where bicameral legislatures exist. Table 3.4 shows us the frequencies with which these alternatives exist in the real world today.

TABLE 3.4

Powers of Second Chambers

Category	Number of Countries
Upper house weaker than lower house	26
Upper house equal to lower house	22
Upper house stronger than lower house	0
Upper house only advisory	1
No upper house	58

Source: Data from Jean Blondel, *Comparative Legislatures* (Englewood Cliffs, NJ: Prentice Hall, 1973), pp. 144–53.

The first relationship, in which the lower house is stronger than the upper house, is the most common relationship today. Because many second chambers are not elected by the public, but are either appointed or hereditary bodies, many theorists argue that in principle upper houses should be weaker than lower houses; they are in essence "undemocratic" institutions.

It must be noted, however, that many of the political settings described in Table 3.4, in which the upper houses are indicated as being legally equal to the lower houses, do not practice this relationship. For example, although the Canadian Senate is in most respects "legally" equal to the House of Commons, and must approve all bills before they become laws, it has been described as having "retained a full set of legislative muscles, but consistently has refused to make real use of them,"[19] and should not be considered as the *de facto* equal of the House of Commons.

In other legislatures, the upper house is both legally and behaviorally an equal partner in the legislative process (although even if it is behaviorally equal, it may not have identical powers). Certainly among the best examples of this type of relationship is the case of the United States Senate. Although the Senate is legally prohibited from certain legislative acts (under the Constitution, for example, it cannot introduce tax bills), overall it is an equal partner in the legislative process. A bill simply cannot become a law without the Senate's approval. Similar situations, both *de jure* and *de facto*, may be found in Italy, Switzerland, Liberia, Mexico, and Jordan.

Although in theory we might find a legislature in which the upper house is actually stronger than the lower house, in practice this is not common today. In some cases people might argue that the U.S. Senate is stronger and more important than the U.S. House of Representatives. The focus of attention, however, must be the question "Can the Senate pass laws without the approval of the House?" The answer is clearly "no." There are no contemporary cases (remember that if we go back far enough in history, at one time the House of Lords dominated the House of Commons in Great Britain, e.g.)[20] in which the power relationship is dominated by the upper house.

Finally, there are a few "variable" cases. Germany is a good example of this. When legislation affects the German Länder, or states, the upper house has an absolute veto over legislation. Members of the upper house, the Bundesrat, are not directly elected by the public, but are chosen by the governments of the German states. If a bill that will affect the states (such as a bill on transportation policy) is not approved by a majority of the representatives of the states in the upper house, it cannot become law. When legislation does not affect the states, such as foreign policy bills, the negative vote of the upper house may be over-ridden by the lower house. We shall examine this process later in this volume.

Some upper houses, then, can be seen to have an **absolute veto** in the legislative process (e.g., the U.S. Senate), in which their refusal to approve legislation results in failure of the legislation in question. Other upper houses can be said to have **suspensory vetoes**; their refusal to approve legislation is only guaranteed to slow the legislative process down a bit. Subsequent repassage by the lower house either with a regular majority (as in Great

Britain) or a special majority (as in Germany) can create laws without the approval of the upper house. Still other upper houses may be said to have **rubber-stamp** power—formal approval—only.

While legislatures vary in terms of the number of houses they have, they also vary in terms of the number of members they have. Houses of legislatures range in size from lows of 16 in the Caribbean island-nation of St. Vincent, and 24 in Barbados, to highs of about 3,000 in China; upper chambers range from 6 in Equatorial Guinea about 830 in Great Britain.[21]

Size of a legislative body may be determined by a number of factors, some philosophical and intentional, others accidental. Some legislative bodies continue to grow until it is clear that there simply is no room for them to grow more, and their size (number of members) is then frozen. The U.S. House of Representatives is a good example of this. The representative-to-population ratio was one for every 30,000 people in 1787; by 1970 was approximately one for every 500,000 people. The ratio has changed because the size of the House was frozen.

In 1787, there were 66 Members in the House of Representatives; there were 242 in 1833. In 1921 a reapportionment based on the 1920 Census would have pushed the size of the House to 483. The House decided at that time to keep its membership at 435, arguing that "the great size of the membership had already resulted in serious limitations on the right of debate and an overconcentration of power in the hands of the leadership."[22] It took eight years until this view was incorporated in law, but in 1929, a law was passed and signed by President Herbert Hoover establishing the maximum size of the House of Representatives at 435 members.

In other settings, the size of a legislative body may be symbolic. The size of the unicameral Israeli Knesset was determined by historic precedent: The Great Assembly—the first supreme legislative authority elected by the Jews in the fourth and fifth centuries B.C.—had 120 members, ten representatives for each of the twelve tribes of Israel. When the modern State of Israel was created in 1949 it was determined that the new national assembly should also have 120 members.[23]

POLITICAL PARTIES IN LEGISLATURES

One of the legislative structures about which we *can* generalize is the political party. Parties are, as a general rule, highly significant structures in legislative systems, in terms of both their organizational influence and their influence over individual legislative behavior.[24]

Parties provide the basis around which formal organization of legislatures takes place.[25] In this context the concept of **party discipline** is central; it relates to the cohesion of the body of party members within the legislature. In a legislature with high party discipline, we can expect legislators to act (and this can include voting, debating, making speeches outside the legislature, introducing bills, or a number of other possible activities as well) in concert with their party leader's directions.[26] In legislatures with low party discipline, the party label is less useful in helping us to predict legislative behavior; individuals will act as they see fit, with little regard for directions from party leaders.

We can cite two examples to illustrate the idea of party discipline. In the British House of Commons, party discipline is strong. Members of the Commons usually vote as their leaders tell them to vote.[27] We would expect all members of the majority Conservative party to vote as a bloc, almost all the time. Any member who votes against his or her party may be subject to (party) sanctions, including withdrawal of campaign funds, being given poor committee assignments in the legislature (or no assignment at all, for that matter), and the like.[28] On occasion "free votes" take place in the House of Commons, during which time the Member of Parliament (MP) may vote as he or she wants. This, however, is the only time the MP is expected to follow his or her own will in voting.

The United States offers a good example of a legislature with considerably *weaker* party discipline. This is not to say that there is *no* party discipline in the Congress, for as a general rule, if we know legislators' party identifications, and if we know the position of the party leaders on a bill, we will be correct more often than we will be incorrect in predicting how legislators will behave. However, it is not at all uncommon to find a group of Southern Democrats voting with Republicans, or a group of liberal Republicans voting with Democrats, although these patterns are less common now than they were a generation ago.

HOW LEGISLATORS ARE SELECTED

There are a number of different "pathways to parliament."[29] Some legislators, of course, are not elected by the public at all, but are appointed by some individual or political body. Others are elected. In this section we want to examine how legislators come to play their roles.[30]

Methods of Selection for Legislatures

1. Direct election by public.
   a. District-based elections, either single-member district or multiple-member-district (this tends to produce a two-party system, and a one-party majority government).
   b. Proportional representation elections (this tends to produce a multi-party system and minority or coalition government).
2. Appointment by head of state.
3. Indirect election by electoral college, convention, local notables, etc.

There are two major methods by which the public elects legislators. One method we can refer to as "district-based" elections; the other method can be called "proportional representation" elections. Each of these methods affects the political system in which it is found.[31] There are a number of variations for each of these general methods (which vary on a country-by-country basis, as we shall see in the next section), but the broad principles are the same.

Single-Member-District Voting

Among the most common forms of district based representation is the **single-member electoral district, plurality voting system**. In this kind of system, the entire nation is divided into a number of electoral districts. Each district corresponds to a seat in the legislative house. Within each district, a contest is held to determine the representative for that district, with the individual receiving the most votes (a *plurality*) being elected. Usually all of the districts in the nation hold their elections on the same day, although special elections may be held to replace a representative who has resigned or died.

The single-member-district, plurality (SMD-P) system, which exists in the United States, Canada, Great Britain, Mexico, Russia, and many other nations, does not usually require that any of the candidates win a *majority* of the vote. (A **majority** is defined as one vote more than 50 percent of the total votes cast.) All that is required for an individual to win is that he or she wins *more* than anyone else (a **plurality**); this is why it is sometimes called a "first past the post" system. So, in a given contest with four candidates, it would be possible for an individual to be elected with only 32 percent of the vote, if the other three candidates each received less (e.g., 25, 23, and 20 percent).

Like other political structures we might examine, the single-member-district system has both advantages and disadvantages. An advantage is that representatives have specific districts that are "theirs" to represent, and people know who "their" representatives are. A disadvantage is that the SMD-P system over-represents majorities, hides minorities, and promotes a two-party system at the expense of third and minor parties. Three examples will help to make this clear.

Let us take four imaginary electoral districts, each with 100 voters, illustrated in Table 3.5. Suppose that in each of these districts, in which, for simplicity's

▶ TABLE 3.5

A Two-Party, Single-Member-District System

District	Party A	Party B	Total
District 1	51	49	100
District 2	51	49	100
District 3	51	49	100
District 4	51	49	100
Total votes	204	196	400
Total seats	4	0	4

TABLE 3.6

A Three-Party, Single-Member-District System

District	Party A	Party B	Party C	Total
District 1	34	33	33	100
District 2	34	33	33	100
District 3	34	33	33	100
District 4	34	33	33	100
Total votes	136	132	132	400
Total seats	4	0	0	4

sake, there are two political parties, Party A wins 51 votes and Party B wins 49 votes. When we total up the results in the four districts, Party A will have won 204 votes to 196 for Party B, a 51–49 percent margin; but Party A will have won 4 seats in the legislature to 0 seats for Party B, a very slight majority in popular votes turning into an overwhelming majority in legislative seats. In short, the votes for Party B will be "unrepresented," or "hidden." This is an extreme mathematical example, yet the principles it demonstrates are not at all uncommon.

The second example, in Table 3.6, illustrates how in a multi-party system (in this case three parties, but the principle would apply to four, five, or more parties) a very small margin—in this case bare pluralities in place of bare majorities—in a number of districts can make a party appear very strong, when, in fact, that is not the case. Here, although the plurality party wins only 34 percent of the popular vote, that 34 percent will yield 100 percent of the seats in the legislature.

The third example, illustrated in Table 3.7, uses the same setting as Table 3.6: four districts of 100 voters, and three parties. We can see that in the most mathematically extreme case a shift of only two votes (or one-half of 1 percent, in this case!), from Party A to Party B, results in Party B winning two seats—that is, 50 percent—in the legislature where it previously had none. In other words, a shift in popular support of as little as one-half of 1 percent of the

TABLE 3.7

A Second Three-Party, Single-Member-District System

District	Party A	Party B	Party C	Total
District 1	34	33	33	100
District 2	34	33	33	100
District 3	33	34	33	100
District 4	33	34	33	100
Total votes	134	134	132	400
Total seats	2	2	0	4

"popular vote" has the potential to change the composition of the legislature by 50 percent. Party C is still shut out of the legislature, despite the fact that it received 33 percent of the vote, one vote out of three, and only one-half of 1 percent less than either Party A or Party B! Clearly this is the most extreme example we could design in a 100-person district, but the principles it illustrates would apply just as forcefully in an electoral district with 100,000 voters.

Although these examples are simpler than the reality of electoral politics, the patterns of bias that they demonstrate are real. In the British general election of May 2005, to take a relatively recent election, the Labour Party won 35.3 percent of the popular vote (down from 40.7 percent in the 2001 election), yet received 55.1 percent of the seats in the House of Commons, a "bonus" of 19.8 percent! On the losing side, the Conservative Party received 32.3 percent of the popular vote yet received only 30.6 percent of the seats in the House of Commons, a "loss" of 1.5 percent. The bias most severely affected the smaller parties, however, as demonstrated in Table 3.8. The Liberal Democrats received 9.5 percent of the seats in the House of Commons in exchange for 22.1 percent of the votes (12.6 percent less than it "should" have received). The "earned less received" losses to many of the very small parties (and there were many other parties that didn't even win a single seat) were not as great as they were for the Liberal Democrats because, as we noted above, many of the other small parties were regionally concentrated (e.g., the Scottish Nationalists, Sinn Fein, or Plaid Cymru), and *where they ran candidates* they won significantly more frequently than did the Liberal Democrats.

TABLE 3.8

The British General Election 2010

Party	% Votes Won	# Seats Won	% Seats Won
Conservative Party	36.1	306	47.1
Labour Party	29.0	258	39.7
Liberal Democrats	23.0	57	8.8
Democratic Unionist Party			
Scottish National Party			
Sinn Fein			
Plaid Cymru			
Social Democratic and Labour Party	11.9	29	4.4
Greens			
Alliance Party of Northern Ireland			
Other			
Total	100%	650	100%

Source: Inter-Parliamentary Union, www.ipu.org/parline-e/reports/2335_E.htm, and British Broadcasting Corporation, www.news.bbc.co.uk/2/shared/election2010/results (last consulted November 2010).

The British 2010 elections resulted in the first parliament without a majority party since 1974. The Conservatives came in first with 306 seats. Labour and the Liberal Democrats followed with 258 and 57 seats, respectively. The remainder went to smaller parties. We can see, though, that the same general phenomenon held: The Conservative Party received 47.1 percent of the seats in the House of Commons in exchange for 36.1 percent of the vote (an 11% "bonus"). The Labour Party received 39.7 percent of the seats in the House of Commons in exchange for 29 percent of the vote (a 10.7% "bonus"), but the third-place Liberal Democrats received 8.8 percent of the seats in the House of Commons in exchange for 23 percent of the vote (a 14.2 "cost").

The problem with the SMD-P system is that if a party can't get more votes than all of the other parties in a district, it might as well not run there, because it will get no representation at all, illustrated by the British Liberal-Democrats. This happened because, although they could count on some votes from many districts, in most districts they did not have more votes than their competitors, so they ended up with no representation. One common by-product of the SMD system is a two-party system, because generally speaking it is extremely hard for third parties to win seats in SMD systems, so two major parties tend to dominate the political landscape.[32]

Proportional Representation Voting

An alternative to the SMD system is called the **proportional representation** (PR) system. The PR system is not based upon districts at all. Rather, the members of the electorate vote for the single *party* they prefer, not for candidates. The proportion of votes that a party receives in the election (e.g., 23 percent of the total votes cast) determines the proportion of seats it will receive in the legislature (e.g., 23 percent of the legislative seats).

An example may help to clarify this. The Israeli system for electing the legislature has a "pure" PR electoral framework. Voters cast their ballots for the political party they support. After the election, if the Labour party has received 25 percent of the votes, it receives 25 percent of the 120 seats (i.e., 30 seats) in the Israeli parliament, the Knesset.

How are the individual winners determined? Prior to the election, parties deposit lists of their candidates with a national election board, and these lists are made public. The parties may submit lists of 120 names—one for each possible seat in the Knesset (even though they can be sure that they will not win 100 percent of the vote). After the election, if Labour has won 30 seats (25 percent of 120 seats), it simply counts down the top 30 names on its electoral list: Positions 1 through 30 are declared elected, positions 31 through 120 are not elected. This system has an added advantage: If a Member of Knesset dies during the term, or if someone resigns, a special election is not necessary; the next name on the party list enters the Knesset.[33]

The PR system, like the SMD system, has its advantages and disadvantages.[34] Its advantages center on the fact that it is highly representative. Parties in Israel need to win only 2 percent of the vote to win a seat in the legislature. This means that groups that are not pluralities can still be represented in the legislature. To take our example in Table 3.5, if all districts in a 100 seat legislature voted in the same 51–49 manner as the four districts we have drawn, in a PR system Party A would receive 51 seats and Party B would receive 49 seats. In a comparable SMD system, Party A would receive 100 seats, and Party B would receive none.

The disadvantage of the PR system is that PR legislatures tend to be multiparty legislatures—since it is so easy for smaller parties to win representation—which means that they tend to be more unstable and to contain more radical and extreme groups than SMD-two-party legislatures. To use our example from Table 3.6, in a PR system Party A would win 34 of 100 seats in the legislature, Party B 33 seats, and Party C 33 seats. This would require the formation of a coalition government, something we shall discuss later in this chapter, since no single party would control a majority of the legislative seats on its own. On the other hand, we might want to argue that this is not really a disadvantage at all—in fact, it is a real advantage, since groups that exist should be represented in the legislature.

Variations on Electoral Models

There are variations on both the SMD and PR models described above. One variation on the SMD-plurality requires a *majority* for election (SMD-M). The single-member-district, majority system invariably involves runoff elections, since, given the many political parties that might exist, few districts give a majority to a candidate on the first round of voting. Voting might be scheduled on two consecutive Sundays (we will see later that this is the case in France), with the top two vote-getters from the first round having a runoff election on the second Sunday. Generally, few districts would elect candidates on the first round (i.e., have candidates that can win majority margins); the other 85 to 90 percent of the districts have runoff elections.

Another variation on the district-based model involves the number of representatives per district. In a number of legislatures we can find **multiple-member districts** (MMD), in which the top vote-getters are elected. In elections for the lower house in Japan (the House of Representatives), each district elects from three to five representatives, depending upon the size of the district. Voters vote for one candidate, and the top three (or four, or five, depending upon the population living in the district) vote-getters are elected. Japan utilizes an even more complex multiple-member-district scheme for its upper house, the House of Councillors.

Technically, American states fall in this "multiple member" category, since each state is represented in the U.S. Senate by two senators and is, therefore, not a single-member district but rather a multiple-member district. The method of selection of U.S. Senators is the SMD method rather than the MMD method, however, since election of senators is "staggered," and only one senator is elected at a time.[35]

LEGISLATIVE FUNCTIONS

There is consensus in the discipline as to many of the structures and functions of legislatures, as well as their common attributes.[36] In general, five functions that legislatures perform for political systems may be sifted from the lists in the literature. These are the following, not necessarily in order of importance:

1. Criticism and control of the other branches of government, most notably the executive
2. Debate
3. Lawmaking or legislation
4. Communication with the public, representation, and legitimation
5. Recruitment, education, and socialization

It is, of course, true that not all legislatures can be said to perform all of these functions. Nor, if they do, can it be said that they perform them all equally well. On the other hand, some legislatures, because of idiosyncratic characteristics of the systems in which they can be found, may be said to perform functions in addition to the five outlined here. Because a legislature fails to perform *all* of these functions does not mean that it performs *none* of them.

Much research on legislatures mentions the *criticism and control* function as being necessary for the maintenance of a stable political system.[37] This function has its roots in seventeenth- and eighteenth-century democratic political theory; at that time the role of the legislature as a check upon the powers of monarchs was first practiced. Legislatures have, in modern times, been less and less able to perform this very important function satisfactorily.[38]

A second function is that of *debate*, or discussion of values for the political system. In many nations the legislature's role in the legislative process is rather modest. It might discuss a bill proposed by the executive or the bureaucracy, but the bill might become law even if it is never actually voted on and passed by the legislature. In such instances, a legislature may appear to be performing both a debating and a legislating function, but *de facto*, its function is limited to debate.[39]

The function most frequently ascribed to legislatures in Western countries is that of *lawmaking*. As Jean Blondel observed, "From the theorists of the 17th Century to those of the contemporary world, it has been held as axiomatic... that the function of legislatures was to make laws."[40] The lawmaking function is no longer considered the litmus test by which a legislature is judged: "in formal terms, the principal function of the Parliament... is to pass legislation. But, legislation is only a part of the Parliament's business."[41]

The fourth function suggested is that of *communication with the public, representation, and legitimation*. The relationship between legislatures and "big business," lobbies, and pressure groups is just as important for democratic government as is the representation of individual views and opinions.[42] The collective actions of legislators in these matters help build support not only for the legislature as an institution but also for the regime itself.[43]

There is a chain of three interconnected concepts at work here. First, legislators are necessarily aware of communications, both supportive and demanding, from their constituents. Second, by performing actions in response to these communications, the legislators can be said to be acting in a representative manner. Finally, by acting in a representative manner, the legislator can contribute significantly to the legitimacy of the governmental structure.

The fifth function that has been attributed to legislatures is that of *recruitment, education, and socialization.* Through the process of attracting individuals to politics, giving them experience, and enabling them to attain higher office, legislatures draw people into the political arena.[44] By serving as role models and by developing and maintaining political norms, legislatures actively participate in the process of political socialization, the transmission of political values.[45]

In some circumstances, legislatures are invested with special functions as a result of a particular constitutional framework or historical background. For example, the British Parliament (and many parliaments like it) also has an elective function—choosing the prime minister. The U.S. House of Representatives has a similar elective function (choosing the president), but because of the nature of the electoral college and historical situations faced by the United States, the House has rarely been called upon to perform this task. The presidential election of 2000 came precariously close to being decided in the House of Representatives; ultimately a decision by the U.S. Supreme Court made the House's participation in the election not necessary.

It was indicated earlier that one of the most important functions usually ascribed to the legislature as an institution is that of *representation.*[46] Whether or not legislatures are truly representative in a demographic sense, the need for legislatures to *appear* representative is central to their mission.

Central to this issue, however, is the very idea of being a "representative." In the late eighteenth century the British Member of Parliament Edmund Burke introduced the idea of "virtual representation," in which he claimed that he could represent the views of the American colonies in the "no taxation without representation" controversy without actually *being from* the colonies. After all, he claimed, he knew what their view was, and he was capable of presenting it to the British Parliament.[47]

Must the distribution of population groups in the legislature accurately reflect their distribution in the general population? It is clear wherever we look that legislatures do not accurately reflect the demographic makeup of their settings.[48] To take the most obvious example, women are systematically underrepresented in their national legislatures.[49]

Table 3.9 shows the disproportionate percentage of seats women fill in a number of nations in each country's government compared with the percentage of the total population women comprise in that country. Women's lack of representation in the world's governments—both low-income and high-income countries—is clearly problematic for those who value representative, democratic government.

TABLE 3.9

Under-Representation of Women in Legislatures

Country	Election Yr	% Women Representatives			Female Population (% Total)
		Lower or Single House	Upper House	I.P.U. Rank	
Rwanda	2008	56.3	34.6	1	51.6
Denmark	2007	38.0	—	13	50.4
Burundi	2010	32.1	46.3	21	51.0
Austria	2008	27.9	29.5	29	51.2
China	2008	21.3	—	56	48.1
United States	2008	16.8	15.3	73	50.7
Guatemala	2007	12.0	—	92	51.3
Malaysia	2008	9.9	28.1	100	49.2
Chad	2002	5.2	—	123	50.3
Bahrain	2006	2.5	25.0	131	47.6

Source: "Women in Parliaments: World Classification," 30 September, 2010, Inter-Parliamentary Union (IPU) *http://www.ipu.org/wmn-e/classif.htm*; Population data from World Bank Group's GenderStats, "Population, Female (% of total)" The World Bank > Data > *http://data.worldbank.org/indicator/SP.Pop.totl. fe.zs.* This table was originally conceived by Kate Thomas.

Similarly, ethnic, religious, and racial minorities tend to be significantly underrepresented in national parliaments. Even in settings in which there are no *legal* barriers to representation, this is a function of educational, financial, career, and other sociological patterns of bias reflected in the electoral machinery of the nation.

Many argue that the important point is not the gender, ethnic identity, age, religious, or racial characteristic of the representative, but the degree to which he or she understands the views of his or her constituency.[50] The true role of the representative, some would argue, is to represent the *interests* of his or her constituency, since obviously one representative cannot actually belong to all of the many demographic groups he or she represents.

The role that legislators play in the generation of legislative output varies in different political systems. A political role, as the term is used here, consists of "a pattern of expected behavior for individuals holding particular positions in a system."[51] One author listed seventeen possible roles that legislators can play; others listed twenty-three.[52] The possibilities are numerous.

Certainly one of the major distinctions in legislative roles comes in the description of a legislator as a **frontbencher** or a **backbencher**. The names derive from positions in the British House of Commons, in which seats were, and still are, arranged in two sets of rows facing each other. Party leaders sit on the front benches of their respective sides; nonleaders, or followers, sit on the back benches—hence, "frontbenchers" for leaders and "backbenchers" for followers.

The prime minister and members of the cabinet sit on the front bench of the Government side of the House. Members who sit on the front bench of the Opposition side of the House are party leaders who *would* be in the cabinet if their party were in power; sometimes these individuals are referred to as members of the **shadow cabinet.**

Although the terms *frontbencher* and *backbencher* are positional terms, designating where one sits, they are also terms of *power*.[53] This is true because as legislators' seniority and power increases, they tend to move to their party's front bench. Those seated on the front bench tend to have more power and influence than those not on the front benches.

Although the British model of the legislature places an emphasis—because of its physical organization—on the "Government versus the Opposition" conflict in the legislature, not all legislatures are organized in this way. We noted in our discussion of ideology that "left" and "right" were simply holdovers from 1792, at which time the French Council of 500 was arranged in a semicircular hall of representatives according to their self-determined place in the political spectrum.[54] Those generally supporting the monarch's policies sat on his right, while those who proposed changes in his policies sat on his left—hence, we noted that "leftists" today tend to favor change and "rightists" tend to prefer the status quo. Like the French Council of 500, American legislative bodies also sit in a semicircular pattern.

Interior of the British House of Commons. General view from the Opposition benches looking toward the Speaker's chair (rear center) and the Government benches (left). The Clerk's Table is in the center.

LEGISLATIVE COMMITTEES

Another of the major structures that we find in legislative bodies is that of the committee.[55] Committees exist to meet a real need in legislatures: Legislative bodies as a whole are often too large to enable complex discussion on highly specialized matters to take place. If, however, the entire legislative body is divided into groups, with each group specializing in a different aspect of the legislature's business, the work of the legislature can be performed more efficiently. The idea of a division of labor and specialization serves as the primary justification for the legislative committee's existence.[56]

Let us imagine a legislature with 200 members. Each legislator could not possibly develop expertise in all of the business of the legislature (everything from weapons systems to tax legislation to national parks policy to agriculture subsidies) to enable the legislature to function at peak capacity. Accordingly, the 200 members will establish, say, 20 committees dealing with the various issues that the legislature must address. Each member may serve on 2 committees, and each committee will have 20 members. It is usually the case, as well, that the individual committees engage further in the "division of labor-specialization" behavior, forming a number of subcommittees so that committee members can specialize in very narrow aspects of the committee's work.

Thus our imaginary legislature might have an Agriculture Committee, a Defense Committee, and a Finance Committee, to take three examples. These committees, as we noted, will have subcommittees. Members of the Agriculture Committee, who will all be generally well informed about all aspects of agriculture, will each be very well informed about some specific aspect of the Agriculture Committee's work (such as the wheat crop, or price subsidies, e.g.).

Legislatures tend to have a number of different types of committees. **Standing committees** (or **permanent committees**) are committees that are established at the opening of the legislative term and which last for the life of the legislature. **Select committees** are committees that tend to be given specific scopes of inquiry, or special problems, to address, as well as specific durations. Some bicameral systems have **joint committees**, which are made up of members from both houses. The **committee of the whole**, often found in legislatures, is a technical device used to establish a different set of procedural rules; a legislative body can "dissolve itself" into a committee of the whole, and without anything physically changing (the same legislators are still sitting in the same seats), there is a different set of rules governing debate time, how motions may be introduced, and so on, that applies to their proceedings.

The relative importance of committees varies on a national basis. In some systems (such as the U.S. legislature), legislative committees are very important and have a significant role in the legislative process. In other systems (such as that of Great Britain), the role of committees is weaker; they are not as active in the "oversight" function as are American committees, and they do not play as significant a role in the legislative process as their American counterparts.[57]

The ability of committees to examine, modify, delay, or even "kill" legislative proposals can be very significant and can be quite important in determining the amount of power the executive branch can exercise over the legislative branch of government.

THE LEGISLATIVE PROCESS

As David Olson has argued, the most common pattern among parliaments in the process of handling legislation is to alternate the focus of activity between the **plenum**—the floor of the legislative house—and committee stages of legislation.[58] Table 3.10 shows the procedures for handling legislation in a typical legislative body; the description is generalized from actual procedures in a number of legislative bodies.

When we speak of legislation, we do not only distinguish between front-benchers and backbenchers, because this would group the Government frontbench with the Opposition frontbench, and the Government backbench with the Opposition backbench. Instead, we leave the Government frontbench standing alone, and group the Government backbench with the Opposition frontbench and backbench. Bills originating in the Government frontbench—where the members of the Cabinet sit—are called **Government bills**. Bills originating from any other member of parliament, either in the Government backbenches or the Opposition frontbenches or backbenches, are called **private members' bills**.[59]

TABLE 3.10

Steps in Legislative Procedure in Selected Countries

Introduction
  First reading: presentation of bill and discussion of its contents
  Debate
  Vote
  To committee(s)

When (and if) bill emerges from committee(s)
  Second reading: often presented by members of committee(s) that held hearings
    on the bill
  Debate
  Vote
  Third reading
  Debate
  Final Vote
In a bicameral system, the bill would then go to the second house, and usually go
through the same procedure there.

In a classic study of the relative difference in efficacy between Government bills and private members' bills, Sheva Weiss and Avraham Brichta found a marked, though predictable, difference in legislative effectiveness between the chances of passage of Government bills and private members' bills.[60] Bills introduced by the Government invariably pass and become law; bills introduced by private members do not usually enjoy the same fate.

LEGISLATURES AND EXECUTIVES

Much has been made in recent years about the "decline of the legislature" as a viable political structure,[61] effectively able to counterbalance the growing structure of the political executive. The argument is made that in the modern political world the executive structure has grown at a dramatic rate in terms of the increase in and centralization of its power, and the legislative structure has correspondingly lost power. This means that the legislature is less able today to provide a meaningful check on the power of the executive.[62]

Some have argued that there is nothing wrong with this scenario at all, and have gone so far as to suggest that the legislature *ought* to expedite this process by voluntarily ceding to the executive many of its own powers. The legislature can remain as an institution, according to these advocates, but it should permit the executive to lead, with the legislature's proper role being to follow.[63]

The question of the relationship between the legislature and the executive is one that can be addressed on two levels. On the normative level, we can ask about what the relationship *should* be. More precisely, which alternative best promotes democratic, representative government? On the empirical level, we can ask about the validity of the observations that legislatures are declining in significance while executives are on the ascent. Is it true? What happens to the executive structure when the legislature loses its power?

Evidence seems to show that the executive institution is winning the battle for power with the legislative branch. There is no way that a legislative body can keep up with a rapidly expanding executive bureaucracy in terms of information, personnel, and ability to formulate policy. To take the example of foreign policy, it simply is not possible for the British House of Commons Committee on Foreign Affairs (with a staff of less than a dozen) to oversee successfully the Ministry of External Affairs (with a staff of literally thousands); the same could be said of the U.S. Senate's Foreign Relations Committee ability to oversee the policy of the U.S. State Department (although the U.S. Senate committees have far more in the way of committee staff than do committees of other national legislatures). In fact, what often ends up happening is that legislative committees become dependent upon executive agencies—whether they are Ministries of External Affairs, Defense, or Agriculture—to supply them with information, and the ability to control the information to which the legislature will have access gives the executive branch of government a permanent and overwhelming advantage in the legislative-executive power competition.

Although it may be the case that legislatures are generally regarded as having lost the battle for expanded power to executives, that does not mean that they have surrendered completely.[64] Indeed, in recent years we have seen a number of calls for reform, and in many instances some changes have been made in the legislative process that were designed to strengthen the legislature in relation to the executive, and to regain some of the traditional powers of the legislature, although there have been some very clear limitations to this reform.[65]

We should note that the subject of legislative reform is not a new one; it has been discussed by legislatures for well over a hundred years.[66] The problem has been, of course, that parliamentary reform—that is, an increase in the *de facto* power of parliament in relation to the executive—is seen as being in a zero-sum game with the executive: Any gains on the part of parliament must come at the expense of the executive. We now turn our attention to an examination of the executive structure.

DISCUSSION QUESTIONS

1. How would you compare Locke's view of legislative institutions with the common view of legislatures today?
2. What do you believe are the most important functions that legislatures perform in their respective political systems today?
3. Which type of legislative system—unicameral or bicameral—seems to you to be most effective? Why?
4. What is the most compelling reason for a legislative system to be bicameral? Why would a system opt to be unicameral?
5. How important are political parties for legislative institutions? Could we have a nonpartisan legislature today?
6. Do you believe that single-member district elections or proportional representation elections are more effective for legislatures? Why?
7. How could legislatures become more accurate in representation of minority groups in society? Is this important?
8. What do legislative committees do in legislative bodies?
9. What are the key "choke points" in the legislative process? If you were redesigning the legislative process, what would you do differently?

KEY TERMS

absolute veto 56
backbencher 66
bicameral legislature 51
committee of the
  whole 68
de facto 52
de jure 52
frontbencher 66
Government bills 69
joint committee 68
legislature 51
lower house 55

majority 59
multiple-member
  districts 63
party discipline 57
permanent committee 68
plenum 69
plurality 59
plurality voting
  system 59
private members'
  bills 69

proportional
  representation voting 62
rubber-stamp
  approval 57
select committee 68
single-member electoral
  district 59
standing committee 68
suspensory veto 56
unicameral legislature 51
upper house 55

SUGGESTED READINGS

Jean Blondel, *Comparative Legislatures* (Englewood Cliffs, NJ: Prentice Hall, 1973). This small book is an excellent introduction to the cross-national study of legislatures. It presents a good deal of data and structural information on similarities and differences of legislative bodies cross-nationally.

Reuven Hazan, *Cohesion and Discipline in Legislatures: Political Parties, Party Leadership, Parliamentary Committees, and Governance* (New York: Routledge, 2006). This is a good example of scholarship that focuses on legislative structures—parties and committees—that includes how legislators operate, and what it is that legislators do.

Gerhard Loewenberg, *Modern Parliaments: Change or Decline* (Chicago, IL: Atherton, 1971). In this volume Gerhard Loewenberg describes the structures of modern legislatures, and especially focuses on legislative relations with key institutions in their environments, most notably political executives.

Gerhard Loewenberg, Samuel Patterson, and Malcolm Jewell, eds., *Handbook of Legislative Research* (Cambridge: Harvard University Press, 1985). This is an edited collection of papers that cover the major research topics related to legislatures, legislative structures and legislative behavior. While it is slightly dated, the volume offers the student an excellent introduction to the key research fields and discussion of previous scholarship.

David Olson and Michael Mezey, *Legislatures in the Policy Process: The Dilemmas of Economic Policy* (New York: Cambridge University Press, 2008). This volume focuses on public policy, the "output" side of the legislative setting, and presents top-rated analysis of how legislatures generate public policy and how they do it.

NOTES

1. In Sir Ernest Barker, ed., *Social Contract: Essays by Locke, Hume, & Rousseau* (New York: Oxford University Press, 1970), p. 73.
2. Ibid., pp. 73–77.
3. What has become a "definitive" resource in the field appeared in 1985 and reviewed the state of the art of legislative studies up to that time. See Gerhard Loewenberg, Samuel Patterson, and Malcolm Jewell, eds., *Handbook of Legislative Research* (Cambridge: Harvard University Press, 1985). A more recent compendium is by M. Steven Fish and Matthew Kroenig, *The Handbook of National Legislatures: A Global Survey* (New York: Cambridge University Press, 2009).
4. Jean Blondel once wrote that "...of the 138 countries which exist in the world today, only five, all in the Middle East, have never had a legislature." In Jean Blondel, *Comparative Legislatures* (Englewood Cliffs, NJ: Prentice Hall, 1973), p. 7. According to the United Nations the count today is 192 nations.
5. The national legislature has been the most common level of study in recent years. Recent examples of such studies include the following: Mark Freeman, *Making Reconciliation Work: The Role of Parliaments* (Geneva: Inter-Parliamentary Union, 2005); Mohamed Abdel Rahim Salih, *African Parliaments: Between Governance and Government* (New York: Palgrave Macmillan, 2005); or Reuven Hazan, *Cohesion and Discipline in Legislatures: Political Parties, Party Leadership, Parliamentary Committees, and Governance* (New York: Routledge, 2006).
6. A very good recent study is that by Philip James Giddings, *The Future of Parliament: Issues for a New Century* (Houndmills, Basingstoke: Palgrave Macmillan, 2005);

or Berthold Rittberger, *Building Europe's Parliament: Democratic Representation Beyond the Nation-State* (New York: Oxford University Press, 2005).

7. Joseph LaPalombara, *Politics Within Nations* (Englewood Cliffs, NJ: Prentice Hall, 1974), p. 177. See also David Farrell and Roger Scully, *Representing Europe's Citizens? Electoral Institutions and the Failure of Parliamentary Representation* (New York: Oxford University Press, 2007).

8. See Scott Morgenstern, *Legislative Politics in Latin America* (New York: Cambridge University Press, 2002); Mohamed Salih, *African Parliaments: Between Governance and Government* (New York: Palgrave Macmillan, 2005), or Gavin Barrett, *National Parliaments and the European Union* (Dublin: Clarus Press, 2008).

9. See for examples of the range of issues that can be affected by legislatures, Roger Congleton and Birgitta Swedenborg, eds., *Democratic Constitutional Design and Public Policy: Analysis and Evidence* (Cambridge: MIT Press, 2006); or David Olson and Michael Mezey, *Legislatures in the Policy Process: The Dilemmas of Economic Policy* (New York: Cambridge University Press, 2008).

10. For discussion of American state legislatures, see Tom Todd, *Unicameral or Bicameral State Legislatures* (St. Paul, MN: Minnesota House of Representatives, 1999). For those who enjoy exceptions to general rules, there are, in fact, *tri*-cameral legislatures, too! To offer one example, the national legislature of the Isle of Man, the oldest continuously operating legislative body in the world, operates in three different situations, a lower house, an upper house, and both houses sitting together as a distinct third house. See also Peverill Squire and Keith Hamm, *101 Chambers: Congress, State Legislatures, and the Future of Legislative Studies* (Columbus, OH: Ohio State University Press, 2005); and Alan Rosenthal, *Engines of Democracy: Politics and Policymaking in State Legislatures* (Washington, DC: CQ Press, 2009).

11. Data come from Jean Blondel, *Comparative Legislatures*, pp. 144–153. To illustrate different nation-counts, note that Michael Curtis says that 47 out of 144 nations in the world are bicameral. See Michael Curtis, *Comparative Government and Politics* (New York: Harper and Row, 1978), p. 195.

12. Valerie Herman, ed., *Parliaments of the World* (London: Macmillan, 1976), p. 3. See also David Arter, *Comparing and Classifying Legislatures* (New York: Routledge, 2009).

13. Herman, *Parliaments of the World*, p. 3.

14. See Donald Shell and David Beamish, *The House of Lords at Work: A Study with Particular Reference to the 1988–1989 Session* (New York: Oxford University Press, 1993). See also Squire and Hamm, *101 Chambers*.

15. See James Madison, *Notes of Debates in the Federal Convention of 1787*, "Introduction" by Adrienne Koch (Athens, OH: Ohio State University Press, 1966), pp. vii–xxiii.

16. These vary on a country-by-country basis.

17. See Jan Erk, *Explaining Federalism: State, Society and Congruence in Austria, Belgium, Canada, Germany, and Switzerland* (New York: Routledge, 2008); or Herbert Obinger and Stephan Leibfried, *Federalism and the Welfare State: New World and European Experiences* (New York: Cambridge University Press, 2005).

18. See Jorg Luther and Paolo Passaglia, *A World of Second Chambers: Handbook for Constitutional Studies on Bicameralism* (Milan: Giuffre, 2007).

19. Allan Kornberg, *Canadian Legislative Behavior* (New York: Holt, Rinehart and Winston, 1967), p. 19; David E. Smith, *The People's House of Commons: Theories of Democracy in Contention* (Toronto, ON: University of Toronto Press, 2007).

20. See *The Work of the House of Lords*, published by the House of Lords Information Office (London, 2005); Kenneth Clarke, *Reforming the House of Lords: Breaking the Deadlock* (London: University College, 2005); or Meg Russell, *Reforming the House of Lords: Lessons from Overseas* (Oxford: Oxford University Press, 2000).
21. Blondel, *Comparative Legislatures*, pp. 144–153. Blondel's data are out of date, and also a bit inaccurate. Caribbean data come from my own research there in 1985; for the British upper house, a publication by the House of Lords itself gives its total membership as about 830. See the Inter-Parliamentary Union "Parline Database," at *http://www.ipu.org/parline-e/parlinesearch.asp*.
22. Robert Diamond, ed., *Origins and Development of Congress* (Washington, DC: Congressional Quarterly, 1976), pp. 127–128.
23. Asher Zidon, *The Knesset* (New York: Herzl Press, 1967), p. 27.
24. See Wouter van der Brug and C. van der Eijk, *European Elections and Domestic Politics: Lessons from the Past and Scenarios for the Future* (Notre Dame, IN: University of Notre Dame Press, 2007), and Reuven Hazan, *Cohesion and Discipline in Legislatures: Political Parties, Party Leadership, Parliamentary Committees, and Governance* (New York: Routledge, 2006).
25. Kaare Strom and Wolfgang Muller, *Delegation and Accountability in Parliamentary Democracies* (Oxford: Oxford University Press, 2006); Richard Katz and William Crotty, *Handbook of Party Politics* (Thousand Oaks, CA: SAGE, 2005).
26. One of the best recent books on the subject is by Magnus Blomgren and Olivier Rozenberg, *Parliamentary Roles in Modern Legislatures* (New York: Routledge, 2010).
27. See J. Richard Piper, "British Backbench Rebellion and Government Appointments, 1945–1987," *Legislative Studies Quarterly* 16 (1991): 219–238.
28. Mark Franklin, Alison Baxter, and Margaret Jordan, "Who Were the Rebels? Dissent in the House of Commons, 1970–1974," *Legislative Studies Quarterly* 11:2 (1986): 143–160.
29. See Larry Diamond and Marc Plattner, eds., *Electoral Systems and Democracy* (Baltimore, MD: Johns Hopkins University Press, 2006). The classic on this subject is Austin Ranney, *Pathways to Parliament* (Madison, WI: University of Wisconsin Press, 1965). A good review of women and elections is in Sue Thomas and Clyde Wilcox, *Women and Elective Office: Past, Present, and Future* (New York: Oxford University Press, 2005).
30. See the collection of articles in the volume edited by Joan DeBardelben and Achim Hurrelmann, *Democratic Dilemmas of Multilevel Governance: Legitimacy, Representation and Accountability in the European Union* (New York: Palgrave Macmillan, 2007).
31. See Anthony McGann, *The Logic of Democracy: Reconciling Equality, Deliberation, and Minority Protection* (Ann Arbor, MI: University of Michigan Press, 2006), and Thomas Lundberg, *Proportional Representation and the Constituency Role in Britain* (New York: Palgrave Macmillan, 2007).
32. For discussions of past British general elections, see Pippa Norris and Christopher Wlezien, *Britain Votes, 2005* (Oxford: Oxford University Press, 2005); and John Bartle and Anthony King, *Britain at the Polls, 2005* (Washington, DC: C.Q. Press, 2006).
33. See Gregory Mahler, *The Knesset: Parliament in the Israeli Political System* (Rutherford, NJ: Fairleigh Dickinson University Press, 1981), especially Chapter 2. On Israeli elections, see Gregory Mahler, *Politics and Government in Israel: The Maturation of a Modern State* (Lanham, MD: Rowman and Littlefield, 2011).

34. See Norman Schofield, *Multiparty Democracy: Elections and Legislative Politics* (New York: Cambridge University Press, 2006), Sarah Birch, *Full Participation: A Comparative Study of Compulsory Voting* (New York: United Nations University Press, 2009).

35. An interesting comparative study of this subject is edited by Lois Duke Whitaker, *Voting the Gender Gap* (Urbana, IL: University of Illinois Press, 2008). See also Mona Lena Krook and Sarah Childs, eds., *Women, Gender, and Politics: A Reader* (New York: Oxford University Press, 2010).

36. Gerhard Loewenberg, *Modern Parliaments: Change or Decline* (Chicago, IL: Atherton, 1971), p. 3.

37. Lord Ponsonby of Shulbrede, "The House of Lords: An Effective Restraint on the Executive," *Parliamentarian* 69:2 (1988): 83–86.

38. See Richard Bauman and Tsvi Kahana, eds., *The Least Examined Branch: The Role of Legislatures in the Constitutional State* (New York: Cambridge University Press, 2006).

39. Michael Mezey, "The Functions of a Minimal Legislature: Role Perceptions of Thai Legislators," *Western Political Quarterly* 25 (1972): 686–701.

40. Blondel, *Comparative Legislatures*, p. 4.

41. Laxmi Singhvi, "Parliament in the Indian Political System," in Allan Kornberg, ed., *Legislatures in Developmental Perspective* (Durham: Duke University Press, 1970), p. 217.

42. See Christopher Grill, *The Public Side of Representation: A Study of Citizens' Views About Representatives and the Representative Process* (Albany, NY: State University of New York Press, 2007), or Tracy Sulkin, *Issue Politics in Congress* (New York: Cambridge University Press, 2005).

43. See Anthony Nownes, *Total Lobbying: What Lobbyists Want (And How They Try to Get It)* (New York: Cambridge University Press, 2006).

44. See Cliff Zukin, *A New Engagement? Political Participation, Civic Life, and the Changing American Citizen* (New York: Oxford University Press, 2006).

45. Eldin Fahmy, *Young Citizens: Young People's Involvement in Politics and Decision Making* (Burlington, VT: Ashgate, 2006), or Jennifer Lawless, *It Takes a Candidate: Why Women Don't Run for Office* (New York: Cambridge University Press, 2005).

46. Malcolm Jewell covers the literature in this area in his essay "Legislators and Constituents in the Representative Process," in Loewenberg, Patterson, and Jewell, *Handbook*, pp. 97–134.

47. For discussion of Burke's views, see George H. Sabine, *A History of Political Theory* (New York: Holt, Rinehart and Winston, 1961), p. 610, or Ian Crowe, *An Imaginative Whig: Reassessing the Life and Thought of Edmund Burke* (Columbia, MO: University of Missouri Press, 2005).

48. A good example of discussion of such an issue is in Johanna Birnir, *Ethnicity and Electoral Politics* (New York: Cambridge University Press, 2007).

49. See Margaret Conway, Gertrude Steuernagel, and David Ahern, *Women and Political Participation: Cultural Change in the Political Arena* (Washington, DC: CQ Press, 2005); or Manon Tremblay, *Sharing Power: Women, Parliament, Democracy* (Burlington, VT: Ashgate, 2005). See also Miki Kittilson, *Challenging Parties, Changing Parliaments: Women and Elected Office in Contemporary Western Europe* (Columbus, OH: Ohio State University Press, 2006); and Louise Chappell and Lisa Hill, *The Politics of Women's Interests: New Comparative Perspectives* (New York: Routledge, 2006).

50. See Gary Segura and Shaun Bowler, eds., *Diversity in Democracy: Minority Representation in the United States* (Charlottesville, VA: University of Virginia Press, 2005); or Christina Wolbrecht and Rodney Hero, *The Politics of Democratic Inclusion* (Philadelphia, PA: Temple University Press, 2005).

51. Raymond Hopkins, "The Role of the M.P. in Tanzania," *American Political Science Review* 64 (1970): 754.

52. LaPalombara, *Politics Within Nations*, pp. 180–182, and Jewell and Patterson, *Legislative Process*, respectively.

53. This is discussed in Trish Payne, *Backbenchers and the Press Gallery* (Canberra: Department of the Parliamentary Library, 1997).

54. Curtis, *Comparative Government and Politics*, p. 158.

55. See Reuven Hazan, *Reforming Parliamentary Committees: Israel in Comparative Perspective* (Columbus, OH: Ohio State University Press, 2001), for one good case study on committees with a very good theoretical introduction. For a good description of the British case, see Patrick Dunleavy, *Developments in British Politics* (New York: St. Martin's Press, 2000).

56. See David Judge, *Backbench Specialization in the House of Commons* (Burlington, VT: Ashgate Publishing, 1982).

57. John Baughman, *Common Ground: Committee Politics in the U.S. House of Representatives* (Stanford, CA: Stanford University Press, 2006).

58. See Walter Oleszek, *Congressional Procedures and the Policy Process* (Washington, DC: CQ Press, 2007), or Jack Davies, *Legislative Law and Process in a Nutshell* (St. Paul, MN: Thomson/West, 2007).

59. See David Marsh and Melvyn Read, *Private Members' Bills* (New York: Cambridge University Press, 1988).

60. See Weiss and Brichta, "Private Members' Bills," p. 25.

61. See William Howell and Jon Pevehouse, eds., *While Dangers Gather: Congressional Checks on Presidential War Powers* (Princeton, NJ: Princeton University Press, 2007), or James Thurber, ed., *Rivals for Power: Presidential-Congressional Relations* (Lanham, MD: Rowman and Littlefield, 2006).

62. See, for an example of this argument, Pendleton Herring, *Presidential Leadership: The Political Relations of Congress and the Chief Executive* (New Brunswick, NJ: Transaction, 2006).

63. See especially the classic argument of Samuel P. Huntington, "Congressional Responses to the Twentieth Century," in *Congress and the President,* ed. Ronald Moe (Pacific Palisades, CA: Goodyear Publishing Co., 1971), pp. 7–31.

64. See John Garrett, *Westminster: Does Parliament Work?* (London: Trafalgar Square, 1993).

65. See for issues related to economic development, Alex Brazier, *Parliament at the Apex: Parliamentary Scrutiny and Regulatory Bodies* (London: Hansard Society, 2003); and Leslie Seidle and David Docherty, *Reforming Parliamentary Democracy* (Montreal: McGill-Queen's University Press, 2003).

66. On this note see David Judge, ed., "Why Reform? Parliamentary Reform Since 1832: An Interpretation," in *The Politics of Parliamentary Reform* (Rutherford, NJ: Fairleigh Dickinson University Press, 1984), pp. 9–36.

Executive Institutions

The traditional "brotherhood" of prime ministers is today increasingly frequently including

INTRODUCTION: THE EXECUTIVE ROLES

When John Locke wrote that the state of nature lacked "power to back and support" the sentence of a national judiciary,[1] he was speaking of an executive power. There is much difference, however, between the kind of executive power that Locke had in mind and the kind of political executive that we find in most contemporary political systems.

What does an executive do in a political system today? In his classic study of the American presidency, Clinton Rossiter listed ten distinct, identifiable

1. Chief of State	6. Chief of Party
2. Chief Executive	7. Voice of the People
3. Commander-in-Chief	8. Protector of Peace
4. Chief Diplomat	9. Manager of Prosperity
5. Chief Legislator	10. World Leader[2]

roles that the president is expected to play in the American political arena, and these roles transfer to the parliamentary system, too:

When we look at this list of duties that the president performs, we must marvel that anyone is able to handle the demands of the office. Indeed, this was one of the major themes of Rossiter's study. Wouldn't a political system be more efficiently run if it hired a *crew* of executives to handle all of these jobs? Actually, the concept of a *multiple executive* is not new; in a number of different contexts in history the multiple executive has been tried. At the Federal Convention in Philadelphia in 1787, where the American Constitution was created, the idea of a multiple executive was suggested. It was rejected, however, because history had shown that it might tend to (1) cause divisiveness when a difficult decision needed to be made, and (2) obscure responsibility, or culpability, since blame for a bad decision might be difficult to attribute to a single individual.[3]

In fact, Rossiter's list of ten roles for the president may be more detailed than is necessary. Political history has shown that we really only need to separate the executive role into two components: a symbolic role, and a political role.[4] In the symbolic role, the executive represents the dignity of the state. The executive lays wreaths on tombs, makes national proclamations, and generally serves a ceremonial function. In the political role, the chief executive "manages the national business," and makes the hard political decisions that need to be made, being the owner of the desk where "the buck stops."[5]

There are, generally speaking, four approaches to the executive institution that are found in political systems around the world, two of which we shall examine at this time. We will see in greater detail in the second part of this text that all political systems have their idiosyncratic differences, but at this stage of our study we are concerned with explaining the general models.

One general type of political executive can be referred to as the *presidential* model of executive, and the other type of political executive can be referred to as the *"Westminster" parliamentary-cabinet* form of executive. Later in this text we will add discussion of the *French parliamentary-cabinet* model and the *collective executive* model (although the model that was developed in the former Soviet Union has become virtually extinct in recent years); these are variations on the two models we shall discuss at this time. As we did with our discussion of legislatures, we will preface our descriptions of executives by saying that what we are about to describe will vary in specific detail from country to country.

THE PRESIDENTIAL AND PARLIAMENTARY EXECUTIVES

The type of political executive that American students know best is the presidential executive. American students are often surprised to learn, however, that the presidential model of executive behavior is in a minority beyond the borders of the United States.

The **presidential executive** model centralizes both political power and symbolic authority in one individual, the president. The president is the individual presiding at ceremonial functions, and it is the president who symbolizes the nation in the eyes of the rest of the world. The president is the head of state. Foreign diplomats present their credentials to him. (Although a number of countries have had women presidents, we will use the masculine pronoun here.) He presents the State of the Union message to the Congress each year. He throws out the first baseball to open the baseball season.[6]

Presidential systems do not separate the symbolic and the business functions of the office. Some have suggested that since the American government has the institution of the vice presidency, which has few constitutional duties and the primary significance of which is not in what it is but in what it might become,[7] a good use of the vice president might be to assign to him or her the ceremonial duties of office and leave the president to important decision-making duties. The problem is that vice presidents do not want to spend all of their time at funerals and ceremonies. Moreover, the public does not accept the idea either; the vice president is, after all, the second officer of American government, not the first, and the public wants to see the president.[8]

The strength of the presidency is in its independence. In the American system, the model for presidential systems elsewhere, the chief executive is elected independently from the legislature. Presidential elections in the United States are held every four years, no more frequently and no less frequently. It is the fixed term of the president and the corresponding security in office that contribute in a significant way to the president's base of power.[9]

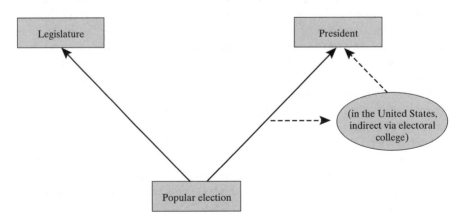

FIGURE 4.1
Presidential Systems' Bases of Power

As indicated in Figure 4.1, the president is independently elected on the basis of popular election. The American political system has an additional structure between the populace and the president, the electoral college, which officially elects the president. The genesis of the electoral college is based upon the Founders' distrust of popular will. The Founders felt that by having voters choose electors, who would subsequently cast ballots for the presidency, their concern could be resolved.[10] Recent American political history—including the quite extraordinary presidential election of 2000—has shown the electoral college to be an anachronistic institution, and efforts are regularly undertaken to do away with the institution and to have the president directly elected by the public. Most other presidential systems do not have an electoral college structure, but instead have voters cast their votes directly for the presidential candidates campaigning for office.

The fact that the American public votes in several different electoral contests—once for the president and vice president (literally for electors for the president and vice president), and once for the House of Representatives (all seats in the House of Representatives come up for reelection every two years), and, where a contest is held, once for the Senate (Senate seats have six-year terms and are staggered so that both seats in any given state are not up for election at the same time)—is quite significant for a number of reasons. First, it gives the president an independent power base. Short of the process of impeachment, which history had shown until the term of President Bill Clinton could be instituted only for high crimes and treason and not simply for reasons of political opposition,[11] the president does not depend upon either the legislature or public opinion for continuation of his four-year term. Once he is in office, this individual remains in office until the term is completed. This allows the president to take actions that may be unpopular with both the public and the legislature in the short term, but which the president feels, nonetheless, are the right actions to take.

A second point to note is that this relationship works in the other direction, too. That is, legislators are chosen by the people, not by the president; as long as they keep their constituencies happy they can act independently of the president, and there is virtually nothing that the president can do to them.[12] As indicated, members of the House of Representatives are elected for two-year terms, and although the president may threaten not to campaign for them in the next election (or even may threaten to campaign against them) if they don't do what he wants, the president cannot directly affect the duration of their time in office. He cannot fire them, as most prime ministers can threaten to do with members of parliament in their political systems. And, their more frequent election allows the public the opportunity to send a message to the government with the more frequent turnover of the House, such as took place in 2010 with the electoral repudiation of some of the policies of President Barack Obama who was elected in 2008.

Senators are elected to six-year terms, and they, in a similar manner, are secure in their office.[13] A president might be angry when a senator from his party fails to support the president's legislation in the Senate, but there is little the president can do to directly punish a recalcitrant senator, short of threatening to withhold future support.[14]

A third significant point to note is that this structural independence of the branches of government (depicted in Figure 4.1) can have negative consequences.

Because both the executive and legislative branches of government have secure tenure in office, they can frustrate each other, but that is all they can do. The president can veto acts of Congress, but Congress can override the presidential veto. (The president of the United States does not have an "absolute" veto that is impossible to override, although presidents in some other systems do possess such absolute vetoes.) Congress can refuse to pass a legislative request of the president, but the president can often try to accomplish his goals through executive decrees, executive agreements, and similar unilateral executive actions.

It is important to recall that the president is not part of the legislative branch of government, and cannot, literally, take part in the legislative process. Only senators can introduce bills in the Senate, and only representatives can introduce bills in the House. If the president is unable to find a legislative "sponsor" for a bill (something that, realistically, is unimaginable!), he would be unable to introduce new legislation. This situation can deteriorate to a point of **immobilism;** each actor has enough power to block the other, but not enough to achieve its own objectives, which means that it is possible that nothing will be accomplished.

This situation is most evident in the United States when the executive and legislative branches of government are controlled by the two major political parties. When Richard Nixon (a Republican) was president he faced a Senate and House controlled by Democrats; the relationship between the two branches of government was often tense.[15] This was repeated during the term of (Republican) Ronald Reagan in the 1980s. For some of that time, Congress was partly controlled by Democrats (a Republican-controlled Senate and a Democratic-controlled House), and for some of that time it was fully controlled by a Democratic majority in both houses. This situation continued through the presidency of George H. W. Bush. Although Nixon, Reagan, and Bush were able to get the support of some Southern (and other more conservative) Democrats, as a general rule much tension existed between the two branches. The same general situation existed with (Democrat) Bill Clinton facing Republican majorities in both Houses of Congress through most of the 1990's.

Following the midterm election of 2010, the Democratic control of the White House and both houses of Congress ended, and the Republican party controlled the House of Representatives with a significant majority. This had significant results in terms of President Barack Obama's ability to press forward with legislation on a strictly partisan basis as he had done during his first two years as president.

Party difference is not a requirement for this kind of tension, however. The four years of Jimmy Carter (a Democratic president with a Democratic Congress) were not terribly productive, either, and often witnessed the same tension, despite the fact that both branches were controlled by Democrats. After his inauguration, Carter proposed an energy program, labeled as "the moral equivalent of war." By the time the Congress acted, (over two years later), Carter's original legislative proposals bore little resemblance to the legislation produced by the Congress.[16]

In brief, although the executive and legislative branches of government in a presidential system *may* pull in tandem, they do not *necessarily* do so, and the structure of the independently selected presidency and legislative branch does enable the state of immobilism to develop.

THE PARLIAMENTARY EXECUTIVE

The **parliamentary executive** is more complex than its presidential alternative, if for no other reason than it is a multiple executive.[17] The ceremonial function and the decision-making function are performed by two different individuals, whose titles vary by political system (see Table 4.1), and to whom we can generically refer as the *head of state* and the *chief executive*, respectively.

The **head of state** symbolizes the state and the dignity of the political regime. The head of state receives ambassadors, hosts receptions, and performs many of the ceremonial tasks government requires. Heads of state, generally, are chosen one of three ways. First, in a number of political systems—about a third of all parliamentary systems—the head of state is a hereditary position, one that "belongs" to a royal family. Certainly among the best-known examples of this manner of selection is the British monarchy, with a clearly delineated line of succession.

A second pattern of selection is one in which the head of state is selected by a governmental body, often the legislature. The president of India is elected by the combined membership of the Indian Parliament, the Lok Sabha and the Rajya Sabha. A third method of selection has been referred to as "self-selection," and is characteristic of political systems in which power has been seized, such as the position of Fidel Castro in Cuba, or the now-toppled position of Idi Amin as president-for-life in Uganda.[18]

The chief executive, on the other hand, is the chief of the executive branch of government.[19] The chief executive is a full-time politician, devoting less time to ceremonial duties of office. Generally speaking, the chief executive in a parliamentary regime performs the same *executive* tasks as the chief executive in a presidential regime, but not the *symbolic* activities. Both executives coordinate government policy-making. Both executives are assisted by cabinets of individuals heading separate departments or ministries of government. Both executives are responsible for the day-to-day operation of government.

TABLE 4.1

Executive Titles

Nation	Model of Government	Head of State	Chief Executive
Australia	Parliamentary	Governor-general[a]	Prime minister
Canada	Parliamentary	Governor-general[a]	Prime minister
Germany	Parliamentary	President	Chancellor
India	Parliamentary	President	Prime minister
Israel	Parliamentary	President	Prime minister
Italy	Parliamentary	President	Prime minister
Japan	Parliamentary	Emperor	Prime minister
Mexico	Presidential	President	President
United Kingdom	Parliamentary	Queen	Prime minister
United States	Presidential	President	President

[a] Serving on behalf of the monarch in his or her absence.

In many political systems, the position of chief executive is totally without *legal* basis, but instead is founded upon years of political custom and tradition—which we have noted can be just as important as written constitutional measures. In other systems the position is legally entrenched and described in detail in constitutional documents.[20] The manner in which the office of the chief executive in parliamentary systems was created is significant in telling us a great deal about both the position of the chief executive and the manner in which that position relates to the position of the head of state.

The Changing Role of the Monarchy

When we discuss the development of parliamentary government, we are, in fact, discussing British political history (just as we are discussing American political history when we speak of the development of the presidential model of government). Although many parliamentary systems today differ from the contemporary British system, the parliamentary system of government as we know it was born in England, and is generally regarded as starting with Robert Walpole as prime minister in 1741. A brief survey of nine centuries of political history may help us to understand and appreciate the role of the monarchy today.[21]

When William, Duke of Normandy, took the English throne in 1066 there existed a political structure called the *witenagemot*, a legislative assembly of sorts, which formally elected him king. William the Conqueror (as he became known) extended and formalized the feudal system during his tenure, and institutionalized the *Curia Regis*, the King's Court, as a political body. At this time there was no distinction among the legislative, executive, and judicial functions of government (John Locke was not to come onto the scene for another 600 years!): All government was the king. The king used the Curia Regis as a source of funds, and in return for members' financial support he listened to their counsel and advice, although he was clearly not bound to accept it.

In 1215, the group of barons of the realm that had made up the Curia Regis drew up a document that was called the *Magna Carta*, describing what the barons considered to be the proper relationship between the king and themselves. It is important to note that this was not a declaration of *new* rights and privileges; rather, it was an expression of what the barons asserted *to have been* the relationship for some time. They argued that the king had been forgetting some of the powers that kings had already given to barons and the public. This "Great Charter" was a significant constitutional document. It expounded upon political obligations of the time: peoples' obligations to the king, the king's obligations to the people, and how law and justice should be administered.

During the thirteenth century the financial resources of the barons of the Curia Regis were not sufficient for the needs of government, and the Curia Regis called upon representatives of towns and counties for "aids"—financial help. In exchange for their financial contributions, representatives of the towns and counties were admitted to the Curia Regis alongside the barons, thus giving the Curia Regis two classes of members: the earlier baronial membership, which became the House of Lords, and its new (and often elected) membership, which became the House of Commons. The term *parliament* (in French the verb *parler* means "to speak") was first used during the thirteenth century to refer to the debating function of these bodies.

Because the king was receiving financial assistance from both groups, he was now obligated to discuss public affairs not only with the baronial nobility, but also with the representatives of the commoners. The public's representatives had an important weapon in their hands to insure that they were listened to: the right to assent, or refuse to assent, to the king's proposals for raising and spending money. Parliament, especially the House of Commons, used this power as a condition with the king: its approval of royal financial proposals in exchange for the king's attention to public grievances. By about the year 1500, the Commons had grown in political strength to the point at which it could introduce proposals on its own to change laws, and could offer amendments to bills that had originated in the House of Lords, the superior house of the legislature.

The seventeenth century saw the legislature's power grow in relation to the monarch, and it was a period of much stress. King James I, who reigned from 1603 to 1625, was an advocate of the **divine right of kings** theory,[22] which argued that the monarch derived his power directly from God, not from the people. James had little need for Parliament as an institution, and he argued that any privileges of Parliament were gifts from the King, not rights of Parliament. During James's twenty-two year reign, Parliament sat for only eight years. On a number of occasions he "dissolved" the House of Commons, declared that they were not "truly" elected, and sent them home—in effect, he fired them. This was the introduction of the monarch's power to "dissolve" the legislature today.

Charles I succeeded his father, James I, in 1625, and followed his father's practice of imprisoning members of Parliament (especially, of course, members of the House of Commons) who opposed him. When Charles could not control a Parliament, he dissolved it and called for new elections after a period of time. By 1640, Charles was in need of funds and convened Parliament to authorize new taxes. The Commons refused; Only three week later Charles again dissolved Parliament. This became known as the "Short Parliament."

Six months later another Parliament assembled; it became known as the "Long Parliament." The issue upon which the election for the House of Commons had been held was the question of whether the king should rule Parliament, or Parliament should rule the king. Within two years an armed struggle ensued (referred to as the English Civil War, 1642–1648) between supporters of the king and supporters of the Parliament. Eventually the royal army was defeated, and Charles was captured and sentenced to death as "a tyrant, traitor, murderer, and public enemy" following a trial in 1649. The Commons dissolved the monarchy and established a republic, led by Oliver Cromwell. In 1660, the Long Parliament dissolved itself, and the Convention that was elected to take its place restored the Stuart family to the throne; Charles II, the son of Charles I, became king of England.

Through the reigns of Charles II (1660–1685) and his brother James II (1685–1688), the tensions between Parliament and the monarch grew again, and in 1688 James II fled, and parliament held that because he had fled the throne was now empty. Parliament then invited William, Prince of Orange, and grandson of Charles I, to rule, and William and his wife, Mary (who was James's older daughter), were proclaimed king and queen by Parliament in 1688.

During the reign of William and Mary, the English constitutional system became much more stable; indeed, it laid much of the groundwork for stable constitutional government to come. The British Bill of Rights (1689)—which asserted that taxes could be raised only with the assent of Parliament, guaranteed the people the right to petition the king, limited the use of the army without the consent of Parliament, guaranteed free elections and freedom of speech and debate in Parliament, limited excessive bail, prohibited "cruel and unusual punishment," and asserted that Parliament ought to meet frequently—became law. Parliament became institutionalized as a significant political actor in the English system of government.

Constitutional Monarchy

Over the last three centuries, the relationship between the monarch and the Parliament has evolved to a point that not even William and Mary would recognize it. *De jure*, under law, most powers of the British government (and in a parallel fashion parliamentary governments, generally) are still exercised in the name of the king or queen (or whatever the title of the head of state is in the political system), but today they are invariably exercised "on the advice" of the chief executive.

In the eighteenth and nineteenth centuries, the king relied more and more on his **cabinet**, a group of advisors, for guidance. In the early eighteenth century the role of the cabinet was only that of providing advice; the king still could do as he pleased. As ideas of democratic and republican government grew over the next two centuries, the power relationship changed so that the king and queen were now *obligated*, although *not* legally required, to accept the advice of their cabinets. The cabinet by now was primarily chosen from the house of Parliament elected by the public, the House of Commons. Now the cabinet was in reality governing in the name of the king or queen, and without consulting him or her.

Among the most striking characteristics of parliamentary government today is the duality of its executive leadership that we referred to earlier. The monarch is the official (*de jure*) head of state, but the active (*de facto*) head of government is the prime minister. Appointments are made, acts of Parliament or the legislature are proclaimed, and all government is carried on in the name of the monarch, although it is the prime minister and his or her cabinet who make all of the selections for appointments, who author or sponsor legislative proposals, and who make the administrative decisions that keep government running.

The legal bases for the prime minister and cabinet are rare, as we noted earlier, and in many political systems both the prime minister and cabinet are (legally) constitutionally nonexistent institutions. In the case of Great Britain (and many Commonwealth nations), the legal claim to power of the cabinet is derived from the fact that, ever since the seventeenth century the monarch has had a **Privy Council** to advise him or her—a kind of present-day cabinet. Today, although the Privy Council is no longer active, cabinet members are first made members of the Privy Council, and then are appointed to the cabinet. The cabinet meets as a "subcommittee" of the (inactive) Privy Council, and acts in the name of the Privy Council, a body that *does* have constitutional and legal status. Discussing the relationship between the Canadian cabinet and the Queen's Privy Council for Canada, R. MacGregor Dawson noted:

> Those appointed to the Privy Council remain members for life, and hence will include not only ministers from the present Cabinet, but also all surviving ministers of past Cabinets as well. The Privy Council would therefore, if active, be a large and politically cumbersome body with members continually at cross-purposes with one another; but it has saved itself from this embarrassment by the simple device of holding no meetings.
>
> The Cabinet, lacking any legal status of its own, masquerades as the Privy Council when it desires to assume formal power; it speaks and acts in the name of the entire Council.[23]

The Selection of the Chief Executive

Although the British monarch may have felt free to chose whomever he or she wanted as advisors in the seventeenth and eighteenth centuries, such is no longer the case today. The process by which the head of state in a parliamentary political system selects the chief executive is another one of those patterns of behavior that may legally (*de jure*) be entirely up to the head of state, but practically and politically (*de facto*) the head of state usually has little or no choice in the matter at all.

In the model found in most parliamentary nations, unlike their presidential counterparts, there is no special election for the **chief executive**.[24] The chief executive is elected as a member of the legislature, just as all of the other members of the legislature are elected. Elections for the legislature are held on a regular basis, which varies with the political system. In Britain, the term of the House of Commons is limited to five years.

After the elections for legislative seats have taken place (a process that we described earlier), it is the duty of the head of state to "invite" someone to create a Government. (It should be noted at this point that the term **Government** with a capital *G* has a specific meaning in this volume: the prime minister and the cabinet; **government** with a lowercase *g* refers to the general structures of the political system.) Although the head of state in most systems is technically free to select whomever he or she wants for the Government, in practice and custom (*de facto*) heads of state are required to invite the leader of the largest political party in the legislature—a recognition of the will of the people—as indicated in Figure 4.2.[25]

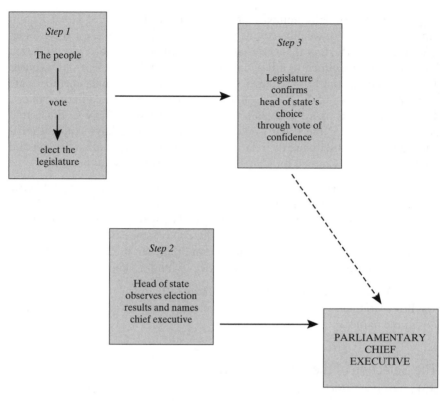

FIGURE 4.2
The Selection of the Parliamentary Chief Executive

Once the head of state designates an individual to create a Government, that individual will subsequently advise the head of state as to whom to appoint to the cabinet. After the new Government (the new prime minister and the new cabinet) has been assembled, in most political systems that Government must first receive a **vote of confidence** from the legislature before it assumes power. The vote of confidence is a vote by a majority of the legislature indicating its confidence in, or support for, the prime minister and his or her cabinet. (Keep in mind that the vote of confidence will typically involve only the lower house of the legislature—the House of Commons in Britain—and will generally not involve the upper house at all.)

In most political systems, if the Government does not receive a vote of confidence—if it receives the support of less than a majority of the legislature in a vote—it cannot take office, and another Government must be designated by the head of state. Britain represents an exception to the general rule that newly designated Governments need votes of confidence. In Britain, and many other Commonwealth nations (the term "Commonwealth" refers to the family of independent nations today that were part of the British Empire), the designation by the head of state *assumes* legislative confidence (i.e., the head of state wouldn't make the appointment without making sure of legislative support first), and the Government assumes power immediately, without first needing an expression of confidence from the legislature.

The institution of the vote of confidence is an indication of **legislative supremacy** in the political system. That is, the legislature "hires" the chief executive (although the head of state may "nominate" him or her) or invests him or her with power. The chancellor in Germany, as well as the prime minister in Japan or India, to cite just a few examples, assumes power only *after* receiving a majority vote of support in their respective legislatures.

This legislative power works in the other direction, too. Just as the legislature "hires" the executive, by expressing support in one of its members forming a Government, it can "fire" the executive by expressing a *lack* of support or confidence in the Government. Whenever the chief executive loses the confidence of the legislature, whenever the legislature passes a resolution of **no confidence** (or, conversely, fails to pass a legislative expression of confidence), the chief executive is, in fact, fired. Even if the legislature expresses a lack of confidence in the chief executive only a week after that person has assumed office, he or she must resign. In some systems this resignation is a legal requirement; elsewhere it is simply a custom that has the force of law.[26] In some systems a vote of no confidence is not even required to fire a chief executive: If the Government is defeated on *any* major piece of legislation, that is considered to be an expression of a lack of confidence in the Government. It should be added that in most parliamentary systems, with their strong tradition of party discipline and the ability of the prime minister to muster a majority, votes of no confidence are very rare. They do, however, happen from time to time, especially if the Government does not control a substantial legislative majority.

When the prime minister resigns, we have a case of the **Government falling**. A Government "falls" when either of two things happens: It loses on a question of confidence or a major piece of legislation, leading the prime minister to resign, or the prime minister resigns for some other reason. The resignation of an individual minister does not cause a Government to fall, but the resignation of the prime minister does cause the Government to fall.[27]

The prime minister in a parliamentary system, then, does not have the job security of a president in a presidential system. The prime minister is selected by the head of state to be chief executive precisely because he or she is typically the leader of the largest party in the legislature. If this individual's party controls a majority of the legislative seats, and if the prime minister can maintain that majority through party discipline, this person should be able to remain prime minister for the entire term of the legislature (and perhaps several terms of the legislature since there are usually no term limits in parliamentary government). If, however, the prime minister does not control a majority, or if the prime minister is not able to retain the support of a majority of the legislature, his or her tenure may be brief.

Of course, if there is a party with a majority, the head of state will have to appoint its leader to be prime minister. (Obviously, if the head of state appointed anyone else, the majority party would make sure that the new Government failed to receive a vote of confidence.) If there is no majority party, one of three situations is possible. First, the head of state may appoint someone to head a **minority government,** one in which the prime minister does not control over 50 percent of the seats in the legislature. Minority governments tend to be short-lived. They usually obtain an initial vote of confidence through a temporary understanding among a number of parties that do not want to have to contest another election right away, and that see a minority government as the least unattractive alternative at the time. These understandings usually break down after a short while and result in a no-confidence vote and the fall of the Government.[28]

A second alternative to a majority party is for the head of state to appoint someone to form a coalition government. A **coalition government** is one in which two or more non-majority parties pool their legislative seats to form a majority parliamentary bloc. There may well be a formal agreement drawn up among the participants in the coalition, in which they agree to team up and create a majority in the legislature to support a Government. We will further discuss coalition governments shortly.

The third alternative, and one usually not taken right away, is for the head of state to not form *any* Government, but instead to **dissolve the legislature**—fire the newly elected legislators—and call for new elections in the hope that the next elections will result in one party winning a clear mandate. This usually is not taken as a first resort, but if the head of state appoints a minority government, which falls within a short period of time, it may be clear to him or her that political stability is simply not possible with the legislature constituted in its current form. If such is the case, the head of state may dissolve the legislature and call for new elections by issuing a **writ of dissolution.**[29]

The chief executive, then, is selected by the head of state *from* the legislature. The chief executive retains his or her position as long as the legislature continues to express support for the Government by approving the proposals of the Government. The concept of party discipline is very important, for it is party discipline that enables the prime minister to control the legislature. There is a circular relationship at work here: The prime minister is selected to be prime minister precisely because he or she is the chosen leader of the largest party in the legislature. This person will remain prime minister as long as he or she can control a majority of the legislature. When a majority cannot be controlled, a motion of no confidence will be passed, and the prime minister will be forced (through either law or custom) to resign.

At this point it is *not* necessary that new elections be held. The head of state must now reassess the situation and may invite someone else (or perhaps even the same person who last failed) to try to form a new Government and receive an expression of legislative confidence. This process—a Government being designated, receiving a vote of confidence, surviving for a period of time, receiving a vote of no confidence and falling, a new Government being designated, and so on—can go on until the term of the legislature is completed, over and over again, until the Head of State decides that there is no point in trying again. At that point the head of state will issue a writ of dissolution, "dissolving" (firing) the legislature (much as we noted Charles I did in 1640), and will call for new elections. Thus the entire process starts again, as indicated in Figure 4.3.

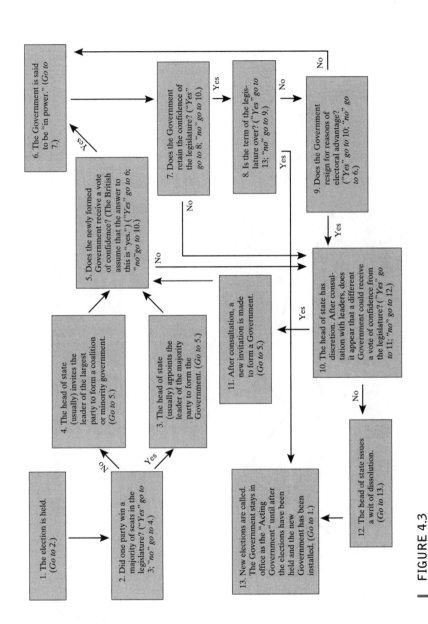

FIGURE 4.3
The Government-Formation Process: A Flow Chart Presentation

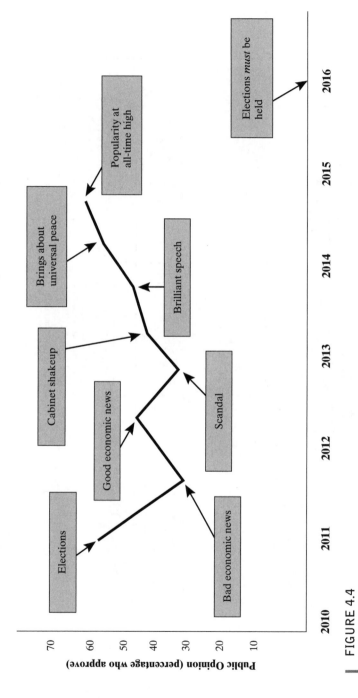

FIGURE 4.4

Government Falling as a Result of Fluctuation in Public Opinion, 2010–2016

It occasionally happens that a chief executive will *cause* his or her own Government to fall, for what we can describe as reasons of *electoral advantage*. Let us suppose that in a hypothetical political system the constitution requires that elections be held at least every five years (as is the case in Great Britain), and elections are held in January of 2011 that result in the Liberal party winning 56 of the 100 seats in the legislature, and the Conservative party winning the remaining 44 seats. The leader of the Liberal party, I. Maginary, becomes prime minister. As time goes by, Maginary's popularity, and correspondingly the popularity of his Liberal party, fluctuates up and down, depending upon economic factors, world events, and so on.

Prime Minister Maginary knows that if the present Government can keep the majority in the legislature satisfied, the constitution will require that elections be held *by* January 2016 (five years after the last election). In early 2014, three years into the term of the legislature but almost two years before elections must be held, Maginary's popularity is at an all-time high, as depicted in Figure 4.4. After some discussion with political advisors, the Maginary Government resigns and asks the head of state to dissolve the legislature and to call for new elections. They do this because they feel that if the elections are held now, they may win control of the legislature by an *even bigger* margin than they did in 2011, and the five-year term of government will start anew. The head of state has no real choice in the matter: Maginary's Liberal party controls a majority in the legislature, and supports Maginary's decision to call for early elections. If the head of state were to refuse to dissolve the legislature, and tried to name some other leader (such as the leader of the opposition Conservative party) to form a Government, the Maginary-Liberal group would vote the new Government down by a 56–44 vote. The head of state, then, grants Prime Minister Maginary a dissolution and calls for new elections to be held, typically in eight to ten weeks. During the interim period, the Maginary Government continues in office as the "Acting" Government, and Maginary's title is "Acting Prime Minister" until the next election is held and a new Prime Minister (likely Maginary) is designated by the head of state.

Although the example just presented is hypothetical, the situation it depicts happens regularly in parliamentary systems. In recent years, dissolutions of this type have taken place in Japan, France, Great Britain, Canada, Belgium, and India, among other nations.

COALITION GOVERNMENTS

In political systems that have more than two major political parties it regularly is the case that no single party controls a majority in the legislature. (Clearly, in a two-party system we don't have this problem. Unless there is a tie—which is quite rare—one of the two parties must, by definition, have more than half of the legislative seats.) Where no party has a majority, as was indicated previously, several options are available to the head of state in the creation of a Government. The most commonly utilized option is the creation of a coalition government.

TABLE 4.2	
A Hypothetical Legislative Composition	
Party A	33 seats
Party B	20 seats
Party C	18 seats
Party D	16 seats
Party E	13 seats

Let us take a hypothetical newly elected legislature to use as an example as we discuss the process of coalition formation. Imagine a 100-seat legislature with five political parties, as described in Table 4.2.

In this instance, the head of state would most likely invite the leader of Party A to form a Government, since Leader A has the largest popular mandate. We should note, however, that in most systems the head of state is not *required* to invite Leader A; the head of state can invite anyone whom she or he feels has the best chance to form a coalition successfully. Leader A needs to find an additional 18 seats in order to form a majority of 51 to support her Government in the legislature. In this case, Leader A could go to either the leader of Party B, or the leader of Party C, to find a partner. As well, of course, Leader A could go to more than one other party, to try to form an ABC coalition, for example.

Usually, Leader A will have to promise the leaders of other parties involved in the coalition some reward for joining the coalition. In most instances, this reward is a cabinet position (or several cabinet positions). Sometimes the payoff is a promise that a certain piece of legislation that the prospective coalition partner has drafted will be passed as part of the Government's program.[30] Sometimes both types of payoff are required.

If Leader A can reach an agreement with one or more partners to form a coalition that will control a majority of the seats in the legislature, then Leader A will receive his or her vote of confidence, and the Government can be said to be installed. If, however, Leader A cannot find sufficient coalition partnership within a constitutionally mandated period of time, usually two to three weeks, then Leader A must return her "mandate" to the head of state and inform the head of state of her inability to form a coalition.

At this point, as indicated earlier, the head of state makes a decision. The head of state could dissolve the legislature and call for new elections, with the hope that in another election a party seeking seats in the next legislature might win a majority, or at least a large enough plurality to be able to form a coalition easily; or the head of state could invite some other party leader to try to form a government. In our hypothetical example, the head of state at this point might turn to Leader B to see whether that person could form a coalition.

The process then goes on and on in this fashion. At each occasion that a Government fails to retain the confidence, or support, of a majority in the legislature—that is, a motion of no confidence introduced by the opposition passes, or a motion of confidence introduced by a Government supporter fails—the head of state must decide whether another leader might be able to succeed. Elections, after all, are expensive, and usually divisive, and one doesn't want to have a national election every six months.

Coalition majority governments tend to be less stable than single-party majority governments in parliamentary systems.[31] In a single-party majority system, the prime minister must be concerned with party discipline keeping followers in his or her party in line. In a coalition system, the flow of power is more diffuse. The prime minister exercises party discipline over his or her party followers, and counts on the leader(s) of the partner coalition party or parties to do the same. Coalitions usually fail because of differences between party leaders—in our example above, because Leader B has a disagreement with Leader A and pulls the support of Party B out of the AB coalition—*not* because of a failure of party discipline within either Party A or Party B.[32]

As might be expected, the complexity of the coalition-formation process is a direct function of the number of political parties in a legislature.[33] In the example in Table 4.3, it is clear that Situation I is most simple, Situation II more complex, and Situation III even more complex. The more parties there are, the more possibilities there are for a winning coalition to form; the more

TABLE 4.3

The Complexity of the Coalition-Formation Process

Party	Seats	Majority Possibilities
Situation I: Simplest		
Party A	44 seats	AB, AC, BC, ABC
Party B	42 seats	
Party C	14 seats	
Situation II: More Complex		
Party A	38 seats	AB, AC, AD, ABC, ABD,
Party B	20 seats	ABE, ACD, ACE, etc.
Party C	17 seats	
Party D	15 seats	
Party E	10 seats	
Situation III: Most Complex		
Party A	30 seats	ABC, ABD, ABE, ABF, ABG
Party B	19 seats	BCDE, CDEFGH, etc.
Party C	12 seats	
Party D	9 seats	
Party E	8 seats	
Party F	8 seats	
Party G	7 seats	
Party H	7 seats	

partners there are in a coalition, the more possibilities there are for intracoalition conflict to cause a coalition to fall apart.

PRESIDENTIAL AND PARLIAMENTARY SYSTEMS: SOME COMPARISONS

Clearly, there are a number of major and significant differences in structure between the presidential and the parliamentary-cabinet system. A question for us to ask at this time is: What are the *behavioral* implications of the differences between the two systems, and how will the two systems differ in terms of policy output and day-to-day operation? Several significant dimensions of difference are mentioned here.

The first distinction has to do with the idea of **responsible government.** Responsible government in this context does not mean trustworthy, or rational government, but instead refers to the Government's *ability* to *deliver* on its promises. Responsible government comes about in parliamentary systems through some of the structural characteristics we have already met. The idea of *party discipline* suggests that legislators will vote (and speak and act) in the manner that their party leader suggests. The selection of the prime minister as leader of the largest party in the legislature and the notion of the *vote of confidence* ensure that the prime minister will always have the support of (and therefore, because of party discipline, be able to control) a majority of the legislature. Consequently, whatever the prime minister wants will have the approval of a majority of the legislature. If the prime minister's proposals do not receive a parliamentary majority, of course, the prime minister will have to resign.

This means that when the prime minister promises the public that his or her Government will act in a certain way, that person is usually in a position to follow through on that promise. In addition to being the leader of the executive branch of government, the prime minister is also (by definition) the leader of the legislative branch of government, controlling the legislative majority.

Contrast this with the presidential system in which the notion of separation of powers and checks and balances—something that explicitly does *not* apply in a parliamentary system—is so important. One of the central principles of presidential government is that the legislature is free to deny requests of the president. Consequently, although a presidential candidate may run for office on the basis of his or her position on a single issue or a number of issues, in most cases the candidate cannot guarantee delivery of campaign promises. To enact policy, the *legislature* must be convinced that the president's policy preferences are the right ones.

Which system is "better"? It is hard to say, and the answer depends upon certain value judgments, since each system has its own strengths and weaknesses. On one hand, the parliamentary system does have a real advantage in rapid policy delivery, through the notions of party discipline and cabinet leadership. On the other hand, if *good* policy can be passed quickly, so can *bad* policy. Many in parliamentary systems bemoan the overwhelming influence of party discipline and corresponding "prime ministerial dictatorship," however, and some have even suggested that their respective systems consider conversion to the presidential model.[34]

The corresponding weakness/strength of the presidential system is precisely its slower, more deliberative legislative process. The argument suggested is that whereas it may (and almost always does) take longer to pass policy, groups that are in a minority in an issue area have more opportunity to protect their interests, and the policy that is ultimately passed (if, indeed, a policy is ultimately passed) is more likely to be a good one. Put slightly more cynically, the policy that is ultimately passed is likely to offend as few as possible. On the other hand, a policy decision that is *urgently needed* may go unanswered for a long period of time while the legislature deliberates and argues with the president.

Another major area of difference between the two systems has to do with stability and tenure of office. In the presidential system, both the president and the legislature have fixed terms of office. They are secure in the knowledge of their fixed terms in these positions, barring extraordinary occurrences (such as impeachment and conviction of the president in the United States, e.g.). This security permits both the president and the legislature to take either an unpopular position or an antagonistic position in relation to the other branch of government if it is believed that such a position is the proper one to take.

The parliamentary system offers no such job security. The chief executive can lose this position at any time, depending upon the mood of the legislature. A chief executive worried about keeping his or her job, then, would be less likely to take a position that is clearly disapproved of by the legislature than would a president, although an individual "out of step" with the legislature would not be likely to be chief executive in a parliamentary system. Moreover, the legislature would be less likely to rebel against executive leadership: Party discipline would tend to force party members to follow the instructions of their leader (and the leader of the majority party, of course, would be the chief executive). If the legislature became too contentious, the chief executive could request a writ of dissolution from the head of state, effectively "firing" the legislature and calling for new elections.

As we indicated earlier, it is easy to see that each of these systems has advantages and disadvantages as far as stability, policy output, protection of minority rights, ability to deliver on campaign promises, responsiveness to public opinion, and so on, are concerned.[35] Some of these values are simply opposites of others: Responsiveness to majority public opinion may infringe on minority rights, for example. What is seen as an advantage to one observer may be a distinct disadvantage to another.

Both the presidential and the parliamentary models of executive structure are conducive to democratic government. Both models can be responsive to public opinion, both can provide effective leadership, and both can provide for the general welfare of the political system. The differences between the two types of systems are differences of structure and process, not ideology. As such, it is difficult to argue that one type of system is, overall, *better* than the other, they are simply *different*.

THE MILITARY

The military is another structure that is part of the executive branch of government and that is significant in both the socialization and recruitment processes. It is sometimes regarded as *the* "elite" in developing nations, and it is also a structure that can be significant on its own in shaping the type and style of political participation that is permitted in the political arena. Although the military is not perceived as a *politically* significant actor in most stable Western democracies, we should not let a pervasive Western ethnocentrism blind us to the fact that the military, as an institution, is a highly significant political actor in many developing regimes.

One need only look at military or military-supported **coups**[36]—military takeovers of the government—or attempted coups in recent history—in Thailand (2006), Mauritania (2005), Nepal (2005), the Central African Republic (2003), or Pakistan (1999), to take but a few examples—to see that in many instances political leaders are more concerned with what the military reaction will be to their decisions than they are with what the reactions of their respective legislatures or courts will be.[37] In fact, even in countries such as India or Guatemala, where civilian governments are clearly in control, the armed forces have been shown to exert considerable political influence.[38] Eric Nordlinger has commented:

> They are symbols of state sovereignty and the primary defenders against possible external or internal attack against the government. Given their prestige, responsibilities, and the material resources needed to fulfill these responsibilities, all military establishments exercise a significant degree of political influence...[39]

The study of what has been called "praetorianism," or military coups, has been justified on many counts, including the fact that such events happen frequently; as Chairman Mao said in China, power "grows out of the barrel of a gun." Among twenty Latin American nations, only two—Costa Rica and Mexico—have not experienced at least one attempted coup since 1945. In one recent study, it was suggested that 57 percent of the Third World states examined had been under military rule for half or more than half of their respective periods of independence.[40] According to one observer, "Between 1945 and 1976, soldiers carried out successful coups in half of the eighteen Asian states," and, more generally, "it turns out that the military have intervened in approximately two-thirds of the more than one hundred non-Western states since 1945."[41]

Although coups may be motivated "for public-spirited reasons on behalf of constitution and nation," research has shown that "almost all coups are at least partly, and usually primarily, inspired by the military's own interests."[42]

One result of a military takeover is almost invariably a significant increase in the defense budget of the regime.[43] Examined more broadly, research shows that "military rule was found to have negative or zero-order correlations with economic development." Moreover, "'politicians in uniform' invariably caused political decay."[44]

The issue of civilian control of the military is a very important one, especially so in developing societies in which (civilian) governments may not yet have acquired the same degree of legitimacy and stability that one finds in the older Western democracies. The key issue involved in the maintenance of civilian control involves finding ways to set limits within which military leaders, and all members of the armed forces, "accept the government's definition of appropriate areas of responsibility."[45]

This does not mean in the final analysis that the military is prohibited from lobbying for policies it supports, but it does mean that the military agrees to do this in acceptable ways, and that the military agrees to accept the consequences of the policy-making process. Thus, the military accepts a subordinate role in the political system. Ironically, in military regimes the leaders face the same problems as previous civilian governments did: How to keep their military underlings loyal and prevent an overthrow of the (military) forces in power at the time.[46]

Remember that the military is a political institution in most countries. The role of the military in a political system is also significantly affected by that country's political culture, history, and tradition: In some Latin American systems the idea of a military coup, if not desirable, is certainly recognized as a statistical possibility—in fact, a probability—over the course of time.

PUBLIC ADMINISTRATION AND THE BUREAUCRACY

Apart from the creation of a cabinet, one of the key functions of the political executive is to administer public policy. In this respect, this volume would be seriously remiss if we did not discuss, albeit briefly, the comparative study of public administration and a comparative analysis of the structure that has come to be called "the bureaucracy."

Public bureaucracies are perhaps the *most common* political structures in the world today; they exist in all political systems, whether they are democratic or authoritarian, "presidential" or "parliamentary," "developed" or "underdeveloped." They are as nearly a universal political structure as one can find: As a specialized structure, "bureaucracy is common to all contemporary nation-states."[47]

The term **bureaucracy** itself is something of a problem because it has a number of definitions, some value-free and some quite judgmental. The scholar whose work is most closely associated with the term, and who contributed most to its development, is Max Weber (1864–1920). Weber's concern was "less with organizational efficiency than with the expansion of bureaucratic power, and with the implications of that expansion for fundamental liberal values."[48]

Weber saw "modern officialdom" as having a number of characteristic patterns of behavior:

1. It has "fixed and official jurisdictional areas," which are "generally ordered by rules or administrative regulations";
2. The authority to give orders is also limited by rules, and officials have "coercive means" that they may use to enforce those rules;
3. The management of the office "is based upon written documents ('the files')," which requires a substantial staff to keep records;
4. Management "presupposes thorough and expert training";
5. Office activity requires the full attention of the official;
6. "The management of the office follows general rules."[49]

Generally, bureaucracies have been studied from several different perspectives.[50] First, they can be studied from an *organizational* perspective, focusing upon structures, organizational charts, lines of communication, hierarchical organization, its formal rules, and how it operates.[51] Second, bureaucracies can be studied from a *behavioral* perspective, seeking to understand what bureaucracies do, how they behave, and what behavioral characteristics distinguish bureaucracies from other hierarchically organized structures.[52] A third approach focuses upon how well bureaucracies *achieve their goals*, and discusses their efficiency, specialization, rational activity, and their role in the framework of democratic government.[53]

Bureaucracies (and here we speak of *public* bureaucracies, although most of what we say about public bureaucracies applies to private bureaucracies as well) are typically complex systems of personnel, usually organized in a hierarchical fashion. That is, bureaucracies are usually *pyramidally* shaped, with the number of employees in higher positions being fewer than those in lower positions.

The nature of a bureaucracy is usually that specialized jobs are performed by different divisions of the organization, and the organization is divided into *functional* categories. Bureaucracies are also well known for having well-institutionalized sets of *rules*, or *procedures*, and a relatively rigid set of *precedents* that govern their behavior.[54]

Bureaucracies often claim to be based upon some kind of merit system, in which one takes an examination to receive a position, or receives a position based upon some perceived objective skills. This is characteristic of more developed nations[55] and is a reaction to practices dating back to the early years of the American Republic. President Andrew Jackson coined the phrase the "spoils system," referring to a chief executive's right to appoint public personnel as one of the "spoils" of an electoral victory.

It is often the case in political bureaucracies that some type of *civil service* system exists that protects the lower-level bureaucrats from political interference in their jobs; if they have been working for several years under the direction of one political party, they do not need to fear that they will lose their jobs should the opposition party gain control of the government. The other side of this coin, of course, is that a party that is new to government does not have the ability to put an unlimited number of its followers into positions of power when it wins an election. They must compete for positions through the established civil service system that already exists. Parties that have been out of power for a long time often claim that the bureaucracy "represents" the interests of the "old order," and that it is "resisting" their proposed changes. Often this is actually the case.

Top-level positions in the bureaucracy often are *political appointments*; there is an expectation that after an election is held all officials at this level will submit their resignations and permit a new cohort of political appointees to direct the administration of policy. Thus in a typical government ministry the minister and the deputy ministers will clearly be political appointments, with the minister being an MP and the deputy ministers being party loyalists, but the director-general (or an official with a similar title) will be a civil servant who remains in office even with a change of administrations.

The function of the bureaucracy is theoretically to *administer* the policy of the executive and to *offer specialized advice* to the executive,[56] not to make policy of its own. As we indicated earlier, however, one of the frequent complaints about bureaucracies is that they do, in fact, make policy in an "irresponsible" way—"irresponsible" because nobody elected them.[57] As society has grown increasingly complex, resulting in the gradual expansion of the executive branch of government over the legislative branch of government—something we discussed in Chapter 3—this administration has required more and more personnel, leading to a rapid growth of public bureaucracies.[58] Often the growth of bureaucracy in modern society is decried, but it has been demonstrated to be necessary to administer more and more complicated social policy.

DISCUSSION QUESTIONS

1. What are the various roles that are played by the political executive?
2. Can you offer a distinction between presidential and parliamentary executive models?
3. What are presidential systems' bases of power?
4. What is the role of political parties in presidential systems?
5. Trace the development of the parliamentary executive structure and the changing role of the monarchy.
6. How would you explain the concept of constitutional monarchy?
7. Explain the selection of the chief executive in a parliamentary government.
8. What is the relationship of power between legislative supremacy and cabinet supremacy?
9. Explain the establishment of coalition governments.
10. How would you compare presidential and parliamentary executive structures? Which is better?
11. What are the potential roles of the military in politics?
12. What is the role of public administration and the bureaucracy in politics?

KEY TERMS

bureaucracy 99
cabinet 86
chief executive 87
coalition government 90
coup 98
dissolve the legislature 90
divine right of kings 85
Government (with
    capital "G") 87

government (with
    lowercase "g") 87
Government falling 89
head of state 83
immobilism 82
legislative
    supremacy 89
minority government 90
no confidence 89

parliamentary
    executive 83
presidential
    executive 79
Privy Council 87
responsible
    government 96
vote of confidence 88
writ of dissolution 90

SUGGESTED READINGS

Daniela Giannetti and Kenneth Benoit, *Intra-Party Politics and Coalition Governments* (New York: Routledge, 2009). Coalition politics can be extremely complicated, and this volume shows how the number of political parties and the behavior of political parties can make the formation and behavior of coalition governments even more confusing.

Dennis Riley and Bryan Brophy-Baermann, *Bureaucracy and the Policy Process* (Lanham, MD: Rowman and Littlefield, 2006). If the bureaucracy is the fourth branch of government (after the legislature, the executive, and the judiciary), this volume is a good introduction to how that branch of government affects the formation and execution of public policy.

Richard Rose, *The Prime Minister in a Shrinking World* (Cambridge: Blackwell Publishers, 2001). This is a good study of one prime ministerial government (Britain) and how the office of the prime minister has evolved in that system. Discusses the prime minister's role in the world today, and how the prime minister's power has changed over time.

Clinton Rossiter, *The American Presidency* (New York: Mentor, 1987). The classic study of the American presidential system of government, focusing on the powers of the president in politics today and how those powers evolved. Includes discussion of presidential relations with the legislative and judicial branches of government.

Rebecca Schiff, *The Military and Domestic Politics: A Concordance Theory of Civil-Military Relations* (New York: Routledge, 2009). This is a good introductory study of the role of the military in political systems, and the relations that exist between military governments and civilian governments cross-nationally.

NOTES

1. See Locke's Section 126 in Sir Ernest Barker, ed., *Social Contract: Essays by Locke, Hume & Rousseau* (New York: Oxford University Press, 1970).
2. Clinton Rossiter, *The American Presidency* (New York: Mentor, 1960), pp. 14–40 passim. A new edition of this was published by the Johns Hopkins University Press in 1987.
3. See James Madison, *Notes on Debates in the Federal Convention of 1787* (Athens, OH: Ohio University Press, 1966), passim.

4. See Joel Aberbach and Mark Peterson, eds., *The Executive Branch* (New York: Oxford University Press, 2005), and Lori Han and Diane Heith, eds., *In the Public Domain: Presidents and the Challenges of Public Leadership* (Albany, NY: State University of New York Press, 2005).

5. "The Buck Stops Here" was an unattributed quote on a sign that was kept on the desk of President Harry Truman.

6. See Sidney Milkis and Michael Nelson, *The American Presidency: Origins and Development, 1776–2007* (Washington, DC: CQ Press, 2008). For descriptions of the American presidency, see John P. Burke, *The Institutional Presidency: Organizing and Managing the White House from FDR to Clinton* (Baltimore, MD: Johns Hopkins University Press, 2000); or Adam L. Warber, *Executive Orders and the Modern Presidency: Legislating from the Oval Office* (Boulder, CO: Lynne Rienner, 2006). A classic study of the presidency can be found in Rossiter, *American Presidency*; or Richard Neustadt, *Presidential Power* (New York: New American Library, 1964).

7. The famous quote by John Adams, the first vice president of the United States, is as follows: "I am possessed of two separate powers, the one *in esse* and the other *in posse*. I am Vice President. In this I am nothing, but I may be everything." Rossiter, *The American Presidency*, p. 131. See also Robert Gilbert, *Managing Crisis: Presidential Disability and the Twenty-Fifth Amendment* (New York: Fordham University Press, 2006).

8. On the powers of the vice-president, see Marilyn Anderson, *The Vice Presidency* (Philadelphia, PA: Chelsea House, 2001). See also Timothy Walch, *At the President's Side: The Vice Presidency in the Twentieth Century* (Columbia, MO: University of Missouri Press, 1997).

9. On presidential elections, see Mark Halperin and John Harris, *The Way to Win: Taking the White House in 2008* (New York: Random House, 2006); Robert P. Watson, *Counting Votes: Lessons From the 2000 Presidential Election in Florida* (Gainesville, FL: University Press of Florida, 2004); and *Presidential Elections, 1789–2004* (Washington, DC: Congressional Quarterly Press, 2005). An interesting approach is found in D. Grier Stephenson, *Campaigns and the Court: The U.S. Supreme Court in Presidential Elections* (New York: Columbia University Press, 1999), a book that is especially interesting since it was written *before* the election the outcome of which was substantially affected by a decision of the Supreme Court.

10. *Federalist* Number 68 by Alexander Hamilton discusses the rationalization of this structure. See *The Federalist Papers* (New York: New American Library, 1961), pp. 411–415. See also John Fortier and Walter Berns, *After the People Vote: A Guide to the Electoral College* (Washington, DC: AEI Press, 2004).

11. There were crimes involved in his impeachment, but there was substantial debate over whether sexual offenses and covering them up were the "high crimes and misdemeanors" suggested by the Constitution. See Leonard Kaplan and Beverly Moran, *Aftermath: The Clinton Impeachment and the Presidency in the Age of Political Spectacle* (New York: New York University Press, 2001); and *Proceedings of the United States Senate in the Impeachment Trial of President William Jefferson Clinton* (Washington, DC: Superintendent of Documents, 2000).

12. See the article in *Facts on File* titled "U.S. Senator Jeffords Leaves Republican Party, Giving Control of Senate to Democrats," *Facts On File* Accession No: 2001214660 Story Date: May 24, 2001.

13. See Steven Calabresi and Christopher Yoo, *The Unitary Executive: Presidential Power from Washington to Bush* (New Haven, CT: Yale University Press, 2008);

and Benjamin Kleinerman, *The Discretionary President: The Promise and Peril of Executive Power* (Lawrence, KS: University Press of Kansas, 2009).

14. See Michael Nelson, *The Powers of the Presidency* (Washington, DC: CQ Press, 2008); and Mark Rozell, *Executive Privilege: Presidential Power, Secrecy, and Accountability* (Lawrence, KS: University Press of Kansas, 2010).

15. See Christopher Kelley, *Executing the Constitution: Putting the President Back into the Constitution* (Albany, NY: State University of New York Press, 2006); Samuel Kernell, *Presidential Veto Threats in Statements of Administration Policy, 1985–2004* (Washington, DC: Congressional Quarterly Press, 2005).

16. See Charles O. Jones, *The Trusteeship Presidency: Jimmy Carter and the United States Congress* (Baton Rouge, LA: Louisiana State University Press, 1988); and Burton Kaufman, *The Carter Years* (New York: Facts on File, 2006).

17. Some good comparative works include Gretchen Bauer and Manon Tremblay, *Women in Executive Power: A Global Overview* (New York: Routledge, 2011); and Arend Lijphart, *Parliamentary vs. Presidential Government* (New York: Oxford University Press, 1992).

18. See the data in Jean Blondel, *Comparative Legislatures* (Englewood Cliffs, NJ: Prentice Hall, 1973), pp. 144–153, column 39.

19. See Richard Rose, *The Prime Minister in a Shrinking World* (Cambridge: Blackwell Publishers, 2001); and Peter Hennessy, *The Prime Minister: The Office and Its Holders Since 1945* (London: Penguin, 2001).

20. See, for example, *The Saint Vincent Constitution Order, 1979* establishing a constitution for the new nation of St. Vincent. Sections 50 and 51 outline the Executive Power: Section 50 states that "The executive authority of Saint Vincent is vested in Her Majesty [and] ... may be exercised on behalf of Her Majesty by the Governor-General...." Section 51 notes that "(1) There shall be a Prime Minister of Saint Vincent who shall be appointed by the Governor-General. (2) Whenever the Governor-General has occasion to appoint a Prime Minister he shall appoint a Representative who appears to him likely to command the support of the majority of Representatives.... (6) The Governor-General shall remove the Prime Minister from office if a resolution of no confidence in the Government is passed by the House and the Prime Minister does not within three days either resign from his office or advise the Governor-General to dissolve Parliament." *Saint Vincent Constitution Order, 1979* (Kingstown, Saint Vincent: Government Printing Office, 1979), pp. 38–39.

21. This section is based upon a much longer discussion of the same subject in the now-classic study by Sydney Bailey, *British Parliamentary Democracy* (Boston, MA: Houghton Mifflin, 1958), pp. 12–20.

22. This argument was expounded at length in his *True Law of Free Monarchies* in 1603.

23. R. M. Dawson, *The Government of Canada* (Toronto, ON: University of Toronto Press, 1965), pp. 184–185.

24. The election in Israel in 1996 created a unique variation on the general parliamentary model after a constitutional change there, one in which the legislature was directly elected by the people (in proportional representation voting), *and* the prime minister was also directly elected by the people. In addition, following the general parliamentary model, the head of state—in Israel called the President—is elected by the Knesset, the legislature. After two elections with this model, Israel changed its constitution again *back* to the model it had used prior to 1996 because it found the changes to be more destabilizing than the older system had been. See Gregory Mahler, *Politics and Government in Israel: The Maturation of a Modern State* (Lanham, MD: Rowman and Littlefield, 2011).

25. In fact, most cabinet members come from the legislative body. See Patrick Malcolmson and Richard Myers, *The Canadian Regime: An Introduction to Parliamentary Government in Canada* (Toronto, ON: University of Toronto Press, 2009).

26. One system with a legal requirement is Barbados. See the *Barbados Independence Order, 1966*: [Section 66 (1)] "The Office of Prime Minister shall become vacant ... [(2)] If the House of Assembly by a resolution which has received the affirmative vote of a majority of all the members thereof resolves that the appointment of the Prime Minister ought to be revoked ...," pp. 62–63.

27. Blondel, *Comparative Legislatures*, pp. 144–153, column 42.

28. See Kaare Strom, "Deferred Gratification and Minority Governments in Scandinavia," *Legislative Studies Quarterly* 11:4 (1986): 583–606.

29. Blondel, *Comparative Legislatures*, pp. 144–153, column 41.

30. Norman Schofield and Itai Sened, *Multiparty Democracy* (New York: Cambridge University Press, 2006). See also Kaare Strom, Wolfgang Moller, and Torbjorn Bergman, eds., *Cabinets and Coalition Bargaining: The Democratic Life Cycle in Western Europe* (New York: Oxford University Press, 2008).

31. See Ian Budge and Hans Keman, *Parties and Democracy: Coalition Formation and Government Functioning in Twenty States* (New York: Oxford University Press, 1990). See also Peter Russell, *Two Cheers for Minority Government: The Evolution of Canadian Parliamentary Democracy* (Toronto, ON: Emond Montgomery Publications, 2008).

32. A very good comparative study is by Simon Hix, Abdul Noury, and Gerard Roland, eds., *Democratic Politics in the European Parliament* (New York: Cambridge University Press, 2007). See also Daniela Giannetti and Kenneth Benoit, *Intra-Party Politics and Coalition Governments* (New York: Routledge, 2009).

33. See Strom et al., *Cabinets and Coalition Bargaining*. See also Josep Colomer, *Comparative European Politics* (New York: Routledge, 2008).

34. See, for example, Avraham Brichta and Yair Zalmanovitch, "The Proposals for Presidential Government in Israel: A Case Study in the Possibility of Institutional Transference," *Comparative Politics* 19:1 (1986): 57–68. See also Alan Arian and David Nachmias, *Executive Governance in Israel* (New York: Palgrave, 2002).

35. Some discussion of this may be found in Jaakko Nousiainen, "Bureaucratic Tradition, Semi-Presidential Rule, and Parliamentary Government, the Case of Finland," *European Journal of Political Research* 16:2 (1988): 229–249.

36. See, for example, George Kieh and Pita Agbese, *The Military and Politics in Africa: From Intervention to Democratic Control* (Burlington, VT: Ashgate, 2004); or Gordon Tullock and Charles Rowley, *The Social Dilemma: Of Autocracy, Revolution, Coup d'Etat, and War* (Indianapolis, IN: Liberty Fund, 2005).

37. See, for example, Anthony F. Lang, *Agency and Ethics: The Politics of Military Intervention* (Albany, NY: State University of New York Press, 2001); or Paul Drake and Ivan Jansic, eds., *The Struggle for Democracy in Chile, 1982–1990* (Lincoln: University of Nebraska Press, 1991).

38. See William Maley and C. J. G. Sampford, *From Civil Strife to Civil Society: Civil and Military Responsibilities in Disrupted States* (New York: United Nations University Press, 2003); Husain Haqqani, *Pakistan: Between Mosque and Military* (Washington, DC: Brookings Institution Press, 2005); and Michael Drake, *Problematics of Military Power: Government, Discipline, and the Subject of Violence* (Portland, OR: Frank Cass, 2002).

39. Eric Nordlinger, *Soldiers in Politics: Military Coups and Governments* (Englewood Cliffs, NJ: Prentice Hall, 1977), p. 3. See also Hasan-Askari Rizvi, *Military, State and Society in Pakistan* (New York: Macmillan, 2000), for example.

40. Talukder Maniruzzaman, *Military Withdrawal from Politics: A Comparative Study* (Cambridge, MA: Ballinger Publishing, 1987), p. 18. See also Jimmy D. Kandeh, *Coups from Below: Armed Subalterns and State Power in West Africa* (New York: Palgrave Macmillan, 2004).

41. Nordlinger, *Soldiers*, pp. 5–6. For examples of this kind of literature see Rebecca Schiff, *The Military and Domestic Politics: A Concordance Theory of Civil-Military Relations* (New York: Routledge, 2009), or Richard Millett and Jennifer Holmes, eds., *Latin American Democracy: Emerging Reality or Endangered Species?* (New York: Routledge, 2009).

42. Nordlinger, *Soldiers*, p. 192. See also Carlos Maria Vilas, *Shaky Democracies and Popular Fury: From Military Coups to Peoples' Coups* (Tampa, FL: University of South Florida, 2004); Michael Kiselycznyk and Phillip Saunders, *Civil-Military Relations in China: Assessing the PLA's Role in Elite Politics* (Washington, DC: National Defense University, 2010).

43. Maniruzzaman, *Military Withdrawal*, p. 3

44. Ibid., p. 205.

45. Claude E. Welch, Jr., *Civilian Control of the Military: Theory and Cases from Developing Countries* (Albany, NY: State University of New York Press, 1976), p. 2; Marcus Mietzner, *Military Politics, Islam, and the State in Indonesia* (Singapore: Institute of Southeast Asian Studies, 2009).

46. Christopher Clapham and George Philip, *The Political Dilemmas of Military Regimes* (Totowa, NJ: Barnes and Noble Books, 1985). See also Risa Brooks, *Shaping Strategy: The Civil-Military Politics of Strategic Assessment* (Princeton, NJ: Princeton University Press, 2008).

47. Ferrel Heady, *Public Administration: A Comparative Perspective* (New York: Marcel Dekker, 1984), p. 59. See also B. Guy Peters and Jon Pierre, *Handbook of Public Administration* (Thousand Oaks, CA: Sage Publications, 2003); Kevin Smith and Michael Licari, *Public Administration: Power and Politics in the Fourth Branch of Government* (Los Angeles, CA: Roxbury Publishing, 2006).

48. David Beetham, *Bureaucracy* (Minneapolis, MN: University of Minnesota Press, 1987), p. 58. More recent works on Weber include Fritz Ringer, *Max Weber: An Intellectual Biography* (Chicago, IL: University of Chicago Press, 2004).

49. Max Weber, "Bureaucracy," in H. H. Gerth and C. Wright Mills, eds., *From Max Weber: Essays in Sociology* (New York: Oxford University Press, 1978), p. 196.

50. This section is based upon much more detailed analysis in Heady, *Public Administration*, pp. 61–64. See Michael Spicer, *In Defense of Politics in Public Administration* (Tuscaloosa, AL: University of Alabama Press, 2010).

51. This is the approach of Edward Schneier, *Crafting Constitutional Democracies: The Politics of Institutional Design* (Lanham, MD: Rowman and Littlefield, 2006). See Patricia Ingraham, Jon Pierre, and B. Guy Peters, eds., *Comparative Administrative Change and Reform: Lessons Learned* (Montreal: McGill-Queen's University Press, 2010).

52. To a substantial degree this approach is illustrated in Walter Kickert, ed., *The Study of Public Management in Europe and the U.S.: A Comparative Analysis of National Distinctiveness* (New York: Routledge, 2008). See also Dennis Riley and Bryan Brophy-Baermann, eds., *Bureaucracy and the Policy Process* (Lanham, MD: Rowman and Littlefield, 2006).

53. An example of this might be J. Michael Martinez, *Public Administration Ethics for the 21st Century* (Santa Barbara, CA: Praeger, 2009). See also B. Guy Peters

and Jon Pierre, *Politicization of the Civil Service in Comparative Perspective* (New York: Routledge, 2004).

54. See Jan-Erik Lane, *State Management: An Enquiry Into Models of Public Administration* (New York: Routledge, 2009).

55. See the discussion by Heady, "Relating Bureaucratic and Political Development" in his *Public Administration*, pp. 409–417.

56. A very good study of the *advising* function is by Norma Riccucci, *Public Administration: Traditions of Inquiry and Philosophies of Knowledge* (Washington, DC: Georgetown University Press, 2010).

57. A very good discussion of some of the philosophical dimensions of this problem, and how democratic control can coexist with bureaucracy can be found in the volume edited by David Rosenbloom, Rosemary O'Leary, and Joshua Chanin, *Public Administration and Law* (Boca Raton, FL: CRC Press, 2010).

58. This point is discussed at some length in the study by Peters in his volume *The Politics of Bureaucracy: A Comparative Perspective*. Peters' second chapter is entitled "The Growth of Government and Administration," and he discusses the growth of administration not only in the executive branch, but also in the legislature and in other areas of the government.

Judicial Institutions

Many judicial institutions rely heavily on ceremony and traditional symbols in their operation. Here Justice Virginia Bell (center) sits with Chief Justice James Spigelman (right) and other Supreme Court judges at her official farewell ceremony at the New South Wales (Australia) Court of Appeal in 2008 in Sydney as she left the Court of Appeal to take up a position on the High Court.

AAP Image/news Ltd pool, Lindsay Moller/AP Photos

- Understand judiciaries as one of the three key Lockean institutions of government.
- Appreciate the comparative study of judiciaries, with their playing significantly different roles in different systems.
- Explain courts as *non*-political institutions.
- Articulate the idea of law as an output of government.
- Describe the different types of law (scientific, moral, natural, positive).
- Evaluate the concept of a legal culture.
- Distinguish between common law legal systems and code law legal systems.
- Appreciate non-Western legal systems and their differences from Western models.
- Explain sources of law.
- Highlight key structures of legal systems.
- Summarize judicial functions in political systems.
- Place the concept of judicial review in its appropriate context in terms of governmental structures.

Having examined the key Lockean political institutions of legislatures and executives, it is appropriate to discuss another group of political institutions that can be very significant for the political systems in which they are found. These institutions, judiciaries, can play absolutely crucial roles in their respective political systems, and there are many, many examples that we can cite of instances in which they are singularly responsible for the success—or failure—of the political system in which they might be found. Although these institutions are less often the focus of comparative political analysis, it is important that students understand the significance they can play in the successful operation of politics around the world.

ON THE COMPARATIVE STUDY OF JUDICIARIES

After our discussion of legislative and executive structures, the structure of government suggested by John Locke in 1690 that remains to be discussed is "a known and indifferent judge, with authority to determine all differences according to the established law."[1] One of the functions that was ascribed to constitutions in our discussion in Chapter 2 was that they serve as an expression of the basic laws of the regime. At this point we should say something about the function of legal systems in political processes and the importance of legal culture in general, as well as something about the role of judges and courts in political systems.

Of the three major Lockean governmental structures—the legislature, the executive, and the judiciary—that can be observed on a cross-national basis, courts and legal systems generally continue to receive the least attention in introductory texts and comparative studies,[2] unless, of course, the study in question explicitly focuses upon the judiciary or the law.[3] Why is this the case? Two possible suggestions can be offered here.

First, as far as systemic characteristics and political institutions go, legal systems and courts may be the most *system-specific*. That is, although both executives and legislatures have structural idiosyncrasies, and have behavior that varies on a country-by-country basis, we can still make a number of useful generalizations about both their structures (e.g., "presidential" systems as compared with "parliamentary" systems) and their behavior (e.g., a system with high party discipline compared with a system with low party discipline). This level of generalization is hard to achieve with legal systems and courts. Although we can speak of constitutional regimes—governments of laws, not ruled by individual whim—we very quickly get to the point at which system-level characteristics of judiciaries must be discussed; consequently generalizability is low.[4]

Second, while executives and legislatures are undoubtedly part of the political process, in many political systems the courts are explicitly *excluded from* the political arena.[5] This is not a refutation of Locke's argument that courts (judges) are necessary to society; it simply limits the role of the judges and the courts to one of arbitration or mediation. They are not, it is claimed, part of the law-making or policy-making process, specifically, or the political arena, generally. (It should be noted, in fact, that Locke suggested the function of the judge was to "determine all differences according to the *established* law" [emphasis added] *not* to actually make the law or public policy.) Accordingly, many political scientists have left the judiciary out of their studies of the political arena and the policy-making process generally.

In explaining the almost-nonpolitical role of the courts, one study has pointed out that courts, "logically and historically, have been undemocratic institutions. An increased role for the courts, then, could render a political order less democratic."[6] Thus, although the courts have often been significant in maintaining individual rights, they have often kept a low profile in their respective polities, thereby generating relatively little scholarship on their *comparative* political impact.

Although courts are often "nonpolitical" in nature, they do play a significant role in political systems. As we shall see, in many systems courts play a role through *judicial review* in shaping the law.[7]

THE IDEA OF LAW

The idea of *law* tends to be assumed whenever we think of politics. That is, there is an implicit (Western, ethnocentric) assumption that political systems are based, to varying degrees, upon the rule of law. This assumption is made because so many of our contacts with government come in relation to governmental rules, regulations, and administrative guidelines. It is almost impossible to think of government existing without laws; the "authoritative allocation of values" with which politics is concerned deals with laws.

Law is generally regarded as one of the greatest achievements of civilization.[8] It is concerned with basic rules of conduct that reflect to some degree the concept of justice. An ideal of **justice** frequently expressed is that the government should be "a government of laws and not of men."[9] What does this mean? It means that there should be some *consistency* in expectations of behavior, and that when deviations from this behavior take place the social response will be more or less consistent. In practice, this ideal is generally interpreted to mean a legal system that treats everyone equally and that is not subject to change through the arbitrary acts of a dictator, or even the whim of transient majorities.[10] Even in the seventeenth century, John Locke saw law as being the principal attraction of society: "Thus mankind, notwithstanding all the privileges of the state of nature, being but in an ill condition while they remain in it, are quickly driven into society....[They] take sanctuary under the established laws of government."[11]

There are a number of different kinds of law to which the interested student can find reference, including positive law, divine law, moral law, natural law, and scientific law,[12] among others. **Scientific laws** refer to observations and measurements that have been empirically determined and that focus upon physical, biological, and chemical concepts, not social questions. **Moral laws** refer to precepts or guidelines that are based upon subjective values, beliefs, and attitudes, focusing upon behavior: the proper (through a particular perspective) way of doing things. **Divine law**, as well, will be seen to vary depending upon the religious or theological conceptual framework from which it is said to be derived. Different types of law are indicated in Table 5.1.

The two major approaches to law with which we as social scientists are concerned are natural law and positive law. **Natural law** refers to a body of precepts governing human behavior that is "more basic than man-made law, and one that is based on fundamental principles of justice."[13] The type of law with which governments are most concerned is **positive law**, which can be said to have three major identifiable characteristics: (1) It is man-made law, (2) it is designed to govern human behavior, and (3) it is enforceable by appropriate governmental action. "Positive law" gets its name not from the fact that it is necessarily "good," but from the fact that it requires *positive action* by people to bring it into being (whereas natural law exists in the state of nature, and religious law is believed to have been given by a higher power).

Conflict has erupted throughout human history when natural law and positive law appear to be in disagreement. Political philosophers from the time of Cicero (106–43 B.C.)—including John of Salisbury, Thomas Aquinas,

> ### TABLE 5.1
>
> **Different Kinds of Law**
>
> - Scientific Law: empirical; observations and measurements
> - Moral Law: subjective: values, beliefs, attitudes
> - Divine Law: religious or theological conceptual framework
> - Natural Law: perceived fundamental principles
> - Positive Law: man-made, governing behavior, enforceable by the state

Thomas Hobbes, John Locke, Jean-Jacques Rousseau, David Hume, Jeremy Bentham, and Karl Marx—through philosophers of the present day have dealt with this thorny issue.[14] What is the individual to do when the law of the state tells one to do one thing, but one's perception of natural law, of the *fundamental* standard of "rightness," says to do something else? Many have argued that human laws (positive laws) that conflict with natural laws (or religious laws) are null and void. St. Augustine's "two sword" theory in the early fifth century was one attempt to resolve this conflict.[15] Augustine argued that natural law and divine law were the same thing: The laws of nature are God's laws. Individuals are required to obey earthly (positive) law only insofar as it does not conflict with natural law. When natural law and positive law conflict, it is the law of God that must be obeyed, according to Augustine.

LEGAL CULTURE

The concept of a "culture" is one that has been developed primarily by sociologists and anthropologists. A legal culture can be considered to be:

> a set of deeply rooted, historically conditioned attitudes about the nature of law, about the role of law in the society and the polity, about the proper organization and operation of a legal system, and about the way law is, or should be made, applied, studied, perfected, and taught. The legal tradition relates the legal system to the culture of which it is a partial expression.[16]

The concept of a **legal culture**, then, focuses upon the beliefs, attitudes, and values of society *relative to the law and politics.*[17]

We mentioned earlier the idea that political systems should be "governments of law and not of men." The reader will recall that in our discussion of constitutions and constitutional government one of the dividing lines between (behaviorally) constitutional and unconstitutional regimes was the degree to which the behavior of regimes was *limited*, controlled by law. Are there limits beyond which the government absolutely may not go? Or, conversely, is the function of law perceived to be primarily that of controlling individual behavior, keeping individuals "under control," while the government may do whatever it wishes?

A nation's legal culture will shape the role that the law and legal institutions play in the political realm. For example, the fact that the United States is "the most litigious country in the world"[18] suggests that Americans are more likely to look to the courts for the resolution of conflict than might citizens of other polities. On the other hand, "the Japanese legal culture puts a premium on informal settlement of legal disputes based on informal controls and social sanction without legal procedure."[19]

Although political cultures do vary on a nation-by-nation basis, there are certain "families" or groupings of legal cultures that may be suggested here for purposes of generalization. These are (1) the Romano-Germanic family; (2) the family of the common law; (3) the family of socialist law; and (4) the non-Western legal families.[20]

The **Romano-Germanic** approach to law, sometimes referred to as "code" law, has developed from the basis of Roman law at the time of Justinian (A.D. 533).[21] This type of law, as contrasted with common law, is based upon comprehensively written legislative statutes, often bound together as "codes." The **Code Napoleon** was just such a bound collection; the Emperor Napoleon (reigned 1804–1815) decided that law throughout his empire needed to be standardized, and he had a single, comprehensive set of laws assembled and disseminated. The Code Napoleon influenced legal structures from Europe to North America to Asia. The French legal system is characteristic of a code law system, and in North America today the legal systems of Louisiana and Québec have similar characteristics, evidence of their (French) colonial heritage.

The **common law** system, found in England and countries modeled on English law (including the United States, generally), is sometimes called "Anglo-American" law,[22] and has been referred to as "judge-made law."[23] This is not to suggest that today's laws in these political systems are not made by the legislatures of those systems or, conversely, that today's laws are made by judges in those systems. Rather, the term suggests that when the science of the law was being developed in England in the twelfth century, it was the judges who made decisions. Today, **judicial precedent** plays a major role in common law nations—the process is referred to as *stare decisis* (to stand by things decided).[24] A judge may use a previously adjudicated case as a guide for his or her decision, but the judge may decide that there are new characteristics involved in the case at hand that require deviation from earlier decisions. Of course, today, the legislature plays a highly significant role in designing the laws that the judge is applying to the specific situation.

The differences between the code law systems and the common law systems can easily be overstated, but two main characteristics should be pointed out. First, judges play a slightly less significant role in decision making in the code law systems, with correspondingly greater influence exercised by the legislature. Second, the common law system, characteristic of Anglo-American nations, tries to minimize the likelihood of an innocent person being convicted by setting up various procedural and substantive safeguards. The code law systems, characterized by the system found in France, "lays more stress on preventing a guilty person from escaping punishment."[25]

Socialist law derives from a different philosophical root.[26] Karl Marx and his philosophy assumed that law was a tool of the state in capitalist societies, and that it was used to oppress the working class. Marx argued that in a perfect socialist state there would be no need for law at all, once the economic ills of society were cured. In fact, of course, things have not turned out to be quite as simple as Marx thought they would. Law in the former Soviet Union, perhaps the best example of such a system, played, if anything, a greater role than in Western democracies.[27]

In the second and third quarters of the twentieth century, Soviet Marxists saw law as a tool of the state, to be used to work toward a socialist society. The state could (and should) use law to further its ends. Law exists to further the interests of citizens. The state knows better than any individuals what the interests of the citizens are. Anything the state does, therefore, must be legal. Thus law becomes simply another instrument of state policy.

In **non-Western legal systems**, such as those of some developing nations, legal cultures are quite different and depend upon (1) local traditions and customs, (2) the legal culture of the colonizing power (if any) that controlled the political infrastructure prior to independence, and (3) the degree to which the colonizing power permitted autonomy and development during the colonial era. In some non-Western systems, religious law, especially Islamic law, now has a major role in the general legal framework of the regime. In others, religious and tribal laws are blended with colonial legal values. Elsewhere, developing nations have completely forsaken their traditional legal cultures and have opted instead for modern legal structures and processes.[28] To take just one example, the legal culture found in Israel today is a blend of Turkish law and British law (former colonial powers in the Middle East), religious law (including Jewish, Muslim, and Christian components), as well as contemporary legal and judicial values.[29]

SOURCES OF LAW

For as long as political systems have been based upon the rule of law, there have been a variety of sources for the laws that have existed. At one point in time, patterns of behavior were governed by *religious* or *moral values*. This kind of law generally comes in entire bodies, often in a specifically delineated set. Thus the Mosaic Law—the Ten Commandments brought down from Mount Sinai by Moses—was a *body* of law. Similarly, the Koran, the sacred book of Islam, contains a *body* of laws. This religious law often is interpreted to be natural law, as we distinguished the terms earlier, although some might argue that religious law may contain elements much more specific than natural law. For example, religious laws may prohibit the consumption of certain foods, regulate men's or women's dress, or govern working on a certain day of the week, when there is no immediately apparent reason why this should be considered to be part of a "law of nature." Depending upon the nature of a society, this type of religious or moral value may become entrenched in the legal framework of a political system.[30]

Some monarchs, notably James I of England (reigned 1603–1625), used religion as a basis of their power. In his *True Law of Free Monarchies*,[31] James I developed his theory of "divine right of kings," arguing that rulers derived their powers from God, and policies that they designed would have the force of law. James I was not the only monarch to believe this, and the *will of the monarch* became a major source of law for a long time.

Another source of law is *tradition* or *custom*. We made the distinction in our discussion of legislatures and executives between *de jure* (in law) and *de facto* (in fact) political power, and argued that tradition may develop the *force of* law, even if it never *becomes* law. The tradition in England, for example, that the monarch selects the leader of the largest party in the House of Commons to be prime minister has become so established that it is taken as part of the "Westminster model" constitutional regime there and elsewhere. Similarly, the tradition that the prime minister "must" resign if he or she receives a vote of no confidence may take on the force of law, even if it hasn't become actual law.

Sometimes traditions are left unwritten, as the parliamentary case of the head of state acting "on the advice" of the chief executive illustrates. On other occasions, traditions are actually formalized and made part of the constitutional or legal framework of a political system. For example, the tradition of American presidents serving only two terms of office was firmly entrenched in American politics prior to World War II. George Washington started the tradition, and if a president did not bow out of politics at the end of his first term of office, he inevitably did so at the end of his second term. When Franklin Delano Roosevelt violated this tradition and ran for a third term, and then a fourth term, some reacted quite strongly. This reaction led to the Twenty-Second Amendment to the Constitution, limiting presidential terms of office.[32]

Certainly, a major source of law in contemporary regimes is *the constitution* of the regime. Some national constitutions include specific legal prescriptions that must be followed in the political system, as well as more general descriptions of the structures and institutions to be found in the regime. The U.S. Constitution, for example, contains a number of specific limitations and guidelines that are not only laws in their own right (e.g., "Congress shall make no law … abridging the freedom of speech…"), but have also generated an entire body of supplementary law.

This happens through yet another source of law, *the judiciary*. Judicial decision making, including the interpretation of constitutional dogma and legislative statutes and the application of judicial precedents to new circumstances, has resulted in a great deal of "judge-made" law.

Another governmental structure directly concerned with the creation of law is, of course, *the legislature*. The legislature as an institution derives its name from the law (*legis*), and certainly one of the functions most commonly attributed to the legislature is the lawmaking function. In some settings the legislature is more important in a political system in some other capacity—its legislative function may be primarily that of a rubber stamp.

More and more often today, we see arguments that legislatures are in a decline as far as their legitimate legislative powers are concerned. The argument suggests that, in both presidential and parliamentary systems of government, legislatures are surrendering their legislative powers to the executive branch in exchange for the rubber-stamp function. The question important to ask is, why is this so?[33]

Theodore Lowi has argued that part of this problem stems from the complexity of modern society and government. It was easy for legislatures in 1690 to perform their legislative tasks—for example, to pass laws forbidding poaching on the king's land. It is much harder for legislatures to address the complex social problems of the twenty-first century that governments must address: For example, how can a legislature fight poverty? It could pass a law making it illegal to be poor, but that would not solve the problem. Lowi suggests in his book *The End of Liberalism* that problems such as these may be beyond the competence of legislatures. Often, the only response to these complex problems that is available to a legislature is to pass leadership on the issue to an executive agency, appropriate adequate funding, and give the executive agency authority to set rules and policy by itself.[34]

This leads to yet another source of law—*administrative decisions*. A legislature may decide, for example, that it does not have either the time or the capacity to make highly specialized policy decisions regarding food and drugs. Its response to this quandary, given a feeling that some regulation in this area is clearly necessary, might be to establish a National Food and Drugs Agency, giving commissioners on the agency authority to set standards and regulations insuring a constant quality of both food and drugs. The actions of a majority of commissioners, then, may have the *force* of law (violations of their decisions and rules could result in fines or imprisonment) and could have the same *effect* as legislated laws, even though the legislature really was not responsible for specific policy set by the agency.[35]

We can see, then, that although positive laws may derive from a number of sources, their effects can be the same. Whether these laws stem from religious or moral values, tradition or custom, a constitution, judicial interpretation, legislation, or administrative actions and decisions, all may serve the functions of regulating behavior in society.

STRUCTURES IN LEGAL SYSTEMS

The heart of a judicial system's structure is to be found in its network of **courts**. Theodore Becker, a significant contributor to the cross-national literature on judiciaries, has characterized courts as having seven components. A court is:

1. An individual or group of individuals;
2. With power to make decisions in disputes;
3. Before whom the parties or their advocates present the facts involved in the dispute and cite principles (in statutes, or other forms) that
4. Are applied by that individual or those individuals;

5. Who *believe* that they should listen to the facts and apply cited principles impartially, and;
6. That they may so decide, and;
7. As an independent body.[36]

The main service of modern courts, then, is to serve as an arena in which controlled conflict may take place. The controls exercised upon this conflict are very rigid, emphasizing verbal, conceptual, legal, and philosophical strengths rather than physical strength. (Let us not forget that at the time of King Arthur, conflicts were often resolved by "champions" in physical combat!)

To process the disputes as smoothly and efficiently as possible, judicial structures are established in political systems. The actual structures of these courts vary tremendously on a system-by-system basis. Federal political systems may have legal infrastructures that reflect their federal makeup; unitary systems may be more simple. Some systems may have very specialized courts as part of their judicial structure, while others may not.

Judiciaries tend to be organized in a pyramidal fashion, with a larger number of courts of initial adjudication, fewer appeals courts, and a single, ultimate, supreme court. In many judicial systems, all cases must begin on the "ground floor" and work their way up through the judicial system. There are instances in some judicial systems, however, in which the appeals courts and supreme court may have some *original jurisdiction*—some cases may actually start at the intermediate or top level, and not have to work their way on appeal to that point.

The question of **jurisdiction,** of which court (or level of court) has authority to adjudicate a specific question, can be complex.[37] For example, in the U.S. judicial system, jurisdiction is divided between federal courts and state courts, reflecting the federal nature of the polity. Sometimes jurisdiction may overlap: In the United States today, for example, it is not a federal crime to rob a bank, but a state crime. It is, however, a federal crime to rob a bank insured by the federal government (and, it turns out, virtually all banks today are federally insured).

So, the individual who robs a federally insured bank actually commits two crimes—robbing a bank (a state crime), and robbing a federally insured bank (a federal crime)—and can, accordingly, face two trials. (Parenthetically, it should be noted that this liability to face two trials is not the same thing as "double jeopardy," against which the individual is protected under the Fifth Amendment to the U.S. Constitution. The Fifth Amendment says that no person shall "be subject for the same offense to be twice put in jeopardy of life or limb...." If a person commits *two offenses*, even in the same act, he or she may be tried twice; he or she may not be tried twice for the same offense.)

The U.S. federal judicial structure, then, consists of a single federal judicial pyramid and fifty separate state judicial pyramids. This double-structured judicial framework was designed to accommodate the federal nature of the American political arena, although it does occasionally make determination of jurisdiction more difficult.

Other federal political systems manage to allow for reflection of their federal character in their judicial systems without this parallel structure. In the case of Canada, for example, there is no "double-pyramid" structure.[38] Courts are "constituted, maintained, and organized" by the provinces in both the areas of civil and criminal law. At the same time, however, to balance the grant of exclusive power over *civil procedure* given to the provinces, the federal government has exclusive jurisdiction over *criminal procedure*, and it is the federal government that controls the appointment, salary, and tenure of the judges in the courts that are established by the provinces. Thus, the Canadian federal judicial structure appears as ten separate provincial pyramids, designed by the provinces and staffed by federal appointments. Civil procedure is established by the provinces (so that, e.g., civil procedures in Ontario might be different from civil procedures in British Columbia, and both are likely to be different from civil procedure in Québec), but criminal procedure will be standardized through its control by the federal government. There is, moreover, a single Supreme Court of Canada that acts as an appeals court for the entire nation.[39]

It can be seen, then, that the actual structural design of judicial systems varies on a nation-by-nation basis. Questions of jurisdiction, appeals, and procedure are so tailored to individual national characteristics that even members of the same legal cultural "families" that we saw earlier—the common law family, for example, or the code law family—may differ significantly in terms of specific political structures. Not only do Canada and the United States differ significantly in the manner in which their judicial structures reflect their federal natures, but even within a nation judicial structures can vary. For example, the court structure in Massachusetts differs from courts in California, and courts in Alberta differ from courts in Newfoundland.

JUDICIAL FUNCTIONS

The judicial function has been characterized by one scholar of comparative politics as consisting of:

> the determination of the meaning of laws and rules, the imposition of penalties for violating those rules, the deciding on the relative rights and obligations of individuals and the community, the determination of the area of freedom to be allowed persons within the political system, and the arbitration of disputes between individuals and officials.[40]

With such a list of functions, it is no wonder that courts or judiciaries are important political structures! Given a focus upon *functions*, it is easy to see that the *structure* of a judiciary can vary, as we have just indicated.

Judges are often in an invaluable position to protect minority rights. Most judicial systems offer some degree of protection for judges, shielding them from the political consequences of their actions. Judges not only can take a nonpolitical view of conflicts, but they are also free to act; in most systems judges cannot be fired for unpopular decisions. Judges have the power to hand down decisions that might be so unpopular, socially or politically, that legislators or executives might hesitate to act, and judges need not be worried about losing their positions. Short of treason or a major criminal offense, judges are often "irresponsible" to majority opinion.

An "irresponsible" judiciary, of course, can be seen as either good or bad, depending upon one's view of the particular policy question under consideration. Some citizens might view a court decision giving individual women the right to decide whether or not to have an abortion as a victory for individual rights and freedom of choice; others might see the same decision as legal toleration of murder. One constituency might cry that a court's decision banning prayer in public school is an act of atheism, while others might argue that the decision has nothing to do with *religion* at all, simply with *religion in school*, and is, therefore, a protection of the rights of a minority in the school who don't want to follow the majority's religious preferences.

JUDICIARIES IN THE POLITICAL ARENA

The judiciary may, in many political systems, engage in a lawmaking function of a sort, by interpreting laws made elsewhere. As a general rule, however, the courts prefer to stay out of the political arena.[41] Even in the United States, where the U.S. Supreme Court is among the most politically active high tribunals in the world, the Court is hesitant to inject itself into the political arena.

Although the U.S. Supreme Court has endeavored to avoid highly visible and highly politicized cases throughout American history, on occasion it has not been possible to avoid the spotlight completely. The presidential election of 2000 was one such instance, in which the Court had to play a highly visible, highly political, and highly significant role in the outcome of the election. While many decried the Court's role as an "undemocratic" institution in making a decision that effectively decided who would be the victor in the election, most commentators were agreed that the *legitimacy* of the Court was highly significant for most Americans in helping to provide a (relatively) swift and definitive outcome to the controversy, even if not all Americans were happy with the substance of the decision. It is worth noting, too, that the legitimacy of the Court was such that its decision did *not* result in widespread civil unrest or civil war.[42]

Clearly, however, the most direct interaction between the courts and other political structures in a regime comes through the pattern of behavior that we refer to as judicial review. **Judicial review** is the process by which courts are in the position to rule upon the propriety or legality of action of the legislative and executive branches of government.[43] More specifically:

> judicial review refers to the judicial power to decide on the constitutionality of activities undertaken by other governmental institutions, most notably those decisions, laws, and policies advanced by executives and legislatures.[44]

> **TABLE 5.2**
>
> **Some Countries Whose Political Systems Include Judicial Review**
>
> | Western Europe and North America | Latin America | Asia and the Pacific | Other |
> |---|---|---|---|
> | Austria | Argentina | Australia | Ghana |
> | Canada | Brazil | India | Israel |
> | Denmark | Colombia | Japan | Nigeria |
> | Ireland | Mexico | Pakistan | |
> | Norway | | Philippines | |
>
> *Source:* Monte Palmer and William Thompson, *The Comparative Analysis of Politics* (Itasca, IL: F. E. Peacock, 1978), p. 136; Theodore Becker, *Comparative Judicial Politics* (Chicago, IL: Rand McNally, 1970), pp. 137, 209, 213, 219–222.

As is indicated in Table 5.2, the concept of judicial review exists in only a clear minority of the nations in the world, and where it does exist, the extent of its scope and ability to review the actions of other governmental structures varies. That is, not all of the courts listed in Table 5.2 are as powerful in their respective political systems as is the Supreme Court in the United States.[45] The idea of judicial review, although most strongly institutionalized today in the United States, was not, as some scholars have suggested, "invented" in American colonial days, or with the decision of Chief Justice John Marshall in the case of *Marbury v. Madison* in 1803.[46] We can go back to the time of Plato to find discussion of judicial review, in a primitive sense, when Plato discussed the establishment of a "nocturnal council of magistrates" to be the "guardians of our god-given constitution."[47]

Although judicial review may not exist at the present time in all judicial systems,[48] there clearly is an ingredient of change at work that we must keep in mind. For example, most studies have taken it as a given that there is no judicial review in Great Britain, and that the fundamental principle underlying the operation of British politics is that of parliamentary supremacy. While this has historically been true, it also has recently been pointed out that the role of the courts in the British political culture has changed, and that this reflects "deep-seated changes occurring in the institutional fabric of British government," especially in the realm of administrative law. It has been shown that "until twenty years ago judges took an extremely restrained position vis-à-vis administrative agencies," but more recently, scholars have noted "an embryonic move toward judicial activism."[49] And, in fact, Britain's political institutions have recently been changed to create a Supreme Court with judicial review functions, something that we will discuss in detail later in this volume. Although this is not meant to suggest that British courts will soon be casually nullifying Acts of Parliament, it does illustrate the fact that all political institutions, courts included, can change over time.

There are two major types of judicial review mechanisms today. One, in the American model, uses the *regular* courts to make decisions. The other major type of judicial review structure comes from Europe and provides a *special* constitutional court or reviewing body to perform the judicial-review function. The Constitutional Court found today in France is a good example of this.[50]

Political systems vary as well in the question of who can initiate suit. In the United States, only someone "injured" by an act can initiate suit. The U.S. Supreme Court will not issue an advisory opinion, or permit an uninvolved party to commence litigation; on the other hand, the Supreme Court of Canada will. In some political systems, those affected by an act are specifically not permitted to initiate a suit. Rather, only specific governmental agencies may apply for judicial review. In still other systems, the access to the judicial review process is very liberal, and anyone can bring a case into the reviewing process. In Colombia, for example, "anyone could introduce a petition of unconstitutionality directly to the Supreme Court, without even having to prove a case or controversy existed, or that he had any real or personal interest in the constitutionality of the law in question."[51]

The justification of judicial review—a practice many condemn as undemocratic in that it permits an (often) unelected and therefore "irresponsible" judiciary to reverse or nullify actions of democratically elected legislators and executives—is basically that there is inevitably some degree of uncertainty about constitutional matters, whether they be powers of an executive or parameters of permissible legislation. As well as being structural blueprints of a regime, constitutions, as we indicated in Chapter 2, in effect provide limitations upon what government may or may not do in a political environment. The authors of a constitution do not have unlimited foresight, and therefore it is inevitable that eventually, even sincere, honest, ethical individuals of good will (not to mention dishonest and unethical individuals) may disagree over what is permissible and impermissible governmental behavior. At that time the court is the appropriate organ of government to step into the picture and help to resolve the conflict.

COURTS IN COMPARATIVE PERSPECTIVE

We began this chapter by observing that courts, as the third of the "standard" three branches of government, tend to not receive the same amount of attention in introductory cross-national studies as either legislatures or executives. It was suggested that this is so primarily because (1) legal systems and legal cultures are more system-specific, and hence more difficult to generalize about, and (2) in many political systems courts and judiciaries are specifically excluded from the political process, and, therefore, not really of direct relevance to discussions of political behavior.

We have seen, however, that judiciaries as well as legal cultures are highly significant to the political systems of which they are a part. The legal culture sets the tone, at a minimum, for the operation of the political regime. Even if the legal culture does not describe specific political structures, it does include the essential philosophical and theoretical principles that will underlie the daily operation of the regime. The judiciary, as a governmental structure, may be more or less political in its operation. Even when it is at its minimum political dimension, however, it is important for the regime in terms of the services it provides in areas of mediation, conflict resolution, and the promotion of regime legitimacy and stability.

DISCUSSION QUESTIONS

1. How do judiciaries interact with the other two key Lockean institutions of government?
2. It has been said that the impact of judiciaries may vary widely in different political systems. How is this so? Where are they most significant?
3. What kind of *non*-political roles do courts play as political institutions?
4. What are the different types of law?
5. What is the importance of the concept of a legal culture?
6. How would you distinguish between common law legal systems and code law legal systems?
7. What are the several sources of law?
8. What do you believe are the key structures of legal systems?
9. Can you place the concept of judicial review in its appropriate context in terms of governmental structures?

KEY TERMS

Code Napoleon   113
common law   113
court   116
divine law   111
judicial precedent   113
judicial review   119

jurisdiction   117
justice   111
legal culture   112
moral law   111
natural law   111
positive law   111

Romano-Germanic
  law   113
scientific law   111
stare decisis   113

SUGGESTED READINGS

John Bell, *Judiciaries within Europe: A Comparative Review* (Cambridge UK: Cambridge University Press, 2010). There is a broad range of judicial behavior across the many nations of Europe, and this volume categorizes and describes the range of judicial behavior in politics and law.

Michael Corrado, *Comparative Constitutional Review: Cases and Materials* (Durham, NC: Carolina Academic Press, 2005). We suggested in the text that the role of courts in judicial review is not even across nations. This volume examines the nature of constitutional review and judicial power cross-nationally, with substantial detail and examples.

Henry Ehrmann, *Comparative Legal Cultures* (Englewood Cliffs, NJ: Prentice Hall, 1976). This is a classic cross-national study of the role of law and legal cultures in nations around the world. This was part of a very strong series published by Prentice Hall on political institutions and political behavior.

Tom Ginsburg and Tamir Moustafa, eds., *Rule by Law: The Politics of Courts in Authoritarian Regimes* (New York: Cambridge University Press, 2008). Law in authoritarian nations is often used as a tool of the state. This volume studies the special case of law in these regimes, and shows how the law is used by the state to support the government of the day.

Thomas Hansford and James Spriggs, *The Politics of Precedent on the U.S. Supreme Court* (Princeton, NJ: Princeton University Press, 2006). The idea of precedent is key to the power and behavior of the U.S. Supreme Court. This volume examines both the historical and current use of the concept of precedent, and shows the role that precedent plays in the current operation of the Court.

NOTES

1. See Locke's Section 125 in Sir Ernest Barker, ed., *Social Contract: Essays by Locke, Hume, & Rousseau* (New York: Oxford University Press, 1970).
2. For example, Joseph LaPalombara's *Politics within Nations* (Englewood Cliffs, NJ: Prentice Hall, 1974), had fourteen chapters, with chapters on legislatures, executives, bureaucracies, interest groups, political parties, participation, and so on, but judiciaries and courts were not discussed.
3. See, for example, Glendon Schubert and David J. Danelski, eds., *Comparative Judicial Behavior* (New York: Oxford University Press, 1969); or Theodore L. Becker, *Comparative Judicial Politics* (Chicago, IL: Rand McNally, 1970).
4. See, for example, Kermit Hall and Kevin McGuire, *The Judicial Branch* (New York: Oxford University Press, 2005); and Hiram Chodosh, *Global Justice Reform: A Comparative Methodology* (New York: New York University Press, 2005).
5. See, for some different types of discussions of this issue, Robert Badinter and Stephen Breyer, *Judges in Contemporary Democracy: An International Conversation* (New York: New York University Press, 2004); or Robert Bork, *Coercing Virtue: The Worldwide Rule of Judges* (Toronto: Vintage Canada, 2002).
6. Jerold Waltman and Kenneth Holland, eds., "Preface," in *The Political Role of Law Courts in Modern Democracies*, (New York: St. Martin's Press, 1988), p. vi.
7. Jerold Waltman, "Introduction," in Waltman and Holland, *Political Role of Law Courts*, p. 5.
8. This is one of the central premises of the work of John Rawls, perhaps the best known of contemporary scholars in this area. See John Rawls, *A Theory of Justice* (Cambridge, UK: Harvard University Press, 1971); and John Rawls, *Justice as Fairness* (Cambridge, UK: Harvard University Press, 2001). See also Ronald Kahn, *The Supreme Court and American Political Development* (Lawrence, MA: University Press of Kansas, 2006).
9. This passage became well known when it was used by John Adams in 1774 in the *Boston Gazette*, number 7. Adams credited this formulation to the philosopher James Harrington (1611–1677), the author of the work *The Commonwealth of Oceana* (1656). See also Austin Sarat and Lawrence Douglas, *The Limits of Law* (Stanford, CA: Stanford University Press, 2005).
10. Herbert Winter and Thomas Bellows, *People and Politics* (New York: John Wiley and Sons, 1977), p. 307. See also Kate Malleson, *The Legal System* (New York: Oxford University Press, 2005); or Mary Sarah Bilder, *The Transatlantic Constitution: Colonial Legal Culture and the Empire* (Cambridge, UK: Harvard University Press, 2008).

11. See Locke's Section 127 in Barker, *Social Contract*, p. 74.

12. For an example of writing on natural law, see Mark Murphy, *Natural Law in Jurisprudence and Politics* (New York,: Cambridge University Press, 2006). On positive law, see James Murphy, *The Philosophy of Positive Law: Foundations of Jurisprudence* (New Haven CT: Yale University Press, 2005). On moral law see Roslyn Muraskin and Matthew Muraskin, *Morality and the Law* (Upper Saddle River, NJ: Prentice Hall, 2001). On divine law see Milner Ball, *The Word and the Law* (Chicago, IL: University of Chicago Press, 1993).

13. Winter and Bellows, *People and Politics*, p. 308.

14. See George Sabine, *A History of Political Theory* (New York: Holt, Rinehart and Winston, 1961), p. 942.

15. Sabine, *History of Political Thought*, pp. 194–196.

16. John Merryman, *The Civil Law Tradition*, quoted in Henry Ehrmann, *Comparative Legal Cultures* (Englewood Cliffs, NJ: Prentice Hall, 1976), p. 8.

17. See Roger Cotterrell, *Law, Culture and Society: Legal Ideas in the Mirror of Social Theory* (Burlington, VT: Ashgate, 2006); or Gad Barzilai, *Communities and Law: Politics and Cultures of Legal Identities* (Ann Arbor, MI: University of Michigan Press, 2003).

18. Kenneth Holland, "The Courts in the United States," in *The Political Role of Law Courts*, ed. Jerold Waltman and Kenneth Holland (Basingstoke, UK: Palgrave Macmillan, 1988), p. 7. See also Michael Grossberg and Christopher Tomlins, *The Cambridge History of Law in America* (New York: Cambridge University Press, 2008).

19. Hiroshi Itoh, "The Courts in Japan," in, *The Political Role of Law Courts*, ed. Jerold Waltman and Kenneth Holland (Basingstoke, UK: Palgrave Macmillan, 1988), p. 211. See also Daniel Foote, *Law in Japan: A Turning Point* (Seattle, WA: University of Washington Press, 2007).

20. Ehrmann, *Comparative Legal Cultures*, p. 13. This and the following several paragraphs are based on more extended material in Ehrmann, and Winter and Bellows, *People and Politics*, pp. 309–10 and 319–22.

21. A good discussion of this can be found in William Gordon, *Roman Law, Scots Law and Legal History: Selected Essays* (Edinburgh, UK: Edinburgh University Press, 2007).

22. A thorough discussion of the assumptions of the Anglo-American legal process can be found in Allan C. Hutchinson, *Evolution and the Common Law* (New York: Cambridge University Press, 2005).

23. On common law more generally, see Hamar Foster, *The Grand Experiment: Law and Legal Culture in British Settler Societies* (Vancouver, BC: University of British Columbia Press, 2008).

24. See Michael Gerhardt, *The Power of Precedent* (New York: Oxford University Press, 2008); or Thomas Hansford and James Spriggs, *The Politics of Precedent on the U.S. Supreme Court* (Princeton, NJ: Princeton University Press, 2006).

25. Winter and Bellows, *People and Politics*, p. 316.

26. See Christine Sypnowich, *The Concept of Socialist Law* (New York: Oxford University Press, 1990), for a full discussion.

27. For discussion of this relationship, see Maria Los, *Communist Ideology, Law, and Crime: A Comparative View of the U.S.S.R. and Poland* (New York: St. Martin's Press, 1988).

28. See Luis Franceschi and Andrew Ritho, eds., *Legal Ethics and Jurisprudence in Nation-Building* (Strathmore, UK: Strathmore University Press, 2005); or Timothy Lindsey, *Law Reform in Developing and Transitional States* (London, UK: Routledge, 2006).

29. See Gregory Mahler, *Politics and Government in Israel: The Maturation of a Modern State* (Boulder, CO: Rowman and Littlefield, 2011), p. 230.

30. On religion and law, see Marci Hamilton, *God vs. the Gavel: Religion and the Rule of Law* (New York: Cambridge University Press, 2005); or Kent Greenawalt, *Religion and the Constitution* (Princeton, NJ: Princeton University Press, 2006).

31. Sydney Bailey, *British Parliamentary Democracy* (Boston, MA: Houghton Mifflin, 1958), pp. 15–16.

32. See Kenneth Thompson, ed., *The Presidency and the Constitutional System* (Lanham, MD: University Press of America, 1990); or Richard Neustadt, *Presidential Power and the Modern Presidents: The Politics of Leadership from Roosevelt to Reagan* (New York: Free Press, 1990).

33. See the references to the "decline of legislatures" literature discussed in Chapter 4. See, for more specific discussion of this issue in the United States, Alan Rosenthal, *The Decline of Representative Democracy: Process, Participation, and Power in State Legislatures* (Washington, DC: Congressional Quarterly, 1999).

34. Theodore Lowi, *The End of Liberalism* (New York: W.W. Norton, 1969), esp. Chapter 5, pp. 128–156.

35. See Alfred C. Aman and William T. Mayton, *Administrative Law* (St. Paul, MN: West Publishing, 2001); or Richard Clements and Jane Kay, *Constitutional and Administrative Law* (London, UK: Blackstone, 2001).

36. Becker, *Comparative Judicial Politics*, p. 13. See John Bell, *Judiciaries within Europe: A Comparative Review* (Cambridge, UK: Cambridge University Press, 2010)

37. There are a number of very good discussions of this issue. See Larry Yackle, *Federal Courts* (Durham, NC: Carolina Academic Press, 2009); or Andrew Harding and Peter Leyland, eds., *Constitutional Courts: A Comparative Study* (London, UK: Wildy and Hill, 2009).

38. See the British North America Act (Canada Act) of 1867, Section 92 (14) for provincial legislative jurisdictions, and Section 91 (27) for federal legislative jurisdiction. The interested student can find this in Robert Jackson and Doreen Jackson, *Politics in Canada: Culture, Institutions, Behaviour and Public Policy* (Scarborough, ON: Prentice-Hall Canada, 1990), pp. 673–755.

39. See Jackson and Jackson, *Politics in Canada*, pp. 197–201.

40. Michael Curtis, *Comparative Government and Politics* (New York: Harper and Row, 1977), p. 102. See Kenneth Miller, *Direct Democracy and the Courts* (New York: Cambridge University Press, 2009).

41. Curtis, *Comparative Government*, p. 107. See Matthew Taylor, *Judging Policy: Courts and Policy Reform in Democratic Brazil* (Stanford, CA: Stanford University Press, 2008).

42. The literature in this area is still growing. See Abner Greene, *Understanding the 2000 Election: A Guide to the Legal Battles That Decided the Presidency* (New York: New York University Press, 2005); Christopher Banks and David Cohen, *The Final Arbiter: The Consequences of Bush v. Gore for Law and Politics* (Albany, NY: State University of New York Press, 2005); Lance Smith-DeHaven, ed., *The Battle for Florida: An Annotated Compendium of Materials from the 2000 Presidential Election* (Gainesville, FL: University of Florida Press, 2005).

43. See Donald Jackson and Neal Tate, eds., *Comparative Judicial Review and Public Policy* (Westport, CT: Greenwood Publishing, 1992); Michael Corrado, *Comparative Constitutional Review: Cases and Materials* (Durham, NC: Carolina Academic Press, 2005).

44. Monte Palmer and William Thompson, *The Comparative Analysis of Politics* (Itasca, IL: F.E. Peacock, 1978), p. 136. See also James Heckman, Robert Nelson,

and Lee Cabatingan, eds., *Global Perspectives on the Rule of Law* (New York: Routledge, 2010).

45. See David O'Keeffe and Antonio Bavasso, *Judicial Review in European Union Law* (London, UK: Kluwer Law International, 2000).

46. Two good references to this decision and its impact can be found in Bernard Schwartz, *A History of the Supreme Court* (New York: Oxford University Press, 1993); and Edward White, *The Marshall Court and Cultural Change* (New York: Oxford University Press, 1991).

47. Becker, *Comparative Judicial Politics*, p. 206. See Tom Ginsburg and Tamir Moustafa, eds., *Rule by Law: The Politics of Courts in Authoritarian Regimes* (New York: Cambridge University Press, 2008).

48. See the new journal published by John Wiley and Sons titled *Judicial Review: Mapping the Developing Law and Practice of Judicial Review*, edited by Michael Fordham in London.

49. Jerold Waltman, "The Courts in England," in *The Political Role of Law Courts*, ed. Jerold Waltman and Kenneth Holland (Basingstoke, UK: Palgrave Macmillan, 1988), pp. 119–120.

50. This is discussed in Andrew Knapp and Vincent Wright, *The Government and Politics of France* (New York: Routledge, 2006): and Susan Milner and Nick Parsons, *Reinventing France: State and Society in the 21st Century* (Basingstoke, UK: Palgrave Macmillan, 2003).

51. Becker, *Comparative Judicial Politics*, p. 208.

Political Behavior and the Political Environment

THE POLITICAL SYSTEM REVISITED

In Chapter 1 we introduced the concept of the political system, a set of related objects connected with one another in an analytic way. We indicated that the relationships of these objects were *perceived* by the observer: Sometimes the links between objects are clear and distinct, but sometimes they are not. The links between the British House of Commons and the British House of Lords are reasonably clear; the links between a particular multinational corporation (e.g., British Petroleum) and a Third World nation's political stability may be less so.

Thus far we have focused our attention upon the central political structures of regimes: constitutional frameworks, legislatures, executives, and judiciaries. We must keep in mind, though, that these political structures, however similar or varied they may be and however they may be related to other constitutional structures in their political regimes, all operate within a political *context* or a political *environment*, not in a vacuum. Although it is possible for us to speak abstractly about constitutional structures, we cannot be content to end our cross-national political analysis at that point; the political environment introduces a broad range of variables into our examination.

There are a number of variables—some at the individual level, and some at the level of the political system—that should be considered to be part of the political environment within which an individual operates in the normal process of political participation. The most general description of these variables would have to include the term *political behavior* to describe our interests: We are interested in understanding how and why the individual acts as he or she does—within a given specific political environment. Questions related to these issues will focus on the development of individual attitudes and values, the process of political socialization, and on the process by which individuals come to be active in politics, the process of political recruitment. We will also describe the nature and function of political elites in the polity, and a very specific kind of political behavior—political violence—and its role in politics. We will also turn our attention to *environmental* factors, such as the general idea of pluralism, the interaction among interest groups in politics, and the role of political parties in the system.

On the individual level, it is appropriate for us to understand how individual political attitudes are developed and passed from generation to generation— the process of *political socialization*—so as to appreciate the political culture of the regime. Moreover, preliminary examination may indicate a need to understand the process of *political recruitment:* How are political leaders and political elites selected from among the ranks of the masses? We also want to understand how some key *types* of characteristics—social class and gender, specifically—can affect opportunities to participate in politics and advance in the political world.

At the level of the political system, we need to understand several other possible influences on political behavior. The subject of political recruitment introduces questions related to the relation of the *political elite* to the masses. We know that the recruitment process serves to separate an elite from the masses, but how "open" is the elite?

We shall also briefly discuss the subject of *political violence*, since it is a type of political behavior that is of significance to the political system in the context of "systems maintenance" that we discussed in Chapter 1.

All of this is a weighty assignment for the beginning student. In the following sections of this chapter, we will briefly discuss the individual and systemic structures and behaviors referred to above. We will discuss their potential impact upon the political systems of which they are a part. They will not, however, be the *primary* foci for our area studies chapters in the second part of this book. Our assumption here is that the student is better prepared for further cross-national study with an introduction emphasizing political structures and political institutions, and placing less emphasis on the many variables in the political environment, than with one that emphasizes the many variables in the political environment, but gives short shrift to the decision-making processes of political regimes.[1]

After brief discussion of several of the factors that may be of significance in the political environment, we will turn our attention in the final chapter of the first part of this book to the "outcomes" of political institutions and political behavior: public policy.

THE STUDY OF POLITICAL SOCIALIZATION AND POLITICAL ATTITUDES

Contemporary studies focusing upon political actors are often based upon the assumption that *who the actors are* affects politics. This includes the study of values, attitudes, beliefs, and skills that actors bring with them to the political arena, and leads us to a discussion of **political socialization**.[2] Many scholars believe that the study of political socialization has value as a factor contributing to a greater understanding of how individual political behavior is motivated.

Interest in political socialization is not a creation of contemporary political scientists. Plato dealt with the problem of political education in his *Republic*, as did Aristotle in his *Politics* and *Ethics*; the debate has continued from the time of Jean-Jacques Rousseau to B. F. Skinner:

> From time immemorial, social philosophers have thought that political education *should* have an early start. For Plato and Rousseau there was also little question about the feasibility of such early instruction; to them it was common sense that young children could be educated in fundamental political matters.[3]

Political socialization has been conceptualized as the process by which "the individual acquires attitudes, beliefs, and values relating to the political system of which he is a member and to his own role as a citizen within that political system."[4] The important thing to note in this conceptualization is that socialization is conceived as a *process*; that is, it is an ongoing action, which is not finished as long as the individual is still able to perceive his or her environment and respond to it.

While the idea of direct, formal political socialization has negative connotations for many because of its similarity to the "indoctrination" of youth in authoritarian political systems, it is nonetheless the case that there are many societal actions that *are* directly politically socializing that exist even in "democratic" regimes—including civics courses and the Pledge of Allegiance, for example.

Many gaps need to be filled in socialization research, and much attention needs to be given to major questions that are still outstanding about the importance of political socialization. In the introductory essay to his now-classic book *Socialization to Politics*, Jack Dennis suggested "ten central problem dimensions" related to socialization research. These include the system relevance of political socialization; varieties of the content of political socialization; socialization across the life cycle and generations; cross- and sub-cultural aspects and variations in socialization; the political learning process; the agents and agencies of political socialization; the extent and relative effects of political socialization upon different individuals; and, finally, problems related to specialized political socialization, especially socialization of political elites.[5]

Dennis suggested over three decades ago that "the question about what effects political socialization has upon political life" is "the most important aspect of political socialization research for the development of a theory of politics."[6] It has been argued that, at a minimum, political socialization is important to the political system because it generates a general support for the political system in which it takes place. What is not known, however, is what proportion of diffuse or general support for a political system may be attributed to socialization. There are other factors that generate diffuse support* in a political system—such as popular leaders, popular decisions or policies, and the like—and it has not yet been sufficiently illustrated that it is the process of political socialization that plays a meaningful and significant role in the creation of diffuse support.[7]

It is interesting to note that *negatively* the effect of socialization upon diffuse support has been illustrated to some degree. In one study, investigators have shown a relationship between the cynicism of parents to government and an increased occurrence of such cynicism in their children, with clear implications for diffuse support for government, generally.[8]

A key question related to the study of political socialization and the development of political attitudes and values is related to the "what" of the process: What is the object, the content, of political socialization that is of significance for the political system? Perhaps the best-known exposition on political culture and the passing of political cultures from one generation to another is to be found in Gabriel Almond and Sidney Verba's classic work *The Civic Culture*.

> When we speak of the political culture of a society, we refer to the political system as internalized in the cognitions, feelings, and evaluations of its population. People are induced into it just as they are socialized into nonpolitical roles and social systems.[9]

Similarly, Gabriel Almond has written elsewhere that political socialization is "the process of induction into the political culture. Its end product is a set of attitudes—cognitions, value standards, and feelings—toward the political system."[10]

---

*Diffuse support is very general support for the regime, not for specific leaders or specific policy, but system-level support.

Political roles, as well as a political culture, are suggested as being among the objects taught by political socialization. As the term is used here, a **political role** is "a pattern of expected behavior for individuals holding particular positions in a system."[11] Roles and role behavior are clearly not established from the time of birth, but are taught phenomena. As such, they are a part of the content of political socialization.

General knowledge of the political system and the manner in which it operates is also included in the content of political socialization. How the system works, the functioning of different branches of the government, the role of political parties in the political system, and so on—all are introduced to individuals through the socialization process.

Another area that has been given considerable attention in investigation is the "when" of the process—a temporal dimension of socialization. Political socialization is a process, and as such is not a phenomenon to be studied merely in individuals at a single age, with no consideration given to earlier and later years. Studies examining the temporal nature of political socialization have focused on such questions as when the process begins, which are the most important years for later political attitudes, and how long the political socialization process can be said to continue.

Research has shown that there is a strong relationship between the *time* of initial socialization to politics and the *agents* of initial political socialization. One study found that legislators could be placed along a bidimensional continuum:

> ranging from those who were socialized early (childhood or grammar school) by the family, through those socialized as adolescents by self (self starters), to those whose socialization was delayed until the post-adolescent period and occurred because of external events and conditions.[12]

While we can say that different agents of socialization are most effective at different times of the age span, problems appear when we try to translate this fact into its effect on legislative behavior, for example.

Different points in the life cycle are significant in terms of *what* will be learned, as well as *by what agent* the socialization will be influenced. It has been demonstrated[13] that children are first aware of executive positions in government, such as the president or a mayor, and not until they grow older do they perceive legislators as anything but "the president's helpers." Jean Piaget has shown that certain concepts are more difficult than others for a child to learn.[14] For example, in one set of studies there was much confusion for young children as to whether they were citizens of Switzerland or citizens of Geneva; it was not until the children reached a later level of cognitive development that they saw that these two possibilities were not mutually exclusive.

Cross-cultural differences and similarities in the socialization process may, in fact, be among the most valuable of the several types of socialization studies, because they have implications for several problem dimensions discussed here.[15] By finding differences in the socialization processes in two different cultural settings, implications can be drawn relating not only to the effectiveness of various agents of socialization, but also to system relevance of the study of political socialization.

Within a single national setting, studies of subcultural and group variations in political socialization may have the same value as cross-cultural research. One good example of this type of research is a classic study by Dean Jaros and others: Through a study of a specific American subculture, in this case the "Appalachian personality," Jaros attempted to not only theorize about the effectiveness of certain agents of socialization in Appalachia as compared with an earlier and comparable study in New Haven, Connecticut,[16] but also to make several theoretical suggestions pertaining to the effects of socialization on the development of political cynicism, and thereby its relevance for system maintenance. Similar studies have been undertaken investigating other subcultural or group characteristics, including race, gender, ethnic group membership, and social class.[17]

The actual question of how learning takes place—the "how" of the socialization question that asks "who learns what from whom, how, and when"—is certainly no less important. This "how" question encompasses several components, and can be seen to often include both the "when" and the "from whom" aspects of socialization theory.

When many people ask how political learning takes place, what they are in fact asking is what the *agents* are that are active in the political learning process, rather than really inquiring about learning theory:

Q.: How did Alden come to believe that?

A.: Oh, she was in the Peace Corps in Jordan and saw that behavior for herself. After the Peace Corps, she was a graduate student at Emory University and read more about that topic. Now she works in the news media, and her views have matured. She also talks about politics with her husband Scott quite a bit.

In many cases this "from whom or what" response to our "how" question is the only response possible. That is, the questioner in this case is not *really* looking for an answer couched in terms of learning theory; the individual is interested in the active elements involved in the process of Alden coming to believe something that she does.

In other instances, the "how" is answered in temporal terms, employing such implicit concepts as maturation, for example:

Q.: How did Darcy come to believe that?

A.: She is now a teacher in elementary school and is much more perceptive of the world around her.

Or an answer in terms of both the "when" and the "from whom":

Q.: How did Darcy come to believe that?

A.: Now that she is married to Chris, who is *very* interested in politics, she talks about politics a great deal. Her daughter Miriam is also teaching her a lot about how children perceive the world around them.

Thus, we can see that often in political socialization research the question being answered, which is ostensibly our "how" question, frequently is not answered in "how" (learning theory) terms at all. Rather, it is answered in terms of either the agents of socialization involved ("from whom or what"), or temporal-chronological factors ("when?"), or both.[18]

By far, the most attention in political socialization research has been given to the "by whom or what" question: The examination of those agents and factors that are most influential in the socialization process. It has been almost traditionally accepted that the family is foremost among the many agents of socialization influential during childhood. Aristotle wrote of the overriding importance of the family in socialization. A more recent author suggests that "the most important source of children's conceptions of authority undoubtedly is the civic instruction which goes on incidental to normal activities in the family."[19]

The literature also shows us that one by-product of the socialization process is that the child is likely to form political impressions, images, and even opinions before he or she has any real political *knowledge* upon which to base those feelings. Children tend to develop party identification early, with no cognitive reason for preferring one party over another. Greenstein wrote that by the fourth grade, more than 60 percent of the children in one study could give a party identification, even if they could not give a satisfactory reason for why they had chosen that party.[20]

Another key set of issues suggested by Jack Dennis concerns the "extent" of political socialization—that is, to what *degree* one is politicized when one is socialized to politics. Does political socialization merely involve imparting a sensitivity or awareness of issues upon an individual, or does it imply a true politicization of the individual? That is, not only is the individual aware of issues, but he or she also has opinions on all the issues involved.

A final area of research involves specialized political socialization. This has focused upon elite socialization, specifically upon those who are politically active, including legislators.[21] By studying the socialization of legislators or other political elites, we know better what kind of individuals attain formal office, for example, and thereby we have some basis for predicting how political elites will perform. As political socialization theory becomes more developed, we should better be able to predict how those political elites will behave once they are in office.

THE STUDY OF POLITICAL RECRUITMENT

The study of **political recruitment** has not been subjected to the same questions of "relevance for the political system" as has political socialization research. Potential critics and challengers have been satisfied that the channels that are open for people to enter the political elite level, and subsequently to become officeholders, influence which people become political elites and subsequent officeholders. This has *de facto* significance for the political system.[22]

Political recruitment research, however, suffers from several of the same theoretical problems as political socialization research. Significant among those problems is that theorists are not in agreement as to exactly what political recruitment is. Although theorists agree that political recruitment is a *process*, definitions suggested in the literature differ. One author, for example, suggested that:

> political recruitment refers to the processes that select from among the several million socially favored and politically motivated citizens comprising the political stratum those several thousand who reach positions of significant national influence.[23]

The most broadly applicable definition is that of Gabriel Almond: He defines recruitment as the function of the political system that draws upon members of the society, inducts them "into the specialized roles of the political system, trains them with political cognitive maps, values, expectations, and affects." Thereby, he writes, the recruitment function "takes up where the general political socialization function leaves off."[24]

Part of the definition problem is that the term *recruitment* is used to cover two actual processes, *initial recruitment to* politics, and *promotion within* the political infrastructure. Lester Milbrath broke down the overall recruitment process into several levels of participation.[25] He argued that there is a hierarchy of political involvement and participation in the United States, ranging from the individual who is merely a "spectator," to a "gladiator" who is actively involved in the political arena, with "transitionals" in the middle. The advantage of this kind of approach is that it allows us to break down the general process into its component parts, and thereby allows us to examine more closely each distinct segment of the overall recruitment process.

A number of studies of political recruitment have been undertaken, with a wide diversity of foci, and several central areas of research may be identified as a basis for an examination of this area (much as we did with the political socialization question). To take one example, Moshe Czudnowski suggested a six-fold framework for the study of political recruitment, including (1) social background characteristics, (2) political socialization and recruitment factors, (3) initial activity and apprenticeship, (4) occupations, (5) motivations, and (6) the selection process itself.[26]

Although this particular framework is made up of several components, a broader examination of the literature seems to indicate the existence of two major foci of study: (1) studies examining the characteristics or backgrounds of those who are recruited, and (2) studies focusing upon the recruitment process itself. It is interesting to note that while most theorists do recognize political recruitment as a process, similar to political socialization, the bulk of the attention in the literature is not focused upon the process—the "how" aspect—of the question, but rather upon the "who" of the question, background studies of those who are recruited.

The rationale for gathering background data is based upon two assumptions. The first is that "relationships exist between social background characteristics and opportunities to gain access to political offices"; the second is that "the social background characteristics are related to variations in the attitudes and behavior of political elites."[27]

Generally speaking, the literature has tended to substantiate the first assumption underlying the study of social background data; there *does* appear to be a relationship between social background characteristics and the opportunity to gain access to political office. It *does* appear to be the case that individuals from the middle and upper classes of some societies tend to be disproportionately recruited in relation to their size in populations as a whole. This bias appears to exist not only in national political office, but also in *all* aspects of the political system, including party work and local-level offices.[28]

One interesting finding of social background research has been the discovery of the strong association between certain occupations and subsequent elective office. The relationship between legislators and the practice of law prior to election has frequently been cited; in the United States "it is proverbial that U.S. Congressmen are lawyers."[29] While the relationship may be "proverbial" in the United States, studies show that this American affinity is not universal. It has been demonstrated that whereas 58 percent of American legislators were lawyers at one point in time, only about 2 percent of Swedish legislators were lawyers. In fact, of twenty-two nations examined in one study, the average percentage of legislators who previously were lawyers was 16 percent, a far cry from a universally "proverbial" relationship.[30]

In addition to the "who" of the recruitment process, considerable attention has been paid to the questions of how and why individuals are recruited. A number of studies have focused on the role that parties and other groups play in the recruitment process. Still others are oriented toward psychological factors involved in the recruitment process, and the roles that the electoral system and opportunity in general play in the process.

Studies focusing on the role played by political parties in recruitment have shown that their significance varies on a country-by-country basis. In the United States, for example, parties have lost much of the influence that they once had over the recruitment process, and they are currently struggling to maintain control over candidate selection. The loss of influence can be attributed to changes in the primary election system and the increased openness of party conventions. As such, the loss of influence varies on a state-by-state basis, depending upon electoral laws in force.[31] Outside of the United States, one need not look too far to see evidence of the importance of the party in the recruitment process, although it, too, varies on a country-by-country basis.[32]

Other groups have been shown to have an impact on the recruitment process, sometimes through the political party itself. Czudnowski demonstrated the conditions under which political parties may become very group-oriented in their selection procedures for candidates for the national legislature, to the extent of permitting groups to dictate who "their" representatives on the party electoral list will be.[33] It was suggested that group-oriented recruitment is positively associated with a proportional representation electoral system.

Yet another important factor that can influence the recruitment process is opportunity. Regardless of the size of the political strata or the number of "self-starters" ready to run for office, recruitment cannot take place if vacancies in office are not present.[34] Moreover, different recruitment rates exist for different offices; in the United States, recruitment to the presidency is more difficult than recruitment to the Senate, because turnover in the Senate is greater, and there are more opportunities there. Similarly, recruitment will be greater for the House of Representatives than for the Senate, and greater for state legislative offices than for national legislative office.

SOME INFLUENCING AGENTS OF POLITICAL BEHAVIOR: SOCIAL CLASS AND GENDER

As we noted above, there are often formal, political, legal barriers that can affect the way individuals behave in political settings. We will note later in this text that the president of Mexico *must* be male. Period. Women need not apply. In some settings there is an age requirement in order to vote, or to hold office. In some settings there are legal restrictions that follow religious lines.

In this section of this chapter we want to discuss some more *indirect* ways of influencing political behavior, and we will specifically focus on three kinds of factors: those related to **social class**, those related to **religion**, and those related to **gender**. Our interest here is *not* to address the formal/legal restrictions that may affect these identifying attributes. Rather, we are interested in social class and gender and their *indirect* influences upon attitudes and behavior.

Social Class

Social class refers to some kind of ordering of groups in society, usually including such objective characteristics as income, education, or occupation.[35] The point of these characteristics is not only to identify the characteristics themselves, but also to give individuals the opportunity to *infer* rankings about individuals: one group is *better than* another in some respects. The importance of a class approach to understanding politics is that it is based upon the notion of *stratification*: some classes have *more* (rights, benefits, resources) than others simply because of their class identity. Certainly one good example of this was the work of Karl Marx,[36] who distinguished between the workers ("the proletariat"), members of a middle class, a group of business workers and self-employed individuals ("the petite bourgeoisie"), and the economic elite ("the bourgeoisie"); one's economic standing affected their power in society and in politics.

It is often the case that social class is strongly associated with ethnic identity.[37] In both developing and underdeveloped nations, ethnic-based conflict has developed based on language, on religion, or on race. Whether we are talking about Third World settings such as the Ibos in Nigeria battling with the Hausa in Nigeria, or the Catholics in Northern Ireland battling with the Protestants in Northern Ireland, ethnic (which would include religious) identity has served as the basis for much violence and much sadness in modern society. In settings where ethnic identity has not resulted in so much *violent* action, such as the United States, it still is possible to identify political competition between and among ethnic groups—Anglo-Saxons, Irish, Hispanic, Jewish, Italian, African-American—that can result in tension in society.

One of the key uses of the construct of *class* is the idea of *class conflict*.[38] This suggests that not only do different classes exist, but that they are in competition with each other to have more power, more access to resources, or more security. The higher classes fight to keep what they have; the lower classes fight to get more of what they don't have. Sometimes these struggles transfer neatly to the political arena (so that British blue-collar workers are more prone to vote for Labour, while British middle- and upper-class voters are more prone to vote for the Conservatives). Sometimes the association between politics and class isn't so neat. It has often been the case that the most intense conflict involving social and economic class has involved the rural poor in developing nations against the landlord class, often well represented in the national government.

Religion

Certainly social class can be affected by religious identity, too.[39] Many societies have dominant religious identities and minority religious identities. The key question is what happens with those identities, are they essentially "private" or "personal" labels, or do they open or close doors of opportunities for individuals. For many years in the United States some of the nation's premier institutions of higher education had quotas on the number of Jewish students they would admit. This was not based upon ability, or likely success, but was an example of social discrimination against a religious group.

Gender

We have already seen in other sections of this text, and we will see again on several occasions in other settings, that *gender* is a significant political construct.[40] That is, it makes a difference in terms of an individual's political behavior whether the individual is a man or a woman in many societies. In most nations women make up more than half of the population. Yet, as we have already seen and will see again, women tend to hold far less than half of the leadership positions in governments. Why is this?

In some societies there is actual *legal* limitation on what women can do.[41] That is, women may be *legally excluded* from participation in some political structures, such as the presidency in Mexico for example, where the law stipulates that the president of Mexico must be a male. In some societies there may be both formal (i.e., legal) and informal (i.e., cultural) limitations placed upon opportunities for women. Although these are examples of gender limiting *behavior*, exactly the same thing can be said for *attitudes*. As individuals—boys and girls—are growing up in society and are developing beliefs and attitudes about politics, about political values, and about potential political behavior, they develop *different* attitudes depending upon their gender. In these settings girls may "learn"— either formally or informally, as we have already described—that political behavior and political leadership is *just not something that girls do*. Other cultures may be gender-blind, and girls may be closer to boys in the kinds of attitudes they develop.

Some scholars have argued that colonialism—whatever its drawbacks for nations and whatever negative things can be said about colonialism as a general phenomenon—played an important role in breaking traditional gender roles in respective colonial systems. Although it is hard to generalize, because different colonial systems had different sets of relationships, some argue that imperialism and colonialism brought increased access to education to women, thereby increasing their relative equality in society.[42] Others argue that the reverse actually occurred, that gender roles were actually more flexible *before* colonial powers appeared and set very rigid social structures into place.

In modern and postmodern societies, gender roles have changed significantly from what we find in the developing world. Women have more opportunities outside of the home. They have more access to education and to career opportunities that they want to pursue. They are more politically active.[43]

Much research has been done on gender and political attitudes. In the early 1990s, the United Nations released a study focusing upon gender, and the annual *Human Development Report* regularly provides data on the situation in which women find themselves in different areas of the world. It is increasingly common that girls have similar opportunities to boys in terms of primary education, and although the equality of the genders decreases as education progresses, this is a pattern that is changing as time goes on.

The 2010 United Nations *Human Development Report* shows that "the disadvantages facing women and girls are a major source of inequality. All too often, women and girls are discriminated against in health, education and the labour market—with negative repercussions for their freedoms." The report further indicates that

- Gender inequality varies tremendously across countries—the losses in achievement due to gender inequality (not directly comparable to total inequality losses because different variables are used) range from 17 percent to 85 percent. The Netherlands tops the list of the most gender-equal countries, followed by Denmark, Sweden and Switzerland.
- Countries with unequal distribution of human development also experience high inequality between women and men, and countries with high gender inequality also experience unequal distribution of human development. Among the countries doing very badly on both fronts are Central African Republic, Haiti and Mozambique.

The *Human Development Report* sorts nations by what it calls the *Human Development Index (HDI)* into four categories, "very high," "high," "medium," and "low."[44] The HDI looks at more than the total amount of wealth in a society, it looks at the *consequences* of that wealth, what we might call the national quality of life. This would include such measures as literacy,

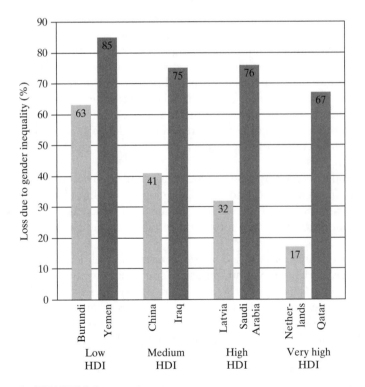

FIGURE 6.1

Loss in Achievement due to Gender Inequality

Source: United Nations, *Human Development Report, 2010.* Online edition found at http://hdr.undp.org/en/mediacentre/summary/gender/ (accessed June 2011).

life expectancy, education, and gross domestic product. It answers the question of whether the wealth created results in a quality standard of living for all. The data show, as indicated in Figure 6.1, above, that even within HDI categories there is still remarkable variation in the degree of loss of achievement due to gender inequality.[45]

We saw in Chapter 2 that one relatively modern ideology, *feminism*, has sought to remove this pattern of behavior in contemporary society.[46] Feminist theory is often used by individuals to explain why politics operates as it does, why political institutions are as they are, and why political behavior has developed as it has developed. Feminists argue that unconscious—and sometimes conscious—attitudes about women held by men that limit their rights and opportunities must be opposed. Feminists advocate removing barriers to the equality of women. The feminist agenda includes a wide range of issues going beyond basic equality and equal rights. Feminists today want more than simply removing *restrictions*: They want true *opportunity*. The agenda includes equal pay for equal work. It includes several health issues, including the abortion issue because it relates to the idea that a woman should have control of her own body. It includes numerous other economic and noneconomic issues, too.

It is worth noting that while women may claim to have a particular problem with full participation in the developing world, progress is being made. Economic development is bringing with it rising opportunity for girls and women, rising educational levels, rising economic opportunities, increasing opportunities to participate in leadership positions in society. While it is true that the majority of women who have become political leaders of their respective nations have *come* to power as either daughters of leaders or widows of leaders, it is increasingly the case that women *are* having opportunities today that were simply not available to them a generation ago.

Group Membership and Attitude Formation

We have seen in the preceding paragraphs that although there are occasionally *legal* barriers to participation by specific groups in society, there are also *informal* barriers to participation, barriers that can be indirect in that they are associated with social characteristics and affect attitudes, which in turn affect behavior. As we look at specific political case studies later in this volume we should keep these factors in mind, and ask whether the explanation for political phenomena is *formal* and *legal*—including political institutions, for example, or rules of behavior—or whether the explanation for political phenomena is *informal*, sometimes *cultural* in nature.

THE ROLE OF THE POLITICAL ELITE

Now that we have briefly examined how the **political elite** *become* the elite, it is important to understand the *role* of the political elite. The "political elite" are those who have relatively high levels of interest in politics and relatively high levels of involvement in the political process. An interesting question is whether "elitism" is compatible with democratic government? How should the elite behave, and how should the masses relate to the elite? Because these are important questions, we will endeavor to highlight some of the most important issues raised by them.[47] The concept of a political elite means different things to different people. On one hand, the term *elite* simply means "best," and there is very little that is objectionable in that. On the other hand, *elite* is sometimes interpreted more broadly to refer to those who wield power in politics, with a distinctively negative connotation.

The question is: How does the existence of a political elite fit in with the idea of democratic government? We know that democracy places many requirements on citizens, including that they be informed, knowledgeable, have principles, and be rational, and we know that not all voters are like that. Fortunately, we have been told that not all voters *need* to have these characteristics for a democratic system to survive.[48] If enough individuals are adequately motivated and informed, the system can continue to operate.

Philosophers who have written about elitism, including Vilfredo Pareto (1848–1923) and Gaetano Mosca (1858–1941), have focused on uneven distribution of power in society. Even more modern theorists, such as Robert Michels (1876–1936), have argued that an uneven distribution of power cannot be avoided; the question is how do organizations (and society) respond to this uneven distribution of power. Perhaps the best known modern study, *The Power Elite* by C. Wright Mills (1956), suggested that politics in the United States was dominated by a small number of military, political, and corporate leaders.

Elite theory suggests that society is not controlled by a wide range of groups, each competing with other groups to have access to power and resources, but suggests instead that society is a closed system controlled by a relatively small group. They might recognize that **pluralism**—having many different groups in society—would suggest that many different groups in society compete for power, but their view is that *real* power is kept controlled by a relatively small group, the same individuals that Mills referred to as the "power elite." In this sense "elite theory" is really about how political power is distributed in society, and about how individuals get control of power.

Is there an association between elitism and political development? Will a politically underdeveloped nation have more, or less, equality in access to power, to resources, and to opportunities? As a general rule, scholars have argued that with economic and political development comes greater opportunity, so that we are more likely to find a more *open* elite, with more opportunities for non-elite individuals to *become* members of the elite, as a country becomes more politically and economically developed.

Elite theory is usually represented as a pyramid of power, as shown in Figure 6.2. This suggests that the number of individuals at the lower levels of the pyramid are large, and as we move up the pyramid—in terms of power and in terms of resources and in terms of opportunity—the number of individuals becomes smaller. At the end of the day, elite theory tells us, political decisions are made by a relatively small number of individuals.

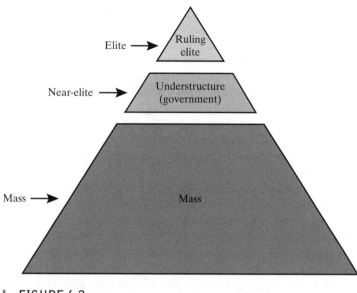

FIGURE 6.2
The Political Elite and the Masses

The key ingredient here is what are called "elite-mass linkages," the patterns of relationships existing between the elite and the masses that allow the elite to govern on behalf of the masses. The elite can govern by force, through coercion, such as we find in military regimes. The political system will be more stable, however, and will have to expend less of its resources on coercive measures if it can govern through a sense of legitimacy on the part of the mass public, and not through a sense of coercion. This will be based upon the degree to which the mass public shares the views of the political and socioeconomic elite.

The existence of elites *can* be compatible with democratic government under the right circumstances.[49] The most important single characteristic appears to be an **open elite**: the possibility for the masses to become part of the elite. Again, this ties in with our discussion of recruitment processes in a regime. Where there are effective recruitment structures, a relatively open elite can exist; where sufficient opportunities do not exist, and where we find a relatively "closed" elite, we will invariably find a system of lower legitimacy and less stability.

POLITICAL PARTICIPATION AND POLITICAL VIOLENCE

The discussion of the role of the military in politics (in Chapter 4) shows that it is not only *participation* that is crucial for regimes, but also the *type* of participation that takes place. There is one kind of participation, which we should mention briefly here, that can be of great significance in the political arena although we have not yet discussed it: political violence.

Violence is one of those terms that means different things to different people.[50] We all might agree that throwing a brick through a window is an act of violence, but there are also other types of violence, as well, that we should keep in mind. Some would argue that there are certain social patterns of behavior—such as racism—that can be referred to as "institutional violence," although others specifically reject "unjust social or political policies" as being "violence" as long as they do not involve physical force.

The range of actions that might be classified as political violence is so broad that constructing a systematic theory is difficult. One recent attempt began with a framework focusing upon "Who" did "What" to "Whom," and subsequently tried to study the "symbolic addressee" of the violence, the claimed "social basis" of the act of violence, the size of the organization undertaking the violence, and "Why" the action took place.[51] (See Table 6.1.)

Among the many types of behavior that we can consider to be examples of political violence might be a riot or a demonstration that turns violent, an assassination, a kidnapping, a mass revolution, a coup d'état, guerrilla warfare, terrorism, and, of course, conventional war. Motivations for these actions might be ideological (e.g., a Marxist revolution or Marxist-inspired coup), religious (e.g, the Islamic revolution in Iran, or the Sikh separatist battles in the Punjab in India), nationalistic (e.g., resistance of the Afghan guerrillas against American military forces), or personal (e.g., an assassination ordered by a leader to remove a potential political competitor). Alternatively, the motivation could come from some combination of these and other reasons.

Consistent with other warnings about ethnocentrism in this text, it is important to remember that American politics in recent years has not been completely

TABLE 6.1

A Typology of Some Relationships in Political Violence

Source ↓ Target →	Individual	Group	State
Individual	Criminal Acts Attitudes Assassination Discrimination	Terrorism Discrimination Tribal Warfare	Riots Coup d'état Revolution
Group	↓	↓ →	Riots Coup d'état Revolution
State	Repression Authoritarianism Totalitarianism	Repression Authoritarianism Totalitarianism	War

confined to peaceful constitutional discourse. Political assassinations, such as the shootings of President John F. Kennedy, presidential candidate Robert F. Kennedy, or civil rights leader Rev. Dr. Martin Luther King, Jr., or the attempted assassinations of President Ronald Reagan or President Gerald Ford were acts of political violence. Much Ku Klux Klan action in the American South involved (and still involves) political violence.[52] Illegal activities by the Federal Bureau of Investigation in the 1960s and 1970s caused "violence" against American citizens. The Ohio National Guard fired on college students at Kent State University who were participating in a demonstration against the Vietnam War in May of 1970, resulting in the deaths of four students.[53] That was political violence, too. This is not meant to suggest that all American politics is violent, but it should serve as a reminder that political violence can exist even in stable, democratic societies.

Because our space is limited here, we shall confine our discussion to a limited number of types of violence. We shall briefly discuss two types of revolution, revolution from "above," the **coup d'état**, and revolution from "below," otherwise known as the *jacquerie*. We shall also briefly discuss guerrilla movements and terrorism, and attempt to point out similarities and differences between the two.

Most simply, a revolution typically involves a dramatic changing of one government, or type of government, for another.[54] One relatively rigid definition that has been offered argues that a revolution involves a "relatively sudden violent and illegal attempt to change the regime of a state or other political organisation, in which large sections of the population are involved as participants."[55] Others might disagree with this view, however, claiming that revolutions often seek to restore legality against a regime that has voided the country's law, and thus cannot be "illegal" actions.

A mass revolution is sometimes referred to as a *jacquerie*, and involves significant and radical changes in the ruling class. Four "great" revolutions of modern times are the American Revolution (1776), the French Revolution (1789), the Russian Revolution (1917–1921), and the Chinese Revolution (1927–1949). See Table 6.2 for a classification of types of political violence.

Another type of revolutionary change, although not one directly involving "large sections of the population," is the *coup d'état*, a sudden seizure of power from above, instead of using the masses from below. Coups are usually carried out by individuals near the center of power who have access to resources and political support. The most common type of coup is called a military coup. The **military coup**, sometimes called a "generals' coup," involves military leaders taking over a polity because of their dissatisfaction with civilian control. This has happened in modern times in Argentina, Thailand, Chad, Pakistan, and Nigeria, among other settings. A coup may also be led by nonmilitary individuals outside of the leadership structure assassinating or deposing the incumbent ruler to substitute themselves as rulers, such as took place recently in Nigeria.

> **▶ TABLE 6.2**
>
> ### Types of Political Violence
>
> Revolution
> - mass revolution (*jacquerie*)
> - *coup d'état*
>   - military coup
>   - palace coup
>   - reform coup
> Terrorism
> Guerrilla Warfare
> Inter-nation Warfare

Other types of coups have been referred to as **palace coups** and **reform coups**. In the former, the forces behind the coup are typically members of a royal family; one member of the royal family tries to push out those in office so that he or she can take power. In the latter case, the sudden political takeover is often done in the name of reform, and the seizure of power may be undertaken by a labor leader or someone holding political office.

The distinction between terrorism and guerrilla action can sometimes become unclear. Generally, we can define **terrorism** as using violence, the threat of violence, coercion, or inducing fear. There is often a symbolic dimension to the terrorist act, as well. The terrorist seeks to influence political behavior of a government through extranormal means, usually having tried and exhausted conventional political options. "Terrorism" is a relatively recent political label in its common usage, although phrases such as "Reign of Terror" (in the French Revolution in 1794) demonstrate that the concept certainly existed long ago.[56]

If we look at groups generally labeled as "terrorists" today, we often find self-ascribed "national liberation" groups. This highlights one very problematic characteristic of the label "terrorist": It is strongly influenced by perspective, as the following example shows.

Menachem Begin, the prime minister of Israel from 1977 to 1984, was once asked how he responded to charges that there was really no difference between his actions against the British in Palestine preceding Israeli independence in 1948—the British referred to him at the time as a "terrorist" and offered a reward of 10,000 pounds sterling, dead or alive, for his capture—and the actions of Yassir Arafat and the Palestine Liberation Organization against Israel in more recent years. Begin's response illustrated the importance of perspective perfectly. He said, "Of course there is a difference. He is a terrorist. I was a freedom fighter."[57]

"Terrorist" is also used as a label for more random acts of violence, such as one finds in the cases of the Japanese Red Army, the Italian Red

Brigade, the West German Baader-Meinhof Gang, and Saddam Hussein's act of "environmental terrorism" in dumping oil in the Persian Gulf as part of Iraq's war effort, and in the yet unused but often discussed context of "nuclear terrorism." In these cases, the terrorist motive is not nationalism, but is instead directed at some policy-related goal, such as the presence of foreign multinationals, environmental concerns, foreign policy issues, the release of "political prisoners," and the like.

We should also note that although objected to by some, the label "terrorism" has also been used in the American context in critical comments about those who use unusual or violent practices to protest against abortions, to protest against logging in the Northwest, to protest the fur industry, or to protest against whaling by the Japanese, to take just a few examples. Again, the use of the label "terrorist" is a very subjective one, and as the example of Prime Minister Begin showed, one man's terrorist can be another man's hero, and *vice versa*.

Guerrilla action, on the other hand, tends to be a bit different in terms of the targets sought by the participants. The usual distinction drawn suggests that guerrillas tend to focus their attention on *government* targets, usually *military* targets, rather than the often random *civilian* targets attacked by terrorists.

These and other types of political violence are of significance for the political system because they offer fundamental challenges to the institutions of the regime. They operate *outside* of the system, as it were, simply rejecting the ability of the institutions and behaviors of the political system to handle their demands.

POLITICAL BEHAVIOR AND ENVIRONMENT IN PERSPECTIVE

It is clear that political structures, like constitutions, cannot be examined in a vacuum. While constitutions might do a great deal to inform us about the behavior of a political regime and the relationships among the various actors and structures within that regime, we know from what we have already seen that there may well be a number of very significant details of the political regime that are not included in the constitution (such as customs, traditions, political culture, political parties, and the like). In this chapter we have seen some of the factors that are key to understanding why individuals participate in politics: those factors that influence not only *who participates* in politics, but *how they come to* believe what they believe. The process of political socialization and political recruitment, the importance of social class and gender, and the role of the political elite, all tell us a great deal about who is active in politics, and why.

We also saw in this chapter that political participation is not always constructive or positive. Political violence is a *kind* of political behavior. Similarly, just studying the constitutional structures of a regime may omit a number of significant political details, and to this extent other variables must be included in area studies to make them complete.

In the next chapter we shall turn our attention to some key organizing structures of politics in contemporary society—interest groups and political parties. Why these types of groups form, and how they form, are key questions that we will meet. As we discuss several different dimensions of what is called "group theory," we will have the opportunity to think about how politics and political behavior is organized, and what the key structures are that help individuals to behave politically.

DISCUSSION QUESTIONS

1. To what does the process of political socialization refer? How is it important for the operation of politics?
2. What are some of the key agents of the political socialization process? How might these differ from one country to another?
3. What do we mean when we refer to the process of political recruitment? To whom does the term apply?
4. How do political institutions and regulations affect the political recruitment process? Give examples from both developed and underdeveloped nations.
5. Who are the political elite? What makes someone part of the political elite? Is this the same in all political settings?
6. Can you describe the relationship between the idea of the existence of a political elite and the existence of a democratic government? Can we have an identifiable political elite in a democracy?
7. What is "political violence"? How do we distinguish (if, indeed, we can) between political violence and "regular" violence? Are there different *kinds* of political violence?
8. What is the difference between a "revolution" and a "coup d'état"?

KEY TERMS

coup d'état   145
gender   137
guerrilla   147
jacquerie   145
military coup   145
open elite   143

palace coup   146
pluralism   142
    political elite   141
political
    recruitment   134
political role   132

political
    socialization   130
reform coup   146
social class   137
terrorism   146

SUGGESTED READINGS

Edward Greenberg, *Political Socialization* (New York: Atherton, 2009). This is an up-to-date edition of one of the classic works of political socialization literature. Greenberg discusses the agents and the actions of political socialization, and discusses the implications of socialization for politics.

Sarah Henderson and Alana Jeydel, *Women and Politics in a Global World* (New York: Oxford University Press, 2010). The premise of this volume is that the political environment and the requirements of political behavior around the world are not the same for women as they are for men. This cross-national study looks at some of the gender-based differences, and discusses the role that women can and do play in politics.

Yeager Hudson and Creighton Peden, *Revolution, Violence, and Equality* (Lewiston, ME: Edwin Mellen Press, 1990). This volume discusses the several types of "nonsystem" political behavior, including revolution and various types of individual-level violence, and describes the impact of these types of behavior for the political systems in which they take place.

Gerhard Loewenberg and Peverill Squire, *Legislatures: Comparative Perspectives on Representative Assemblies* (Ann Arbor, MI: University of Michigan Press, 2002). Loewenberg and Squire offer an extremely broad and comprehensive examination of legislatures, and in doing so show *how* individuals come to be members of legislatures, the process of political recruitment.

Robert Putnam, *The Comparative Study of Political Elites* (New York: Prentice Hall, 1976). Putnam examines who the political elite are, how they get to be elite, what characteristics separate them from non-elites, and what the significance of what they do is for the political system.

NOTES

1. An example of the latter is G. Almond and G. Bingham Powell, eds., *Comparative Politics Today: A World View* (Boston, MA: Little, Brown, 1980).
2. Jean Blondel, *Comparative Legislatures* (Englewood Cliffs, NJ: Prentice-Hall, 1973), p. 76. Two interesting recent works that touch upon the importance of socialization research are by Alan S. Zuckerman, *The Social Logic of Politics: Personal Networks as Contexts for Political Behavior* (Philadelphia, PA: Temple University Press, 2005); James Gimpel, Celeste Lay, and Jason Schuknecht, *Cultivating Democracy: Civic Environments and Political Socialization in America* (Washington, DC: Brookings Institution Press, 2003).
3. David Easton and Jack Dennis, *Children in the Political System* (New York: McGraw Hill, 1969), p. 76. See also Bjorkman Bennich, *Political Culture under Institutional Pressure: How Institutional Change Transforms Early Socialization* (New York: Palgrave Macmillan, 2007).
4. Edward Greenberg, *Political Socialization* (New York: Atherton, 2009), p. 3. See also Robert Hess and Judith Torney-Purta, *The Development of Political Attitudes in Children* (New Brunswick, NJ: Aldine Transaction, 2006).
5. Jack Dennis, ed., *Socialization to Politics* (New York: John Wiley, 1973), p. 4. See also Rosalee Clawson and Zoe Oxley, *Public Opinion, Democratic Ideals, and Democratic Practice* (Washington, DC: CQ Press, 2008).
6. Dennis, *Socialization*, p. 5.
7. See David Easton, *A Framework for Political Analysis* (Englewood Cliffs, NJ: Prentice Hall, 1965), pp. 124–125.
8. Dean Jaros, and others, "The Malevolent Leader: Political Socialization in an American Subculture," *American Political Science Review* 62 (1968): 564–575. See Eldin Fahmy, *Young Citizens: Young People's Involvement in Politics and Decision Making* (Burlington, VT: Ashgate, 2006).

9. Gabriel Almond and Sidney Verba, *The Civic Culture* (Boston, MA: Little, Brown, 1965), p. 14. Some more recent work that has built upon Almond and Verba's scholarship includes David Jackson, *Entertainment and Politics: The Influence of Pop Culture on Young Adult Political Socialization* (New York: Peter Lang, 2009).

10. Almond, "Introduction," in *The Politics of the Developing Areas*, ed. Gabriel Almond and James Coleman (Princeton, NJ: Princeton University Press, 1960), p. 27. See also Eric Shiraev, *People and Their Opinions: Thinking Critically about Public Opinion* (New York: Pearson/Longman, 2006).

11. Raymond Hopkins, "The Role of the MP in Tanzania," *American Political Science Review* 64 (1970): 754–771.

12. Allan Kornberg and Norman Thomas, "The Political Socialization of National Legislative Elites in the United States and Canada," *Journal of Politics* 27 (1965): 761–775.

13. See, for example, Jens Qvortrup, *Studies in Modern Childhood: Society, Agency, Culture* (New York: Palgrave Macmillan, 2005); or Orit Ichilov, *Political Learning and Citizenship Education under Conflict: The Political Socialization of Israeli and Palestinian Youngsters* (New York: Routledge, 2004).

14. The classic article is by Jean Piaget and Anne-Marie Weil, "The Development in Children of the Idea of the Homeland," *International Social Science Bulletin* 3 (1951): 561–578. More recent work includes Sonia Livingstone and Kirsten Drotner, eds., *International Handbook of Children, Media, and Culture* (London, UK: SAGE, 2008).

15. An example of such a study is John Schumaker and Tony Ward, *Cultural Cognition and Psychopathology* (Westport, CT.: Praeger, 2001).

16. Jaros and others, "The Malevolent Leader," pp. 564–575; and Greenstein, "The Benevolent Leader," pp. 934–943.

17. Other studies include Gary Segura and Shaun Bowler, *Diversity in Democracy: Minority Representation in the United States* (Charlottesville, VA: University of Virginia Press, 2005); or Russell Francis Farnen, *Political Culture, Socialization, Democracy, and Education: Interdisciplinary and Cross-National Perspectives for a New Cenutry* (New York: Peter Lang, 2008).

18. Alan Zuckerman, ed., *The Social Logic of Politics: Personal Networks as Contexts for Political Behavior* (Philadelphia, PA: Temple University Press, 2005). See also Li Bennich-Bjorkman, *Political Culture: How Institutional Change Transforms Early Socialization* (New York: Palgrave Macmillan, 2008).

19. Greenstein, *Children and Politics*, p. 44.

20. Ibid. p. 71.

21. For illustrations of this type of literature, see Sue Thomas and Clyde Wilcox, *Women and Elective Office: Past, Present, and Future* (New York: Oxford University Press, 2005); Ronald Keith Gaddie, *Born to Run: Origins of the Political Career* (Lanham, MD: Rowman and Littlefield, 2004); and Margaret Conway, *Women and Political Participation: Cultural Change in the Political Arena* (Washington, DC: CQ Press, 2005).

22. See Michael Hartmann, *The Sociology of Elites* (New York: Routledge, 2007); Volker Perthes, *Arab Elites: Negotiating the Politics of Change* (Boulder, CO: Lynne Rienner, 2004).

23. Robert Putnam, *The Comparative Study of Political Elites* (New York: Prentice Hall, 1976), p. 46. See also Masamichi Sasaki, *Elites: New Comparative Perspectives*

(Boston, MA: Brill, 2008); and Andrew Roth, *Parliamentary Profiles* (London, UK: Parliamentary Profiles, 2004).

24. Almond, "Introduction," p. 31. See also Katherine Opello, *Gender Quotas, Party Reform, and Political Parties in France* (Lanham, MD: Lexington Books, 2006).

25. Milbrath, *Political Participation*. See also Marian Sawer and Manon Tremblay, *Representing Women in Parliament: A Comparative Study* (New York: Routledge, 2006).

26. Czudnowski, "Political Recruitment," pp. 178–229.

27. Harold Clarke and Richard Price, eds., "Political Recruitment: Theoretical Overview and Review of the Literature," in *Recruitment and Leadership Selection in Canada* (Toronto, ON: Holt, Rinehart, and Winston, 1976), p. 7.

28. See, for examples of such studies, the following: Mino Vianello and Gwen Moore, *Gendering Elites: Economic and Political Leadership in 27 Industrialized Societies* (New York: Macmillan, 2000).

29. M. Pederson, "Lawyers in Politics: The Danish Folketing and United States Legislatures," in *Comparative Legislative Behavior: Frontiers of Research*, ed. Samuel Patterson and John Wahlke (New York: Wiley, 1972), p. 25.

30. Patterson and Wahlke, *Comparative Legislative Behavior*, p. 25. See also Peter Siavelis and Scott Morgenstern, eds., *Pathways to Power: Political Recruitment and Candidate Selection in Latin America* (University Park, PA: Pennsylvania State University Press, 2008).

31. See Roger Davidson and Walter Oleszek, *Congress and Its Members* (Washington, DC: CQ Press, 2006); Gerhard Loewenberg and Peverill Squire, *Legislatures: Comparative Perspectives on Representative Assemblies* (Ann Arbor, MI: University of Michigan Press, 2002).

32. A very good review of the literature on political parties can be found in Frank Belloni and Dennis Beller, eds., *Faction Politics: Political Parties and Factionalism in Comparative Perspective* (Santa Barbara, CA: A.B.C. Clio, 1987).

33. Moshe Czudnowski, "Sociocultural Variables and Legislative Recruitment," *Comparative Politics* 4 (1972): 561–587; and Moshe Czudnowski, "Legislative Recruitment under Proportional Representation in Israel: A Model and a Case Study," *Midwest Journal of Political Science* 14 (1970): 216–248.

34. Malcolm Jewell and Samuel Patterson, *The Legislative Process in the United States* (New York: Random House, 1973), p. 88.

35. See Marjorie Cohen and Jane Pulkingham, *Public Policy for Women: The State, Income Security, and Labour Market Issues* (Toronto' ON: University of Toronto Press, 2009).

36. See John Seed, *Marx: A Guide for the Perplexed* (New York: Continuum, 2010); Paul Hirst, *Marxism and Historical Writing* (New York: Routledge, 2010); or Miguel Abensour, Max Blechman, and Martin Breaugh, *Democracy against the State: Marx and the Machiavellian Moment* (Malden, MA: Polity, 2011).

37. Thomas Barfield, *Afghanistan: A Cultural and Political History* (Princeton, NJ: Princeton University Press, 2010); Roland Hsu, *Ethnic Europe: Mobility, Identity, and Conflict in a Globalized World* (Stanford, CA: Stanford University Press, 2010); Neal Jesse and Kristen Williams, *Ethnic Conflict: A Systematic Approach to Cases of Conflict* (Washington, DC: CQ Press, 2011).

38. Irene Thomson, *Culture Wars and Enduring American Dilemmas* (Ann Arbor, MI: University of Michigan Press, 2010); or Thomas Bramble and Rick Kuhn, *Labor's Conflict: Big Business, Workers and the Politics of Class* (New York: Cambridge University Press, 2011).

39. See Brian Grim and Roger Finke, *The Price of Freedom Denied: Religious Persecution and Conflict in the 21st Century* (New York: Cambridge University Press, 2011); or Richard Brian Miller, *Terror, Religion, and Liberal Thought* (New York: Columbia University Press, 2010).

40. See Mona Lena Krook and Sarah Childs, *Women, Gender, and Politics: A Reader* (New York: Oxford University Press, 2010); or Sarah Henderson and Alana Jeydel, *Women and Politics in a Global World* (New York: Oxford University Press, 2010).

41. Jennifer Lawless and Richard Fox, *It Still Takes a Candidate: Why Women Don't Run for Office* (New York, UK: Cambridge University Press, 2010); or Anna Manasco Dionne, *Women, Men and the Representation of Women in the British Parliaments: Magic Numbers?* (Manchester: Manchester University Press, 2010).

42. See Georgina Waylen, *Gender in the Third World* (Boulder, CO: Lynne Rienner, 1996).

43. See Ronald Inglehart and Pippa Norris, *Rising Tide: Gender Equality and Cultural Change around the World* (Cambridge, UK: Cambridge University Press, 2003).

44. United Nations, Human Development Report, 2010, "Indices," available at *http://hdr.undp.org/en/statistics/hdi/* (accessed June 2011).

45. United Nations, Human Development Report, 2010, "Media," available at *http://hdr.undp.org/en/mediacentre/summary/gender/* (accessed June 2011).

46. Jonathan Dean, *Rethinking Contemporary Feminist Politics* (New York: Palgrave Macmillan, 2010); Catherine Redfern and Kristin Aune, *Reclaiming the F Word: The New Feminist Movement* (New York: Palgrave Macmillan, 2010).

47. See, for examples of recent work in this area, Richard Zweigenhaft and G. William Domhoff, *Diversity in the Political Elite: How It Happened, Why It Matters* (Lanham, MD: Rowman and Littlefield, 2006).

48. Jocelyn Evans, *Voters and Voting: An Introduction* (Thousand Oaks, CA: SAGE, 2004); Charles Kadushin, *The American Intellectual Elite* (New Brunswick, NJ: Transaction, 2006); Martin Wattenberg, *Where Have All the Voters Gone?* (Cambridge, MA: Harvard University Press, 2002).

49. A very good discussion of these issues can be found in Peter Bachrach, ed., *Political Elites in a Democracy* (New York: Atherton, 1973). See also G. William Domhoff, *Who Rules America? Power and Politics and Social Change* (Boston, MA: McGraw Hill, 2006).

50. For examples of recent discussion of this issue, see Fernando Coronil and Julie Skurski, *States of Violence* (Ann Arbor MI: University of Michigan Press, 2006); or Virginia Held, *How Terrorism Is Wrong: Morality and Political Violence* (New York: Oxford University Press, 2008).

51. Merkl, *Political Violence*, pp. 32–33. See Beverley Milton-Edwards, *Islam and Violence in the Modern Era* (New York: Palgrave Macmillan, 2006).

52. Two interesting sources on this topic are by David Mark Chalmers, *Backfire: How the Ku Klux Klan Helped the Civil Rights Movement* (Lanham, MD: Rowman and Littlefield, 2003); and Bill Stanton, *Klanwatch: Bringing the Ku Klux Klan to Justice* (New York: Dutton, 1992).

53. See Kim Sorvig, *To Heal Kent State: A Memorial Meditation* (Philadelphia, PA: Worldview Press, 1990). See also Brad Lucas, *Radicals, Rhetoric, and the War: The University of Nevada in the Wake of Kent State* (New York: Palgrave Macmillan, 2006).

54. See Yeager Hudson and Creighton Peden, *Revolution, Violence, and Equality* (Lewiston, ME: Edwin Mellen Press, 1990).

55. John R. Thackrah, *Encyclopedia of Terrorism and Political Violence* (London, UK: Routledge and Kegan Paul, 1987), p. 215. See also David Whittaker, *The Terrorism Reader* (New York: Routledge, 2007).

56. Edgar O'Ballance, *Language of Violence: The Blood Politics of Terrorism* (San Rafael, CA: Presidio Press, 1979), pp. 1–8. See also Philip Herbst, *Talking Terrorism: A Dictionary of the Loaded Language of Political Violence* (Westport, CT: Greenwood Press, 2003).

57. Interview with the author in the Knesset, April 3, 1975. The distinction between being a hero of national liberation and being a terrorist is often one of perspective, as this interview indicated. See Gerald Cromer, *A War of Words: Political Violence and Public Debate in Israel* (New York: Frank Cass, 2004).

Pluralism, Parties, Interest Groups, and Social Movements

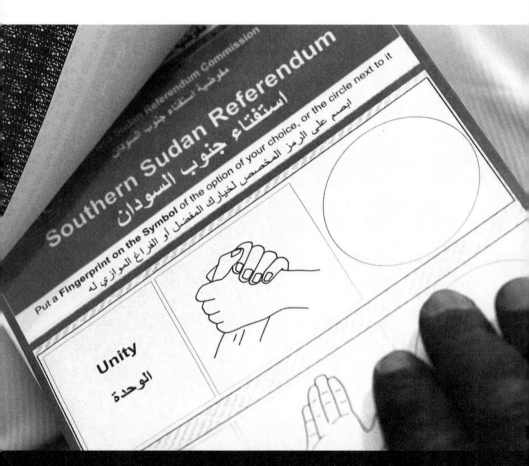

Citizen participation in decision-making—one example of which is voting—can be crucially important in the political system, both for the system's creation as well as for specific decisions made by structures that are part of the political system. Here an electoral worker counts referendum votes in Khartoum, capital of Sudan, in January of 2011, in the election that determined South Sudan's secession from Sudan.

Zhang Chuanqi/XinHua/Xinhua Press/Corbis

INTRODUCTION

In this chapter we will investigate some of the ways that the political environment is organized in its operation, as distinct from the material that we examined in the last chapter that focused on how attitudes and behavior of individuals can be influenced. We will begin with some discussion of a *pluralist* theory of democracy, and discuss the relationship between *pluralism* and *corporatism* in politics. We will then discuss the concept of *collective action*, and the way that it might influence the operation of politics and individual political behavior, followed by some attention given to the distinctions between democratic and nondemocratic rule, and the implications of those concepts for the political environment.

At that point we will turn our attention to two major organizing structures in the political environment, the *interest group* and the *political party*. Both of these structures play key roles in both democratic and nondemocratic politics, and both affect in significant ways the political contexts within which they operate. After we have completed this examination we will be prepared to turn our attention, in the next chapter, to a discussion of the *outputs* of the political process, public policy.

PLURALISM AND CORPORATISM

Among the most basic concepts in modern political science is the idea of **pluralism**. The idea suggests that "multiple, competing elites (including interest groups) determine public policy through bargaining and compromise."[1] Although referred to as "factions" and not called "pluralism" at the time, this topic was debated during the establishment of American political institutions as the theme of one of James Madison's contributions to *The Federalist Papers*, Number 10.[2] Central to the concept of pluralism is the idea of individual rationality, individual choice, and the premise that a rational individual will act in his or her own self-interest.

According to what is called "pluralist theory,"[3] interest groups could be called **advantage groups**: People join them because they see an advantage to doing so. Policy outcomes are perceived as a result of group competition, not necessarily a product of majority rule: A well-organized minority can defeat a less-well-organized majority in the process of competition for policy outcomes.

The original group theorist was Arthur Bentley, whose 1908 work[4] was very popular in the 1950s; it was expanded upon by David Truman, whose 1951 book *The Governmental Process* became one of the classics of political science. Truman took the idea of interest groups farther than had Bentley, suggesting that individuals belong to several different interest groups, the group loyalties reflecting different aspects of their interests and personalities: This gave rise to Truman's idea of "overlapping" group affiliations. According to Truman:

> "Interest group" refers to any group that, on the basis of one or more shared attitudes, makes certain claims upon other groups in the society for the establishment, maintenance, or enhancement of forms of behavior that are implied by the shared attitudes.[5]

Not only did Truman consider organized interest groups as part of what he called "the governmental process," but he also considered *potential* interest groups part of the process.

Mancur Olson's work *The Logic of Collective Action*, as we will note shortly, helped to explain the problems with Truman's theory, because Olson pointed out that it was not logical, or rational, for an individual to invest his or her time or effort in joining an organization if that organization was working for a **collective good**. He defined a "collective good" as "any good such that, if any person X in a group ... consumes it, it cannot feasibly be withheld from the others in that group."[6] By this definition, it would not be "rational" for an individual to contribute funds to and work hard for a clean air fund, because if the goal was achieved it would also be available to individuals who had not contributed. And, if enough other people supported the goal, then the individual might share in the rewards (i.e. the good public policy of clean air) without having to absorb *any* of the costs. Olson's work demonstrated that if there already was an interest group to further a certain goal, it might *not* be the case that all individuals interested in that goal would join the group: They could enjoy the benefits of the group without contributing to the efforts of the group.

Another collection of theories regarding political interaction among groups of individuals involves **corporatism**. The idea of corporatism implies for many a too-close interaction of groups and government. For some it further suggests "a situation where the interest organizations are integrated in the governmental decision-making process of a society."[7] Modern development of the idea of corporatism, called neo-corporatism, "emphasizes the characteristics of the interest associations entering a relationship with the state apparatus, and the nature of this relationship, i.e., the ways in which they are recognized and granted a representational monopoly by the state."[8]

A theory of **neo-corporatism** takes up where the theory of pluralism leaves off. It suggests that groups are significant for the political system, although it accepts Olson's suggestion that not all individuals with shared interests will necessarily join those groups. There are a number of common elements in the several variations of neo-corporatist theory today:

1. Monopolies of interest representation exist and are important to explain political behaviour and policy outcomes.
2. Hierarchies emerge among associations, and they may subordinate and coordinate the activities of whole economic sectors and/or social classes.
3. Membership in associations is not always voluntary ... arrangements exist both to bind members to "their" associations and to prevent the emergence of competing ones.
4. Interest associations are not just the passive recipients of already formed member interests, but may play an active role in identifying and forming those interests.
5. Interest associations do not merely transmit member preferences to authorities, but may actively and coercively govern the behaviour of their members, especially through devolved responsibility for the implementation of public policy.
6. The state may not be either an arena for which interests contend or another interest group with which they must compete, but a constitutive element engaged in defining ... the activities of associations...
7. Interest associations are not always autonomous entities pressuring the state from without and seeking access wherever they can find an opportunity....[9]

The idea of *conflict* is found at the center of neo-corporatist theory just as it is found at the center of pluralist theory.[10] This conflict involves disagreement among different groups regarding social, economic, and political goals—what the goals should be, and how they should be achieved. Pluralism and corporatism (or neo-corporatism) are at different ends of a continuum, because both argue for the significance of the *group* in the political process. Where they differ is on the relationship between government and groups—perhaps put another way, the degree to which the government establishes a patron-client relationship with specific interest groups.

THE LOGIC OF COLLECTIVE ACTION

One of the key assumptions of democratic politics is that individuals will participate when given the opportunity to do so. They *will* communicate with the government to be certain that their preferences come about. They *will* vote. They *will* participate in other ways. We know, however, that this is empirically not correct. People often, commonly in fact, do *not* participate in politics, even when they can, and even when it is relatively easy to do so in stable and secure democratic regimes. We might be able to understand why someone would refrain from participating in situations of danger (such as being shot at in a demonstration, or when voting against the government), or great expense (such as having to pay huge fees to participate). Why, however, do individuals not participate when there is no threat to them personally and there is essentially no cost?

One now-classic study of American politics examined political participation, and found that nearly 30 percent of American adults knew virtually nothing about politics. These individuals were labeled "apathetic." Another 60 percent of adults paid some attention to politics, but participated only moderately. They were called "spectators." Only about 5 to 7 percent of the public were active participants in politics, routinely engaging in discussion and participation in presidential election years, and this number fell to 1 to 2 percent in nonpresidential election years. These individuals were referred to as "gladiators."[11] Why were there so few "gladiators"?

This question can be expanded to focus on the broader political landscape. Why is it when it is so easy to vote that individuals do not vote in some nations? Why do individuals not invest the modest time and effort necessary to participate in democratically choosing their leaders when given the opportunity to do so?

One of the best explanations for why this is the case, as we suggested above, was offered by Mancur Olson in his seminal book *The Logic of Collective Action*, published in 1965.[12] Olson argued that although the traditional interpretation of democratic government is that people will participate when given the opportunity to do so, by joining political parties or operating in interest groups, in fact individuals usually do not do this. Further, Olson argued that this inaction was a *rational* position to take: Personal inaction often makes more sense than participation in collective action through political parties or interest groups.

Olson argued in terms of what is called **rational choice theory**. Individuals will participate when it is in their personal interest to do so, when their individual participation will make a difference in terms of benefits (e.g., public policies) to them, personally. In his work Olson suggested that individuals will be rational actors in deciding whether to participate or not, and will ask some version of the question: Are the potential benefits of this action greater than the potential costs of this action? If the anticipated benefits of an action (e.g., voting, or demonstrating) are not greater than the anticipated costs (e.g., time spent, possible arrest), then an individual might not participate, even if he or she *could* do so.

If the individual thinks that the costs of a potential action could be very high, and the benefits relatively lower, she might not participate. If a group is already going to participate in the direction that the individual would prefer, and he perceives that his participation wouldn't make a significant difference in any event, he might not participate. It is all a matter of costs and rewards, calculated very objectively.

From the perspective of the logic of collective action, participation often is wasted energy. This is especially true in what can be called **collective goods**, either material goods or nonmaterial goods that are *shared* by a number of people or that will be available to all. Should I join a group that is going to work hard to clean up a polluted lake? While it may be a good thing to do so, the rational perspective may say "no," and be happy to let the group go ahead. If the group is successful in cleaning the lake, then the benefits of the clean lake are available to all without having worked. If the group is not successful in cleaning the lake, then their efforts were wasted, and the nonparticipating citizen didn't incur the cost of time and effort that being a member of the group would have demanded.

There are many different forms of political participation, ranging from joining a group to voting to organizing to protest a government action to even more violent and dangerous options. Each of these types of participation can be examined from a *rational choice* perspective: Is my personal participation likely to make a difference that will benefit me? It certainly may be the case that from a *philosophical* perspective participation is a good and necessary thing. Democracy will only work if the people (the *demos*) actually participate. On the other hand, while some individuals may derive enough satisfaction from participation alone to make the participation worthwhile to them, others participate only out of a sense of citizen *duty*, and for them the costs may exceed the benefits relatively easily. An individual who doesn't care a good deal about politics may be willing to walk to the nearby polling station to vote out of a sense of duty, but if the weather is especially bad, she or he might decide to stay home. An individual who feels moderately pleased about new democratization and elections taking place might be willing to stand in line for hours to vote, until he or she sees gangs attacking potential voters. Participation, in short, is not always automatic.

DEMOCRATIC AND NONDEMOCRATIC RULE

The perspective of rational choice theory reminds us of a very important point: The act of political behavior is a function of its context. In some settings it is very easy to participate. Elsewhere it is much more difficult. Sometimes the costs are low or nonexistent. Other times the costs may be extremely high, including imprisonment, or even death. The same *act*, for example walking into a voting booth and casting a vote, can have very different implications in two different systems, and very different consequences, too. Voting in the United States may take some time, but is extremely likely to be safe. We do not hear of individuals being killed while voting. Voting in the recent election in Haiti, or in the recent election in Zimbabwe, could easily result in an individual's being killed, or at least badly injured, by individuals trying to prevent voters from voting against the incumbent.

There are many kinds of political structures in democratic nations that are designed to serve as **linkage mechanisms** to connect the voice of the people to the political leaders of the regime. A list of these structures might include (a) interest groups, (b) political parties, (c) *ad hoc* social movements, and (d) nongovernmental organizations (NGOs). In a democratic government, these structures listen to the public and pass along some message to the leaders in a way that in some manner parallels the formal legislative representative relationship.

In nondemocratic regimes the government is usually not interested in encouraging individual political participation from the public, at least not much *free* individual participation. The government does want people to participate—it wants them to obey laws, to pay taxes, to come to political rallies, to cheer at parades, and so on—but it doesn't want them doing so *on their own* or *without government sanction*. Some of these regimes have structures that roughly approximate structures in democratic settings, including elections, political parties, interest groups, and so on, but the structures are clearly controlled by the government, and spontaneous behavior or political expression is not encouraged.[13]

Nondemocratic regimes are usually defined as political systems in which power is controlled by a small group that exercises power without being *responsible* to the public.[14] In this sense the word *responsible* means "answerable": The people do not have an opportunity to remove the leaders from office, and the public often does not play a key role in selecting the leaders to hold office in the first place. Leaders in nondemocratic regimes may come to power through a military, palace, or reform *coup*, and among their primary concerns is staying in power. We generally observe that nondemocratic regimes limit individual freedom in order to stay in power. While this usually results in limitations on individual freedom of behavior, it is not the same thing as curtailing all political participation.

Authoritarian governments, in fact, *encourage* public participation in order to develop legitimacy for themselves. They will claim a 100 percent participation rate in elections—contrasted with less than two-thirds turnouts in most democratic countries—thereby showing that they are *more* democratic than Western democratic nations. They will have larger legislatures, to show that more individuals are elected to office. They have active political parties (often only one is allowed). They have active and productive, but tightly controlled, media structures. In short, it is not the *level* of participation that differs from Western democratic regimes, but the *nature* of the participation and the *freedom* of the individual.

It turns out that there is a strong association between modernization and democracy. Societies that do not have modern institutions—such as urbanization, education, equal rights, and the like—are not likely to have democratic rule. Modernization is not the same thing, of course, as equal access to resources. These associations are not absolute, however. It is possible to find high standards of living in both democratic and nondemocratic nations, and it is possible to find low standards of living in both democratic and nondemocratic nations.

THE NOTION OF CIVIL SOCIETY

This brings us back to the idea of **civil society**. Civil society can be defined as the way that the population of a nation organizes into associations or organizations that are independent of formal institutions of the state, the way that people organize groups to define their interests.[15] Civil society includes traditional interest groups (that we will discuss shortly), as well as social movements and nongovernmental organizations. The most important point to note about what is included in civil society and what is not included in civil society is that civil society is *distinct from the government institutions*. It really refers to organizations that citizens form on their own, without governmental "guidance" or regulation. Some of these groups may have political goals or interests (and we will discuss them below when we discuss interest and pressure groups), and some may have no political goals at all. The point is that citizens become involved in society and organize with other citizens to form groups and networks that permit them to interact with others.

In this way civil society is a key ingredient of a democratic political culture, providing some of the networks and support mechanisms that permit democratic political behavior to take place. The idea of a "loyal opposition" developed in Britain in the early nineteenth century to suggest that it was possible to *oppose* the government of the day but still be *loyal* to the monarch.[16] In much the same way, the concept of a civil society *permits* criticism of a particular regime while still being committed to operating *within* the particular regime.

Two of the pioneers in scholarship in this area in the 1950s were Gabriel Almond and Sidney Verba, who did field research in a number of nations and concluded that there was something that they called a *civic culture* that could be found in democracies, a term that referred to individuals' accepting both the "rules of the game" of the political system and also the individuals who were their leaders. A civic culture and a civil society are two kinds of sets of relationships that make it possible for government to work in a stable way, even if individuals may be unhappy with individual political decisions from time to time. Whether we are talking about religious organizations, sports organization, fraternal organizations, or other kinds of networks, these gathering structures are important to politics because they help individuals to articulate what is important to them and to interact with others.

A more contemporary study of the notion of civil society was undertaken at the very end of the twentieth century by Robert Putnam. In *Bowling Alone* Putnam sought to understand the state of American civil society, and he showed that there had been in the preceding years a consistent decline in membership in a wide range of associations, everything from educational associations to bowling leagues (hence the title of his book). Putnam argued that this suggested a serious decline of American *social capital*, a decline in social networks and the social trust that is developed in them.

INTEREST GROUPS

Although political systems may contain political structures designed to ensure popular representation in the governmental policymaking process, most notably the legislature, it is entirely likely that the formal governmental (constitutional) structures of representation will not prove to be sufficient for representing all shades of public opinion.

Two additional structures are available in the political environment to supplement the formal (constitutional) representative structures, and they are quite effective in many political regimes. Both the **interest group** and the **political party** can play significant roles in political systems in assisting formal-legal structures in the processing of political demands and the communication of public beliefs, attitudes, and values.

Although interest groups and political parties have a number of characteristics and functions in common,[17] we should be very careful to distinguish between them, for they really are quite different. As we indicated earlier, group theory suggests that all public opinion can be described in group terms and that individual opinion is essentially unimportant, save for the fact that individuals make up groups. All public opinion either originates with groups or is articulated by groups, so we do not really need to worry about individual representation as long as a mechanism for group representation exists.[18]

Interest groups are collections of individuals who share common beliefs, attitudes, values, or concerns. The shared concern(s) may focus upon a variety of issues, such as concern about nuclear weapons, gun control, air pollution, or about minimum wage or work conditions. The shared concern(s) may also be a bit more frivolous, such as (with due apologies to any offended!) love of miniature schnauzers, Parker fountain pen collecting, or appreciation of antique wall clocks.

Interest groups come into existence because individuals see something to be gained by such an association, either material gains (higher wages by joining a union, or free auto towing and maps by joining an automobile club); psychological gains (a feeling of "brotherhood" from joining a fraternity, or a sense of religious satisfaction by joining a church); recreational gains (lower ski-lift fees by joining a ski association); humanitarian gains (helping to promote civil rights by contributing to a civil rights organization), and so on.[19]

Interest groups may be highly organized, loosely organized, or not formally organized at all, for that matter.[20] Their scope of concern may be quite broad, or quite narrow. Groups might be open to anyone interested, or limited in membership. They may, in short, vary greatly. Interest groups can be more or less active, and more or less effective, depending upon several different constraints on their behavior. These constraints include the group's *resources*, the group's *objectives*, and the *political environment* within which the group is operating.[21]

Different interest groups have different levels of *resources*, although the types and natures of these resources can vary greatly. Financial resources can affect what a group can do in terms of activity, media, publicity, travel, and outreach. The number of individuals who participate in the interest group is important, too. Groups that are small generally have less impact than groups that are very large. It should be noted in this regard that the degree that a group is tightly organized can make up for smaller numbers; the National Rifle Association's ability to generate mass mailings to the U.S. Congress is legendary in explaining its ability to influence legislation, even though its number of members isn't that large. The relationship between the interest group and key social and political institutions can affect how important an interest group will be. American labor unions have had for decades a close relationship with the Democratic Party in the United States; when the Democrats control government, the union agenda is much more likely to be enacted than with the Republicans.

The group's *objectives* make a difference in how effective the group is. There is a wide range of subjects of interest of interest groups, and a wide range of objectives. Some seek to influence a tax code. Others seek to regulate individual behavior. Others may seek to entrench religious law as the law of the political system. "Green" organizations may be concerned about establishing public policy that is concerned with environmental issues. Some organizations may work for international peace. Others may simply be content to promote a group of individuals gathering once a week to play a game of checkers. In short, the goal of the interest group may be easier to achieve or more difficult to achieve.

Finally, the *political environment* within which the interest group operates makes a difference. As we have suggested earlier, in nondemocratic regimes the government is far more concerned with social order and stability than it is concerned with individual freedom and interests. This may make it much more difficult for interest groups to organize and operate without the blessing of the regime. On the other hand, democratic regimes may be nearly wide open in terms of the organization and operation of interest groups, and may offer no resistance to the interest group at all.

Group theorists suggest that interest groups play a very important function in the political arena. (See Figure 7.1.) They can be important as *linkage mechanisms*, some argue, because they are very effective communicators of segments of public opinion.[22] Because interest groups generally are of limited scope, they are able to communicate their collective opinion more effectively than can individuals. The National Rifle Association (NRA) and the American Medical Association (AMA) are two examples of interest groups that, although numerically not

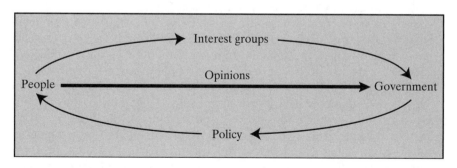

FIGURE 7.1
Interest Groups and Political Linkages

overwhelmingly large, are very effective in exerting political pressure in the areas of concern to their members.

The argument for interest group utility suggests that political (formal, constitutional, legislative) representatives simply cannot represent *all* of their constituents. On any given issue in relation to which a legislator takes a position, it is almost inevitable that he or she will alienate some group. An American legislator voting in favor of gun control, for example, is going to irritate constituents who oppose gun control. What is more, once "their" representative has come out on the opposite side of an issue, the anti-gun-control constituents (to use the same example) are no longer—strictly speaking—represented by their representative in the legislature. The existence of an interest group, in this case the NRA, affords these individuals recourse to an alternative representational structure, that will voice their concerns and act on their collective behalf.

Many political scientists use the terms *interest group* and *pressure group* interchangeably. Others, however, make a distinction between the two terms, and the student should be aware of the distinctions that are drawn.[23] Pressure groups, simply put, are said to be a subset of interest groups that are organized exclusively for the purpose of political lobbying. Thus we can say that all pressure groups are interest groups, but not all interest groups are pressure groups.

There are many kinds of interest groups ("collections of individuals who share a common belief, attitude, value, or concern") whose activities are oriented around nonpolitical themes. A fountain pen collectors' club may meet once a month to have fountain pen shows and competitions, give prizes and award ribbons, and discuss articles of interest in the widely read publication *Pen World*. Their group is obviously a nonpolitical concern. Other interest groups are usually nonpolitical. The American Automobile Association (AAA) has its primary *raison d'être* auto safety, and provides its members with a number of benefits: maps, car insurance, tow service, and so on. On occasions, however, the AAA has become politically active, such as when the Congress was considering an extra tax on gasoline. The AAA, acting on behalf of its members (drivers), lobbied effectively against such a tax.

Still other interest groups are *exclusively* political, having as their primary reason for being a policy objective, for example a group to end American involvement in Afghanistan, or a group lobbying for reproductive rights. These groups, **pressure groups**, are narrower in scope—usually related to a single issue—and ostensibly temporary. Once their policy objective is achieved, they no longer have a reason for being. General interest groups, on the other hand, are much longer-lived, and their reason for being is not as transient. Pressure groups will often support *any* candidate—from whatever political party—who will pledge to support their particular cause. Pressure groups are usually *single-issue* groups, and orient all of their political behavior around "their" issue. This is very different from the behavior of political parties.

POLITICAL PARTIES

This leads to our next distinction, the difference between interest groups (and here the term includes our pressure-group subcategory) and political parties. Many differences between parties and interest groups have been pointed out in detailed studies, including permanence and levels of organization (political parties tend to be more permanent and institutionalized than interest groups), and breadth of issue concerns (parties almost invariably are concerned with a large number of issues, while interest groups usually focus upon a more narrow range of issues).

The single most important difference between parties and interest groups, however, relates to the *goals* of the organization. The goal of the interest group is to *satisfy its members*, either through the organization itself (for example, with the Fountain Pen Collecting Club), or through political pressure resulting in a specific policy outcome (for example, the National Rifle Association helping to defeat gun-control legislation). The goal of a political party is to *win control of political office*, gain political power, and thereby control the policy-making process.[24] The interest group does not care which party or which individual wins an election as long as its specific policy concern prevails. The political party is much broader in scope, and seeks to hold power (to the point of perhaps modifying some of its issue positions if that will help it to control power); the interest group is not so much concerned with power as with policy outcome.

Parties have been said to derive from a number of different sources.[25] One source is factions within a national legislature. American political parties are examples of this; they originally formed as groups of legislative supporters of Thomas Jefferson and Alexander Hamilton, which subsequently established formal organizations leading to the creation of the Jeffersonian-Democrats and the Federalists.[26] A second source of party organization is labor movements. The British Labour Party is a good example of this,[27] in which an already existing labor organization (itself an interest group) decides to develop a political identity, seeking not only to influence labor policy but also to control power. Still another point of origin of political parties is the national-liberation movement. The Congress Party in India was not primarily a political party under British rule; rather, it was organized to help achieve Indian independence, and to help drive the British from of India. Once the British left, the conversion from liberation movement to political party was a logical next step.[28] Finally, parties may be created for ideological reasons, being created to represent a viewpoint not otherwise represented in the polity.[29]

As organizations, political parties vary greatly in a number of different respects, including membership and size, and structure of organization, not to mention variation in the number of parties active in the system itself.[30] One of the primary structural distinctions among parties is whether they are "mass" parties or "cadre" parties. Maurice Duverger, in his classic work *Political Parties*, suggested that "the difference involved is not one of size but of structure." For mass parties, the recruiting of members is a fundamental activity, "the members are therefore the very substance of the party, the stuff of its activity. Without members, the party would be like a teacher without pupils."[31] Also, mass parties are *financially* based upon the mass; the party finances are, to a large extent, based upon member dues.

The cadre party is of a different sort. As Duverger suggested, "what the mass party secures by numbers, the cadre party achieves by selection; ... it is dependent upon rigid and exclusive selection." Sometimes the distinction between mass and cadre parties is made less clear because the cadre parties may admit numbers of the mass in imitation of a mass party; there are few pure cadre parties today. Contemporary American parties, for example, are disguised cadre parties. They have democratic constitutions and permit mass participation, but are really steered by a much smaller group of individuals. Generally, then, cadre parties correspond to more caucus-organized types of parties, usually decentralized, while mass parties tend to correspond to parties based on branches, more centrally organized and "firmly knit."

The number of political parties in an electoral system is a function of several factors, including ideology, political culture, electoral laws, and methods of election.[32] Duverger noted that the relationship between the electoral regime and the number of political parties is direct: "The simple-majority single-ballot system favours the two-party system."[33] There are a number of different-sized party systems: single-party systems, two-party systems, two-party-plus systems, and multiparty systems. The term *party system* refers not to a single party, but instead to the framework of parties operating in a given nation. It discusses the number of parties that are competitive in a system (not the absolute number that can be said to exist, because that typically includes many parties that are grossly unrealistic in competition).

This is significant because the number of parties "realistically" competing in a political system (that is, that have a realistic chance of being elected and organizing power) tells us about that system. Countries that only permit a single party are less likely to be "democratic" by objective measures than countries with several parties. Countries with several parties, none of which can control a majority in the legislature, are more likely to be politically unstable than others. We want to know whether a political system is a *single-party* system, a *two-party* system, or a *multiparty system*, if possible, to better understand the context within which political institutions are operating.

We should note at this point that the terms *single-party* and *two-party* are not meant to be taken literally. Even authoritarian "single-party" systems may have several parties that are active in elections. Party systems that we call "two-party" systems often have far more than two parties active and extant. What we are really asking about is the *likelihood of winning elections* in electoral competition. Typically, single-party systems are systems in which one party will regularly win more than 65 percent of the vote, two-party systems suggest that the two (or two-plus such as Britain or Canada) parties will receive over 75 percent of the vote, and multiparty systems suggest that the two largest parties have a total of less than 75 percent of the vote.[34]

Single-party systems are often associated with nondemocratic rule, where "the party" and "the state" are often seen as the same. Authoritarian regimes, such as that found in China, Cuba, or formerly the Soviet Union or Nazi Germany, are examples of single-party systems. But single political parties may also operate in developing nations that are essentially democratic, with the single dominant party being the party that was associated with independence and freedom, for example the Kenyan African National Union in Kenya, or the Congress Party in India.

We will see later in this volume, however, that Mexico's single-party system has evolved into a competitive two-party system, with the PRI candidate coming in *third* in the last presidential election.[35] The Congress Party has split and resplit in India, and has lost national elections in recent years, and although it still exists and is a major player, it does not dominate national politics in the manner it did at India's independence or during India's early years.[36]

Two-party systems, or two-party-plus systems, are often the consequence of electoral systems, as we have seen earlier in this book. Where we have a single-member-district, plurality voting, electoral system, we tend to have two political parties, or series of two political parties. The Canadian political system, as we will see later in this volume, has one system of party competition at the national level, and a number of different systems of party competition at the provincial level. Thus any given electoral contest may be a two-party or three-party competition, but there are a number of different parties in existence in Canada.

Political parties are an important part of a theory of pluralism. If "political pluralism," as one author has put it, highlights the "existence of a 'plurality of groups that are both independent and non-inclusive,'" then parties are an important part of that pluralistic model.[37] Parties are absolutely crucial as an organizing structure in legislatures; obviously, party discipline (which we have discussed in an earlier chapter) could not exist in a legislative body without political parties, and it is party discipline that is the vehicle for responsible government, a government being able to deliver on its promises.[38]

Internal party organization varies on a party-by-party basis.[39] Some parties are highly unified, while others are collections of factions that may not have a great deal in common except their commitment to share power. Some parties are very democratic organizations, while others permit no internal competition at all and are simply organizations dedicated to following and supporting a single individual's political advancement.

Political parties, much like interest groups, serve a number of important functions in the political regime. They are, among other things, rather elaborate personnel services, serving as a mechanism for assisting in the hiring of political leaders.[40] They help to organize political groups. They help to articulate political demands.[41] They serve as a point of reference for bewildered voters who are overwhelmed by the political world: Party label is often the only clue available to voters to guide their behavior, and it is widely used as such.

Another important function served by the political party as an organization is in the process of political development.[42] Parties are important vehicles in the process of political recruitment, helping to bring individuals into the political arena by offering a convenient vehicle for participation to the masses.

Parties also serve as structures that mobilize the electorate—"get out the vote" and participation—through competition between parties (or within a party in one-party systems).[43] Through this action they contribute to a sense of "national integration,"[44] thus helping to develop a sense of political nationhood on the part of the masses.[45]

In short, research has shown that political parties can play significant roles in five important respects in the process of political development. First, parties encourage and facilitate political participation. Second, they help to stimulate a sense of governmental legitimacy through the campaign process and the debate that ensues. Third, they contribute to the development of a sense of national integration. Fourth, they play an important role in conflict management within the polity, providing a vehicle by which differences of opinion over policy preferences can be peacefully resolved. Fifth, and finally, political parties play an important role in the political socialization function in society, helping to transmit attitudes and values from one generation to another.

Much as the interest group was seen to be a political structure that assists in the representation function in the political world, so too the political party serves as a "linkage mechanism"[46] in passing along public opinions from various groups in the electorate to government officials. Of course, the degree to which parties serve these several functions depends upon the individual party organization and the political system within which it is found. Depending upon the number of political parties in a system, the degree of party discipline found in the political system, and the ideology and constituency of the party in question, the role of the party will vary.

Scholars have speculated about the future of political parties, and whether they can continue to be as central a political structure in their respective political systems as they have been in the past. The continual growth of executive power in political systems all over the world, combined with greater public attention to politics and increasingly aggressive media, means that traditional assumptions about political parties and political party behavior have to be rethought.[47]

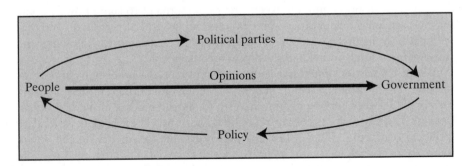

FIGURE 7.2
Political Parties and Political Linkages

SOCIAL MOVEMENTS

Social movements can be defined as broad groups of individuals who share an interest in a given social issue. How do social movements differ from interest groups or political parties? Interest groups generally are organized, and (as we suggested earlier) are "collections of individuals who share common beliefs, attitudes, values, or concerns." They are what can be called **advantage groups**, which come into existence because a number of individuals see something to be gained (either materially or psychologically) by doing so. And they serve as linkage mechanisms between the public and the state. We said that pressure groups were a subset of interest groups that are organized exclusively for the purpose of political lobbying (and thus all pressure groups are interest groups, but not all interest groups are pressure groups). We distinguished between interest groups and political groups, but noted that the most important difference is the breadth and the ultimate goal of the organization: The political party seeks to hold power, and is broader in scope, than the interest group.

As a general rule, we can say that social movements share many of the characteristics of interest groups, in that they articulate group interests and seek to influence the government (rather than to hold power themselves). A key difference, however, is that social movements are likely to be *less organized* than an interest group, and possibly have a broader constituency, one that doesn't correspond to a particular political structure. They also, in a manner similar to our description of interest groups, want to *influence* public policy, but *not control power and exercise policy* themselves. Another characteristic that social movements have in common with interest groups is that they are inclusive and that they help individuals to bring their concerns to the attention of political and social leaders *outside of* the political structures of the regime.

Anthony Giddins has argued that there are five general categories of social movements in modern society:

1. democratic movements that work for political rights;
2. labor movements that work for control of the workplace;
3. ecological movements that are concerned with the environment;
4. religious movements that work with more or less outreach;
5. peace movements that work toward peace and less global conflict.[48]

We might argue that many interest groups flow out of, or conversely help to create, social movements. What can be called The Women's Movement has created many interest groups over time and around the world, and in some political systems even political parties dedicated to issues focusing upon women. The same can be said for the gay rights movement and the right-to-life movement. The "Environmental Movement" has similarly created many interest groups, and political parties for that matter (such as the Greens in Germany). The civil rights movement in the United States created several interest groups (the National Association for the Advancement of Colored People, among others).

Nationalist movements can be seen as a special case of social movements, in which a group of individuals that is articulating a common set of beliefs (for example, that India should become independent of Britain) starts to act within the political system to influence political policy. These movements create interest groups, and sometimes political parties, that work toward the common goal of the individuals involved.

We cannot write about social and political movements at this time without mentioning the series of demonstrations that became known as the "Arab Spring," that took place from December of 2010 through the summer of 2011. Protests first began in Tunisia. They flared up in Egypt on January 25, 2011, and ran for over two weeks. They spread through Libya, Bahrain, Syria, Jordan, to as far west as Morocco. Almost no country in the region was untouched. This was a wave of protest that was a political movement in the purest sense of the term; organization was almost spontaneous, made possible by advances in technology and the ubiquity of cell phones. Although the protest in Tunisia started with an instance of self-immolation by an individual angry at being mistreated by the police, it rapidly—extremely rapidly—spread throughout the region (even including relatively stable countries such as Turkey) protesting against authoritarian rule and crying for democratic government.[49]

Social movements emerge as a result of one of several possible causes. One theory ("social deprivation theory") suggests that people create social movements because they feel deprived of some resource, and they start to coalesce with others who share the feeling of deprivation related to that resource.[50] A second theory ("mass-society theory") argues that social movements are made up of individuals in large societies who feel insignificant or socially detached. Social movements, according to this theory, provide a sense of empowerment and belonging that the movement members would otherwise not have.[51] Yet a third idea ("structural strain theory") suggests that people believe that society has problems, and this is what draws them together in a common movement.[52]

One of the major scholars in the field of social movements today is Ronald Inglehart, who has written about the proliferation of social movements in contemporary society. His view is that traditional political parties are no longer adequate organizationally to represent citizen concerns, and that more *ad hoc* group activity is forming in response to the issues of the day. This activity, he suggests, is finding its outlet in social movements, rather than political parties.[53]

PLURALISM, PARTIES, INTEREST GROUPS, AND SOCIAL MOVEMENTS

The terms *groups*, *parties*, and *movements* are central in any discussion of democratic politics, and are even central in discussion of political participation in systems that may not, at a given time, be democratic. After all, the existence of over a million Chinese students in Beijing in May, 1989, showed the potential impact of an interest group: The "critical mass" that was present at the time was so large that even calling in the Chinese Army was not able to control students' behavior for quite a period of time. The recent Arab Spring protests and democracy movement is another example of how spontaneous political movements may arise even in repressive and authoritarian contexts. Political parties, interest groups, and social movements are primary vehicles by which collective public opinion is communicated to the political elite in most political systems.

We have seen in this chapter that a pluralistic approach to the study of politics suggests that we need to look at (some kind of) political groups to understand how much political behavior takes place. We saw in Chapter Six how individuals develop their political beliefs and attitudes, and how the political elite comes to be the political elite. It is necessary to add to this—as we have done in this chapter—some understanding of pluralism theory, interest groups, political parties, and social movements to get a broad vision of what influences political behavior and how that political behavior appears in the political environment.

At this point in our study of comparative politics, we will turn our attention to the *output* of the political process—the product of the political process—that we call public policy. Now that we have some idea about how people develop their political attitudes and come to be active in politics, and now that we've seen in this chapter how they channel their political activity through groups, parties, or movements, it is appropriate to look at *what* it is they do with that activity. It is to a study of public policy that we now turn our attention.

DISCUSSION QUESTIONS

1. What is the importance of political behavior for the political system?
2. What are the key components of the political environment within which political structures operate?
3. Explain the difference between "pluralism" and "corporatism." What is the significance of both terms for the political system?
4. What is "rational choice" theory, and how does it explain individual behavior?
5. What is the importance of the concept of "civil society"?
6. What are the key differences between political parties and interest groups (and pressure groups)? How are they different in democratic politics?
7. What are the differences between social movements and interest groups?

KEY TERMS

advantage groups   156
civil society   160
collective goods   159
corporatism   157
interest group   162

linkage mechanisms   159
nationalist
  movements   170
neo-corporatism   157
pluralism   156

political parties   162
pressure groups   164
rational choice
  theory   158
social movements   169

SUGGESTED READINGS

William Galston, *The Practice of Liberal Pluralism* (New York: Cambridge University Press, 2005). Galston offers a comprehensive cross-national examination of what pluralism is and how it is found in various forms around the world. This is a good example of scholarship dealing with the concept of pluralism and its significance.

Richard Katz and William Crotty, eds., *Handbook of Party Politics* (Thousand Oaks, CA: SAGE, 2005). This volume offers a wide range of data on political parties around the world, including both national data and categorization of *types* of party structures.

Kay Lawson, *Political Parties and Democracy* (Santa Barbara, CA: Praeger, 2010). Lawson has been publishing on political parties for years. This volume describes the importance of political parties for democratic government, and offers numerous examples and much data on the variation in structures of political parties in the systems in which they are found.

Juan Linz, *Totalitarian and Nondemocratic Regimes* (Boulder, CO: Lynne Rienner, 2000). Linz offers both a typology of nondemocratic regimes as well as a thorough description of the role of nondemocratic regimes in the world. He describes the importance of political structures and institutions for government stability.

Mancur Olson, *The Logic of Collective Action: Public Goods and the Theory of Groups* (Cambridge, MA: Harvard University Press, 1965). This is a classic volume that has been the point of generation of a huge amount of scholarship over the last half-century. The idea of "collective action" and its role in democratic politics is very important, and this volume is an essential starting point for this kind of discussion.

NOTES

1. Harmon Zeigler, *Pluralism, Corporatism, and Confucianism: Political Association and Conflict Regulation in the United States, Europe, and Taiwan* (Philadelphia, PA: Temple University Press, 1988), p. 3. See also William Galston, *The Practice of Liberal Pluralism* (New York: Cambridge University Press, 2005).
2. Alexander Hamilton, James Madison, and John Jay, *The Federalist Papers* (New York: New American Library, 1961), pp. 77–83.
3. This section is based upon a much longer analysis in Zeigler, *Pluralism*, pp. 4–11. See also Douglas Farrow, *Recognizing Religion in a Secular Society: Essays in Pluralism, Religion, and Public Policy* (Montreal, QC: McGill-Queen's University Press, 2004).
4. Arthur F. Bentley, *The Process of Government: A Study of Social Pressures* (Chicago, IL: University of Chicago Press, 1908).
5. David Truman, *The Governmental Process* (New York: Knopf, 1951), p. 33. See also Michael Peletz, *Gender Pluralism: Southeast Asia since Early Modern Times* (New York: Routledge, 2009).
6. Mancur Olson, *The Logic of Collective Action: Public Goods and the Theory of Groups* (Cambridge, MA: Harvard University Press, 1965), p. 14.
7. O. Ruin, "Participatory Democracy and Corporatism: The Case of Sweden," *Scandinavian Political Studies* 9 (1974): 171–186, as cited in Gerhard Lehmbruch and Philippe Schmitter, eds., *Patterns of Corporatist Policy-Making* (Beverly Hills, CA: SAGE, 1982), p. 4. See also Colin Crouch and Wolfgang Streeck, *The Diversity of Democracy: Corporatism, Social Order, and Political Conflict* (Cheltenham, UK: Edward Elgar, 2006).

8. See Stein Larsen, ed., *The Challenges of Theories on Democracy: Elaborations over New Trends in Transitology* (New York: Columbia University Press, 2000); and George Fredrickson, *Diverse Nations: Explorations in the History of Racial and Ethnic Pluralism* (Boulder, CO: Paradigm, 2008).

9. Philippe C. Schmitter, "Reflections on Where the Theory of Neo-Corporatism Has Gone and Where the Praxis of Neo-Corporatism May be Going," in Lehmbruch and Schmitter, *Patterns*, pp. 260–261.

10. Two examples of research dealing with corporatism and group conflict are Bernard Grofman and Robert Stockwell, *Institutional Design in Plural Societies: Mitigating Ethnic Conflict and Fostering Stable Democracy* (Irvine, CA: University of California Center for the Study of Democracy, 2001); and Marina Ottaway and Amr Hamzawy, *Getting to Pluralism: Political Actors in the Arab World* (Washington, DC: Carnegie Endowment for International Peace, 2009).

11. Lester Milbrath, *Political Participation* (Chicago, IL: Rand McNally, 1965).

12. Mancur Olson, *The Logic of Collective Action* (Cambridge, MA: Harvard University Press, 1965).

13. One of the classic studies of this subject is by William Kornhauser, *The Politics of Mass Society* (Glencoe, IL: Free Press, 1959).

14. A good discussion of nondemocratic rule is offered by Juan Linz, *Totalitarian and Nondemocratic Regimes* (Boulder, CO: Lynne Rienner, 2000).

15. Karen Hagemann and Sonya Michel, *Civil Society and Gender Justice: Historical and Comparative Perspectives* (New York: Berghahn Books, 2008). See, for other examples of this literature Jon Shefner, *The Illusion of Civil Society: Democratization and Community Mobilization in Low-Income Mexico* (University Park, PA: Pennsylvania State University Press, 2008); or Wanda Krause, *Women in Civil Society: Women, Islamism, and Networks in the UAE* (New York: Palgrave Macmillan, 2008).

16. On the development of the concept of a "loyal opposition," see Gerald Schmitz, "The Opposition in a Parliamentary System," published by the Political and Social Affairs Division of the Parliamentary Information and Research Service of the Parliament of Canada. It can be found at *http://www.parl.gc.ca/Content/LOP/researchpublications/bp47-e.htm#GOV* (accessed June 2011).

17. One of the classics in this area is Norman Luttbeg, ed., *Public Opinion and Public Policy* (Homewood, IL: Dorsey Press, 1974), esp. pp. 1–10, 109, and 187. More recent work includes Christine Barbour et al., *Keeping the Republic: Power and Citizenship in American Politics* (Washington, DC: CQ Press, 2006); or Paul Collins, *Friends of the Supreme Court: Interest Groups and Judicial Decision Making* (New York: Oxford University Press, 2008).

18. Truman, *The Governmental Process*, esp. pp. 129–139, offers the classic articulation of this argument.

19. See Robert Alexander, *The Classics of Interest Group Behavior* (Belmont, CA: Thomson/Wadsworth, 2006).

20. One of the classic typologies developed for the study of interest groups was developed by Gabriel Almond, and can be found in his introduction to G. Almond and J.S. Coleman, eds., *The Politics of the Developing Areas* (Princeton, NJ: Princeton University Press, 1960), p. 33ff.

21. This three-fold framework was offered by James Danziger, *Understanding the Political World: A Comparative Introduction to Political Science* (White Plains, NY: Longman, 1996), pp. 68–69.

22. There has been a great deal of work in this area. Among more recent work would be included the following: Laura Woliver, *From Outrage to Action: The Politics of*

Grass-Roots Dissent (Urbana, IL: University of Illinois Press, 1992). See also Luttbeg, pp. 187–188. The articles reprinted in this section of this reader that deal with the pressure groups model of political linkage are all very well done and provide illustrations of the linkage suggested by the theory.

23. This distinction is developed in Luigi Grazio, *Lobbying, Pluralism, and Democracy* (New York: Palgrave, 2001). See also Paul Herrnson, Ronald Shaiko, and Clyde Wilcox, eds., *The Interest Group Connection: Electioneering, Lobbying, and Policymaking in Washington* (Washington, DC: CQ Press, 2005).

24. See Richard Katz and William Crotty, eds., *Handbook of Party Politics* (Thousand Oaks, CA: SAGE, 2005). For further distinctions, see Curtis, pp. 143–44. See also Louis Sandy Maisel and Jeffrey Barry, eds., *The Oxford Handbook of American Political Parties and Groups* (New York: Oxford University Press, 2010).

25. One of the classic essays in this area is by J. LaPalombara and M. Weiner, eds., "The Origin and Development of Political Parties," in *Political Parties and Political Development* (Princeton, NJ: Princeton University Press, 1966), pp. 3–6.

26. A good discussion of this is found in James Sterling Young, *The Washington Community: 1800–1828,* (New York: Harcourt, Brace and World, 1966). See also Morton Keller, *America's Three Regimes: A New Political History* (Oxford, UK: Oxford University Press, 2007).

27. See Meg Russell, *Building New Labour: The Politics of Party Organisation* (New York: Palgrave Macmillan, 2005). See also David Rubinstein, *The Labour Party and British Society: 1880–2005* (Brighton, UK: Sussex Academic Press, 2006).

28. This is discussed in Stanley Wolpert, *Shameful Flight: The Last Years of the British Empire in India* (Oxford, UK: Oxford University Press, 2006).

29. One of the best illustrations of ideological parties, of course, involves communist and Marxist parties. Arun Jana and Bhupen Sarmah, *Class, Ideology and Political Parties in India* (Colorado Springs, CO: International Academic Publishers, 2002).

30. Probably the best single reference book was compiled and edited by Richard Katz and William Crotty, titled *Handbook of Party Politics* (London, UK: SAGE, 2005). See also D.J. Sagar, *Political Parties of the World* (London, UK: Harper, 2009).

31. This and material in the next paragraph come from Maurice Duverger, *Political Parties* (New York: John Wiley, 1963), p. 63.

32. See David Farrell, *Electoral Systems: A Comparative Introduction* (New York: Palgrave, 2001).

33. Duverger, *Political Parties*, p. 217.

34. This framework is offered by Marcus Ethridge and Howard Handelman, *Politics in a Changing World: A Comparative Introduction to Political Science* (New York: St. Martin's Press, 1994), p. 133.

35. Larissa Adler de Lomnitz et al., *Symbolism and Ritual in a One-Party Regime: Unveiling Mexico's Political Culture* (Tucson, AZ: University of Arizona Press, 2010).

36. Paul Wallace and Ramashray Roy, *India's 2009 Elections: Coalition Politics, Party Competition, and Congress Continuity* (Thousand Oaks, CA: SAGE, 2011).

37. Giovanni Sartori, *Parties and Party Systems: A Framework for Analysis* (Cambridge, UK: Cambridge University Press, 1976), p. 15.

38. See Stephen Taylor and David Wykes, *Parliament and Dissent* (Edinburgh, UK: Edinburgh University Press, 2005); or Reuven Hazan, *Cohesion and Discipline in Legislatures: Political Parties, Party Leadership, Parliamentary Committees and Governance* (London, UK: Routledge, 2005).

39. One example of a study of internal party structure is by Richard Katz and William Crotty, *Handbook of Party Politics* (Thousand Oaks, CA: SAGE, 2005).
40. One of the classics in this area is the work of Austin Ranney, *Pathways to Parliament: Candidate Selection in Britain* (Madison, WI: University of Wisconsin Press, 1965).
41. See Kay Lawson, *The Comparative Study of Political Parties* (New York: St. Martin's Press, 1976), pp. 136–161; or her newer *Political Parties and Democracy* (Santa Barbara, CA: Praeger, 2010).
42. See Victor Tonchi and Albertina Shifotoka, *Parties and Political Development in Namibia* (Johannesburg, SA: EISA, 2005); Dafydd Fell, *Party Politics in Taiwan: Party Change and the Democratic Evolution of Taiwan, 1991–2004* (New York: Routledge, 2005).
43. In an American context this is discussed at some length by Donald P. Green and Alan Gerber, *The Science of Voter Mobilization* (Thousand Oaks, CA: SAGE, 2005); and in David Brady and Mathew McCubbins, *Party, Process, and Political Change in Congress* (Stanford, CA: Stanford University Press, 2007).
44. Myron Weiner and Joseph LaPalombara, "The Impact of Parties on Political Development," in *Political Parties and Political Development*, p. 413.
45. See Stein Rokkan, "Electoral Mobilization, Party Competition, and National Integration," in *Political Parties and Political Development*, LaPalombara and Weiner, eds., pp. 241–266. See also Anika Gauja, *Political Parties and Elections: Legislating for Representative Democracy* (Burlington, VT: Ashgate, 2010).
46. Luttbeg, *Public Opinion*, pp. 109–186. See also Kay Lawson, "When Linkage Fails," in *When Parties Fail: Emerging Alternative Organizations*, ed. Kay Lawson and Peter Merkl (Princeton, NJ: Princeton University Press, 1988), pp. 13–40.
47. An example of this kind of study is the work by Louis Sandy Maisel and Paul Sacks, eds., *The Future of Political Parties* (Beverly Hills, CA: SAGE, 1975).
48. Anthony Giddens, *The Nation-State and Violence.* (Cambridge, UK: Polity Press, 1985).
49. See the article by Ray Takeyh in the *New York Times*, "A Post-American Day Dawns in the Mideast," *New York Times*, June 8, 2011, available at *http://www.nytimes.com/2011/06/09/opinion/09iht-edtakeyh09.html?scp=3&sq=arab%20spring&st=cse* (accessed June 8, 2011).
50. Denton Morrison, "Some Notes toward Theory on Relative Deprivation, Social Movements, and Social Change." in *Collective Behavior and Social Movements*, ed. Louis E. Genevie (Itasca, IL: Peacock, 1978), pp. 202–209.
51. William Kornhauser, The Politics of Mass Society (New York: Free Press, 1959).
52. Neil Smelser, *Theory of Collective Behavior* (New York: Free Press, 1962).
53. Ronald Inglehart, *Culture Shift in Advanced Industrial Society* (Princeton, NJ: Princeton University Press, 1990), pp. 363–368.

Public Policy

Foreign policy is one of the most important types of policy to be created by a national government. Here U.S. Secretary of State Hillary Rodham Clinton, left, prepares to shake hands with Indian Foreign Minister S. M. Krishna at the end of a joint press conference in New Delhi, India.

INTRODUCTION

In the first half of this volume, we have seen a focus on *political institutions* and *political behavior*, but before we turn our attention in the second half of the book to our case studies, we need to look at some of the *outputs* of political systems: what they do, what they produce, and what the impacts of these outputs are. This leads us to a discussion of public policy, more generally, and more specifically to some discussion of some of the broad policy areas included in that general topic.

There are many different ways that we might approach a preliminary conversation about public policy. These might include a *regional* approach (e.g., Asian public policy as distinct from Latin American public policy), or a *developmental* approach (e.g., policy in the developing world as distinct from policy in the developed world), or even a *chronological* approach (e.g., public policy in the nineteenth century as distinct from public policy in the twentieth century). In this volume we have chosen to examine—albeit briefly—a variety of public policies in terms of the *focus of their activity*, that is, whether they involve domestic issues or international issues. Any one of these approaches might be equally effective for an initial examination of this material, but this approach seems to fit best with the institutional perspective that we take in this volume.

A recent study of comparative public policy noted that this kind of examination has become increasingly difficult in modern times.

> Many of the key cornerstones of public policy analysis have become problematic as processes of globalization have disrupted the traditional analytical and conceptual frameworks through which policymaking and implementation have been understood. The reorientation of the role of the state, the increasing variety of terrains and actors involved in the making of public policy, and the transition from government to governance are all aspects of a changing environment, the implications of which need to be captured within contemporary analysis.[1]

We saw earlier in this volume that the study of politics often involves the idea of *pluralism*, or the assumption that there are many different groups in society, with competing interests and demands and that those groups have to use the governmental process to determine what policy is finally enacted. One of the major approaches to the study of politics sees democracy as "a contest among interest groups carried out under particular kinds of rules, which makes the contest 'democratic.'"[2] Democratic government uses conflict resolution mechanisms and deliberative procedures and institutions to manage these conflicting demands and policy preferences, and to (it is hoped) peacefully arrive at effective public policy.

One of the first modern political scientists to specifically discuss public policy, as such, was Charles Merriam, a University of Iowa Ph.D. who taught at the University of Chicago. In 1922 Merriam published a book titled *The American Party System: An Introduction to the Study of Political Parties in the United States*[3] (Macmillan) that was important both because of its reliance on *data*, and because of its interest in *outputs* of politics: what political institutions *did*. Merriam is credited with being one of the leading figures in the development of the study of public administration and public policy.

KINDS OF PUBLIC POLICY

As we noted in earlier chapters, governments are often called upon to resolve problems, to provide as we noted in Chapter 1 an "authoritative allocation of values" about how issues should be resolved. This is true whether the issues at hand are military issues (e.g., "should South Korea attack North Korea?"), economic issues (e.g., "should the more wealthy pay more taxes than the less wealthy?"), educational issues (e.g., "how do we guarantee all citizens equal access to a quality education?"), transportation issues (e.g., "what needs to be done to protect the air travel industry against terrorism?"), health issues (e.g., "what needs to be done to assure all citizens access to medical care?"), and so on.

In the last seven chapters we have seen that not all governments are structured identically. We have seen remarkable differences in governmental structures, in terms of executive structures, in terms of legislative structures, in terms of judicial structures, in terms of electoral institutions, federal/unitary organization, and so on.[4]

A recent study of public policy drew the distinction between **government by network** and **government by market**.[5] In the former, the bureaucracy "is replaced by a wide variety of other kinds of institutions. The government stops trying to do everything itself and funds other organizations that do the actual work the government wants done." This often comes about because the government feels that other structures can act more quickly, or more effectively, than it can by itself. "The defining characteristic is that [the organizations] are all contracted by a state entity using state money for something that the private market would not produce, to the extent required, on its own."[6]

While the "government by network" model suggests that "much of the public's work is paid for by the government even though it is not performed by government employees and not constrained by all a government's protocols and central-control mechanisms," in the "government by market" model the government's work involves little in the way of either public money or public employees. "The government uses state power to create a market that fulfills a public purpose." This is especially important in policy areas where substantial behavior change is needed,

> Government by market is the best, and sometimes only, realistic implementation option when a policy consensus is reached that requires many hundreds of businesses or many thousands of people to change their behaviors. Government by market is especially important in an era where citizens place a high value on personal choice and in an era in which scientific and technological changes happen so quickly that the law cannot keep up.[7]

Many worry, however, that the government's relinquishing policy-making power and the ability to undertake policy-making initiatives to the private sectors will cripple the ability of the government to act where only it can act. This is especially true in the area of foreign policy. As we shall see later in this chapter, national governments have lost a good deal of their control over multinational corporations in the last few decades, but the need for governments to act in the international arena is still crucially felt.[8]

In the preceding chapters, we have described a number of institutional structures that are used to arrive at these "authoritative allocations of values." As we have tried to make clear, there are different approaches to institutional responses, different styles of legislatures, different styles of executives, different styles of judiciaries, different styles of bureaucracies, and on and on, and there is no evidence that one *style* of institution necessarily produces a better *product*, or *output*, than another. That is, there is no evidence that presidential systems of government produce qualitatively better policy (however we might measure that concept!) than parliamentary systems of government, or that a unicameral legislature is wiser than a bicameral legislature, or that district-based representation is more intuitive than functional representation.

We noted in our discussion of legislatures that the legislative process (which is just one of a number of possible ways policies might be determined, along with judicial decisions, executive proclamations, bureaucratic decisions, and more) can be affected at a number of points. Individual legislators will try to shape public policy. Legislative committee hearings provide options to shape public policy. The actual implementation by government departments also provide options for shaping public policy.

Having said that, the challenge is relatively straightforward: *Governments*—however they are structured—are faced with *problems*—what we called "demands" earlier in this book, expressions by groups in society that something needs to happen, whether that "something" involves health issues, transportation issues, economic issues, or something else—and they need to arrive at what is called a *policy* in relation to the problem, a statement about what (if anything) the government intends to do about the problem, how it will take that action, and what it hopes to accomplish in the action.

STAGES IN THE POLICY-MAKING PROCESS

When we look at public policy-making, we can identify three distinct phases that are part of the policy-making process. First, we look at what can be called **agenda setting**. Following agenda setting comes a process that seeks to determine the **formulation of options**. Finally, we turn to a discussion of **implementation** of those options. Along the way many discussions and debates will need to take place to determine whether the policy issue at hand will merit any government response at all, and how many resources (e.g., how much money) will be devoted to responding to that problem area.

Agenda Setting

One of the most "political" dimensions of the policy-making process involves the setting of the policy agenda. Governments cannot do everything, both because the resources are not available and because there isn't adequate time, and one of the first challenges they face is deciding what their political agenda is going to be. All governments need to decide—among a *very* long list of public demands and wishes—which several issues they are going to try to pursue, and which (often very intensely held) issues they are not going to try to pursue. This does not mean, of course, that the question is settled, because the process of the government making decisions has many potential points of influence, and organized groups will try to have "their" issues taken up at many different stages.

The setting of a government's agenda is a crucial stage in making public policy, because the government is prioritizing some issues, some questions, some challenges, some conflicts, above others. Government leaders will enter office with a set of priorities, but this list will be modified by the demands of the time and by other actors in the governmental process. After a great deal of discussion, a government will set a legislative and a policy-making agenda, although as we have already noted this agenda of the government can be influenced and affected to varying degrees by other, nongovernmental, actors.

A variety of individual actors, interest groups, and less-organized collections of actors will attempt to convince the government that *their* issues are the most pressing and most important issues of the day. Different political systems have different points of access, and some systems' agendas may be modified more easily than others. More open democratic governments are certainly more malleable than more closed authoritarian governments, for example. At the end of the day, some of these efforts at influence will succeed, and the government will find the policy-making agenda being modified on a regular basis.

We noted earlier that issue-advocacy through political parties and interest groups, among other structures, seeks to influence public policy through education, lobbying, or political pressure. What are called advocacy groups attempt to educate the public as well as government policy makers about the nature of problems, what legislation is needed to address problems, and the funding required to provide services or conduct research.

The Formulation of Options

After a policy agenda is determined, the question of *how* policy options are to be determined comes to the fore. Policy options are often formulated in executive agencies (the Ministry of Transportation in Britain, for example, or the Department of Transportation in the United States), and proposed policy may be sent to the legislature via appropriate channels. Alternatively, policy options may originate in the legislature, as a result of interest groups working with legislators to get a policy approved by the government.

The legislature is often key in this stage, because alternative solutions are considered, and public discourse takes place about what the best outcomes might be. One model for doing this is work that takes place in legislative committees and subcommittees, which eventually might modify the original policy recommendation of the executive branch or an individual legislator.

In other cases, a policy recommendation might be handled entirely within the government bureaucracy, such as in the American political system when a policy decision is made on the role of federal regulation of prescription drugs. An announcement will be distributed by an administrative agency, such as the Food and Drug Administration (F.D.A.), public hearings will be held, and eventually a policy will be handed down by the F.D.A. that has the force of law, even though the legislative branch of government has had no actual role in the determination of the specific policy at hand.

Implementation

Once a decision has been made about a specific policy, it moves to the implementation phase of the policy-making process. Implementation may take hours, or it may take weeks, or it may take months or years, depending upon the complexity and the political implications of the policy.

In December of 2010 both the U.S. Senate and the House of Representatives approved repeal of the "don't ask, don't tell" policy that had applied to the U.S. armed forces: Gay and lesbian soldiers, sailors, and aviators could only serve in the military if they kept their lifestyle choices a secret. The repeal of the "don't ask, don't tell" policy would permit these individuals to "come out" and remain on active duty, where previously if they had openly spoken of their preferences they would have been discharged from the armed forces. The nature of this policy was complex, however, and it was approved with the condition that the armed forces would need to undertake further study about *how* the new policy would be implemented, so that implementation could take place in a way that would not adversely affect the operational capabilities of the armed forces.

DOMESTIC POLICY

At its most basic level, questions related to domestic policy have to do with whether the government of the day will or will not regulate in certain areas. We could make a long list of areas of contentious public policy—including, for example, religious policy, environmental policy, health policy, military policy, national security policy, transportation policy, housing policy, education policy, and on and on—and for each of these areas we could describe why the government has chosen to act, or why the government has chosen to not act.

Earlier in this volume we discussed the liberal-conservative ideological continuum in terms of government activity in the economy, and most public policy can be described in similar terms: Does the government feel that it is appropriate for it to regulate a specific area of concern (e.g., housing, transportation, health resources) in order to meet its obligations to the public. In many cases the liberal position urges governmental action, and the conservative position urges governmental *inaction.*[9] Examples of some possible issues that could be raised are included below in Table 8.1, where

TABLE 8.1			
Making Domestic Public Policy			
Policy Area	Why might regulation be needed?	A liberal position might suggest	A conservative position might suggest
Education policy	There is uneven quality of educational opportunities for children.	The government should play an active role in regulating public education so that all Americans have an opportunity to have a quality education.	The government should not intervene, but should let local school districts determine what happens in their local schools.
			(continued)

(continued)

Policy Area	Why might regulation be needed?	A liberal position might suggest	A conservative position might suggest
Environmental policy	Business interests will not worry about long-term environmental concerns, but will do whatever they need to do to maximize profits.	The government should play an active role in regulating industries that affect the environment to protect the environment from business greed and shortsightedness.	The government should not intervene, but should let the free market and the industries involved determine environmental practices.
Health Insurance Policy	Health insurance benefits are unevenly available in society, with some having good health insurance and some without any insurance at all.	The government should play an active role in regulating the health insurance industry to make sure that all members of society have access to medical care.	The government should not intervene, but should let the free market and the health care industries determine options.
Housing policy	An unregulated housing market will permit racial and ethnic discrimination and unfair financing practices.	The government should play an active role in overseeing home financing industries and preventing discrimination.	The government should not intervene, but should let the free market and the industries involved determine housing practices.
Transportation policy	The government needs to have guidelines to insure that airplanes (for example) are properly maintained and that air safety is assured. If the government doesn't do this, industry will "cut corners" to maximize profits and put people at risk.	The government should play an active role in safety inspections and in establishing guidelines for safe practice by airline pilots.	The government should not intervene, but should let the free market determine best practices for safe operation and maintenance of equipment.

we can see that the general conservative position is to have the government not be involved in regulating, controlling, requiring, limiting, or in some way affecting policy, but rather suggests that private industry should be permitted to find an appropriate policy outcome to respond to public needs. The general liberal response is that given a free hand the free market will not always decide fairly, or safely, or appropriately.

Social policy is sometimes referred to by critics as "welfare policy," because of the perspective of social conservatives that government guarantees of benefits in relation to income, housing, medical care, education, and the like are degrees of being "on welfare." Indeed, the term *welfare* itself has become pejorative for many, indicating an *inappropriate* level of government activity in a given area. This differential use of the term *appropriate* shows how an individual's personal ideology can affect their view of policy. What is "appropriate" governmental action for one person could well be *in*appropriate for another, and *vice versa*. What is *reasonable* profit-making by the private health sector for one observer may be seen as price gouging by another. What is *responsible care* of the environment exercised by the private sector to one participant may be criminally negligent behavior to another.

Sometimes, it can be argued, the private sector is simply *incapable* of responding to pressing problems. There are clearly examples that could be cited of recent events that have demonstrated the inability of the private sector to respond to crises in a timely or appropriate way, for example the British Petroleum oil-drilling catastrophe in the Gulf of Mexico in the summer of 2010. The behavior that led to inadequate safety practices in this case seems to be a good example of what happens when the private sector is not adequately regulated and is permitted to take risks to maximize its profits.[10]

On the other hand, the United States federal government has not had a perfect policy-making record or record of responding to crises in recent years either. After Hurricane Katrina in New Orleans, the U.S. federal government appeared to be no more capable of responding to very short-term crises—such as providing drinking water to those affected—than many developing nations. It is instructive that Walmart was able to act more effectively in some areas (such as shipping in truckloads of drinking water) than was the federal government.[11]

In other cases, a policy issue in question may appear on its face to be more capable of being regulated by the government. Both the case of cybersecurity[12] and the case of organ donor programs[13] seem to be areas in which the government could, in fact, contribute some regulation and some known and agreed-upon processes to the marketplace.

The role played by the private (business) sector in the public policy debate has been the key focus in recent years where, as we suggested above, the preference of the private sector is often for government to stay out of the policy business and to let the private marketplace—whether in transportation, health care, education, or other areas—determine what happens, while the opposing viewpoint has been that the private sector will not think about these questions in an unselfish manner, and that only government will be concerned with those who do not have power in the political arena.

There is another dimension to the debate, however, which involves the increasing role of the *global* marketplace, and the fact that national powers (i.e., governments) are no longer really sovereign. Even the great powers and superpowers of years past are unable to control multinational corporations' behavior when it comes to investments, jobs, and a significant sector of the marketplace. In a recent study Kevin Farnsworth looked at the changing nature of corporate power and the growing influence of business in shaping policy interventions around the world, concluding that business power and influence has grown significantly in the international marketplace in recent years, and that governments that were at one time sovereign (such as the governments of Western Europe and North America, among others, not to mention smaller governments of developing nations) are no longer immune to the influence of the private sector.[14]

DOMESTIC POLICY-MAKING IN THE DEVELOPING WORLD

Although we have examined public policy-making by policy area, and not by region or developmental or functional grouping, a word about different abilities should be included here. We should make perfectly clear at this point in our discussion that some nations have more policy alternatives available to them than do others. The United States may choose to offer its citizens universal health insurance; India could not do so even if it wanted to do so. Why? Because the United States has a resource base that is significantly different from the resource base available to India.

In order to be fair in our comparative approach to policy-making, we have to explicitly note that most of the developed world has had a substantial number of years to get to the economic and social policy position in which it is found today. Most nations of the developing world have been independent only a relatively short period of time—many only since the end of the Second World War—and the years of their independent existence have been much more challenged by global conflict and resource shortages than were the challenges faced by the nations of the developed world when they were, in fact, becoming developed nations.

In short, some of the policy alternatives that we discussed earlier in this chapter are viable possibilities in some settings, whereas they are simply not viable possibilities in other settings. It is precisely because of the relative wealth of the United States that it is so shocking to see the relative academic performance of American students compared to students of other countries that are not as resource-rich. The "have" nations of the world have options when it comes to public policy that are not options for the "have not" nations of the world.

BOX 8.1

Developing Nations

Frequently, the term *developing nations* is used interchangeably with "the Third World"; strictly speaking, these are not the same thing.* During the 1960s the term *Third World* referred to nations that were not in the Western, capitalistic, industrial, and (generally) democratic states, including the United States, Britain, France, Japan, and so on (the "First World"), and *also* not in what used to be called the East European Marxist-Leninist states, including the former Soviet Union, and its satellites (the "Second World").

Developing nations include the low- and middle-income nation-states. The World Bank defines as "low-income" those nations with a per capita GNI of $1,005 or less. Middle-income nations are in turn divided into two groups. Lower-middle-income nations were defined by the World Bank as those having $ 1,006–$3,975 GNI per capita. Upper-middle-income nations were defined by the World Bank as those having $3,976–$12,275 GNI per capita. The high-income category includes all countries with a per capita GNI of more than $12,276.**

One author has suggested that the term *Third World* implies a number of characteristics including a colonial history; a relatively underdeveloped economy and level of technological development, especially when compared to the United States or Europe; a lack of interest and/or success in developing "modern" (that is, European) social, cultural, and economic institutions; and a commitment to work for greater world equality in the realm of economic and social policy.*** Elsewhere, six common characteristics have been suggested as being typical of developing nations: (1) low levels of living standards; (2) low levels of productivity in work; (3) high rates of population growth; (4) high and rising levels of unemployment and underemployment; (5) dependence on agricultural production and "primary product exports"; and (6) dependence and vulnerability in international relations.**** ■

---

* See Benjamin F. Bobo, *Rich Country, Poor Country: The Multinational as Change Agent* (Westport, CT: Praeger, 2005); or Howard J. Wiarda, *Political Development in Emerging Nations: Is There Still a Third World?* (Belmont, CA: Thomson/Wadsworth, 2004).

** The World Bank, "How We Classify Countries," available at http://data.worldbank.org/about/country-classifications (accessed July 2011).

*** Jacqueline Braveboy-Wagner, *Interpreting the Third World: Politics, Economics, and Social Issues* (New York: Praeger, 1986), p. 2.

**** Michael P. Todaro, *Economic Development in the Third World* (New York: Longman, 1989), p. 27. See also Mitchell Seligson and John Passe-Smith, *Development and Underdevelopment: The Political Economy of Global Inequality* (Boulder, CO: Lynne Rienner, 2003).

INTERNATIONAL AND FOREIGN POLICY

Most citizens probably think first of *domestic* affairs when they think about public policy. There are many different kinds of issues—which we have described above—that have direct and immediate effects upon individuals' lives in the domestic realm. It is also true, however, that *international* public policy affects all of us, too, whether we come from "have" or "have not" nations. Probably the first kind of public policy that we think of in the international realm involves armed conflict and war; even if the fighting does not directly affect us, it does *indirectly* affect us because huge sums of money are being spent on armaments that could be spent in other ways. International policy is important in nonwarfare areas, too, because these policies can *prevent* war, and the loss of life, through economic relations, trade issues, and a variety of other economic dimensions. Thus, **international policy** is important for all nations, and we should briefly discuss three different realms of such policy here: military policy, economic policy, and development/political policy.

As one scholar has noted, "domestic politics usually takes place within a context of generally settled order, whereas international politics takes place in a state of relative anarchy." That is, "in domestic affairs, the state assumes a 'monopoly on the *legitimate* use of force, [meaning] that public agents are organized to prevent and to counter the private use of force.'"[15] Because there is no monopoly of force in international relations, Kenneth Waltz describes the international arena as one in which nations engage in "self-help," where "each nation must look to its own security because there is no higher authority that can consistently and effectively do this for them."[16]

In the next section of this chapter we will discuss some other very important dimensions of international policymaking that can affect people in significant ways: approaches to international trade and international development assistance. A nation's international policy affects the degree to which it is inclined to offer assistance to other nations, assistance for such broad purposes as public health and public education. As we shall see, the budgets for these purposes are huge; yet even with these huge budgets the relative misery of the developing world—as measured by such indicators as infant mortality, undernourishment, disease, life expectancy, and other similar measures—is great. So much international effort is devoted to these efforts, yet so much more is needed. These, indeed, are a very concrete indicator of the power of international policy to do good.

One of the key policy questions that affects international assistance is whether development aid should be "tied" or "untied" in nature. **Tied foreign aid** is usually defined as aid—whether loans or grants—that must be spent in the donor nation. **Untied aid,** then, is aid that the recipient nation can spend anywhere. What is the difference? From the donor's perspective, the advantage of tied aid is that it can have some economic impact in the home nation. The U.S. Government, for example, can give aid but insist that tractors be American-made tractors, or grain be American-grown grain. This gives the recipient nation the product, but keeps jobs in the United States. From the recipient's perspective, the advantage of untied aid is that the nation can look for cheaper tractors, or grain, and may even build that tractor factory in its own territory, thus getting both tractors *and* jobs. Table 8.2 shows data on poverty in the contemporary world, something that can be affected by foreign aid.

The Organization for Economic Cooperation and Development (OECD) has studied the question of tied versus untied aid at great length. In a 1991

TABLE 8.2

Poverty in the World

	Net Official Development Assistance Per Capita (2007)	% of Children under 5 Malnourished (2007)	Under 5 Mortality per 1000 Births(2007)	HIV Prevalence % of Population Aged 15–49 (2007)	% Population Living below $2 / Day (2007)
Argentina	2	2.3	16	0.5	11.3
Cameroon	104	15.1	148	5.1	57.7
Haiti	73	18.9	76	2.2	72.1
Jordan	88	3.6	24	n.a.	3.5
Kenya	34	16.5	121	n.a.	39.9
West Bank/ Gaza	504	0	27	n.a.	n.a.

Source: The World Bank, World Development Report, 2010 (Washington, D.C.: The World Bank, 2010), Selected World Development Indicators, Tables 1–5, pp. 378–386.

study the OECD recognized that tying aid could make foreign assistance more politically palatable to a donor nation (because it would help to create jobs by requiring that money be spent "at home"), but argued that while there might be political benefit from tying development aid, the actual economic impact in the donor nation of tying development assistance might not be economically significant. It also concluded that the tying of aid could increase development costs by as much as 20 to 30 percent.[17]

FOREIGN POLICY DECISION-MAKING

Although the study of warfare often dominates discussion of foreign policy decision-making, the study of the *process* of making foreign policy has become increasingly recognized as being important in recent years. How are foreign-policy decisions made, whether they are decisions about going to war or decisions about giving foreign aid?

One of the most comprehensive presentations of a theory of foreign policy decision-making to be offered in recent years was put forward by Michael Brecher a number of years ago. Although this study of the *process* of making foreign policy happened to be focused on Israel, the *theory* upon which his work was based is certainly applicable to other nations, too. In his study called *The Foreign Policy System of Israel*,[18] Brecher suggested that the foreign policy system of Israel is divided into three parts: "inputs," "process," and "outputs." The "inputs" segment is in turn made up of three components, the "operational environment," "communication," and the "psychological environment." The "process" segment deals with the formulation of strategic and tactical decisions, along with the way these decisions are implemented by various structures of government. The "outputs" segment pertains to the substance of decisions and actions by the government. Each of these parts of the overall process deserves individual comment, for each makes its separate contribution to our understanding of the entire scheme.

The **external environment** suggested by Brecher includes a general consideration of the global environment, or, as he puts it, the "total web of relationships among all actors within the international system (states, blocs, organizations)."[19] All of these relationships can affect the manner in which Israel acts in any given situation. Regional relationships, or what Brecher terms "subordinate systems," focus primarily upon the Middle East, for obviously this environment has a direct bearing upon foreign policy decisions. Other bilateral relationships, especially those with the superpowers/great powers, such as the relations between Israel and the United States or Israel and Russia, must also be taken into consideration in the formulation of Israeli foreign policy.

The **internal environment** is composed of the domestic factors that can influence foreign policy. Among the many factors that would be included in this category are military capability, economic strength and resources, the current political environment, and the context within which decisions are made (i.e., public opinion, government coalitions, and other short-term domestic political considerations). The degree of interest-group involvement in the political system and how divided or agreed these various segments of the public are over foreign policy options is a very significant part of the study of public opinion, as is an understanding of who the competing elites are and of their respective strengths.

The views, or "inputs," of these various actors in the international and domestic environments are communicated to decision-making elites through a variety of communications outlets, including the mass media, the press, books, radio, television, and the bureaucracy. These decision-making elites, then, become what Brecher refers to as the "core decision-making group" of the foreign policy system, consisting of the head of Government, the foreign minister, and a relatively narrow range of other political actors.[20]

As this "core decision-making group" tries to make foreign policy decisions, its individual members must operate within their own psychological environments. Each decision maker brings with him or her a set of attitudes about the world, other nations in the foreign policy setting, ideology, tradition, and the desirability of a variety of policy alternatives. Decision makers also bring in their psychological predispositions a set of images of the environment and their perceptions of reality in the political world. These images may be more or less realistic and flexible and can color the information that the decision makers receive from the external and internal operational environments.

After the elements making up the operational environment have been communicated to the elite and then filtered through the psychological screens of individual decision makers, the policy-making process itself helps to determine what policy is chosen and how that policy is implemented. Factored in here would be the number of individuals involved in the decision-making process, the chain of command or power relationship among these individuals, whether a given policy decision is seen as a political decision, the degree to which it must be openly debated and discussed, and a variety of other factors in the Israeli political world.

THE POLICY-MAKING PROCESS AND PUBLIC POLICY

While it is true that states remain crucially important actors in regulating and directing economic and political globalization, their unambiguous power in the policy-making process is rapidly changing. As Jon Pierre noted in his 2000 volume titled *Debating Governance: Authority, Steering, and Democracy*,

> The overarching question is what significance or meaning remains of the liberal democratic notion of the state as the undisputed centre of political power and its self-evident monopoly of articulating and pursuing the collective interest in an era of "economic" globalisation, a hollowing out of the state, decreasing legitimacy for collective solutions, and a marketisation of the state itself. Is it the decline of the state we are witnessing, or is it the transformation of the state to the new type of challenges it is facing at the turn of the millennium?[21]

The international context of globalization and governance are clearly inter-related processes, and each one of these affects the other one. Nations want to retain their domestic autonomy, but they also want the ability to expand their own markets into *other* nations' spheres of domestic autonomy. This means that while they want sovereignty in their own spheres, they also do not want to be regulated by other nations' sovereignty. Domestic governance will inevitably come into conflict, then, with global interaction, and this will be true as much for the major powers as it is true for the developing nations. As Patricia Kennett has noted, however, in a global era states with the ability to exercise power both economically and politically should not be construed as the "unchallenged masters of the global economy."[22]

DISCUSSION QUESTIONS

1. What are the kinds of challenges that can be resolved by public policy-making? What are the limits of these policies? Are there any policies that the government *cannot* resolve?
2. How do different governmental structures affect public policies? Give examples for different types of executive, legislative, and judicial structures? How could different electoral systems affect public policy-making?
3. What are the different stages in the policy-making process?
4. Can you give illustrations of specific challenges of domestic political issues and the limitations of domestic politics in responding to policy needs?
5. What are examples of specific challenges that governments in the developing world face in making public policy?

6. What kinds of issues are important in the formulation of international and foreign policy?
7. What are the most important influences in the foreign policy decision-making process? What are the key actors and behaviors that play a significant role in the formulation of foreign policy?

KEY TERMS

agenda setting 180
external environment 189
formulation of options 180
government by market 179
government by network 179
internal environment 189
international policy 187
social policy 184
tied foreign aid 187
untied aid 187

SUGGESTED READINGS

Roger Congleton and Birgitta Swedenborg, eds., *Democratic Constitutional Design and Public Policy: Analysis and Evidence* (Cambridge, MA: MIT Press, 2006). There is a range of different structures in democratic nations that affect public policy. This volume examines different political structures in different settings and analyzes how those different structures influence the type of policy that is created.

Patricia Kennett, ed., *Governance, Globalization, and Public Policy* (Northampton, MA: Edward Elgar, 2008). This collection of essays focuses on the range of patterns of government behavior around the world and how the government structures of those nations affect the policy that their governments produce.

John McCormick, *The European Union: Politics and Policies* (Boulder, CO: Westview Press, 2008). Although there is a range of behavior in terms of public policy formation in the many nations of Europe, it is possible to discuss similarities and differences between and among the many nations there. This volume focuses exclusively on public policy in Europe and presents analysis of the assumptions underlying the policy-making process there.

Martin Painter and John Pierre, *Challenges to State Policy Capacity: Global Trends and Comparative Perspectives* (New York: Palgrave Macmillan, 2005). There are limitations to what states can do in terms of public policy. This volume offers a comparative examination of the range of those limitations, and how the public policy in the nations concerned is affected by the political institutions of those nations.

Jon Pierre and Guy Peters, *Governing Complex Societies: Trajectories and Scenarios* (New York: Palgrave Macmillan, 2005). The process of government is complicated, and it is influenced by many different factors in different settings. This volume examines what some of those different factors are and their relative importance where they are found.

NOTES

1. Patricia Kennett, ed., "Introduction: Governance, the State and Public Policy in a Global age," in *Governance, Globalization, and Public Policy* (Northampton, MA: Edward Elgar, 2008), p. 3. See also Martin Painter and John Pierre, *Challenges to State*

Policy Capacity: Global Trends and Comparative Perspectives (New York: Palgrave Macmillan, 2005).

2. Xavier de Souza Briggs, *Democracy as Problem Solving: Civic Capacity in Communities across the Globe* (Cambridge, MA: MIT Press, 2008), p. 28. See also Robert Schoeni, *Making Americans Healthier: Social and Economic Policy as Health Policy* (New York: Russell Sage Foundation, 2008); or Bjorn Gustafsson, Shi Li, and Terry Sicular, eds., *Inequality and Public Policy in China* (New York: Cambridge University Press, 2008).

3. Charles Merriam, *The American Party System: An Introduction to the Study of Political Parties in the United States* (New York: MacMillan, 1922).

4. Roger Congleton and Birgitta Swedenborg, *Democratic Constitutional Design and Public Policy: Analysis and Evidence* (Cambridge, MA: MIT Press, 2006); and Walter Kickert, ed., *The Study of Public Management in Europe and the U.S.: A Comparative Analysis of National Distinctiveness* (New York: Routledge, 2008).

5. Elaine C. Kamarck, *The End of Government... as We Know It: Making Public Policy Work* (Boulder, CO: Lynne Rienner, 2007), pp. 17–21. See also William Genieys and Marc Smyrl, *Elites, Ideas, and the Evolution of Public Policy* (New York: Palgrave Macmillan, 2008).

6. Kamarck, p. 17.

7. Ibid, p. 20.

8. See Allison Stanger, *One Nation under Contract: The Outsourcing of American Power and the Future of Foreign Policy* (New Haven, CT: Yale University Press, 2009).

9. See David Reisman, *Health Care and Public Policy* (Northampton, MA: Edward Elgar, 2007).

10. A very comprehensive review of the events leading to the disaster appeared in the *New York Times* on December 6, 2010, titled "Deepwater Horizon's Final Hours," by David Barstow, David Rohde, and Stephanie Saul.

11. A very good source for this was the volume edited by Manning Marable and Kristen Clarke (New York: Palgrave Macmillan, 2008).

12. See, for example, the Congressional Hearings "Cybersecurity: a review of public and private efforts to secure our nation's Internet infrastructure: hearing before the Subcommittee on Information Policy, Census, and National Archives of the Committee on Oversight and Government Reform, House of Representatives, One Hundred Tenth Congress, first session, October 23, 2007."

13. See the Congressional Hearings "Utilizing public policy and technology to strengthen organ donor programs: hearing before the Subcommittee on Information Policy, Census, and National Archives of the Committee on Oversight and Government Reform, House of Representatives, One Hundred Tenth Congress, first session, September 25, 2007."

14. See Kevin Farnsworth, "Governance, Business and Social Policy: International and National Dimensions," in *Governance, Globalization, and Public Policy*, ed. Kennett, pp. 35–55. See also Otto Holman, "Transnational Governance and National Employment Regulation: The Primacy of Competitiveness," in *op. cit.*, ed. Kennett pp. 56–76. A European focus can be found in John McCormick, *The European Union: Politics and Policies* (Boulder, CO: Westview Press, 2008).

15. Kenneth Waltz, *Theory of International Politics* (New York: McGraw Hill, 1979), pp. 102–104.

16. Ibid.

17. See Catrinus Jepma, "Development Studies Center Study: The Tying of Aid," *Organization for Economic Cooperation and Development*, 1991, available at *http://www.oecd.org/LongAbstract/0,3425,en_2649_33959_29412506_119699_1_1_1,00.html/*. See also Takatoshi Ito and Anne O. Krueger, eds., *East Asia Seminar on Economics: Governance, Regulation, and Privatization in the Asia-Pacific Region* (Chicago, IL: University of Chicago Press, 2004).

18. Michael Brecher, *The Foreign Policy System of Israel: Setting, Images, Process* (New Haven, CT: Yale University Press, 1972).

19. Ibid., p. 5

20. Ibid., p. 11.

21. Jon Pierre, *Debating Governance: Authority, Steering, and Democracy*, (Oxford, UK: Oxford University Press, 2000), p. 2. See also Jon Pierre and Guy Peters, *Governing Complex Societies: Trajectories and Scenarios* (New York: Palgrave Macmillan, 2005).

22. Kennett, p. 13.

The British Political System

The prime minister is the single most important individual in British politics. Here Prime

LEARNING OBJECTIVES

- Explain the relationship between "England" and "Great Britain" and "United Kingdom."
- Understand the concept of an "unwritten constitution" and how the British constitutional system developed.
- Apply the parliamentary model of government that we studied earlier in this volume to the British system.
- Understand the evolution of the split between the Head of State role and the Chief Executive role.
- Discuss the power relationship between the prime minister and other actors in British politics.
- Explain the crucial role that Margaret Thatcher played in modern British politics.
- Clarify the relationship between the House of Commons and the House of Lords, and their different roles in British politics.
- Appreciate the importance of the concept of party discipline in a parliamentary setting.

The British political system is regarded by many as the "mother" of modern democracies. The institution of Parliament developed in Great Britain, and the role of the monarchy in Britain devolved to a point at which it could exist in harmony with democratic political norms. The Westminster model of parliamentary government to which we have referred again and again in this book is derived, of course, from the parliamentary system that evolved in Britain at Westminster. It seems logical, therefore, that the subject of our first area studies chapter should be the United Kingdom.

Many students are confused about the names England, (Great) Britain, and the United Kingdom. These three names are not interchangeable; they refer to different political systems. The United Kingdom is a country in Western Europe

UNITED KINGDOM

Total Area (rank)	243,610 sq km (79)
Population (rank)	62,689,362 (22)
Population Growth Rate (rank)	0.557% (148)
Urban Population	80%
Life Expectancy at Birth (total population) (rank)	80.05 (28)
Literacy	99%
Government Type	Constitutional monarchy
Legal System	Common Law
Head of Government	Prime Minister David Cameron
Chief of State	Queen Elizabeth II
Gross Domestic Product (GDP)	$2.247 trillion
GDP Per Capita (rank)	$34,800 (37)
GDP Real Growth Rate (rank)	1.3% (164)
Unemployment Rate (rank)	7.9% (86)

UNITED KINGDOM

N

ATLANTIC
OCEAN

North
Sea

SCOTLAND

Wick

Inverness

Aberdeen

Glasgow

Edinburgh

NORTHERN
IRELAND · Belfast

Irish Sea

NORTH

NORTH
WEST

Leeds

Liverpool

Manchester

Sheffield

EAST
MIDLANDS

Norwich

ENGLAND

EAST
ANGLIA

WEST
MIDLANDS

Birmingham

WALES

SOUTH
EAST

Cardiff

London

UNITED KINGDOM

SOUTH WEST

Portsmouth

0   100   200   300 Miles

Plymouth

English Channel

0   100   200   300 Kilometers

with a population of nearly 61 million people and a national capital in London. The formal name of the **United Kingdom** (usually abbreviated UK) is the United Kingdom of Great Britain and Northern Ireland. (Prior to 1922, when Ireland was divided into Northern Ireland and the Republic of Ireland, the formal name of the UK was the United Kingdom of Great Britain and Ireland.) **Great Britain** is the principal island of the United Kingdom, and it includes England, Scotland, and Wales. **England** is an administrative unit of the United Kingdom of Great Britain and Northern Ireland. It occupies most of the southern half of the island of Great Britain, Wales is to the west, and Scotland is to the north. Having said all of this we should note that today the term *Britain* is generally used interchangeably with "United Kingdom" or "England," even though they do not refer to the same thing.

THE BRITISH CONSTITUTIONAL SYSTEM

Earlier we discussed the distinction between governments with written constitutions and those with "constitutional government," and pointed out that a political system need not have a written document in order to be referred to as a constitutional regime. Indeed, the example that we used at that time was the case of Britain. Students of British politics agree that for all intents and purposes there *is* a British Constitution, in the sense that there is a body of fundamental precepts underlying the British political regime, and consequent British political behavior. The fact that Britain does not have a specific document called a constitution has led some to say that Britain has no constitution. This error "confuses the constitution with what is usually only one of its sources."[1]

Britain's lack of a written constitution is not a result of British inexperience with the writing of constitutions. The British government has written constitutions for many former possessions that are today independent nations, most in the **Commonwealth of Nations.** For example, in 1867, the British North America Act was passed by the British Parliament. It united what was then called Canada (today Ontario and Québec) with Nova Scotia and New Brunswick to form the Dominion of Canada. Australia received its constitution in 1901. The Union of South Africa Constitution was passed in 1909. New Zealand was granted responsible government in 1852.[2] India's independent status and relations with the British Commonwealth were defined at the London conference of prime ministers in April of 1949, and its new constitution became effective in January of 1950.[3] Many constitutions have been written for newly independent countries—formerly members of the British Empire—since that time.

Constitutions of political regimes can frequently be said to have several components: (1) written charters or collections of historic documents, (2) legislative statues of "constitutional" significance, (3) judicial interpretation, and (4) customs and precedents.

> The "written" constitutions acquire many unwritten parts and through the years they become overlaid with legislative amplifications, judicial interpretations, and customary provisions. The "unwritten" ones usually have important parts committed to paper as charters or broad constitutional statues. In the course of time the two types come more and more to resemble one another.[4]

One scholar of the British Constitution has suggested that there are essentially three sources from which the British Constitution emanates: statutory law (Acts of Parliament), common law and judicial decisions, and "the customs of the Constitution."[5] Although there is no single document that can be called the British Constitution, scholars agree that fundamentally this is not significant; whether there is a single document or not, Britain *has* a constitution in the sense that there are fundamental principles underlying British government and limiting the behavior of the British government.

Statutory law is law that derives from Acts of Parliament. We should note that while not all Acts of Parliament can or should be regarded as constitutional acts, "there is scarcely a session of Parliament that does not contribute to the constitutional structure statutes that add to or alter the basic law of the land."[6] Acts that are usually considered to be part of the **unwritten British Constitution** are the Magna Carta (1215), the Petition of Right (1626), the Habeas Corpus Act (1679), the Bill of Rights (1689), the Act of Settlement (1701), the Acts of Union with Scotland (1707) and Ireland (1800), the Great Reform Act (1832), the Parliament Act (1911), and the Statute of Westminster (1931), among many others.[7]

Common-law sources of constitutional doctrines are harder to pin down. Common law, by definition, is concerned with customs; according to **William Blackstone**, the eighteenth-century scholar whose work on British law is seen as being authoritative, law of this nature is "not set down in any written statute or ordinance, but depending on immemorial usage for their support."[8] Many judicial decisions eventually become part of the body of common law, and acquire "constitutional" status over time. Generally speaking, judicial interpretation is of less significance in Britain than in America. Because Britain operates under a system of legislative supremacy, with no judicial review of legislative statutes, the British judiciary has a lower profile than its American counterpart. As one observer has noted: "The British courts, however, in interpreting and clarifying the law frequently declare what the constitution is. The civil liberties of British subjects are largely embedded in the common law and thus have been defined and protected by the courts."[9]

The third source of British constitutional doctrine has been referred to as "*customs of the Constitution*." A number of these customs may be highlighted here:

1. The Cabinet consists of members of, and is responsible to, Parliament.
2. The Sovereign [today, the Queen] does not attend Cabinet meetings.
3. The Sovereign does not withhold assent from (veto) Bills which have passed the two Houses of Parliament.
4. The Speaker (presiding officer) of the House of Commons takes no part in political controversy.[10]

These four points illustrate the customs of behavior that have evolved over the years in Britain and are referred to as being "constitutional" in nature today. Although the monarch today may *legally* retain the right to veto or withhold assent from an act of the British Parliament, it would be regarded as *unconstitutional* for her to do so.[11] Similarly, while the monarch *legally* can appoint anyone she wants to be prime minister, *constitutionally* she can only appoint someone who can command the support of a majority of the House of Commons. This distinction may strike many as being curious, that an action may be at the same time both *legal* and *unconstitutional*. It is nonetheless the case, however, that in the United Kingdom the *law* may permit an action that has, through *custom* over time, become impermissible. This is a valid distinction, and important one to recall.

It is important to distinguish "between the Constitution and the principles that underlie it. The Principles are in one sense more important than the Constitution itself."[12] Constitutions may change, through statutory acts, common law, judicial decisions, or custom—but principles remain. Two fundamental principles underlie the British Constitution. The first principle involves the *rule of law*. Citizens are entitled to the protection of law, and both individuals and the government of the state are to be limited in what they can do by the law of the regime. The second principle is **Parliamentary sovereignty**, a principle that we suggested earlier in this chapter. This point can be further stated to mean that (1) there is no law of an earlier Parliament that the current Parliament cannot change if it wishes to do so; (2) there is no clear distinction between "constitutional" Acts of Parliament and Acts of Parliament that are not "constitutional"; and (3) no person or body (for example, the courts) can nullify an Act of Parliament on the grounds that the act is opposed to the Constitution.[13] Anything the British Parliament does, by definition, is constitutional, even though it is possible to imagine legislation that it might—legally—pass that individuals might see as violating customs and traditions to the extent that they might call the legislation "unconstitutional."

A number of structural characteristics of the British political system can be regarded as almost "constitutional" in their significance for the regime.[14] First, the United Kingdom is a *unitary* political system, not a federal system, a point to which we shall return shortly. Centralized power is something that is, and has been, part of British constitutional life.

In addition to the United Kingdom being a unitary political system, the second structural characteristic, as we noted earlier in this text, is that the **Westminster model** generally is composed of four parts. First, the chief executive is not the same as the head of state. Second, the executive powers of government are exercised by the chief executive and his or her cabinet, not the Head of State. Third, the chief executive and the cabinet come from and are part of the legislature. Fourth, the chief executive and the cabinet are responsible to, and can be fired by, the legislature. This Westminster model of government differs significantly from the American system in that there is *no* clear separation of powers between the legislative and executive branches of government in the British setting, which is so important to the American political culture. The concern of the American Founders over "checks and balances" simply is not found in the Westminster political structure. The political executive is actually *part of* the legislature, and the courts do not have the power to limit what the legislature does.

A third political structure identified with the British Constitution, which was suggested in the preceding paragraph, is that the prime minister and cabinet are drawn from and are responsible to the national legislature. ("Responsible to" here means "answerable to"—the legislature has the right to hire and fire the prime minister.) Although occasionally some cabinet members may not be from the legislature, the prime minister and the bulk of the cabinet will invariably be from the House of Commons (or whatever the name of the lower, elected, house of the national legislature is in other systems modeled after the British Parliament). They remain in office as long as they continue to be supported by a majority of the lower house of the national legislature.

A fourth major significant political structure in the British system is that of political parties. Political parties are so much a part of the British political system that we cannot imagine British politics operating in their absence. Institutions and patterns of behavior such as "responsible government," "party discipline," and "votes of confidence," among others, require healthy political parties. Parliamentary government could not exist without a rigorous system of political parties.

UNITARY GOVERNMENT IN BRITAIN

Britain is **unitary**. There is no "sharing" of sovereignty between the national government and some intermediate level of government; there are no sovereign intermediate levels of government in the United Kingdom to correspond to states in the United States or provinces in Canada or Länder in Germany (although there *are* administrative units of government that exist). This is significant in that Parliament thereby becomes more relevant to the daily routine of life in Britain because it influences many aspects of life affected by intermediate levels of government in other political systems.

We should note, however, that in 1997, the start of a **devolution of power** from Westminster to the regions took place. Two different referenda were held in the United Kingdom to give Scotland and Wales an opportunity to reclaim some of the political power that had developed in Westminster over the years. The Government of **Tony Blair** was committed to giving the Scots and the Welsh the option of having their own parliaments with wide—but not exclusive—powers to govern in their respective areas. Blair pledged in the 1997 parliamentary campaign to institute a broad devolution of powers from the central government at Westminster in London to Scotland, Wales, and Northern Ireland.[15]

The constitutional structures of the United Kingdom are reflected in the governmental structure. Welsh affairs are handled at the British national level by the secretary of state for Wales, working with Members of Parliament elected from Wales. The secretary of state for Scotland is also a cabinet member, who works with Members of Parliament from that area. A secretary of state for Northern Ireland works with its eighteen Members of Parliament to represent that territory.

In September of 1997 referenda were held in both Scotland and Wales on the issue of *devolution*.[16] In Scotland, voters responded to two questions: Did they want to set up their own parliament in Edinburgh with wide powers, and did they want this parliament to have the power to raise extra taxes. Seventy-four percent of the voters said "yes" to the first question, and sixty-three percent said "yes" to the second.

A week later the Welsh voted on a single question: Did they want their own assembly with the power to administer public services? The assembly would not have the power to levy taxes or pass laws, so it was not called a parliament. The Welsh voted 50.3 percent "yes," which was enough for Prime Minister Blair to claim support for this policy and indicate that he would pursue that direction in future policy.

On December 2, 1999, Britain officially created a new provincial government in Northern Ireland, and devolution took another step forward. Northern Ireland on that day received home rule for the first time in many years. The devolution issue in relation to Northern Ireland had been wrapped up in the history of religious violence there, with Protestant and Catholic paramilitary groups there fighting since 1922, so devolution could proceed only as far as the status of the peace process would permit it. Under what was called the **Mitchell Agreement**— named after former U.S. Senator George Mitchell who chaired a committee that worked on a peace agreement for Northern Ireland—much authority over policy in Northern Ireland would move from London to Belfast, and government of the province would come from a new local assembly and cabinet.[17]

EXECUTIVE STRUCTURES

The British case is the source of the "split executive" parliamentary model that we described earlier in this text. The role of the monarch is one that has evolved over a long period of time; its function is one of both substance and style. George Orwell, the noted English author, observed in 1944 that:

> in a dictatorship the power and the glory belong to the same person. In England the real power belongs to unprepossessing men in bowler hats: the creature who rides in a gilded coach behind soldiers in steel breast-plates is really a waxwork. It is at any rate possible that while this division of functions exists a Hitler or a Stalin cannot come to power.[18]

The Monarch

In our discussion of the political executive earlier, a brief outline of the evolution— and perhaps (a different use of the term) *devolution* is the more appropriate term— of the power of the British monarchy was presented. We saw that while at one point the monarch had absolute power to promulgate laws, fire the legislature, and imprison political opponents, the situation changed radically (but gradually) over time. As democratic institutions became popular, they also became powerful, and the ability of the monarch (who happened to be in power at the time) to resist reform diminished. Monarchs more sympathetic to liberal ideas, such as William and Mary (proclaimed king and queen by Parliament in 1688), helped the process to maintain, and to increase, its momentum.

Today, not even William and Mary would recognize the relationship between the monarch and the Parliament. *De jure*, under law, most powers of British government are still exercised in the name of the king or queen, but in reality today they are exercised "on the advice" of the chief executive, the prime minister.

In the eighteenth century, the king relied more and more on his cabinet—a group of advisors—for guidance. In the early eighteenth century, the role of the cabinet was *only* that of providing *advice*; the king still did as he pleased.

As ideas of democratic government grew over the next two centuries, the power relationship changed so that the king was *obligated* in terms of history and culture (although not *legally required*) to accept the advice of his cabinet. Cabinet members now were exclusively drawn from the house of Parliament that was chosen by the public, namely the House of Commons. Now the cabinet was in reality governing in the name of the king without consulting him.

> The monarch has the constitutional right, as Bagehot put it, to be consulted, to advise, and to warn. When Anthony Eden resigned as Foreign Secretary in 1938, King George VI protested to Neville Chamberlain, the Prime Minister, that he had not been kept properly informed. It is clearly a valuable safeguard that Prime Ministers should be under such an obligation, and should have to bear it in mind when they may be tempted to arbitrary action. Cabinet papers, Foreign Office dispatches from overseas posts, and major departmental memoranda are sent to the Monarch.[19]

"The elaborate pretense that the Queen is still the real ruler of Britain still decorates the machinery of British government," noted one observer. Two examples of what can be called a **royal pretense** can be offered here by way of illustration. All Royal Commissions begin with a message from the monarch: "Greetings! Now Know Ye That We, reposing great trust and confidence in your knowledge and ability...." Legislative acts begin with the words "Be it enacted by the Queen's most Excellent Majesty, by and with the advice and consent of the Lords Spiritual and Temporal, and Commons, in this present Parliament assembled...."[20] While both of these messages *seem* to be indicating that the monarch really is considering alternatives, in fact that is not the case, and the monarch has no real decision in the matter at all.

One of the most visible examples of the "royal pretense" occurs on an annual basis when the Queen opens the session of Parliament, seated on her throne in the House of Lords. She "summons the Commons" to the chamber of the House of Lords and reads her **Speech from the Throne**, in which she outlines the plans she has for "her" government, what she wants "her" government to do in the coming parliamentary session. The fraud here, of course, is that the speech that she reads is in reality written by the prime minister and cabinet; like a puppet, she says what she is told to say.[21]

The Selection of the Chief Executive

Among the most striking characteristics of British parliamentary government today is the **duality of its executive leadership**. The monarch is the official or legal (*de jure*) head of state, the head of state in law, but the active (*de facto*) head of government, the head of government in fact, is the prime minister. Appointments are made, acts of Parliament are proclaimed, policy is proposed, and all government is carried on in the name of the monarch. It is the prime minister and his or her cabinet, however, who make all the *selections* for appointments, who author or sponsor legislative proposals, and who make the administrative decisions that keep government running.

The legal claim to power of the cabinet rests in the fact that, since the seventeenth century, the monarch has had a **Privy Council** to advise him or her—a kind of present-day cabinet. In earlier days of British government, the Privy Council was the focus of governmental power, but as the British Constitution has evolved over the years, so too has the Privy Council. Today, although the Privy Council is no longer active, cabinet members must *first* be made members of the Privy Council, and *then* are appointed to the cabinet.[22] There are today over 520 Privy Councilors, since appointment to the Privy Council is a lifetime designation.[23] Cabinet membership may change frequently, and individuals may leave the Cabinet; they do not leave the Privy Council. Today the Privy Council continues to meet, but its day-to-day business is done by Cabinet members.

The cabinet meets as a subcommittee of the (inactive) Privy Council and acts in the name of the Privy Council.

> The Privy Council has survived as the formal machinery through which the monarch exercises her prerogative powers when necessary. Although membership of the Privy Council is extensive ... its working character is that of a small number of ministers who are called together to witness the signature by the monarch of some formal document.[24]

Although the British monarch was free to choose whomever he or she wanted as advisors long ago, this is no longer the case today. As soon as election returns are in, if an incumbent prime minister's party has lost its majority that person submits his or her resignation to the Queen, and subsequently the new majority leader in the House of Commons is "invited" to form a government. Symbolically the act is described as "the Queen has invited Mr. Cameron to form a Government," or "the Queen has invited Mrs. Thatcher to form a Government." This is not a realistic description of the process today; there really is no alternative for the Queen to the invitation that is issued.

"In theory, the Queen has the right both to dissolve parliament and to choose the prime minister"—however, the first power has not really been exercised in the past hundred years; the second power "only recently has become a fiction."[25] This lack of real power in the selection of a prime minister is the result of clear majorities existing in the House of Commons with "obvious" prime ministerial choices. Should some future election produce an inconclusive result, with no clear majority present in the House of Commons, the monarch may again be called upon to take a meaningful and substantive part in the selection process.

The Cabinet and the Prime Minister

In his classic work on the British Cabinet, Sir Ivor Jennings wrote in 1951 that "it is a peculiarity of our Constitution that the principles governing the formation and working of the Cabinet and its relations with Parliament can be stated with hardly any reference to the law."[26] In 1937, the British Parliament finally took statutory notice of the cabinet when it passed the Ministers of the Crown Act, naming a number of "cabinet rank" positions.[27]

The development of the position of prime minister has followed the evolution of the cabinet itself. The earliest of cabinets were collections of advisors to monarchs. Cabinet members held little power, and none was first among the group of equals. George I (who ruled from 1714 to 1727) started the practice of having his cabinet meet in his absence. The result of this:

> was to transform what had been a mere inner group of royal advisors into a board of government with an independent existence of its own. Having lost its natural president [the King], it was inevitable that it should find one of its own, a "prime minister" in fact, upon whom would fall the task of coordinating policy, which before had been the King's.[28]

The first "modern" British prime minister is usually cited as being Sir Robert Walpole, who held office from 1721 to 1742. Ever since World War II, the styles of prime ministers have varied, and the range of roles played by the prime minister "has prompted a long-running debate about the power of the Prime Minister between 'the presidential school' and 'the chairmanship school.'"[29]

The prime minister is first minister of the cabinet, but the power of that position varies widely depending upon the political environment of the time. Some British prime ministers have had much power, others have simply been in the role of "chairman of the board," coordinating action among a number of powerful actors. "Viewed from the top, British government looks more like a mountain range than a single pyramid of power. The Prime Minister is preeminent among these peaks, but the political significance of this preeminence is ambiguous."[30]

Although the prime minister has traditionally received the bulk of the attention of scholarship related to the executive branch of government in Britain, there has been some scholarship in recent years focusing upon the cabinet itself. It is the ministers, after all, who are responsible for gathering resources for public programs. It is the ministers who are in a position to oversee and—to some degree—direct the vast civil service, a subject to which we shall return shortly.[31]

The individual ministries are also important because they serve as a step on the way to the prime ministership for a given individual. Some ministries have (such as Treasury or Defense) more status than others (such as Agriculture, or the Welsh Office).[32] In any event, it is rare that individuals become prime minister without having served in other cabinet capacities first.

Individual ministers have several different constituencies that must be kept in mind as they perform their jobs. First, they must direct their own ministries, thus being in a position of responsibility for a vast network of civil service employees. Second, they must be aware of and responsible to Parliament, for the Government as a whole is responsible to Parliament for what it does. Third, they must respond to the needs and desires of the public outside of Westminster, including their own political parties, trade unions, chambers of commerce, professional organizations and interest groups, as well as international factors.[33]

The cabinet has varied in size in this century, ranging from just over a dozen to over two dozen members. At the time of this writing it has twenty-three full members,[34] although in 2009 under Labour Prime Minister Gordon Brown it reached thirty-one members in size and was criticized as being "too big to make decisions."[35] Current membership of the cabinet

TABLE 9.1

The British Cabinet

Prime Minister, First Lord of the Treasury, and Minister for the Civil Service, The Rt. Hon. David Cameron MP

Deputy Prime Minister, Lord President of the Council, The Rt. Hon. Nick Clegg MP

First Secretary of State, Secretary of State for Foreign and Commonwealth Affairs, The Rt. Hon. William Hague MP

Chancellor of the Exchequer The Rt. Hon. George Osborne MP

Lord Chancellor, Secretary of State for Justice The Rt. Hon. Kenneth Clarke QC MP

Secretary of State for the Home Department, Minister for Women and Equality The Rt. Hon. Theresa May MP

Secretary of State for Defence The Rt. Hon. Dr. Liam Fox MP

Secretary of State for Business, Innovation and Skills The Rt. Hon. Dr. Vince Cable MP

Secretary of State for Work and Pensions The Rt. Hon. Iain Duncan Smith MP

Secretary of State for Energy and Climate Change The Rt. Hon. Chris Huhne MP

Secretary of State for Health The Rt. Hon. Andrew Lansley CBE MP

Secretary of State for Education The Rt. Hon. Michael Gove MP

Secretary of State for Communities and Local Government The Rt. Hon. Eric Pickles MP

Secretary of State for Transport The Rt. Hon. Philip Hammond MP

Secretary of State for Environment, Food and Rural Affairs The Rt. Hon. Caroline Spelman MP

Secretary of State for International Development The Rt. Hon. Andrew Mitchell MP

Secretary of State for Northern Ireland The Rt. Hon. Owen Paterson MP

Secretary of State for Scotland The Rt. Hon. Michael Moore MP

Secretary of State for Wales The Rt. Hon. Cheryl Gillan MP

Secretary of State for Culture, Olympics, Media and Sport The Rt. Hon. Jeremy Hunt MP

Chief Secretary to the Treasury The Rt. Hon. Danny Alexander MP

Leader of the House of Lords, Chancellor of the Duchy of Lancaster The Rt. Hon. The Lord Strathclyde PC

Minister without Portfolio (Minister of State) The Rt. Hon. The Baroness Warsi PC

Source: Government of the United Kingdom, Prime Minister's Office, 10 Downing Street, available at http://www.number10.gov.uk/news/latest-news/2010/05/her-majestys-government-49840 (accessed June 2011).

is illustrated in Table 9.1. The prime minister is guided in cabinet selections by a number of factors:

1. the need to include as many of the leading members of his party as possible and to represent the various groups and shades of opinion;
2. by the convenience of having a reasonable number of reliable friends and close supporters;
3. by the need to achieve adequate coordination between departments;
4. the desirability of avoiding friction and jealousy between the "ins" and the "outs" as well as to silence potential critics.[36]

The role of the prime minister in the British political system can be analytically broken down into seven different components.[37] First, the prime minister is concerned with *party management*. The prime minister holds that office precisely because he or she is head of his or her party in the House of Commons, and prime ministers must be careful to maintain party support. One way to do this is through party patronage—appointments to either cabinet-level or subcabinet-level positions. A majority of the 650 members currently serving in the House of Commons is 326; by the time a prime minister appoints about 20 MPs to cabinet positions, and another 60 to subcabinet rank positions, and yet another two to three dozen to positions of parliamentary private secretary, this individual has a block of almost one-third of the votes necessary for remaining in office.

The Government exists because it controls a majority in the House of Commons. The ultimate weapon of the Government to keep its party members in control is the power of dissolution, but this is too severe a threat to bandy about lightly. "The majority must be treated with respect and given reasonably full information in response to questions.... Even the strongest Governments have been known to bow to 'the sense of the House.'"[38]

The second major job of a prime minister involves the *timing and winning of a general election*. Winning a national election is necessary for a prime minister to retain his or her power. (The current prime minister, David Cameron, attained power through a general election, not in the middle of a parliamentary session.) Only the prime minister has the power to choose a date for a national election (and to advise the queen to dissolve Parliament and call for an election on a given day). Prime ministers want to set election dates such that balloting day corresponds to their parties' popular periods, not with inevitable slippages in popularity.

A third dimension of activity for the prime minister involves his or her *image in Parliament*. Contacts in both the majority and opposition parties must be nurtured. Until World War II, the prime minister was personally "Leader of the House of Commons." Since that time other requirements have prevented the prime minister from holding this position personally, but the prime minister must still be aware of, and concerned with, happenings in the House of Commons.

Related to this is a fourth facet of the prime minister's role, participating in **parliamentary question time**. Twice a week the prime minister appears in the House of Commons to answer parliamentary questions, primarily from the members of the Opposition. Prime ministers take this activity seriously, as a poor performance can affect both their image in Parliament and their image with the public. One student of this phenomenon indicated that "on two nights a week the Prime Minister receives up to three boxes of files in preparation for the next day's ordeal, reading these ahead of Cabinet papers or Foreign Office telegrams."[39]

Yet another dimension of the prime minister's activity involves *debating policy*. Research has shown that in a typical year the prime minister will participate in only six major debates, which are usually on only three issues: international affairs, the economy, and the business of the Government.[40] As far as general debate is concerned, the prime minister usually has ministers in charge of relevant departments articulate the Government's position in a debate.

Prime ministers are also concerned with *press publicity*. The prime minister, after all, must worry about the general image of his or her Government. Generally speaking, the press is happy to oblige the prime minister with media attention; this is an example of a symbiotic relationship in which both the prime minister and the press profit from media coverage of the prime minister.

The seventh and final component of behavior of the prime minister is one to which we have already alluded: *chairing the cabinet*. The once or twice a week that the prime minister sits down with the heads of the various departments of government allows for crucial policy discussion to take place, as well as for communication of problems from ministers to the prime minister. All cabinet members are affected by the principle of "collective responsibility." This means that the cabinet as a whole is responsible for acts of the Government, and no member of cabinet may attack or criticize actions of the Government after a collective policy decision has been made.

Margaret Thatcher and "Thatcherism"

The arrival of Margaret Thatcher as prime minister in May 1979 affected British politics significantly and "changed the nature of contemporary Conservatism."[41] Thatcher's strong antisocialist and antiunion style was *not* an example of a consensual style of leadership: She knew what she wanted to accomplish, and she worked in a determined manner to accomplish it. She introduced a style to contemporary British politics that came to be known first as "conviction politics," and subsequently as **Thatcherism**.[42] If this meant engaging in an ideological battle within her own party, she was quite willing to do so. Indeed, many observers of British politics indicated that "the main feature of the first Thatcher administration was the Prime Minister's near total dominance over economic policy formation."[43]

When Thatcher moved into 10 Downing Street in 1979 the British economy was weak. She sought to turn the economy around, to a substantial degree through legislation nullifying many of the socialist policies that had been directing the economy for years, and engaging in direct conflict with the powerful labor unions.[44]

The Thatcher government **privatized** a number of government-owned industries, for instance, overseeing the conversion of British Telecom from a government-run business to being a private corporation with stockholders.[45] The government cut subsidies, reduced services, and fought with local governments that—often still controlled by the Labor opposition party—sought to move into policy areas vacated by the central government.

Ultimately, Thatcher's "conviction style" of politics—specifically her insistence on new taxes and her opposition to further integrating Britain into the European economy—alienated even most of her supporters in the Conservative party. In November 1990, Thatcher's leadership of the Conservative party was challenged by former (Conservative) Defense Minister Michael Heseltine. Heseltine received enough votes on the first ballot of the party leadership vote to convince Thatcher that she would not win, and she indicated that she would resign as leader and prime minister once the party selected a new leader. On the next ballot, it was not Heseltine, but Thatcher's hand-picked successor, John Major, who was elected leader of the Conservative party. The day after that vote, Margaret Thatcher visited the Queen to submit her resignation, and the Queen "invited" John Major to form a Government.

Between that time and May of 1997, John Major tried to steer a more moderate Conservative line, and the Conservative party was re-elected under Major's leadership in April of 1992. His re-election in April of 1992—the fourth straight win for the Conservative Party—showed that a substantial proportion of the British public supported his record.

Unfortunately for Major and the Conservatives—perhaps simply as a result of the Conservative Party being in power for so long—the public's support for Major's Government and his leadership started to decline, sharply, by the middle 1990s. This trend was intensified by the change in the leadership of the Labour Party and the very skillful campaigning of **Tony Blair** as a "new" (that is, moderate) Labour leader. Blair called for a "national renewal," and moved the Labour Party closer to the political center of British politics. He emphasized that after eighteen years of rule the Conservative Party "was tired," and worked hard to tie John Major to the policies of Margaret Thatcher. At the time of the 1997 election, he was able to convince a substantial majority of British voters that Labour no longer represented the "threat" to Britain that Margaret Thatcher had described years earlier, and that Labour would be more responsive to the contemporary needs of the British public than the entrenched leadership of the Conservative Party. Labour won the 1997 election handily, and Mr. Blair became, at age forty-three, the youngest prime minister since the early nineteenth century, serving until June of 2007.[46]

Blair was a successful prime minister, serving as prime minister longer than any other Labour Party PM (the next-longest Labour PM was Clement Attlee, who served from 1945 to 1951), and leading the party to three consecutive general election victories. He presided over a moderated Labour Party, which likely was why he managed to stay in power for as long as he did. Although the government increased spending on health and education during his tenure in office, it was also careful about significant tax increases during his time in office, too. Blair also opposed adopting the euro as the currency to replace the British pound, an opposition that was supported by the British public. Blair oversaw the signing of the Belfast Agreement, a peace agreement and framework for government of Northern Ireland. Other significant acts during Blair's term as Prime Minister included constitutional change with the Human Rights Act of 1998, devolution of power with a Scottish Parliament and a Welsh Assembly, and the removal of most hereditary peers from the House of Lords in 1999. He emphasized the importance of the National Health Service and public education.

In 2007, after serving two full terms as Prime Minister (1997–2001, 2001–2005, and being re-elected in 2005 for a third term), Blair announced that after ten years he thought he had served long enough, and stepped down in September 2007, succeeded by Gordon Brown. As had been the case with his Conservative predecessor, Blair's longevity in office was bound to be limited; in local elections held in May of 2006 the Labour Party lost over 300 local council seats around the UK, and Blair felt that it was time that he step down.

Blair was succeeded as Labour leader and prime minister by Gordon Brown, who had served as Blair's Chancellor of the Exchequer. Unfortunately for Brown, despite his being a different individual from Tony Blair, the public was ready for a change in party leadership. In May of 2008 Labour was dealt another clear blow in local elections, suffering its worst loss in over four decades and receiving only 24 percent of the vote.[47] In April of 2010 Brown asked the Queen for an early dissolution of Parliament and new elections, which led in May of 2010 to a coalition government—the first **hung parliament**, in which no party has received a majority, since 1974—led by **David Cameron** of the Conservative Party and Nick Clegg of the Liberal Democratic Party.

LEGISLATIVE STRUCTURES

In the British case, a bicameral national legislature is not a function of a federal regime as is the case in the United States, Germany, India, Australia, or Canada. Instead, it is a result of a class-conscious society and political evolution. For a brief period of time, 1649 to 1660, the House of Commons declared that the House of Lords "was useless and dangerous" and it was accordingly "wholly abolished and taken away."[48] The House of Lords was revived in 1660, and since that time the relationship between the two houses has passed through three distinct phases. The first phase, from 1660 to 1810, saw a period of general predominance of the House of Lords, although the House of Commons was not without influence.

Between 1811 and 1911 a number of changes took place that affected the relationship between the two houses. The Reform Acts of 1832, 1867, and 1884 strengthened the House of Commons in relation to the House of Lords. The increased acceptance of the idea that the cabinet should be responsible to the House of Commons (and should, therefore, resign if the House of Commons should fail to support its policies) clearly limited the future role of the House of Lords.

When the House of Lords rejected a number of Government bills that had passed the House of Commons in 1910, the Government pushed through The Parliament Act of 1911, which limited the power of the Lords in two aspects: (1) Money bills could only be delayed for one month after being approved by the House of Commons, and then they became law even without the approval of the Lords; and (2) other public bills could be delayed for up to two years, after which time they would become law with only the approval of the Commons. (This period was shortened to one year by the Parliament Act of 1949). The Parliament Act of 1911, which institutionalized these two radical limitations on the power of the House of Lords, was approved by the Lords only after it became clear that if they failed to do so the king was prepared to appoint enough new peers sympathetic to the bill to guarantee its passage.[49]

The third phase, from 1911 to the present time, has seen the House of Commons as the clearly dominant power in the relationship. The House of Lords no longer challenges major legislative policy of the Government. It may occasionally revise or amend bills, and has been known to oppose outright acts of the Commons, but under the Parliament Act of 1911 its power to influence policy of the Government is severely limited.[50]

The House of Lords

One of the major roles of the House of Lords historically has been not legislative at all, but judicial.[51] The House of Lords inherited a number of judicial functions from the *Curia Regis*, and until 2009 (when the Supreme Court of the United Kingdom came into existence) it served as the supreme judicial tribunal of the United Kingdom. Originally, the entire House of Lords acted as an appeals court; in 1876 an act was passed (the Appellate Jurisdiction Act of 1876) allowing for the appointment to the House of Lords of "Lords of Appeal in Ordinary," holding peerage for life. They were required to have held high judicial office for at least two years or to have been practicing for at least fifteen years. Their membership in the House of Lords was only for those individuals, and would not be hereditary and thereby passed to their children.

The functions of the House of Lords today can be said to have four components:

1. The examination and revision of Bills brought from the House of Commons....
2. The initiation of Bills dealing with subjects of a comparatively non-controversial character....
3. The interposition of so much delay (and no more) in the passing of a Bill into law as may be needed to enable the opinion of the nation to be adequately expressed upon it....
4. Full and free discussion of large and important questions....[52]

According to the House of Lords' information, much of its time is devoted to the review of legislation, as indicated in Table 9.2.

TABLE 9.2

Tasks of the House of Lords

Key functions of the House of Lords include:
- Making effective laws for the people of the United Kingdom
- Questioning and debating the work of government
- Investigating and influencing public policy
- Reaching out to connect people with the House of Lords
- Representing the United Kingdom on the international stage

How time is spent:
Legislation: 55 percent (bills 47%, statutory instruments 8%)
Scrutiny: 41 percent (debates 30%, questions 8%, statements 3%)
Other: 4 percent

Source: House of Lords, *The Work of the House of Lords, 2009–2010* (Westminster, 2010), p. 28, *available* at http://www.parliament.uk/documents/lords-information-office/hol-woth200910.pdf (accessed June 2011).

Early in its existence, prior to the seventeenth century, "there were usually between seventy and one hundred persons who sat in the House of Lords in response to the King's writ of summons."[53] As of June 2011, there are "around 830" members of the House of Lords, according to the House of Lords Information Office, made up of three groups: Elected Hereditary Peers, Archbishops and Bishops, and Life Peers, as indicated in Table 9.3.

One response to the demand for reform has been the introduction of **life peerages**. Since the late nineteenth century, more and more members of the House of Lords have been appointed as Life Peers. They serve as members of the House of Lords as long as they live, but their titles are not passed to their heirs as is the case with normal peerages. The Life Peerages Act of 1958 resulted in a great increase in the number of Life Peers in the House of Lords, with few new hereditary peerages being created since 1964. As noted in Table 9.3, the appointment of *Hereditary* Peers—where children would inherit their parents' seats in the Lords—to sit in the House of Lords was ended in 1999 by the *House of Lords Act*, but at that time 92 of the over-700 members were elected by their fellow Lords to stay as members for the duration of their terms (their lives).[54]

One idea proposed in 1948 was that women should be permitted to serve in the House of Lords, but the tradition-conscious House of Lords opposed the idea. Peeresses, women who inherited a seat in the House of Lords from their fathers in the absence of a male heir, were forbidden from sitting and voting in the House of Lords. This policy has since been changed, and today there are a number of peeresses in the Lords.[55]

Only since 1963 has it been possible for individuals to resign from the House of Lords, to renounce their peerages. Traditionally, one could not renounce one's title, and since the law forbade individuals from serving in both Houses of Parliament, if a member of the House of Commons had a father who

TABLE 9.3

The House of Lords, June 6, 2011

Party	Hereditary-Elected (vacant)	Archbishops and Bishops	Life Peers (Vacant)	Total (Vacant)
Conservative	47	0	170	217
Labour	4	0	239	243
Liberal-Democrat	4	0	88	92
Crossbench	31	0	152	183
Bishops	0	24	0	24
Other	2	0	27	29
Total	88(2)	24	676(38)	788(40)

Women: 147 (20.05 percent)

The classification used by the House of Lords is as follows:

Elected Hereditary Peers: The right of hereditary Peers to sit and vote in the House of Lords was ended in 1999 by the House of Lords Act but 92 Members were elected internally to remain until the next stage of the Lords reform process.

Archbishops and Bishops: A limited number of 26 Church of England archbishops and bishops sit in the House, passing their membership on to the next most senior bishop when they retire. The Archbishops of Canterbury and York traditionally get life peerages on retirement.

Life Peers: Appointed for their lifetime only, these Lords' titles are not passed on to their children. The Queen formally appoints life Peers on the advice and recommendation of the Prime Minister.

Source: Government of the United Kingdom, House of Lords web page, http://www.parliament.uk/about/mps-and-lords/about-lords/lords-types/ (accessed June 2011). See also http://www.parliament.uk/mps-lords-and-offices/lords/lords-by-type-and-party/ for party affiliations (accessed June 2011).

was a peer in the House of Lords, and his father died, that Commons member had to resign his seat in the Commons and take his father's seat in the Lords. He could not simply renounce his new peerage and stay in the Commons. In 1948, party leaders in Parliament agreed to allow peers to renounce their positions, thus allowing members of the House of Commons who "accidentally" became peers to retain their elected positions. [56]

Reform of the House of Lords has continued over time. In 1999 the House of Lords Act removed the right of most hereditary peers to remain as members of the House, and reduced the size of the Lords from 1,330 (October 1999) to 669 (March 2000). An amendment to that Act permitted 92 hereditary peers to remain until the House was fully reformed. Today there are several different ways that an individual can become a member of the House of Lords, including:

A. House of Lords Appointments Commission: Set up in May 2000, this independent, public body recommends individuals for appointment as non-party-political life peers and vets nominations for life peers to ensure the highest standards of propriety.

B. Dissolution Honours: Takes place at the end of a Parliament, when peerages can be given to MPs—from all parties—who are leaving the House of Commons.

C. Resignation Honours: Resigning prime ministers can recommend peerages for fellow politicians, political advisors, or others who have supported them.

D. Political lists/ "working Peers": Lords appointed to boost the strengths of the three main parties. Regular attendance in the House is expected, usually on the frontbench as a spokesman or whip. The media has dubbed these Members "working Peers."

E. Ad hoc announcements: Used to announce someone appointed as a Minister who is not already a Lord.

F. Archbishops and bishops: The number of bishops in the House has been limited to 26 since the mid-nineteenth century. If a vacancy comes up, the most senior serving bishop is appointed. The Archbishops of Canterbury and York usually get life peerages on retirement.

G. Speakers: Traditionally, peerages are awarded to former Speakers of the House of Commons. [57]

The House of Commons

We saw earlier that the original reason for being of the House of Commons was a fund-raising one; the king needed to raise more money than the House of Lords could provide, and politically he could do so only by summoning representatives of the public to Parliament. Early Parliaments were primarily concerned with two tasks: First, they agreed to requests from the king for money; second, as a *quid pro quo* for giving the king money, they presented the king with petitions of grievances.

The nineteenth century was a century of reform for the House of Commons. The Reform Act of 1867 allowed all householders to vote, as well as all persons occupying lodgings of an annual value of £10 or more. Similar measures were enacted for Scotland and Ireland in 1868. The Ballot Act of 1872 brought secret voting, and a Reform Act of 1884 further expanded suffrage. (Women over 30 were first allowed to vote in 1918; in 1928 requirements for women to vote were made the same as those for men.)[58]

The development of the cabinet in the eighteenth century greatly changed the role of the House of Commons.[59] The Speaker was originally perceived as the king's representative in the House; by 1640 the Speaker was the representative of the House of Commons to the king. Today, the Speaker has great power to control debate and legislation. Speakers are elected by a new House of Commons immediately after a general election. The majority party nominates a candidate who invariably wins on a party-line vote.

LEGISLATION

There are a number of different types of legislation in the British House of Commons. We can initially distinguish between *Government bills* and *private members' bills*. Government bills are bills that are introduced and sponsored by the cabinet, and to which strong party discipline is applied. Private members' bills are proposals for legislation that are introduced by noncabinet members (including members of the majority party who are not in the cabinet, as well as by members of all of the opposition parties).

Private members' bills are legally restricted in only one way: they may not deal with money, either raising it or spending it. Moreover, private member bills are placed on a separate calendar, usually handled only on Friday afternoons, and few members of Parliament even have the opportunity to introduce their own proposals over the course of a legislative session due to the limitation of time.[60]

Since there would not be time in a legislative session for all members of Parliament who wanted to submit private members' bills of their own to do so, a "ballot," or drawing, is held at the beginning of each session to determine which members of Parliament will have the opportunity to introduce their own pieces of legislation.[61]

Besides distinguishing between bills on the basis of who introduces them in the House of Commons, we can also distinguish between bills in terms of their scope: What do the proposed pieces of legislation intend to do? *Public bills* are drafts of new laws that would affect the country as a whole, such as tax law, criminal law, regulation policy, and so on. *Private bills* have individual application only, such as a special act of citizenship, for instance.[62]

The legislative process in the House of Commons involves the "standard" parliamentary procedure that we covered earlier in this text.[63] After bills are passed in the House of Commons they are sent to the House of Lords. As indicated above, if the House of Lords does not approve a bill, it no longer can kill the bill, but can only delay its eventual passage.

A final, special, procedure should be mentioned here that relates again to the "royal pretense" that was mentioned earlier. Bills approved by both Houses of Parliament must be given the Royal Assent (approval by the queen) before they become law. Ever since 1707 this Royal Assent has not been refused to a bill that has passed both Houses of Parliament. The monarch has not given the **Royal Assent** in person since 1854; today it is done by a Commission.

> The title of each Bill which is to receive the Assent is read, and the Assent is signified by the Clerk of the Parliaments. The assenting formula is still given in Norman French. For Public Bills, and Private Bills of a local character, is it "La reine le veult" (the Queen wishes it). For Private Bills of a personal character the formula is "Soit fait comme il est desire" (let what is desired be done). The formula for Bills granting supply or imposing taxation is "La reine remercie ses bons sujets, accepte leur benevolence, et ainsi le veult" (the Queen thanks her good subjects, accepts their benevolence, and so wishes it). The formula for refusing the assent was formerly "La reine s'avisera" (the Queen will consider the matter).[64]

THE CIVIL SERVICE

The civil service is an integral part of British government and politics. When cabinet ministers seek to have policy put into operation, it is through the civil service that they operate. The civil service is, ostensibly, nonpolitical, and its function is to administer the policies of the government of the day.[65]

Over time it has been made clear that the civil servant is an apolitical employee of the government. At the end of the twentieth century nearly 600,000 civil servants work for the British government (down from a high of 732,000 in 1979), about one-sixth of them working in the Inner London area.[66] Only a small proportion of them are high-ranking policymakers; the vast majority are individuals working in offices of government agencies around the nation. Recent Governments have been concerned with the higher ranks of the civil service because "civil service and administrative reforms have been seen as intimately linked to the 'sharp end' of the Government's policy outputs."[67] The high-ranking civil servants, sometimes referred to as "Mandarins" (the term comes from China where "Mandarens" were Manchu officials), play an important role in government.[68] One study of this relationship has concluded that "civil servants have more influence, and ministers less, than constitutional theory suggests."[69]

LOCAL GOVERNMENT

Another level of government in Great Britain that cannot be ignored is the local level. Although we earlier referred to Britain as a unitary and not a federal government because all sovereignty was based at Westminster, while ultimate sovereignty resides at Westminster, the central government has decentralized many governmental functions, and local government is often significant in Britain.

A significant role for **local government** has a long history in Britain, going back to the early nineteenth century. The role of local government became more political after the arrival of Thatcherism began to reshape many fundamental domestic policies of the central government. In regions of Britain where Thatcher's Conservative Party was very unpopular, local governments sought to continue many of the programs that Thatcher was discontinuing or cutting back at the national level.[70]

We noted earlier that local elections often serve as popularity tests for prime ministers between times of national elections. Both Tony Blair and Gordon Brown suffered significant Labour Party losses in local elections between the third election of Blair as prime minister in 2005 and Brown's ultimate defeat to David Cameron in 2010.

THE SUPREME COURT OF THE UNITED KINGDOM

The Supreme Court of the United Kingdom was created in the Constitutional Reform Act of 2005, and took effect in October of 2009. Through this legislation the new court took over the functions that had been exercised by the House of Lords for over six hundred years, more precisely exercised by the subgroup of the House of Lords referred to as the **Law Lords,** who were appointed specifically for that purpose. The role of the Supreme Court is to "play an important role in the development of United Kingdom law," as well as being the final court of appeal in the United Kingdom. According to the Supreme Court itself, its role includes the following:

- it is the final court of appeal for all United Kingdom civil cases, and criminal cases from England, Wales, and Northern Ireland;
- it hears appeals on arguable points of law of general public importance;
- it concentrates on cases of the greatest public and constitutional importance;
- it maintains and develops the role of the highest court in the United Kingdom as a leader in the common law world.[71]

The transfer of judicial functions from a subgroup of the House of Lords to an independent Supreme Court was meant to be significant in British constitutional development. "The Supreme Court was established to achieve a complete separation between the United Kingdom's senior Judges and the Upper House of Parliament, emphasizing the independence of the Law Lords and increasing the transparency between Parliament and the courts."[72] It even moved out of the building where the Law Lords had been sitting to a new site in its own building, across Parliament Square from the House of Lords.

The separation of the Supreme Court from the House of Lords did not change one very important characteristic of British politics, however: There still is no power of judicial review exercised by the Supreme Court, and laws passed by Parliament cannot be nullified by the Court. Many educated observers of the British (unwritten) constitution believe, however, that this birth of a new constitutional structure in the United Kingdom is opening the door for major constitutional change. As one commentator has noted,

> No one suggests yet that the UK Supreme Court will follow its namesakes in the United States and Israel by declaring statutes unconstitutional. It is worth remembering, however, that the US Supreme Court justices did so in 1803 without explicit powers under their country's constitution and so did their Israeli counterparts in 1995, without a written constitution at all. Lord Collins, however, one of the law lords who will move to the new court in October, predicts that his colleagues will evolve over time into a different type of body—"perhaps not so pivotal as the American Supreme Court, but certainly playing a much more central role in the legal system and approaching the American ideal of a government of laws and not of men."[73]

POLITICAL PARTIES AND ELECTIONS

It has been suggested by a noted scholar that "British government is **party government.**"[74] Parties organize electoral activity, including the selection of candidates in elections, the construction of programs, and the operation of election campaigns. In the general elections, voters vote not so much for the individual candidates whose names appear on the ballot papers, but rather for the party "team" with which the candidate is affiliated.

Politics in Britain has also often been referred to as "the politics of class,"[75] so it should come as no surprise that support for political parties in Britain has frequently been explained in terms of class allegiances. In recent years the allegiances have been described as "Labour, representing the working community, versus the Conservatives, representing capital."[76]

Parties are "unknown to the constitutional law."[77] Parties originally developed in Britain over the issue of royal power, with the Tories (later to be called the Conservatives) favoring the royalty, and the Whigs (later to become the Liberals) opposing the royalists. Around the time of their development, in 1688 or so, neither the Tories nor the Whigs could have been called political parties in the contemporary sense of the word.[78]

One of the early developmental problems of British political parties involved the question of opposition to the monarch.[79] The concept of a "loyal opposition" developed slowly, and not without a great deal of friction, because early on it was difficult for many to accept the notion that it was possible to be *against* a government in power without being against the regime *itself.*[80]

By the middle of the eighteenth century the concept of a "loyal opposition" was accepted. Edmund Burke, a great British politician of the time, argued that to combine to oppose or topple the government was not treason: "when bad men combine, the good must associate; else they will fall, one by one...."[81] Parties contribute a great deal of stability to the political system, by providing the basis for the formation of Governments and by "enabling the Government, as leaders of the most powerful party in the House of Commons, to secure the passage of their programme of legislation."[82]

In the past, Britain has usually been regarded as a two-party political system. Strictly speaking, though, this is not correct. In years past, Britain could be said to have a two-party system by one measure only: The number of political parties that had formed a Government since 1945 are two— Conservative, and Labour. This changed in 2010, however, with the participation in the coalition government of the Liberal Democratic Party. So, by any measure today we would have to say that Britain has a multiparty system. Indeed, an examination of election results from the 2010 election shown in Table 9.4 shows that there are *many* more than two political parties active in British elections!

This misperception about the British party system is largely a result of the relationship between electoral systems and party systems, which we discussed earlier. Britain has a single-member-district, plurality voting electoral system— what we earlier called a first past the post system. It doesn't matter whether a given candidate receives a *majority* of votes in a constituency as long as he or she has a *plurality*—more votes than any other candidate.

TABLE 9.4

The 2010 British General Election

Party	% of Votes Received	Seats Won	% of Seats Won	Difference (% seats won)— (% vote received)
Conservative	36.1	307	47.2	+ 11.1
Labour	29.0	258	39.7	+ 10.7
Liberal-Democratic	23.0	57	8.8	− 14.2
Democratic Unionist	0.6	8	1.2	+ 0.6
Scottish Nationalists	1.7	6	0.9	− 0.8
Sinn Fein	0.6	5	0.8	+ 0.2
Plaid Cymru (Welsh)	0.6	3	0.5	− 0.1
Others	8.5	7	1.1	+ 2.6
Total	100.1	650	100.0	—

Turnout: 65.1% Women: 143 (22%)

Note: The number of seats in the House of Commons increased in the 2010 election to 650. The 650 single-member districts are allocated 533 to England, 59 to Scotland, 40 to Wales, and 18 to Northern Ireland.

Source: http://www.ipu.org/parline-e/reports/2335_E.htm, and The British Broadcasting Corporation, "Election 2010," accessed on the web at http://news.bbc.co.uk/2/shared/election2010/results/ (accessed June 2011).

In the period immediately prior to the 2010 national election there was much discussion in Britain about electoral reform.

In February 2010, the House of Commons approved government plans to hold a nationwide referendum on changing the electoral system from "first-past-the-post" to "alternative votes." ... The Labour Party, which had pledged electoral reform in its 1997 election manifesto, argued that the new voting system was needed to restore trust in politics. The Liberal Democrats led by Mr. Nick Clegg, which have historically been a strong proponent of electoral reform, supported the plan. On the contrary, the Conservative Party argued that the current system had ensured a stable government and kept out extremists. It pledged to abolish the referendum plan if it won the general elections. Finally, the outgoing House of Commons was dissolved before the Bill could become law.... In the alternative votes system, voters rank candidates in order of preference. A candidate obtaining more than 50 per cent of the first choice votes is declared elected. If no candidate secures more than 50 per cent of the votes, the candidate with the fewest number of votes is eliminated and voters' second choices are allocated to the remaining candidates. This process continues until a winner emerges.[83]

There has not been a single political party that has won over half of the votes in a British parliamentary election since 1935. The closest that any party has come to a majority of the votes was in 1955 when the Conservative party won 49.7 percent of the vote. The extreme bias of the single-member-district, plurality system can be illustrated by the October 1974 election in which the Labour party won a bare majority in the House of Commons of 319 seats (out of 635, a *bare* majority) with 39.2 percent of the vote, while the Liberal party had 18.3 percent of the vote (almost half of the Labour vote), and yet received only 13 seats in the House of Commons (4 percent of the Labour total).[84]

The same general phenomenon happened in the 1997, 2001, and 2005 elections, too. In all of these elections, Labour received substantial majorities in terms of the seats in the House of Commons, but considerably less popular support. To take just one illustration, in the 2005 election results, Labour received almost 55 percent of the seats in the House of Commons in exchange for 35 percent of the popular vote, while the Liberal Democratic Party received less than 10 percent of the seats in exchange for over 20 percent of the votes!

As can be seen from Table 9.4, this bias of vote concentration continues to exist. The Labour party received 29 percent of the vote and received 258 seats in the House of Commons, while the Liberal-Democratic party received 23 percent of the vote (80 percent of the number of votes that Labour received) and received 57 seats in the House of Commons (22 percent of the number of seats that Labour received).

There was some shock following the election, because the British are used to majority governments, not having had a **hung Parliament** since 1974, but following several intense rounds of conversations the leader of the plurality party—David Cameron of the Conservatives—announced that he had reached an agreement with Nick Clegg of the Liberal-Democratic Party and that together a Conservative/Liberal-Democratic bloc with 364 seats would govern, considerably more than a bare majority of the 650 seats in the House of Commons.

Constitutionally, elections for the House of Commons must be held at least every five years. As we have seen, however, since the British Constitution is "unwritten," the constitutional parameters relating to elections are whatever the House of Commons says they should be. In 1694, the Commons passed the Triennial Act, setting the maximum term of the House at three years; in 1716 the maximum term was extended to seven years by the Septennial Act. It wasn't until 1911 that the present five-year constitutional limitation was set. Since 1911 it has usually been the case that elections have been called before the five-year limit on the life of a Parliament. There have been two noteworthy exceptions to this, however. During both the World War I and World War II, Parliament decided—and legislated accordingly—to postpone elections because of the feeling that electoral uncertainty would not help the war efforts. Consequently, "the Parliament chosen in 1910 was not dissolved until the end of 1918, and there was no general election in Britain between 1935 and 1945."[85]

Essentially it can be argued that one person, the prime minister, decides when a national election will take place. Although since 1911 the constitution has required (with the two exceptions noted) that elections be held at least every five years, in point of fact the prime minister has felt free over the years to request that the monarch dissolve Parliament and call for new elections at a time earlier than required that is an advantage to the Government in power. Tradition requires (although technically the law does not) that the monarch grant a dissolution when one is requested by the prime minister.

One of the most remarkable differences between the British electoral process and many other electoral processes is the relative brevity of the campaign period in Britain. In the American system, for example, primaries sometimes start as much as eleven months before elections, and informal campaigning may begin significantly before that. In Britain, the Government's ability to call a "surprise" election may be a real strategic advantage; "approximately three weeks after a dissolution, the entire electorate of Britain goes to the polls."[86] Vacancies arising between general elections are filled through by-elections, elections that take place in individual "ridings," or electoral districts, as needed.

THE BRITISH SYSTEM IN PERSPECTIVE

This chapter presented few major deviations from what we learned in earlier chapters. The British political system *is* the Westminister Model that we met earlier. In this presentation of the major structures in the British political system, we have briefly shown the manner in which it is possible to look at a political system using the general approach we introduced at the beginning of this text.

We have seen in this chapter that in a nation's constitutional makeup, customs and traditions may be just as important as written statutes, if not more so. The fact that it is even possible to imagine actions in the British political system that might be *legal*, yet *unconstitutional* attests to the relative importance of the unwritten law of tradition. Britain offers a clear example of a political system in which one must be familiar with the political environment and political history of a nation before one can seriously attempt to understand how public policy is made there.

DISCUSSION QUESTIONS

1. How would you explain to someone who has never studied this region the relationship between "England" and "Great Britain" and "United Kingdom"? Do they refer to the same thing? What are the differences?
2. What are the especially important components of the British "unwritten constitution"? What would be the significance if Britain had a written constitution? What would be different?
3. Britain is the model for the parliamentary model of government. What are the key components of the British model?
4. The positions of Head of State and Chief Executive evolved over a long period of time in British politics. Which is most significant today? Why?
5. What is the political role of the prime minister in British politics? How does the prime minister relate to other actors?
6. What would you say was the most important way that Margaret Thatcher played a crucial and possibly transformative role in modern British politics?
7. What are the differences in roles between the House of Commons and the House of Lords? Does the House of Lords play any important functions in British politics today?
8. Give an example of the importance of the concept of party discipline in British parliamentary government today.

KEY TERMS

Blackstone, William   199
Blair, Tony   201
Cameron, David   210
Commonwealth of Nations   198
devolution of power   201
duality of executive leadership   203
England   198
Great Britain   198
hung parliament   210

Law Lords   217
life peerages   212
local government   217
Mitchell Agreement   202
parliamentary question time   207
parliamentary sovereignty   200
party government   218
privatized industry   209
Privy Council   204

Royal Assent   216
royal pretense   203
Speech from the Throne   203
Thatcherism   208
unitary   201
United Kingdom   198
unwritten British Constitution   199
Westminster model   200

SUGGESTED READINGS

Vernon Bogdanor, *The British Constitution in the Twentieth Century* (Oxford, UK: Oxford University Press, 2003). The British Constitution today is a product of historical practice and accident. This volume describes the evolution of the practice of politics in Britain, and how the "unwritten" British Constitution developed over time.

Jonathan Bradbury, *Devolution, Regionalism and Regional Development: The UK Experience* (New York: Routledge, 2008). This is a very good study of the issue of devolution in the United Kingdom, and how the drive toward devolution developed strength and eventually resulted in greater political power for regional authorities.

J.A. Chandler, *Local Government Today* (New York: Manchester University Press, 2009). How do local governments operate in a unitary political system? If all political sovereignty resides at Westminster, how are the duties of local governments determined, and how effectively do they operate?

Dennis Kavanagh and Anthony Seldon, *The Powers Behind the Prime Minister: The Hidden Influence of Number Ten* (London, UK: HarperCollins, 2008). The British prime minister is clearly the most important actor in the British political system, but much of his power derives from informal structures, and much of his power is exercised informally as well.

Michael Rush, *The Role of the Member of Parliament Since 1868: From Gentleman to Players* (Oxford, UK: Oxford University Press, 2001). Parliament has evolved over the years considerably, as a consequence of a number of different factors. This volume examines the change and growth of the role of the Member of Parliament over the years, and shows how it has evolved as a result of a number of specific actions and events.

NOTES

1. Max Beloff and Gillian Peele, *The Government of the United Kingdom* (New York: W.W. Norton, 1980), p. 10. See also Elizabeth Wicks, *The Evolution of a Constitution: Eight Key Moments in British Constitutional History* (Portland, OR: Hart Publishing, 2006).

2. George W. Keeton, *Government in Action in the United Kingdom* (London, UK: Ernest Benn, Ltd., 1970), pp. 29–30. See also Peter Oliver, *The Development of Constitutional Theory in Australia, Canada, and New Zealand* (Oxford, UK: Oxford University Press, 2004); and Rodney Brazier, *Constitutional Reform* (Oxford, UK: Oxford University Press, 2008).

3. See Zoya Hasan and Eswaran Sridharan, *India's Living Constitution: Ideas, Practices, Controversies* (London, UK: Anthem, 2005).

4. Hiram Stout, *British Government* (New York: Oxford University Press, 1953), p. 19. See also Kenneth Morgan, *The Oxford Illustrated History of Britain* (New York: Oxford University Press, 2009).

5. Sydney D. Bailey, *British Parliamentary Democracy* (Boston, MA: Houghton Mifflin, 1958), p. 2.

6. Stout, *British Government*, pp. 20–21. See also Ellis Wasson, *A History of Modern Britain: 1714 to the Present* (Malden, MA: Wiley-Blackwell, 2009).

7. Stout, *British Government*, p. 20. See also Richard English and Charles Townshend, *The State: Historical and Political Dimensions* (London, UK: Routledge, 1999).

8. Beloff and Peele, *Government*, pp. 10–11; and Bailey, *Parliamentary Democracy*, p. 3.

9. Stout, *Government*, p. 21. See also Vernon Bogdanor, *The British Constitution in the Twentieth Century* (Oxford, UK: Oxford University Press, 2003); and Robert Hazell, *Britain's Constitution to 2020* (New York: Palgrave Macmillan, 2008).

10. Bailey, *Parliamentary Democracy*, p. 4.

11. See *The Monarchy in Britain* (London, UK: Her Majesty's Stationery Office, 1981), pp. 8–11. See also Charles Douglas-Home and Saul Kelly, *Dignified and Efficient: The British Monarchy in the Twentieth Century* (Brinkworth, Wiltshire, UK: Claridge Press, 2000).

12. Bailey, *Parliamentary Democracy*, p. 5.

13. Ibid., p. 6.

14. Stout, *Government*, pp. 26–27. See also John Garrard, *Democratization in Britain: Elites, Civil Society and Reform Since 1800* (New York: Palgrave, 2001).

15. In July of 1997 the British Government released plans to create a 129-seat Scottish parliament to be located in Edinburgh, as well as plans to create a 60-seat Welsh legislative assembly, to be located in Cardiff. The Scottish parliament would be more powerful than the Welsh body because it would have some taxation and legislative powers—including the power to decide whether to raise or lower income taxes by up to 3 percent—while the Welsh body would not have taxation powers, but would be able to legislate on issues such as health, transportation, the environment, and education. This devolution plan would not have permitted either the Scottish or Welsh bodies to vote on full independence. See "Great Britain: Plans for Scottish, Welsh Home Rule Set," *Facts on File* Accession No. 1997072130 (July 24, 1997).

16. See Michael O'Neill, *Devolution and British Politics* (New York: Pearson/Longman, 2004).

17. See "British Parliament Transfers Authority Over Northern Ireland to Provincial Government," in *Facts on File* Accession No. 1999156480 (December 2, 1999). See also Christopher McCrudden, "Northern Ireland, the Belfast Agreement, and the British Constitution," in *The Changing Constitution*, eds. Jeffrey Jowell and Dawn Oliver (Oxford, UK: Oxford University Press, 2004).

18. Anthony Sampson, *The New Anatomy of Britain* (New York: Stein and Day, 1972), p. 215.

19. Max Nicholson, *The System* (New York: McGraw Hill, 1967), p. 158. See Charles Douglas-Home and Saul Kelly, *Dignified and Efficient: The British Monarchy in the Twentieth Century* (Brinkworth, UK: Claridge Press, 2000).

20. Sampson, *New Anatomy*, p. 215.

21. Ibid. See also Bill Jones and Dennis Kavanagh, *British Politics Today* (New York: Manchester University Press, 2003), especially Chapter 12: "The Monarchy and the House of Lords." The text of the Throne speech of Queen Elizabeth II that was delivered on November 15, 2006, can be found on the British Broadcasting Corporation web page: *http://news.bbc.co.uk/1/hi/uk_politics/6150274.stm* (accessed June 2011).

22. Stout, *Government*, pp. 70–71.

23. See the website maintained by the Government of the United Kingdom on the Privy Council at *http://privycouncil.independent.gov.uk/privy-council/privy-council-members/* (accessed June 2011). A list of members of the Privy Council and the dates they became members can be found at *http://privycouncil.independent.gov. uk/privy-council/privy-council-members/privy-counsellors/* (accessed June 2011).

24. Beloff and Peele, *Government of the United Kingdom*, p. 67.

25. Sampson, *New Anatomy*, pp. 217–218.

26. Sir Ivor Jennings, *Cabinet Government* (Cambridge, UK: Cambridge University Press, 1951), p. 79.

27. Stout, *Government*, p. 77. See also Simon James, *British Cabinet Government* (London, UK: Routledge, 1999); and Dennis Kavanagh and Anthony Seldon, *The Powers Behind the Prime Minister: The Hidden Influence of Number Ten* (London, UK: HarperCollins, 2008).

28. K.R. MacKenzie, *The English Parliament* (New York: Penguin Books, 1950), p. 81.

29. James Barber, "The Power of the Prime Minister," in *British Politics in Perspective*, ed. R.L. Borthwick and J.E. Spence (New York: St. Martin's Press, 1984), p. 73. See also Thomas Poguntke and Paul Webb, *The Presidentialization of Politics: A Comparative Study of Modern Democracies* (New York: Oxford University Press, 2005); and Peter Hennessy, *The Prime Minister: The Office and Its Holders Since 1945* (New York: Palgrave, 2001).

30. Richard Rose, "British Government: The Job at the Top," in *Presidents and Prime Ministers*, eds. Richard Rose and Ezra Suleiman (Washington, DC: American Enterprise Institute, 1980), p. 1.

31. Richard Rose, *Ministers and Ministries: A Functional Analysis* (Oxford, UK: Clarendon Press, 1987), p. 4.

32. A table ranking the political status of the many cabinet portfolios can be found in Rose, *Ministers and Ministries*, p. 86.

33. Peter Hennessy, *Cabinet* (Oxford, UK: Basil Blackwell, 1986), pp. 1–15.

34. See the web page from the Prime Minister's Office at 10 Downing Street that lists all full members of the Cabinet and those who also attend Cabinet meetings. The list can be found at *http://www.number10.gov.uk/news/latest-news/2010/05/her-majestys-government-49840* (accessed June 2011).

35. David Barrett, "Cabinet 'Too Big to Make Decisions,'" the *Telegraph*, June 20, 2009, available at *http://www.telegraph.co.uk/news/politics/5586956/Cabinet-too-big-to-make-decisions.html* (accessed June 2011).

36. H. Victor Wiseman, *Politics in Everyday Life* (Oxford, UK: Basil Blackwell, 1966), pp. 167–169.

37. Rose, "The Job at the Top," pp. 3–26. See also Andrew Blick and G.W. Jones, *Premiership: The Development, Nature, and Power of the British Prime Minister* (Charlottesville, VA: Imprint Academic, 2010).

38. Wiseman, *Politics*, p. 159.

39. Rose, "The Job at the Top," pp. 12–13. See also Peter Riddell, *The Unfulfilled Prime Minister: Tony Blair's Quest for a Legacy* (London, UK: Politico's, 2005).

40. Rose, "The Job at the Top," pp. 12–13. See also Tony Blair, *A Journey: My Political Life* (New York: Alfred Knopf, 2010).

41. Martin Holmes, *The First Thatcher Government, 1979–1983: Contemporary Conservatism and Economic Change* (Boulder, CO: Westview Press, 1985), p. 1. See also Eric Evans, *Thatcher and Thatcherism* (New York: Routledge, 2004).

42. Peter Jenkins, *Mrs. Thatcher's Revolution: The Ending of the Socialist Era* (Cambridge, MA: Harvard University Press, 1988), p. 81.

43. Indeed, the Thatcher government's goal of lowering inflation at almost any cost "brought about a fundamental division of opinion within the Conservative Cabinet, backbench MPs and the party itself. The conflict between the political monetarists, or dries, and the left-wing Conservatives, or wets, was a marked feature of the whole of the period from 1979 to 1983." Holmes, *Thatcher Government*, pp. 74, 199.

44. A good description of this relationship is in Dave Marsh and Jeff King, "The Unions Under Thatcher," in Lynton Robins, ed., *Political Institutions in Britain: Development and Change* (New York: Longman, 1987), pp. 213–229.

45. On recent directions of policy, see Tony Baldry and Jane Ewart-Biggs, *Social Policy* (London, UK: Wroxton Papers in Politics, 1990).

46. See Philip Stephens, *Tony Blair: The Making of a World Leader* (New York: Viking, 2004).

47. See "Brown 'disappointed' by poll loss," *BBC News* May 2, 2008, available at *http://news.bbc.co.uk/2/hi/uk_news/politics/7372860.stm* (accessed June 2011).

48. Bailey, *Parliamentary Democracy*, p. 35. See also Janice Morphet, *Modern Local Government* (London, UK: SAGE, 2008); and J.A. Chandler, *Local Government Today* (New York: Manchester University Press, 2009).

49. Frank Stacey, *British Government* (London, UK: Oxford University Press, 1975), p. 72.

50. Bailey, *Parliamentary Government*, pp. 36–37, 41. See Meg Russell, *Reforming the House of Lords: Lessons from Overseas* (New York: Oxford University Press, 2000).

51. See Maxwell Barrett, *The Law Lords: An Account of the Workings of Britain's Highest Judicial Body and the Men Who Preside Over It* (Hampshire, UK: Macmillan, 2000). See also A.P. LeSueur, *Building the UK's New Supreme Court: National and Comparative Perspectives* (New York: Oxford University Press, 2004); and Louis Jacques Blom-Cooper, Brice Dickson, and Gavin Drewry, eds., *The Judicial House of Lords* (New York: Oxford University Press, 2009).

52. Bailey, *Parliamentary Government*, p. 38. See also Emma Crewe, *Lords of Parliament: Manners, Rituals and Politics* (New York: Manchester University Press, 2005); and Peter Dorey and Alexandra Kelso, *House of Lords Reform Since 1911: Must the Lords Go?* (New York: Palgrave Macmillan, 2011).

53. Bailey, *Parliamentary Government*, p. 42.

54. Nicholson, *The System*, p. 153. See also the study by the Government of Great Britain, *A House for the Future: A Summary* (London, UK: Royal Commission on the Reform of the House of Lords, 2000); and Meg Russell and Robert Hazell, *Next Steps in Lords Reform: Response to the September 2003 White Paper* (London, UK: University College, London, 2003).

55. Keeton, *Government in Action*, p. 63.

56. Nicholson, *The System*, p. 153. See also Frank Pakenham, Earl of Longford, *A History of the House of Lords* (London, UK: Sutton, 1999).

57. See the House of Lords web page, "How Do You Become a Member of the House of Lords?" available at *http://www.parliament.uk/about/mps-and-lords/about-lords/lords-appointment/* (accessed June 2011).

58. Bailey, *Parliamentary Democracy*, pp. 65–69. The evolution of the institution is chronicled in Michael Rush's book *The Role of the Member of Parliament Since 1868: From Gentleman to Players* (Oxford, UK: Oxford University Press, 2001). See also John Robert Maddicott, *The Origins of the English Parliament, 924–1327* (New York: Oxford University Press, 2010); and Philip Norton, *Parliament in British Politics* (New York: Palgrave Macmillan, 2005).

59. A very good description of the development of parliamentary government and the role of the Parliament can be found in Michael Rush, *Parliamentary Government in Britain* (New York: Holmes and Meier, 1981), pp. 19–47. See also Anna Manasco Dionne, *Women, Men and the Representation of Women in the British Parliaments: Magic Numbers?* (Manchester, UK: Manchester University Press, 2010).

60. Wiseman, *Politics*, p. 147.

61. Stacey, *British Government*, p. 56. See also Robert Hazell and Richard Rawlings, *Devolution, Law Making and the Constitution* (Charlottesville, VA: Imprint Academic, 2005).

62. Stout, *British Government*, pp. 128–137.

63. Wiseman, *Politics*, p. 148. See, for a very good cross-national treatment of this subject, David Olson, *The Legislative Process: A Comparative Approach* (New York: Harper and Row, 1980), p. 346.

64. Bailey, *Parliamentary Democracy*, p. 108.

65. See Gavin Drewry and Tony Butcher, *The Civil Service Today* (Oxford, UK: Basil Blackwell, 1988), pp. 1–8. A good general treatment of this is in the volume by Andrew Gray and William Jenkins, *Administrative Politics in British Government* (New York: St. Martin's Press, 1985). See also David Marsh, David Richards, and Martin J. Smith, *Changing Patterns of Governance in the United Kingdom: Reinventing Whitehall?* (New York: Palgrave, 2001).

66. See John Gretton and Anthony Harrison, eds., *Reshaping Central Government* (New Brunswick, NJ: Transaction Books, 1987), p. 2. See June Burnham and Robert Pyper, *Britain's Modernised Civil Service* (New York: Palgrave Macmillan, 2008).

67. John R. Greenaway, "The Higher Civil Service at the Crossroads: The Impact of the Thatcher Government," in *Political Institutions in Britain: Development and Change*, ed. Lynton Robins (New York: Longman, 1987), p. 49. See also Rodney Lowe, *The Official History of the British Civil Service: Reforming the Civil Service* (New York: Routledge, 2011).

68. Anthony Sampson as quoted in Drewry and Butcher, *The Civil Service Today*, p. 151. See Richard Chapman, *Ethics in the British Civil Service* (London, UK: Routledge, 2010).

69. John Greenwood and David Wilson, *Public Administration in Britain* (London, UK: Allen and Unwin, 1984), p. 84.

70. A very good essay discussing this problem is by Mike Goldsmith and Ken Newton, "Central-Local Government Relations: The Irresistible Rise of Centralised Power," in *Change in British Politics*, ed. Hugh Berrington (London, UK: Frank Cass, 1984), pp. 216–233. See also Colin Copus, *Party Politics and Local Government* (New York: Manchester University Press, 2004); and Jonathan Bradbury, *Devolution, Regionalism and Regional Development: The UK Experience* (New York: Routledge, 2008).

71. See the Supreme Court web page, "The Role of the Supreme Court," available at *http://www.supremecourt.gov.uk/about/role-of-the-supreme-court.html* (accessed, June 2011).

72. See the Supreme Court web page, "Significance to the UK," available at *http://www.supremecourt.gov.uk/about/significance-to-the-uk.html* (accessed June 2011).

73. See Joshua Rozenberg's column in *The Times/The Sunday Times Times Literary Supplement* titled "Britain's New Supreme Court: Why Has a Fundamental Change in the Constitution Been So Little Reported and Debated?" printed September 2, 2009, available at *http://entertainment.timesonline.co.uk/tol/arts_and_entertainment/the_tls/article6818434.ece* (accessed June 2011).

74. Richard Rose, *Politics in England* (Boston, MA: Little, Brown and Co., 1980), p. 249. See also Declan McHugh and F.F. Ridley, *Reflections on British Parliamentary Democracy* (Oxford, UK: Oxford University Press, 2004).

75. Derbyshire, *Politics in Britain*, p. 5. See also Paul Webb, *The Modern British Party System* (Thousand Oaks, CA: SAGE, 2000).

76. Derbyshire, *Politics in Britain*, p. 5. There is a much longer discussion of the nature of the interparty differences in economic and social policy here, pp. 6–14.

77. Keeton, *Government in Action*, p. 90. See also David Boothroyd, *Politico's Guide to the History of British Political Parties* (London, UK: Politico's, 2001).

78. Stout, *British Government*, p. 163.

79. A very good discussion of the evolution of British parties can be found in H.M. Crucker, "The Evolution of the Political Parties," in *British Politics in Perspective*, eds. R.L. Borthwick and J.E. Spence (New York: St. Martin's Press, 1984), pp. 104–121.

80. Bailey, *Parliamentary Democracy*, p. 138.

81. Ibid.

82. Keeton, *Government in Action*, p. 93. See also Paul Whiteley and Patrick Seyd, *High-Intensity Participation: The Dynamics of Party Activism in Britain* (Ann Arbor, MI: University of Michigan Press, 2002); and Colin Copus, *Party Politics and Local Government* (New York: Manchester University Press, 2004).

83. Inter-Parliamentary Union, *PARLINE* database, "United Kingdom-House of Commons," available at *http://www.ipu.org/parline-e/reports/2335_E.htm* (accessed June 2011). See also Adam Boulton and Joey Jones, *Right Honourable Housemates: The 2010 Election and the Coalition Government* (New York: Simon and Schuster, 2010).

84. Rose, *Politics*, p. 256. See also Christopher Kam, *Party Discipline and Parliamentary Politics* (New York: Cambridge University Press, 2009); and Dennis Kavanagh and Philip Cowley, *The British General Election of 2010* (New York: Palgrave Macmillan, 2010).

85. Stout, *British Government*, p. 200. See also Stephen Ingle, *The British Party System: An Introduction* (New York: Routledge, 2008); and Simon Griffiths and Kevin Hickson, *British Party Politics and Ideology after New Labour* (New York: Palgrave Macmillan, 2010).

86. Stout, *British Government*, p. 211.

The French Political System

France offers a presidentially-dominated parliamentary government. Here Nicolas Sarkozy

- Understand how French political history in the Third and Fourth Republics helped to shape the creation of the Fifth Republic.

- Appreciate the unique role of Charles de Gaulle in the creation of the Fifth Republic.

- Understand the particular nature of French unitary government.

- Explain the special characteristics of the French presidency, and understand its particular powers.

- Understand how the role of political parties has changed in France over time, and how the coalition nature of French politics affects the way public policy is made.

- Compare the French legislature and legislative process to those of other democratic systems and appreciate unique characteristics that exist in France.

We saw in Chapter 9 that the constitutional system of Great Britain is the product of a gradual process that took place over a period of several hundred years; the same cannot be said of the French constitutional system. In the British case, we can point to specific dates of constitutional significance—for instance the signing of the Magna Carta in 1215—but the general constitutional *system* has remained intact and has changed only slowly over a long period of time. The French system is more properly characterized as experiencing a number of (more or less) sudden and severe alterations of the entire political regime, not merely evolutionary modifications of aspects of the system.

Total Area (rank)	643,801 sq km (42)
Population (rank)	65,312,249 (21)
Population Growth Rate (rank)	0.5% (151)
Urban Population	85%
Life Expectancy at Birth (total population) (rank)	81.19 (13)
Literacy	99%
Government Type	Republic
Legal System	Civil Law
Head of Government	Prime Minister François Fillon
Chief of State	President Nicolas Sarkozy
Gross Domestic Product (GDP)	$2.583 trillion
GDP Per Capita (rank)	$33,100 (39)
GDP Real Growth Rate (rank)	1.5% (161)
Unemployment Rate (rank)	9.5% (104)

FRANCE

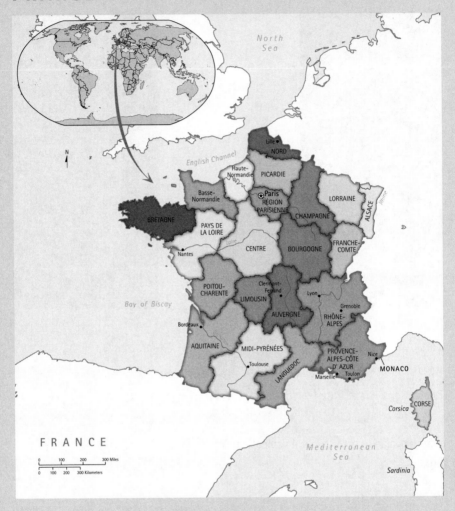

FRENCH CONSTITUTIONAL HISTORY

We refer to the current system of government in France as the Fifth Republic. This suggests, and properly so, that earlier republics have come and gone. Many of these arrivals and departures have not been slow and moderate, but have been abrupt and violent substitutions of one system of government for another— revolutions in fact, if not in name. It behooves us at this point to examine briefly the recent constitutional history of France that has led to the establishment of the Fifth Republic.

The Third Republic

We begin our discussion of modern French political structures with the **Third Republic,**[1] which has been referred to by some as a "republic by default."[2] Although the Third Republic dates from 1870, its constitution was not assembled until 1875. Its bicameral parliament was composed of a Chamber of Deputies and a Senate, the deputies elected by the people and the senators elected indirectly and over-representing rural areas.[3] The combined legislature, called the National Assembly, elected a president for a seven-year term. Ministers were responsible to the legislature, and with the consent of the Senate the president could dissolve the Chamber of Deputies before its four-year term expired.

The fact that the Third Republic lasted as long as it did—seventy years, from 1870 until 1940—is an anomaly of French political history. One should not deduce from the relative longevity of the Republic that its life was placid and stable; such was not the case. A number of crises arose on several different occasions during the life of the Republic that caused many people to fear that the Republic was in danger of extinction.[4]

Interestingly, World War I did not appear to have a deleterious effect upon the regime. By contrast, the economic depression in Europe after the war severely affected the Government. In 1935, a temporary electoral alliance of a number of political parties helped elect Leon Blum as premier. The Spanish Civil War in 1936 affected the stability of the Blum regime, as did a number of other social issues, and the Government resigned after a year.

From 1936 through 1940 several governments were created and dissolved. The Spanish Civil War, the Munich Agreement of 1938 between Neville Chamberlain (the British prime minister) and Adolph Hitler over the annexation of Czechoslovakia by Germany, the Nazi-Soviet Nonaggression Pact of 1939, and the German invasion of Norway and the Low Countries, all left French governments powerless to act.

The phenomenon that most people associate with French politics under the Third and Fourth Republics is no doubt **ministerial instability**, the frequent turnovers of cabinets. The phenomenon can be illustrated by comparing the number of French and British cabinets and premiers (or prime ministers) during similar periods, as indicated in Table 10.1.

The major explanation for the frequency of new cabinets in France during the Third Republic can be found in the Chamber of Deputies. There were

TABLE 10.1

Ministerial Instability in France: A Comparative Perspective

	Third Republic, France	Britain	Fourth Republic, France	Britain
	1879–1940	1880–1940	1947–1958	1945–1963
Number of cabinets	94	21	18	5
Average cabinet life	8 mos.	36 mos.	8 mos.	43 mos.
Number of premiers	44	11	15	4
Average tenure of premier	16 mos.	60 mos.	9 mos.	54 mos.

Source: Adapted from material in Roy Pierce, *French Politics and Political Institutions* (New York: Harper and Row, 1968), pp. 19–21.

usually eight to ten parties in the legislature, which invariably meant that coalitions were necessary to form government majorities. These coalitions (as we have seen is often the case with coalitions) were not able to withstand the short-term pressures brought about by rapidly evolving political events, which resulted in the collapse of government after government.

In June of 1940 a new cabinet was formed that was led by the World War I hero, Marshal Henri Petain. The hope of many was that Petain, as a military hero, would be able to provide strong leadership in the face of powerful external pressure from Hitler's Nazi Germany. He did provide leadership, but in an unexpected direction. Immediately after taking power on June 16, 1940, Petain opened negotiations with the Nazis; less than a week later (on June 22) he signed an armistice with Germany dividing France into an occupied northern half, and an unoccupied southern half, governed from the city of Vichy. From this time until November of 1942, when Germany occupied all of France, the Vichy regime governed the southern half of France without a constitution, a legislature, or presidential elections. The Third Republic was dead.[5]

The Fourth Republic

When France was liberated in 1944, General Charles de Gaulle, who had led a National Council of Resistance from London during the War, became head of the new Government.[6]

In October of 1945, "French voters by an overwhelming majority of 18,600,000 to 700,777 decided to leave the Third Republic in its grave."[7] The first postwar legislature was subsequently elected, and one of its first tasks was to construct a new constitution for the **Fourth Republic**; this combination legislature-constitutional convention was called the Constituent Assembly. There was no agreement, however, on the direction that should be followed in France's constitutional future.[8]

The first draft constitution was presented to the voters in May of 1946 for ratification, and was rejected by a narrow margin: 10,584,539 to 9,454,034. This plan proposed abolition of the Senate as an essentially "undemocratic" institution (since it was not directly elected by the public), and proposed a weak executive, with virtually all powers vested in a unicameral National Assembly. The draft had the support of the left parties, the Communists and the Socialists, but was opposed by moderate parties and a new political organization, the Popular Republican Movement (MRP).

The second Constituent Assembly, elected in June 1946, produced a draft constitution that resembled the first proposal in many respects. It placed almost complete authority in the elected National Assembly, a term previously used to designate the entire two-house parliament, with a weak Council of the Republic as a second legislative house.

Members of the National Assembly were to be elected from *multimember* districts, averaging five deputies per district, by proportional representation. The executive was to remain weak. In October of 1946, this plan was presented to the French public, and it received an unenthusiastic approval: 9,297,470 votes in favor, 8,165,459 against, with 7,775,893 eligible voters not voting. General de Gaulle and his supporters, who had argued for a stronger executive and opposed the plan, claimed that the new constitution would never last since it was supported by only slightly more than a third of the electorate.[9]

A number of devices were included in the constitution to promote governmental stability, such as the 1954 change making the investiture of a prime minister easier by requiring a relative, or simple, majority (a majority of those present and voting) rather than an absolute majority (a majority of all members of the legislature). Despite this, however, the multiparty system encouraged by the electoral framework of proportional representation led to an *absence* of stable parliamentary majorities, producing a change in cabinets averaging once every six months.

Although domestic issues were the primary source of political conflict in the early postwar years, by the mid-1950s it was international events that consumed governmental attention. The Government was able to handle almost all of the crises it faced. The War in Indochina (Vietnam) was ended in 1954. France accepted West Germany into the North Atlantic Treaty Organization (NATO) in 1957, and joined the European Economic Community (the Common Market). Both Morocco and Tunisia were granted independence in 1956. Also in 1956 the French Government passed legislation to "set France's African colonies south of the Sahara on the road to real, and not sham, self-government."[10] The question of Algeria, however, proved to be too much for the Government.

In April 1958 the French army stationed in Algeria supported a revolt launched by European settlers in Algiers and called for the formation of a "Government of Public Safety" in Paris. They demanded that the present Government resign, and that General de Gaulle be called out of political retirement to take power.[11] The Government in power accepted General de Gaulle as "the only possible savior-assassin of the regime. On June 1, 1958, by a vote of 329 to 224, the Assembly accepted de Gaulle as prime minister, and the next day empowered him to supervise the drafting of a new constitution."[12] The Fourth Republic was dead.

THE FRENCH CONSTITUTIONAL SYSTEM OF THE FIFTH REPUBLIC

When on June 1, 1958, the National Assembly invested de Gaulle as prime minister, many deputies in the Assembly were suspicious of de Gaulle and feared that his selection would lead to the creation of another Napoleon-like empire. In June of 1946 de Gaulle had delivered in the town of Bayeux what would prove to be one of his most famous speeches. He set forth his notion of the type of strong, vigorous executive leadership that he thought France needed.[13]

In spite of de Gaulle's protestations that at the age of 67 he did not pose a threat to French liberty, when the legislature authorized him to draft a new constitution it attached two significant conditions to the authorization: First, the constitution of the new Fifth Republic *had to retain* the two distinct offices of the president and the premier. Second, the new constitution would *have to retain* the characteristic of having the premier "responsible to" the legislature: That is, the legislature would have the power to fire the premier. The latter requirement was included on the assumption that de Gaulle himself would seek the premier's office, and thus the legislature would still have some degree of control over any future acts of de Gaulle.

It is interesting to note that although de Gaulle was given authority by the legislature to draft a new constitution that he would subsequently submit to the public in a referendum for approval, many argued that this grant of power was illegal. The constitution of the Fourth Republic, in effect when de Gaulle worked on his draft constitution, provided that constitutional amendments could be initiated only in parliament. Thus, it has been argued by anti-Gaullists that the de Gaulle Constitution of the Fifth Republic was simply a "coup d'état that had only a thin veneer of legality."[14]

The **de Gaulle constitution** does not fit neatly into either of the two major models of executive leadership (presidential or parliamentary) that we introduced earlier in this text. The presidential model has a single individual playing both the roles of head of state and chief executive, elected independent of the legislature, with a base of power independent of the legislature. The parliamentary model separates the two executive roles: the weak figurehead chosen by one of a number of different mechanisms (such as heredity or election) and the powerful chief executive coming from, being a part of, and being responsible to, the legislature. The de Gaulle constitution bridges the two systems, and is accordingly sometimes referred to as either a **quasi-presidential** or a **quasi-parliamentary** system.

The de Gaulle constitution brought together elements of both the Bonaparte era and the Republican era. "The Constitution established a strong Executive in the form of a president with independent power to govern and a cabinet headed by a prime minister responsible to a popularly elected assembly."[15] To put the institution of the French president in a comparative perspective, the president of France had both in theory *and in practice* the power that the British prime minister had in practice, *but not* in theory. The French model, unlike the standard Westminster-model power relationship, produced a politically significant head of state and a weak chief executive.

The so-called de Gaulle constitution of 1958 was actually drafted by a small group of individuals, led by Michel Debré, the future prime minister.[16] No person other than de Gaulle had more influence on the 1958 constitution than Debré. The new constitution was submitted to a Constitutional Advisory Committee, primarily made up of legislators, and subsequently presented to the public for approval in a national referendum.

A strong presidency, coupled with some structural changes in the powers of the legislature, was the major thrust of changes that the Fifth Republic would make to the political system of the Fourth Republic. This was clearly in response to what was seen as the fundamental weaknesses of the Fourth Republic: a lack of leadership, and parliamentary instability.

UNITARY GOVERNMENT IN FRANCE

French Politics is built on three levels of government: the commune, the départements, and the national government.[17] Just as French parliamentary government is a variation of the "normal" parliamentary model, so too the French style of unitary government appears to be different from other unitary governments.

Remember that while unitary governments and federal governments both have local *as well as* national levels, they differ in the existence of an *intermediate* level of government. The United States, Canada, and Germany are examples of federal governments in which power is shared (to different degrees) between the "central" or "national" governments and the intermediate governments—states, provinces, or Länder. The primary alternative to the federal system is the unitary regime, in which there is *no* intermediate level of government. The "typical" unitary government (if such can be said to exist) is found in Great Britain, in which a national government and a local government divide functions that would be of concern to the intermediate level of government in a federal regime, although all sovereignty resides with the national government.

The French system includes 22 administrative regions containing 96 départements (this is usually referred to as **metropolitan France**). There are also four overseas **départements** (Guadeloupe, Martinique, French Guiana, and Reunion Island), five overseas territories (New Caledonia, French Polynesia, Wallis and Futuna Islands, and French Southern and Antarctic Territories), and two "special status" territories (Mayotte, and St. Pierre and Miquelon).

The 1982 law affecting the twenty-two administrative regions—setting up elected regional councils with the power to elect their executives—also gave the regional authorities many powers that had previously belonged to the national government.

The French system is an odd form of unitary government, because although there is much sharing of power between the national and local levels of government, there are intermediate levels of government designed to assist in the *administration* of policy.[18] Locally, the mayor and municipal council deal with two kinds of decisions: how to carry out and finance state-mandated services, and priority-setting decisions in areas not controlled by the state. The *commune*, the lowest level political organization of the state, is the central administrative unit of the state.

The second level of French government is the *département*. The *prefect* is the representative of national government in the département. This individual has "wide-ranging powers over local government."[19] A good deal of the commune's legislation cannot go into effect without the prefect's approval. There are ninety-five départements in France, most of which have the same borders today that they did at the time of the French Revolution in 1789.

Départements are governed by a council (*conseil général*); for purposes of administration, départements are divided into subunits called *cantons*, and each canton elects one member to the département council. Like the commune, the department is both a self-governing structure and an administrative level of the state. The chief executive of government at the département level is not an elected official at all, but is the prefect, who is appointed.

It can be seen, then, that although France is invariably—and correctly—classified as a unitary regime, it is a unitary regime with many characteristics that might be thought to be more appropriate for a federal system than a unitary system. Départements and cantons both exist above the local (commune) level, and we will see later, particularly in regard to the Senate, that they play a significant role in the French political system.

EXECUTIVE STRUCTURES

The Presidency

When de Gaulle returned to power in 1958, it was generally expected that the presidency would be crucial.[20] It was by making the president—usually the weak figurehead actor in split-executive parliamentary systems—the keystone of the system, rather than the prime minister—usually the dominant figure in parliamentary systems—that de Gaulle and the coauthors of the new constitution were able to put so much power in the hands of a single political actor and yet still be able to stay within the conditions set down by the Fourth Republic legislators permitting a new constitution to be written and submitted to the public for approval.

The system of executive power in the Fifth Republic is similar in many respects to those found today in Austria, Finland, Ireland, and Iceland, in which the president is popularly elected. In those systems, however, the president is significantly weaker than in the French system, "because his role is circumscribed by his being subject to ouster by Parliament (as in Iceland), by strong legislative powers that Parliament possesses (as in Finland), or by the role of strong, disciplined parties (as in Austria). The French president, in contrast, suffers from none of these limitations."[21]

We suggested earlier in this volume that constitutions are often written in response to political regimes of the past. This is certainly true in France: the Constitution of the Fifth Republic was written in response to French political history.

De Gaulle's goal in designing the constitution was "to free the executive from legislative domination and so to make possible greater governmental stability."[22] The president was given absolute power, without needing the consent of either the Government or the Parliament, to:

1. Appoint the prime minister
2. Dissolve Parliament
3. Assume Emergency Powers under Article 16
4. Ask Parliament to reconsider a law just passed
5. Refer a law to the Constitutional Council for judgment on its constitutionality
6. Preside over the Council of Ministers (the Cabinet)
7. Serve as Commander-in-Chief
8. Exercise the right of Pardon
9. Decide whether or not to submit a bill to popular referendum when the Parliament or the prime minister suggest it.[23]

We should especially note the presidential power to dissolve the National Assembly (the lower house of the bicameral legislature) at any time the president wishes, except while exercising emergency powers under Article 16 (see later) or if the National Assembly has already been dissolved once within a year. It is not unusual to find this power in the hands of the head of state in other political systems; the British monarch has the same power. The difference, and a significant one, is that although *de jure* (in law) the British monarch may use this power at any time, *de facto* (in fact) she will use it *only* "on the advice" of the prime minister. The French president possessed this power both *de jure* and *de facto*—in law and in fact—and French presidents since the time of de Gaulle have used the power on their own initiative, without seeking approval of, or acting on request of, the prime minister and cabinet.

A major set of presidential powers included in the de Gaulle constitution of the Fifth Republic dealt with **emergency powers of the president. Article 16** of the constitution stated that "when the institutions of the Republic, national independence, the integrity of national territory, or the application of international commitments are threatened in a serious and immediate fashion, and the normal functioning of public institutions is interrupted," the president is authorized to "take the measures required by these circumstances."[24]

The measures that the president could take were virtually unlimited. The only checks on his (or her) power were that (1) the president must consult with the prime minister, the presidents of the two houses of legislature, and the Constitutional Council; and (2) the legislature must remain in session during the period of the declared emergency. It should be noted that the first item required the president only to *consult* with others, not seek their approval or permission, so these "checks" really did nothing to limit what the president did.

Article 16 has been used only once during the Fifth Republic. In April 1961 a group of French generals in Algeria who opposed governmental policy leading to Algerian independence from France threatened to invade the French mainland and take over the Government. De Gaulle acted under Article 16, announced that "the institutions of the Republic" were threatened, and declared a state of emergency. The attempted coup was put down within a very few days, but de Gaulle let his Article 16 powers remain in force for more than five months; only the president decides when to deactivate the Article 16 emergency powers.

There really are no "checks and balances" in the traditional sense over the president's use of the emergency powers in Article 16. The president needs no countersignature, no "advice and consent," no one's permission to declare the state of emergency; and the state of emergency remains until the president, and only the president, decides to declare the emergency over.

Yet another set of powers exclusively reserved for the president had to do with justice-related issues. Again, without the permission or countersignature of either the Government or the legislature, the president had the power to appoint three of the nine members of the Constitutional Council, which will be further discussed later. Moreover, the president had the right of pardon.

Beyond these powers, anything the president wanted to do in the French political system could only be done in collaboration with others. For example, only the president has the power to call for a **referendum,** to submit a political issue to the voters, but theoretically he may call a referendum *only* if asked to do so by either the Government or the legislature. In September of 2000, a question put before the French voters in a referendum was overwhelmingly approved; in that ballot 72 percent of the voters approved a measure to shorten the president's term of office from seven to five years. Only about 30 percent of the voters participated in the referendum, however, the lowest turnout ever recorded for a referendum.[25]

This theoretical control over the referendum was in response to the history of its use—or *abuse*—in French politics. Napoleon frequently used the referendum, often to achieve a goal that the legislature would not permit, and the public at the time did not prove to be terribly discriminating in its approval of Napoleon's ideas. The founders of the Fifth Republic, while giving the president great emergency powers, did not want to give a charismatic president license to regularly circumvent the duly elected legislators in the policy-making process.

Given that the president has only the above-mentioned powers (even though they are significant powers), which he can perform independently of all others, what has caused the French political leadership system to evolve to a point at which it has been argued it resembles the American presidency as much as, if not more than, the Westminster model of parliamentary government?

The answer can only partially be attributed to the constitutional grant of special powers to the president. There is in French politics a "fundamental difference between the role which the constitution and those who actually drafted it assigned to the presidency and the actual significance which the office has taken on in the process of decision making."[26]

Certainly a major reason for the evolution of the presidency as a significant political institution was the first holder of the office, Charles de Gaulle.[27] De Gaulle was a charismatic leader who favored strong executive leadership, and in the same way that initial incumbents of many political offices leave lasting impressions on the institutions they helped to create, de Gaulle's role in the development of the French presidency cannot be overstated.

A second reason for the growth of the relative power of the French presidency can be found in the constitutional amendment of October 1962, which established the *direct popular election* of the president.[28] In the 1958 constitution, the president was to be elected by an electoral college made up of local and provincial officials and national legislators. By having the president directly elected by the people, and therefore responsible to them and not to the legislators, de Gaulle gave the presidency a tremendous infusion of power and legitimacy.

As a result of the 1962 referendum, the president's term of office was seven years, making him one of the most secure chief executives in any Western democracy. The September 2000 referendum, in which the term was shortened from seven years to five years, was seen as the most radical change to the French constitution in decades.[29]

The issue of whether the seven-year term for the president should be shortened had been on the political agenda since Georges Pompidou assumed the presidency in 1969, but most presidents opposed having their terms shortened and would not submit the issue to a referendum or to parliament in a special session. Jacques Chirac, the president at the time of the referendum, had been on record as opposing the change in the length of the presidential term until the summer before the vote. The new policy went into effect at the end of Chirac's term, in 2002; some reporters suggested that Chirac believed that his chances to win re-election would be increased if voters knew that he would not serve seven more years, but only five.[30]

Direct popular election "endowed the presidency with the legitimacy of a direct popular vote, which, it was hoped, would accrue to the office when it was occupied by a less charismatic personality than General de Gaulle."[31] The apparent similarity to the American system can be overstated, however. Apart from the strong head of state, which is a single deviation from "normal" parliamentary systems, the French system is still much closer to the parliamentary model than to the American presidential model. This is so for a number of reasons:

1. By holding the power of dissolution (Article 12) over parliament, the French president can "interfere directly" with parliamentary organization and activity. The American president, of course, cannot.
2. By dissolving parliament the French president can, like the British prime minister, create a plebiscitory situation to receive popular support for his actions. The American president, of course, cannot dissolve the legislature.
3. The president has vast emergency powers under Article 16, with no judicial oversight as exists in the United States with the judicial review of the Supreme Court.[32]

The Prime Minister

The role of the prime minister in the Fifth Republic is of less significance than in most parliamentary systems. (It should be noted that the formal title of the chief executive in France is "prime minister," not "premier." "Premier" was used in the Third and Fourth Republics, and is still often used today as an incorrect holdover from former regimes.)

The role of the prime minister "has been limited to a joint formulation of policy with the President (in which the premier has played an increasingly subordinate role) and to manage the legislature so that it will accept the government's program."[33] One student of the French political system has suggested that in the Fifth Republic the prime minister is "merely the 'head of government', while the president is the actual decision-maker. He leaves to the premier the role of being a link between the president and Parliament, particularly on matters the president is not interested in."[34]

The President, Prime Minister, and "Cohabitation"

The model of French politics described above seemed to operate reasonably well until the election of 1986. To understand the significance of the 1986 election it is necessary to go back to April and May of 1981, at which time François Mitterand was elected president, the first time a Socialist had been elected president of France. One of his first actions was to dissolve the National Assembly (at that time conservative-dominated) and call for new elections, producing a Socialist-dominated legislature. At that point he appointed a Socialist prime minister, Pierre Mauroy, and everything continued normally with a Socialist president, a Socialist prime minister, and a Socialist-controlled legislature until the next elections.

By the time of the next elections for the National Assembly, the Socialists had lost much of their glamour, and they captured only 216 out of 577 seats in the Assembly. (Socialist) President Mitterand invited Jacques Chirac, leader of the largest party within the majority (conservative) coalition to become prime minister. He and Chirac agreed to a new power-sharing arrangement between the (Socialist) president and the (conservative) prime minister, something that came to be called *cohabitation*—"living together."[35] For the duration of Mitterand's term as president, his powers were considerably reduced from their pre-1986 level, and, correspondingly, the powers of Prime Minister Chirac were considerably greater than the powers of the prime minister had been previously.[36]

This practice has continued in recent years, and the current situation in France can be more accurately characterized as one with two more equally powerful (although *not* equal) actors, rather than a situation essentially dominated by the president, as was the case during the first two decades of the Fifth Republic.[37]

LEGISLATIVE STRUCTURES

The Legislature and the Government

The executive branch dominates the legislative process in a number of ways. Two of these are functions of direct limitation on the power of the legislature. First, the legislature cannot propose "increasing expenditures or lowering revenue in relation to the details of and total range of government budgetary proposals."[38] Second, the legislature can only pass laws dealing with matters that are specifically delegated to it in the constitution.

The budgetary process in any political system is a point of vulnerability for the Government. Governments that are unable to have their budgets passed find themselves at the mercy of their respective legislatures, literally unable to carry on the business of governing. The Fifth Republic's constitution places strong restrictions on the legislature's ability to obstruct or delay the Government in the budgetary arena.[39]

The knowledge that the essence of the Government's budget will become law in any case, and the limitations imposed upon the legislature in terms of changes it can and cannot propose to the Government's budget, place the legislature at a severe disadvantage in relation to the Government.

In addition, the 1958 constitution departed from "the traditional French republican principle of unrestricted parliamentary sovereignty" by specifically listing the legislative powers of parliament (Article 34), indicating those areas in which parliament could legislate; fields not specifically reserved for the legislature were left to the Government "to decide by decree."[40]

There are a number of other ways in which the executive is able to influence the legislative process. First, the Government controls the agenda of the National Assembly, and "by means of its power to determine the agenda the government can insure that its bills have priority over private members'." The Government also has the power to stipulate which portions of its legislative proposals can be amended, and how much time can be spent on each section of the bill. Moreover, the Government can call for a **blocked vote** requiring the legislative chambers to vote on a bill in its original text "incorporating only those amendments proposed or accepted by the government."[41]

As a more severe action, the Government can announce that it is making the passage of a bill into a question of confidence. If it does this, the bill automatically passes "unless a censure motion is filed by one-tenth of the deputies within 24 hours and an absolute majority of the deputies vote in support of censure."[42]

The question of the relation between the Government and the National Assembly over the concept of "censure" or "confidence" is interesting, because it is another area in which the usual vulnerability of the executive branch to the will of the legislature has been modified from the standard model. Although some texts declare that "if a motion of censure is adopted by the National Assembly, the Government must resign,"[43] history has shown that this rule of thumb has not always been followed.

The censure process is more difficult to operate in France than it is in many parliamentary systems, although it is not as difficult as we shall see to be the case with the German "positive vote of no confidence" in the next chapter. Opposition members can introduce motions of censure if the motion is signed by one-tenth of the deputies of the National Assembly (totaling 491). After the motion is introduced, 48 hours must pass before it can be debated and voted on; in order for it to pass, the motion must receive an absolute majority of deputies' support (half plus one of the 491 deputies), not just a majority of deputies present and voting. Opposition members who sign a motion of censure are enjoined from being co-signatories of another such motion during the same legislative session; this is designed to prevent a constant stream of motions that are sure to be defeated.[44]

The Senate

In 1947 the founders of the Fourth Republic decided to do away with the Senate as the second half of the legislative body in the (then-) new regime. Their argument was that the Senate was (1) undemocratically selected, since it was not directly elected by the people; (2) overrepresentative of rural areas; and (3) either redundant or antidemocratic—if it agreed with the lower house it was redundant and therefore unnecessary, and if it disagreed with the popularly elected lower house it was antidemocratic, since the lower house *was* popularly elected and the Senate was not. After some discussion, a weak "Council of the Republic" was substituted for the Senate in the Fourth Republic. In 1958 Charles de Gaulle brought back the second house to the French legislative system.

The Senate is sometimes referred to as the "agricultural" chamber of the legislature, because it over-represents rural areas of France. As we noted earlier, the unit of representation in the Senate is the département; the number of senators representing a given département varies from one or two to over five, depending upon the size and population of the département.

Generally speaking, the Senate is the inferior of the two legislative bodies in France today. This inferior position can be measured in a number of ways.

For instance, the Senate meets less frequently than does the Assembly. As another indicator we can look at the number of bills becoming laws and their point of origin; in one classic study, only 23 percent of bills originated in the Senate.[45]

However, the Senate sometimes can be an effective legislative body in terms of its ability to provide a "sober second thought" to legislative proposals, especially to Government proposals.[46] This is true for very much the same reason as it is for the House of Lords in Great Britain. Because the Government is responsible to the lower house, and can be fired by the lower house, party discipline will keep criticism in that body to a minimum. The upper house, to which the Government is *not* responsible, often has more freedom to inquire and discuss and criticize than does the lower house. An additional basis of power for the Senate in France is more parallel to the upper house in Germany (the Bundesrat) than to the House of Lords in Great Britain; although France is not a federal regime, senators represent geographical districts, or départements, and when Government bills deal with regional issues, agriculture, or similar questions, the Senate is likely to play a more significant role in the legislative process than it otherwise would.

The Legislative Process

The Senate of the Fifth Republic is not an equal partner in the legislative process. The legislative process is clearly dominated by the Government in the National Assembly, with the Senate often not much more than an after-thought in the process.

> As in the Fourth Republic, and in Britain, West Germany, and Italy, a distinction is made between government bills (*projets de loi*) and private members' bills (*propositions de loi*), with the former accounting for most of the bills introduced in the Assembly. When a bill is introduced, it is sent first to the *bureau*; and the speaker, who heads that unit, transmits the bill directly to a legislative committee. When the committee has done its work, the *rapporteur* formally reports the bill to the floor for what is technically the initial "reading" of it. The ensuing debate, which provides an opportunity for the introduction of amendments, is followed by a vote. After its passage by the Assembly, the bill is transmitted to the Senate. If that chamber accepts the original version of the bill, it is sent to the government for signature. If the Senate rejects the bill, the subsequent procedure varies. There can be a resort to the shuttle (*navette*)—the sending of a bill back and forth between the two chambers until a common version is achieved; second, the government may request the establishment of a conference committee (*commission mixte paritaire*); third, the government may ask each chamber for a "second reading," (i.e., a reconsideration and new vote on the original bill); and fourth, if disagreement persists, the government may ask the Assembly to determine the final version of the bill by simple majority vote.[47]

The Government's ability to select among these several options when interchamber disagreement arises in the legislative process gives it a great deal of power. Ultimately, the Government can choose to simply ignore the Senate and ask the National Assembly to determine the final version of a bill. If the National Assembly wants to pass a bill that the Government does not want, it can simply let the *navette* go on endlessly, or keep the bill off the agenda. Finally, of course, if the Government finds both chambers noncompliant, it has the ultimate power to couple a "blocked vote" with a question of confidence to force its proposals through the legislative process.

THE CONSTITUTIONAL COUNCIL

As is the case in most parliamentary systems of government, France has no active tradition of judicial review in politics.[48] In spite of this, the **Constitutional Council** of the Fifth Republic was designed (Articles 56–63 of the Constitution) "to ensure that constitutional provisions would possess a certain superiority over ordinary laws." Its function is to rule on the standing orders of the legislature and, on request of the Government majority (but not a legislative minority), to determine the boundaries of executive and legislative competence and "whether laws...or treaties are in conformity with the constitution."[49] It also is required to supervise presidential and parliamentary elections, as well as referenda.

Many in 1958 feared the creation of a Constitutional Council because it sounded very much like the U.S. Supreme Court; the powers of the U.S. Supreme Court were thought to be too sweeping to transplant to the French system. The fears of an activist judiciary have not been realized, however, primarily because the members of the Constitutional Council were generally sympathetic to Government policy. Three of the nine regular judges are appointed by the president, three by the president of the National Assembly, and three by the president of the Senate. The nine judges serve nine-year terms. Former presidents of the Republic are on the Constitutional Council for life terms, as well.

The bulk of the Constitutional Council's work has been in adjudicating jurisdictional disputes between the presidency and the legislature "over boundaries of law and regulation." The Constitutional Council so consistently ruled on behalf of the president's point of view that it became perceived as an "auxiliary of executive authority."[50]

The Council is most frequently consulted today on the questions of the constitutionality of legislation. This is one dimension of its power that has grown in recent years, increasing the status of the Constitutional Council to more nearly that of the U.S. Supreme Court.

POLITICAL PARTIES AND ELECTIONS

There have traditionally been a number of political parties active in the French political system. In modern times, it was not until the Fifth Republic that a true majority party existed in France, the UNR-UDR (Union for a New Republic-Democratic Union for the Republic).[51] Throughout French history, the political party systems that existed failed to provide a basis for stable elections; the parties failed to govern.[52]

General Charles de Gaulle, in his criticisms of the Government in the Fourth Republic, described this anarchic situation of no responsible government and no responsible opposition as *"le regime des partis."*[53] It was strictly speaking, a regime *with* parties, not a regime *of* parties. Party *control* (in the sense of stable party government) of the regime did not come until de Gaulle's supporters won parliamentary majorities in the Fifth Republic.

Gaullism and Presidential Leadership

Certainly among the most significant phenomena in the French party system was the rise of the Gaullist "nonparty" that became the significant political organization of the regime. Originally, **Gaullism** was a movement of support for Charles de Gaulle that claimed to be an alternative to divisive political parties; both organizationally and ideologically it insisted upon being regarded simply as a following for de Gaulle. Its ideology was the ideology of de Gaulle; its organization was designed to further the interests and goals of de Gaulle. It "pretended not to be a party at all, but rather a national *movement*, an alternative to parties."[54]

The Gaullist ideology was perceived as a rightist ideology, but was able to draw from the political left as well as the right, because of de Gaulle's antiparliamentary attitudes shared with the Communist party (the PCF), his positive view of the Church, which was shared with the Popular Republican Movement (MRP), and his commitment to plebiscitory democracy and frequent referenda, generally a left-wing attitude. In 1962 the Union for a New Republic (UNR), in fact the Gaullist party of its day, combined with a generally conservative working-class party called the Democratic Union of Labor to form the Democratic Union for the Republic (UDR).

When de Gaulle left the political scene and Georges Pompidou, his former prime minister, became president, the Gaullist movement weakened somewhat, but not as much or as rapidly as many had predicted would be the case.[55] Many had claimed that the UDR—the Democratic Union for the Republic, the descendent of the UNR—and Gaullism in general, were simply personalistic followings for de Gaulle; as soon as de Gaulle left politics, the critics said, the Gaullists as a political bloc would fall apart.

Pompidou reigned over the demise of the UDR between 1970 and 1974. By the time of the parliamentary elections in 1973, the UDR had so weakened that it joined with the Independent Republicans and the Center of Democracy and Progress (CDP) in an electoral alliance called the Union of Republicans for Progress (URP), but even with that its parliamentary representation fell from 273 seats in 1968 to 185 in 1973.

With the election of Valérie Giscard d'Estaing as president in 1974, the UDR became an "also-ran." Giscard, an Independent Republican, drew a good deal of what was left in the UDR to his party, the Independent Republican party.

The Giscard years were associated with economic liberalism, a theme of national unity, and a "more liberal functioning of institutions,"[56] the latter including a slight increase of the power of the parliament compared to earlier regimes.

The year 1981 saw the rise to prominence of the Socialist party under President François Mitterand. In the 1981 campaign many of the principle issues were economic, and Mitterand was able to convince a majority of the French voters that they should give the political left a chance to lead France. Mitterand became the first Socialist to be elected president, and as was indicated earlier, he immediately dissolved the National Assembly and called for new elections so that he could have a Socialist-dominated Assembly to help enact his program. The Socialists, riding on the coattails of the newly elected president, won a clear majority (262 of the 491 seats), and with their non-Communist allies controlled 285 seats in the National Assembly. With a clear majority in the legislature, Mitterand was able to implement a number of socialist policies.[57]

The perception at the time was that the "intention of the French Socialist administration, presided over by Mitterand, was 'to give the state back to the people.'"[58] Mitterand believed that centralization had been necessary in the *creation* of France, but at the time of his election *de*centralization was necessary for the *future* of France. Mitterand was a political realist, recognizing that the forces which elected him were as much a response to the economic climate of the time as they were indications of fundamental agreement with his ideology.[59]

Public reaction against the Mitterand Government and some of its policies led to a decline in public support for the Socialists. In local elections in 1982 and 1983, many of the supporters who had worked so hard for Mitterand in 1981 supported conservative candidates, and the conservative parties made great progress. In the long view, "the years of socialist government did not produce the revolution of which many of its supporters dreamed." Social inequality and injustice did not disappear; the economy did not expand as promised.[60]

In March of 1986 the "French socialist experience"[61] came to an end with a conservative victory in the elections for the National Assembly, resulting in the *cohabitation* arrangement between Socialist President Mitterand and conservative Prime Minister Chirac discussed earlier. The conservatives thought that this was a foreshadowing of a presidential victory for their candidate in 1988, but such was not the case: President Mitterand, with a much more economically moderate and ideologically toned-down campaign than he had run in 1981, defeated Prime Minister Chirac, who was running against him for the presidency, and won re-election in 1988.

Mitterand's term in office was followed in 1995 by the election of M. Chirac as president. Chirac ran for office promising tax cuts, but the economy did not cooperate, and he and his prime minister, Alain Juppé, were not able to honor their campaign promises. In 1997 Chirac dissolved parliament prematurely and called for early elections in a bid to increase support for his economic program. Unfortunately, the public did not approve of this course of action, and the strategy backfired; in the subsequent election of 1997 the Socialist Party and other parties on the left defeated Chirac's conservative allies, forcing Chirac into a new period of cohabitation with Socialist leader Lionel Jospin as prime minister.

In 2002, at age 69, Chirac ran for a second term as president. He received the support of less than 20 percent of the voters in the first round of voting in April 2002. Most observers had expected that he would face incumbent (Socialist) Prime Minister Lionel Jospin in the second round of voting; instead, the candidate receiving the second-highest vote total in the first round was controversial far-right politician Jean-Marie Le Pen of the law-and-order, anti-immigrant National Front. When the second round took place, Chirac won re-election by a landslide, receiving over 80 percent of the vote; most parties outside the National Front had called for opposing Le Pen, even if it meant voting for Chirac. Following his re-election, Chirac sought to reorganize politics on the right, establishing a new party, initially called the Union of the Presidential Majority, then the Union for a Popular Movement (UMP), to take the place of the former Rally for the Republic. The UMP won the parliamentary elections that followed the presidential poll with ease, a point to which we shall return shortly.

The 2007 election was seen as a generational election. Both **Nicolas Sarkozy** (UMP) and Ségolène Royal (Socialist) were born after World War II. The results of the first round of voting saw Sarkozy and Royal qualify for the second round with Sarkozy getting 31 percent and Royal 26 percent.

In the voting for the second round, Sarkozy received 53 percent of the votes to Royal's 47 percent.

French Political Parties

Most contemporary texts dealing with French politics[62] discuss the party system in terms of component parties, and move from left to right (or right to left) along the political spectrum describing the respective ideologies and policy positions of the many contemporary French parties.[63] Because of the nature of the electoral system—a point to which we shall turn shortly—many parties have decided that although they are not going to merge permanently with one another, their views are sufficiently similar so that they should not compete against each other in elections. This kind of attitude gave rise to the Union of Republicans for Progress (URP) in 1973, leading to a coordination of candidacies around France among the Independent Republican Party, the Democratic Union for the Republic (UDR), and the Center for Democracy and Progress (CDP). The same thing happened in the elections of 1978 and 1981 with the French Democratic Union (UDF) resulting from coordination between the Republican Party (PR, formed by Giscard from the Independent Republican Party in 1977), the Center for Social Democrats (CDS, a new party organized from the earlier CDP), and some others. In both 1988 and 1993 the Union for French Democracy and the Rally for the Republic contested the elections jointly as the Union of the Rally and of the Center (URC). Subsequently, many of the various right-wing parties joined the URC prior to the second ballot.

Another more recent phenomenon involved the development of the National Front (FN) led originally by Jean-Marie Le Pen and now by his daughter Marine Le Pen.[64] The National Front has been variously labeled as "extreme right" and "neo-Nazi," and has campaigned strongly in favor of statism, and against foreigners. As noted earlier, although its strength today is not nearly what it was, its leader Le Pen did make it to the final two in the 2002 presidential election.[65]

ELECTIONS TO THE NATIONAL ASSEMBLY

If France were a "typical" parliamentary system, we would have only elections to the national legislature to study at this point, because the selection of the head of state would not be politically significant, and the selection of the chief executive would automatically follow the leader of the majority in the lower house of the national legislature. However, because of the 1962 referendum—to have the president directly elected by the citizenry rather than indirectly elected by a complex electoral college—any discussion of French elections must include both presidential and parliamentary elections. We begin our brief discussion with the National Assembly, move to the presidency, and conclude with a discussion of selection of senators.

French elections for the National Assembly are for terms of five years (or less if the Assembly is dissolved early) and for the most part have been based upon a *majority* approach to voting rather than a *plurality* approach (the latter being the case in Great Britain or the United States). That is, in electoral contests for the National Assembly the initial question that is asked on election day after the polls close is *not* "Who received the most votes?" The reader will recall that in single-member district, plurality voting systems, the candidate who receives the most votes is the winner; if there are six candidates and the candidate with the most votes receives only 25 percent of the total vote, that candidate is elected even though 75 percent of the public did not vote for him or her. In majority-based elections, unlike the plurality-based elections, to win a race on the first ballot one must receive a *majority* of the vote, one more than half of the votes cast.

We said earlier that French elections for the National Assembly have "for the most part been based upon a majority approach" because for about one year—from March of 1986 until June of 1987—the electoral system was changed from universal direct election as described further below to a proportional representation electoral system. (That is, proportional representation within départements, not nationally, with a 5 percent threshold necessary for election.)[66] Proportional representation replaced the single-member district model when it became clear to President Mitterand that his Socialist party faced an overwhelming rejection by the voters in the election of March 1986.

With the majority voting system and only a 30 percent level public opinion support, the Socialists would very likely have become a tiny minority in the Assembly. With a change of the rules for elections to a system of proportional representation voting, the Socialists won 206 out of 577 seats in the National Assembly, but the parties of the right still controlled a majority in the Assembly, and a conservative government was formed. This resulted in the period of *cohabitation* we referred to earlier. The system of proportional representation elections angered the political elite, and brought about a commitment by the new government to get rid of it again. Within a year of the election the new conservative-dominated government restored the former electoral system.

When the presidential elections were held in April and May of 1988 and President Mitterand was re-elected, he again—much as he did immediately after his first electoral victory seven years earlier—dissolved the National Assembly and called for new elections. Again, as in 1981, the French public gave the left a majority in the Assembly, although the Socialist party alone did not receive the outright majority in 1988 that it did in 1981, and it had to make arrangements with the Communists[67] to maintain a majority.

Two years after being elected president in 1995, President Jacques Chirac decided to dissolve the National Assembly in 1997 and call for early elections—a year before their "normal" time—feeling that he could revitalize the right-of-center majority in the National Assembly. The Right believed that in taking the Left by surprise they could minimize their losses and hold on to a clear majority for a new five-year term, enough time to meet the challenges of moving France into the European Union and meeting the strict criteria set up by the Maastricht Treaty for countries to gain entry to the single European currency. As noted earlier, the strategy did not work, and the 1997 Assembly was dominated by the Socialists.

In December of 2000 the National Assembly—three years into its five-year term and controlled by the Socialist Party—voted to reverse the order of the next scheduled elections that had been planned for the spring of 2002, having the presidential election precede the parliamentary election rather than the other way around. As noted earlier, in the September 2000 referendum the voters of France decided to reduce the presidential term from seven years to five years. One of the arguments in favor of this change was that since the elections for parliament and the president would be held in the same year (with both the National Assembly and the president having five year terms, the assumption was that they would be held at nearly the same time), the likelihood was that *cohabitation* would disappear since it would be less likely that one party would win the presidency and a different party would control the Assembly.

Analysts suggested that if the presidential election were held first the Socialists would be more likely to win, thereby increasing the likelihood that they would also control the Assembly. They also suggested that the (conservative) Rally for the Republic (RPR) was more like to gain control of the Assembly if the elections for that body were held first, thereby helping the RPR to continue to control the presidency.

As noted earlier, because of the appearance of Jean-Marie LePen in the race, M. Chirac was overwhelmingly re-elected to a second term, and he restructured the party system on the political Right to replace the RPR as the major Right political party with a new organization called the Union for a Presidential Majority, later called the Union for a Popular Movement .[68]

Given the number of political parties in the French electoral system, it is clear that with a majority-based electoral system few candidates will win majorities outright. This has led to France's unique two-ballot "simple majority" system of voting.[69] The first election is held on a Sunday, and a candidate who receives an absolute majority (50 percent of the vote plus one vote) of the total votes cast in his district is elected on the first round of voting, provided she or he receives the votes of at least one-quarter of the number of registered voters in the constituency.[70] If no candidate wins a majority on the first ballot—which is the case in most constituencies—a second ballot is held on the following Sunday. At that time, whichever candidate receives a *plurality* (that is, more votes than anyone else) of the votes is declared the winner. (See Table 10.2.)

Being elected to the National Assembly on the first ballot is the exception rather than the rule. In the Assembly election of 2007, the most recent elections, only 110 of the 577 races were resolved in the first round of voting, a bit under 20 percent of the total; only five of these deputies were elected for the first time, and the other 105 first-ballot victors were re-elected.[71]

When the second round of elections are held, no new candidate for office may register. In order to contest the second ballot, a candidate must have received 12.5 percent of the vote on the first round. (This was raised from 10 percent in the 1978 election.) If only one candidate receives over 12.5 percent of the votes cast on the first ballot, the person who receives the second-largest number of votes on the first ballot may also participate in the second ballot, in which only a simple majority is needed to win. Although this means that technically several candidates could compete in the second round of voting (since more than two candidates could receive 12.5 percent of the vote on the first round), most second ballots turn out to be duels between two parties because of the alliances that we mentioned earlier.

Preelectoral alliances/agreements have had the effect in many cases of turning the first ballot into a type of primary election, in which a number of candidates from the left may compete, and a number of candidates from the right may compete, with the understanding that the top vote-getter from the left will "represent" the left, and the top vote-getter from the right will "represent" the right.

The bias of the electoral system that we have discussed in general earlier in this text—more specifically in regard to Britain—appears again in the French election for the National Assembly. Table 10.2 shows that while the UMP received 98 seats in exchange for 40 percent of the vote on the first ballot, the Socialist party received only 1 seat in exchange for 25 percent of the vote. (That is, the Socialists received over 60% of the UPM's votes, and received 1 percent of the UPM's seats!)

TABLE 10.2

The Parliamentary Election of June 10 and June 17, 2007

Party	Abbreviation	% Votes in First Round (Seats)		% Votes in Second Round (Seats)		Number of Seats After Second Round (% Total)
Union for a Popular Movement	UMP	39.54	(98)	46.36	(215)	313
Presidential Majority	MAJ	2.37	(8)	2.12	(14)	22
[Other Right]	—	2.47	(2)	1.17	(7)	9
Movement for France	MPF	1.20	(1)	0.50	(0)	1
Socialist Party	PS	24.73	(1)	42.26	(185)	186
Left Radical	RG	1.32		1.63	(7)	7
Union for French Democracy	UDF	7.61		0.49	(3)	3
Regionalist	—	0.51		0.52	(1)	1
Others	—	11.94		0.16	(1)	1
Communist Party	PC	4.29		2.28	(15)	15
[Other Left]	—	1.97		2.47	(15)	15
Greens	V	3.25		0.45	(4)	4
Totals		101%	(110)	99.1%	(467)	577 (99.8%)

Turnout: Round One: 60.42% (26.5 million of 43.9 million eligible)
Round Two: 59.99% (21.1 million of 35.2 million eligible)

Source: Inter-Parliamentary Union, "France—Assemblée Nationale," http://www.ipu.org/parline-e/reports/2113_A.htm (accessed May, 2011).

Presidential Elections

In presidential elections a candidate must receive an absolute majority of the votes in order to win on the first ballot. This has never happened in Fifth Republic France; the most votes that Charles de Gaulle ever received on the first ballot was 44 percent of the total votes cast. As can be seen in Table 10.3, in the 2007 election to replace Jacques Chirac as president for a five year term, the winner, Nicolas Sarkozy, received just over 30 percent of the first-ballot votes. The second ballot is limited to the top two vote-getters from the first round, and takes place two weeks after the first round of voting.

Election of Senators

The selection of senators differs from the single-member-district, majority voting selection of deputies to the National Assembly. Senators are intended

TABLE 10.3

The Presidential Election of April 22 and May 6, 2007

Registered voters: 44,472,733

Voters: 37,342,004

First Round, April 21, 2002

Nikolas Sarkozy, Union for a Popular Movement, 31.18%

Ségolène Royal, Socialist Party, 25.87

François Bayrou, Union for French Democracy, 18.57

Jean-Marie Le Pen, National Front, 10.44

Olivier Besancenot, Revolutionary Communist League, 4.08

Philippe de Villiers, Movement for France, 2.23

Marie-George Buffet, French Communist Party, 1.93

Dominique Voynet, The Greens, 1.57

Arlette Laguiller, Workers' Struggle, 1.33

José Bové, Alter-Globalization, 1.32

Frédéric Nihous, Hunting, Fishing, Nature, Tradition, 1.15

Gérard Schivardi, Workers' Party, 0.34

Total 100.01 (36,719,396 votes cast)

Second Round, May 5, 2002

Nikolas Sarkozy, Union for a Popular Movement, 53.06%

Ségolène Royal, Socialist Party, 46.94

Total 100.0 (35,773,578 votes cast)

Source: Government of France web page, "The Presidency," http://www.elysee.fr/president/la-presidence/le-president-de-la-republique/l-investiture-des-presidents-de-la-republique/decision-du-10-mai-2007-portant-proclamation-des.9542.html (accessed May, 2011).

to represent the administrative/territorial units of France, and the method of their selection reflects this. They are elected by *grands électeurs*—individuals who hold elected office in some other governmental structure (e.g., mayors, members of the National Assembly, local councillors, and the like)—and thus Senators are only indirectly representative of the population.

The French Senate is currently going through an evolutionary transformation, moving from a structure in the past in which senators were elected for nine-year terms and one-third of the Senate was elected every three years, to a structure in which Senators will serve a six-year term and one-half of the chamber will be replaced every three years.

Senators are elected from départements by electoral colleges. These electoral colleges range from 270 electors in smaller départements, to over 6,000 electors in the larger départements, depending upon the population of the départements. Deputies in the National Assembly from districts in a given départements, départemental councillors, and delegates chosen by municipal councils—all comprise these electoral colleges. Thus, the Senate is elected by the 577 National Assembly deputies, about 3,000 *conseillers généraux*, and about 100,000 delegates from the municipal councils.[72] (See Table 10.4.)

> ◤ **TABLE 10.4**
>
> ### The Senate After the September 21, 2008 Election by Political Group
>
> | | |
> |---|---|
> | Groupe Communiste Republicain et Citoyen and Left Party | 24 |
> | Group Union Centriste—UDF | 29 |
> | Group du Rassemblement Democratique et Social Europeen | 18 |
> | Groupe Socialiste | 115 |
> | Group Union pour un Mouvement Populaire | 148 |
> | Senators not on other lists | 7 |
> | Total | 341 |
> | Women: 75 (21.9% of total) | |
>
> *Source:* Government of France, Senate, "List of Senators by Political Groups," online at http://www.senat.fr/senateurs/grp.html.
>
> According to the Inter-Parliamentary Union, "Until the renewal in 2004 inclusive, senators had been elected for a nine-year term by using series A, B and C, for the renewal of one third of the Senate every three years. The term has been shortened to six years starting from the 2007 renewal. As a transitional measure to introduce the new series 1 and 2, under which half of the Senate is renewed every three years, the mandate of the senators whose term would have normally expired in September 2007, 2010 and 2013 has been shortened or extended to be renewed in September 2008, 2011, and 2014 respectively (cf. law No. 2005-1562 of 15 December 2005). The series 1 and 2 will be first applied to the renewals of 2011 and 2014 respectively. Thereafter, all senators will serve a six-year term." See Inter-Parliamentary Union web page, "France" > "Sénat," http://www.ipu.org/parline-e/reports/2114_A.htm accessed May, 2011. a six-year term." See Inter-Parliamentary Union web page, "France" >

The larger départements (seven in all) elect five or more senators; smaller départements choose fewer. In the départements that choose five or more senators, senators are chosen by proportional representation voting: Electors vote for a party list, and parties receive a number of senatorial positions corresponding to the proportion of the vote they received. In the smaller départements, senators are elected on a two-ballot system very similar to elections for the National Assembly: A majority is required on the first ballot, and a plurality is required on the second ballot.

The Senate is often referred to as an "agricultural chamber" because of its malrepresentation of the French population. "Rural France is overrepresented and urban France is underrepresented in the Senate." For example, "the eight departments of the Paris Region, plus five other départements which each had more than one million inhabitants...contain one-third of the French population, and while they have 32 percent of the...seats in the National Assembly, they have only 26 percent of such seats in the Senate."[73]

THE FRENCH SYSTEM IN PERSPECTIVE

We have seen in this chapter that the French political system can almost be seen as a variation of the Westminster model of government in several respects, many of them quite significant. The dual executive, although resembling the

British model on paper, is quite different in its actual day-to-day behavior and power structure. The French president is virtually unique in the parliamentary world (except for political systems modeled after France), having both in theory and in practice all of the power that the British monarchy has only in theory.

The French Constitution is partially responsible for this. When Charles de Gaulle and his colleagues designed the constitutional structures of the Fifth Republic, they took pains to provide for strong executive leadership—to a large extent to compensate for years of weak executives and strong, and uncontrollable, legislatures. The fact that the legislatures in both the Third and Fourth Republics were unstable foundations upon which to base a government was not lost on the founders of the Fifth Republic.

The legislative bodies of the Fifth Republic are typical of other parliamentary legislatures in a number of respects. First, of course, they are inferior to the executive branch of government. The legislature is *not* expected to be a major policy-making body in the political system. Its function is to approve the policies of the executive, and, if the executive becomes too unpopular, to replace the Government. Second, the upper house of the legislature is inferior to the lower house of the legislature. Ultimately, the Senate can have only a suspensory veto over the actions of the National Assembly; it can slow down the actions of that house, but it cannot prevent National Assembly legislation from becoming law.

French elections differ from elections in other political systems because of the single-member-district, majority voting system used for the National Assembly, and the two-wave voting for the presidency. Again, we can see that the structure of the electoral system can have an impact upon the political party system in a country. France has a number of political parties, not just one or two, and these parties do their best to operate within the rules of the Fifth Republic's electoral system.

In the case of France, then, we have been able to see a number of applications of the material we described in the first part of this text. Constitutions, executives, legislatures, electoral systems, and political parties all matter in the day-to-day operation of a political regime. We will continue to see in the chapters that follow that some of the idiosyncratic features of political regimes are of tremendous significance in the daily operation of government.

DISCUSSION QUESTIONS

1. What were the political behaviors from the Third Republic that France particularly wanted to avoid in the Fifth Republic? What from the Fourth Republic? Was there agreement on the problems of the earlier regimes?
2. How was de Gaulle's role in the creation of the Fifth Republic special? How did the "de Gaulle Constitution" particularly reflect the values of de Gaulle? What were the issues that were most important to him?
3. What are the special characteristics of unitary government in France? How is French unitary government different from unitary government in Britain, for example?

4. How does the French executive structure compare with other parliamentary executives? What are the powers of the French president that are usual for Parliamentary heads of state? What are the president's most unusual powers?
5. How has the operation of "cohabitation" affected the way that French politics has operated in recent years? Is this a structure that is good for France?
6. How would you compare the French legislative process to the legislative process of Britain? Is the French model more or less efficient? Why?

KEY TERMS

Article 16   239
blocked vote   243
cohabitation   243
Constitutional
   Council   246
de Gaulle
   constitution   236
départements   237

direct popular election of
   the president   241
emergency powers of the
   president   239
Fourth Republic   234
Gaullism   247
metropolitan France   237

ministerial
   instability   233
navette   245
quasi-parliamentary   236
quasi-presidential   236
referendum   240
Third Republic   233

SUGGESTED READINGS

David Scott Bell, *Presidential Power in the Fifth Republic France* (New York: Berg, 2000). This is a very thorough study of the power of the president in the Fifth French Republic. The power and role of the president has changed considerably over the years, and this volume describes those changes and what led them to take place.

Andrew Knapp, *Parties and the Party System in France: A Disconnected Democracy?* (New York: Palgrave Macmillan, 2004). This is a good analysis of the political parties in contemporary France. It discusses the nature and the roles of political parties, their positions on key issues, and how they have operated in recent French politics.

Michael S. Lewis-Beck, *The French Voter: Before and After the 2002 Elections* (New York: Palgrave Macmillan, 2004). This is an empirically-oriented study of voting behavior in France through the 2002 election. Lewis-Beck places voting results in historical contexts, and explains the importance of specific elections for the overall development of French politics.

Kenneth Moure and Martin Alexander, *Crisis and Renewal in France, 1918–1962* (New York: Berghahn, 2002). This is a good historical examination of France through the Third and Fourth Republics and into the Fifth Republic of DeGaulle.

Vincent Wright and Andrew Knapp, *The Government and Politics of France* (New York: Routledge, 2006). A very good introductory volume describing both the historical and structural changes that have characterized the development of Fifth Republic France.

NOTES

1. For discussion of French political history prior to the Third Republic, see William Fortescue, *The Third Republic in France, 1870–1940: Conflicts and Continuities* (London, UK: Routledge, 2000).

2. William Safran, *The French Polity*, 2nd ed. (New York: Longman, 1985), p. 5.

3. John Ambler, *The Government and Politics of France* (Boston, MA: Houghton-Mifflin, 1971), p. 7. See also Robert Young, *An Uncertain Idea of France: Essays and Reminiscence on the Third Republic* (New York: P. Lang, 2005).

4. Further discussion of this period can be found in Gwendolen Carter, *The Government of France* (New York: Harcourt, Brace, Jovanovich, 1972), pp. 22–23, and Ambler, *The Government and Politics of France*, p. 7. See also James Lehning, *To Be a Citizen: The Political Culture of the Early French Third Republic* (Ithaca, NY: Cornell University Press, 2001).

5. See Robert Paxton, *Vichy France: Old Guard and New Order, 1940–1944* (New York: Columbia University Press, 2001). See also Michael Curtis, *Verdict on Vichy: Power and Prejudice in the Vichy France Regime* (New York: Arcade, 2002).

6. Carter, *The Government of France*, p. 25. See also Kenneth Moure and Martin Alexander, *Crisis and Renewal in France, 1918–1962* (New York: Berghahn, 2002).

7. Ambler, *The Government and Politics of France*, p. 10.

8. The best general discussions of problems and performances of the Fourth Republic are to be found in two sources: Philip Williams, *Crisis and Compromise: Politics in the Fourth Republic* (New York: Doubleday, 1966); and Duncan MacRae, *Parliament, Parties, and Society in France: 1946–1958* (New York: St. Martin's Press, 1967).

9. Ambler, *The Government and Politics of France*, p. 11.

10. Pierce, *French Politics and Political Institutions*, p. 44. See Tony Chafer, *The End of Empire in French West Africa: France's Successful Decolonization?* (New York: Berg, 2002).

11. Safran, *The French Polity*, p. 11. On the crisis in Algeria, see Martin S. Alexander and John F.V. Keiger, *France and the Algerian War, 1954–62: Strategy, Operations, and Diplomacy* (Portland, OR: Frank Cass, 2002). On de Gaulle, see Daniel Mahoney, *DeGaulle: Statesmanship, Grandeur, and Modern Democracy* (London, UK: Transaction Publishers, 2000). De Gaulle's autobiographical *The Complete War Memoirs of Charles de Gaulle* (New York: Carroll and Graf, 1998), is also worth noting.

12. Ambler, *The Government and Politics of France*, p. 13.

13. See the text of de Gaulle's Bayeux speech in Martin Harrison, ed., *French Politics* (Lexington, MA: DC Heath, 1969), pp. 24–28.

14. Safran, *The French Polity*, p. 59. See Cindy Skach, *Borrowing Constitutional Designs: Constitutional Law in Weimar Germany and the French Fifth Republic* (Princeton, NJ: Princeton University Press, 2005).

15. Roy C. Macridis, *French Politics in Transition* (Cambridge, MA: Winthrop, 1975), p. 6. See also David Scott Bell, *Presidential Power in the Fifth Republic France* (New York: Berg, 2000).

16. On the origins and drafting of the new constitution, see Nicholas Wahl and Stanley Hoffman, "The French Constitution of 1958," *American Political Science Review* 53 (1959): 332–382.

17. Suzanne Berger, *The French Political System* (New York: Random House, 1974), p. 126. Much of the material in this section, and all quotes unless otherwise noted, derive from Berger, pp. 126–131. See Nicholas Atkins, *The Fifth French Republic* (New York: Palgrave Macmillan, 2004).

18. See John A. Rohr, "French Constitutionalism and the Administrative State: A Comparative Textual Study," *Administration and Society* 24:2 (1992): 224–240.

19. Berger, *The French Political System*, p. 127. See also Vincent Wright and Andrew Knapp, *The Government and Politics of France* (New York: Routledge, 2006).

20. Henry Ehrmann, *Politics in France* (Boston, MA: Little, Brown, 1976), p. 267. See also Jean Chalaby, *The de Gaulle Presidency and the Media: Statism and Political Communications* (New York: Palgrave Macmillan, 2002).

21. Safran, *The French Polity*, p. 128. See also Robert Elgie, *The Changing French Political System* (Portland, OR: Frank Cass, 2000).

22. Leslie Derfler, *President and Parliament: A Short History of the French Presidency* (Boca Raton, FL: University Presses of Florida, 1983), p. 169.

23. Ambler, *The Government and Politics of France*, p. 126.

24. For the full text of the Constitution, see Pierce, *French Politics and Political Institutions*, pp. 227–254, or Ambler, *The Government and Politics of France*, p. 237–248.

25. John-Thor Dahlburg, "French Deliver a Yawn on Shorter Presidential Term," *Los Angeles Times*, September 25, 2000, available at *http://articles.latimes.com/2000/sep/25/news/mn-26504* (accessed May 2011).

26. Ehrmann, *Politics in France*, 268.

27. See de Gaulle's essay "Charles de Gaulle and the Presidency," in *French Politics*, ed. Harrison, pp. 48–54.

28. On the change to a five-year term of office, see Olivier Duhamel, *France's New Five-Year Presidential Term* (Washington, DC: Brookings Institution, 2001).

29. Olivier Duhamel, "France's New Five-Year Presidential Term," *Brookings*, March 1, 2011, available at *http://www.brookings.edu/articles/2001/03france_duhamel.aspx* (accessed May, 2011).

30. Ibid.

31. Ehrmann, *Politics in France*, 269. See also Michael S. Lewis-Beck, *The French Voter: Before and After the 2002 Elections* (New York: Palgrave Macmillan, 2004).

32. Ehrmann, *Politics in France*, pp. 270–272.

33. Carter, *The Government of France*, p. 81. See also Serge Berstein and Jean-Pierre Rioux, *The Pompidou Years, 1969–1974* (New York: Cambridge University Press, 2000).

34. Safran, *The French Polity*, p. 130; or Carter, *The Government of France*, p. 83.

35. See John Frears, "Cohabitation," in *France at the Polls*, ed. Penniman, pp. 228–236. See also David Scott Bell, *Francois Mitterand: A Political Biography* (Malden, MA: Polity, 2005).

36. A good description of this period can be found in Ian Derbyshire, *Politics in France: From Giscard to Mitterand* (London, UK: W & R Chambers, 1987), pp. 105–114.

37. See Christiane Gouaud, *La cohabitation* (Paris: Ellipses, 1996).

38. Carter, *The Government of France*, p. 75. See also Connie Doebele and Kevin King, *French Politics and the French Parliament* (West Lafayette, IN: C-SPAN Archives, 2003).

39. Carter, *The Government of France*, p. 75. See also Pierce, *French Politics and Political Institutions*, p. 87.

40. Pierce, *French Politics and Political Institutions*, pp. 78–79.

41. Philip E. Converse and Roy Pierce, *Political Representation in France* (Cambridge, MA: Harvard University Press, 1986), p. 533.

42. Carter, *The Government of France*, p. 72.

43. Pierce, *French Politics and Political Institutions*, p. 91.

44. Carter, *The Government of France*, p. 72. See also Pierce, *French Politics and Political Institutions*, p. 91.

45. Safran, *The French Polity*, pp. 171–172.

46. See Paul Smith, *A History of the French Senate* (Lewiston, NY: E. Mellen Press, 2005–2006).

47. Safran, *The French Polity*, p. 165.

48. See Alec Stone, "Where Judicial Politics Are Legislative Politics: The French Constitutional Council," *West European Politics* 15:3 (1992): 29–43; or Carter, *The Government of France*, p. 324.

49. Carter, *The Government of France*, pp. 32–33.

50. Berger, *The French Political System*, p. 57; or Pierce, *French Politics and Political Institutions*, p. 80.

51. Carter, *The Government of France*, p. 39. See Andrew Knapp, *Parties and the Party System in France: A Disconnected Democracy?* (New York: Palgrave Macmillan, 2004).

52. J.R. Frears, *Political Parties and Elections in the French Fifth Republic* (New York: St. Martin's Press, 1977), p. 12. See also Robert Elgie, *The Changing French Political System* (Portland, OR: Frank Cass, 2000); Ehrmann, *Politics in France*, pp. 223–224; David Scott Bell, *Parties and Democracy in France* (Brookfield, VT: Ashgate, 2000).

53. Frears, *Political Parties*, p.12. See D. L. Hanley, *Party, Society, and Government: Republican Democracy in France* (New York: Berghahn Books, 2002).

54. Safran, *The French Polity*, p. 68. See also Alistair Cole, Patrick Le Galès, and Jonah D. Levy, *Developments in French Politics 3* (New York: Palgrave, Macmillan, 2005).

55. D.L. Hanley, A.P. Kerr, and N.H. Waites, *Contemporary France: Politics and Society Since 1945* (Boston, MA: Routledge and Kegan Paul, 1979), p. 41. See also Berstein and Rioux, *The Pompidou Years, 1969–1974*.

56. J.R. Frears, *France in the Giscard Presidency* (London, UK: Allen and Unwin, 1981), p. 162. See also the volume edited by Vincent Wright, *Continuity and Change in France* (London, UK: Allen and Unwin, 1984), for a collection of essays offering a general description of the Giscard years.

57. A very good book (in French) about François Mitterand written before his candidacy is that by C.L. Manceron and B. Pingaud, *Francois Mitterand: L'Homme, Les Idees, Le Programme* (Paris, France: Flammarion, 1981).

58. Michael Keating and Paul Hainsworth, *Decentralisation and Change in Contemporary France* (Brookfield, VT: Gower, 1986), p. 15.

59. Maurice Larkin, *France Since the Popular Front: Government and People, 1936–1986* (Oxford, UK: Clarendon Press, 1988), p. 356; and John Tuppen, *France Under Recession: 1981–1986* (Albany, NY: State University of New York Press, 1988), p. 1.

60. Tuppen, *France Under Recession*, p. 257.

61. Sonia Mezey and Michael Newman, eds., *Mitterand's France* (London, UK: Croom Helm, 1987), p. 4.

62. See David Hanley, *Party, Society, Government: Republican Democracy in France* (Oxford, UK: Berghan Press, 2001).

63. A very good survey of French parties is that edited by David S. Bell, *Contemporary French Political Parties* (New York: St. Martin's Press, 1981). See also Richard Gunther, Jose Montero, and Juan Linz, *Political Parties: Old Concepts and New Challenges* (New York: Oxford University Press, 2002).

64. See N. Mayer and Pascal Perrimeau, "Why Do They Vote for Le Pen?" *European Journal of Political Research* 22:1 (1992): 123–137; on Marine Le Pen, see the article in *The Economist* titled "France's Far Right: The Rise of Marine Le Pen," *The Economist*, March 9, 2011, available at *http://www.economist.com/blogs/dailychart/2011/03/frances_far_right* (accessed May 2011).

65. See the discussion of the National Front's performance in the 2002 legislative elections in the Inter-Parliamentary Union's analysis, "France–Last Election,"

http://www.ipu.org/parline-e/reports/2113_E.htm. See also Roland Cayrol, *The 2002 French Elections: A Drama in Five Acts* (Washington, DC: Brookings Institution, 2002).

66. The exact operation of this P.R. system can be found in John Frears, "The 1986 Parliamentary Elections," in *France At the Polls, 1981 and 1986: Three National Elections*, ed. Howard Penniman (Durham, NC: Duke University Press, 1988), pp. 211–214.

67. A very good article on the French Communist party is that by George Ross, "Party Decline and Changing Party Systems: France and the French Communist Party," *Comparative Politics* 25, no.1 (1992): 43–62.

68. Government of France, France Diplomatie, "The French Political System: From 'Cohabitation' to a Five-Year Term," *http://www.diplomatie.gouv.fr/en/france_159/ institutions-and-politics_6814/the-french-political-system_6827/from-cohabitation-... to-five-year-term_12291.html* (accessed May 2011).

69. See Inter-Parliamentary Union, "France: Elections," *http://www.ipu.org/parline-e/ reports/2113_B.htm*.

70. Unless turnout is very small and the candidate has received the votes of less than one-quarter of all of the registered electors.

71. See the most recent electoral data from the Assemblée Nationale, "Élections Législatives des 10 et 17 Juin 2007," *http://www.assemblee-nationale.fr/elections/2007/resultats/ LDD1_NOM.csv.asp* (accessed May 2011).

72. Frears, *Political Parties*, p. 224. Each department has a council, called the *conseil general*, which consists of from twenty to seventy members who are elected from subdivisions of the department called *cantons*. Elections of departmental councillors (*conseillers generaux*) are called *elections cantonales*. Each city and town in France has a municipal council. Election of municipal councillors are called *elections municipales*. See Pierce, *French Politics and Political Institutions*, p. 75.

73. Pierce, *French Politics and Political Institutions*, p. 75.

The German Political System

The chancellor is the leader of a parliamentary majority in Germany. Here Chancellor Angela Merkel attends a European Union summit in Brussels, Belgium, in 2010.

Thierry Tronnel/Corbis

THE GERMAN CONSTITUTIONAL SYSTEM

When World War II ended in 1945, the four Occupying Powers (the United States, the United Kingdom, France, and the Soviet Union) agreed to work toward a reunification of occupied Germany. By December 1947, however, at the London Conference of the Council of Foreign Ministers of the four Occupying Powers, it was clear to the British, French, and Americans that the Soviet Union was not prepared to move to a reunification of Germany. Accordingly, the three western powers decided to move forward and attempt to restore normal civilian government on their own.

Many German leaders were concerned about this; they believed that such an action would result in a permanent division of Germany, with the Soviet Union controlling the eastern quarter of the country. Many West German leaders opposed the creation of a West German constitution until such time as Germany was reunified. After some discussion, a compromise was reached: The West Germans agreed to construct a "temporary" constitution until Germany was reunified.

GERMANY

Total Area (rank)	359,022 sq km (62)
Population (rank)	81,471,834 (16)
Population Growth Rate (rank)	−0.208% (212)
Urban Population	74%
Life Expectancy at Birth (total population) (rank)	80.07 (27)
Literacy	99%
Government Type	Federal Republic
Legal System	Civil Law
Head of Government	Chancellor Angela Merkel
Chief of State	President Christian Wulff
Gross Domestic Product (GDP)	$3.32 trillion
GDP Per Capita (rank)	$35,700 (33)
GDP Real Growth Rate (rank)	3.5% (111)
Unemployment Rate (rank)	7.4% (78)

GERMANY

In September 1948, the Parliamentary Council met in Bonn and drafted a document called the **Basic Law** for the three Western Occupied Zones. According to its preamble, the Basic Law was to "give a new order to political life for a transitional period," and was not only for the West Germans, but also "on behalf of those Germans to whom participation was denied." Article 146 stated that the Basic Law "shall cease to be in force on the day on which a constitution adopted by a free decision of the German people comes into force."[1] The document was drafted by representatives of the three western Occupying Powers and West German leaders acceptable to the Occupying Powers.

The construction of the Basic Law was finally completed in May 1949. To avoid the appearance of establishing a permanent political system, it was never submitted to the West German people for ratification. Rather, it was submitted to legislatures of the West German states, the **Länder**, winning the endorsement of all of the West German Länder except Bavaria.[2] The West German Basic Law was finally approved on May 23, 1949. And, just as many of the West German leaders had feared, the German Democratic Republic (East Germany) came into existence less than a month later.

Just over forty-one years later, on October 2, 1990, East and West Germany reunited after four decades of partition. The early years of the separation included a blockade of West Berlin; the most dramatic sign of the partition was a wall dividing the East and West parts of the city of Berlin. The reunited Germany, now the most populous and economically powerful nation in the European Community, adopted West Germany's constitutional system; the highly centralized political structures of communist East Germany disappeared. Many Germans were excited about the prospect of reuniting East and West Germany, but at the same time they were concerned about the costs of reunification.[3] In fact, among the challenges facing the nation was the task of bringing the standard of living of Germans in the former German Democratic Republic (East Germany) up to that of the Federal Republic of Germany (West Germany). They also feared that their reunification and their new role as the largest and most economically powerful European nation might engender concern among other European nations.

Many details can be pointed out that distinguish the 1949 Basic Law from the 1919 Constitution of the **Weimar Republic**—the parliamentary republic established in Germany in 1919 to replace the imperial government that preceded it. One of the major perceived shortcomings of the Weimar Constitution was that it promoted internal discord through a number of supposedly democratic structures, especially the power of the presidency and the mass plebiscites that were so frequently utilized. The Basic Law sought, through a number of political structures, to remedy the defect of "too much democracy"[4] in the earlier regime.

The Basic Law sought to modify German direct democracy, while at the same time emphasizing the protection of human rights, individual liberty, and division of powers in a federal structure. Except in extraordinary circumstances, elections would be held every four years. Moreover, the public would vote *only* for representatives to the lower house of the legislature. The president, the chancellor, and members of the upper legislative house would all be chosen indirectly. Structures were established to make it more difficult to overthrow chancellors—the chief executive in Germany.

Although the Basic Law sought to "dampen" many of the (perceived) "overly democratic" structures of the Weimar regime, it did *not* intend to restrict individual freedoms or rights. To the contrary: Articles of the Basic Law that deal with civil and political rights (Articles 1–19) are given a "preferred position"; as one scholar noted, "for the first time in German history, there were no loopholes left in the protection of individual rights."[5] Both Article 1, which focuses on human dignity, and Article 20, which guarantees Germans the "right to resist any person or persons seeking to abolish [the German] constitutional order," *cannot* be amended. Other articles dealing with civil and political rights cannot be suspended except after a ruling by the Federal Constitutional Court (Article 18).[6] The Basic Law can be amended by a two-thirds majority vote of each house of the federal legislature (subject to the limitations mentioned above), and "has been altered more often in twenty-five years than the American [Constitution] in two hundred."[7]

Germany today has five key constitutional bodies that are significant in the political process. These are the Federal Constitutional Court, the Federal President, the Federal Cabinet and Chancellor, and the two chambers of the legislature, the **Bundestag** and the **Bundesrat**. After a brief discussion of German federalism we shall discuss each of these institutions here.

FEDERALISM IN GERMANY

Germany is the only major state of Western Europe that has a federal rather than a unitary political structure.[8] However, the fact that Germany is a federal system should not be a surprise. This is so for several reasons, including (1) a general fear of centralized government that developed during the Nazi period; (2) a history of federal and confederal relations in Germany, with the exception of the centralized Nazi era, going back to 1871 when the German Reich was formed and "composed of twenty-five 'historic' German states that 'voluntarily' entered into a federation";[9] and (3) the pattern of administration of the Occupying Powers from 1945 to 1949 that led to the creation of seven of today's sixteen states or Länder (the singular of *Länder* is *Land*). Three of today's Länder existed as separate political entities prior to 1945.[10] German federalism was "a device which perpetuated into the era of a single national state the particularist habits and traditions of the dynasties and estates which were dominant in the separate states of Germany."[11]

The federal nature of Germany has resulted in wide disparities among the intermediate levels of political organization. The Länder vary greatly in size

TABLE 11.1

Länder in the German Federal System

Land	Area (Sq. Mi.)	Population	Bundesrat (upper chamber) Seats	Parties in Land (State) Government
Baden-Wurttemberg	13,739	10.75 million	6	CDU/FDP
Bavaria	27,114	12.53 million	6	CSU/FDP
Berlin [a]	184	3.45 million	4	SPD/Die Linke
Brandenberg [a]	10,036	2.51 million	4	SPD/Die Linke
Bremen	155	0.66 million	3	SPD/Greens
Hamburg	287	1.78 million	3	SPD
Hesse	8,113	6.07 million	5	CDU/FDP
Lower Saxony	18,127	7.92 million	6	SPD/CDU
Mecklenburg-Vorpommern[a]	8,685	1.64 million	3	CDU/FDP
N.Rhine-Westphalia	13,084	17.85 million	6	SPD/Greens
Rhineland-Palatinate	7,621	4.01 million	4	SPD
Saarland	987	1.02 million	3	CDU/FDP/Greens
Saxony[a]	6,562	4.15 million	4	CDU/FDP
Saxony-Anhalt[a]	9,650	2.34 million	4	CDU/SPD
Schleswig-Holstein	6,018	2.83 million	4	CDU/FDP
Thuringia [a]	5,983	2.24 million	4	CDU/SPD

[a]Formerly part of the German Democratic Republic.

Sources: Most recent data come from the Government of Germany web page dealing with the Bundesrat, http://www.bundesrat.de/cln_179/nn_11400/EN/organisation-en/stimmenverteilung-en/stimmenverteilung-en-node.html?__nnn=true (accessed April 2011).

and in population, as illustrated in Table 11.1, and these disparities increased significantly following unification of East and West Germany in 1990.[12]

There are both advantages and disadvantages to the German style of federalism. The drawbacks are that policy can vary from state to state, providing unequal opportunities across the nation. It is a complex system, resulting in a situation in which "it is far from easy for the citizen to form an accurate picture of the seventeen different decision-making centres in the Federal Republic of Germany.[13] It is time consuming, requiring more discussion between government actors in the process of making policy. And, it is more costly, because there is a required level of redundancy that doesn't exist in unitary systems. The advantages of federalism are that political power is divided, thus making it easier to protect against abuse of power. It is more democratic. It offers the public more choices where the selection of leadership is concerned. And, it "guarantees a multiplicity of centres of economic, political and cultural influence."[14]

The German federal system, often referred to as an example of "cooperative federalism,"[15] gives the intermediate-level components of the regime, the Länder, a great deal of political power—far more power than is found in American states, for example. Article 28 of the Basic Law requires that the Länder "conform to the principles of republican, democratic, and social government based on the rule of law," but leaves questions of specific governmental structure up to the state governments. The state of Bavaria has a bicameral legislature; all others have unicameral legislatures. States are allowed to determine their own electoral structures.

It can be suggested that a major reason that the Länder are as powerful as they are in the German political system is due to the different types of legislation discussed in the Basic Law. The Basic Law essentially balances centralized and decentralized powers by distinguishing among *three different types* of legislation.

Article 73 gives exclusive *federal jurisdiction* over legislation involving foreign affairs, citizenship, money, customs, federal railroads, telecommunications, federal employees, copyrights, and cooperation of the central government and Länder in criminal matters. The *Länder* are given **residual** powers in Article 70: "The Länder shall have the right to legislate insofar as this Basic Law does not confer legislative power on the Federation." Finally, Articles 72 and 74 list twenty-three specific areas in which jurisdiction is **concurrent**: The Länder may legislate in these areas "as long as, and to the extent that, the Federation does not exercise its right to legislate." Among areas of concurrent jurisdiction are civil and criminal law; registration of births, deaths, marriages; issues related to public welfare; labor laws; regulation of education; road traffic and highways; and some health-related matters.[16]

The Länder have maintained a great deal of influence in the German political system for several reasons. One is that there are many legislative powers left residually to them. Another is the constitutional provision that stimulates **cooperative federalism** by requiring that the states administer most national policy, although this does not include foreign affairs and defense matters.[17]

Certainly another factor that must be considered is the political role of the upper house of the federal parliament, the Bundesrat. This is a structure that we will discuss later in this chapter; here we mention that all deputies in the upper house are chosen by the Länder legislatures, not the general electorate, and are correspondingly perceived to represent the Länder governments.

Legislation within the federal jurisdiction that affects the Länder, even if the Länder themselves cannot legislate on the issue, must be approved by a majority of the Land representatives in the Bundesrat, or it does not become law. The Länder, therefore, have *sole* jurisdiction through the residual clause of Article 70 over any subject matter not given to the federal government. They have *concurrent* (shared) jurisdiction over a number of subject matters in areas specified by the Basic Law. Even in the areas that are described in the Basic Law as exclusively federal jurisdiction, the Länder are not without influence, because issues that might affect them must be approved by their representatives in the Bundesrat.

The Constitutional Court

Another structure in Germany that reinforces the federal nature of the polity is the Constitutional Court. Unlike the Supreme Court of the United States, the Constitutional Court of Germany is not a court of appeal for either criminal or civil cases. Rather, the Constitutional Court.

> is a watchdog for the Basic Law. Its mission is not only to defend individual liberty and civil rights but to protect the legislature from the courts applying laws incorrectly. The Court is the final arbiter of disputes between the federal executive and the Bundes tag, between the federal government and the states, between the different states, and between other courts.[18]

On a number of occasions over the years, the Constitutional Court has ruled against the federal government, supporting an interpretation of the Basic Law favoring expansion of the powers of the Länder.[19]

Germany has an independent judicial structure reflecting its federal character, with (in addition to the Constitutional Court) a High Court of Justice and four systems of courts with jurisdictions in administrative, financial, labor, and social issues. While all courts have the ability to review the constitutionality of government action and legislation in their particular areas of jurisdiction, only the Constitutional Court can declare legislation unconstitutional. If the other courts find a constitutional problem, they must refer the case to the Constitutional Court.

EXECUTIVE STRUCTURES

The Parliamentary Council that drafted the Basic Law in 1948 felt that the institution of the presidency in the Weimar period was, to some degree, responsible for the weakness of the chancellor at that time, and thus responsible for the use of "emergency rule" that led to the rise of Hitler and the corresponding abuse of law. Thus, when the members of the Parliamentary Council met in 1948 to construct new political structures, there was little sense that a strong head of state was necessary. Their goals with respect to executive powers were straightforward, and dealt with a "neutralized" presidency, a strengthened chancellorship, and controls on Parliament.[20]

First, members of the Parliamentary Council believed that the president should be "neutralized," which meant that she or he should have few, if any, significant political powers, and should play the figurehead role in office that the constitutional monarchs of Britain or Scandinavia play. This meant that the presidency should be an explicitly nonpolitical office.

Second, members felt that the position of the head of the government, the **chancellor**, should be strengthened. The chancellor should not be as vulnerable to short-term political pressures as he had been in the Weimar regime, and his or her base of power should be more secure.[21]

Third, members of the council wanted to design a structure in which there would be "penalties" imposed on the legislature if it started to use its power in relation to the chancellor "irresponsibly." "Irresponsibly" in this case refers to the type of behavior observed in the Weimar regime in which several small parties would get together to vote no confidence in a chancellor and subsequently not be able to agree on a replacement. The "penalty" structure designed was part of a "constructive" vote of no confidence, described below.

The Federal President

Articles 54 through 61 of the Basic Law deal with the office of the federal president. The president is elected by a Federal Convention made up of members of the Bundestag (the lower house of the federal legislature) and an equal number of members elected by the legislative assemblies of the states. The vote in the special convention must be by an absolute majority of the delegates on the first two ballots; if no one wins a majority on either of the first two ballots, the candidate receiving a plurality on the third ballot is elected.

The federal president has very few real powers. Orders and decrees of the federal president *must* be countersigned by the federal chancellor or an appropriate federal minister to be valid. This is significantly different from the relationship between most heads of state and their chief executives and cabinets: In most systems, legally (*de jure*) the head of state has a great deal of power, although actually (*de facto*) it is recognized that the head of state will only act "on the advice" of his or her chief executive. In Germany, the head of state is *legally* (*de jure*) restricted to the passive role. That the head of state must have all orders and decrees countersigned is a legal acknowledgment of his or her lack of power. The two exceptions to the countersignature rule are (1) the appointment and dismissal of the federal chancellor and (2) the dissolution of the Bundestag, both of which we will address later.

The president appoints and dismisses ministers, federal judges, and civil servants, promulgates laws, represents the federation in its international relations, and concludes treaties, all "on the advice," of course, of the federal chancellor. Above all, the federal president is expected to be "above politics," to be nonpartisan, and to represent Germany to the world.

The Chancellor and the Cabinet

What is officially referred to as "the Federal Government" in Germany refers to the federal chancellor and his or her cabinet (the first female chancellor, Angela Merkel, was elected in 2005).[22] The present cabinet is composed of the chancellor and fifteen ministers.[23] The chief executive in Germany is the chancellor, and it is the chief executive, not the head of state, to whom we must turn to see the real locus of power in the political arena. The chancellor "has been seen as the keystone of the political system, the guarantee of stability and coherence in the democratic structure of German politics."[24] The chancellor is more powerful than most parliamentary chief executives, primarily because the chancellor has greater job security than most. This has led the German system to be referred to as "Chancellor Democracy."[25]

Elections are held for the Bundestag at least every four years. According to Article 39, "The Bundestag...term shall end four years after its first meeting or on its dissolution. The new election shall be held during the last three months of the term or within sixty days after dissolution." The Bundestag must assemble within thirty days after the election. The Bundestag determines the termination and resumption of its meetings, but may be called into special session by the federal president, the federal chancellor, or one-third of the Bundestag members.

After the elections of the members of the Bundestag, the president proposes a chancellor-designate, which in the German case has either been the leader of the majority party in the Bundestag (in 1957) or has been the leader of the apparent majority coalition. Article 63 of the Basic Law states that "the Federal Chancellor shall be elected, without debate, by the Bundestag upon the proposal of the Federal President."

If the federal president makes a designation not supported by a majority in the Bundestag, the Bundestag has the power to reject the candidate. If the person proposed by the president is not supported by a majority, "the Bundestag may elect within fourteen days of the ballot a Federal Chancellor by more than one-half of its members."

If the Bundestag rejects the federal president's nominee, and cannot agree on majority support for its *own* candidate within fourteen days, a new vote in the Bundestag must be taken "without delay, in which the person obtaining the largest number of votes shall be elected." If this person has been elected by a majority of Bundestag members, the federal president *must* appoint him or her within seven days. If this person has *not* been elected by a majority, but only by a plurality, the federal president must *either* appoint him or her within seven days, or else dissolve the Bundestag and call for new elections within sixty days. (To date, all chancellors have been those approved as initial presidential designations, indicating the degree to which federal presidents make only "realistic" nominations.)

Once a chancellor has been confirmed by the Bundestag, it is *extremely* hard to fire that individual. One of the major distinctions between presidential and parliamentary systems that we observed earlier in this text was in respect to tenure, or job security: Presidents generally have fixed terms of office, whereas prime ministers can lose their positions at any time through votes of no confidence by the legislature. The Parliamentary Council of 1948 did not want the chancellor to be in a vulnerable position and developed a new political structure to help protect the chancellor's job security: the **positive** or **constructive vote of no confidence.**

The positive vote of no confidence is described in Article 67 of the Basic Law:

> The Bundestag can express its lack of confidence in the Federal Chancellor only by electing a successor with the majority of its members and by requesting the Federal President to dismiss the Federal Chancellor.

The Federal President must comply with this request and appoint the person elected.... Forty-eight hours must elapse between the motion and the vote thereon.

In short, having a majority of members of the Bundestag express their lack of confidence in a chancellor is *not* sufficient to dismiss that chancellor; they must at the same time (actually, prior to that time) agree on a successor that a majority of the Bundestag can support. This can be a very difficult task, and has helped the federal chancellor weather strife and complaints that might have much more serious consequences—such as causing the Government to fall—in other political systems.

This positive vote of no confidence has led some to refer to the German political system as a "semi-parliamentary system" rather than a parliamentary system, arguing that a "genuine parliamentary system, in the sense of enforceable responsibility of the executive to parliament, existed in Germany only as long as the Weimar Constitution functioned."[26] The difficulty of obtaining a positive vote of no confidence is so great that the Government is virtually no longer responsible to the Bundestag.

In September 1982, for the first time, such an unusual incident did arise. After constant feuding within the Social Democratic/Free Democratic party coalition, the Free Democratic Party (FDP) minor partner decided to withdraw its support for the Government of Helmut Schmidt.[27] In itself, this guaranteed only a *simple* **vote of no confidence**, and not a *positive* vote of no confidence. After consultation, however, it became clear that the leader of the more conservative Christian Democratic/Christian Socialist Union (CDU/CSU) bloc—Helmut Kohl—was willing to make policy concessions to the Free Democrats that convinced the FDP deputies to join with the CDU/CSU deputies in a positive vote of no confidence, voting Helmut Schmidt out and Helmut Kohl in.[28]

In addition to the unlikelihood that the chancellor will be thrown out of office, the chancellor has the added leverage of being able to *use* a vote of confidence as a weapon. Article 68 states that if the chancellor *asks* for a vote of confidence, and does not receive it, he or she can ask for a dissolution of the Bundestag and call for new elections. This has been used in the past by chancellors either to (1) push a piece of legislation through the Bundestag that might have difficulty otherwise by referring to the vote on the bill as a question of confidence, or (2) bring about an early dissolution for electoral gain. Newly-selected chancellor Kohl used this vehicle after his accession to the chancellorship in September 1982 to seek a popular mandate from the German people, since his party had not won a majority with him as leader. He received the mandate he sought in the March 1983 elections.

Unlike other political systems, in Germany the head of state does not possess the legal power to dissolve the Bundestag at will. (We did point out, of course, that although most heads of state have this power legally, they really only exercise it "on the advice" of their chief executives. In Germany the head of state does not even possess the power merely legally.) The federal president can dissolve the Bundestag only under one of two circumstances: first, if her nominee for chancellor is not approved by the Bundestag, and the chancellor eventually chosen by the Bundestag does not have majority support and is not acceptable to the president; and second, if the chancellor requests a vote of confidence in the Bundestag, and the Bundestag fails to give him or her one, *and* the chancellor subsequently requests a dissolution.

Chancellors who know that elections must be held within the next year or so, and who see their popularity as being very high, have been known to use the "confidence mechanism" to secure an early dissolution. They do this by asking for a vote of confidence *and instructing their own party supporters to vote against them*, thereby insuring that they will lose the vote of confidence. (Note, however, that this is not the same as a positive vote of no confidence; the Bundestag has not agreed on a replacement for the chancellor.) The chancellor's supporters will go along with this, of course, since it is in their own interest to have elections held at a time when their party and their leader are both popular.

We can see, then, that the German chancellor is stronger in her political system than virtually any other parliamentary chief executive we can imagine. The chancellor not only has the usual tool of party discipline at her disposal, but she *also* has the resources of (1) being extraordinarily difficult to dismiss and (2) being able to threaten the legislature with dissolution if it is not cooperative.

Ministers in the Federal Republic share in collective responsibility, as do ministers in other parliamentary regimes, but they have more individual authority because they tend to manage their individual departments "on their own responsibility," with less collective input than in many other parliamentary systems. The cabinet tends to be smaller than in many nations; recent cabinets consisted of fifteen or sixteen members. The major limitation on the cabinet as a policymaker has been that governments have involved coalitions, and in many instances the coalition partners have not been able to agree in cabinet and "many policy issues have to be prepared outside the Government."[29]

LEGISLATIVE STRUCTURES

Several aspects of the federal legislature have already been introduced. We have seen in earlier chapters of this book how the members of the Bundestag (the "federal diet," the lower house of the legislature) are elected.[30] We have seen the relationship between the Bundestag and the federal chancellor; the chancellor is dominant and is beyond the normal reach of the legislature in terms of the usual meaning of "responsible government." We also saw in a very introductory manner that the Bundesrat (the "federal council," the upper house of the legislature) is important in the federal structure of the regime, although some discussions of German politics do not consider it a significant chamber of the legislature since it is not elected.

The Bundestag, the Lower House

The Bundestag is perceived in the Basic Law to be the center of legislative activity in German politics. The German political system is essentially designed to be managed by the chancellor and her cabinet. The job of the Bundestag is to choose its leader; once this is accomplished, it is expected that the Bundestag will permit itself to be led by the Government. The difficulty of the passage of a *positive vote of no confidence* is an indication that the framers of the Basic Law did not *intend* for the Bundestag to exercise its role as the ultimate authority in the regime very often.

The Bundestag is today composed of 622 members. The Bundestag nominally has 598 members, of whom 299 are elected in fixed single-member districts, and another 299 are elected by statewide party proportional lists. The complex electoral system also allows for some *extra* seats to be created—called "overhang" seats, and in the current Bundestag there are 24 of these, bringing the total to 622 members.

The Bundesrat, the Upper House

Article 50 of the Basic Law indicates that "the Länder shall participate through the Bundesrat in the legislation and administration of the Federation." The Bundesrat, the upper house, is important insofar as the federal distribution of powers is concerned. As seen in Table 11.1, the sixteen Länder each have either three, four, five, or six deputies in the Bundesrat, depending upon their size, yielding a total of 69 members. A majority in the Bundesrat is 35 votes. Article 51 of the Basic Law indicates that every Land shall have at least three seats in the Bundesrat; Länder with between 2 and 6 million inhabitants shall have four, Länder with between 6 and 7 million inhabitants shall have five, and Länder with more than 7 million inhabitants shall have six votes.[31]

This difference in the size of Bundesrat delegations, however, does not alleviate disproportionate representation. To take two examples, the city-state of Bremen (with three delegates) has one Bundesrat representative for each 220,000 people, and the state of North Rhine-Westphalia (with six delegates) has one Bundesrat representative for each three million people.

The Land governments (the legislative assemblies of the Länder) choose their three, four, five, or six delegates to the Bundesrat. Since the Bundesrat delegates are chosen by the Land governments, they will all be of the political party that controls the majority in the Land legislature. Bundesrat delegates from a Land *must* cast their votes as a bloc; they may not divide their three, four, five, or six votes.

The role of the Bundesrat in the German legislative process varies, depending upon the specific piece of legislation involved. According to the Basic Law (Articles 77 and 78), bills intended to become federal laws require adoption by the Bundestag. Bills can be introduced in the Bundestag by either the Bundesrat, the Bundestag, or the federal Government (the chancellor and the cabinet).

The Legislative Process

The legislative process is complex.[32] All bills begin their legislative journey in the Bundestag. Bills introduced by the Bundesrat (a small number) go first to the Government for comment before being introduced in the Bundestag.[33] Bills being introduced by the Government (more than half of the total)[34] go first to the Bundesrat for comment before being introduced in the Bundestag. In each of these cases, *scrutiny* is implied, not *veto* power; the goal is for government actors to let other government actors know what is happening. Bills starting in the Bundestag (almost half) are simply introduced there; they do not go to either the Bundesrat or the Government for advance scrutiny. Currently almost 50 percent of all laws passed require the approval of the Bundesrat.[35]

Once bills are introduced, they first go through the "Bundestag phase" of the legislative process, including a first reading, a vote in the Bundestag, assignment to a committee, followed by a committee report, a second reading and vote in the Bundestag covering specific details of the proposed legislation, followed by a third reading and vote.

If a bill passes the Bundestag phase of the legislative process—and many do not—it goes to the Bundesrat. This is the first opportunity for the Bundesrat to see bills that were initiated in the Bundestag (other bills either were initiated in the Bundesrat or were initiated in the Government and first sent to the Bundesrat for review and comment prior to going to the Bundestag). The Bundesrat can either approve the bill, in which case it is sent on to the federal president to sign and to the chancellor or appropriate minister to countersign, or within two weeks the Bundesrat may ask for a meeting of the Bundestag-Bundesrat Mediation Committee to try to find a compromise.

At this point an important distinction must be made. Bills that "affect the Länder" *require the approval* of the Bundesrat: It has an *absolute veto* over this kind of legislation; if it doesn't approve, the bills don't pass.[36] Bills that do not directly affect the Länder—for example, questions dealing with foreign policy—do not require Bundesrat approval; over these bills the Bundesrat has only a *suspensory veto*.

In cases over which the Bundesrat has an absolute veto, and in which it does not approve of the Bundestag bill, a compromise must be reached by the Mediation Committee and must be approved by both houses before it can be handed down as law. Failing this, the bill does not become law. Laws that affect the interests of the states are called "consent bills" because they cannot come into force unless the Bundesrat explicitly consents to them. "Objection bills" are bills that can come into effect over the objection of the Bundesrat because they do not directly affect the interests of the states.[37]

In cases over which the Bundesrat does *not* have an absolute veto, and in which the Bundesrat does not approve of the Bundestag bill,

> it may enter a suspensive veto, but only after an effort at compromise through the Mediation Committee has been made.... If the Bundesrat enters its objection by a vote of a majority of its members, then the

Bundestag can override it by the same majority; if the Bundesrat has entered its objections by a vote of two-thirds of its members, it can only be overridden in the Bundestag by a vote of two-thirds of the Members present, but these two-thirds must also constitute at least a majority of the total membership. If the Bundesrat fails to act within the prescribed time limits, bills which do not specifically require its approval are ready for promulgation.[38]

The structure of the Mediation Committee is modeled after the conference committee of the U. S. Congress. Members are appointed from *each* house of the legislature. Unlike the American conference committee, however, which is only a temporary political structure and which is created *de novo* for each bill over which a compromise is necessary, the Mediation Committee is a standing committee—permanent for the life of the legislature. It is composed of Bundesrat members (one from each Land) and Bundestag members, divided proportionally to reflect party distribution in that house. The Bundesrat, then, while not having an absolute veto in all cases, as is the case with the United States Senate, is a reasonably powerful upper house.

Over the years the Bundesrat's veto power has expanded to include a substantial proportion of all federal legislation. To some degree this expansion has occurred through judicial decisions. Article 84 of the Basic Law gave the states the task of administering much federal legislation; the states argued before the courts—successfully—that since they had to *administer* the law, they were *affected by* the law, and accordingly the Bundesrat should have absolute veto power. Accordingly, states currently argue that even if a law affects them only because they must administer it, the entire law may be vetoed by the Bundesrat in the legislative process.

POLITICAL PARTIES AND ELECTIONS
The Electoral Process

Germany is a political system with many political parties, but one that has been dominated by just a few parties over the last sixty years;[39] the system has evolved since the 1949 election to become a two-coalition, if not a two-party, system. In the elections of October 5, 1980, although twenty political parties appeared on West German ballots, the five major parties (CDU, CSU, FDP, SPD, Greens) won 99.5 percent of the votes; in the March 6, 1983, elections, the five major parties again won 99.5 percent of the votes; in the January 1987 elections, the five major parties won 98.7 percent of the votes; in the December 1990 election—the first election after unification—these five parties won 92.2 percent of the votes.[40] In the October 1994 election, these five parties won 91.1 percent of the total votes, in September of 1998 they won 88.9 percent of the total, in September of 2002 they won 93 percent of the total, in September of 2005 the five parties won 87.3 percent of the votes, and in the 2009 election they won almost 90 percent of the total, because a new party ("The Left") appeared and won 11 percent of the votes.[41] The reasons for this are complex, and to explain the pattern of the parties' election returns over the years we must know something of the manner in which the German electoral system operates.

In 1949, at the time of the creation of the Federal Republic, each citizen voted only once in each election. This system was changed in 1953 when a second vote for each citizen in each election was added.[42] When Germans go to the polls, they receive a ballot with two columns, as illustrated on page 279. In the left-hand column, known as the "first vote," the citizen votes directly for a candidate who has been nominated by a local political party organization (there are no primary elections in Germany), in a single-member-district, plurality voting electoral framework. This is sometimes referred to as the **constituency vote.** Germany is now divided into 299 single-member districts[43] from which deputies are selected by simple plurality margins: Whichever candidate in a district receives the most votes wins. If two or more candidates receive the same number of votes, the returning officer (the official in charge of administering the election) for the electoral district draws lots to decide the winner. (We should note that this has never happened yet.)

In the right-hand column the citizen casts a "second vote" for a political party, not a candidate, in a proportional representation electoral competition. Parties receive seats on the basis of the percentage of votes they receive in the election. At least another 299 deputies are elected to the Bundestag through this electoral route, bringing the total number of seats in the Bundestag to at least 598. An illustration of a ballot for Bundestag elections is found in Figure 11.1.

Some argue that the second ballot is in many ways more important than the first, "direct," ballot, because it is the second ballot that determines the final proportion of parliamentary seats that each party will receive in the Bundestag. In each Land, every party is entitled to the number of seats that corresponds to its share of the second votes. The number of "district" seats is subtracted from the total number of seats due to the party on the basis of its performance in the proportional representation elections, determining the number of "at large" seats the party will receive. For example, if a party wins 25 percent of the vote on the proportional ballot—thus earning a total of 150 seats in the new Bundestag (25 percent of 598 total "normal" official seats available yields 164 seats)—and it wins 70 district seats, it will be awarded 80 at-large seats to bring its total to the percentage it earned in the election. Individual candidates will be selected, in order, from party lists that have already been filed with the government.

There may, however, be more than the "normal" 598 seats elected to the Bundestag. Indeed, as we noted earlier, today there are 622 members. What are called "overhang mandates" are awarded when parties win more seats on the first ballot in the constituencies than they are entitled to according to the "second vote" proportions. In the 1994 election, sixteen

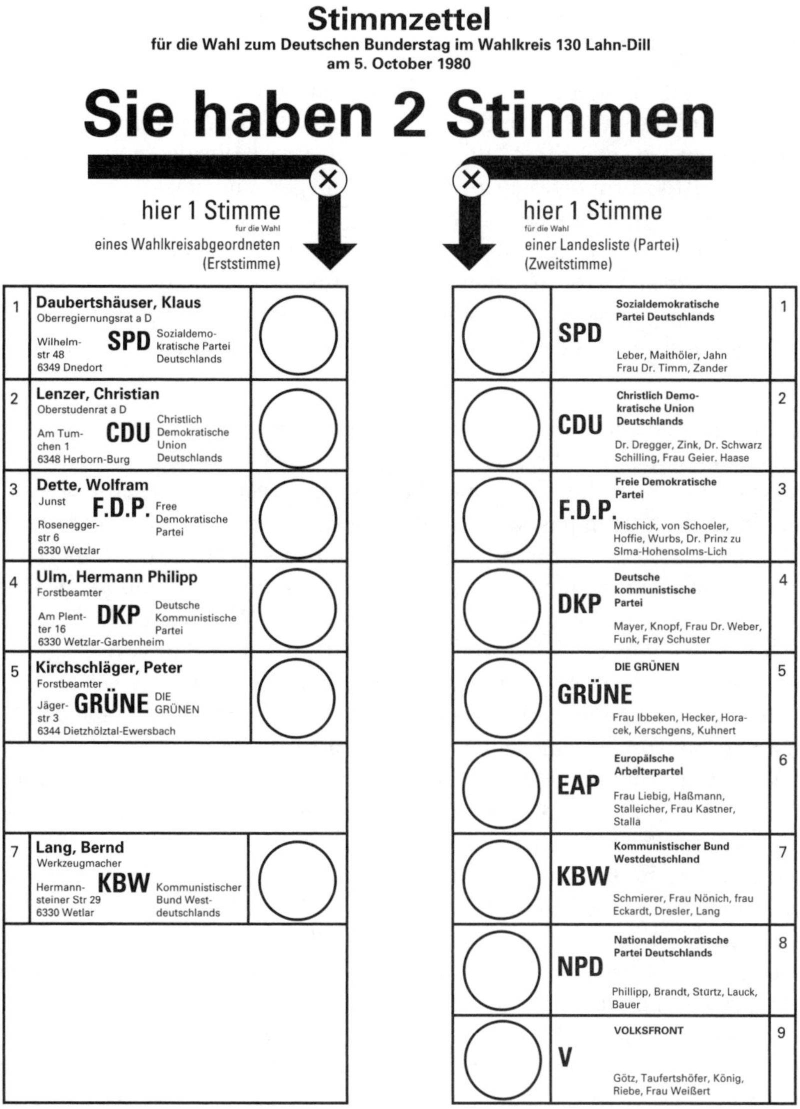

Stimmzettel
**für die Wahl zum Deutschen Bunderstag im Wahlkreis 130 Lahn-Dill
am 5. October 1980**

Sie haben 2 Stimmen

hier 1 Stimme	hier 1 Stimme
fur die Wahl	für die Wahl
eines Wahlkreisabgeordneten	einer Landesliste (Partei)
(Erststimme)	(Zweitstimme)

Erststimme (left column):

1	Daubertshäuser, Klaus — Oberregierungsrat a D — Wilhelmstr 48, 6349 Dnedort — **SPD** Sozialdemokratische Partei Deutschlands	◯
2	Lenzer, Christian — Oberstudenrat a D — Am Tumchen 1, 6348 Herborn-Burg — **CDU** Christlich Demokratische Union Deutschlands	◯
3	Dette, Wolfram — Junst — Roseneggerstr 6, 6330 Wetzlar — **F.D.P.** Free Demokratische Partei	◯
4	Ulm, Hermann Philipp — Forstbeamter — Am Plentter 16, 6330 Wetzlar-Garbenheim — **DKP** Deutsche Kommunistische Partei	◯
5	Kirchschläger, Peter — Forstbeamter — Jägerstr 3, 6344 Dietzhölztal-Ewersbach — **GRÜNE** DIE GRÜNEN	◯
7	Lang, Bernd — Werkzeugmacher — Hermannsteiner Str 29, 6330 Wetlar — **KBW** Kommunistischer Bund Westdeutschlands	◯

Zweitstimme (right column):

◯	**SPD** Sozialdemokratische Partei Deutschlands — Leber, Maithöler, Jahn, Frau Dr. Timm, Zander	1
◯	**CDU** Christlich Demokratische Union Deutschlands — Dr. Dregger, Zink, Dr. Schwarz Schilling, Frau Geier, Haase	2
◯	**F.D.P.** Freie Demokratische Partei — Mischick, von Schoeler, Hoffie, Wurbs, Dr. Prinz zu Sīma-Hohensolms-Lich	3
◯	**DKP** Deutsche kommunistische Partei — Mayer, Knopf, Frau Dr. Weber, Funk, Fray Schuster	4
◯	**GRÜNE** DIE GRÜNEN — Frau Ibbeken, Hecker, Horacek, Kerschgens, Kuhnert	5
◯	**EAP** Europälsche Arbeiterpartei — Frau Liebig, Haßmann, Stalleicher, Frau Kastner, Stalla	6
◯	**KBW** Kommunistischer Bund Westdeutschland — Schmierer, Frau Nönich, frau Eckardt, Dresler, Lang	7
◯	**NPD** Nationaldemokratische Partei Deutschlands — Phillipp, Brandt, Stürtz, Lauck, Bauer	8
◯	**V** VOLKSFRONT — Götz, Taufertshöfer, König, Riebe, Frau Weißert	9

| FIGURE 11.1
A Sample Ballot for Bundestag Elections

"surplus" seats were awarded—12 to the CDU and 4 to the SPD—as opposed to six in the previous (1990) election, bringing the total seats in the Bundestag today to 672. In the 1998 election thirteen "surplus" seats were awarded—all going to the SPD—bringing the total to 669. In the 2002 election there were five overhang mandates (4 SPD, 1 CDU/CSU). In the 2005 election there were 16 overhang mandates (9 SPD and 7 CDU), and in the 2009 election there were 24 overhang mandates, 21 won by the CDU, and 3 won by the CSU. [44]

> The second ballot provision made the system basically proportional, with two important exceptions. A party had to secure at least five percent of the second ballot vote, or win three "direct" district (first ballot) contests in order to share in the proportional distribution of parliamentary seats. Secondly, if a party won more district contests (first ballot) than it was entitled to according to its totals on the second ballot, it was allowed to keep the extra seats and the parliament was enlarged accordingly. In the last West German parliament, for example, there was one of these "excess mandates" and the Bundestag had 497 members in addition to 22 from West Berlin.[45]

The rationale behind the two-vote electoral system is that it allows for the accuracy of proportional representation, while still allowing for the "personal representation" of the single-member-district electoral structure. Another function of the system has to do with interest groups and representation. One study has suggested that for individual candidates who seek to enter parliament from outside of political party organizations, it is "virtually impossible to gain nomination as a party candidate for a direct seat,"[46] that is, for a seat for which voters ballot directly for an individual candidate. However, significant interest groups may have sufficient influence at the Länder level to be able to influence the Länder political parties to include "their" candidates on the party's "proportional representation" part of the ballot.

Voting turnout is regularly high; 89 percent of the electorate voted in 1983; 84.3 percent voted in 1987; in the first election after unification 77.8 percent of the eligible voters participated; 78.9 percent voted in 1994; 82.2 percent voted in 1998; 79.1 percent voted in 2002; in 2005 77.7 of the eligible voters voted; and in the most recent election in 2009 70.8 percent of the eligible voters voted.[47] Every citizen over the age of 18 years has a vote, and eligibility certificates are mailed by the Federal Board of Elections to lists of eligible voters prepared by the local census bureau.

We might think that the proportional representation component of the electoral system would encourage a large number of political parties to flourish in the Federal Republic of Germany, as was the case in Weimar Germany. There was much discussion about this possible consequence when the authors of the Basic Law met in 1948; the structure that has evolved to prevent the proliferation of minor parties in Germany is called the Five Percent Clause.

Proportional representation electoral systems, as we saw earlier in this text, can have the negative effect in a political system of providing *too much* representation. If every party that receives, say, 1 percent of the vote is given representation in the legislature, we may find a legislature with so many political parties that coalition governments are always necessary, leading to what we saw can be less stable governments. (This is the case in Israel, which has a "pure" proportional representation electoral system that regularly results in over a dozen political parties in the Knesset, Israel's unicameral parliament.)

Under the Weimar Constitution, which preceded World War II, a proportional representation system existed that resulted in a large number of political parties. In fact, fourteen different parties successfully competed for the Reichstag election of September 14, 1930. Many Germans thought that it was wrong that although nine parties had less than 5 percent of the total vote, they still took part in deciding who was to form the government.[48]

There is a difficult trade-off involved in this policy, one that we discussed earlier. On the one hand, single-member districts fail to represent small minority blocs in electoral districts; on the other hand, proportional representation systems many result in too much influence for minor parties. To limit the danger of tiny parliamentary blocs gaining a disproportionate amount of political influence and resulting in political instability through resultant coalition governments, the Federal Election Law introduced the **Five Percent Clause**.[49]

The Five Percent Clause indicates that parties can win seats from the proportional representation "second votes" *only* if they poll at least 5 percent of the second votes, or (1) if they have won at least three constituency seats, or (2) if they represent an officially registered "national minority" (such as the party of the Danish minority in Schleswig-Holstein).[50]

The Five Percent Clause has been of significance for Germany. In the first Bundestag in 1949 there were ten parties represented, but ever since the Five Percent Clause was introduced, there have been only four until the 1983 election added a fifth. The 1990 postunification election expanded this slightly. The Five Percent Clause serves as a real psychological barrier for voters that dampens enthusiasm for new parties, as well as serves as a legal or structural barrier; many voters feel that voting for a minor party is "throwing away" their votes, since the minor parties will probably *not* win 5 percent of the vote. The major parties usually can be counted upon to remind the voters of this principle. This is undoubtedly why we have not seen the appearance of many new parties in the Bundestag since the Five Percent Clause came into force.

When East and West Germany were reunified in 1990, there was concern expressed by many parties in (what had been) East Germany that they would not be able to compete with the larger, better organized parties in (what had been) West Germany in the 1990 elections. The Supreme Court then, in fact, threw out the Five Percent Clause as unconstitutionally discriminating against the smaller (formerly) East German parties. On the advice of the Supreme Court, the law was amended at that time so that political parties in the former German Democratic Republic (East Germany) could form alliances and run on joint tickets, and so that votes for the proportional seats would be counted separately in the what was once East Germany and West Germany,[51] thereby allowing smaller East German parties to compete against smaller East German parties, and not have to compete against the larger West German parties.

Political Parties

As is the case in most democratic systems, it is impossible to discuss the German political system without an explicit discussion of political parties.[52]

Unlike many democracies, however, in Germany parties are *constitutionally* included in the political system: The Basic Law specifically refers to political parties, and in Article 21 "guarantees the legitimacy of parties and their right to exist—if they accept the principles of democratic government."[53] The Federal Republic has thoroughly institutionalized political parties, and we describe the working of the German politics as "party government," as we do other parliamentary democracies.

Although a large number of political parties have consistently competed in German elections, various structures in the political system—most notably the Five Percent Clause we just discussed—have made it extremely difficult for minority or splinter parties to form and flourish. The Five Percent Clause has been successful in this goal.

In 2005, the Christian Democratic Union (CDU) party won 180 seats. The CDU's sister party in Bavaria, the CSU, won 46 seats. The CDU/CSU bloc, with 226 seats, had very slightly more seats than the Social Democratic Party (SPD) of then-Chancellor Gerhard Schröder, which won 222 seats. After a very long postelection negotiation period, the (conservative) CDU/CSU bloc formed a **Grand Coalition** with the (liberal) SPD, and **Angela Merkel** became Germany's first female Chancellor.[54]

The Grand Coalition had difficulty governing, however, because the CDU (and CSU) and the SPD disagreed on many issues. In the 2009 elections, Chancellor Merkel's CDU hoped to win by a larger margin so that either it could govern by itself or so that it would be able to form a coalition government with the Free Democratic Party (FDP), ideologically more similar to its goals. The FDP is a more business-oriented party, and had been a member of the CDU-led coalition government between 1982 and 1998.

In the 2009 campaign, Chancellor Merkel argued for a continuation of the *status quo*. During the campaign the CDU and the SPD were very, very close to each other. The results were surprising, however. The CDU gained 14 seats over its results in 2005, going from 180 to 194, while the partner CSU held constant at 45 seats. The CDU/CSU's hoped-for partner, the FDP, increased its results by 50 percent, winning 93 seats rather than 61. This gave the CDU/CSU/FDP coalition a comfortable majority of 332 in the Bundestag. On the other hand, the SPD had its worst election since the end of the Second World War, winning only 146 seats, down 76 from its 2005 performance. The Green Party slightly increased its population, from 51 to 68, and the Left Party went up from 54 seats to 76 seats.

In the September 2009 election for the Bundestag, twenty-nine parties competed for the voters' attention. There were 43.2 million valid votes cast. The parties received from 32 percent of the first votes cast (the Christian Democratic Union, receiving 13.8 million votes) to less than 1 percent of the first votes cast (seventeen parties received less than one percent of the vote, for instance, "The Center" receiving 369 votes, total).[55] Results of the 2009 election are found in Table 11.2.

Four political parties have proven over time to play a significant political role in the German political system, all participating in government coalitions

> **TABLE 11.2**
>
> **Federal Election Results in Germany, September 27, 2009**
>
> | | Total Seats Won, 2009 (2005) | Constituency Seats Won, 2009 (2005) |
> |---|---|---|
> | SPD | 146 (222) | 64 (145) |
> | CDU | 194 (180) | 173 (106) |
> | FDP | 93 (61) | 0 (0) |
> | The Left Party | 76 (54) | 16 (3) |
> | Alliance 90/The Greens | 68 (51) | 1 (1) |
> | CSU | 45 (46) | 45 (44) |
> | Total | 622 (614) | 299 (299) |
>
> Turnout: 70.78% of eligible voters (77.7% in 2005)
>
> *Note*: The total number of seats won includes the "overhang" seats. The simple number of seats to be elected is 598.
>
> *Source*: Bundestag web page, "Official Results for the 2009 Bundestag Election," http://www.bundestag.de/htdocs_e/bundestag/elections/results/index.html (accessed April 2011).

at one point or another. A fifth party, the Greens, has regularly won seats, but has not yet participated in government. From 1949 through 1956, and from 1961 through 1965, West Germany was governed by a coalition of the Christian Democratic Union (CDU) and Christian Socialist Union (CSU) parties (the CSU is the CDU in the state of Bavaria—they act as one party in the government), and the Free Democratic Party (FDP). In 1957 the CDU/CSU had an outright majority in the Bundestag, the only time an outright majority has been obtained by a political party, and formed a government without a coalition, which lasted until elections in 1961. From 1965 through 1969 a "grand coalition" existed, in which all the major parties including the Social Democratic Party (SPD) participated in the Government. From 1969 until 1982, all governments were SPD and FDP coalitions.[56]

In September 1982, as we have already discussed, primarily as a result of economic pressure exerted on the Government, the FDP/SPD coalition came apart, and the FDP gave its support instead to the CDU/CSU bloc. Accordingly, Chancellor Schmidt of the Social Democratic Party resigned, and Helmut Kohl of the Christian Democratic Union/Christian Socialist Union bloc became chancellor. This coalition stayed in power until 2005 when a new "Grand Coalition" came into existence, headed by Angela Merkel and the conservative CDU/CSU party.

The CDU/CSU bloc is a conservative party, and was founded in 1945 based upon Christian, conservative, social principles.[57] The CSU was also founded in 1945 and appears on the ballot only in Bavaria, while the CDU is a more national party, appearing on *all* ballots *except* in Bavaria. The CDU and CSU are almost always in agreement on major issues, and are considered as one party in the Bundestag, although each party maintains its own structure. The Christian Democratic Union has a federal party conference at least every two years, consisting of 1,001 delegates from the local, regional, and state associations, as well as delegates from foreign associations. The federal party conference comes to a decision as what the basic principles of the party's platform will include.[58] The Christian Socialist Union is divided into 10 district associations, 108 area associations, and about 2,900 local associations. The CSU is present in practically every Bavarian municipality. It is Bavaria's strongest party and the most powerful force in the municipalities.[59]

The Free Democratic Party (FDP) is the liberal-center party in Germany, and is much more active in the German political system than its relatively small size might suggest. It has been referred to as the "party of coalition,"[60] having served as a coalition partner with both the CDU/CSU and the SPD. It is perceived as a centrist party, mainly composed of middle- and upper-class Protestants who consider themselves "independents" and thus has been in most elections the only acceptable partner for the more conservative CDU/CSU and for the more liberal SPD. The 2005 election was an exception to this pattern. Although the SPD did well—receiving 9.8 percent of the vote and 61 federal deputies—because the CDU/CSU did less well than predicted, the FDP-CDU/CSU bloc didn't have enough support in the Bundestag to form a new government. Instead, the CDU formed a "Grand Coalition" with the SPD, and the FDP entered the opposition.[61] In 2009, as we have seen, the FDP reappeared as a "natural" partner to the CDU/CSU plurality winner.

The Social Democratic Party (SPD) dates back to the 1860s, is one of the oldest political parties in the world, and was a traditional working class social democratic party.[62] The SPD is a left-of-center political party. Historically the SPD was associated with Marxist policies, but since 1959 this association has been less clear. Its economic policies are a very moderate version of socialist thought, more sympathetic to free-market economic policies than to Marxist thought. The SPD first participated in a cabinet in the Grand Coalition of 1965; in 1969 the SPD led the cabinet formation process for the first time, joining in a coalition with the FDP. This alliance continued through the elections of 1972, 1976, and 1980, dissolving in October 1982, as indicated above.[63] The SPD, as we have noted above, was a partner in the Grand Coalition with the CDU/CSU following the 2005 election, but following the 2009 election was back in the opposition.

As already stated, the Green Movement in Germany became a parliamentary political party only in recent years.[64] The Green Movement emerged in Germany in 1975, and for many years existed as a lobby in West Germany opposing expanded use of nuclear power, opposing NATO strategy, and applying pressure for changes in society which "did not pose an immediate threat to the established 'people's' or 'catch-all' parties."[65] Membership in the Greens rose from 3,000 in October 1979, to over 10,000 in January 1980; in March 1980 the Greens met to formulate a formal political party program.[66]

The Greens were especially important as a demonstration that views that were outside the mainstream of West German political thought could win representation in parliament.[67] Although there had been several protest movements with various degrees of popular support in West Germany between the formation of the Federal Republic and 1983,[68] the Greens' victory in 1983 offered the first instance of parliamentary political victory for an organization that could be called a "protest movement."

The Greens have not been a typical German party, and their parliamentarians have not been typical legislators, in either behavior or demeanor.[69] The average Green legislator was almost ten years younger than other legislators, and "six of the ten youngest deputies in Parliament were Greens."[70]

In the 1980 federal elections the Greens did not cross the threshold required for representation. In the 1983 federal election they received 5.6 percent of the vote, and entered the federal Parliament for the first time.[71] They increased their voter support in 1987 with 8.4 percent of the vote.[72] The (former West German) Greens did not get enough votes in the 1990 election to clear the 5 percent threshold and win any seats in the new legislature, but the (former East German) Alliance 90/Greens did win sufficient votes to be represented, so the Green movement continued to be represented in the federal legislature. In 1994 the Greens from East and West returned to the Bundestag with over 7 percent of the vote, winning 49 seats; this figure held almost constant at 47 seats and 6.7 percent of the votes in the 1998 election. The Greens' support increased to almost 9 percent of the vote in 2002, although in the 2005 election their support dropped slightly to just below 7 percent of the vote. It increased to almost 11 percent in 2009.

THE GERMAN POLITICAL SYSTEM IN PERSPECTIVE

We see in Germany, then, a political system that is *similar to* others that we have already seen, but one that differs in a number of aspects from those other systems. Although many idiosyncratic structural and procedural differences exist between Germany and other nations, the most significant differences that we have highlighted in this chapter number four.

First, Germany is federal, and the role of the states (Länder) in the German political system is quite significant. Through the veto power of the Bundesrat, the Länder exercise a great influence in the policy-making process generally, and in the legislative process specifically. The federal distribution of power makes Germany unlike any other European political system we will see here.

Second, the "normal" responsibility of the chief executive to the (lower house of the) legislature is different in the German political system. The political structure of the "positive vote of no confidence" has many implications for the degree to which the chancellor must worry about the likelihood that she will be dismissed by the Bundestag.

Third, the German electoral structure offers a unique blend of methods of selection for a national legislature. By combining single-member-district with proportional-representation selection, the Germans have attempted to blend the advantages of each: the minority representation of proportional representation with the stability and orientation of district-based representation.

Moreover, by establishing the Five Percent Clause the Germans have attempted to resolve the major drawback of proportional representation—namely a proliferation of political parties and the ensuing political instability of the regime.

Fourth, from a legislative point of view the German case is quite interesting. In some political systems (such as that of the United States) the upper house has, both in law (*de jure*) and in fact (*de facto*), an absolute veto. Laws cannot be made without the approval of the upper house. In other political systems (such as those of Britain and France) the upper house has only a suspensory veto, in both law and in fact. If both the Government and the lower house want a piece of proposed legislation passed, it will become law, and the most that the upper chamber can do is to slow down the process. In Germany, on the other hand, in both law and in fact, the upper house sometimes has an *absolute veto*, and sometimes has a *suspensory veto*, depending on the focus of legislation under consideration.

This brief discussion of the German political system, then, although only covering a small portion of all of the significant structures of the political regime, points out some of the interesting, significant, and, in some cases, unique characteristics of the German polity. We will see in several of the following chapters that many of these political structures that are so appropriate to the German political culture would not work elsewhere. Other regimes have developed their own mechanisms and structures for processing political demands and supports.

DISCUSSION QUESTIONS

1. What were the most important changes that had to be made in West Germany to allow for the addition of East Germany to the German constitutional system?
2. What are the special federal institutions and political practices in Germany? How do they influence German politics?
3. What is special about the German chancellor? What special powers does she have? What is special about her relationship with the German parliament?
4. What is the relationship between the Bundestag and the Bundesrat in the legislative process in Germany? Do they have equal roles? What is particularly representative of the principle of federalism in their procedures?
5. Is the German coalition-formation process substantially different from coalition-formation in other democratic nations? How? Why?

KEY TERMS

Basic Law   266
Bundesrat   267
Bundestag   267
chancellor   270
concurrent legislative
  jurisdiction   269
constituency vote   278

cooperative
  federalism   269
Five Percent
  Clause   281
grand coalition   282
Länder   266
Merkel, Angela   282

positive or constructive vote
  of no confidence   272
residual powers of the
  Länder   269
simple vote of no
  confidence   273
Weimar Republic   266

SUGGESTED READINGS

Gert-Joachim Glaessner, *German Democracy: From Post–World War II to the Present Day* (New York: Berg, 2005). This is a good historical study of the development of German democracy from the end of World War II to the present time.

Arthur Gunlicks, *The Länder and German Federalism* (New York: Manchester University Press, 2003). German federalism is unique, and the specific German brand of federalism affects the political power of both the German Länder and the central government in Bonn. This volume describes the relations between the two levels of government and how these relations affect the types of policy produced in Germany.

Eric Langenbacher, ed., *Launching the Grand Coalition: The 2005 Bundestag Election and the Future of German Politics* (New York: Berghahn Books, 2006). The Grand Coalition was a crucial political outcome of a key political challenge in modern German politics. This volume describes the context and structures that existed in German politics prior to the creation of the Grand Coalition, and how the Grand Coalition was created.

Charles Lees, *Party Politics in Germany: A Comparative Politics Approach* (New York: Palgrave Macmillan, 2005). This volume offers a thorough analysis of the evolution of political parties in modern Germany and discussion of the role that they play in the German political system. It includes discussion of party politics both before and after German unification.

Geoffrey Roberts, *German Electoral Politics* (Manchester, UK: Manchester University Press, 2006). German elections are a key structure in the German political system, and this volume offers a very thorough discussion of the factors that make up the electoral system of Germany.

NOTES

1. Guido Goldman, *The German Political System* (New York: Random House, 1974), pp. 157, 214. The full text of the Basic Law can be found here. See also Gert-Joachim Glaessner, *German Democracy: From Post–World War II to the Present Day* (New York: Berg, 2005).

2. According to Hancock, a majority of the members of Bavaria's parliament opposed the Basic law "because it provided for a more centralized form of government than they would have wished. Nonetheless, the Bavarian Landtag endorsed the Basic Law as binding on the state." See M. Donald Hancock, *West Germany: The Politics of Democratic Corporatism* (Chatham, NJ: Chatham House, 1989), pp. 29–30; Margaret Crosby, *The Making of the German Constitution: A Slow Revolution* (Oxford, UK: Berg, 2004).

3. See, for a brief discussion of the costs of reunification and problems immediately following unification, "Economic Affairs of Germany" in "Germany", *Europa World Yearbook 1993*, p. 1208. See also Stephen Redding and Daniel Sturm, *The Costs of Remoteness: Evidence from German Division and Reunification* (London, UK: Centre for Economic Policy Research, 2005).

4. On this note, an interesting study was published in 1966 by Karl Jaspers, a well-known German philosopher, who argued that "the Federal Republic of Germany is well on its way to abolishing parliamentary democracy and may be drifting toward some kind of dictatorship...." See Karl Jaspers, *The Future of Germany* (trans. E. B. Ashton) (Chicago, IL: University of Chicago Press, 1967), p. v.

5. Klaus von Beyme, *The Political System of the Federal Republic of Germany* (New York: St. Martin's Press, 1983), p. 12.

6. See Goldman, *The German Political System*, pp. 157–164. All quotes from the Basic Law are taken from the text in Goldman, and will not be given individual citations.

7. Lewis Edinger, *Politics in West Germany* (Boston, MA: Little, Brown, 1977), p. 11.

8. See Raoul Blindenbacher and Abigail Ostien, *Dialogues on Distribution of Powers and Responsibilities in Federal Countries* (Montreal, QC: McGill-Queen's University Press, 2005).

9. David Conradt, *The German Polity*, 3rd ed. (New York: Longman, 1986), p. 210.

10. The three were Bavaria, Hamburg, and Bremen. See Conradt, *The German Polity*, p. 212.

11. Johnson, *State and Government*, p. 7. See also Arthur Gunlicks, *German Public Policy and Federalism: Current Debates on Political, Legal, and Social Issues* (New York: Berghahn Books, 2003).

12. See Simon Green and William Paterson, eds., *Governance in Contemporary Germany: The Semisovereign State Revisited* (New York: Cambridge University Press, 2005); or Arthur Gunlicks, *The Länder and German Federalism* (New York: Manchester University Press, 2003).

13. See the CIA *World Factbook Online*, at *https://www.cia.gov/cia/publications/factbook/geos/gm.html#Govt* (accessed April 2011). See also R. Daniel Keleman, *The Rules of Federalism: Institutions and Regulatory Politics in the EU and Beyond* (Cambridge, MA: Harvard University Press, 2004).

14. Ibid.

15. Hancock, *West Germany*, p. 49. See also Jan Erk, *Explaining Federalism: State, Society, and Congruence in Austria, Belgium, Canada, Germany, and Switzerland* (New York: Routledge, 2008); and Sergio Ortino and Mitja Zagar, eds., *The Changing Faces of Federalism: Institutional Reconfiguration in Europe from East to West* (New York: Palgrave, 2005).

16. See John M. Quigley and Konrad Stahl, *Fiscal Competition and Federalism in Europe* (Amsterdam, The Netherlands: North-Holland Press, 2001). On Europe more broadly, see Florentina Harbo, *Towards a European Federation: The EU in the Light of Comparative Federalism* (Baden-Baden, Germany: Nomos, 2005).

17. Hancock, *West Germany*, p. 49. See also Wilfried Swenden, *Federalism and Second Chambers: Regional Representation in Parliamentary Federations: The Australian Senate and German Bundesrat Compared* (New York: Peter Lang, 2004).

18. Peter Katzenstein, *Policy and Politics in West Germany: The Growth of a Semisovereign State* (Philadelphia, PA: Temple University Press, 1987), pp. 17–18. See also Florian Profitlich, *The Federal Constitutional Court of Germany* (London, UK: Springer, 2004).

19. See Tom Ginsburg and Robert Kagan, eds., *Institutions and Public Law: Comparative Approaches* (New York: P. Lang, 2005); Alec Stone Sweet, *The Judicial Construction of Europe* (New York: Oxford University Press, 2004).

20. Johnson, *State and Government*, pp. 49–50. See also Ludger Helms, *Presidents, Prime Ministers, and Chancellors: Executive Leadership in Western Democracies* (New York: Palgrave Macmillan, 2005)

21. See the discussion of "The Elevation of the Chancellor" in *Democracy in Western Germany: Parties and Politics in the Federal Republic* , ed. Gordon Smith (New York: Holmes and Meier, 1986), p. 56; or the chapter by Thomas Poguntke, "A Presidentializing Party State? The Federal Republic of Germany," in *The Presidentialization of Politics: A Comparative Study of Modern Democracies*, eds. Thomas Poguntke and Paul Webb (New York: Oxford University Press, 2005).

22. Johnson, *State and Government*, p. 50. A very good profile of Angela Merkel, Germany's first female Chancellor, can be found on the British Broadcasting Corporation website at *http://news.bbc.co.uk/2/hi/europe/4572387.stm* (accessed April 2011).

23. See the Government of Germany web page with information on the cabinet and the federal chancellor, *http://www.bundesregierung.de/Webs/Breg/EN/Federal-Government/federal-government.html* (accessed April 2011).

24. Johnson, *State and Government*, p. 54. See also the web page of the Federal Government that discusses the role of the Chancellor and the Cabinet in German government, *http://www.bundesregierung.de/Webs/Breg/EN/Federal-Government/Function AndConstitutionalBasis/function-and-constitutional-basis.html* (accessed April 2011).

25. For example, see Conradt, *The German Polity*, p. 162. Again, see the Federa Government web page description of the role of the Chancellor, "Role of the Chancellor," *http://www.bundesregierung.de/Webs/Breg/EN/Federal-Government/FunctionAnd ConstitutionalBasis/function-and-constitutional-basis.html* (accessed April 2011).

26. John Herz, *The Government of Germany* (New York: Harcourt, Brace, Jovanovich, 1972), p. 123. See also Katja Ziegler and Denis Baranger, eds., *Constitutionalism and the Role of Parliaments* (Oxford, UK: Hart, 2007).

27. A good analysis of this period can be found in Gert-Joachim Glaessner, *German Democracy: From Post–World War II to the Present Day* (New York: Berg, 2005).

28. This is discussed in some detail in Hancock, *West Germany*, pp. 121–124.

29. Johnson, *State and Government*, pp. 68–9. See also Eric Langenbacher, ed., *Launching the Grand Coalition: The 2005 Bundestag Election and the Future of German Politics* (New York: Berghahn Books, 2006).

30. Articles 38, 39 of the Basic Law. See also Klaus von Beyme, *The Legislator: German Parliament as a Centre of Political Decision-Making* (Brookfield, VT: Ashgate, 1998).

31. See the Bundesrat web page at *http://www.bundesrat.de/EN/Home/homepage__ node.html?__nnn=true* (accessed April 2011). See also Arthur Gunlicks, *The Länder and German Federalism* (New York: Manchester University Press, 2003); and Wilfried Swendon, *Federalism and Second Chambers, op. cit.*

32. See the Bundestag web page: *http://www.bundestag.de/htdocs_e/bundestag/function/ legislation/index.html* (accessed April 2011).

33. See Gerhardt Loewenberg, *Parliament in the German Political System* (Ithaca, NY Cornell University Press, 1967), p. 269.

34. Ibid., p. 270.

35. See the section on the Bundesrat in the Government of Germany's publication *Facts About Germany*, *http://www.tatsachen-ueber-deutschland.de/en/political-system/ main-content-04/the-bundesrat.html* (accessed April 2011).

36. Loewenberg writes that about 60 percent of important measures require Bundesrat approval. The Basic Law sections that determine which subjects are subject to Bundesrat approval are "scattered over many sections of the document." Lowewnberg, Parliament, pp. 365–366, n. 214.

37. A good discussion of the role of the Bundesrat in the passage of legislation can be found on the web page of the Bundestag, in English, *http://www.bundestag.de/ htdocs_e/bundestag/function/legislation/index.html* (accessed April 2011).

38. Loewenberg, *Parliament*, p. 366.

39. See Geoffrey K. Roberts, *Separate and Equal? Some Controversial Features of the German Federal Electoral System* (Manchester, UK: University of Manchester Press, 1999); or Geoffrey Roberts, *German Electoral Politics* (Manchester, UK: Manchester University Press, 2006).

40. *Germany: Elections, Parliament, and Political Parties* (New York: German Information Center, 1990), pp. 20–21. Results of the December 1990 election were

published in *The Week in Germany*, December 7, 1990 (New York: German Information Center), p. 1.

41. The results of the 2009 election can be found at the Bundestag web page "Official Result for the 2009 Bundestag Election," *http://www.bundestag.de/htdocs_e/ bundestag/elections/results/index.html* (accessed April 2011). An archive of past results that can be found on the Inter-Parliamentary Union web page, *http://www .ipu.org/parline-e/reports/2121_arc.htm* (accessed April 2011).

42. von Beyme, *The Political System of the Federal Republic of Germany*, p. 26.

43. In the electoral term of the Bundestag (1990–1994) the number of constituencies was increased from 248 to 328 as a consequence of the unification of Germany in 1990 and the increase in population and electoral size. As noted earlier, the number of districts was changed in 2001 from the 656 seats of the previous Bundestag (328 district representatives, and 328 electoral list representatives) by the Federal Electoral Law of 27 April 2001. Today it is 299 single-member constituencies and a "normal" 299 proportional seats, although the latter can change. See the web page of the Bundestag that describes the electoral system, *http://www. bundestag.de/htdocs_e/bundestag/elections/electionresults/election_mp.html* (accessed April 2011).

44. See the Bundestag web page, which offers some background on this complex topic: *http://www.bundestag.de/htdocs_e/bundestag/elections/results/index.html* (accessed April 2011). A list of the specific overhang seats can be found on the Bundestag web page. See also the web page of the Inter-Parliamentary Union, "Germany: Last Elections," *http://www.ipu.org/parline-e/reports/2121_E.htm* (accessed April 2011).

45. David P. Conradt, *Unified Germany at the Polls: Political Parties and the 1990 Federal Election* (Baltimore, MD: Johns Hopkins University Press, 1990), pp. 23–24.

46. Eva Kolinsky, *Parties, Opposition, and Society in West Germany* (New York: St. Martin's Press, 1984), p. 40.

47. See the Bundestag web page, "Official Result of the 2009 Bundestag Election," *http://www.bundestag.de/htdocs_e/bundestag/elections/results/index.html* (accessed April 2011). A wonderful reference resource is the web page of the International Institute for Democracy and Electoral Assistance, which keeps (among other things) records of voting turnout in all democratic elections. See the IIDEA's web page at *http://www.idea.int/vt/country_view.cfm?CountryCode=DE* (accessed April, 2011). See also David P. Conradt, Gerald Kleinfeld, and Christian Soe, *A Precarious Victory: Schroeder and the German Elections of 2002* (New York: Oxford University Press, 2004); and Eric Langenbacher, *Launching the Grand Coalition: The 2005 Bundestag Election and the Future of German Politics* (New York: Berghahn Books, 2006).

48. Helmut Gobel and Herbert Blondiau, eds., *Procedures, Programmes, Profiles: The Federal Republic of Germany Elects the German Bundestag on 5 October, 1980* (Bonn, Germany: Inter-Nationes, 1980), p. 13.

49. For a discussion of the evolution of this point, see Karl H. Cerny, ed., *Germany at the Polls: The Bundestag Election of 1976* (Washington, DC: American Enterprise Institute, 1978), pp. 3–17.

50. Gobel and Blondiau, *Procedures*, p. 13.

51. "Germany: Elections, Parliament, and Political Parties," p. 8.

52. See Charles Lees, *Party Politics in Germany: A Comparative Politics Approach* (New York: Palgrave Macmillan, 2005); and Simon Green and William Paterson, *Governance in Contemporary Germany: The Semisovereign State Revisited* (New York: Cambridge University Press, 2005).

53. Russell J. Dalton, *Politics: West Germany* (Boston, MA: Little Brown, 1989), p. 246.

54. See the report by the British Broadcasting Corporation, "Merkel Becomes German Chancellor," appearing on November 22, 2005, on the BBC, *http://news.bbc.co.uk/2/hi/europe/4458430.stm* (accessed April 2011).

55. See the results of the election at the Inter-Parliamentary Union web page, *http://www.ipu.org/parline-e/reports/2121_E.htm* (accessed April 2011).

56. There is much good discussion of the evolution of the party system in the chapter by Gerhard Loewenberg, "The Remaking of the German Party System," in *Germany at the Polls*, ed. Karl Cerny (Washington, DC: American Enterprise Institute, 1990).

57. See Geoffrey Pridham, *Christian Democracy in Western Germany* (New York: St. Martin's Press, 1977). Another good source on Christian Democratic movements is by Thomas Keselman and Joseph Buttigieg, *European Christian Democracy: Historical Legacies and Comparative Perspective* (Notre Dame, IN: University of Notre Dame Press, 2003).

58. See the CDU web page at *http://www.cdu.de/en/3440.htm* (accessed April 2011).

59. See the CSU web page at *http://www.csu.de/partei/international/english.htm* (accessed April 2011).

60. See Christian Soe, "The Free Democratic Party," in *West German Politics in the Mid-Eighties*, eds. H. Peter Wallach and George Romoser (New York: Praeger, 1985).

61. See the discussion of coalition negotiation in the British Broadcasting Corporation coverage of the event on November 15, 2005: "Analysis: German Coalition Deal," *http://news.bbc.co.uk/2/hi/europe/4438212.stm* (accessed April 2011).

62. See the Social Democratic Party web site: *http://www.spd.de/aktuelles/* (accessed April 2011). Unfortunately the party no longer maintains a web page in English.

63. A very good study of the role of the Social Democrats while in power can be found in the work by Dan Hough, Michael Koss, and Jonathan Olsen, *The Left in Contemporary German Politics* (New York: Palgrave Macmillan, 2007).

64. See Gerd Langguth, *The Green Factor in German Politics: From Protest Movement to Political Party* (Boulder, CO: Westview Press, 1986); and Werner Reutter, *Germany on the Road to 'Normalcy'" Policies and Politics of the Red-Green Federal Government (1998–2002)* (New York: Palgrave Macmillan, 2004).

65. Elim Papadakis, *The Green Movement in West Germany* (New York: St. Martin's Press, 1984), p. 13.

66. Ibid., pp. 159, 161.

67. Rob Burns and Wilfried van der Will, *Protest and Democracy in West Germany: Extra-Parliamentary Opposition and the Democratic Agenda* (New York: St. Martin's Press, 1988), p. 230.

68. Among these might be included the opposition to remilitarization and nuclear weapons (1950–1969), the movement of students against authoritarianism (1965–1969), the women's movement (1968 to 1985), environmentalism (1970s and 1980s), and mass opposition to nuclear arms (1980 to 1986). See Burns and van der Will, *Protest and Democracy*, with chapters on each of these protest movements.

69. A good analysis of the Greens can be found in Werner Hulsberg, *The German Greens: A Social and Political Profile*, trans. Gus Fagan (London, UK: Verso, 1988), especially in Chapter 7, "The Greens: A Preliminary Assessment," and Chapter 8, "The Crisis of Orientation." See the web page of the Green party at: *http://www.gruene.de/startseite.html* (accessed April 2011). Unfortunately the web page is not available in English.

70. Dalton, *Politics: West Germany*, p. 293 n. 15.

71. Papadakis, *The Green Movement*, p. 196.

72. Hulsberg, *German Greens*, p. 247. In Appendix I of his study Hulsberg provides election results for the Greens in Land and Federal elections between 1978 and 1987.

The Canadian Political System

LEARNING OBJECTIVES

- Explain how Canada's bi-national history affected Canada's constitutional development.

- Understand the unique federal balance of powers in Canada.

- Appreciate the role that regionalism plays in the day-to-day politics of Canada and the balance of powers that exists there.

- Compare the role of the Canadian prime minister with the roles of prime ministers in other democratic regimes to appreciate both similarities and differences.

- Explain the relationship between the House of Commons and the Senate, and explain the role of the Senate in the Canadian parliamentary democracy.

- Understand the role that political parties play in Canadian democracy, and discuss how this has changed over time.

Although there are many respects in which the Canadian political system is similar to the British political system, such as its parliamentary form of government, or single-member district voting for the lower house and an appointed upper house, it will become apparent that in spite of these similarities many significant structural and behavioral differences exist between the two nations. In this chapter we shall discuss the nature of the Canadian political system, including its constitutional framework, its special federal and bi-national character, its political institutions, its party system, and the power relationships that exist between and among actors in the political system.

CANADA

Total Area (rank)	9,984,670 sq km (2)
Population (rank)	34,030,589 (37)
Population Growth Rate (rank)	0.794% (136)
Urban Population	81%
Life Expectancy at Birth (total population) (rank)	81.38 (12)
Literacy	99%
Government Type	Federal parliamentary constitutional monarchy
Legal System	Common law except in Québec, which has civil law
Head of Government	Prime Minister Stephen Harper
Chief of State	Queen Elizabeth II
Gross Domestic Product (GDP)	$1.574 trillion
GDP Per Capita (rank)	$39,400 (22)
GDP Real Growth Rate (rank)	3.1% (123)
Unemployment Rate (rank)	8% (89)

CANADA

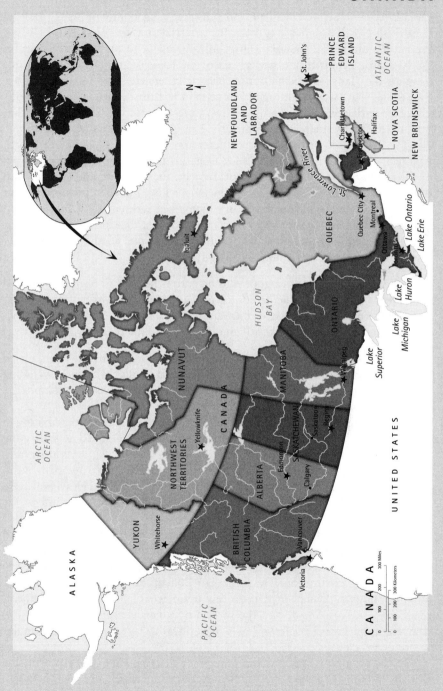

THE CANADIAN CONSTITUTIONAL SYSTEM

Canada became an independent and self-governing dominion as a result of the **British North America Act** (hereafter referred to as the **BNA** Act) of 1867. From 1867 until 1982 Canada was technically independent. However, because the basis of its constitution was an act of the British Parliament, any amendment to the Canadian Constitution had to be enacted not by Canada, but by Britain. This was traditionally done by the British Parliament whenever Canada's Parliament so requested.[1] Thus, from 1867 until 1982 it was said that "the BNA Act, as amended," formed the basis of the Canadian Constitution.

The **BNA Act** provided for the creation of a federal union in North America, and thereby dealt with such topics as language, the explicit powers of the provinces and the national government, the structure and composition of Parliament, and so on. One of the document's broadest but most important phrases was found in the preamble, in which it was written that Canada would have a government "... similar in principle to that of the United Kingdom."[2]

It has been suggested that the **"similar in principle" clause** was for many years the source of many Canadian civil liberties:

> ...because the United Kingdom has no entrenched Bill of Rights, the actual extent of the rights and freedoms of Canadians is enshrined only in the many centuries of British legal tradition—a fact which, while not a restriction on our liberties, makes them difficult to define precisely.[3]

In other areas of constitutional evolution, the "similar in principle" clause may be seen as a basis for much of the broader Canadian political culture, including such characteristics as representative and parliamentary government, a powerful cabinet, majoritarianism, and so on.[4]

Additionally, several wholly Canadian statutes were seen as contributing to the Canadian Constitution. Among these statutes were included acts affecting the creation of the western provinces, for example. As well, several statutes that were called "organic laws"[5] were usually considered to be included in the constitution. These laws involved basic principles of the regime, and were simply acts of the Parliament; as such they could be amended or altered by other acts of the Parliament.

Since the federal nature of the Canadian government left a great deal of legislating to the individual provinces, many suggested that there was a large body of provincial legislation that needed to be included when one referred to the Canadian Constitution. The Canadian Constitution, then, was until 1982 an amorphous document in that it drew upon acts of the British Parliament, the Canadian Parliament, and the several provincial Parliaments, as well as drawing upon British common law and political culture through the "similar in principle" clause.

In the spring of 1982, at the request of the Canadian Government, the British Parliament passed the Canada Act (1982), which put the Canadian Constitution under Canadian control for the first time in Canada's history.[6] This was referred to as the **patriation**—"bringing the Constitution home"— of the Constitution. The Canada Act had a number of major consequences for Canadian constitutional evolution. First, by passing the Canada Act the British Parliament changed the name of the British North America Act to the **Constitution Act.** (Thus, the British North America Act of 1867 is now referred to as the Constitution Act of 1867; the British North America Act of 1886 is now referred to as the Constitution Act of 1886, and so on.)

Second, included in the passage of the Canada Act was a new Charter of Rights that was to be added to the Canadian Constitution. Canada had never had a Charter of Rights before, relying for the basis of its citizens' civil rights as we noted earlier upon the "similar in principle" clause in the preamble of the BNA Act and the British constitutional heritage that this implied.

Third, in the Canada Act the British Parliament added an amending formula to the British North America Act. Previously, whenever Canada wanted to amend its constitution it had to ask the British Parliament to pass a new British North America Act; many Canadians felt that the time had come to stop this anachronistic practice. Now Canada would be able to amend its constitution on its own.

Fourth, finally, by passing the Canada Act the British Parliament renounced the right ever again to legislate for Canada. Where previously Canada might have been *de facto* an independent nation, *de jure*, legally, it was dependent upon Britain for its constitutional structure. Henceforth, Canada was to be both *de facto* and *de jure* independent.[7]

The British heritage of Canada comes not only from the fact that Britain administered Canada prior to Canadian independence, but as well from the fact that much of Canadian political culture was rooted in British history. Indeed, the majority of the population in Canada in the nineteenth and twentieth centuries was of Anglo-Celtic stock, and Britain was a correspondingly important source of values, attitudes, and culture. Additionally, of course, Britain has been a major source of immigrants for Canada, thus insuring that a large proportion of the Canadian population would continually be aware of, and interested in, British cultural values.[8]

The "similar in principle" clause would not have been so important if the Canadian people had not been oriented to the British political culture to begin with; its vagueness certainly would have permitted greater deviation from the British model than exists today had Canada wanted it. The clause draws its real importance from the fact that Canadians are already oriented toward the Westminster Model, and willingly adopt structures and culture implied by the clause.

FEDERALISM IN CANADA

Structurally, the BNA Act created a federal government, giving most major legislative power to the national government, but reserving for the provincial governments a number of areas of sovereignty. The provinces have not lost their powers to the national government over the years, partly because of the restraint exercised by successive national governments, and partly "because judicial interpretation of the provincial powers to regulate property and civil rights greatly expanded the scope of provincial authority."[9]

The Canadian political system has evolved over the past 145-plus years to the form in which it is found today. The concept of federalism existed in Canada prior to the creation of the British North America Act of 1867, and was used as the basis of the act, drawing upon experiences of Canada and of other nations.[10]

> In contrast to the Constitution of the United States, which had just endured the war between the States, the BNA Act assigns both the general and residual powers of government to the Dominion (national government), not the Provinces.... But it was not to be so. It is commonly known that the decisions of the Judicial Committee of the Privy Council (the highest judicial organ in Canada until the Supreme Court of Canada was made the final judicial body [in 1949]) abridged the general powers of the Dominion governments and enhanced the legislative powers of the Provinces.[11]

Relevant sections of the British North America Act (now the Constitution Act) are worth noting. **Section 91** of the Act indicates that the national legislature will have the jurisdiction "to make Laws for the Peace, Order, and good Government of Canada" in relations to all matters not "assigned exclusively to the Legislatures of the Provinces." It then offers "for greater Certainty, but not so as to restrict the Generality of the foregoing Terms of this Section" a list of thirty-one powers (originally twenty-nine powers) of the federal government.

Section 92 deals with the Provinces: "In each Province the Legislature may exclusively make Laws in relation to Matters coming within the Classes of Subject next herein-after enumerated," and lists sixteen specific areas of jurisdiction, one of which (Section 13) is "Property and Civil Rights."

The problem for Canadian government today is that many aspects of governmental responsibility that have developed since 1867 have been interpreted first by the (British) Judicial Committee of the Privy Council—which acted as the ultimate judicial body for Canada in Canada's early years—and later by the Supreme Court of Canada, to fall under the "Property and Civil Rights" clause of Section 92 rather than the "Peace, Order, and good Government" clause of Section 91, giving legislative authority over them to the provinces rather than the federal government.

In apparent disregard of the passage of Section 91 stating, "but not so as to restrict the generality of the foregoing Terms," the judicial bodies of Canada have ruled that since the Founders put a list of powers for the Dominion into Section 91, those (*and only* those) must be the powers they intended for the Dominion government, and nothing more (in spite of the fact that they explicitly said that restricting the generality of Section 91 was not their intention). In several instances, the Justices have denied that the "Peace, Order and good Government" clause gave the Dominion broad jurisdiction, and apparently doubted "that the Dominion could have any power at all except those specifically enumerated in Section 91."[12]

So, at the same time that the Supreme Court in the United States was making decisions that resulted in *greater* federal jurisdiction at the expense of the states, decisions in Canada were going in the other direction, ruling that policy jurisdiction belonged to the provinces, not the Dominion. What kept the Dominion government in a position of some influence was money. Specifically, the provinces could not *afford* all of the jurisdictions that the courts were ruling were their responsibility, so the Dominion government was able to regain much of its lost influence through its "power of the purse" and a variety of what were called "tax-renting," revenue sharing, and conditional grant schemes.[13]

Certainly one of the major underlying questions in Canadian politics in modern times has to do with where, on a central-peripheral scale similar to that which we observed earlier in this volume, Canadian federal-provincial jurisdictions can be found.[14] Many have argued that federalism has been the saving grace of the Canadian political arena for the last hundred years or so.[15] Others argue that federalism has had a great deal to do with the problem of national unity that Canada has experienced. One author has gone so far as to suggest that the separatist issue in Québec is related to general problems of federalism, and has added that "to the extent that separatist opinion may be understood as a concern about the necessary conditions of political community, the question posed by separatism becomes for us a question about federalism."[16]

In each of the ten provinces, the power of the Crown—today the **Queen of Canada** (the same person as the Queen of the United Kingdom)—is represented by a Lieutenant-Governor, appointed by the Governor-General-in-Council (the governor-general, acting on the advice of the prime minister). Provincial legislatures are all unicameral, elected for maximum terms of five years, and are composed of a legislature called the Legislative Assembly (in Québec it is called the "Assemblée Nationale," the "National Assembly") and the Lieutenant Governor, who serves the provincial head-of-state role. Like the federal House of Commons, the term of a provincial assembly may not exceed five years. Similarly, like the federal House of Commons, government in the provinces is based upon a parliamentary system of government in which the Lieutenant Governor appoints the leader of the majority in the legislative assembly to be premier (the parallel role to the national prime minister), and the premier serves in that position as long as she or he is able to maintain the support of a legislative majority, or until the term of the legislature expires.

Today the three northern territories are under the constitutional power of the federal government. The Yukon Act, the Northwest Territories Act, and the Nunavut Act serve as the statutory authority for the three territories. The territories have elected assemblies, executive councils, and individuals who serve the role of lieutenant governor who are appointed by the Minister of Indian and Northern Affairs.

It may be that much of the indecision about the precise power distribution that should exist in the Canadian polity (e.g., should the Dominion [the national government] or the provinces be dominant?) can be attributed to the fact that Canadian history has seen both of these power relationships exist.[17] This phenomenon has led, Alan Cairns has argued, to the "other crisis" in Canadian politics, "the crisis of a political system with a declining capacity for the effective use of the authority of government for the attainment of public goals."[18] It does appear to be true that with the growth of power of the Supreme Court of Canada in recent years there has been a broader interpretation of federal powers; for example the Supreme Court of Canada has determined that the federal government should have jurisdiction over radio, telecommunications, and nuclear energy.

REGIONALISM AS A SOURCE OF TENSION

We know what questions of *federalism* imply. How does **regionalism** differ? Canada is a very large nation, and although we will see in a moment many of the issues that are significant for a specific group in Canada—the French Canadians, who primarily live in Québec—we should not forget that there are *many* groups in Canada, and much geography to exacerbate tensions that might develop.

Canadian federalism was originally based upon regionalism. "The West" had representation, and "the Maritimes" had representation, along with Ontario and Québec, in the original Confederation agreement. There are, in fact, several different ways to conceive of regionalism in Canada. One source approaches a conception of Canadian regionalism working with six regions in Canada: the Atlantic provinces (Newfound and Labrador, Nova Scotia, New Brunswick, and Prince Edward Island); Québec; Ontario; the Prairie provinces (Manitoba, Saskatchewan, and Alberta); British Columbia; and the North (Yukon, Northwest Territories, and Nunavut).[19]

The units haven't gone away, and Western alienation is a theme that often is visible in discussion of Canadian politics today. Westerners have felt that Canadian politics is dominated by the Center, by Ontario, and that Ontario pays more attention to the unhappiness of Québec than it does to the population and issues of the West. Richard Simeon and David Elkins argued many years ago that Canada embraced *several* regional political subcultures, which together made up Canada.[20] More recently, several Western provincial leaders, among them Ralph Klein of Alberta, argued for institutional responses including a restructuring of the Canadian Senate to better represent the interests of the West; some even called for Western separatism from Canada.[21]

FRENCH CANADA AND QUÉBEC

Since before Confederation in 1867 the question of the relation between Québec and the rest of English Canada has been one of the major points of contention—if not *the* major point of contention—in the Canadian political system. Whatever the policy issue in question, whether it involves health policy, energy policy, education policy, or labor policy, to take just a few examples, it seems to be more intensely debated in Québec than in any other Canadian province. This is because, some have argued, Québec approaches many debates not only as *federal-provincial* conflicts, but also as *nationalistic* conflicts involving a very real feeling of *nationalism* for French Canadians,[22] manifested as **Québec nationalism,** where "nationalism" can be defined as a sense on the part of a population that it wants to pursue territorial sovereignty or self-government.

We should note that the term *French Canadian* is not, strictly speaking, the same as *Québécois*, since there are French Canadians living outside of Québec, primarily in Ontario and New Brunswick.[23] However, it is true that the overwhelming majority of Canada's French-speaking population lives in the Province of Québec, and that Québec is approximately as unilingual and French as the rest of Canada is unilingual and English.

At the time of Confederation, Québec had significant concerns about join-ing the English-dominated union, but fear of attack from its neighbor to the South (the United States, just finishing a Civil War) motivated it to act despite these factors. Québec insisted, however, on a decentralized *federal* system in which it would retain control over policies most important to its unique char-acter, especially language and education.[24] Ever since Confederation, politics in Québec have varied from more to less militantly nationalistic, and at times over the last hundred and forty-five years the situation has even become vio-lent. While the issue of Québec nationalism is too complex to adequately resolve here, we can highlight some of the issues that have figured prominently in debates over the years.[25]

Culture. The government of Québec has jealously guarded areas of policy that are especially important to French Canadian nationalism over the years, focusing especially on language, culture, education, and religion. Before the "Quiet Revolution" of the 1960s, the Québec political culture was

> generally very traditional, conservative, patronage-oriented, authoritarian, backward, rural, corrupt, and heavily influenced by the Roman Catholic Church. [Later], it has become progressive, if not radical, urban, demo-cratic, modern, secularized, and bureaucratized. The only feature appar-ently common to the two periods, the importance of nationalism, has even changed in nature. Rather than nationalism of survival, it has become ... one of expansion and growth, which is outward-looking and aggressive.[26]

During the **Quiet Revolution,** the people of Québec made it clear that they would no longer accept a second-class citizenship,[27] and that they wanted significant changes in their society. These changes took place with remarkable speed, and Québec society today is quite different from Québec society of the 1950s and early 1960s.

"Special Status." Québec has argued that it is *not* simply one of ten prov-inces—not a province "comme les autres," like the other nine. Many Québécois support a "two nations" theory of Canadian federalism,[28] suggesting that Canada is a federation of two nations, an English nation and a French nation, and that the English nation can be subdivided into nine units that correspond to nine of Canada's provinces today, while the French nation corresponds to Québec. In all issues, they suggest, Québec should be treated as a *partner* with (all of) the rest of Canada.

In recent constitutional discussions and debates, Québec has insisted on a constitutional recognition that it has a "special status" in the federal system, although the precise meaning of that phrase has never been made clear. This has resulted in a wide range of responses from the other provinces to Québec's demand, ranging from moderate support to furious opposition. In May of 1980, Québec Premier René Lévesque, the leader of the Parti Québécois, brought about a referendum on a new relationship between Québec and the rest of Canada, one called "sovereignty-association." The referendum failed by a 60–40 percent margin, but the issue came up again later. In fact, Québec has not yet ratified the present—1982— national Constitution, and has said that it will not do so until its "special status" is adequately recognized in that document through an appropriate amendment.[29]

Decentralized Federalism and Public Policy. Québec has consistently favored a decentralized federalism for Canada's national government, with most power remaining in the control of the provincial governments, not in the control of the federal government. Québec's government has traditionally argued that the provinces should have primary competence in virtually all policy areas, ranging from education to many foreign aid programs, and in many instances Québec has refused conditional grant programs from the federal government[30]—turned down millions of dollars—because those grants often would give the federal government policy-making power and because of its desire to keep the federal government from expanding the range of programs it controls or influences in contemporary society.

This debate over the optimal balance of Canada's constitutional structures has been long and at times heated. Québec has had more than one referendum in modern times on the nature of its relationship with the rest of the federation and whether it should move in the direction of sovereignty, once in 1980 and once in 1995.[31] The 1980 referendum was defeated by about a 60 percent to 40 percent margin; the 1995 referendum was defeated by about 50.5 percent to 49.5 percent (with nearly a 93 percent voter turnout!), a much narrower margin! More than one study of what the financial and cultural effects of secession would be have been undertaken.[32] Despite this fact, Québec continues as a member of the federal system and continues to work with the rest of Canada to discover a new "balance" for Canadian federalism that feels best to all of Canada's components.

One response to the 1980 referendum was that Canada "patriated" its constitution in 1982, referred to by many as "unilateral patriation," bringing it completely under its own control rather than having to ask the British Parliament to make changes, and began to renew its efforts to bring Québec back into Confederation. To date those efforts have not succeeded. A number of agreements, and attempts at agreements, have been tried, including the 1987–1990 **Meech Lake Accord process** and the 1992 **Charlottetown Agreement** process, among others.

The Meech Lake process, led by Prime Minister Brian Mulroney, specifically recognized Québec as a "distinct" society and allowed for Québec to have "renewed federalism," but at the end of the day the document that was agreed upon by all ten premiers and the prime minister was not approved because it required unanimous provincial ratification, and both Manitoba and Newfoundland failed to pass the needed approval legislative resolutions. This left Québec feeling frustrated at the inability of the rest of Canada to give it the recognition it felt it deserved, and left the rest of Canada frustrated at Québec's unwillingness to accept what (they felt) was fundamentally a good arrangement.

The 1992 Charlottetown process slightly modified the Meech Lake agreement to make it more palatable to other provinces, and made a major modification: *All* provinces would have a veto over future changes to Canadian political institutions. (This was a response to the criticism of some provinces that the Meech Lake package contained too many special powers for Québec.) The package included a "Canada Clause" to discuss Canadian values and entrench them in constitutional law, it further decentralized many federal powers, it made progress on more self-government for Native peoples, and proposed a number of institutional changes for federal political institutions, including changes in the House of Commons and the Senate. This agreement, too, was not approved, and in a national referendum (only the third national referendum in Canadian history) in which over 70 percent of the electorate voted, Canadians turned down the package of agreements by a 54 percent to 45 percent margin.

In 1995 and 1996 the Canadian Parliament passed legislation that it hoped would resolve the problem, by agreeing to a statement that Québec was "a distinct society" in Canada, by creating a structure so that Québec, Ontario, British Columbia, and any two Maritime or Prairie provinces could veto any further constitution change, and by committing the federal government to not use its spending power to create new shared-cost programs with the consent of the majority of the provinces. This, too, was not sufficient for Québec.

In 1995 a referendum took place in Québec dealing with its role in the federation. The referendum was controversial, and was criticized by many for being deceptive and confusing.[33] The referendum question was as follows:

> Do you agree that Quebec should become sovereign, after having made a formal offer to Canada for a new economic and political partnership, within the scope of the Bill respecting the future of Quebec and the agreement signed on June 12, 1995.

Critics said that the wording of the question was unfair. It asked for a "yes" response, that was more comfortable for voters than a "no" response. It suggested goodwill to Canada, but wasn't clear what that goodwill really entailed. And, it made no mention that *separation* was the goal of the referendum. Ultimately the Québec voters turned out in huge numbers—over 93 percent of registered voters participated—and very narrowly rejected the referendum, by a 50.6 to 49.4 margin.

Federal Prime Minister Jean Chrétien decided to take a twofold approach to the 1995 referendum, involving what became known as "Plan A" and "Plan B." The former emphasized cooperation and a willingness to consider increased *devolution*, or transferring more power from the federal government to provincial governments. This would possibly result in looser federal arrangements, with *all* provinces—including Québec—having relatively more power. The latter position, Plan B, was one that involved more confrontation and hard dialogue, challenging the right of Québec to secede and showing the voters of Québec what the costs of separation would be.

Plan B did not claim that Québec's voters did not have the right to vote in referenda, but did question whether the government of Québec could unilaterally act upon the results of such a referendum if a referendum advocating sovereignty and/or independence were to pass. The federal government's position was that any change in the federal arrangement between Québec and the rest of Canada would have to be negotiated between Québec and the other governments (the other nine provinces and Ottawa). Further, Ottawa argued that Québec might not fare as well in those negotiations as many assumed, that Québec's borders might not remain the same as they currently are, that Québec would have to assume a portion of the national debt (putting a huge financial burden upon its citizens), that Québec would not have a right to continue to use the Canadian dollar, that Québec would not be protected by the Canadian armed forces, and so on. Automatic membership in the North American Free Trade Agreement was also disputed, with Ottawa suggesting that a new government of Québec would have to apply for admission in the same way that many Latin American nations were going to do, and that for its part Ottawa was not at all sure that it would support such an application for membership by Québec. In other words, if Québec were to pull out of Canada such an action would not be cost-free.

In the days since the 1995 referendum, the strength of Québec nationalism has ebbed and flowed. In 1999 the Federal government passed the *Clarity Act*, which said that the federal government would not enter into negotiations with a province over separation unless (a) the referendum question was "clear," and (b) a "clear" expression of will had been obtained by a "clear" majority of the population.[34] In 2003, following Parti Québécois premiers Lucien Bouchard and Bernard Landry, Jean Charest became premier, and the Liberal party took control of the Québec National Assembly following many years of Parti Québécois (PQ) dominance. In the 2007 Québec election, the PQ came in *third* place, behind the first-place Liberals and the second place Democratic Action of Québec Party.

The issues of Canadian nationalism, Québec nationalism, and Canadian national unity have been debated since well before the 1867 Confederation agreement. Unlike other federal systems, however, in Canada the issue of the future of the national arrangement has regularly been high on the agenda of contentious and disputed issues of the day.

EXECUTIVE STRUCTURES

Under the BNA Act the national legislature was to be bicameral, and the executive power of the government was to be maintained by the governor-general, the representative of the Crown in Canada. Today the executive power is vested in the prime minister and the cabinet—nowhere mentioned in the BNA Act. The governor-general is primarily a figurehead,[35] and is appointed by the Queen of Canada (the same person as the Queen of the United Kingdom) to serve as her representative when she is not there[36]—almost all of the time—acting on the advice of the prime minister of Canada for what is typically a five-year term of office.

The cabinet is the repository of the true executive powers in Canadian government today. Although its formal (*de jure*, legal) function is to advise the sovereign, or the sovereign's representative, over the years power has come to rest *in the cabinet itself* rather than remain in the hands of the governor-general.[37]

The cabinet provides a link between the legislative power of the nation and the executive power of the nation in that virtually all members of cabinet are members of Parliament, and the cabinet itself is *responsible* to the House of Commons in the way we used the term in our earlier study of legislative institutions. The cabinet, therefore, "...is a legislative, executive, and administrative body,"[38] and is central in the Canadian governmental system. The crucial factor in this linkage between the executive and the legislative powers in the cabinet is the need for members of cabinet to hold positions in the House of Commons or the Senate, because this overlap insures that the cabinet will not forget its responsibility to the Parliament.

The leader of the cabinet is the prime minister, who is more than simply a "first among equals." He or she appoints others to the cabinet (appointments are of course actually technically made by the governor-general "on the advice" of the prime minister), and may ask for their resignations if he or she wishes; although cabinet decisions are theoretically reached by a consensus of the cabinet, the prime minister may impose a policy upon his or her cabinet colleagues. It is the prime minister who decides how best to balance the cabinet, both geographically and ideologically, when he or she "suggests" cabinet appointments to the governor-general.

It has been suggested that the prime minister has certain built-in advantages over his or her cabinet colleagues. First, the size of the prime minister's staff has greatly increased over time, giving him or her an advantage over other cabinet members with smaller staffs. Second, through his or her power to assign colleagues to cabinet committees, the prime minister has a great deal of leverage over the individual ministers, as well as influence. Third, cabinet members must spend a great deal of their time administering their various portfolios, and thus are more involved with detailed work than the prime minister, who has greater control over his or her own calendar and schedule. Finally, in spite of the fact that the cabinet is collectively responsible to the Parliament, each member of cabinet is individually responsible to the prime minister, since the

> ### TABLE 12.1
>
> **Minority Governments in Recent Years.**
> **Seats Controlled by Minority Governments in the House of Commons**
>
> | Years | Parliament/ Prime Minister | Party |
> |---|---|---|
> | 1972–1974 (109 of 264; 23 short) | 29th / Pierre Trudeau | Liberals |
> | 1979–1980 (136 of 282; 5 short) | 31st / Joe Clark | Conservatives |
> | 2004–2006 (135 of 308; 19 short) | 38th / Paul Martin | Liberals |
> | 2006–2008 (124 of 308; 30 short) | 39th / Stephen Harper | Conservatives |
> | 2008–2010 (143 of 308; 12 short) | 40th/ Stephen Harper | Conservatives |
>
> Source: Parliament of Canada, "Duration of Minority Governments, 1867 to Date," http://www.parl. gc.ca/ParlInfo/compilations/parliament/DurationMinorityGovernment.aspx?Language=E (accessed June 2011).

prime minister "suggested" his or her appointment to the governor-general, and thus the prime minister has another source of influence or leverage over individual cabinet members.[39]

Excluding from consideration minority and coalition governments, which have been few in modern Canadian history, although more frequent in recent years,[40] the Canadian prime minister has typically been the leader of the majority party in the House of Commons, and thus has selected members of his or her cabinet from among his party colleagues, being required to "balance" the cabinet according to many varied criteria, including regional, cultural, religious, ethnic, and economic criteria.[41] A list of recent minority government, and the number of seats controlled in the House of Commons by minority governments, can be found as Table 12.1.

Parliamentary government in Canada today could more realistically be called cabinet government; the true role of members of Parliament is to react to their leaders' ideas, to support or oppose cabinet proposals. This situation has, as one might imagine, resulted in criticism of the cabinet and the prime minister as being dictatorial and domineering. In fact, however, it is not at all unusual, as we have already seen in other instances. Defenders of the system contend that this situation is not unique to Canada, and that it is a normal by-product of a responsible-party, parliamentary system of government.[42]

The office of the **governor-general** is still the repository for most of the *formal* powers that were lodged there in 1867, the *de jure* executive powers that we referred to earlier in this book. The governor-general's loss of real or *de facto* power is as much a result of British parliamentary development as it is a result of Canadian parliamentary development; most major changes in the evolution of the office were made prior to Canadian independence in 1867. Today the governor-general plays a political role very similar to that of the heads of state in other parliamentary regimes. He or she "acts on the advice" of the cabinet and the prime minister, and may assent, or refuse to assent, to bills passed by both Houses of Parliament (although precedent has established that the power to refuse to assent to legislation is no longer a practicable option open to him or her).

LEGISLATIVE STRUCTURES

The BNA Act provided for a bicameral legislature, a Senate and a House of Commons. The Senate was to be appointed and to resemble other "upper" Houses of the time (1867), in that it was to provide a check on the elected House of Commons, be more representative of property, and guarantee provincial and regional representation in the government's policy-making process.

Provinces are not represented in the Canadian Senate in the same manner that states in the American Senate are represented by two senators each; as noted earlier, the Canadian Senate was constructed to represent the different geographical *regions* equally, not provide equal representation for each of the provinces, thus providing that the membership of the upper house was not based upon population. The provinces of Québec and Ontario each have twenty-four senators. All of the western provinces together have twenty-four senators, giving six each to British Columbia, Alberta, Saskatchewan, and Manitoba. All of the Maritime Provinces, prior to 1949, together had twenty-four senators, giving ten to New Brunswick, ten to Nova Scotia, and four to Prince Edward Island. When Newfoundland was admitted to Confederation in 1949, it received six senators of its own. The Northwest Territories, Nunavut, and the Yukon each have one senator, bringing the total to 105. The Constitution provides for four or eight extra senators to be appointed under special circumstances (up to a maximum of 112 senators, to allow for the breaking of a deadlock within the Senate and the Commons), too. (See Table 12.2.)

The Senate has historically been hampered in its legislative task by two major factors. First, the Senate suffers from a type of personnel problem. Although senators must now retire at the age of seventy-five years, many senators are inactive in the Senate's affairs due either to illness, old age, or lack of interest. Additionally, since appointment to the Senate is a political honor, many senators see the position *only* as one of honor and attend the work of the Senate only very rarely, instead spending their time in business outside of the Senate. Senators need only attend once every two years in order to keep their seats. This situation results in a small core of senators having to do the work of the entire House, making it virtually impossible for the body to perform up to its potential.

A second major factor hampering the Senate's performance of its legislative task is that most legislation, and *all* financial legislation, originates in the House of Commons, and consequently the Senate has little work to do early in its session and a great deal of work to do later when bills from the Commons are sent to the Senate for passage. This leaves the Senate little time for serious consideration of the bills themselves.

Many observers note that the strength of the Senate has traditionally been found in its committees.[43] The Senate, through its committees, has become a major screening point for much private legislation in the Canadian political system, in part because similar opportunities are not readily available in the House of Commons. Indeed, scrutiny of the executive in many respects can be *better* performed in the Senate than in the Commons, since, due to

TABLE 12.2

The Senate of Canada
Membership as of June 2011

Party	Seats	
Conservative	54	
Liberal	45	
Independent	2	Men: 66 Women: 37 (35.9%)
Progressive Conservative	2	
Vacant	2	Québec (1); Newfound and Labrador (1)
Total	105	

Source: Government of Canada, Parliament of Canada, The Senate, http://www.parl.gc.ca/
SenatorsMembers/Senate/PartyStandings/ps-E.htm (accessed June 2011).

party discipline and the "responsibility" of the Government to the House of Commons, the Commons cannot feel as free to criticize the executive part of the government: Too much criticism of the Government in the Commons could embarrass the Government, since it must maintain the confidence of the Commons. The same is not the case in the Senate.

The Senate has been the subject of much criticism in the Canadian political arena. The debate has long gone on as to whether the Senate should be left as it is, be reformed, or simply be abolished.[44] If the Senate acts against the will of the House of Commons and the Government, it is criticized as being antidemocratic. If it acts supporting the will of the House of Commons and the Government, it is criticized as being a useless expense.

In recent years, however, the movement for Senate reform has become increasingly popular in Canada. The movement took on its most formal power when the province of Alberta passed a law indicating that the citizens of Alberta would vote for nominees for the Senate; subsequently, the prime minister would be morally bound (the law suggested) to advise the governor-general to appoint the individual(s) who had been elected by the people of Alberta when an opening came about in the Senate. Early after having been elected prime minister in 2006, Stephen Harper announced that his government would pursue "comprehensive Senate reform." Its proposals for reform—that would have included a method to ascertain the preferences of electors on appointments to the Senate, and a way to limit the tenure of senators—never got past the first reading in the House of Commons, and never even *got* to a reading stage in the Senate. The cries for Senate reform continue to be heard across Canada, and most students of the institution are in agreement that there *will*, indeed, eventually, be significant reform of the Senate in the future.[45]

Several topics related to the House of Commons and its role in the Canadian political system are important in our inquiry here, inasmuch as they may affect legislative behavior in the Parliament. The legislative process itself has been discussed at length in several different places, and it is not necessary to repeat a description of the legislative process at this point.[46] Rather, we shall discuss some of the characteristics of Parliament that are relevant to our study, characteristics that include the role of political parties in the Commons, formal Commons structures and their impact upon legislative behavior, and the role of the backbencher in the House of Commons, generally.

The party's role vis-à-vis parliamentary action is significant in the Canadian political system. In a manner similar to that of other parliamentary nations, party discipline exists in the House of Commons. That is, once parties have decided what their policy is to be, party members are expected to support that policy in the House, through their speeches or their votes. If a member does not follow the party lines, he or she can expect the party to react in an appropriate manner.

Voting in the Commons reflects the existence of a disciplined responsible-party system, as well as Canada's federal system of government.[47] Whether the party members in the House of Commons vote in line with their party's policy out of fear, pragmatism, or for normative reasons, the end result is the same: The political party is a significant factor in the House of Commons.

The House of Commons is the source of the authority of the executive power of the prime minister and his or her cabinet. The governor-general traditionally invites the leader of the largest party in the House of Commons to form a Government, which is responsible to (i.e., must maintain the support of a majority in) the House of Commons. Only on rare occasions, when no single party has controlled a majority in the House, has the prime minister not directly led a majority, and in those instances informal "understandings" existed between the major (plurality) party and a "partner" party. For example, on more than one occasion the Liberal Party led by Pierre Elliot Trudeau had an "understanding" with the New Democratic Party that permitted the Liberals to govern; the NDP preferred the Liberals in power to the Conservatives. In the period from 2006 through 2011, Conservative Party leader **Stephen Harper** survived as Prime Minister with the serial assistance of the other parties in the House, the Liberals, the New Democrats, or the Bloc Québécois.

The powers and structures of the Canadian House of Commons are very similar to those that we met in the British situation. What has been referred to as the Canadian "Parliamentary Life-Cycle"[48]—from the governor-general summoning both Houses of Parliament together for the Speech from the Throne, through normal business during the parliamentary session, through a *vote of no confidence* or the termination of Parliament due to the expiration of its term of office—follows the Westminster Model very closely.

The stages of the legislative process in Canada follow the British model in a similar manner. Different calendars exist for Government business and Private Members' business, with a limit on the amount of time each day that can be spent on Private Members' business. *Government Bills*[49] typically begin in Cabinet, where policy discussion leads to a recommendation for legislation. Legislation is drafted (typically by the Department of Justice) and approved by the appropriate minister and subsequently the entire Cabinet before it is actually introduced in Parliament. Bills are introduced in either house of Parliament, but Government bills invariably are first introduced in the House of Commons, where they receive a first reading and brief discussion, a second reading (with a debate and a vote on the principles of the bill), and are referred to legislative committee for detailed examination. When (and if) the bill is reported out of committee, it receives a third reading and vote, and if it passes this hurdle, the bill goes to the other House of Parliament for a repetition of the legislative process there. Bills must pass both houses in identical form before they can be assented to by the Governor-general.

Debate in the House of Commons is vigorous, and the daily Question Period in the House—when Members of Parliament from both sides of the House, Government and Opposition, can address questions to all members of the Cabinet—can be extraordinarily lively and tense. Unlike the British case in which the prime minister responds to questions only twice a week, for fifteen minutes at a time, the Canadian prime minister must be prepared to respond to questions *every* day of the week during Question Period. These questions are designed to elicit information from the Government, bring issues to the attention of the Government, and embarrass the Government, and the prime minister and other members of the Cabinet must be prepared to answer a very wide range of inquiries.

Thus, as in the other parliamentary systems we discussed earlier in this book, while the executive branch of government *leads* the legislative branch, in that the leaders of the executive branch are also the leaders of the largest party in the legislative branch, the executive is also *of* the legislative branch, and thereby responsible to it.

COURTS

Canada's federal system is also reflected in the way its system of courts operates.[50] Canadian courts, like courts in most other democratic nations, are independent of the executive branch of government, and are thereby shielded from direct political pressure. Provinces have their own police, county, and superior courts, with the right to appeal to higher provincial courts and, ultimately, to the federal Supreme Court of Canada. Court structures are operated by the provinces in both the areas of civil and criminal law. At the same time, however, to balance the grant of exclusive power over *civil procedure* given to the *provinces*, the *federal* government has exclusive jurisdiction over *criminal procedure*, and it is the federal government that controls the appointment, salary, and tenure of the judges in the courts that are established by the provinces. Thus, the Canadian federal judicial structure appears as ten separate provincial pyramids, designed by the provinces and staffed by federal appointments, with civil procedure established by the provinces (so that, for example, civil procedures in Ontario might be different from civil procedures in British Columbia), but criminal procedure will be standardized through its control by the federal government.

There is a single Supreme Court of Canada that acts as an appeals court for the entire nation,[51] both in civil and criminal cases. The Supreme Court also advises on questions referred to it by the Governor-General in Council (that is, on the advice of the prime minister). Such issues might include issues of the constitutionality of federal or provincial law, or questions about Parliament's powers or the powers of a provincial legislature. An example of such a referral was the question of whether the *Assemblée Nationale* of Québec had the power to organize a binding referendum on Québec's position in the Canadian federation.

In civil cases the Supreme Court may hear cases if the Court believes that a "question of public importance" is involved, one that goes beyond the personal interests of the parties involved in the litigation. In criminal cases the Court may choose to hear cases where there is a question about a significant point of law.

The Federal Court of Canada is a special federal court that has jurisdiction in claims against the Crown, claims by the Crown, or a variety of issues related to Federal Boards, Commissions, or other federal issues, including taxes, citizenship, interprovincial works, and the like. The Federal Court of Appeal hears appeals from trial courts, and appeals from Federal Boards and Commissions. While the Court sits only in Ottawa, it has offices throughout Canada.

In Canada today, the judges of the respective courts, from the Supreme Court of Canada and the Federal Court of Canada through the provincial high courts, are quite secure in their positions. Only upon request of both Houses of Parliament to the governor-general of Canada can a judge be removed from office, and then only after a major formal investigation by a judicial inquiry body, including all of the chief justices in Canada. This has never happened in Canadian history.

POLITICAL PARTIES AND ELECTIONS

Members of the House of Commons are elected by plurality voting in single-member districts. As we have seen to be the case elsewhere, there is a relationship between electoral systems and party systems (i.e., certain electoral systems may promote or retard the growth of political parties). The Canadian electoral system has had a good deal of impact upon the Canadian party system, and both deserve some comment here.

The Canadian party system is literally a multiparty system, but can be called a **two-party-plus system.**[52] One political scientist has argued that the present electoral system in Canada may have negative consequences for elections because of the manner in which it influences the party system.[53] Specifically, he suggested that in many modern elections the electoral system either did not produce a majority government or produced such a majority that the opposition was left ineffective. Although his work does not include the most recent federal elections, the consequences of elections that he described prior to that time have continued to exist in recent years.

The results from recent federal elections demonstrate the importance of *electoral concentration* of vote. Parties that received electoral support that was sufficiently concentrated won substantial numbers of seats in specific regions of the country. A negative version of this is demonstrated by the Progressive Conservative Party, which suffered from what could be called the weakness of "diffused support." The PC Party had controlled 153 seats in the Parliament elected in 1988, but won *only* 2 seats in the election of 1993, despite winning a substantial (16 percent) proportion of the vote. This was because its vote was spread out too thinly, so. candidates routinely came in second—sometimes third—in their electoral contests. The reader will recall that the bias of single-member district voting is that coming in second provides no representation at all. This pattern was repeated in the 1997 federal election in which the Progressive Conservatives received 19 percent of the vote, yet received less than 7 percent of the seats in the House of Commons.

The data from the 2011 election show this same phenomenon, this time working *in favor* of the Conservative Party of Canada. The Conservatives won 39.6 percent of the vote, but that translated into over 50 percent of the seats in the House of Commons because the Conservative support was geographically concentrated, so that they often won seats with *less than* a majority of the votes in a district. On the other hand, the Liberals received almost 19 percent of the vote yet won just over 10 percent of the seats in the House, because their strength was not sufficiently concentrated; they often came in second, or third, thus diluting the strength of their support.[54] (See Table 12.3)

Third and fourth parties have played an important role in Canadian politics in the past, regardless of their strength in the federal House of Commons, both because of their ideologies, and because they often control political office at the *provincial* level, which has given them a substantial base of power in the particular Canadian federal structure. As Mallory has argued, third parties can afford to experiment with new ideas, and can play the necessary role of innovator in the party system.[55] They may also be valuable in that they may attract people to the political system who are not attracted by the major parties. The roles of the Reform Party and the Alliance (especially) in the province of Alberta, and the Bloc Québécois in the province of Québec demonstrate that a firm basis on the provincial level can be enough to catapult a party to national significance. Although the electoral system has tended to unduly support some parties and weaken others in terms of representation in Commons, these parties have managed to survive and to make themselves heard in Parliament, and across the nation, and have thereby performed a function for the political system as a whole.[56]

The importance of the Canadian electoral system is obvious: The system makes it difficult for smaller parties to exist and function at the national level, much as proportional representation systems make it easy for smaller parties to exist and function. In systems with proportional representation, a party may need only have 1 or 2 percent of the national vote in order to be represented in the legislature. In Canada, on the other hand, a party must have a plurality of votes in a single district.

TABLE 12.3

The House of Commons, May 2, 2011 Election

Party	% of vote	# of seats	% of seats	Electoral bias
Conservative	39.6	166	53.9	+14.3
New Democratic Pty	30.6	103	33.4	+ 2.8
Liberal	18.9	34	11.0	− 7.9
Bloc Québécois	6.0	4	1.3	− 4.7
Green	3.9	1	0.3	− 3.6
Total	99.0	308	99.9	

Members: 308; women: 76 (24.7 %)

- 106 members from Ontario
- 75 from Québec
- 36 from British Columbia
- 28 from Alberta
- 14 each from Manitoba and Saskatchewan
- 11 from Nova Scotia
- 10 from New Brunswick
- 7 from Newfoundland and Labrador
- 4 from Prince Edward Island
- 1 from the Northwest Territories
- 1 from Nunavut
- 1 from Yukon

Source: Inter-Parliamentary Union, *Parline,* "Canada: House of Commons," http://www.ipu.org/parline-e/reports/2055_E.htm (accessed June, 2011).

This makes it more difficult to win a seat; not only must the party have a certain level of support nationally, but the support must be sufficiently *concentrated* in order to have the party win even a single seat and be represented by even one person in Parliament. This will have an effect not only upon the ease with which a party can reach majority status in Parliament but also upon recruitment to Parliament: Fewer party organizations are able to take part in legislative behavior.

The formal structure of parties in Canada is different from party structures in Britain, partially because of the differences suggested between a unitary (e.g., Britain) and a federal (e.g., Canada) governmental system. The federal nature of the Canadian political system has, in past years, been reflected in the party system, in which provincial party organizations were not run directly by the national party organizations. The relative independence of the provincial party organizations has left these parties in the position of being able to criticize policies of the national party organizations, if they see fit to do so. This allows sectionalism to have some voice within a national party organization, something with both positive and negative consequences.[57]

Traditionally, the national and provincial executives of political parties have met at least annually, and their role in the party policy-making process has been somewhat ambiguous. Jackson and Jackson have noted that "parties at the federal and provincial levels may bear the same name but act quite independently," showing that the Liberals "have separate federal and provincial wings in the four largest provinces—Québec, Ontario, Alberta, and British Columbia—that are informally linked to varying degrees." This "informal linkage" sometimes makes it very difficult for a party to be effectively organized, or to compete effectively.[58] Van Loon and Whittington have suggested that "the feeling persists, especially in the caucus, that the executive exists to administer the party machinery, and the caucus to determine party policy."[59] Thus, some tension has existed within the respective party organizations as to who, in fact, should have influence upon the policy-making decisions that must be made.

Party organization in the Parliament is most evident in the party caucus. There, policy questions are discussed, although these discussions vary in liveliness depending upon whether the given party is in or out of power. When a party is out of power, there is likely to be greater freedom in discussion. When a party is in control of the government, the opposite is likely to be the case.

Another link that the Canadian parties have with the public is that of the party convention.[60] Party conventions may be used to increase party morale, to help formulate party policy, or to choose new leadership. Conventions vary in frequency. The New Democratic party holds a regular convention every two years to discuss its leadership and the issues it believes are most important to its political future.[61] The Liberal and Progressive Conservative parties are supposed to hold conventions every two to four years, or so their platforms indicate. However, if the party is functioning well, or if there is little public desire for such a participatory event, the party is likely to postpone the convention until such demands occur. On the other hand, conventions may be called *early* to respond to special party needs or to respond to electoral weaknesses of party leaders, as well.

THE CANADIAN SYSTEM IN PERSPECTIVE

We began this chapter with the statement that although the Canadian political system could be seen to have a great many similarities to the British political system, it would be seen in the course of the chapter that many significant structural and behavioral differences exist between the two nations. This has been shown to be the case.

The federal nature of the Canadian political system has many significant ramifications for the practice of Canadian politics. Because Canadian federalism is significantly different from other federal power relationships, such as the German, Australian, or American cases, provinces have a great deal of power in Canada and the Dominion government is weaker in relation to the provinces than are many other federal national governments in relation to the governments of their component parts.

Beyond this, the special bi-national character of the Canadian national identity, and the particular conflicts that exist in Canadian society as a result of English–French tensions, have added a dimension to Canadian political debates that simply does not exist in other systems. Questions dealing with the special role of Québec in the Canadian federal system, the "special status" of Québec in the Canadian constitutional system, and the future role of a French–Canadian nation within Canada are all unique challenges to political stability in a future Canadian polity.

We observed several structural factors that are different in Canada from what they are elsewhere. A written Constitution with an entrenched Charter of Rights and Freedoms and an active system of judicial review clearly separate Canada from the British system of government that served as the original model for Canadian politics.

A number of legislative distinctions exist, too. The ability of the back-bencher to introduce legislation without the formal permission of his or her party whip is of no little significance in terms of the autonomy of individual legislators. Similarly, rules governing debate, the introduction of motions, and so on, are all more flexible and permissive in Canada than they are in many other parliamentary systems. The system of committees, and other recent changes in parliamentary procedure designed to give individual legislators a more significant role in the legislative process clearly set Canada apart from other "Westminster" parliamentary systems.

One of the most significant structural characteristics observed in the Canadian political system is the electoral system itself. The existence of single-member districts with a multiparty system is unusual, and the system has been shown to have a bias when electoral results are examined.

Although Canada began as a British territory, and in its early years developed a political and constitutional system "similar in principle" to that of the United Kingdom, we have seen that there are a significant number of respects in which Canada is significantly different from Britain. The political institutions, and corresponding political behaviors, which have evolved over the past century-and-a-quarter, have demonstrated that Canada is, indeed, a mature, independent nation; while Canada may have started out as a "child" in the British "family," modeling governmental institutions and political practices after the practice of the British "adults," over time institutions and behaviors have developed that demonstrate a uniquely Canadian way of addressing political challenges and problems.

DISCUSSION QUESTIONS

1. Why did Canada not have a written constitution originally? What changed in Canada's political environment to make the "patriation" of a constitution important?
2. How is Canadian federalism different from that in Germany or the United States? What powers do Canadian provinces have that their counterparts in other nations do not? Does this make policymaking in Canada more or less efficient?

3. What is the role of *geography* in Canadian politics? How has regionalism been manifested in Canadian political institutions historically? Does this still apply today?

4. Does the Canadian prime minister have more or less power than his British counterpart? Why? How would you compare the Canadian prime minister with the German chancellor? Why?

5. What is the role of the Senate today? Should it continue to exist? Why? How would you compare it with the upper houses of Britain and Germany? What is the added value that it brings to the Canadian legislative process?

6. How has the competition between Canada's major political parties changed over the years? What are the key differences between the role of parties in Canada today and their historical role?

KEY TERMS

British North America Act (BNA) of 1867 296
Charlottetown Agreement 302
Constitution Act 297
decentralized federalism 302
governor-general 306
Harper, Stephen 309

Meech Lake Accord 302
patriation 296
Québec nationalism 301
Queen of Canada 299
Quiet Revolution 301
regionalism in Canada 300
Section 91 of BNA Act 298

Section 92 of BNA Act 298
similar in principle clause 296
special status 301
two-party-plus system 311

SUGGESTED READINGS

William Coleman, *The Independence Movement in Québec, 1945–1980* (Toronto, ON: University of Toronto Press, 1984). Québec plays a special role in the Canadian federal system. This book describes the role of Québec in the Canadian federation, and how that role has evolved over the years to the position it occupies today.

Alan Gagnon and Brian Tanguay, *Canadian Parties in Transition* (Peterborough, ON: Broadview Press, 2007). As is the case in other Western democracies, political parties play a crucial role in Canadian politics. This volume describes the Canadian political party system on both the national level and the provincial level, and offers a context within which their role can be evaluated.

Robert J. Jackson and Doreen Jackson, *Politics in Canada: Culture, Institutions, Behaviour and Public Policy* (Toronto, ON: Pearson, 2009). This is an introductory textbook on Canadian politics, and has been *the* definitive textbook on Canadian politics for years. It covers all Canadian political institutions and political behavior.

Patrick James, *Constitutional Politics in Canada after the Charter: Liberalism, Communitarianism, and Systemism* (Vancouver, BC: University of British Columbia Press, 2010). A comprehensive and up-to-date examination of the role of the constitution in Canada and the relationship of constitutional law and policy to the practices and principles of traditional Canadian political culture.

David E. Smith, *Federalism and the Constitution of Canada* (Toronto, ON: University of Toronto Press, 2010). Canadian federalism poses challenges for both the central government in Ottawa and the provincial governments. This volume examines the special nature of federalism in Canada and describes the ways in which it makes the creation of public policy more difficult than it might otherwise be.

NOTES

1. In 1965, Minister of Justice Guy Favreau indicated in a review of practices of amending the Constitution of Canada that although an enactment by the United Kingdom is necessary to amend the BNA Act, such action is taken only upon formal request from Canada. No Act of the United Kingdom Parliament affecting Canada is, therefore, passed unless it is requested and consented to by Canada. Conversely, every amendment requested by Canada in the past has been enacted. See Guy Favreau, *The Amendment of the Constitution of Canada* (Ottawa, ON: Queen's Printer, 1965), p. 44. See also Patrick James, *Constitutional Politics in Canada after the Charter: Liberalism, Communitarianism, and Systemism* (Vancouver, BC: University of British Columbia Press, 2010).

2. Robert Jackson and Michael Atkinson, *The Canadian Legislative System* (Toronto, ON: Macmillan, 1974), p. 76.

3. Richard Van Loon and Michael Whittington, *The Canadian Political System* (Toronto, ON: McGraw-Hill, 1971), p. 111. See also John Redekop, ed., "Continentalism: The Key to Canadian Politics," in *Approaches to Canadian Politics* (Scarborough, ON: Prentice Hall, 1983), p. 35.

4. Van Loon and Whittington, *The Canadian Political System*, p. 100. See the publication by the Government of Canada, *A Consolidation of the Constitution Acts, 1867 to 1982* (Ottawa, ON: Department of Justice, Canada), 1999.

5. Robert Dawson, *The Government of Canada* (Toronto, ON: University of Toronto Press, 1954), p. 63.

6. The history leading up to the new constitution was long and arduous, and hotly debated. For discussion of the process, as well as the significance of the new document, see Gregory Mahler, *New Dimensions of Canadian Federalism: Canada in Comparative Perspective* (Rutherford, NJ: Fairleigh Dickinson University Press, 1987), Chapter 3: "Canadian Federalism and Constitutional Amendment and Reform in Canada," pp. 57–83. See also David E. Smith, *Federalism and the Constitution of Canada* (Toronto, ON: University of Toronto Press, 2010).

7. There has been an explosion of literature on the Canadian Constitution in the last many years as a result of the revision and "patriation" of the Constitution. See *inter alia* Michael Behiels, ed., *The Meech Lake Primer: Conflicting Views of the 1987 Constitutional Accord* (Ottawa, ON: University of Ottawa Press, 1989); Raymond Breton, *Why Meech Failed: Lessons for Canadian Constitutionmaking* (Toronto, ON: C.D. Howe Institute, 1992); and James B. Kelly, *Governing with the Charter* (Vancouver, BC: University of British Columbia Press, 2005).

8. One of the best studies of this area is that by David Bell, *The Roots of Disunity: A Study of Canadian Political Culture* (Toronto, ON: Oxford University Press, 1992). The major cultural cleavage in Canada, of course, one to which we shall return later in this chapter, is that between English Canada and French Canada, primarily in Quebec. On this, see Kenneth McRoberts, *English Canada and Quebec: Avoiding the Issue* (North York, ON: York University Press, 1991).

9. Allan Kornberg, *Canadian Legislative Behavior* (New York: Holt, Rinehart, and Winston, 1967), p. 17. The provinces are still very much significant players in the Canadian political system, far more important, in fact, than are states in the United States. See Jennifer Smith, *The Meaning of Provincial Equality in Canadian Federalism* (Kingston, ON: Institute of Intergovernmental Relations, Queen's University, 1998). More recent studies would include the following: Herman Bakvis and Grace Skogstad, *Canadian Federalism in the New Millennium: Performance, Effectiveness, and Legitimacy* (Toronto, ON: Oxford University Press, 2001).

10. For a historical approach to the topic of federalism, see William Ormsby, *The Emergence of the Federal Concept in Canada: 1839–1845* (Toronto, ON: University of Toronto Press, 1969). See also Garth Stevenson, *Federalism in Canada* (Toronto, ON: McClelland and Stewart, 1990); and David E. Smith, *Federalism and the Constitution of Canada* (Toronto, ON: University of Toronto Press, 2010).

11. Steven Muller, "Federalism and the Party System in Canada," in A. Wildavsky, ed., *American Federalism in Perspective* (Boston, MA: Little Brown, 1967), p. 147. A volume on the role of the Judicial Committee in the shaping of Canada's Constitution is that by Christopher Manfredi, *Judicial Power and the Charter: Canada and the Paradox of Liberal Constitutionalism* (Toronto, ON: McClelland and Stewart, 1992).

12. See Magnusson, Soberman, and Lederman, *Canadian Constitutional Dilemmas Revisited, op. cit.* A very good study is that by Ivan Bernier and André Lajoie, *The Supreme Court of Canada as an Instrument of Political Change* (Toronto, ON: University of Toronto Press, 1986).

13. See Harvey Lazar, ed., *Toward a New Mission Statement for Canadian Fiscal Federalism* (Montreal, QC: McGill-Queen's University Press, 2000). See also Thomas McIntosh, *Federalism, Democracy and Labour Market Policy in Canada* (Montreal, QC: McGill-Queen's University Press, 2000); and Robert B. Asselin, *The Canadian Social Union: Questions about the Division of Powers and Fiscal Federalism* (Ottawa, ON: Library of Parliament, 2001).

14. See Edwin Black, *Divided Loyalties: Canadian Concepts of Federalism* (Montreal, QC: McGill-Queen's University Press, 1975), especially pp. 1–21. See also Duane Adams, *Federalism, Democracy, and Health Policy in Canada* (Kingston, ON: Institute of Intergovernmental Relations of Queen's University, 2001). A good debate can be found in two volumes: Gordon DiGiacomo, *The Case for Centralized Federalism* (Ottawa, ON: University of Ottawa Press, 2010); and Gilles Paquet, *The Case for Decentralized Federalism* (Ottawa, ON: University of Ottawa Press, 2010).

15. For example, see Gilles Lalande, *In Defense of Federalism: A View from Quebec* (Toronto, ON: McClelland and Stewart, 1978).

16. William Mathie, "Political Community and the Canadian Experience: Reflections on Nationalism, Federalism, and Unity," *Canadian Journal of Political Science* 12 (1979): 19. It has already been observed that in many respects the "central" problem of federalism in Canada has to do with the question of Québec and its relation with the federal government, a topic to which we shall return later in this chapter. See Guy LaForest, *What Canadian Federalism Means in Québec* (Edmonton, AB: University of Alberta Press, 2010).

17. See the very good essay by Howard Cody, "The Evolution of Federal-Provincial Relations in Canada" for a discussion of this history. See also Alan Cairns, "The Other Crisis of Canadian Federalism," *Canadian Public Administration* 22 (1979): 176–177.

18. Cairns, "The Other Crisis," p. 175.

19. Robert J. Jackson and Doreen Jackson, *Politics in Canada: Culture, Institutions, Behaviour and Public Policy* (Toronto, ON: Pearson, 2009), p. 94. See also Brett McGillivray, *Canada: A Nation of Regions* (New York: Oxford University Press, 2010).

20. Richard Simeon and David Elkins, "Regional Political Cultures in Canada," *Canadian Journal of Political Science* 7, no. 3 (1974): 397–437. See Roger Biggins and Loleen Berdahl, *Western Visions, Western Futures* (Peterborough, ON:

Broadview Press, 2003); and Nelson Wiseman, *In Search of Canadian Political Culture* (Vancouver, BC: University of British Columbia Press, 2007).

21. See Roger Gibbins, *Prairie Politics and Society* (Toronto, ON: Butterworths, 1980); Larry Pratt and Garth Stevenson, eds., *Western Separatism* (Edmonton, AB: Hurtig, 1981), or Janice Gross Stein et al., *Uneasy Partners: Multiculturalism and Rights in Canada* (Waterloo, ON: Wilfrid Laurier University Press, 2007).

22. See Dominique Clift, *Québec Nationalism in Crisis* (Montreal, QC: McGill-Queen's University Press, 1982) for a very good historical discussion of nationalism in Québec. See also Robert Chodos, Michel Venne, and Louisa Blair, *Vive Québec! New Thinking and New Approaches to the Québec Nation* (Toronto, ON: James Lorimer, 2001).

23. See Jonathan Vance, *A History of Canadian Culture* (New York: Oxford University Press, 2009) for a discussion of this distinction. See Alain Gagnon and Rafaele Iacovino, *Federalism, Citizenship and Québec: Debating Multinationalism* (Toronto, ON: University of Toronto Press, 2007).

24. This is a very interesting dimension of Canadian history, and is covered very nicely in Edgar McInnis' volume *Canada: A Political and Social History* (Toronto, ON: Holt, Rinehart and Winston of Canada, 1969). A very good discussion of "the constraints of history" in Québec can be found in the volume by Guy Lachapelle, Gérald Bernier, Daniel Salée, and Luc Bernier, *The Québec Democracy: Structures, Processes, and Policies* (Montreal, QC: McGraw-Hill Ryerson, 1993).

25. See A. Brichant, *Option Canada: The Economic Implications of Separatism for the Province of Québec* (Montreal, QC: The Canada Committee, 1968); Louis Balthazar, *Québec: A Political Retrospective, 1979–1998* (Plattsburgh, NY: Center for the Study of Canada, 1998). Very good general discussions of these issues include David Cameron, ed., *The Referendum Papers: Essays on Secession and National Unity* (Toronto, ON: University of Toronto Press, 1999); and George Sherman, *Past and Future of the Separatist Movement in Québec* (Plattsburgh, NY Center for the Study of Canada, 1997).

26. Rand Dyck, *Provincial Politics in Canada* (Scarborough, ON: Prentice Hall of Canada, 1991), p. 215.

27. One of the classic works of this period was by Pierre Vallières, titled *White Niggers of America* (Toronto, ON: McClelland and Stewart, 1971). See also Louis Balthazar and L. Haenens, *Images of Canadianness: Visions on Canada's Politics, Culture, Economics* (Ottawa, ON: University of Ottawa Press, 1998).

28. This is clearly explained in Edwin Black, *Divided Loyalties: Canadian Concepts of Federalism* (Montreal, QC: McGill-Queen's University Press, 1975).

29. Discussion of the "Meech Lake" Agreement, named after the site at which initial agreement was reached, has been the subject of a massive literature in recent years. See, *inter alia*, Andrew Cohen, *A Deal Undone: The Making and Breaking of the Meech Lake Accord* (Vancouver, BC: Douglas and McIntyre, 1990); or Pierre Trudeau, *Pierre Trudeau Speaks Out on Meech Lake* (Toronto, ON: General Paperbacks, 1990).

30. This would be a grant in which the federal government might say, to take an example from the field of education, "we know that you have the authority to develop a network of community colleges and we do not, but if you will develop a network of colleges according to our specifications, we'll pay for the overwhelming percent of the cost of the development." While many of the provincial governments have accepted these types of offers—on the grounds that they're getting something (such

as a network of community colleges) for a significantly lower cost than otherwise might be the case—Québec has opposed these offers on the principle that the federal government shouldn't be involved *at all* in issues over which provinces have jurisdiction. See Richard Simeon, *Federal Provincial Diplomacy*, op. cit. See also Alain Noel, *Without Québec: Collaborative Federalism with a Footnote?* (Montreal, QC: Institute for Research on Public Policy, 2000).

31. See the two essays by Gregory Mahler, "Canadian Federalism and the 1995 Referendum: A Perspective from Outside of Québec," *American Review of Canadian Studies* 25, no. 4 (1995): 449–476; and "The 1995 Québec Referendum and Canadian Unity: A Perspective from One Year's Distance," *American Review of Canadian Studies* 26, no. 4 (1996): 641–646. See also Anne F. Bayefsky, *Self-Determination in International Law: Quéebec and Lessons* (The Hague, The Netherlands: Kluwer Law International, 2000).

32. See William Coleman, *The Independence Movement in Québec, 1945–1980* (Toronto, ON: University of Toronto Press, 1984); or John Fitzmaurice, *Québec and Canada: Past, Present, and Future* (New York: St. Martin's Press, 1985).

33. Jackson and Jackson, *Politics in Canada*, p. 235

34. Ibid., p. 244.

35. A good description of the evolution of this power in Canada can be found in James Mallory, *The Structure of Canadian Government* (Toronto, ON: MacMillan, 1971), pp. 11–21. See also Jackson and Jackson, *Politics in Canada*, pp. 268–271.

36. Of course the Queen is *not* in Canada most of the time. Typically the Queen will visit Canada no more than once a year. See Adrienne Clarkson, *Media Information: Installation of the Governor General, October 7, 1999* (Ottawa, ON: Canadian Heritage, 1999).

37. Jackson and Atkinson, *The Canadian Legislative System*, p. 53.

38. Allan Kornberg and William Mishler, *Influence in Parliament: Canada* (Durham, NC: Duke University Press, 1976), p. 34.

39. Kornberg and Mishler, *Influence in Parliament*, pp. 35–36. Good work on the power of the prime minister would include Gordon Donaldson, *Eighteen Men: The Prime Ministers of Canada* (Toronto, ON: Doubleday, 1985); and Archives Canada, *Prime Ministers of Canada: The Prime Minister in Canadian Life and Politics* (Ottawa, ON: Library and Archives Canada, 2009).

40. Stephen Harper's Conservative-led minority government that was elected in 2006 was only the 11th minority government to be formed in 39 Canadian general elections through 2006.

41. For discussions of the Cabinet and its formation, see Robert Dawson and W.F. Dawson, *Democratic Government in Canada* (Toronto, ON: University of Toronto Press, 1971), pp. 46–54.

42. The classic study in this area is that by Thomas Hockin, *Power: The Prime Minister and Political Leadership in Canada*, 2nd ed. (Scarborough, ON: Prentice-Hall Canada, 1977).

43. See the Senate publication *Fundamentals of Senate Committees* (Ottawa, ON: The Senate of Canada: 1999). See also Serge Joyal, ed., *Protecting Canadian Democracy: The Senate You Never Knew* (Montréal, QC: McGill-Queen's University Press, 2003).

44. See David E. Smith, *The Canadian Senate in Bicameral Perspective* (Toronto, ON: University of Toronto Press, 2003). A less positive perspective is characterized by Claire Hoy's volume *Nice Work: The Continuing Scandal of Canada's Senate* (Toronto, ON: McClelland and Stewart, 1999).

45. There is a substantial literature on Senate reform. A good recent effort is that by Jennifer Smith, *The Democratic Dilemma: Reforming the Canadian Senate* (Montréal, QC: McGill-Queen's University Press, 2009); and Bruce Hicks and André Blais, *Restructuring the Canadian Senate Through Elections* (Montréal, QC: Institute for Research on Public Policy, 2008).

46. A very good review essay of recent scholarship on the Canadian Parliament can be found in the piece by Michael Atkinson and Paul Thomas, "Studying the Canadian Parliament," *Legislative Studies Quarterly* 18, no. 3 (1993): 423–451.

47. See Christopher Kam, *Party Discipline and Parliamentary Politics* (New York: Cambridge University Press, 2009).

48. Jackson and Jackson, *Politics in Canada*, pp. 315–316. See Alain Lanoix, *Elections in Canada* (Ottawa , ON: Library of Parliament, 2000).

49. A very good discussion of types of bills—private vs. public, Government vs. Private Members', money vs. nonfinancial, and supply vs. ways-and-means—can be found in Jackson and Jackson, *Politics in Canada*, p. 317.

50. See the British North America Act (Canada Act) of 1867, Section 92 (l4) for provincial legislative jurisdictions, and Section 91 (27) for federal legislative jurisdiction. The interested student can find this in Jackson and Jackson, *Politics in Canada*, pp. 178–182. See also Beverley McLachlin, *The Canadian Judicial System in the 21st Century* (Ottawa, ON: Supreme Court of Canada, 2000); and Ian Greene, *The Courts* (Vancouver, BC: University of British Columbia Press, 2005).

51. See Jackson and Jackson, *Politics in Canada*, pp. 179–180. See also Peter James McCormick, *Supreme at Last: The Evolution of the Supreme Court of Canada* (Toronto, ON: James Lorimer & Co., 2000). See also R. Martin, *The Most Dangerous Branch: How the Supreme Court of Canada Has Undermined Our Law and Our Democracy* (Montréal, QC: McGill-Queen's University Press, 2003).

52. A very good study of the current electoral system is found in the volume by Henry Milner, *Making Every Vote Count: Reassessing Canada's Electoral System* (Peterborough, ON: Broadview Press, 1999). See also William Cross, *Political Parties, Representation, and Electoral Democracy in Canada* (Don Mills, ON: Oxford University Press, 2002); and the eighth edition of a classic, Hugh Thorburn, *Party Politics in Canada* (Toronto, ON: Prentice-Hall of Canada, 2001).

53. Alan Cairns, "The Electoral and the Party System in Canada," *Canadian Journal of Political Science* 1 (1968): 61–75. See also Cameron D. Anderson, *Voting Behavior in Canada* (Vancouver, BC: University of British Columbia Press, 2010); and André Blais, *To Keep or to Change First Past the Post? The Politics of Electoral Reform* (New York: Oxford University Press, 2008).

54. A good general work on Canadian elections is by Harold Clarke, Allan Kornberg, and Thomas Scotto, *Making Political Choices: Canada and the United States* (Toronto, ON: University of Toronto Press, 2009). See also Cameron Anderson and Laura Stephenson, *Voting Behaviour in Canada* (Vancouver, BC: University of British Columbia Press, 2010).

55. Mallory, *The Structure of Canadian Government*, p. 202. See also R. Kenneth Carty, et al., *Rebuilding Canadian Party Politics* (Vancouver, BC: University of British Columbia Press, 2000).

56. For a good general discussion of parties and regionalism, see William Cross, ed., *Political Parties, Representation and Electoral Democracy in Canada* (Don Mills, ON: Oxford University Press, 2002); and John Courtney, *Elections* (Vancouver, BC: University of British Columbia Press, 2004).

57. See Alan Gagnon and Brian Tanguay, *Canadian Parties in Transition* (Peterborough, ON: Broadview Press, 2007); or Keith Archer and Lisa Young, *Regionalism and Party Politics in Canada* (Don Mills, ON: Oxford University Press, 2002).

58. Jackson and Jackson, *Politics in Canada*, p. 407.

59. Van Loon and Whittington, *The Canadian Political System*, p. 243. See also William Cross, *Political Parties* (Vancouver, BC: University of British Columbia Press, 2004).

60. See George Perlin, ed., *Party Democracy in Canada: The Politics of National Party Conventions* (Scarborough, ON: Prentice-Hall Canada, 1988).

61. See John Richards, Robert Cairns, and Larry Pratt, eds., *Social Democracy Without Illusions: Renewal of the Canadian Left* (Toronto, ON: McClelland and Stewart, 1991).

The Russian Political System

Russia's two national leaders are often seen together at public events. Here President
Medvedev (right) and Prime Minister Putin (left) leave an event at the Tomb of the

The study of politics in Russia, as well as Russia's political heritage, requires a deviation from the normal pattern of the "area studies" chapters preceding this one. Our fundamental premise in this volume has been that if we study the basic constitutional structures of a political regime we can develop some understanding of how the regime operates.

This is not to suggest that the detailed study of political parties in Britain, for example, would not contribute a great deal to a deeper understanding of the operation of the British political system. It would. What we have suggested, however, is that it is *possible* to understand how the British political system generally operates without a detailed examination of the Labour and Conservative parties. Similarly, it is possible to become *acquainted* (and remember, our area studies do not claim to be comprehensive, but are simply designed as introductions) with the other political systems we have examined without detailed knowledge of their respective political parties.

Total Area (rank)	17,098,242 sq km (1)
Population (rank)	138,739,892 (9)
Population Growth Rate (rank)	−0.47% (223)
Urban Population	73%
Life Expectancy at Birth (total population) (rank)	66.29 (162)
Literacy	99.4%
Government Type	Federation
Legal System	Civil Law
Head of Government	Premier Vladimir Putin
Chief of State	President Dmitry Medvedev
Gross Domestic Product (GDP)	$1.465 trillion
GDP Per Capita (rank)	$15,900 (71)
GDP Real Growth Rate (rank)	4% (100)
Unemployment Rate (rank)	7.6% (82)

RUSSIA

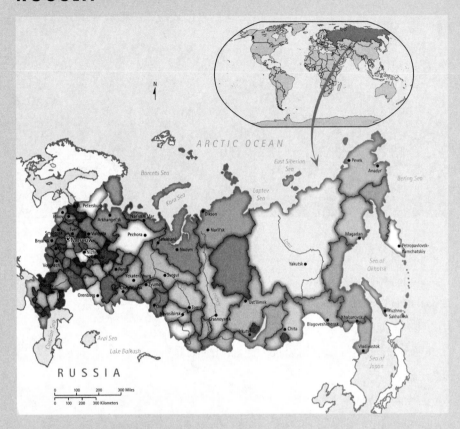

This is all said by way of introduction to the chapter on the Russian political system because the Russian case poses an exception to the general patterns described above, one that will be paralleled by the case of China later in this volume. While we can understand the essential pattern of operation of these other political systems by confining our examination to what might be called "constitutional political structures," such an examination of the Russian political system would likely give us an inadequate image of political operations there. The Russian political system, while it has an extensive history, is a very *new* system in many important respects; we must appreciate its newness, and the circumstances from which it emerged, if we are to understand its operation.

Accordingly, after an examination of the Russian political heritage, we will turn our attention to a tentative examination of the new constitution and the system of constitutional political structures in the new political system that is called Russia. We must recall that modern Russia does *not* have a democratic history upon which to draw at moments of stress, and does not have numerous democratic precedents to use as examples during moments of political crisis. Thus, while we may describe a number of (relatively new) political institutions, only time will tell us the degree to which they will either endure or be effective.

RUSSIAN CONSTITUTIONAL HISTORY

For many years—from 1917 through the breakup of the Soviet Union in 1991—the name "Russia" was used interchangeably by many with "the **Union of Soviet Socialist Republics**," the USSR, despite the fact that such a usage was incorrect. Russia was a *part* of the USSR—one of fifteen "independent" republics—but not the *same as* the USSR. The USSR was geographically the largest country in the world, making up nearly one-sixth of the earth's land mass—"more than twice the size of the United States, almost as big as the United States, Canada, and Mexico put together...only slightly smaller than the whole continent of Africa."[1] (This kind of comparison was slightly misleading, however, because a careful study of the Soviet map would have shown that a significant portion of the USSR was "not conducive to protracted habitation for sizeable populations."[2]) The Russian Federation today is an area of 6.5 million square miles, just under twice the size of the United States, and upon the demise of the USSR in 1991 the Russian Federation became the largest of the successor states to the USSR and inherited its permanent seat in the United Nations.

THE RUSSIAN POLITICAL HERITAGE

Russia has existed for more than eleven centuries, under a variety of names and a variety of rulers. Under the Soviet regime many suggested that there were historical factors that had proven to be significant in influencing Soviet development in a non-Western direction;[3] clearly, the same thing can be said about Russia. Patterns of behavior such as the "persistent tradition of absolutism in government, the recurrent use of revolutionary violence to solve political problems, and the lack of experience with democratic institutions and constitutional procedures,"[4] all contributed to a political tradition in the Soviet Union—and now Russia—that was distinctly different from that shared by most Western (democratic) nations. (See Table 13.1)

TABLE 13.1

Some Important Landmarks in Russian History

1237–1240	Mongol (Tatar) conquest of Russia begins 200 years of Mongol rule
1480	Ivan III frees Muscovy from Mongol rule
1712	Peter the Great moves capital of Russia to St. Petersburg for a "window to the West"
1861	Emancipation of the serfs by Alexander II
1905	Revolution forces Nicholas II to grant reform, including establishment of a parliament (the Duma)
1917	March Revolution overthrows monarchy and establishes socialist government
1917	November Revolution brings Lenin's Bolsheviks to power
1917–1921	War Communism
1921–1928	New Economic Policy
1924–1938	Death of Lenin in 1924 leads to a struggle for power. Stalin emerges on top and then ruthlessly consolidates his control
1953	Death of Stalin
1957	Consolidation of power by Nikita Khruschev
1964	Khruschev ousted; replaced by Leonid Brezhnev and Alexander Kosygin
1982	Brezhnev dies; succeeded by Yuri Andropov
1984	Andropov dies; succeeded by Konstantin Chernenko
1985	Chernenko dies; succeeded by Mikhail Gorbachev Gorbachev elected to new Presidency of Soviet Union
1991	Boris Yeltsin elected President of Russia (June); Attempted *coup d'état*/overthrow of Gorbachev (August 19); Gorbachev resigns from Communist Party (August 24); Commonwealth of Independent States Treaty Signed (December 21); Breakup of USSR; Gorbachev resigns as USSR President (December 25)
1993	Current Russian Constitution promulgated
1996	Yeltsin reelected as President (June)
2000	Vladimir Putin elected as President (March)
2004	Vladimir Putin re-elected as President (March)
2008	Dmitry Medvedev elected as President, and appoints Vladimir Putin as premier

One major pattern in the Russian past was the history of revolutions, which led to the Revolution of 1917.[5] Among the earliest acts that can be called revolutions in Russian history was a shake-up in government led by Ivan the Terrible in 1564. Ivan was rebelling not against the government (*he* was *Tsar* at the time!) but against the nobles in his regime, claiming that they were evil and traitorous. He agreed to maintain the throne only under the condition that he be given control of a secret police network called the Oprichnina, which he used to destroy the power of the nobles by arresting them, exiling them, and taking over their estates. Ivan's actions served to neutralize any threat that the nobility had posed to the power of the Tsar.

The Revolt of December 1825, known as the Decembrist Uprising, was an attempt by the Tsar's guards to overthrow the Tsar (Nicholas I, 1825–1855) and do away with the restrictive, autocratic government of Russia. Partially because of the uncertainty of the revolutionaries, who could not agree on the kind of regime that they wanted to replace the Tsar, the revolt was suppressed, and an increase in governmental repression took place at the hand of the Tsar.

The oppressiveness of the Tsar, however, did not check the spread of revolutionary ideas. Although the Tsar freed the serfs in 1861 as a gesture to placate public unrest, revolutionary fervor continued to spread. Political organization was begun by a revolutionary intelligentsia, primarily organized in the Narodnik movement. The Narodniki were originally intellectually based—drawn from student and intellectual groups. The movement had as its goal the promotion of a socialist society, maintaining that the traditional Russian village was socialist in orientation. The Narodniki argued that "once the aristocratic system and the feudal order were destroyed, Russia would spontaneously be recognized as a vast association of agrarian cooperative communities."[6]

The first Marxist organization in Russia, called the Emancipation of Labor, was founded in 1883 by a group led by George Plekhanov. Between 1883 and 1894 this kind of group was formed in most major Russian cities, including one formed in St. Petersburg in 1895 led by a young revolutionary known as Vladimir Lenin (whose real name was Ulyanov). Both Joseph Stalin (whose real name was Joseph Dzhugashvili) and Leon Trotsky (whose real name was Leon Bronstein) became active in politics during this period. In 1898 the first Russian Social Democratic Party convention was held in Minsk, its goal being to consolidate various factions of Marxists.

The second Russian Social Democratic Party convention was held in 1903, meeting first in Brussels (because it was not permitted in Russia), then moving to London. In London the party divided into two factions over the issue of organization. Some party members wanted a European-style Social Democratic Party. Lenin argued against that form of party, saying that the Tsar's secret police would not permit such an open party to operate freely. He argued in favor of a restricted, tightly organized party of dedicated revolutionaries. The party split into two factions over this question on a 33–18 vote.[7] Lenin was leader of the majority faction, called the Bolsheviks. The labels **Bolshevik** (majority) and **Menshevik** (minority) stuck to the two factions of the party, and the two factions of the Russian Social Democratic Party were thereafter known as the Bolsheviks and the Mensheviks.

At this time Lenin presented his proposals, which he had introduced in his earlier publication, titled *What is To Be Done?* (published in 1902). In that work he called for a new kind of nonelectoral party organization, designed not so much to compete for power in elections, but "to seize power on behalf of the working class and to establish a 'dictatorship of the proletariat.'"[8]

At the turn of the twentieth century, Russia was again near the point of revolution. Strikes and industrial unrest spread throughout the country as a result of yet another economic crisis. On January 9, 1905, a day that came to be known as "Bloody Sunday," soldiers fired on a procession of workers bringing a list of grievances to the Tsar (Nicholas II), killing hundreds and causing a revolt. Workers' councils, called soviets, were formed in many cities to direct strike activities. Leon Trotsky, a leader of the St. Petersburg soviet, issued a call for constitutional reforms, free elections, a parliament, and freedom for political parties to form.

The Tsar managed to put down the revolt, but acceded to many of the requests as an effort to promote the stability of his regime. In the **October Manifesto**, he promised a national parliament (the Duma), a constitution, free elections, and protection of civil liberties. After 1905 Russia was a much more liberal and less oppressive society than it had been previously, although the Tsar was still the most significant political actor because of his power of absolute veto over the Duma and his power to dismiss the Duma at will.[9]

The year 1917 saw new revolution in Russia. Russia's performance in World War I, coupled with continued poor economic growth and increased governmental repressiveness, led to more rebellions. The tsar was overthrown in March of 1917, and the Duma became the Provisional Government, granting amnesty to most of the Bolshevik leaders who had been exiled (like Lenin) or sent to Siberia (like Stalin) by the Tsar, and allowing them to return to the political scene. From the beginning of the Revolution, the workers' councils, the *soviets*, played central roles in the coordination of revolutionary activity. The Petrograd (the new name for St. Petersburg) soviet, in fact, rivaled the Provisional Government (the Duma) as a source of leadership.

In April 1917, Lenin returned to Russia and issued his April Theses, calling for the overthrow of the Provisional Government and the transformation of the "bourgeois democratic revolution" into a revolution sponsored by the "proletarian class."[10] The Provisional Government, headed by Alexander Kerensky, opposed Lenin's policies, but in the end could not stand up to the Bolshevik organization. On the nights of November 6–7, 1917, all members of the Provisional Government were arrested by the Red Guard, on order of Lenin. Lenin announced that the former government was dissolved, and that the Petrograd Soviet, headed by its Central Executive Committee, was now in control. The new government was headed by a Council of Peoples' Commissars, led by Lenin as chairman, Stalin as commissar of nationalities, and Trotsky as commissar of foreign affairs.

From 1917 through 1991 the Soviet Union existed as a Marxist-Leninist political system, moving through a number of different leaders, through varying degrees of authoritarian government, and through varying degrees of aggressiveness about spreading the doctrine of **Marxism-Leninism** to other political systems.[11] With the coming to power of **Mikhail Gorbachev** in 1985, a new era began. This included a gradual relaxation of the degree to which the Communist Party of the Soviet Union ran the government and, equally important, a corresponding increase in human rights tolerated by the central government as well as a corresponding diminution in the amount of control Moscow insisted on having over the fifteen "independent republics" of the Soviet Union.[12]

In November of 1989 the Wall dividing Germany's East and West Berlin was opened, and shortly thereafter physically came down.[13] In 1990, East and West Germany were reunified. This reunification, combined with other effects of the centrifugal forces of nationalism had a critical impact upon the Soviet Union and its satellite governments in Eastern Europe. In 1991, under Mikhail Gorbachev, discussions were undertaken about a restructuring of the Soviet Union into a new confederation, giving more power—returning sovereignty—to the individual republics. This led, as we shall further discuss below, to the creation of the Commonwealth of Independent States (CIS) and the death of the Union of Soviet Socialist Republics. It was, indeed, a "new world order."[14]

The Devolution of the Soviet Union

The USSR was composed of fifteen union republics—hence the name *Union of Soviet Socialist Republics*. The Soviet nation consisted

> of more than a hundred large and small ethnic groups with their own distinct cultural heritages. Many, but not all, ethnic groups [had] their own territories within the USSR. These territories were designated, in descending order of importance, as "Union Republics" [15] "autonomous republics" [11], "autonomous regions" [8], and "autonomous areas" [10].[15]

In the late 1980s the heterogeneous nature of the Soviet Union became the cause of tension—and open violence—in Soviet politics. The "nationality question"[16] was the cause of many deaths in 1989 as various ethnic groups protested that they were not receiving adequate attention from Moscow.[17] The goals of these ethnic groups were often territorial, but occasionally involved unhappiness with religious, political, or economic policies. According to the U.S. State Department, about thirty-five borders within the Soviet Union were being disputed between different national groups in the Soviet Union in early 1989, including conflicts in Armenia, Azerbaijan, Kazakhstan, Uzbekistan, Lithuania, and Georgia, to name just a few.[18]

The largest single geographic component of the USSR was the Russian Soviet Federative Socialist Republic (RSFSR), making up over three-fourths of the USSR. The fourteen other union republics apart from Russia were each called Soviet Socialist Republics (SSRs). They included Armenian SSR, Azerbaidzhanian SSR, Belorussian SSR, Estonian SSR, Georgian SSR, Latvian

TABLE 13.2

The Composition of the Former USSR

Name of Union Republic	Date Created	Capital	Area (Sq.Mi)	Population (In Millions*)
Russian SSR	Nov 1917	Moscow	6,592,800	146.1
Ukraine SSR	Dec 1917	Kiev	233,100	49.2
Belorussian SSR	Jan 1919	Minsk	80,200	10.4
Azerbaidzhan SSR	Apr 1920	Baku	33,400	7.7
Armenian SSR	Nov 1920	Erevan	11,306	3.4
Georgian SSR	Feb 1921	Tbilisi	26,911	5.0
Turkmenian SSR	Oct 1924	Ashkabad	188,417	4.5
Uzbek SSR	Oct 1924	Tashkent	172,700	24.8
Tadzhik SSR	Oct 1929	Dushambe	54,019	6.4
Kirgiz SSR	Dec 1936	Frunze	76,642	4.7
Kazakh SSR	Dec 1936	Alma-Ata	1,049,200	16.7
Lithuanian SSR	Jul 1940	Bilnius	26,173	3.6
Latvian SSR	Jul 1940	Riga	24,695	2.4
Estonian SSR	Jul 1940	Tallin	17,413	1.4
Moldavian SSR	Aug 1940	Kishinev	13,012	4.4

* This was the population of the Republic in 2000, at the time of the breakup of the Soviet Union.

SSR, Lithuanian SSR, Kazakh SSR, Kirghiz SSR, Moldavian SSR, Tadzhik SSR, Turkmen SSR, Ukrainian SSR, and Uzbek SSR. Member republics making up the former USSR are listed in Table 13.2.

The 1936 Soviet Constitution, and later the 1977 Soviet Constitution, both suggested that the USSR was a *federal* political system. The federal relationship, as it has been described earlier in this book, proved to be more imaginary than real, however. In reality, the Soviet Union was a very centralized unitary system with a number of component units that had no real powers of their own, and thus which could not be called "federal" in any meaningful sense of the term.

Soviet federalism was developed by Lenin and Stalin as a vehicle for controlling many of the "independent republics" that had been included in the Russian Empire. In the Revolution of 1917 the Bolsheviks had promised self-determination to the various national minorities, and military conquest did not appear to them to be a preferential strategy, if they had any choice. By making the new state a "federation" it was possible to at least maintain the impression that the member units retained some token autonomy.

The Constitution of 1924 contained a number of clauses reflecting the "federal" nature of the regime. In addition to the "usual" powers granted federal governments (found in federal regimes of the day including Canada, West Germany, the United States, and Australia, for example), such as the power to coin money, to have an army, and the like, the Soviet Constitution gave the federal government a great number of economic planning powers, central to Marxist ideology. The constitution had no bill of rights and no electoral laws, leaving these areas of concern, as well as the areas of civil and criminal law, to the member republics.[19] In practice, however, things didn't work out this way.

It is interesting to note that the 1977 constitution, in an early draft, suggested doing away with the Soviet federation and creating a unitary state. The plan was turned down, and deleted from the final draft of the constitution. The 1977 constitution, referred to the USSR as a "unitary, federal, and multinational state, formed on the basis of the principle of socialist federalism and as a result of the free self-determination of nations and the voluntary union of equal Soviet Socialist Republics."[20]

The Soviet federal structure was partially reflected in the constitutional structure of the government in one of the two houses of the Soviet legislature, the Supreme Soviet. Under the 1988 amendment to the constitution, 750 members of the Supreme Soviet were to be elected on the basis of governmental units, with each of the country's republics having the same representation in the legislature; thus Estonia's 1.5 million citizens had the same number of representatives as the Ukraine's 50 million.[21]

As we noted above, by 1991 the gradually increasing spirit of nationalism that had begun to reassert its presence in a variety of the "independent" republics was too strong to ignore any longer. The Union of Soviet Socialist Republics was dissolved,[22] and a new structure of association, the **Commonwealth of Independent States**, emerged to replace the USSR as a vehicle for the association of a number of truly independent republics, all of which had been Union Republics within the USSR.[23]

Not all of the former components of the USSR chose to join the CIS; Estonia, Latvia, and Lithuania, the Baltic Republics of the USSR, were not interested in prolonging a formal association with the other states. They left. The other states had been willing in 1991 to stay within the USSR and to create a looser confederation, still calling the association the Union of Soviet Socialist Republics. Following an attempted overthrow of the government in Moscow in 1991 by ultra-conservative forces opposed to these changes,[24] however, and the resignation of President Gorbachev from the Communist Party,[25] the other republics decided that *more* independence from Moscow, rather than less, was the better course to follow in the future. The CIS did not prove to be a terribly effective political structure to succeed the USSR, however, and coordination of policy among the former Soviet republics was not consistent. This is not inconsistent with our discussion earlier in this volume about the relative advantages and disadvantages of various forms of federalism and confederation; the CIS was much more similar to a *confederation* than to a *federation*, with all of the advantages and disadvantages this suggests.

THE RUSSIAN CONSTITUTIONAL SYSTEM

For the student of American politics, the American Constitution is a highly significant document. In contrast, studies of Soviet politics traditionally did not spend a great deal of time or attention explaining the Soviet Constitution, because it was *not* a meaningful or significant document in the Soviet political regime.

The Russian constitutional system following its most recent constitutional modification in 1993 is one that is developing a number of democratic political structures.[26] This development, however, is often slow, and frequently painful. As we will see later in this chapter, a pluralistic system of political parties is in the process of developing in Russia today, and debate over what *should be* the new constitutional institutions of the regime is very intense and visible in the public arena, even to the point of leading to public violence.

Indeed, part of the violence in Russia in mid-1993, including what the leaders of Parliament referred to as a *coup d'état* by President **Boris Yeltsin**, and what Boris Yeltsin referred to as *unconstitutional behavior* by the leaders of Parliament, was caused precisely because *both* sides of the debate were firmly committed to what *they* called *constitutional government*; they simply couldn't agree on what *kind* of constitution Russia ought to have.[27]

Thus, we should note that it is very clear that the new generation of Russian leaders consider their constitutional institutions to be very important, even if they cannot agree on precisely what those institutions should be.

One problem that has made the development of constitutional consensus more difficult in Russia is that there has been no *tradition* of stable constitutional government in Russia or the Soviet Union.[28] Yet, it is clear that the *existence* of a constitution must have been important to the Bolsheviks, and to their political successors: The Soviet Union had a number of constitutions, and political leaders would not have invested the effort to create the constitutions if they did not feel that the exercise would be worth their while. Indeed, in the fall of 1988 the Soviet government devoted significant time and effort to the process of constitutional reform.

Since the revolution of 1917 there have been six constitutional eras in the USSR and Russia. First, on July 10, 1918, a new constitution was put into force in Russia. This was followed by the second era, with the arrival of the first constitution of the USSR in January 1924. In 1935 a third era came about when a constitutional commission was appointed and instructed to draft a new constitution for the USSR, to replace its original 1924 constitution. The new constitution was approved late in 1936.

After Stalin's death, movements were launched to create a new constitution, but progress was slow. In 1962 Khrushchev began efforts to draft a new constitution, but his ouster in 1964 stalled the project. Although Brezhnev became chairman of the Constitutional Commission, the project was not a high priority for him at the time. A fourth constitutional era came when, "without the usual advance clues, there came the abrupt announcement in May, 1977 that the new draft constitution would soon be published for nationwide discussion."[29]

Under Mikhail Gorbachev a new constitutional balance of power, a fifth era, was brought about in 1988 and 1989 with a new Supreme Soviet and Soviet Presidency, which will be described later. With the resignation of President Gorbachev[30] and the dissolution of the Soviet Union in 1991, a new constitutional era began for Russia, although it was still evolving in September of 1993 when some argued that a civil war was narrowly averted involving a conflict between Boris Yeltsin[31] and the more conservative Russian Parliament.

By September of 1993, Yeltsin and the Russian Parliament had been in conflict for a good while, with the Parliament controlled by Communist conservative elements—those not supporting Yeltsin's efforts to reform the system both in terms of economic policy and in terms of efforts to speed up democratization. After some supporters of the Parliament tried to mount an armed uprising, Yeltsin called out the army to recapture the parliament building from the rebels. Yeltsin remained in control, with his power stabilized for the time being.[32]

In November of 1993 President Yeltsin announced that a new constitution would be placed before the Russian voters on December 12, 1993, to replace the constitution originally adopted in April of 1978 but that had been amended on numerous occasions since that time. At the same time, Yeltsin indicated that Russian voters would be asked to vote for members of the new parliament. The new constitution would give the president the right, under limited conditions, to issue decrees having the force of law, to dissolve parliament, to declare a state of emergency, and to temporarily curb civil rights; it would also give Russians a number of unprecedented guarantees of personal freedoms and entrench a number of reforms of Communist-era economic policies.

In the December 1993 election, the new constitution was approved by a significant majority of voters in a nationwide plebiscite, but Yeltsin's party did not win a majority in the new parliament.[33] While many debated whether this was a result of the unpopularity of his economic policies, his ineffective campaigning before the election, or a personal rejection of Yeltsin himself, the outcome was a state of uncertainty. Although Yeltsin vowed to press on with his economic and political reforms, it appeared that his policies would have as much difficulty in the new parliament as they had experienced in the old one.

In the 1993 "Yeltsin" constitution, the president has a great deal of power.[34] The president nominates the prime minister, who must be confirmed by the Duma. However, if the Duma rejects the president's nominee three times, he then has the power to dissolve the Duma and call for new elections. Although some claimed that the 1993 constitution would not last long following its promulgation, at the time of this writing (2011) it has endured, and although we will argue later in this chapter that the presidency has become extremely powerful, the constitutional system itself has endured.

The question can be asked, "Why did Soviet leaders continue for so many years the 'constitutional ruse' as it could be called, having constitutions that were primarily of symbolic significance?" The answer appears to be that the Soviets had an ambivalent attitude toward constitutions. On one hand, in terms of Marxist ideology, they saw both the state and its structures such as a constitution as evils. On the other hand, they were willing to recognize constitutions as *necessary* evils, necessary for providing external and internal legitimacy, and for helping to run the regime in the "transitional period" during which time the state "evolves" from capitalism to socialism to communism.

Even though Lenin and his fellow revolutionary leaders were in the middle of a significant domestic battle with other Soviet political leaders, they still believed that it was important to have a constitutional framework for their new government.[35] The role of the constitution in the USSR was to give "legal expression to the basic ideological norms of Soviet doctrine."[36]

FEDERALISM IN RUSSIA

As we noted earlier, there is a long and well-entrenched history of federal structures in Russia. Long before the Soviet Union was created in the early years of the twentieth century as a federal structure, Russia could be characterized as a more or less federal regime. Even when it was ruled by the Czar as the Russian Empire, there were characteristics of federal government that could be seen, although whether it was *actually* federal government—in the sense of shared sovereignty—is really a different matter; the history of the nation is a history of centralized power, whether it was called unitary government or whether it was called federal government. The appearance of federal-like structures was, as we suggested earlier in this book, often the case in extremely large nations, because of the sheer size and heterogeneity of Russia. It was not possible to govern all of Russia from a completely centralized perspective, simply because of geography and distance.

When the Union of Soviet Socialist Republics was created, the USSR *had* to operate under a model of being federal because the "independent" republics that were drawn into the USSR would not voluntarily come otherwise. While some might argue that the member republics did not come voluntarily in any event, it was far more politically palatable to the actors involved to use the language of federalism to describe the nature of government in the USSR. Many of the member republics were themselves "federative socialist republics," reflecting the fact that each republic, in turn, was made up of member units with which power was shared.

Once the Soviet Union dissolved, and the member republics decided to walk away from the Union, Russia maintained its federal governmental structure. Today, the Russian Federation is made up of eighty-three "federal subjects," each represented in the Federal Council of the legislature. There are forty-six *oblasts* (provinces), twenty-one component *republics* (nominally autonomous with its own constitution, president, and legislature), nine *krais* (territories), geographic regions, and four *autonomous okrugs* (districts), one *Jewish Autonomous Oblast*, and two *federal cities* (Moscow and St. Petersburg) that function as separate governmental regions. The eighty-three federal subjects are grouped into eight federal districts, each administered individually by a representative of the Russian President.[37]

IDEOLOGY

The political regime that was referred to as the USSR had an ideological foundation officially referred to as **"Marxism-Leninism."**[38] Ultimately, Marxism-Leninism was based upon the *Communist Manifesto* (written in 1848) and subsequent writings of Karl Marx and Friedrich Engels. More directly, however, political ideology in the Soviet Union could be explained as Marxism interpreted and applied by Soviet leaders of the day, including Lenin, Stalin, Khrushchev, and Brezhnev. Each of these leaders in turn interpreted and revised Marx's ideas so that the particular version of Marxism would support the regime of the day and provide a rationalization for the policies of the government in power.[39]

The perspectives of Marx were, in fact, different from those of Lenin, Stalin, Khrushchev, Brezhnev, or even Gorbachev. Marx was a theorist, dealing with economics, philosophies, and ideas. Lenin and his followers were pragmatists, political actors, interested in the philosophy suggested by Marx, but faced with the challenge of putting the theories into concrete form, of operationalizing the ideology.

As the economic, social, and political characteristics of the Soviet Union changed, Marx's ideas had to be revised to fit the times. Lenin, for example, revised Marxian theory to justify its relevance to the conditions of the Soviet Union during the period between 1917 and 1924.[40] Lenin died in January, 1924. Following his death there was a major power struggle to decide who would be the next leader. The two major contestants were Joseph Stalin and Leon Trotsky. Stalin's position emerged as the dominant of the two; as secretary-general of the Communist Party of the Soviet Union he had been able to build a strong base of power.

In 1936 Stalin had a new constitution written that he proclaimed to be the most democratic in the world. He created a new parliament, and a bill of rights (although it did not effectively protect individual rights from governmental abuses), and at the same time centralized power to guarantee that no one would be able to challenge his control. After securing his hold on power, Stalin claimed that the Marxist revolution was completed within the USSR.[41] Stalin, accordingly, turned his attention away from the revolution within the state, to revolution in other states, looking at the concept of revolution in the world. After the USSR had developed into a militarily powerful regime, Stalin felt that the Soviet system could assist Marxist revolutions in other parts of the world.

In terms of major modifications of Marxism (or of "Marxism-Leninism-Stalinism" as he preferred to call it), Stalin's contributions were neither as many nor as significant as those of Lenin. However, he did make some contributions to the Soviet polity, including the creation of the structure of the five-year plan to direct the development of the Soviet state and the introduction of the concept of "enemy of the people" into Soviet ideology.[42]

Nikita Khrushchev emerged as Soviet leader in 1957. In a manner similar to Lenin and Stalin, Khruschev was said by students of Marxism to have contributed several major theoretical modifications to the Marxism-Leninism-Stalinism of his day.[43]

Less than ten years later, while Chairman and First Secretary Khruschev was vacationing, he was "deposed" by a team headed by Leonid Brezhnev and Alexi Kosygin in October 1964. The post-Khrushchev leadership, primarily Leonid Brezhnev, undertook somewhat of a retrenchment following the ouster of Khrushchev. The liberalization by Khrushchev of restrictions in the areas of arts, literature, and education, was again tightened; the Soviet Union's apparent relaxation of its control over its satellites also was reversed, with the 1968 crushing of the Czechoslovakian uprising.[44]

Following the death of Leonid Brezhnev in November of 1982, the future direction of Soviet ideology was uncertain. Yuri Andropov, former head of the KGB (the State Security Committee) and Politburo member was selected to take over as secretary-general of the Communist party, but his period of leadership was brief and did not contribute anything in the way of ideological significance, primarily due to his age and illness.[45] When Andropov died in 1984, he was replaced by Konstantin Chernenko, another senior party leader, who also died in office after a very brief period of leadership. The accession to office of Mikhail Gorbachev in 1985 suggested the promise of significant change in what, exactly, a "Marxist" ideology meant,[46] but in 1985 *no* observer of the Soviet system would have imagined the degree of change that would come within the next decade, through the Gorbachev years and into the period of leadership of Boris Yeltsin.[47]

STRUCTURES OF THE GOVERNMENT

The Former Congress of People's Deputies

The idea for the Congress of People's Deputies was first suggested by Mikhail Gorbachev in the late fall of 1988 as part of a package of reforms for the Soviet government. One observer noted that Gorbachev had become

> increasingly frustrated and angry at the resistance being mounted to his reforms by Party and state bureaucrats. He holds these officials to blame for the economic stagnation and moral decline from which his country suffers, and accuses them of stifling the initiative of the population.[48]

This legislative body, the first elections for which were held in March, 1989, was intended to be a more active legislature than had been the case with the Supreme Soviet in the past; its members would be elected from competitive elections, and it would elect from among its 2,250 members 542 members of a new, much more active and more powerful, Supreme Soviet.

The exact role of the new Congress of People's Deputies was still being negotiated at its first meeting in June of 1989. Among the agreements which were reached at that time were that: (a) the congress would convene twice a year instead of once, as originally proposed by Gorbachev; (b) deputies of the (2,250-member) Congress who were not elected to the (542 member) Supreme Soviet or its commissions or committees could participate in the sessions and have access to the information and documents made available to the Supreme Soviet, and (c) the Congress would retain the "right to cancel or change any document, any legislative act, and any decision taken by the Supreme Soviet."[49]

The Former Supreme Soviet

Prior to the constitutional amendment proposed by Mikhail Gorbachev in late 1988, the Supreme Soviet was a very weak, essentially rubber-stamp legislative body that approved whatever legislation was placed before it by Communist Party officials, despite the fact that it was described (in Chapter 15 of the constitution) as "the supreme body of state power in the USSR... empowered to resolve all questions placed within the jurisdiction of the USSR by this constitution."[50]

The Supreme Soviet was a bicameral body, composed of the Soviet of the Union and the Soviet of Nationalities, members of which were all elected at the same time for four-year terms. Members of the Soviet of the Union were elected on the basis of population. Members of the Soviet of Nationalities, represented the "federal" nature of the political system, with each union republic having thirty-two seats, each autonomous republic having eleven seats, each autonomous region having five seats, and each national area having one seat. The two houses of the Supreme Soviet had over 1,500 representatives.

As noted earlier, in 1988 Mikhail Gorbachev proposed a fundamental change in the institution, asking the Supreme Soviet to abolish itself,[51] and to create a new institution in its place, the new *Congress of People's Deputies*. As part of his package of proposals, Gorbachev proposed that the Congress would elect from among its own members a *new* Supreme Soviet, one that would "act as a full-time legislature for the nearly eight months it will be in session,"[52] meeting for two sessions each year, one in the spring and one in the fall, each lasting three or four months. On paper, at least, the new Supreme Soviet was to be much more active, and important, than its predecessor had been.[53]

At the same time that new institutions were being created at the level of the USSR government, new institutions were proposed and created for Russian government, too. Institutions of the Russian Republic were essentially parallel to those of the Soviet government, with a Russian Federation Supreme Soviet made up of a Council of the Republic and a Council of Nationalities. The executive branch was to be led by a president, assisted by a Government (a chairman and a number of ministers) drawn from the Supreme Soviet. In essence the Russian government was very much a French-model government led by a strong president.[54]

The New Federal Assembly

In the fall of 1993 when Boris Yeltsin won his "battle for supremacy between the executive and legislative branches," and called for new legislative elections, he also ordered replacement of all of the regional and territorial legislatures, demanding that they "submit to new elections and face a drastic reduction in their size...." The new councils were called state dumas—a term used in Tsarist Russia—and were to be made up of fifteen to fifty full-time legislators. They replaced the existing councils, called soviets.[55] The precise nature of Russian federalism today is still evolving in terms of the balance of power between the central government and the regional and local governments. The Russian Federation today has 89 units, including two federal cities, Moscow and St. Petersburg.

Yeltsin's new legislative structure[56] included an upper house, called the Federation Council, and a lower house called the State Duma. The State Duma had 450 members, elected for a four-year term. Of these, 225 members were elected by simple majority from single-member district constituencies. The other 225 members were elected by a party-list proportional representation system, in which the entire nation would be treated as a single constituency, with only federal lists receiving at least 5 percent of the popular vote eligible to receive seats. Voters cast two separate ballots for the two groups of legislators.

The electoral system was changed for the State Duma elections that took place on December 2, 2007. Under the new system, designed by President Vladimir Putin, elections were completely based upon proportional representation, replacing the mixed electoral system initiated by Boris Yeltsin. The term for the Duma was also changed from four years to five years. In this PR system a party has to obtain at least 7 per cent of the votes (up from 5 per cent) to win representation in the State Duma. At the time of the election thirty-five political parties applied to contest the elections, but the Central Electoral Commission (CEC) permitted only eleven parties to participate. Critics of the new electoral system with 7 percent threshold argued that the measures prevented small parties from entering the parliament,[57] but President Putin insisted the tougher standard were necessary to stop extremist parties from running for elections.

At the time of the election the turnout was moderate, with just under 64 percent of the voters participating—69.5 million individuals casting votes out of 109.1 million registered voters—and the party that won the most votes was the United Russia party. As noted, eleven parties competed for a share of the 450 places in the State Duma.[58] The election yielded the distribution of seats indicated in Table 13.3.

The Council of the Federation has 178 appointed members, with 89 multi- (two-) member constituencies that correspond to the various units of the Russian Federal government. Two members are appointed by the executive and legislature of each of the units of the government, the regions, and the local governments.

TABLE 13.3

The Duma Election of 2007

Political Group	% Votes	Seats
United Russia	64.3	315
Communist Party	11.6	57
Liberal Democratic Party of Russia	8.1	40
A Just Russia	7.7	38
Total	91.7	450
Number of women = 63/445, or 14 percent		

Source: Inter-Parliamentary Union, *PARLINE*, "Russian Federation: State Duma," http://www.ipu.org/parline-e/reports/2263_E.htm (accessed June 2011).

The New Presidency

Until the 1989 changes in the power of the Supreme Soviet, one of its most important structures was the Presidium (its full title was the Presidium of the Supreme Soviet of the USSR), which had thirty-nine members, including a chairman, a first vice-chairman, fifteen vice-chairmen (one from each union republic supreme soviet), a secretary, and twenty-one members. Members of the Presidium were elected by the USSR Supreme Soviet "at a joint meeting of its chambers," from among its members in both houses. The Presidium was referred to as "the continuously functioning agency of the USSR Supreme Soviet, accountable to the latter for all its activity, and exercising...the functions of supreme body of state power of the USSR in intervals between sessions of the Supreme Soviet."[59]

Thus, although the legislative function may have rested *de jure* with 1,517 member Supreme Soviet, it was possible to say that this function was *usually* exercised by the Presidium's Chairman and a few assistants *in the name of* the Presidium, carrying out "most of the legislative functions of the government."[60] The chairman of the Presidium was the most visible of the thirty-nine members, however, and he usually acted in the name of the complete body. Until 1989 the chairman of the Presidium was often referred to by western media as the president of the USSR. In October of 1988, Andrei Gromyko was forced to retire from the position of chairman of the Presidium, and was replaced by Mikhail Gorbachev. As part of Gorbachev's package of reforms for the Supreme Soviet, he suggested the creation of a new position of an executive president, called the chairman of the USSR Supreme Soviet, who would be elected by the Congress of People's Deputies. Gorbachev "made no secret of his intention to become the first holder of the new, extremely powerful post of executive president." On May 23, 1989, Gorbachev was nominated in the newly-created Council of People's Deputies for the new position, and on May 26 he was elected President by 96 percent of the Deputies voting.[61]

The *Russian* presidency occupied by Boris Yeltsin, as we noted above, was created at the same time as Gorbachev's Soviet presidency. Yeltsin was elected president of Russia on June 12, 1991.[62] Much of his effort in his first two years in office was spent fighting with the Russian parliament, many members of which were remnants from the days of Communist control of the institutions of the Soviet Union. Following his battle with the Parliament in the fall of 1993, Yeltsin was confident that the elections in December of 1993 would produce a new constitution with increased power for the president, and a Parliament more sympathetic to his economic and political goals. The constitution was approved; the sympathetic parliament, however, did not come into being.

Yeltsin was re-elected in a two-part election on June 16, 1996. In the first stage of the election he barely won a plurality of the votes. In the run-off election between the two top vote-getters, he received a majority of the votes and won a second term in office. His term was troubled by serious domestic and economic problems. The bureaucracy was huge and had to be significantly cut back. There was a serious challenge to the government by "mob"-like racketeers, and many reports indicated that the government was unable to enforce the law over the racketeers. The Russian economy virtually collapsed, with the ruble being halved in value and imports falling by nearly 45 percent.[63] In August of 1998, the government floated the ruble, significantly devaluing it, imposed strong currency controls, and tried to regain control of the economy. This caused an enormous backlash as Russians criticized the government and indicated that they had been better off under an oppressive Communist state, but Yeltsin stayed the course.

Yeltsin had numerous challenges as the end of the decade arrived. In 1999, the former Russian satellites of Poland, Hungary, and the Czech Republic all joined the North Atlantic Treaty Organization (NATO), something that Russia took to be a challenge, since accepting these nations as equal international partners emphasized the change in Russia's status in the preceding decade. This was exacerbated when it was made clear that Lithuania, Latvia, and Estonia, all of which had also at one time been part of the Soviet Union, wanted to join the organization in the future. In addition, just three years after the Chechen-Russian war (1994–1996) ended in a virtual stalemate, the fighting started again in 1999, with Russia launching air strikes and following up with significant deployments of ground troops. By the end of November 1999, Russian troops had surrounded Chechnya's capital, Grozny, and about 215,000 Chechen refugees had fled to neighboring territories.

These challenges in Russia's strategic environment, combined with Yeltsin's significant health problems in his second term in office, led him to announce that he intended to step down at the end of his term of office. This was seen by many outside of Russia as a real test of the democratic system established by Yeltsin, based upon the foundation laid by Gorbachev: Would the system be able to handle a transition to someone who was not intimately involved with the creation of the current Russian democratic institutions?

The answer was, apparently, "yes." In the presidential election of April 7, 2000, over 68 percent of registered voters participated in the contest, and **Vladimir Putin** won the election with a significant margin of victory, approximately of the same magnitude on the first ballot that Yeltsin had won on the second round of the election of 1996. Putin had a number of serious economic and political challenges to face immediately after assuming office, and while he clearly was not able to resolve all of the problems that had been in existence for literally decades, he did make a real contribution[64] to the goal of having a stable transition from one government to another and demonstrating to the Russian population as well as those watching from elsewhere in the world that stable government in Russia could be achieved.

During his first term, Putin moved to recentralize power and cut back the positions of regional governments and big business. He also pushed forward an ambitious program of domestic reforms, particularly in the economic sphere, including banking reforms, tax reform, anti-money-laundering legislation, and administrative and judicial reform.

Putin was elected to a second term as Russian president by a landslide in March 2004 with over 70 percent of the vote. His nearest rival, the Communist candidate, drew less than14 percent. As Putin's second term drew to an end, outside observers were convinced that he was not going to give up power easily

> **TABLE 13.4**
>
> **The Presidential Election of 2008**
>
> | Candidate | Percentage |
> |---|---|
> | Dmitry Medvedev | 70.2 |
> | Gennady Zyuganov | 17.7 |
> | Vladimir Zhirinovsky | 9.4 |
> | Andrey Bogdanov | 1.3 |
> | (others) | 1.4 |
> | *Total* | *100 %* |
>
> *Source:* Central Intelligence Agency, *The World Factbook* "Russia," https://www.cia.gov/library/publications/the-world-factbook/geos/rs.html (accessed June 2011).

and were watching closely to see what he would do. As things turned out, Putin followed the letter of the law in the constitution, and did not stand for re-election in the 2008 presidential election. As the election approached, he announced that his first deputy Prime Minister, **Dmitry Medvedev**, was his preferred choice to be the next president of Russia, and he campaigned for Medvedev in the elections.[65]

Immediately after being endorsed by Putin, Medvedev announced that if he were elected in 2008 he would appoint Putin to be his premier, and Putin announced that he would accept that position if it were offered. Although the constitution did not permit Putin to serve a third consecutive term as President, it did *not* bar him from serving as premier, in which role he could continue to play an extremely influential role in Russian government.

Medvedev was elected President on March 2, 2008, as shown in Table 13.4, and promptly appointed Putin to be his premier.

During Medvedev's presidency there was much speculation about the power relationship between Medvedev and Putin, and whether Medvedev was simply a four-year "place-holder" for Putin, allowing him to stay at the center of power until he would be eligible to be president again. (In changes made to electoral law during Putin's second term as president, the length of a term of office of the President would increase from four years to five years, effective with the president elected in 2012.) In the summer of 2011 Putin announced that he would, indeed, run for the presidency in the 2012 election, and Medvedev announced that he would support Putin.

THE RUSSIAN CONSTITUTIONAL COURT

The **Constitutional Court** of the Russian Federation has been described as "the first independent court to be established in Russia since the Bolshevik Revolution."[66] The Court was established in October of 1991 by the Fourth Russian Congress of People's Deputies. While the law that created the Court indicated that it was "prohibited from considering political questions," it was frequently caught in the middle of explicitly political quarrels between President Yeltsin and the Russian Parliament. The Court is authorized in the 1995 constitution to rule on violations of constitutional rights, to hear appeals from lower courts, and to participate in impeachment proceedings against the president.

In fact, although the Court initially tried to walk a very narrow line and offend neither the Parliament nor the president, its decisions favored the Parliament significantly more frequently than they did the president.[67] Yeltsin suspended the Constitutional Court in October of 1993, but reconvened it in March of 1995.

POLITICAL PARTIES AND ELECTIONS

In the "old" Soviet system, when thinking of political parties one thought only of the Communist Party of the Soviet Union. The Communist Party of the Soviet Union (hereafter referred to as the CPSU) was *virtually* a governing organization in the USSR, and was "by far the most important political institution in that country."[68] While the role of the Communist Party of the Soviet Union went over a relatively short period of time from one of absolute dominance to one of being outlawed,[69] the structure of the political party has come to play a much more realistic role in Russian politics.

In recent years, a number of significant political parties and movements have come into existence, some more democratically oriented than others.[70] Some of these parties have roots in earlier democratic movements. Other parties, however, are direct descendants of the CPSU itself. It is clear from recent presidential and legislative elections, however, that the Communist Party is no longer the dominant force in Russian politics that it was only a couple of decades ago.

The dominant political party in recent years has been the party of Vladimir Putin, The United Russia Party. Although other parties do exist in Russia, and do compete in parliamentary elections, the United Russia Party is clearly the dominant party of the era. The Liberal-Democratic Party of Russia (LDPR) is an ultranationalistic party, led by the Deputy Speaker of the Duma, Vladimir Zhirinovsky. The Communist Party of the Russian Federation (CPRF), headed by Gennady Zyuganov, continues to support the traditional economic policies of the old Communist regime. The Communist Party is especially strong in rural areas of Russia, and campaigns with the platform that it will nationalize key industries and improve health care, public education, and public housing. Another major party is the Russian United Democratic Party (YABLOKO), led by Grigory Yavlinsky, which claims that it is the party of "Freedom and Justice." The other major party is the pro-Western Union of Right-Wing Forces (SPS), led by Nikita Belykh and former deputy prime minister Boris Nemtsov, which calls for economic and administrative reform, emphasizing the importance of building "a free, democratic, strong and humane State" that would be respected and "not feared."[71]

POLITICAL SUCCESSION, RUSSIAN STYLE

The issue of the **succession of leadership** in the Soviet Union and Russia illustrates the problem that we mentioned earlier about a lack of established democratic traditions and commitment to peaceful democratic transitions from one leader to another.[72]

Leonid Brezhnev was able to arrange the ouster of Nikita Khruschev through political alliances in the Politburo; in 1977 he expanded his base of power by acquiring the position of Chairman of the Presidium of the Supreme Soviet in addition to his position as General Secretary of the Communist Party. The leaders who followed Brezhnev to the post of Party General Secretary, Yuri Andropov and Konstintin Chernenko were both old party functionaries, and because of their ages (79 and 82 years, respectively) and accompanying illness, their opportunities to lead and to suggest significant policy innovations were few.

Many Sovietologists were keenly interested in what would happen in the process of succession of Brezhnev. Some thought it would introduce conflict and instability, some thought it would simply maintain the *status quo*, and some thought that it would open up significant avenues for reform in Soviet politics.[73]

Andropov's ill health made him a weak leader, and he placed a special emphasis on what was called "collective leadership" during his brief time in office. He was not able to create a new cabinet to reflect his own preferences, but was forced to permit the existing members of the Politburo, the Party Secretariat, and most top government functionaries to retain their positions. This was to no small degree because he "owed his election as general secretary primarily to [Defense Minister Marshal] Ustinov and [Foreign Minister Alexi] Gromyko". As well, he "also had to show consideration for that part of the 'Brezhnev faction,'…who had voted for him".[74]

When Chernenko succeeded to the General Secretary position, he was able to arrange for himself to be elected chairman of the Presidium of the Supreme Soviet relatively quickly, in June of 1983. As with Andropov, however, his health very quickly limited his ability to exercise the potential power of his office. At this time Mikhail Gorbachev rose to the position of second secretary of the Central Committee, and frequently substituted for Chernenko whose health forced him to take lengthy breaks from activity.

While Mikhail Gorbachev assumed the USSR's top position in the spring of 1985, some suggested that his assumption of power might "well prove to be a major turning point in Soviet history;"[75] others asked if he would "make a difference" in the way the Soviet regime functioned.[76] As we have already noted, he introduced a number of very significant structural changes in his first few years in office, even though he continued to face strong resistance from the entrenched bureaucracy to his call for a new kind of society.

Gorbachev led Soviet politics from 1985 through 1991, and the *perestroika* ("restructuring"), *glasnost* ("openness"), and *demokratizatsiya* ("democratization") that were associated with his regime were highly significant in changing the tenor and direction of Soviet—and post-Soviet—politics. Under his leadership, the fundamental structural changes of USSR governmental institutions discussed in this chapter took place, including changes in legislative and executive structures and a significant change in the role of the Communist Party in the political system.

In 1990, the Congress of the Russian Soviet Federated Socialist Republic declared that its laws would take precedence over Soviet laws. This contributed significantly to the demise of the USSR. In April of 1991, the Russian Federation created the position of president, and two months later Boris Yeltsin became Russia's first democratically-elected president.

Yeltsin's political fortunes varied drastically between the date he came to power in June of 1991 and the end of the decade. While at times both he and the political and economic reforms he advocated had wide support, at other times his governments suffered dramatically. Indeed, the conflict between Yeltsin and the Russian Parliament that took place in September of 1993—to which we have already referred—was illustrative of some of the problems from which his government suffered.

The most remarkable legacy of the Yeltsin presidency, however, may be what came after Yeltsin's term: a peaceful transition to a democratically elected successor. It is customary to observe that in a country that is new to democracy it is not the *first* democratic election that is crucial to watch, but the *second*. A despot may decide to bring about reform and may order a "democratic" election to take place, and it may be the case that the culture will not support that reform and in the election after the one ordered by the authoritarian ruler serious problems will develop. While Putin's campaign and election were not without problems and charges of improprieties, the international observers who were on hand indicated that the election was free and fair and that the election of Putin was a legitimate one.

We noted, above, that Putin "finessed" the Russian electoral law by designating a hand-picked successor—Dmitry Medvedev—who, in turn, promised to appoint Putin to serve as premier during his term of office as president. Putin's 2011 announcement that he intended to run for President in the 2012 election offered support for the theory that Medvedev's succession to power was simply part of a ruse, as many observers labeled it, to permit Putin to stay in power and "guide" Medvedev for four years as required by the Russian constitution, and then to constitutionally return to power for up to ten more years (two five-year terms) in 2012.[77]

THE RUSSIAN SYSTEM IN PERSPECTIVE

The Russian system provides an interesting case study, both in its own right and in a comparative perspective. Russia is a political system that is actively evolving from one period and style of politics to another. We can see that the changes from *Soviet* institutions and political behavior to *Russian* institutions and behavior has been, and will continue to be, both dramatic and traumatic.

Indeed, no one knows at this point in time whether Russia's recent experiences with democracy will, in fact, endure.

The Russian case is an illustration of a society without a history of democratic institutions and political behavior attempting to establish democratic institutions and behavior. The transition to stable, Western-style parliamentary democracy will not come without a long period of tension and effort on the part of the Russian people, but if they can achieve all of the goals they are seeking to achieve, much will have been accomplished.

In short, the Russian system is quite different from other political systems we have met. Nations in flux, as we see in the case of Russia, are nations with significant *potential*, but ones that have to worry about the potential for violence and self-destruction as well as the potential for accomplishment. The *single most important* lesson we should draw from our studies is that we cannot walk into any new political study with the assumption that all politics operate in the same fashion as they do in the United States. In this manner, we can see the values of cross-national political inquiry. Our new perspectives provide us with a better ability to make our own observations in the future and to draw our own conclusions as we continue our studies.

DISCUSSION QUESTIONS

1. How did the long and difficult history of governmental transitions affect the current Russian political system? What do you think were the most significant historical events in this evolution?
2. We have seen that constitutions may be more or less significant in a political system. Has the role of Russia's constitution varied over time? What is its role today?
3. Is Russia federal in the same way that Germany and Canada are federal? What are the differences that you see? How is Russia different? How does this affect the power of the president of Russia?
4. The Soviet Union was born in a complex and rigid ideological context. How would you characterize the role of ideology in the creation of Russia? Was ideology the driving force, or was it pragmatic politics? How much is ideology steering policy and politics in Russia today?
5. What are the key differences between Russian political institutions today and the political institutions of the Union of Soviet Socialist Republics and the Commonwealth of Independent States that preceded it? Should Russia be classified as a parliamentary regime, a presidential regime, or something else? Why?
6. What *is* the relationship between President Medvedev and Prime Minister Putin today? How can we tell who is really in charge in Russia? Does it make a difference?
7. Given the importance of political parties to the Soviet Union, are parties as important to Russia? What is the role of political parties in Russia today?

KEY TERMS

Bolshevik   329
Commonwealth
  of Independent
  States   333

Constitutional
  Court   343
devolution of Soviet
  Union   331

Gorbachev, Mikhail   331
Lenin, Vladimir   329
Marxism-Leninism   331
Medvedev, Dmitry   343

SUGGESTED READINGS

Jeffrey Kahn, *Federalism, Democratization, and the Rule of Law in Russia* (New York: Oxford University Press, 2008). Russian federalism is significantly different from federalism in Western democracies. This volume describes the development, evolution, and current status of federalism in Russia and how it affects the operation of politics in Russia.

Julie Newton and William Tompson, eds., *Institutions, Ideas and Leadership in Russian Politics* (New York: Palgrave Macmillan, 2010). This is a very good single-volume introduction to politics in Russia, describing ideology, behavior, and political institutions there.

Kevin O'Connor, *Intellectuals and Apparatchiks: Russian Nationalism and the Gorbachev Revolution* (Lanham, MD: Lexington Books, 2006). Many wonder how Mikhail Gorbachev managed to rise to power and why he did what he did once he controlled power. This volume provides answers to those questions and is a very good choice for an understanding of that period of time.

Nicholas Riasanovsky, *A History of Russia* (New York: Oxford University Press, 2011). A very comprehensive history of Russia, before, during, and after the Soviet Union period. This volume provides needed background for an understanding of the political development of the institutions of Communism.

Gordon Smith and Robert Sharlett, *Russia and Its Constitution: Promise and Political Reality* (Boston, MA: Martinus Nijhoff, 2008). The role of the constitution in Russia is different from comparable situations in Western democracies. This volume describes the constitution and explains its evolution and its place in the Russian political system.

NOTES

1. Vadim Medish, *The Soviet Union* (Englewood Cliffs, NJ: Prentice Hall, 1981), p. 1.
2. John S. Reshetar, *The Soviet Polity* (New York: Harper and Row, 1978), p. 21.
3. Geoffrey Hosking, *Russia and the Russians: A History* (Cambridge, MA: Harvard University Press, 2001), is a good reference in this area. See also Nicholas Riasanovsky, *A History of Russia* (New York: Oxford University Press, 2011).
4. Gwendolen M. Carter, *The Government of the Soviet Union* (New York: Harcourt, Brace, Jovanovich, 1972), p. 14. See also A. I. Polunov, Thomas Owen, and L. G. Zakharova, *Russia in the Nineteenth Century: Autocracy, Reform, and Social Change, 1814–1914* (Armonk, NY: M.E. Sharpe, 2005).
5. This section is based upon a much longer section written by Vernon V. Aspaturian, "Soviet Politics," in Roy C. Macridis, *Modern Political Systems: Europe* (Englewood Cliffs, NJ: Prentice Hall, 1978), pp. 335–340. See also the discussions of Russia's revolutionary heritage in S. A. Smith, *The Russian Revolution: A Very Short Introduction* (New York: Oxford University Press, 2002).
6. Aspaturian, "Soviet Politics," p. 336.
7. Michael G. Roskin, *Countries and Concepts* (Englewood Cliffs, NJ: Prentice Hall, 1982), p. 219.

8. Aspaturian, "Soviet Politics," p. 338. Some good recent studies of Lenin include the following: Christopher Read, *Lenin: A Revolutionary Life* (New York: Routledge, 2005); and Stephen Lee, *Lenin and Revolutionary Russia* (New York: Routledge, 2003).

9. Adam B. Ulam, *The Russian Political System* (New York: Random House, 1974), p. 27.

10. See David Marples, *Lenin's Revolution: Russia, 1917–1921* (Harlow, UK: Longman, 2000).

11. A very good general history is by Theodore Link, *Communism: A Primary Source Analysis* (New York: Rosen Publishing Group, 2005). More specialized studies are by Adam B. Ulam, *The Bolsheviks: The Intellectual and Political History of the Triumph of Communism in Russia* (Cambridge, MA: Harvard University Press, 1998); and Terry Fiehn and Chris Corin, *Communist Russia Under Lenin and Stalin* (London: John Murray, 2000).

12. A good history looking at the relative impact of Mikhail Gorbachev in historical context is by Kevin O'Connor, *Intellectuals and Apparatchiks: Russian Nationalism and the Gorbachev Revolution* (Lanham, MD: Lexington Books, 2006). See also M. S. Gorbachev, *Gorbachev: On My Country and the World* (New York: Columbia University Press, 1999). See Iulia Shevchenko, *The Central Government of Russia: From Gorbachev to Putin* (Burlington, VT: Ashgate, 2004); and Jonathan Harris, *Subverting the System: Gorbachev's Reform of the Party's Apparat, 1986–1991* (Lanham, MD: Rowman and Littlefield, 2005).

13. See David Marples, *The Collapse of the Soviet Union: 1985–1991* (New York: Pearson, 2004); and Ruth Starkman, *Transformations of the New Germany* (New York: Palgrave Macmillan, 2006).

14. In September of 1990 President George H. W. Bush discussed the Persian Gulf crisis and international relations in a speech entitled "Toward a New World Order." (*U.S. Department of State Dispatch* September 17, 1990, v. 1 no. 3 p. 91). More recently, and related to the Soviet Union, in May of 1991 Bush spoke of "The Possibility of New World Order, Unlocking the Promise of Freedom" (*Vital Speeches* May 15, 1991, v. 57 n. 15, p. 450). A recent study of Russia is that by J. L. Black, *Vladimir Putin and the New World Order: Looking East, Looking West?* (Lanham, MD: Rowman and Littlefield, 2004).

15. Medish, *The Soviet Union*, pp. 29–30.

16. Ronald Grigor Suny, "The Nationality Question," in Janet Podell and Steven Anzovin, eds., *The Soviet Union* (New York: H. W. Wilson, 1988), p. 136.

17. Indeed, "in his closing speech to the first session of the new Congress of People's Deputies, Mikhail Gorbachev commented that no single issue had been so widely discussed by the Congress as that of interethnic relations." *Radio Liberty: Report on the USSR* 1, no. 24 (June 16, 1989), p. 21.

18. Celestine Bohlen, "The Soviets and the Enmities Within," *New York Times* April 16, 1989, Section E, p. 1.

19. John N. Hazard, *The Soviet System of Government* (Chicago, IL: University of Chicago Press, 1980), pp. 98–99.

20. See Robert Sharlet, *The New Soviet Constitution of 1977* (Brunswick, OH: King's Court Communications, 1978), p. 97. This has a copy of the complete text of the constitution.

21. Felicity Barringer, "Soviets Draft Plans for Government Change," *New York Times* October 22, 1988, p. 3.

22. Adam Ulam's essay "Looking at the Past: The Unraveling of the Soviet Union," *Current History* 91, no. 567 (1992): 339–347 is very good in this regard. See Nick Bisley, *The End of the Cold War and the Causes of Soviet Collapse* (New York: Palgrave Macmillan, 2004).

23. "Commonwealth of Independent States Treaty Signed," *New York Times*. December 23, 1991, p. A. 10. On the CIS, see Zbigniew Brzezinski and Paige Sullivan, *Russia and the Commonwealth of Independent States: Documents, Data, and Analysis* (Armonk, NY: M.E. Sharpe, 1997).

24. "Soviet Coup Started," *Los Angeles Times*, August 30, 1991, p. A1. See also Andrew Langley, *The Collapse of the Soviet Union: The End of an Empire* (Minneapolis, MN: Compass Point Books, 2006).

25. "Gorbachev Resigns from C.P.S.U.," *New York Times*, August 25, 1991, p. 1.

26. Michael McFaul, Nikolai Petrov, and Andrei Riabov, *Between Dictatorship and Democracy: Russian Post-Communist Political Reform* (Washington, DC: Carnegie Endowment for International Peace, 2004).

27. See Steven Erlanger's article "Now Yeltsin Must Govern: Struggle with Hard-Liners Over for Now, Talk Is of 'A Second Russian Revolution,'" *New York Times*, October 10, 1993, p. 1. See also Thomas Remington, *The Russian Parliament: Institutional Evolution in a Transitional Regime, 1989–1999* (New Haven, CT: Yale University Press, 2001).

28. Ulam, *The Russian Political System*, p. 59.

29. Sharlet, *The New Soviet Constitution of 1977*, pp. 4–6.

30. "Resignation of President Mikhail Gorbachev," *Vital Speeches* 58, no. 7 (January 15, 1992), p. 194.

31. See Leon R. Aron, *Yeltsin: A Revolutionary Life* (New York: St. Martin's Press, 2000); Roy Medvedev, *Post-Soviet Russia: A Journey Through the Yeltsin Era* (New York: Columbia University Press, 2000).

32. See Boris Kagarlitsky, *Russia Under Yeltsin and Putin: Neo-Liberal Autocracy* (Sterling, VA: Pluto Press, 2002). On the new Russian Constitution, see Gordon Smith and Robert Sharlet, *Russia and Its Constitution: Promise and Political Reality* (Boston, MA: Martinus Nijhoff, 2008); or Jane Henderson, *The Constitution of the Russian Federation: A Contextual Analysis* (Portland, OR: Hart, 2010).

33. See Anton Steen and Vladimir Gelman, *Elites and Democratic Development in Russia* (New York: Routledge, 2003).

34. Eugene Huskey, *Presidential Power in Russia* (Armonk, NY: M.E. Sharpe, 1999).

35. Reshetar, *The Soviet Polity*, p. 172.

36. Aspaturian, "Soviet Politics," p. 401. See also Sharlet, *The New Soviet Constitution of 1977*, pp. 73–132.

37. On Russian federalism, see Jeffrey Kahn, *Federalism, Democratization, and the Rule of Law in Russia* (New York: Oxford University Press, 2008); or Cameron Ross and Adrian Campbell, *Federalism and Local Politics in Russia* (New York: Routledge, 2009). A more focused study is by Katherine Graney, *Of Khans and Kremlins: Tatarstan and the Future of Ethno-Federalism in Russia* (Lanham, MD: Lexington, 2010).

38. A very good collection on ideology in the former Soviet Union is Stephen J. Lee, *Russia and the USSR, 1855–1991: Autocracy and Dictatorship* (New York: Routledge, 2006). Archie Brown's book *The Rise and Fall of Communism* (New York: Ecco, 2009), traces the origins of the communist ideology through its collapse.

39. Sam C. Sarkesian and James Buck, *Comparative Politics* (Sherman Oaks, CA: Alfred Publishing Co., 1979), pp. 97–98. Marxism is a highly elaborate theoretical

framework, too extensive to analyze here in detail. See Gustav Wetter, *Soviet Ideology* (New York: Praeger, 1962), for a very good introduction to the ideas of Marxism as interpreted in the Soviet Union.

40. Medish, *The Soviet Union*, pp. 67–8.
41. Sarkesian and Buck, *Comparative Politics*, p. 101. Recent analyses of Stalin would include Robert Service, *Stalin: A Biography* (Cambridge, MA: Harvard University Press, 2005).
42. Ibid. See also Aspaturian, "Soviet Politics," p. 356.
43. Aspaturian, "Soviet Politics," p. 358. On Khruschev, see William Taubman and Sergei Khrushchev, *Nikita Khrushchev* (New Haven, CT: Yale University Press, 2000); Nikita Sergevich Khrushchev, *Memoirs of Nikita Khrushchev* (University Park, PA: Pennsylvania State University, 2004).
44. Carter, *The Government of the Soviet Union*, p. 13. See also Matthew Ouimet, *The Rise and Fall of the Brezhnev Doctrine in Soviet Foreign Policy* (Chapel Hill, NC: University of North Carolina Press, 2003).
45. Volkogonov and Shukman, *Autopsy for an Empire, op. cit.*; and John W. Parker, *Kremlin in Transition*, vol. 1, *From Brezhnev to Chernenko, 1978 to 1985* (Boston, MA: Unwin Hyman, 1991).
46. See Christopher Xenakis, *What Happened to the Soviet Union? How and Why American Sovietologists Were Caught by Surprise* (Westport, CT: Praeger, 2002). See also Thomas Remington, *Politics in Russia* (New York: Longman, 2008).
47. George W. Breslauer, *Gorbachev and Yeltsin as Leaders* (New York: Cambridge University Press, 2002); or Stephen Kotkin, *Armageddon Averted: The Soviet Collapse, 1970–2000* (New York: Oxford University Press, 2008). See also Jonathan Haslam, *Russia's Cold War: From the October Revolution to the Fall of the Wall* (New Haven, CT: Yale University Press, 2011).
48. Elizabeth Teague, "Gorbachev's First Four Years," *Radio Liberty: Report on the USSR* l, no. 9 (March 3, 1989), pp. 3–4.
49. See Dawn Mann, "The Opening of the Congress," *Radio Liberty: Report on the USSR* l, no. 23 (June 9, 1989), pp. 1–2.
50. Sharlet, *The New Soviet Constitution of 1977*, p. 108.
51. Paul Quinn-Judge, "Gorbachev Dominance Displayed in Parliament," *Christian Science Monitor*, December l, 1988, p. 1.
52. David Remnick, "New Soviet Congress Tackles Procedure," *Washington Post*, May 27, 1989, p. A15.
53. Bill Keller, "A Guide to the Election Process," *New York Times*, March 26, 1989, p. E3. See also Dawn Mann and Julia Wishnevsky, "Composition of Congress of People's Deputies," *Radio Liberty, Report on the USSR* l, no. 18 (May 5, 1989), p. 6.
54. See *Radio Free Europe/Radio Liberty Research Report* 2, no. 20 (May 14, 1992), pp. 112–119.
55. Celestine Bohlen, "Yeltsin Orders Replacement of Legislatures of Regions," *New York Times*, October 9, 1993, p. 9. See also Richard Sakwa, *Russian Politics and Society* (New York: Routledge, 2008).
56. See Tiffany Troxel, *Parliamentary Power in Russia, 1994–2001: President vs. Parliament* (London: Palgrave Macmillan, 2003). See also Julie Newton and William Tompson, eds., *Institutions, Ideas and Leadership in Russian Politics* (New York: Palgrave Macmillan, 2010).
57. See "OSCE Slams 'Unfair' Russian Elections," *Der Spiegel*, December 3, 2007, available at *http://www.spiegel.de/international/world/0,1518,521063,00.html* (accessed June 2011).

58. See Radio Free Europe/Radio Liberty, "The Russian Federation Votes: 2003–2004," *http://www.rferl.org/specials/russianelection/parties/unified.asp.*

59. Sharlet, *The New Soviet Constitution of 1977*, p. 112.

60. Little, *Governing the Soviet Union*, p. 157.

61. Teague, "Gorbachev's First Four Years," p. 4. See also Michael Parks, "Party Picks Gorbachev as Nominee for President at People's Congress," *Los Angeles Times*, May 23, 1989, p. 8; and Michael Parks, "New Russian Congress Elects Gorbachev to Presidency," *Los Angeles Times*, May 26, 1989, p. 1.

62. See "Yeltsin Elected President," *U.S. News and World Report* 110, no. 21 (June 17, 1991), pp. 36–38. On the presidency, see Richard Rose, *Russia Elects a President* (Glasgow, UK: Centre for the Study of Public Policy, 2000). On Yeltsin, see Timothy Colton, *Yeltsin: A Life* (New York: Basic Books, 2008).

63. See Barry Turner, ed., *The Statesman's Yearbook* (Basingstoke, UK: Palgrave, 2000), pp. 1329–1330.

64. See Peter Baker, *Kremlin Rising: Vladimir Putin's Russia and the End of Revolution* (New York: Scribner, 2005). See also Michael Stuermer, *Putin and the Rise of Russia* (New York: Pegasus Books, 2009). On Putin's power, see Stephen White, *Politics and the Ruling Group in Putin's Russia* (New York: Palgrave Macmillan, 2008); and Richard Sakwa, *Power and Policy in Putin's Russia* (Abingdon, UK: Routledge, 2009).

65. See BBC News, "Putin Sees Medvedev as Successor," December 10, 2007, available at *http://news.bbc.co.uk/2/hi/europe/7136347.stm* (accessed June 2011). See also Richard Sakwa, *The Crisis of Russian Democracy: The Dual State, Factionalism, and the Medvedev Succession* (New York: Cambridge University Press, 2011).

66. This section is based upon a more detailed discussion in *Radio Free Europe/Radio Liberty Research Report* 2, no. 20 (May 14, 1992), p. 14. See also Alexei Trochev, *Judging Russia: Constitutional Court in Russian Politics: 1990–2006* (New York: Cambridge University Press, 2008).

67. *Radio Free Europe/Radio Liberty Research Report, op. cit.*

68. Ronald Hill and Peter Frank, *The Soviet Communist Party* (London, UK: Allen & Unwin, 1981), p. 1.

69. See Rita DiLeo, "The Soviet Communist Party, 1988–1991: From Power to Ostracism," *Coexistence* 29, no. 4 (1992), pp. 321–334. See also S. P. Roberts, *Putin's United Russia Party* (New York: Routledge, 2011).

70. See the essay by Roy Medvedev, "After the Communist Collapse: New Political Tendencies in Russia," *Dissent* 39, no. 4 (Fall, 1992), pp. 489–498.

71. See IPU PARLINE database, *http://www.ipu.org/parline-e/reports/2263_E.htm* (accessed June 2011). On elections see Richard Sakwa, *Putin: Russia's Choice* (New York: Routledge, 2008); or Neil Munro and Richard Rose, *Russian Elections Since 1991* (Aberdeen, UK: University of Aberdeen Press, 2009).

72. Much of the material in the next few paragraphs is based upon much more extensive analysis in Boris Meissner, "Implications of Leadership and Social Change for Soviet Policies," in Kinya Niiseki, ed., *The Soviet Union in Transition* (Boulder, CO: Westview Press, 1987), pp. 50–56.

73. Timothy Colton, *The Dilemma of Reform in the Soviet Union* (New York: Council on Foreign Relations, 1986), pp. 68–69.

74. Meissner, "Leadership," p. 52.

75. Herbert J. Ellison, "Gorbachev and Reform: An Introduction," in Lawrence W. Lerner and Donald W. Treadgold, eds., *Gorbachev and the Soviet Future* (Boulder, CO: Westview Press, 1988), p. 1.

76. There is an absolutely massive literature on Gorbachev. See, *inter alia*, A. S. Cherniaev, Robert English, and Elizabeth Tucker, *My Six Years with Gorbachev* (University Park, PA: Pennsylvania State University Press, 2000); and Jack F. Matlock, *Reagan and Gorbachev: How the Cold War Ended* (New York: Random House, 2004).

77. See Tony Halpin, "'Puppet President' Dmitri Medvedev takes power in Putin job swap," [London] *Times*, May 7, 2008, available at *http://www.timesonline.co.uk/tol/news/world/europe/article3882798.ece* (accessed June 2011). See also Stuart Goldman, *Russia's 2008 Presidential Succession* (Washington, DC: Congressional Research Service, 2008).

The Chinese Political System

Party roles and state roles often merge in China. Here Communist Party leader
and President Hu Jintao holds a child at Yumin Village in Shenzhen.

China, as will become clear right away, is different from other political systems we have seen and will see in this book. China is a political system with which the contemporary student of politics should be familiar, if for no other reason than over one-fifth of the population of the planet lives within its borders. It is noteworthy, then, that for so many years (and still today) so many people have known so little about China.

CHINA

Total Area (rank)	9,596,961 sq km (4)
Population (rank)	1,336,718,015 (1)
Population Growth Rate (rank)	0.493 (152)
Urban Population	47%
Life Expectancy at Birth (total population) (rank)	74.68 (95)
Literacy	92.2%
Government Type	Communist state
Legal System	Civil law influenced by Soviet system
Head of Government	Premier Wen Jiabao
Chief of State	President Hu Jintao
Gross Domestic Product (GDP)	$5.878 trillion
GDP Per Capita (rank)	$7,600 (126)
GDP Real Growth Rate (rank)	10.3% (6)
Unemployment Rate (rank)	4.3% (41)

A discussion of China in a textbook that puts an emphasis on political institutions and political structures is exceedingly problematic. We need to indicate at the outset that this chapter will not be parallel to all of the other country-studies chapters in this volume, primarily because such an approach to understanding Chinese politics would *not* lead to an understanding of Chinese politics. China's political structure, and its political history, can be characterized as being dominated by charismatic and powerful individuals, and it has been those individuals and the patterns of behavior they have demonstrated that have guided and shaped Chinese political history.

China today is a strongly ideologically-based system. What does this mean? Don't all nations have political ideologies at their foundations? Yes, they do, but those foundations are also influenced by the political structures that rest upon those foundations. In the case of China, while there is a clear foundation of Marxist-Leninist-Maoist ideology, that ideology has been interpreted by the leaders of the day—a relatively small number of extremely powerful individuals—rather than by the structures and institutions of the regime.

Scholars who specialize in the study of China and Chinese politics have long suggested that China must be studied in a different way from the way other nations can be studied; its unique history has created a political culture and political institutions that are not directly comparable to those of other nations. This will result in a relatively longer discussion of Chinese history and culture in this chapter than we have provided in other chapters, and a relatively shorter discussion of Chinese institutions and political structures than have been provided elsewhere.

THE "MIDDLE KINGDOM" AND MODERN CHINESE HISTORY

The history of China goes back over 3,300 years, and China has been argued to be "imprisoned by her history."[1] China has been referred to as the "**Middle Kingdom**," *Zhōngguó* in Mandarin Chinese, which can also be translated as "the center of civilization," and this perspective of Chinese culture has shaped the way China has seen its own role in the world. One historical characteristic of China has been its isolation from the rest of the world, and especially from the West, and this has had an effect upon Chinese political development.

Many names have been used to describe China and eras of government and society in China as it has evolved through dynasties, a republican period, and into and during the current Communist period. The history of China as a significant region is a very long and complex one, as illustrated in Table 14.1.

China's early dynasties were an important part of the growth of Chinese civilization, and they played an important role in the development of civilized society. Over the almost three thousand years leading up to the collapse of the Qing dynasty in 1911, there were twenty-five dynastic changes in China; they created the basis for an *expectation* that stable society required authoritarian rule.[2] Through the Xia and Shang Dynasties the idea of Chinese nationhood

TABLE 14.1

Eras in Chinese History

B.C. ca. 21st–16th century	Xia
B.C. 1700–1027	Shang
B.C. 1027– 221	Zhou
B.C. 221–207	Qin
B.C. 206 –220 A.D.	Han
220–588	Period of instability
618–907	Tang
907–960	Five Dynasties
960–1279	Song
1279–1368	Yuan
1368–1644	Ming
1644–1911	Qing
1912–1949	Republic of China (in mainland China and Taiwan)
1949–	Republic of China (in Taiwan)
1949–	People's Republic of China (on mainland)

Source: Adapted from Robert L. Worden, Andrea Matles Savada and Ronald E. Dolan, eds., *China* (Federal Research Division, Library of Congress, 1987), http://lcweb2.loc.gov/frd/cs/cntoc.html (accessed July 2011), "Table A: Chronology of Chinese Dynasties."

developed. It was during the Zhou Dynasty that China's great schools of intellectual thought—Confucianism, Legalism, Daoism, Mohism, and others—developed.

> Since the beginning of recorded history (at least since the Shang Dynasty), the people of China have developed a strong sense of their origins, both mythological and real, and kept voluminous records concerning both. As a result of these records, augmented by numerous archaeological discoveries in the second half of the twentieth century, information concerning the ancient past, not only of China but also of much of East, Central, and Inner Asia, has survived.[3]

Of the many influences upon Chinese culture, the teachings of **Confucius** (Kung Fu-tzu, approximately 551–479 B.C.) may be the best known in the West. While the emperors based their power on "a mandate of heaven,"—a Chinese variation on what would be known in Europe much later as "the divine right of kings" theory—Confucian theory suggested that even emperors had to follow ethical principles, including moral leadership.

Over the years the identity of a "Chinese" nation and culture developed. Assimilation and conquest helped China expand, and two general characteristics of the various imperial dynasties can be identified here that had implications for future (and present) Chinese attitudes and behavior. One of these generalizations was that an important characteristic of Chinese society and culture has been its *agrarian* nature, and "the unceasing struggle of the largely agrarian Chinese against the threat posed to their safety and way of life by non-Chinese peoples on the margins of their territory."[4] This is what gave rise to the image of China as the "middle kingdom," or "central nation," standing up to periodic invasion from outside. The Great Wall of China, we should recall, was a *defensive* structure, designed to keep outsiders out.

Another general legacy of China's past has been that China has had a history of *strong rulers*, and *not* democratic government.[5] Chinese emperors have often been characterized in the literature as being authoritarian[6]—sometimes "ruthless"—and this was significant:

> This tradition stretches back at least to the first emperor of the Qin Dynasty...who unified China in 221 B.C.E. A ruthless ruler, the emperor ended feudalism in China, starting China on a path remarkably different from that of Europe or Japan. The legacy of this crushing of local autonomy has been a powerful belief that China can be unified only under strong, central rule; the idea of federalism, although now advocated by some intellectuals, is alien to China's political tradition.[7]

As the Qing dynasty weakened in the late nineteenth century the global political environment was beginning to intrude on China in a way that had not happened in earlier years. Beginning with the **Opium War** (1839–1842), outside forces pressed Chinese authorities to make concessions (primarily for reasons of expanded trade) that resulted in China suffering from increasing foreign domination and interference in its domestic policy. The Opium War ended with China having to cede Hong Kong to the British, as well as agree to grant **extraterritorial rights** to foreigners in China, which meant that foreigners could operate under their own national legal systems while in China, and not have to operate under Chinese law.[8] From 1850 to 1865 a major peasant uprising took place, the Taiping Rebellion, which sought to overthrow the Qing dynasty; the rebellion was ultimately defeated by the government of the day, but estimates suggest that 20 million Chinese may have been killed in the process. These signs of imperial weakness led many to start to question what form of government should come in China's future.

Chinese who had been exposed to Western education and Western politics were interested in taking advantage of the weakening Qing dynasty to undertake fundamental changes in China. **Sun Yat-sen** was typical of these individuals: born middle-class, exposed to Western ideas, including Christianity, and educated overseas. A new class of political leaders was emerging, one that was not interested in a continuation of the old order.

When Chinese imperial rule ended in 1911, and the **Republic of China** was established led by Sun Yat-sen (1866–1925), there were still many who wanted to restore the throne to an emperor. However, a Western-style parliamentary democratic republic was established in 1912, one that struggled to provide stability for the regime; Japan, especially, was supporting those who were not interested in the success of the new regime. From 1912 through 1928 China struggled with weak republican government that was unable to effectively control the nation. A network of **warlords** was developed that dominated politics in that era, using private armies of regionally powerful individuals.

Sun Yat-sen turned to the new Soviet Union for assistance, which provided advisers to the **Nationalist Party** (known as the **Guomindang**, GMD). At the same time, a group of Chinese who were inspired by Marxist theory and the Soviet Revolution formed the Communist Party of China in 1921. In addition to supporting Sun and the Nationalists, however, Moscow was *also* providing advice and support to the new **Chinese Communist Party** (CCP) being established by **Mao Zedong**. There was, apparently, some thought that perhaps the CCP and the Nationalists would unite and create a new government. For a period of time (starting in 1923) they did join together under the auspices of the Communist International—*Comintern*—in China, led by Mikhail Borodin, who ordered the CCP to merge with the GMD, to fight the warlords and establish stability in China. "The GMD was the larger, older, and better-known party, while the CCP brought in a core of highly dedicated young activists—as well as foreign aid from the Soviet Union."[9]

Sun Yat-sen died in 1925, and was succeeded by **Chiang Kai-shek,** who broke with the Communists and the Soviet Union, and who militarily united China by 1927 by turning against the Communist Party organization. In April of 1927, the GMD attacked their CCP allies in Shanghai; fighting lasted until 1930, referred to as the era of "White Terror." Ultimately several hundred thousand Communists and sympathizers were killed by the Nationalists. From 1927 to 1938 China was governed by the Nationalists from Nanjing (which means "southern capital"; Beijing means "northern capital").[10]

After the 1927 split between Chiang Kai-shek and the CCP, the CCP started to engage in armed resistance against the Nationalists. Mao Zedong, its leader, argued that unlike the Soviet Union's Marxist model (which called for the oppressed industrial workers to unite and lead the Communist struggle), China needed a different revolutionary model because it did not have a class of oppressed industrial workers to lead the Communist struggle: The CCP needed to organize the *peasants* to perform this task. In 1931 the CCP announced the establishment of the Chinese Soviet Republic, under the leadership of Mao Zedong, based in Jiangxi Province in south-central China. The forces of Chiang moved against Mao, and because the Communist forces were no match for the Nationalists, Mao and his **People's Liberation Army** fled from Jiangxi and in 1934–1935 undertook the "**Long March**" to Shaanxi Province in the north to a new political base.

Although the Long March was a military disaster for the CCP, during which it lost most of its strength (some say as much as 90 percent), it was significant for Chinese politics for three important reasons. First, in this period Mao strengthened his hold over the CCP, becoming Chairman of the Party in January of 1936, a role he continued to control until his death in 1976. The development of other future leaders of China was significant, too; indeed, all Chinese leaders through Deng Xiaoping were drawn from that leadership pool. Second, during this period Mao reshaped the Communist Party as a militarized body, and closely linked it with the Red Army. "Rural guerrilla struggle and the eventual encirclement of the cities, rather than the organization of the urban working class, became the formula for Communist victory."[11] Third, the Long March played a huge role in Chinese political *mythology,* providing the CCP with legends to support its leadership for years to come.[12]

From the early 1930s through 1946, China was focused on political tension with Japan and what was to become the Second World War, and from 1937 to 1945 the GMD and the CCP were again acting as if they were allies. Japan invaded Manchuria in 1931, and established a puppet government in what they called Manchukuo in 1932. Japan then pressed south into mainland China, and active conflict between China and Japan began in July of 1937. Japan quickly conquered Shanghai, and then in an effort to crush the Nationalist government undertook what was called the "**Nanjing massacre**" in December of 1937, killing over 57,000 Chinese prisoners of war in one day; China reports over 340,000 deaths and 20,000 women raped in that campaign.[13]

When, following the American victory over Japan, the war with Japan was ended in 1945, civil war between the Nationalists and the CCP broke out, eventually resulting in the Nationalists being driven off the mainland to the island of Taiwan in 1949 where the Republic of China was declared. Mao and the CCP established the new capital of the **People's Republic of China** in Beijing on October 1, 1949.

Once the CCP had driven the Nationalists off of the mainland, their primary goal became the establishment of a Marxist-Leninist government. The government that was established was an authoritarian and highly centralized structure, one that remains highly centralized and tightly controlled today (although much less so than under Mao).

THE CHINESE CONSTITUTIONAL SYSTEM

China ratified its most recent constitution in 1982. We noted in Chapter Two that constitutions play a number of different roles in their respective systems, including serving as (a) expressions of ideology, (b) expressions of the basic laws of the regime, (c) organizational frameworks for governments, (d) statements about how government is organized, and (e) statements about how constitutions can be changed, with an amendment clause. We noted that different constitutions perform these several tasks differently. In the Chinese case, the most important role of the constitution is clearly ideological; as we shall see throughout the rest of this chapter, basic laws and structures of the regime are changed as needed to meet the needs of the Chinese Communist Party. The importance of the Constitution of the People's Republic of China is to serve as a document of educational and symbolic value for the nation.

In earlier chapters, when we have discussed the constitutional system we have focused on the political structures that are established to assist in the operation of state government. In China, although those state institutions and structures exist, they are clearly secondary to the political institutions, structures, and ideology of the Chinese Communist Party. As Figure 14.1 shows, the unofficial and informal linkages from the Party structure to the State structure are the key determinants of power.

In describing the Chinese constitutional system, we can note that China is a unitary and socialist state based upon Marxist-Leninist thought modified by "Mao Zedong Thought and Deng Xiaoping Theory."[14] The Preamble to the Constitution states, "The basic task of the nation in the years to come is to concentrate its effort on socialist modernization," and that it will operate "under the leadership of the Communist Party of China and the guidance of Marxism-Leninism and Mao Zedong Thought."

We will see below that Chinese political structures include a 3,000-member National People's Congress, elected indirectly from regional congresses, which in turn elects a president and a state council (the Chinese equivalent of a cabinet), which in turn selects a premier. Those structures in themselves are not so very different from structures we have met in other political systems, and they *sound* like a variation on a typical parliamentary model government, but their operation and importance *is* radically different from those of other nations, for reasons that we will see below.

The major difference in Chinese constitutional operation is the role of the Chinese Communist Party (CCP), which in fact is the key political institution in the regime. Essentially all political decisions are made and undertaken with the guidance and approval of the CCP, and not only the state constitution but also the CCP constitution must be considered in an understanding of how Chinese politics works.

> Both constitutions stress the principle of democratic centralism, under which the representative organs of both party and state are elected by lower bodies and in turn elect their administrative arms at corresponding levels. Within representative and executive bodies, the minority must abide by decisions of the majority; lower bodies obey orders of higher-level organs. In theory, the National Party Congress ranks as the highest organ of party power, but actual power lies in the CCP Central Committee and its even more exclusive Political Bureau. At the apex of all political power are the members of the elite Standing Committee of the Political Bureau.[15]

UNITARY GOVERNMENT IN CHINA: THE CHINESE COMMUNIST PARTY IN POLITICS

The Chinese Communist Party is the core of Chinese politics today.[16] China's 1982 Constitution declares, "The People's Republic of China is a unitary multi-national state," and indicates that its philosophical orientation is "under the leadership of the Communist Party of China and the guidance of Marxism-Leninism and Mao Zedong Thought."[17] Accordingly, rather than discussing the Party's structures later in this chapter, it is appropriate to discuss it here in the context of China's approach to unitary government and its vehicle for organizing all governmental and political activity. The Chinese Communist Party (CCP) is so close to being *equivalent* with the Chinese state in power and scope that the two institutions are, for all intents and purposes, the same thing. In December of 2010 the CCP had a membership of 80.27 *million* members and 3.3 *million* branches of the Party![18] This is not a political party in the same sense of the word as political parties in Britain, France, the United States, or even Russia.

In its philosophy, the Chinese Communist Party states that it follows "Marxism-Leninism and Mao Zedong Thought."[19] In a major speech at the sixteenth meeting of the National Congress of the Chinese Communist Party in June of 2006, **Jiang Zemin,**[20] who was General Secretary of the Communist Party of China from 1989 to 2002, as well as president of the People's Republic of China from 1993 to 2003, added to this traditional characterization by saying that the party must "adhere to the important thought of **Three Represents.** This thought is a continuation and development of Marxism-Leninism, Mao Zedong Thought and Deng Xiaoping Theory."[21] Jiang's "Three Represents" meant that China would follow the basic writings of Marx as interpreted by Lenin, but also modify those principles in their application to China by examining the writings and theories of both Mao Zedong and Deng Xiaoping.

Maoist thought has several key components. James Hsiung has suggested that in traditional Chinese political culture, morality and authority are inseparable, and thus Marxist-Leninist thought as interpreted by Mao was a key *moral* foundation of the Communist Party in China.[22] Mao's view of society ascribed a key role to the peasants. It was rigidly egalitarian, and many actions of the government later (such as the Great Leap Forward, which will be further discussed below), turned out to be disastrous precisely because Mao insisted in treating all members of society equally, too equally in fact. Mao believed that even when Communists were in power they needed to be "ever vigilant against the dangers of bourgeois (capitalist) influences."[23] The class struggle was a *continuing* struggle.

China's unitary government is highly centralized, and most decisions that are made develop under the auspices of appropriate levels of leadership of the CCP. The CCP is highly hierarchical, and is led by the **Supreme Leader,** who is the center of the party. The Supreme Leader has *traditionally* held the position of **General Secretary of the Party,** but in recent years it has been possible that someone else could be the General Secretary of the Party; the Supreme Leader continues to be a member of the **Politburo Standing Committee,** a subgroup of the Politburo that is at the center of power. The most important political group within the CCP is the **Politburo,** most of whose members also hold other important offices in the formal state governmental structures. The actual *powers* of the Politburo and the *functions* of the Politburo as a policy-making group have varied over time, depending upon the individuals involved. The members of today's Politburo Standing Committee are indicated in Table 14.2.

There has traditionally been a great deal of overlap between formal *party* position and formal *state* position, although this is not legally required. Mao Zedong was president (a state position) and also chairman of the CCP (a party position). Deng Xiaoping was Supreme Leader (a party position), but never

> **TABLE 14.2**
>
> **Members of the Politburo Standing Committee**
> **of the Communist Party of China**
>
> 1. Hu Jintao: general secretary of the CPC, president of the People's Republic of China (PRC), chairman of the Central Military Commission
> 2. Wu Bangguo: chairman of the standing committee of the National People's Congress
> 3. Wen Jiabao: premier of the state council of the People's Republic of China
> 4. Jia Qinglin: chairman of the National Committee of the Chinese People's Political Consultative Conference
> 5. Li Changchun: "Propaganda Chief"
> 6. Xi Jinping: top-ranked secretary of CPC Secretariat, vice president of the People's Republic of China, vice chairman of the Central Military Commission
> 7. Li Keqiang: first-ranked vice premier of the State Council of the People's Republic of China
> 8. He Guoqiang: secretary of the Central Commission for Discipline Inspection
> 9. Zhou Yongkang: secretary of Political and Legislative Affairs Committee
>
> *Source*: ChinaToday.com, "The Communist Party of China," http://www.chinatoday.com/org/cpc/ (accessed July 2011).

held either the General Secretary position (also a party position) or the presidency (a state position). Today, **Hu Jintao** is president of the People's Republic of China and also general secretary of the Communist Party of China, as well as chairman of the Central Military Commission.

Each member of the Politburo Standing Committee is responsible for a specific function—if the Politburo is the Communist Party equivalent of the Cabinet, then each member would have equivalent responsibilities within the Party organization of a Cabinet minister in the government—such as the military, agriculture, industry, legal affairs, international relations, and so on. The nine members of the Politburo Standing Committee are elected by members of the Politburo, which is composed of about twenty individuals and which is itself selected by the **Central Committee of the Chinese Communist party.** The Central Committee of the CCP is a body of about 200 individuals—most recently documented at 204 members[24]—elected by the **Party Congress,** which is supposed to meet every five years but meets irregularly. The Party Congress is designed to represent the lower levels of party organization, and consists of 4,000 to 5,000 members who come together for a few days at a time, every five years or so, to ratify actions of the Central Committee (which, in fact, ratifies actions of the Politburo) and to elect members of the Central Committee.

Thus, we can see that while in *formal* organization the Chinese Communist Party is organized from the lower level to the higher level—village committees electing county committees, county committees electing provincial committees, provincial committees participating in the Party Congress, the Party Congress selecting the Central Committee, the Central Committee selecting the Political Bureau (Politburo) of the Central Committee, and the Politburo selecting its own Standing Committee—in fact *real* power and decision making flows in the opposite direction: individuals with power are on the Politburo, they decide who will be on the Central Committee in important positions (along with many others who are not politically significant), and so on.

This reflects a Chinese version of a Marxist-Leninist-Stalinist practice of **democratic centralism.** Democratic centralism means that key decisions are made at the center, and then moved out to the more democratic bodies and structures to be ratified. Article 3 of the 1982 Constitution says that "The state organs of the People's Republic of China apply the principle of democratic centralism."[25] Although it is theoretically possible in this kind of setting for the larger, lower, body to say "no" to plans that come down from above, this almost never happens. Democratic centralism is far more *central* than *democratic* in nature.

The CCP meets at National Congresses, and it is at those meetings that the national leadership sets the stage for the next several years. Since its founding in 1921 there have been seventeen meetings of the **National Party Congress,** as shown in Table 14.3. In recent years, the Party has met fairly regularly, approximately every five years, usually immediately before the meeting of

TABLE 14.3

Meetings of the National Congress of the Chinese Communist Party

Congress	Date	Location
1	July, 1921	Shanghai
2	July, 1922	Shanghai
3	June, 1923	Guangzhou
4	January, 1925	Shanghai
5	April, 1927	Shanghai
6	June, 1928	Moscow
7	April, 1945	Yanan
8	September, 1956	Beijing
9	April, 1969	Beijing
10	August, 1973	Beijing
11	August, 1977	Beijing
12	September, 1982	Beijing
13	October, 1987	Beijing
14	October, 1992	Beijing
15	September, 1997	Beijing
16	November, 2002	Beijing
17	October, 2007	Beijing

Source: ChinaToday.Com, "The Communist Party of China," http://www.chinatoday.com/org/cpc/ (accessed July 2011).

the National People's Congress (the national legislature). Many members of the National Party Congress are *also* elected representatives to the National People's Congress.

The Seventeenth National Congress of the Communist Party of China was held in October of 2007. At that time party representatives from all over the nation assembled in Beijing for several days of Party business. President Hu Jintao gave the major address to the Congress that the President or General Secretary normally gives at that time.[26]

Although China is a unitary political system, it is divided into many *administrative* districts because of the scale of government that is necessary. Article 30 of the 1982 Constitution states:

> The administrative division of the People's Republic of China is as follows: (1) The country is divided into provinces, autonomous regions and municipalities directly under the Central Government; (2) Provinces and autonomous regions are divided into autonomous prefectures, counties, autonomous counties and cities; (3) Counties and autonomous counties are divided into townships, nationality townships and towns. Municipalities directly under the Central Government and other large cities are divided into districts and counties. Autonomous prefectures are divided into counties, autonomous counties, and cities. All autonomous regions, autonomous prefectures and autonomous counties are national autonomous areas. (Article 30)

China has twenty-two provinces (*sheng*), five autonomous regions (*zizhiqu*), and four municipalities (*shi*). China also has two **special administrative regions** (SARs): Hong Kong, which reverted from British control in 1997; and Macau, which reverted from Portuguese control in 1999. Beijing also claims Taiwan as a province, although Taiwan rejects this and that relationship is still a tense one as the United States continues to support Taiwan diplomatically and with military aid.

The governors of China's provinces and autonomous regions and mayors of its centrally controlled municipalities are appointed by the central government in Beijing, although these positions, too, require approval from the National People's Congress. The political leadership of both Hong Kong and Macau have more local autonomy than the "normal" Chinese regions, since they have separate governments, legal systems, and basic constitutional laws, but they come under Beijing's control in matters of foreign affairs and national security, and their chief executives are handpicked by the central government.[27]

POLITICAL CULTURE AND POLITICAL PARTICIPATION

Chinese political behavior and political thought is often referred to as "Mao Zedong Thought," although as we have noted this has been modified to include "Deng Xiaoping Theory" as well. Mao's approach to Marxism-Leninism was to be *pragmatic*, and he actively practiced what analysts have referred to as the "**Sinification of Marxism**" over the years, rooting the abstract formulations of Marxism-Leninism in the specific reality of China.[28] Deng carried this even farther. This included such strategies as *mass mobilization*—using groups of people to carry the message of the revolution to the population—and the idea of *a united front*—the idea of trying to bring the majority of people together in an initiative and thereby isolate those who were in opposition.

One of the manifestations of Mao's commitment to a Chinese version of Marxism was the collectivization of industry and agriculture in 1955–1956, when the CCP decided to eliminate private ownership of land. Across China some 110 million farms were converted to about 300,000 "cooperatives" run by the party; the party similarly took over factories and private businesses in cities, as well. This was followed in 1957 by the **Hundred Flowers Movement,** based upon a saying of Confucius, "Let a hundred flowers bloom, let a hundred schools of thought contend," and suggested that the free and open exchange of ideas would be supported by Mao.[29]

Unfortunately for those who decided to freely exchange ideas that were critical of the government, Mao was apparently shocked by the amount of criticism that the government received under the Hundred Flowers Movement, criticism about collectivization, criticism about taking away private property and industry, and criticism about the decline of democratic rights and practices. Mao labeled the critics "rightists"—suggesting that they were antirevolutionaries—and launched an Anti-Rightist campaign to clamp down on complaints against the government.[30]

During the years that Mao led China, Chinese popular culture suffered from several major dislocations, including three that should be specifically mentioned here: the Great Leap Forward, the "Red Versus Expert" Debate, and the Cultural Revolution. The **Great Leap Forward** was the name given to a five-year plan announced in 1958 that was Mao's attempt to increase Chinese self-sufficiency and radically grow the Chinese economy by transforming the economy from an individualized agrarian one to an effective collective agricultural and industrial one.[31] The Great Leap Forward intended to rapidly grow agriculture and industry by collective efforts, and by dividing China into **communes** of about 5,000 families that would work together for greater efficiency than had been the case. Communes were in turn subdivided into working teams of twelve families, with twelve teams in a brigade. By the end of 1958, 700 million people had been placed into 26,578 communes.[32] Private property was banned.

The Great Leap Forward was not a success, however; it turned out to be a disaster, in fact. While the idea of decentralization had some merit, the overall plan had taken many workers away from their fields, so food shortages developed. Since workers were not trained for industrial tasks and supplies were irregular, industrial production fell drastically. More important were the dimensions of terror and authoritarianism that developed, with mass propaganda sessions commonplace, and killings not uncommon if groups of individuals didn't meet their assigned goals. Reports described individuals tortured or killed if they failed to meet their grain quotas.[33] Having so many decentralized groups meant that there was no coordination in providing resources, and material shortages were frequent. The first phase of collectivization that took place resulted in widespread famine. The official toll of deaths resulting from the Great Leap Forward is 14 million, but in 1987 some scholars estimated the number of victims to be between 20 and 43 million.[34] One of the most-often cited examples of failed policy in this era was the policy that required the development of backyard furnaces to produce steel:

> The campaign to develop backyard furnaces came to symbolize the wastefulness of the GLF. Determined to surpass England and catch up with the United States in steel production, Chinese leaders called for the creation of thousands of small-scale iron smelters. By late 1958, there were several hundred thousand small blast furnaces scattered throughout the country. Into these furnaces went every bit of scrap steel that peasants could locate—sometimes including their own cooking implements.
>
> The result was wasteful in the extreme. The quality of the iron produced was so poor that most of it had to be discarded. In many instances, perfectly good iron and steel products had been dumped into the blast furnaces only to produce useless lumps of iron. Moreover, forests were destroyed in this ill-fated effort to industrialize, causing an ecological disaster from which China has yet to recover.[35]

The **Red versus Expert debate** was one of the most divisive issues in China in the early 1960s. The more pragmatic Party leaders were labeled as the "experts," and the more radical supporters of Mao and the People's Liberation Army (PLA) were labeled as the "Red" faction, and they disagreed over the appropriate strategy for China's ongoing economic development after the Great Leap Forward failed. The moderates—the "experts"—had managed to roll back some of the more extreme polices of the Great Leap, so that by 1962 peasants were again permitted their own private plots and farm animals. Premier Liu Shaoqi and Vice-Premier Deng Xiaopig felt that Communist purity was less important than what actually *worked*: Deng's famous quote of the day was "it doesn't matter whether a cat is black or white as long as it catches mice."[36]

Although the "experts" brought calm and some economic stability back to China, Mao and his more ideological supporters were troubled by the pragmatic approach. They felt that allowing private farming would inevitably lead to the kind of conflicts that were developing at the time in Eastern Europe (in East Germany, Poland, and Hungary, where criticism of Communism was increasing and demonstrations were taking place). The Reds felt that the Experts were not sufficiently committed to the CCP. At the end of the day, the Red faction proved victorious. Liu and Deng were removed from their posts in the party and government and placed under house arrest.

The **Cultural Revolution** took place between 1966 and 1976, and had as a goal further advancing socialism by removing aspects of capitalism from Chinese society, as well as more effectively imposing Maoist orthodoxy within the Chinese Communist Party.[37] In August of 1966 Mao called for a Great Proletarian Cultural Revolution, more commonly known as the Cultural Revolution, to seek out and remove bourgeois (Western) influence from Chinese culture, and to push capitalist tendencies out of Chinese society. To do this, he organized youth groups, **Red Guard** groups, to be formed around the country. Their job was to purge society of individuals who were deemed to be deviating from the "true" socialist path; this frequently focused on teachers, artists, intellectuals, and individuals who were too oriented to non-Chinese values, but included literally tens of thousands of others, too.[38]

> Under the banner of opposing the "four olds" (old customs, old habits, old culture, and old thinking), Red Guards ransacked people's homes, confiscating or destroying anything deemed "feudal" in nature (including old books, paintings, and ceramics), persecuting individuals deemed "bourgeois" or "rightist," and denouncing party leaders who were accused of opposing Chairman Mao.[39]

One observer has noted that "just as the Great Leap Forward was an economic disaster, the Cultural Revolution was a political disaster."[40] A consequence of the Cultural Revolution was great damage, both societal and individual. Over 70 percent of the CCP Central Committee was removed from their positions, and Red Guard units were notorious for arresting, beating, and killing Chinese who had done little to deserve punishment.[41] Literally millions of people were persecuted, imprisoned, and lost their homes and their property and their jobs. There is a massive literature by survivors who were forcibly displaced.

The Cultural Revolution ended officially in 1969, although its effects lasted for years after that, through the arrest of the Gang of Four (one of whom was Mao's wife), who were charged with treasonous crimes and for criminal excess during the Cultural Revolution. One result of the disaster of the Great Leap Forward was a re-examination of the role that Mao played in China, and a review of the "cult of personality" that surrounded him. Mao stepped down as State Chairman of the People's Republic of China in 1969, although he did remain as chairman of the CCP.

One of the conclusions that we can reasonably draw from even a cursory examination of Chinese political history is that China has not developed institutions that can *gradually* respond to a need for change. Countries that are able to address problems gradually, while the problems are developing and before a major crisis comes about, are able to respond to issues more successfully than nations that have to lurch from crisis to crisis, undertaking major systemic modification at each lurch. We can see that both the Great Leap Forward and the Cultural Revolution were attempts to resolve a large number of issues in one package. The Chinese Communist Party looked for broad-ranging policies (e.g., the Great Leap Forward) that could respond to complex social problems (economic development, equitable distribution of goods, social equality) in simple ways (i.e., collectivization), and those responses did not work What was clear from both the Great Leap Forward and the Cultural Revolution was that social challenges are *too complex* to be solved by this kind of all-encompassing policy, and what is most likely to happen is that disastrous policy will be applied in a disastrous way with disastrous results.

POLITICS AND POLITICAL STRUCTURES

China's political tradition of having strong executive leadership over the years has resulted in the executive branch of the formal political system being much more important than the legislative branch, although it must be said that the National People's Congress (NPC, not to be confused with the National Congress of the Communist Party of China), the legislature, which is the highest organ of state power according to the Chinese constitution, has become more active and visible in recent years.

In theory, formal governmental administrative structures are completely separate from structures of the Chinese Communist Party. In reality, however, there is a huge overlap between party membership and formal state political leadership positions, and as one moves higher up the state political hierarchy the overlap becomes stronger and stronger, until it is complete at the upper levels of political participation. Thus, an official organizational chart of the leadership of the People's Republic of China would be unhelpful without a description of the *un*official leadership, too. Individuals with the most political power *may* hold formal positions of power, but that need not always be the case. As one observer has noted, "sometimes leaders have remained in seemingly insignificant positions yet exercised enormous power. This is easier in an authoritarian system than in a democratic one, for in the former, the public has virtually no way of protesting the accretion of power in a particular individual or institution."

A good example of this is the case of Hua Guofend: from 1977 to 1980, Hua simultaneously held the three most powerful institutional positions in China (CCP Chairman, Premier of the State, and CCP's Chairman of the Military Affairs Commission), whereas Deng Xiaoping held the position of a mere Vice-Premier. Yet, by 1979, Deng exercised far greater power than Hua, and was even able to shift the locus of power away from the CCP Chairman (a position Deng was powerful enough to abolish) to the CCP's General Secretary, who at that point was a long-time ally of Deng's.[42]

Figure 14.1 shows the official *state* government leadership on the left, and the *party* leadership on the right. The president of the People's Republic of China today is Hu Jintao, who replaced Jiang Zemin in March of 2003 and was re-elected in 2008. Although the position of president is symbolically important, Hu's more important base of power is that he *also* serves as General Secretary of the CCP and chairman of the Party's Central Military Commission, the top Party/military position.

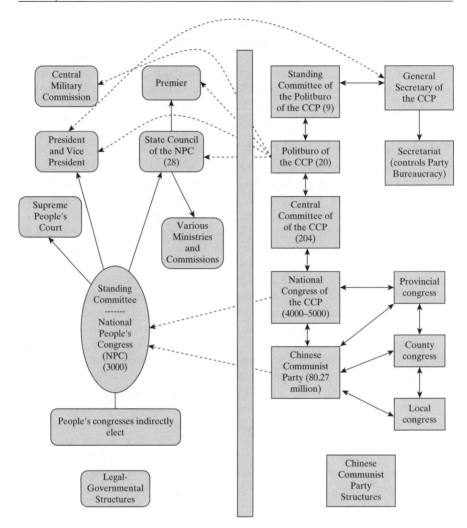

FIGURE 14.1
How China is Ruled

Executive Branch

The executive branch of government is led by the **State Council,** the equivalent of the Cabinet in most Western democratic governments. The State Council is chaired by the **premier,** who is formally reviewed by the National People's Council after being appointed to office by the president. The State Council also typically has four or five *vice-premiers,* as well as several *state councilors,* ministers in charge of ministries, the auditor-general, and the secretary general of the Chinese Communist Party. Other members of the State Council are nominated by the premier and reviewed by the NPC or its Standing Committee, and appointed and removed by the president. Today's State Council has 28 members, with the premier. Members of the State Council have a term of office concurrent with the term of the NPC. State Council members are limited to no more than two consecutive terms on the State Council.[43]

As is the case with members of cabinet in Western nations, the members of the State Council each oversee the work of a ministry. A list of ministries and Commissions that make up the State Council can be found in Table 14.4.

The position of president of the People's Republic of China is described in the Constitution as having the same term as that of the NPC. Moreover, the president is constitutionally prohibited from serving more than two consecutive terms. The president is elected by the NPC. His duties described in Arti-

---

TABLE 14.4

Ministries and Commissions Represented on the State Council

Ministry of Foreign Affairs

Ministry of National Defense

National Development and Reform Commission

Ministry of Education

Ministry of Science and Technology

Ministry of Industry and Information Technology

State Ethnic Affairs Commission

Ministry of Public Security

Ministry of State Security

Ministry of Supervision

Ministry of Civil Affairs

Ministry of Justice

Ministry of Finance

Ministry of Human Resources and Social Security

Ministry of Land and Resources

Ministry of Environmental Protection

Ministry of Housing and Urban-Rural Development

Ministry of Transport

Ministry of Railways

Ministry of Water Resources

Ministry of Agriculture

Ministry of Commerce

Ministry of Culture

Ministry of Health

National Population and Family Planning Commission

People's Bank of China

National Audit Office

Source: GOV.cn, Chinese Government Web Portal, "Ministries and Commissions Under the State Council," http://english.gov.cn/2005-08/05/content_20741.htm (accessed July 2011).

cles 80 and 81 are unremarkable: "in pursuance of decisions of the National People's Congress and its Standing Committee," he

- promulgates statutes;
- appoints and removes the Premier, Vice-Premiers, State Councillors, Ministers in charge of Ministries or Commissions, and the Auditor- General and the Secretary-General of the State Council;
- confers state medals and titles of honour;
- issues orders of special pardons;
- proclaims martial law;
- proclaims a state of war;
- issues mobilization orders;
- receives foreign diplomatic representatives on behalf of the People's Republic of China;
- appoints and recalls plenipotentiary representatives abroad; and
- ratifies and abrogates treaties and important agreements concluded with foreign states.

Legislative Branch

There is no doubt that legally, constitutionally, the **National People's Congress** (NPC) is the legislative branch of the national government of the People's Republic of China. The question that needs to be asked is: What does it *do*? What is the relationship between the NPC and the parallel, although unofficial, body of the National Congress of the Chinese Communist Party? The answer is that since its creation in 1954, the NPC has played a variety of roles, none central, some less important than others. It has never *really* been a significant body, but it has seen its role change from being less to more frequently cited as a symbolic player in Chinese politics. Through the Mao-driven campaigns of the Great Leap Forward (1958–1960) and the Cultural Revolution (1966–1976), power was very centralized in Mao's hands, and the NPC was really irrelevant. Since Mao's death in 1976, however, the NPC has become more visible, it has been convened regularly, and its involvement in law-making, oversight, and constituency representation has increased.[44]

Under China's 1982 Constitution, the National People's Congress is the "highest organ of state power."[45] The primary function of the National People's Congress is *ratification* and *legitimation* of Party decisions. The NPC exercises "the legislative power of the state," but actually what it does is to meet on an annual basis for two or three weeks and approve actions that either have *already* been taken in its name, or to approve proposals coming from the CCP for actions that *will* be taken in its name.

When the NPC is *not* in session (which is typically fifty weeks out of each year), every two months or so the **Standing Committee of the NPC** will meet to "supervise" the government and to approve proposals that cannot wait until the next regularly scheduled meeting of the NPC. The NPC Standing Committee consists of a chairman, 15 vice chairmen, a secretary general, and

153 members, so in fact the Standing Committee looks like a small national legislative body, which is what it is. Standing Committee members are often senior CCP and former state leaders and officials. The Standing Committee is elected for the same term as the National People's Congress (Article 66), and acts in the name of the NPC when it is not in session.

The members of the NPC are elected for terms of five years, according to Article 60 of the Constitution. It is constitutionally charged to meet in session once a year, and has the statutory responsibility (Article 62):

1. To amend the Constitution;
2. To supervise the enforcement of the Constitution;
3. To enact and amend basic statutes concerning criminal offences, civil affairs, the state organs, and other matters;
4. To elect the President and the Vice-President of the People's Republic of China [previously translated as Chairman and Vice-Chairman of the People's Republic of China—translator's note.];
5. To decide on the choice of the Premier of the State Council upon nomination by the President of the People's Republic of China, and to decide on the choice of the Vice-Premiers, State Councillors, Ministers in charge of Ministries or Commissions and the Auditor-General and the Secretary-General of the State Council upon nomination by the Premier;
6. To elect the Chairman of the Central Military Commission and, upon his nomination, to decide on the choice of the other members of the Central Military Commission;
7. To elect the President of the Supreme People's Court;
8. To elect the Procurator-General of the Supreme People's Procuratorate;
9. To examine and approve the plan for national economic and social development and the reports on its implementation;
10. To examine and approve the state budget and the report on its implementation;
11. To alter or annul inappropriate decisions of the Standing Committee of the National People's Congress;
12. To approve the establishment of provinces, autonomous regions, and municipalities directly under the Central Government;
13. To decide on the establishment of special administrative regions and the systems to be instituted there;
14. To decide on questions of war and peace; and
15. To exercise such other functions and powers as the highest organ of state power should exercise.

Elections of members to the NPC are indirect. Deputies are elected by people's congresses in twenty-three provinces, five autonomous regions, and four municipalities directly under the central government. Representatives are also chosen from special administrative regions (Hong Kong and Macau) and by the armed forces. The minimum number of deputies from provinces or regions is fifteen, but the number varies with the population of the unit being represented. Elections take place in a multicandidate format (i.e., there are always more candidates than seats to be filled); top vote-getters in each race are elected.

> The allocation of the number of Deputies to the NPC—which may not exceed 3,000—is decided by its Standing Committee in accordance with the principle that the number of citizens represented by each rural Deputy is four times that represented by each urban Deputy (880,000 people to 220,000). The number of Deputies elected by minority nationalities—which, according to the Constitution, are all entitled to appropriate representation—is also allocated by the Standing Committee, in light of the population and distribution of each nationality; they are chosen by the respective people's congresses and their number totals approximately 12% of that of the NPC. Nationalities with exceptionally small populations have at least one Deputy.[46]

The Legal System

China has a very conventional system of courts, with the highest level of court being the **Supreme People's Court** in Beijing.[47] Other courts include the Higher People's Courts in provinces, autonomous regions, and special municipalities, as well as Intermediate People's Courts at the prefecture level and in parts of provinces, autonomous regions, and special municipalities. A series of Basic People's Courts also exist in counties, towns, and municipal districts.

The Supreme People's Court supervises the administration of justice by local courts and special courts, while courts at higher levels oversee the administration of courts at lower levels. At each level, the courts are "responsible to the organs of state power which created them." Judges are limited to two consecutive terms running concurrently with the National People's Congress or local people's congresses.

The court system is paralleled by a hierarchy of prosecuting organs called people's procuratorates; at the apex stands the Supreme People's Procuratorate. The procurators serve as prosecutors, or district attorneys, and are limited to two consecutive terms running concurrently with the NPC or local people's congresses.

One of the legal characteristics that the People's Republic of China has taken directly from the Marxist-Leninist model of the old Soviet Union is that it sees the value of a close interaction of the legal system with its ideological and political cultural system. China is a system in which *law* is very important, as a way for the state to regulate the behavior of citizens, but *lawyers* and *litigation* are not at all as common or visible as in the West, since "the Chinese have historically had a distaste for lawyers and for resorting to law to settle disputes."[48]

A key characteristic of the Marxist-Leninist model was that law was seen to be *a tool of the state*. Marx's view was that in capitalist societies, despite what the governments said, the legal system was not equitable in terms of the resources available to the different actors involved, with the workers having far fewer resources than the property-owning class, and that it was therefore appropriate in a Marxist state for the state to *use* the legal system to further the goals of the state. In China, as in the Soviet Union, law is used as a tool of the state to further the goals of the state.

> In short, while in the American legal system the emphasis is on process, in China it is on serving the state and society. Murderers must be executed, regardless of how evidence was acquired, because the protection of societal interests takes precedence over the rights of any single individuals.[49]

This means, unfortunately, that protection of individual rights and liberties is not a high priority for either the legal system or the government more broadly conceived. As we noted in Chapter Two when we talked about written and unwritten constitutions and the role of law, in a system in which the law serves as a tool of the state, and in which the dominant political party can be identified with the state, the goals of the party can start to become identified as the law, and individuals who come in conflict with these goals can find themselves subject to what may seem to be arbitrary enforcement of the law. Many felt that the treatment of the participants in the **Tiananmen Square** demonstrations in 1989 was a gross miscarriage of justice, and that the violent response of the government to the demonstrations by the participants was the real crime at the time, and this has led to much discussion about the state of civil society in China today.[50]

BOX 14.1

The Tiananmen Square Massacre, 1989

During the 1980s the Chinese government was interested in economic expansion and growth, and was less concerned about political reforms. By the mid-1980s many in China, especially students and intellectual leaders, were frustrated at government policy and the pace of political and social reform. In 1986, a group of university students in Shanghai began a series of public demonstrations about student living conditions, and these demonstrations grew to include other criticism of the government and government policy in other areas.

The immediate cause of the Tiananmen Massacre was a demonstration that was sparked by the death on April 15, 1989 of Hu Yaobang, the former General Secretary of the CCP who had been associated with *support* of political liberalization but who had been forced from his position because he was too supportive of reform. Huge popular demonstrations developed to protest past repressive government decisions and to call for further political reform. Although the demonstrations were focused on inflation and government corruption, the government at the time saw the real focus of the demonstrations as the overthrow of the government. As the demonstrations increased, the focus of the

(continued)

(*continued*)

demonstrations shifted and included fundamental changes in China's political system, labor unions, and even the removal of Li Peng (the premier) and Deng Xiaoping (the vice-premier).

By the time of Hu's funeral, it was estimated that 100,000 people were in Tiananmen Square. The demonstrations lasted seven weeks after Hu's death. Premier Li Peng declared martial law on May 20, but took no other action. Finally, late on June 3, 1989, the government clamped down on the demonstrators with a sudden and surprisingly extreme response to the peaceful mass protest. Tanks and People's Liberation Army troops were summoned to Tiananmen Square in central Beijing, and hundreds (700 was the estimate most commonly used) of peaceful demonstrators were shot dead by seeming random firing from the troops. An iconic photograph of a lone student standing in the Square in front of a tank came to symbolize the tragedy, despair, and rage associated with the event.

Sources: James Miles, *The Legacy of Tiananmen: China in Disarray* (Ann Arbor: University of Michigan Press, 1997), p. 28; Merle Goldman, "The 1989 Demonstrations in Tiananmen Square and Beyond: Echoes of Gandhi," in Adam Roberts and Timothy Garton Ash, eds., *Civil Resistance and Power Politics: The Experience of Non-Violent Action from Gandhi to the* Present (New York: Oxford University Press, 2009), pp. 247–259; and Jean-Philippe Béja, *The Impact of China's 1989 Tiananmen Massacre* (New York: Routledge, 2011). See also The British Broadcasting Corporation, "1989: Massacre in Tiananmen Square," http://news.bbc.co.uk/onthisday/hi/dates/stories/june/4/newsid_2496000/2496277.stm (accessed July 2011).

POLITICAL REFORM AND LIBERALIZATION

One of the patterns of Chinese politics that we identified at the outset of this chapter is the pattern of strong—sometimes overly strong—leadership that has resulted in modern times in authoritarian leadership. We have seen the consequences of the Great Leap Forward, and the Cultural Revolution, two illustrations of Maoist policy that were disastrous for the nation.

The modern Chinese leader most closely associated with reform was **Deng Xiaoping.** In 1977, Deng Xiaoping (who had been purged during the Cultural Revolution) was restored to his position as vice-premier, and led China in discussion of modernization. From 1977 through 1985 the most radical groups in the CCP were either moved out of power or purged completely from CCP positions, and by 1981 public pronouncements were being made that were critical of past actions:

A 1981 pronouncement by the Communist Party Central Committee called the Cultural Revolution "the most severe setback [to]...the Party, the state and the people since the founding of the People's Republic." It assigned Mao chief responsibility for the disaster and accused the once-revered leader of arrogance.[51]

During the 1980s, many problems were identified by Chinese leaders along with issues inherited from the Mao era that needed to be reformed.[52] These included the problem of the overconcentration of political power, the lack of development of formal institutions, the state of health of the Chinese Communist Party, a weak bureaucracy, and the need for a reconciliation of the CCP and the public.

We have noted above several instances of too much political power resting in the hands of Mao. While this may have been consistent with the way Chinese leaders have exercised political power for literally thousands of years, by the 1980s it was seen to be increasingly problematic for modern times. The Chinese attempted to resolve this by doing away with the title of Party Chairman, in the hope that it might provide some modest diminution of power held by the Party leader, although it is not clear that General Secretary is a significantly weaker title, and the more basic problem of the Chinese Communist Party exercising control on the organs of state government was not touched at all.

The Chinese tradition of having power exercised by strong individuals rather than flowing through stable and regulated political institutions has also been a concern in modern times. Mao clearly preferred to rule by virtue of his personal charisma, so formal state titles and lines of organizational reporting were not significant in his era. In the time since Mao, there have been some efforts made to restore standing to formal political bodies, with greater consultation of the National People's Congress and the Politburo, for example. This, too, only resulted in very marginal change, since the political leaders of the day, from Deng through Hu, have consistently held on to their own personal political power. This has continued to change in post-Deng years, though, and today China has more discussion that looks like Western policy debate than ever before.[53]

By the time that Deng took control of the Chinese Communist Party, party members "on the whole were too old, too uneducated, and too radical."[54] The Party saw this as a major challenge, and set upon a new path of recruitment of members to the party. By 2005 almost one quarter of members were under the age of thirty-five (when less than 5 percent were under twenty-five when Deng assumed power), and over 56 percent had a high school or higher level of education (compared with under 18 percent in 1984).

During the early Deng years a variety of reforms started to appear, including a reduction of CCP ideological positions and a corresponding increase in more pragmatic policy. The state began to liberalize its views about privacy, individual rights, communication, education, and a variety of different areas that affected individuals.[55] This reform began to put great stress on the system—because China was still not a democracy, by any means—and in 1989 violence developed in Tiananmen Square as was described above.

The significance of the liberalization of the Deng years, however, is that in the contemporary world the Chinese population wants to move even farther forward.[56] Although the government of the day clamped down on the

Tiananmen Square demonstrators, it was relatively shortly thereafter when liberalization started again. What Bruce Gilley has called a "democratic break-through" has been imagined by the public, and while the political leadership of the CCP has the power to regulate individuals' *behavior* at the present time, it does not have the power to regulate what the individuals *think*. While it can regulate *some* of their communication, it cannot regulate *all* of their communication. As quickly as the government blocks web pages and tries to censor e-mail, individuals develop techniques for getting around the government barriers. Gilley imagines what China will look like without the Chinese Communist Party in control, noting that

> The CCP will have ruled China for 60 years in 2009. The previous records for a party's unbroken tenure in office were just over 70 years by both the Russian Communist Party and Mexico's Institutional Revolutionary Party. Whatever the exact date of democratic transition, the CCP will go down in history as one of the world's longest lived ruling parties. It will be a reign that ends for the same reason that other dynasties in China ended: the court lost touch with the people, was starved of resources, and finally rotted from the inside.[57]

The Chinese bureaucracy needed help, too, since it suffered from many of the same problems as did the CCP. In the Deng years the government actively recruited for the state bureaucracy, seeking young and more highly educated officials.

Finally, the Party has tried to help restore relations between itself and the public through less regulation of individuals. Certainly in recent years the Party has opened the doors to capitalism, to private property, and to many different manifestations of Western behavior—including music, art, and so on. The Chinese government has established special economic zones to encourage foreign investment and employment, and has vigorously encouraged Western investment in China.[58]

The post-Mao economic goals of the Chinese government have been wildly successful. China's leaders wanted to develop technology and become competitive with the West. They also wanted to develop a middle class, and create material prosperity in China. "In the post-Mao period, China's leaders have based their legitimacy on their ability to create economic growth and better living standards rather than on political correctness."[59]

THE CHINESE SYSTEM IN PERSPECTIVE

The final chapter of a recent collection of essays on contemporary Chinese politics began with the observation that

> China seems to be a paradox: on the one hand, it has a thriving capitalist economy; on the other hand, the catalyst behind its phenomenal growth has been none other than the Chinese Communist Party. Economic liberalization and socialist authoritarianism have marched hand in hand.

Unlike many ailing post-Soviet states with weakly institutionalized democratic structures and fragile economies, the Chinese Communist Party has unleashed a tide of economic entrepreneurialism, raising living standards and making China a major economic global player, while at the same time maintaining territorial power.[60]

We have seen in this chapter that the institutional approach that we have used in this text for understanding the way that political systems operate in other parts of the world doesn't work in China. The Chinese approach to politics—involving a highly ideological regime and highly personalistic following of executive-centered leadership—does not recognize the important role for political institutions that is the key to understanding politics elsewhere. Whereas in *most* nations—developed and underdeveloped, Northern and Southern, Eastern and Western—it is important to know what a constitution says, and how the political structures of the regime are organized, in China both of these factors take a decidedly secondary role to the behavior of the One Party State, the ideology of Chinese Communism, and the attitudes of the Supreme Leader of the day.

But it is important to understand and appreciate that Chinese politics is changing, and changing relatively rapidly. The opening to a market economy that was undertaken—or at least tolerated—by Deng Xiaoping has had, and will continue to have, terribly significant consequences for the Chinese regime. It appears to be inevitable that *doing business* with the West means *having more social and cultural contact* with the West, and this in turn is going to result in increased demands by the Chinese public for more *political rights and liberties*.

Recent months and years have shown that this increased contact with the West is, indeed, having an effect upon Chinese society and culture. There is a vibrant and growing middle class in China today, not only in the largest cities but indeed growing across the nation. The middle class is, increasingly, in touch with the West electronically—sometimes to the consternation of the Chinese government, which tries to regulate communication between Chinese citizens and those outside of China—and that contact is resulting in greater demand for Western-style freedoms. Although the pressures of the Arab Spring* did not ignite in China, there is no doubt that the Chinese government is aware of the patterns of behavior that are flourishing around the world, and this is being reflected in the government's increasing sensitivity to the need for *political*, as well as *economic* reform in the way the Chinese government operates.

---

*This refers to the pattern of demonstrations and protests and demands for increased democratization that broke out across the Arab world in the period from January through June of 2011. Several governments in the Middle East were toppled—including Tunisia and Egypt— while others were moved to make what could be significant political reforms—including Jordan and Morocco—while others started and continue to be in revolutionary turmoil—including Libya, Syria, and Yemen.

DISCUSSION QUESTIONS

1. What would you suggest are the four most important themes in Chinese history that have shaped Chinese politics today?
2. Identify several major crises in the development of the Communist Party of China. What were the effects of each of these crises?
3. How would you compare the formal state institutions in China and those in Western nations? Do Western models work in China? Why or why not?
4. What are the key structures of the Communist Party of China, and how does power flow both up and down in the Party?
5. What is the relationship between the structures of the Communist Party of China and the Chinese national government? Where is the more important base of power? Why?
6. What is the relationship between political institutions and political leaders in China? Do individuals have power because of the positions they hold, or do they hold certain positions because they control power?
7. What are the forces that are pressing toward economic and political liberalization in China today?

KEY TERMS

Central Committee of the Chinese Communist Party 365
Chiang Kai-shek 361
Chinese Communist Party (CCP) 361
communes 368
Confucius 359
Cultural Revolution 370
democratic centralism 366
Deng Xiaoping 378
extraterritorial rights 360
General Secretary of the Party 364
Great Leap Forward 368
Guomindang (GMD) 361
Hu Jintao 365
Hundred Flowers Movement 368

Jiang Zemin 364
Long March 361
Mao Zedong 361
Middle Kingdom 358
Nanjing Massacre 362
National Party Congress 366
National People's Congress 374
Nationalist Party 361
Opium War 360
Party Congress 365
People's Liberation Army 361
People's Republic of China 362
Politburo 364
Politburo Standing Committee 364
premier 372
Red Guard 370

Red versus Expert debate 369
Republic of China 360
Sinification of Marxism 368
special administrative regions 367
Standing Committee of the National People's Congress 375
Standing Committee of the Politburo 372
State Council 372
Sun Yat-sen 360
Supreme Leader 364
Supreme People's Court 376
Three Represents 364
Tiananmen Square 378
warlord 361

SUGGESTED READINGS

Paul Clark, *The Chinese Cultural Revolution: A History* (New York: Cambridge University Press, 2008). The Cultural Revolution was one of the key periods of time of modern Chinese history, and shaped the future of Chinese politics. Mao's leadership during this period had very significant implications for millions of people.

Frank Dikötter, *The Age of Openness: China before Mao* (Berkeley, CA: University of California Press, 2008). History has played an extraordinarily important role in China, and the history of China leading up to the period of Mao's domination explains a good deal of how and why Mao was as successful as he was. This volume, by one of the leading scholars in the field, examines the period of history prior to Mao's rise to power.

Rebecca Karl, *Mao Zedong and China in the Twentieth-Century World: A Concise History* (Durham, NC: Duke University Press, 2010). Mao Zedong was the dominant figure in modern Chinese politics. This volume describes Mao's rise to power and his operation—and domination of—Chinese politics in modern times.

Michael Palmer, *The Constitution of the People's Republic of China: A Contextual Analysis* (Oxford, UK: Hart Publishing, 2007). The role of the constitution in China is different in Chinese politics from the role of constitutions in other polities. This volume describes the cultural and structural factors in the environment that affect the Chinese constitution and that limit the role of the Chinese constitution to primarily symbolism.

Tony Saich, *Governance and Politics of China* (New York: Malgrave Macmillan, 2011). This is a very good single volume describing the institutions and behaviors that are important in modern Chinese politics.

NOTES

1. John K. Fairbank, *China: The People's Middle Kingdom and the U.S.A.* (Cambridge, MA: Belknap Press, 1967), pp. 3–4. See John K. Fairbank and Merle Goldman, *China: A New History* (Cambridge, MA: Harvard University Press, 2006); Paul S. Ropp, *China in World History* (New York: Oxford University Press, 2010); Mark Edward Lewis, *China Between Empires: The Northern and Southern Dynasties* (Cambridge, MA: Harvard University Press, 2009); or Rinn-Sup Shinn and Robert Worden, "Historical Setting," in Robert L. Worden, Andrea Matles Savada, and Ronald E. Dolan, eds., *Country Profile: China* (Federal Research Division, Library of Congress, 1987), *http://lcweb2.loc.gov/frd/cs/cntoc.html* (accessed July 2011).

2. Charles Hauss, *Comparative Politics: Domestic Responses to Global Challenges*, Chapter 11, "China," (Belmont, CA: Wadsworth/Thomson Learning, 2000), p. 297. See Nicola Di Cosmo, *Military Culture in Imperial China* (Cambridge, MA: Harvard University Press, 2009).

3. Robert L. Worden, Andrea Matles Savada, and Ronald E. Dolan, eds., *Country Profile: China* (Federal Research Division, Library of Congress, 1987), "Updated Profile, August 2006," p. 2, *http://lcweb2.loc.gov/frd/cs/profiles/China.pdfp.2* (accessed July 2011).

4. Worden et al., *Country Profile: China – Updated Profile*, p. 2.

5. Bruce J. Dickson, "China," in Michael J. Sodaro, ed., *Comparative Politics: A Global Introduction* (New York: McGraw-Hill, 2008), p. 656.

6. A good essay on contemporary authoritarianism is by Yan Jiaqi, "The Nature of Chinese Authoritarianism," in Carol Lee Hamrin and Suisheng Zhao, eds., *Decision-Making in Deng's China: Perspectives from Insiders* (Armonk, NY: M.E. Sharpe, 1995), pp. 3–14.

7. Joseph Fewsmith, "The Government of China," in Michael Curtis, ed., *Introduction to Comparative Politics* (New York: Pearson, 2003), p. 452.

8. James Townsend and Brantly Womack, *Politics in China* (Boston, MA: Little, Bown, 1986), p. 46. A history of China prior to the rise to power of Mao can be found in the work by Frank Dikötter, *The Age of Openness: China before Mao* (Berkeley, CA: University of California Press, 2008). See also Peter Zarrow, *China in War and Revolution, 1895–1949* (London, UK: Routledge, 2005).

9. Fewsmith, "The Government of China," p. 456. On the influence of Russia at this time, see Bruce Elleman, *Moscow and the Emergence of Communist Power in China, 1925–1930: The Nanchang Uprising and the Birth of the Red Army* (New York: Routledge, 2009); Robert Service, *Comrades! A History of World Communism* (Cambridge, MA: Harvard University Press, 2007); or S. A. Smith, *Revolution and the People in Russia and China: A Comparative History* (New York: Cambridge University Press, 2008).

10. Maurice Meisner, *Mao's China and After* (New York: Free Press, 1987), p. 27. Two good references are by Jay Taylor, *The Generalissimo: Chiang Kai-shek and the Struggle for Modern China* (Cambridge, MA: Harvard University Press, 2009); and Suisheng Zhao, *A Nation-State by Construction: Dynamics of Modern Chinese Nationalism* (Stanford, CA: Stanford University Press, 2005).

11. Marcus Ethridge and Howard Handelman, *Politics in a Changing World: A Comparative Introduction to Political Science* (New York: St. Martin's Press, 1994), p. 412.

12. In Edgar Snow's book *Red China Today* he notes that Premier Zhou Enlai and other leaders looked back on the Long March as their personal struggle. See Edgar Snow, *Red China Today* (New York: Vintage, 1970), pp. 111–112. See also Shuyun Sun, *The Long March: The True History of Communist China's Founding Myth* (New York: Doubleday, 2006).

13. See Diana Lary, *The Chinese People at War: Human Suffering and Social Transformation, 1937–1945* (Cambridge, UK: Cambridge University Press, 2010).

14. The full text of the Chinese Constitution can be found on its website. See the website of the Chinese Constitution, "The Constitution of the People's Republic of China," "Preamble," *http://english.peopledaily.com.cn/constitution/constitution.html* (accessed July 2011). See Michael Palmer, *The Constitution of the People's Republic of China: A Contextual Analysis* (Oxford, UK: Hart Publishing, 2007); or the edited collection by Stéphanie Balme and Michael Dowdle, *Building Constitutionalism in China* (New York: Palgrave-Macmillan, 2009). See also Arif Dirlik, *Marxism in the Chinese Revolution* (Lanham, MD: Rowman and Littlefield, 2005).

15. Worden et al., *Country Profile: China* update August, 2006, p. 26.

16. The website of the Chinese Communist party is *http://english.cpc.people.com.cn/*.

17. See the web site of the Chinese Constitution, "The Constitution of the People's Republic of China," "Preamble," *http://english.peopledaily.com.cn/constitution/constitution.html* (accessed July 2011).

18. Chinatoday.com, "The Communist Party of China," *http://www.chinatoday.com/org/cpc/*.

19. Ibid.

20. Jiang Zemin became leader in China following the Tiananmen Square protests of 1989. With the waning influence of Deng Xiaoping and the other members of China's senior leadership, Jiang effectively became the Supreme Leader in the 1990s.

21. Communist Party of China, "News of the Communist Party of China," "The Three Represents," *http://english.cpc.people.com.cn/66739/4521344.html* (accessed July 2011).

22. James Chieh Hsiung, *Ideology and Practice: The Evolution of Chinese Communism* (New York: Praeger, 1970), p. 107.
23. Ethridge and Handelman, *Politics in a Changing World*, p. 414.
24. See the web page of the 17th National Congress of the Communist Party of China, "List of Members of the 17th CPC Central Committee," *http://english.people.com.cn/90002/92169/92187/6287697.html*.
25. Constitution, Article 3. See Pierre F. Landry, *Decentralized Authoritarianism in China: The Communist Party's Control of Local Elites in the Post-Mao Era* (Cambridge, UK: Cambridge University Press, 2008).
26. Communist Party of China, "News of the Communist Party of China," online, "The 17th National Congress of the Communist Party," "Full Text of President Hu Jintao's Report at 17th Party Congress," *http://english.cpc.people.com.cn/66102/6290205.html* (accessed July 2011).
27. Worden, et al., *Country Profile: China*, pp. 25–28. The issue of local administration is described in Chae-ho Chong and Tao-chiu Lam, eds., *China's Local Administration Traditions and Changes in the Sub-National Hierarchy* (New York: Routledge, 2010). A very interesting approach to the study of Chinese unitary government is the chapter by Steven Phillips, "The Demonization of Federalism in Republican China," in Emilian Kavalski and Magdalena Zolkos, eds., *Defunct Federalisms: Critical Perspectives on Federal Failure* (Burlington, VT: Ashgate, 2008).
28. Fewsmith, "The Government of China," p. 457. A good analysis of the impact of Mao on China can be found in Rebecca Karl, *Mao Zedong and China in the Twentieth-Century World: A Concise History* (Durham, NC: Duke University Press, 2010); and Chang-tai Hung, *Mao's New World: Political Culture in the Early People's Republic* (Ithaca, NY: Cornell University Press, 2011).
29. See Harry Harding, *Organizing China: The Problem of Bureaucracy, 1949–1976* (Stanford, CA: Stanford University Press, 1981), Chapter 5: "The First Crisis: The Hundred Flowers, 1956–1957," pp. 116–151.
30. Dickson, "China," p. 667.
31. See Frank Dikötter, *Mao's Great Famine: The History of China's Most Devastating Catastrophe, 1958–1962* (New York: Walker and Co., 2010); or Harding, *Organizing China*, Chapter 6: "The Great Leap Forward and Its Aftermath, 1957–1962," pp. 153–194.
32. Chris Trueman, "The Great Leap Forward," in *China: 1900–1976*, *http://www.historylearningsite.co.uk/great_leap_forward.htm* (accessed July 2011).
33. Benjamin Valentino, *Final Solutions: Mass Killing and Genocide in the Twentieth Century* (Ithaca, NY: Cornell University Press, 2004), p. 127.
34. Dikotter, *Mao's Great Famine*, p. 70. *Time* magazine said, "It is now established that at least that number [20,000,000] died in China during the famine that followed the Great Leap between 1959 and 1961." See Jonathan Spence, "Mao Zedong," *Time* magazine, April 13, 1998, available at *http://www.time.com/time/magazine/article/0,9171,988161-1,00.html* (accessed July 2011).
35. Fewsmith, "The Government of China," p. 461.
36. Ethridge and Handleman, *Politics in a Changing World*, p. 416
37. See Paul Clark, *The Chinese Cultural Revolution: A History* (New York: Cambridge University Press, 2008); Hui-yun Zhuang, *Idealism and the Abuse of Power: Lessons from China's Cultural Revolution* (Burlington, VT: Ashgate, 2010); Roderick MacFarquhar and Michael Schoenhals, *Mao's Last Revolution* (Cambridge, MA: Harvard University Press, 2006); or Harding, *Organizing China*, Chapter 8: "The Second Crisis: The Cultural Revolution, 1966–1968," pp. 235–265.

38. There is a large literature on the Cultural Revolution. See, *inter alia*, K. S. Karol, *The Second Chinese Revolution* (New York: Hill and Wang, 1974).

39. Fewsmith, "The Government of China," p. 462.

40. Dickson, "China," p. 669.

41. Ethridge and Handelman, *Politics in a Changing World*, p. 417.

42. Lawrence Mayer, John Burnett, and Suzanne Ogden, *Comparative Politics: Nations and Theories in a Changing World* (Upper Saddle River, NJ: Prentice-Hall, 1996), p. 309.

43. See the Government of China website, GOV.cn, "The State Council," *http://english .gov.cn/2005-08/05/content_20763.htm* (accessed July 2011). See also Tony Saich, *Governance and Politics of China* (New York: Malgrave Macmillan, 2011).

44. Kevin O'Brien, *Reform Without Liberalization: China's National People's Congress and the Politics of Institutional Change* (New York: Cambridge University Press, 1990).

45. Constitution, Article 57.

46. Inter-Parliamentary Union, PARLINE database, "China: National People's Congress," *http://www.ipu.org/parline-e/reports/2065_B.htm* (accessed July 2011).

47. This section is based upon a much more detailed discussion in Worden, et al., *Country Profile: China*, pp. 25–28. See also Daniel C. K. Chow, *The Legal System of the People's Republic of China in a Nutshell* (St. Paul, MN: Thomson/West, 2009).

48. Mayer, et al., *Comparative Politics*, p. 312. A very good study of the Chinese legal system is by Victor Li, *Law Without Lawyers: A Comparative View of Law in China and the United States* (Boulder, CO: Westview, 1978). See also Pitman Potter, ed., *Domestic Law Reforms in Post-Mao China* (Armonk, NY: M.E. Sharpe, 1994); and Zhu Sanzhu, "Reforming State Institutions: Privatizing the Lawyers' System," in Jude Howell, *Governance in China* (Boulder, CO: Rowman and Littlefield, 2004), pp. 58–77.

49. Mayer et al., *Comparative Politics*, p. 313. See also Xiaobing Li, *Civil Liberties in China* (Santa Barbara, CA: ABC-CLIO, 2010); and Margaret Y. K. Woo and Mary Elizabeth Gallagher, eds., *Chinese Justice: Civil Dispute Resolution in Contemporary China* (New York: Cambridge University Press, 2011).

50. See Baogang He, *The Democratic Implications of Civil Society in China* (New York: St. Martin's Press, 1997); and Jude Howell, "New Directions in Civil Society: Organizing Around Marginalized Interests," in Jude Howell, ed., *Governance in China* (Boulder, CO: Rowman and Littlefield, 2004), pp. 143–171.

51. Ethridge and Handelman, *Politics in a Changing World*, p. 419. See also Xudong Zhang, *Postsocialism and Cultural Politics: China in the Last Decade of the Twentieth Century*. Durham, NC: Duke University Press, 2008).

52. This section is based upon a much longer discussion in Dickson, "China," pp. 672–674.

53. See John P. Burns and Stanley Rosen, eds., *Policy Conflicts in Post-Mao China: A Documentary Survey, with Analysis* (Armonk, NY: M.E. Sharpe, 1986). See also David Shambaugh, *China's Communist Party: Atrophy and Adaptation* (Berkeley, CA: University of California Press, 2009).

54. Dickson, "China," p. 673. On the decline of Communism, see X. L. Ding, *The Decline of Communism in China: Legitimacy Crisis, 1977–1989* (New York: Cambridge University Press, 2006); and Kjeld Erik Brødsgaard and Yongnian Zheng, *The Chinese Communist Party in Reform* (New York: Routledge, 2006).

55. A very good discussion of how the human rights agenda squares with traditional Chinese values can be found in William Theodore de Bary, "Confucianism and Human Rights in China," in Larry Diamond and Marc Plattner, eds., *Democracy in East Asia* (Baltimore, MD: Johns Hopkins University Press, 1998), pp. 42–54.

56. See Joseph Fewsmith, *China Since Tiananmen: The Politics of Transition* (New York: Cambridge University Press, 2001). See also Cheng Li, ed., *China's Changing Political Landscape: Prospects for Democracy* (Washington, DC: Brookings Institution Press, 2008).

57. Bruce Gilley, *China's Democratic Future: How It Will Happen and Where It Will Lead* (New York: Columbia University Press, 2004), especially p. 136. Another good source is Lowell Dittmer and Guoli Liu, eds., *China's Deep Reform: Domestic Politics in Transition* (Lanham, MD: Rowman and Littlefield, 2006).

58. Yumei Zhang, *Pacific Asia: The Politics of Development* (New York: Routledge, 2003), p. 34. See also Kerry Brown, *Friends and Enemies: The Past, Present, and Future of the Communist Party of China* (New York: Anthem Press, 2009).

59. Dickson, "China," p. 677. And see Chae-ho Chong, ed., *Charting China's Future: Political, Social, and International Dimensions* (Lanham, MD: Rowman and Littlefield, 2006).

60. Jude Howell, "Getting to the Roots: Governance Pathologies and Future Prospects," in Jude Howell, ed., *Governance in China*, p. 226. See also See Willy Wo-Lap Lam, *Chinese Politics in the Hu Jintao Era: New Leaders, New Challenges* (Armonk, NY: M.E. Sharpe, 2006).

The Mexican Political System

The president has an extraordinary amount of power in the Mexican political system. Here Felipe Calderon holds a press conference at the 2011 World Economic Forum in Davos, Switzerland.

Yu Yang/XinHua/Xinhua Press/Corbis

- Appreciate Mexico's political stability in the context of Third World nations and the political context of Latin America within which it operates.

- Discuss Mexican federalism, both in terms of its effect upon policy-making in Mexico and in terms of its similarity to and difference from other federal systems.

- Understand Mexico's version of a presidential executive, and the position he holds in the political system.

- Describe the relation between Mexico's two legislative chambers, and explain how they compare with corresponding legislature structures elsewhere.

- Understand the operation of political parties in Mexico today.

- Appreciate the economic progress that Mexico has made over the last two decades.

Mexico—formally the United Mexican States—represents many variations from other nations we have already examined in this book. It is our first Latin American nation. It is the first presidential (as distinct from parliamentary) nation. And, although it is a "developing" nation, it is a developing nation that has achieved a remarkable level of political stability over the years. These characteristics—among others—guarantee that in this chapter we shall note several differences in both political structure and political behavior from those we have observed.

MEXICO

Total Area (rank)	1,964,375 sq km (15)
Population (rank)	113,724,226 (11)
Population Growth Rate (rank)	1.10% (105)
Urban Population	78%
Life Expectancy at Birth (total population) (rank)	76.47 (72)
Literacy	86.1%
Government Type	Federal Republic
Legal System	Civil Law
Head of Government	President Felipe Calderón Hinojosa
Chief of State	President Felipe Calderón Hinojosa
Gross Domestic Product (GDP)	$1.039 trillion
GDP Per Capita (rank)	$13,900 (85)
GDP Real Growth Rate (rank)	5.5% (61)
Unemployment Rate (rank)	5.6% (55)

MEXICO

THE MEXICAN POLITICAL HERITAGE

Although Mexico has not had a revolution since early in the previous century (1910–1921), this should not be taken to suggest that there have been no issues of controversy in Mexican politics since that time, or that there has not been any significant political instability in domestic politics. Such is not the case. Indeed, Mexico's political culture is fragmented, and there are many issues of conflict.[1]

Mexico has, even in recent years, experienced some very tense moments in the political arena. In 1968 several hundred students were killed in Mexico City while demonstrating against the government; massive land expropriation was undertaken in 1976; and an economic crisis struck Mexico in 1982. Indeed, many claimed that the 1988 presidential election was "stolen" by the forces of President **Carlos Salinas de Gortari** when it was clear that the candidate of the Institutional Revolutionary Party (PRI) might actually lose a presidential election for the first time in modern history. The same was true for the July 2006, election for president that resulted in a highly contested electoral outcome when the Federal Electoral Court declared **Felipe Calderón** of the Partido Accion Nacional (PAN) the winner of the election and president-elect.[2]

In the campaign for the August 1994 presidential election, the Institutional Revolutionary Party (PRI, the party of the government) candidate for the presidency associated with political reform, Luis Donaldo Colosio, was assassinated; another reform-oriented party leader, the secretary general of the PRI, was assassinated in September, 1994, shortly after the election. In both of these cases, the individuals identified as the assassins were tried and convicted, but suspicions persist in Mexico that the full story behind the killings has not yet come out, and links with former President Carlos Salinas de Gortari (because of the involvement of his brother) continue to worry many.

Another significant point of instability relates to violence that broke out in the south of Mexico in the state of Chiapas in January of 1994. The insurrection dealt with concerns about social issues—specifically, land reform—and President de Gortari had to send the army against members of the Zapatista movement when they seized their state's second-largest city, San Cristobal de las Casas, and three other sizable towns.[3] De Gortari eventually promised amnesty for the rebel leaders and government action on the issues related to poverty and land reform, but all of Mexico was shaken that such a level of violence took place. The government unilaterally declared a cease-fire in 1994, and active guerrilla warfare ended. In December of 1997 a massacre of forty-five peasants took place in the state of Chiapas, again increasing tensions in the state. We shall return to further discussion of these issues later in this chapter.

In the early 1970s Mexico seemed to have entered an era of rapid development and increasing prosperity. Mexico's oil industry was rapidly expanding, and became the fourth-largest in the world. Later, however, primarily as a result of the decline in world oil prices, Mexico's economy became a shambles, and domestic politics reflected the economic tensions.[4]

Mexico's political history falls into several broad eras.[5] Prior to 1521 Mexico was ruled by a series of Indian empires. Between 1521 and 1810, Mexico lived under Spanish colonial rule. Mexico first revolted against the Spanish on

September 16, 1810; the struggle went on until 1821, when a stable independent government was installed. Between 1821 and 1877 there were a number of emperors, dictators, and presidents in power, and Mexico lost Texas (1836) and later (1846–1848) lost what today are California, Nevada, Utah, most of Arizona and New Mexico, and parts of Wyoming and Colorado, to the United States.

In 1855, the Indian leader Benito Juárez began to introduce political reforms in Mexico, but his leadership was short-lived, and between 1861 and 1867 Mexico fell under the rule of European powers. In 1867 Juárez again took power as president and executed Maximilian of Austria, who had become emperor of Mexico in 1864.

From 1877 to 1911 Mexican politics were dominated by the long, dictatorial presidency of Porfirio Diaz (1876–1880, and 1884–1911). The Diaz regime led to the social revolution of 1910–1921, which is regarded by most Mexicans as the beginning of modern Mexican politics. "The commonly accepted and most convenient symbol for the beginning of Mexico's modernization process is the Mexican Revolution of 1910."[6]

POLITICAL STABILITY

Over the last several decades, Mexico's **stability** has been the single most visible characteristic distinguishing it from other Latin American nations. It has continued to operate under the same political structures for nearly eighty years, and is the only major Latin American political system not to have had a military coup since the end of World War II. Also an exception to the general Latin American pattern, every president elected since 1934 has served out his full six-year term and participated in a peaceful transition of power rather than having his power seized by a *coup* of one kind or another.

"Stability," as we use the term here, does not mean that Mexican society has not had social tensions, however. As recently as 1997 significant social tensions—including insurrection—have taken place. Here, "stability" is used in a more restrictive sense to indicate the continuity of major political structures. One important example of this relative stability is the relation between the Mexican military and the civilian government. Whereas military coups are common in Central and South America, such is not the case in Mexico.[7]

Among the aspects of Mexican culture contributing to this pattern of stability is the process of political socialization. It has been suggested, however, that Mexico's socialization patterns have transformed in recent years, resulting in changes in the socialization process.[8] These include an expansion of mass education—today nearly one-third of Mexicans are in school, and an increasingly educated mass public wants to have more education. Student groups see increasing educational opportunities not only as avenues for advancement, but also as means to further develop governmental expertise and legitimacy.[9]

For those who were adolescents in the early years of the twentieth century, the revolution was an event of overwhelming significance; for the "postrevolutionary generation" the most important characteristic of the environment in which they were reared was the prevalence of violence and instability. Thus, a stable contemporary regime is an important factor in the lives of most Mexican political elites today.

THE MEXICAN CONSTITUTIONAL SYSTEM

Mexico's contemporary political system was born in revolution. The new constitution, amending the constitution of 1857, was announced in February 1917 and has been the constitution of Mexico since then. Three key characteristics reflected in the constitution are representative democracy, presidential dictatorship, and corporatism.[10]

Mexico's leadership in 1917 believed in the virtues of classical liberalism and established a constitution based upon **representative democracy**, guaranteeing equal rights for all citizens; providing for separation of powers in the legislative, executive, and judicial branches of government; and establishing representative government based upon popular sovereignty. A centralized federal government has developed with significant political powers; for example, permitting the government to nationalize the petroleum industry in 1938 and allowing it to restrict foreign ownership of land in Mexico.[11]

While some aspects of the constitution clearly were based upon fundamental principles of representative democracy, others were less benign. Indeed, some have suggested that Mexico today has virtually a **presidential dictatorship**. The president has the right to issue executive decrees, which have the force of law; despite the notion of separation of powers the president is permitted to introduce proposals in the legislature on his own authority (something that the American president, for example, is not permitted to do). This gives him direct legislative power, in addition to his executive power. The president also has the power to appoint and remove judges, giving him clear judicial power as well. Thus, the president's power

> [i]s such that it absorbs and is complementary to the powers of the other two branches of government. In addition, the sovereignty of the states is found to be extremely limited by the Federation and subject to the discretionary powers of the president. The result is the establishment of a constitutional dictatorship of the presidential variety.[12]

The third theme of Mexican politics is **corporatism**, which we defined earlier in this book as implying a "close interaction of groups and government," where "organizations are integrated in the government decision-making process." As the government's financial planning has come under increased pressures in recent years, tensions have begun to develop in the government-business relationship, and the government has anxiously sought ways to smooth over the sources of tension.[13]

Mexican labor law recognizes classes in society, and the Courts of Conciliation and Arbitration are given authority to resolve conflicts between labor and owners. There are many governmental boards and commissions that provide industrial and interest groups with a role in policy making. These commissions can be referred to as "corporate" because through appointment of leaders of different social and economic groups to membership on the boards, these groups are, indeed, integrated in the government decision-making process.[14]

FEDERALISM IN MEXICO

Mexico is a federal system, including thirty-one states and one federal district, each of which has some policy jurisdiction. However, the Mexican states do not have the degree of power in relation to Mexico City, for example, that the German Länder have in relation to Berlin. Each state has its own constitution and has the right to pass its own laws, within clearly defined parameters. Each state elects its own governor, who holds office for a term of six years. The state legislatures have three-year terms of office.[15]

It should be noted that despite the pre-eminence of the federal president, governors are significant political actors in Mexican politics, and charges of electoral fraud have been regularly leveled in gubernatorial elections as well as elections for the national presidency and congress.

The overwhelming power of the president in the Mexican political system has done a great deal to weaken Mexican federalism. The president exercises control over state governments, much as he exercises control over other branches of the federal government, through both constitutional and traditional justifications.[16]

Most frequently, however, the major source of presidential power, rather than coming exclusively from legal or constitutional structures, emanates from practical sources, such as the president's control (through legislation) of grant programs, federal financial aid to the states, and similar sources.

BOX 15.1

Political Development and Political Modernization

Individual nation-states do not spring fully-mature into the contemporary political world. *Political development* and *modernization* are processes, and sometimes these processes are effectuated speedily, while at other times they take longer. Sometimes the evolution involved is gradual, other times it is abrupt, violent, and painful.*

Often the terms *modernization* and *development* are used interchangeably to refer to the movement of a nation-state from one evolutionary stage to another. Some scholars, however, distinguish between the two terms:

[Development is] an evolutionary process in which indigenous institutions adapt and control change and are not simply caught up in imitating and reacting to outside forces. Modernization is often contemporary, imported, and creates a dependency on the technologically advanced urban-industrial centers without helping local political and social institutions to grow and adapt. Development means that a system has some ability to be selective in the type and pace of changes, often imported, that occur in a country.**

* A very good recent work in this area is by Harry Eckstein, *Regarding Politics: Essays on Political Theory, Stability, and Change* (Berkeley: University of California Press, 1992).
** Herbert Winter and Thomas Bellows, *People and Politics* (New York: Wiley, 1977), pp. 352–353.

In recent years there has been an increasing policy of administrative decentralization in Mexico. Many believe that this has been a necessary response to recent "hyper-urbanization" in Mexico—the rush of so many rural residents to the urban area surrounding Mexico City, a topic to which we shall return later in this chapter. The government realizes that educational, cultural, and health resources simply must be made available over a far broader geographic area; if not, some experts say, the rush to the urban areas will continue.[17]

Mexico's approach to federalism is, as noted above, far more centralized than what we observed in Germany. Indeed, "the central government bureaucracy, dominated by the presidency, is the main source of public policy."[18] Although states and state governments should be kept in mind, our attention can remain focused on the *national* level of government if we are seeking an understanding of how political institutions and political behavior operate in Mexico.

EXECUTIVE STRUCTURES

Simón Bolivar once observed that the new republics of the Americas needed kings who could be referred to as presidents, and added that, in Mexico at least, these kings were kings for six-year periods.[19] Mexican presidents are elected by direct popular vote and can hold office for a single six-year term, after which they can never be re-elected. The president must be at least thirty-five years of age, and must be a native-born Mexican who is the son of native-born Mexicans.[20] He cannot be a clergyman of a religious group. If he has been in either the military or in the cabinet (as all recent presidents have been), he must have retired from that position at least six months prior to the election. The president is the single most powerful individual in Mexican politics.[21]

POWER

Much of the president's power comes from his constitutional role in government; the president "encounters no effective restraint *within* government."[22] In that role he has very wide power to appoint and remove government officials (much broader fiscal powers than, say, the American president), the capacity to initiate and veto legislation, and the power to control the military. (Since the revolution, the military has been reorganized, and today it is restricted in its power to influence policy.) Although legislators in Mexico have the power to introduce legislation, legislation is typically introduced by the president.[23]

Nomination and Selection

The presidential election of 1988 was the first Mexican presidential election in modern history in which the outcome was truly in doubt, although by the time the votes were all counted (and, opposition leaders charged, rigged) the PRI candidate again won.[24] While the PRI's hold on power continued thereafter, it was shaken, and in the election of 2000, after seventy-one years of the PRI being the party of power, another party won the presidency with the victory of the PAN party's Vicente Fox. The 2006 election saw the PRI finish *third* in the presidential race, so in hindsight the election of 2000 must be seen as the beginning of a manifestation of a truly competitive Mexican electoral system.[25]

The usual practice within the PRI through the 2000 election was to have the incumbent president hand-pick his successor, invariably from among those individuals who have been active cabinet members. As noted above, the constitution requires that a cabinet officer seeking the presidency must resign from office at least six months before the presidential elections, but this has not provided any difficulties for recent candidates. There are some socioeconomic characteristics that are apparently valued by presidents when selecting their successors, including physical appearance, a neutral position in relation to organized religion, a middle-class background, coming from a large state, and having a wife who "has a moderate interest in public affairs."[26] (For a list of recent presidents of Mexico, see Table 15.1.)

When recent incumbent presidents neared the final year of their six-year term of office, pressures began to be exerted on them to "name" a successor. Incumbents have tried to resist this pressure for as long as possible, however, because once an incumbent names the "heir apparent," he loses much of his own political power and will not be able to accomplish as much as he previously could. One scholar, in fact, has identified nine different stages in the process of the selection of a new president.

1. President consults with advisors and colleagues as to acceptability of possible nominees.
2. The President announces his choice.
3. Power-seekers and political leaders in the PRI praise the candidate-designate.
4. Candidate is officially nominated at the PRI Rally.
5. The Campaign takes place.
6. The Election takes place.
7. The winning candidate officially accepts the election results.

TABLE 15.1

Some Recent Mexican Presidents

Gustavo Diaz Ordaz	1964–1970	Institutional Revolutionary Party (PRI)
Luis Echeverría Alvarez	1970–1976	Institutional Revolutionary Party (PRI)
José López Portillo	1976–1982	Institutional Revolutionary Party (PRI)
Miguel de la Madrid Hurtado	1982–1988	Institutional Revolutionary Party (PRI)
Carlos Salinas de Gortari	1988–1994	Institutional Revolutionary Party (PRI)
Ernesto Zedillo Ponce de Leon	1994–2000	Institutional Revolutionary Party (PRI)
Vicente Fox Quesada	2000–2006	National Action Party (PAN)
Felipe Calderón Hinojosa	2006–2012	National Action Party (PAN)

8. The new president selects his advisors.
9. The new president selects an advantageous time to announce his appointments.[27]

Once the outgoing president "nominated" his successor—who in recent elections had been a member of the Cabinet and has thus immediately resigned from the Cabinet—the nominee of the PRI was expected to travel all over the country campaigning for office, meeting leaders of interest groups, local leaders, business leaders, community politicians, and so on, and in fact improve his knowledge of local problems at the same time that he was increasing his own visibility in the eyes of the electorate. Past experience has shown that even the most isolated of Mexican villages was visited over the course of the campaign—if not by the candidate himself, then by one of his campaign workers.

This process was violently disrupted in 1994 when the PRI candidate for the presidency Luis Donaldo Colosio, who had been hand-picked by outgoing President Salinas de Gortari, was assassinated in early March as he was campaigning around the country. Picking Colosio's successor was especially difficult for the PRI because of a legal requirement that candidates could not have held public office during the six-months period before the election, which eliminated most of the possible candidates for the position. In late March of 1994 the PRI nominated Ernesto Zedillo Ponce de Leon, a former cabinet minister and someone who had been Colosio's campaign manager, to serve as the party's new presidential candidate.

Some once questioned why Mexico should even go through this ritual if the results of the election were certain. Of course, since 2000 the response to this question has been that the results of the election were *not* certain: **Vicente Fox Quesada** of the Alliance for Change (which included the National Action Party (PAN) and the Mexican Green Ecologist Party (PVEM)) won the 2000 presidential election. Even before this upset of the PRI, however, there were at least two reasons why the national campaign was useful, even if it contained no surprises. First, the act of campaigning itself helped to create support for the regime, and thereby afforded the government greater legitimacy than it might otherwise have had. Second, the presidential campaign could make a significant difference to candidates for the Senate and the Chamber of Deputies who were running for office, either on the same side as the presidential candidate or on an opposition ticket.

In the presidential election of August 1994, President **Ernesto Zedillo Ponce de Leon** of the Institutional Revolutionary Party was elected by a substantial margin, and was sworn in on December 1, 1994. Zedillo was educated as an economist, with degrees from Yale, and had served in the prior Salinas Administration as Secretary of Programming and Budget as well as Secretary of Education prior to receiving the nomination for the presidency and running for the office.

President Zedillo pursued several goals as soon as he took office. Among these was to continue to "open" Mexico's political system so that groups and political parties that had in the past been shut out of participation could participate. He also targeted reform of the justice system, control of narcotics traffic, cutting corruption, and economic reform as needing a great deal of attention.

Six years later the situation was different. In July of 1999, as the term of President Zedillo was coming to a close, one of the key questions in Mexican politics had to do with the issue of fraud and the PRI; the PRI was heartened, and its election chances were greatly increased, when a report was released at the end of July clearing the PRI of fraud. The opposition had hoped that the PRI would face serious charges that would affect its chances in the campaign. The leadership of the National Action Party (PAN) and the Party of the Democratic Revolution (PRD), however, saw that victory might still be possible if they could pool their resources to support a candidate together. By September it was clear that their policy preferences, and the fact that they each had a strong leader who wanted to be the nominee of the combined party, would prevent a coalition, and talks ended.

In November of 1999 the PRI chose its candidate, Francisco Labastida, and PRI supporters were confident that victory would again be theirs. Within a week of receiving the PRI leadership position the former interior minister left on his first official tour abroad as the PRI presidential candidate, travelling to Argentina, Brazil, Uruguay, and Chile.

In December of 1999, the head of the National Action Party (PAN), Vicente Fox, indicated that he wanted to renew efforts to create a national opposition alliance, and although Labastida and the PRI were in a comfortable leading position, Fox and his supporters continued to be enthusiastic. In April of 2000, Fox was declared to be the winner of a six-way presidential debate, and his energy level and the energy level of his campaign increased; a month later he moved ahead in the opinion polls for the first time, and gave increasing credibility to his claim that the PRI could be defeated if the opposition pulled together.[28]

On election day the unthinkable happened, and the PRI lost, for the first time since 1929. Fox was sworn in on December 1, 2000. This was not only the first non-PRI president in Mexican history, but also "the first peaceful democratic transfer of power ever in Mexican history."[29]

A year after his election, however, all was not going well for Fox. He had not made great progress on his campaign promises, and was being seen as an ineffective leader. One commentator noted: "After Fox had brazenly predicted 7 percent economic growth this year, Mexico's economy has skidded to zero growth. After promising to create 1.3 million jobs, at least 250,000 jobs have been lost."[30] These were challenges that continued to face the Mexican president, and by the time of the presidential campaign in 2006 the PAN was in trouble.

The 2006 election was the closest in Mexican political history, and it took over two months for a definitive result to appear—and even then it was not "definitive" to all. The Justices of the Federal Electoral Institute—the government agency in charge of organizing the election—ruled that the election was fair,

> ## TABLE 15.2
>
> ### The Presidential Election of July, 2006
>
> | Candidate | Vote % |
> |---|---|
> | Felipe Calderón Hinojosa (PAN) | 35.89 |
> | Andres Manuel López Obrador (PRD) | 35.31 |
> | Roberto Madrazo (PRI) | 22.26 |
> | Other | 6.54 |
> | Total | 100.00 |
>
> **Party Abbreviations**
> PAN: National Action Party
> PRD: Party of the Democratic Revolution
> PRI: Institutional Revolutionary Party
>
> *Source*: U.S. Government, Central Intelligence Agency, *World Factbook*, https://www.cia.gov/library/
> publications/the-world-factbook/geos/mx.html (accessed May 2011).

and that the conservative candidate, former energy minister Felipe Calderón Hinojosa of the National Action Party, had won. The Party of the Democratic Revolution candidate Andres Manuel López Obrador came in a razor-close second, and the candidate of the Institutional Revolutionary Party, the party that had controlled power from 1929 to 2000 without stop, came in third.[31] Results of the July, 2006 presidential election can be found in Table 15.2.

LEGISLATIVE STRUCTURES

The Mexican Congress is bicameral, and consists of a Chamber of Deputies and a Senate. The Congress is inferior to the president in the structures of governmental power, and its consent to presidential legislative proposals can be counted upon. In fact, recent scholarship has indicated that presidential proposals have been approved unanimously 80 to 95 percent of the time in recent years, and are normally opposed by less than 5 percent of the members of the Congress.[32]

The Senate

Senators are elected for six-year terms, and the Senate is "frankly regarded in Mexico as a rubber stamp for presidential policy,"[33] and accordingly is not looked upon as a highly significant structure. Senators are elected by direct popular vote. The voting system is innovative, and reflects Mexico's concern with making sure that significant minorities have some representation in the government. With the understanding that district-based representation tends to over-represent plurality parties and "hide" minority parties, the new electoral system was designed to make sure that significant minorities have representation by *reserving seats* for those minority parties.

The Senate has a total of 128 members, as reflected in Table 15.3, with thirty-two multimember constituencies of four Senators representing each of the thirty-one states and the Federal District. (This is a new Senate structure; until recently the Senate had 64 members.) Three of the four Senators for each constituency are directly elected by the people, with a plurality vote (that is, the top three vote-getters are elected); the fourth seat is given to the minority party, which did the best in the vote. The most recent election was on July 2, 2006.

The Senatorial election of 2006 was held simultaneously with elections for a new president, the House of Representatives, and other local elections. Voters elected all 128 members of the Senate. The National Action Party (PAN)—the party of newly-elected President Calderón—won 52 seats.

The main issues in the 2006 elections were the high crime rate, poverty and undocumented Mexican workers in the United States. The PAN endorsed Mr. Felipe Calderon as its presidential candidate and presented tough policies on crime, including life sentences for kidnappers. The PRD, led by the former Mayor of Mexico City, Mr. Manuel Lopez Obrador, formed an alliance, called the "Alliance for the Good of All", with the Labour Party and the Convergence Party. The alliance fought the elections under the slogan "For the Good of All, the poor first", pledging to improve healthcare and education. The Alliance for Mexico coalition was composed of the PRI and the Green Party of Mexico. The PRI, led by former senator Mr. Roberto Madrazo, pledged to create nine million jobs inside Mexico to prevent Mexican workers migrating to the United States.[34]

TABLE 15.3

Senate Membership, 2006–2012

Political Group	Total	Majority	Minority	PR
National Action Party	52	32	9	11
Alliance for Mexico (PRI + Green)	38	10	19	9
Alliance for the Good of All (PRD)	36	22	4	10
Social Democratic and Peasant Alternative Party	1	0	0	1
New Alliance Party	1	0	0	1
Total	128	64	32	32

Source: Inter-Parliamentary Union, "Mexico: Last Elections," http://www.ipu.org/parline-e/reports/2212_E.htm (accessed May, 2011).

The Chamber of Deputies

The 500 Deputies are elected for three-year terms according to a system of single-member-district voting and **partial proportional representation,** under which 200 of the 500 seats in the Chamber are elected by proportional representation, while the other 300 seats are elected from single-member districts.

The 300 single-member-district seats are based upon population, but the constitution guarantees each state at least two deputies. Although each state's *number* of seats is based upon the state's total population as a share of the national population, there is no constitutional provision that forces the states to divide their quota of seats into equally populated districts.

Electoral reform was introduced in 1977, raising the number of deputies from about 200 (the exact number depended upon how many minority party deputies were elected)[35] to 400, and this reform became effective with the 1979–1980 legislative session. For the 1988 election the total number of seats was raised to 500; the number of seats has remained 500 through the most recent—July 2009—election. Of these seats, 300 were elected by a single-member-district, majority-vote system, with those districts based upon population similar to electoral systems we have seen in Britain, or Germany (see Table 15.4).

Mexico's electoral system strengthens the voice of the opposition parties in the Chamber of Deputies; the majority party is not permitted to hold more than 300 seats in the 500-seat legislature, unless it wins over 60 percent of the votes, in which case it can hold up to 315 seats. The 200 at-large seats are distributed by proportional representation on the basis of the proportion of the national vote won by each party. All of the opposition parties together are guaranteed at least 150 of these 200 at-large proportional seats.

▶ TABLE 15.4

The July 5, 2009, Election for the Chamber of Deputies

Political Group	Total Seats	Majority Seats	Proportional Seats	Number of Women
Institutional Revolutionary Party (PRI)	237	184	53	53
National Action Party (PAN)	143	70	73	48
Democratic Revolutionary Party (PRD)	71	39	32	21
Green Party of Mexico (PVEM)	21	4	17	9
Labour Party (PT)	13	3	10	4
New Alliance Party (NA)	9	0	9	4
Convergence Party (CONV)	6	0	6	2
Total	500	300	200	141

Source: Inter-Parliamentary Union, "Mexico: Last Elections," http://www.ipu.org/parline-e/reports/2211_E.htm (accessed May 2011).

Thus, 30 percent of the seats in the Chamber of Deputies are guaranteed to opposition parties, *as well as* those seats they can win in the 300 district-based electoral races. This means that although the power of the Chamber of Deputies is limited, the opposition is *guaranteed* a presence there. Several smaller parties have benefited from the at-large proportional seats.[36]

In the election of July 2009, in a different manner from the results for the Senate elections, the National Action Party of President Calderon came in second in the Chamber of Deputies to the Institutional Revolutionary Party, dropping almost 60 seats from its previous 206, while the PRI increased by almost 120 seats. President Calderon indicated that he believed that the fact that the Chamber of Deputies was going to be led by the Opposition party would not interfere with his ability to do his job. These figures are indicated in Table 15.4.

THE BUREAUCRACY

By the mid-1970s, the Mexican federal public sector included 1,075 agencies with nearly 3.4 million employees—nearly 17 percent of the country's total workforce. The administration of President de la Madrid sought to decentralize some of this bureaucracy, emphasizing regional programs and the increased participation of state and local governments in programs, especially those dealing with health care and education.[37]

We noted earlier that there are many quasi-governmental organizations in Mexico that complement the federal and state governments' efforts to enact policy. A recent study listed 123 decentralized agencies, 292 public enterprises, 187 commissions, and 160 development trusts, as well as 18 regular ministries and departments of state making up the federal bureaucratic infrastructure.[38]

As we shall discuss below, although the federal government has sought to decentralize the bureaucracy somewhat in recent years, it is still the case that massive bureaucracy affects the ability of the central government to enact policy, especially in central industrial areas such as oil, petroleum exploration and distribution (PEMEX), steel (SIDERMEX), fertilizers (FERTIMEX), and food purchasing, processing, and distribution (CONASUPO).[39]

POLITICAL PARTIES AND ELECTIONS

A strong relationship exists between the dominant political party and the state in Mexico, but there remains a clear difference between the two. The primary function of the dominant party is to mobilize support and to legitimize the state.[40]

Although Mexico was often thought of as a one-party nation because of the history of the dominance of the PRI, such is no longer the case; the last two elections, especially, have shown that not only is it possible to defeat the PRI, but it can be done on a widespread scale.[41] Indeed, as noted above, the

PRI candidate for President finished *third* in the 2006 election. There are many opposition groups in society, made up of peasants, students, and workers.[42]

In the state and local elections of 1983, the major opposition party of the day, the National Action Party (PAN), won in a record number of state capitals and major cities, and many were asking what the future held for the dominant party, the PRI. After the loss of the presidency in the 2000 and 2006 elections, this question will certainly become asked even more frequently in the future. To a large degree the problems of the PRI have been anchored in its clear identification with the Mexican *status quo*; it was, after all, the party that was in power for seven decades.[43]

The PRI was the major party in Mexico from the 1920s through the 2000 election. It was so well entrenched and central to the operation of the government that through the end of the 1990s it had been seen as serving "as a subordinate extension of the presidency and central government bureaucracy."[44] The PRI had three major factions, an agrarian faction, a labor faction, and a "popular" faction, and was governed by a national party congress called the National Assembly. Each of the three factions of the PRI vied for power on the Executive Committee, and although these three factions were ostensibly all on the same side in an election, there was often great competition between and among them for formal party leadership positions.

The PRI continues to play a very important role in Mexican politics, although given its second presidential loss in two elections in 2006 its future is far less certain than it was a decade ago.[45] Its leaders were encouraged by its performance in the 2009 election for the Chamber of Deputies and its ability to win control of that legislative body, and they hope to be able to develop that success further for the 2012 presidential election. In the recent past, the topic of fraud is one that was frequently associated with the PRI, and elections at all levels, presidential, Congressional, and state office as well, and it will be interesting to see if the PRI can build upon its 2009 performance to become a nationally competitive party again. The emphasis in the 2000 election was on having a "clean" election, and the rapid concession of the election by the PRI leaders can be seen as an effort to show that the elections were open and free of fraud. And, it will be recalled, the PRI lost that election.

In the 2006 presidential election the theme of **fraud** reappeared, with hundreds of thousands of Mexicans demonstrating in the Zocalo, Mexico City's main square, crying that the election had been stolen from the PRD's Obrador by the forces of the PAN's Calderon; ironically, the PRI was not involved in the crisis at all because its candidate had finished *third* in the voting and was clearly *not* going to be the winner in the election.[46]

The National Democratic Front (FDN) was a new competing party in the 1988 election. Its roots were not new, however; they included the Mexican Communist Party (PCM),[47] which changed its name to the Unified Socialist Party of Mexico (PSUM) in 1981 when it joined with several smaller parties in a left-of-center coalition. The PSUM was able to provide the PRI with serious competition at the state level, although it was not very effective in federal elections until 1988.[48] The FDN is regarded by many as not really a true party, but rather an electoral coalition whose roots include not only the

Communist PCM or PSUM, but also a healthy non-Communist tradition. The FDN competed as the PRD, the Party of the Democratic Revolution later, and was favored for a long while to win the 2006 presidential election, losing by less than one-tenth of 1 percent.

The major right-of-center parties include the Mexican Democratic Party (PDM) and the National Action Party (PAN). Both parties became more successful in elections following the 1977 reforms, which created at-large proportional representation in the Chamber of Deputies, and they offered the PRI serious competition at the state level through the end of the 1990s. The PDM was considered "the most conservative party with registration in Mexico,"[49] and has its strongest political support in the countryside.

The PAN is considered the major party of the political right in Mexico today,[50] and certainly after its victory in the 2000 and 2006 presidential elections and in so many state legislative elections it is likely to continue to be the significant player in Mexican politics in the future. The major difference between the PAN and the PRI included the PAN's greater criticism of the United States, and the PAN's desire to support the Catholic Church.[51] Thus, the president and the PRI were able to increase their perceived legitimacy by encouraging the opposition parties, without giving up any real political power at all.[52]

Even though the PRI had—until the 2000 presidential election—won nearly every federal election held since 1929, the broader Mexican electoral arena involved real electoral competition through 2000; with the PRI having lost both the 2000 and 2006 presidential elections, it is certainly safe to say that the electoral arena is an open and competitive one today. And, as we noted earlier, with recent electoral reforms there seems to be progress being made in offering Mexican voters real choices in the electoral setting.[53]

A record 78 percent of registered voters participated in the 1994 presidential election, and 65 percent voted in 2000. Almost 60 percent participated in the 2006 election. Turnout for the 2009 legislative elections was expected to be very low, approaching 30 percent (although it should be noted that "off-year" elections in the United States—elections that take place in years when there is no presidential election to stimulate voters' interest—often have less than a 30 percent participation rate).[54]

The reforms of 1977 and 1988, alluded to earlier, were designed to increase political participation and to stimulate electoral competition. By just about any measure, the reforms have been effective; ever since they were enacted, in fact, opposition to the PRI has increased, and the PRI has moved from being the dominant party in the nation to being an also-ran.[55]

POLITICAL DEVELOPMENT AND ECONOMICS

Two distinct problem areas confront the government today. Both of these problems are a function of the economic crisis in Mexico.[56] One of these concerns urban migration, especially the unique set of problems facing Mexico City. The massive pattern of **migration** from rural Mexico to the capital city is putting intolerable demands upon the infrastructure of Mexico City and has already had significant effects upon the quality of life there. The second problem has an international dimension, and concerns the implications of the (illegal and) massive flow of Mexican population across its northern border with the United States.

Mexico City has suffered the same problems of urban migration as have the major cities of many developing nations, sometimes referred to as **hyperurbanization.**[57] The crises of poverty and high unemployment often serve to push significant populations from rural areas to the urban capital area in search of jobs and better living conditions. To show how significant this population movement to urban areas has been, see Table 15.5. In 1910, 28.7 percent of Mexico's population lived in an urban setting. In 2030 this is predicted to be 82.9 percent![58]

Ironically, the migrants usually find neither jobs nor better living conditions; rather, these migrations contribute to greater unemployment and worse living conditions.[59]

Mexico City represents the worst of this general problem. With a 2009 population estimate of 8.84 million residents (and the greater metropolitan region has 21.2 million residents), in 2009 approximately 23 percent of Mexico's entire population lived in the greater Mexico City area—an increase of almost 3 percent from the year 2000, and a publication by the U.S. Department of State refers to Mexico City as "the largest concentration of people in the world."[60]

Mexico City faces a wide range of environmental challenges. Over 2 million of its residents have no running water, sometimes living more than three city blocks from the nearest faucet. Over 3 million of its inhabitants have no sewage facilities. The city produces over 14,000 tons of garbage *every day*, but can process only 8,000 tons. Breathing the polluted air of Mexico City, (caused by 3 million cars, 7,000 buses, and over 13,000 factories) has been likened to smoking two packs of cigarettes a day, and the combination of chemical and biological poisons has been estimated to kill over 30,000 children annually through respiratory and gastrointestinal disease. "Overall," one study has noted, "pollution may account for the deaths of nearly 100,000 people a year."[61]

It is this type of situation that has led many Mexicans to leave their homeland and head north to a country where, they have heard, there are jobs for those who want them and a better life for those who are willing to work for it. About half of Mexico's population are under 21 years of age, and many of these see a future in the America as preferable to a future in Mexico. The Mexican–American border

▶ **TABLE 15.5**								
Mexico's Urban Population								
Year	1950	1960	1970	1980	1990	2000	2005	2015 (pred)	2030 (pred)
Urban pop (%)	42.7	50.8	59.0	66.3	72.5	74.7	76.0	78.8	82.9

Source: Globalis, "Mexico: Urban Population," http://globalis.gvu.unu.edu/indicator_detail.cfm?IndicatorID=30&Country=MX (accessed May 2011).

is nearly 2,000 miles long, and issues such as smuggling, illegal immigration, and the border's ecology (including air and water pollution) have proven to be a source of irritation in Mexican–American relations.[62]

The **North American Free Trade Agreement**, ratified in November of 1993, was designed to do something about this latter problem. The Agreement, negotiated by the governments of Mexico, the United States, and Canada, was designed to lower tariffs among the three nations and to improve trade opportunities among the three North American neighbors. One result of this Agreement would be increased job opportunities in Mexico, with higher salaries offered to Mexican workers, helping them decide to stay in Mexico rather than look to the north for their futures.

American critics of the Agreement argued that while it might benefit Mexico, it would result in a significant loss of American jobs, as well as having a generally negative effect upon the continental environment because Mexican environmental standards were significantly lower than American ones. Businesses, they said, would move from the United States to Mexico to find cheaper labor and less stringent environmental regulations.

Supporters of the plan countered that Mexico had promised to strengthen its environmental regulations so that there would be no "belt" of environmental disasters along the Mexican–American border. In addition, they argued, although some American jobs might be lost to Mexicans, the corresponding increase in American jobs because of the expanded market open to Americans would more than make up for the losses.

On balance, NAFTA has helped Mexico a great deal. According to one source, since the inception of NAFTA the trade relationship between the United States and Mexico has tripled, making Mexico the United States' second-largest business partner.[63] And, recent data has shown a significant decrease in the number of young Mexicans trying to illegally cross the border to find jobs in the United States; the growth of good jobs on the Mexican side of the border has been a very effective way of keeping young educated Mexicans in Mexico.

These trade-related problems were to some degree a function of Mexican economic stagnation.[64] The 1993 World Bank report indicated that where Mexico's external debt was $57.4 billion in 1980, by 1991 it had increased to $101.7 billion. This 1991 debt was equal to 36.9 percent of Mexico's GNP, a staggering debt burden. By 1993 the external debt had grown to $165.7 billion, 69.9 percent of Mexico's G.N.P.[65] See Box 15.2

The situation was so bad by December of 1994 that the United States decided that it had to respond positively to Mexico's requests for extraordinary assistance to what was called the "Peso crisis." A package of loans was assembled by the United States—under a Presidential Order of Bill Clinton, over some significant opposition from those in Congress who were afraid that the Mexican government would never be able to repay the loans—totaling nearly 50 billion dollars.[66] Using these resources the Government of Mexico was able to significantly improve its economic situation and paid the loans back to the United States *in full, and ahead of schedule.*[67]

BOX 15.2

Mexican Debt in Perspective

The inequality between and among nations in their wealth and economic viability has led to a growing system of *international dependence*, in which the "have-not" nations have come to rely more and more upon the aid programs of the "have" nations in order to survive. In many respects "the history of the Third World is to a large extent the history of its incorporation into a global economy dominated by the 'core' industrialised countries of Western Europe and the United States."* The programs of these core nations include grants, loans, and in-kind assistance (such as wheat or tractors).

The economic dependence of the developing nations upon the developed nations has grown into a major international problem in recent years as the international debts of some of the have-not nations have skyrocketed, and the likelihood that they will ever be able to repay their loans has decreased. It is easy to see that Ecuador, a country with an external debt of over 23 percent of its Gross Domestic Product ** is going to have serious problems repaying its debts. Jamaica has worse problems, with an external debt of 77.8 percent of its Gross Domestic Product.***

* Paul Cammack, David Pool, and William Tordoff, *Third World Politics: A Comparative Introduction* (Baltimore: Johns Hopkins University Press, 1988), p. 250.
** The World Bank, *World Development Indicators,* "Data: Ecuador," http://data.worldbank.org/country/ecuador (accessed July 2011).
*** The World Bank, *World Development Indicators,* "Data: Ecuador," http://data.worldbank.org/country/jamaica (accessed July 2011).

Mexico today is a country of contrasts. It is clearly a nation in which the vast majority of the resources are controlled by a small minority of the population.[68] In the World Bank's *World Development Report, 2011*, the data show that in 2008 (the most recent year for which there is data), the poorest 10 percent of the population accounted for only 1.8 percent of the income, while the highest 10 percent of the population account for 41.4 percent of the income.[69] See Table 15.6 for the growth of Mexico's economy.

TABLE 15.6

The Growth of the Mexican Economy

Year	Gross Domestic Product
1999	$ 865.5 billion
2010 (est)	1,004.0 billion

Source: U.S. Government, Central Intelligence Agency, *World Factbook,* "Mexico," "Economy," https://www.cia.gov/library/publications/the-world-factbook/geos/mx.html,

THE MEXICAN SYSTEM IN PERSPECTIVE

We have seen, albeit briefly, in this chapter that the Mexican case provides us with the opportunity to view a different type of political system from others we have met in this volume—in many respects a significantly different system. Mexico was born in revolution and social upheaval, and in recent years has been endeavoring to establish the kinds of social and political institutions that would ensure domestic stability and social harmony.

To a substantial degree, especially if we compare Mexico with her neighbors to the south, the endeavors have been successful if for no other reason than Mexico has not experienced the regular military *coups d'état* experienced by so many Latin American nations.

Nevertheless, Mexico is still suffering many of the problems faced by other nations in developing world. Economic problems, distributional problems, and technological problems have meant that the general quality of life in Mexico has not been able to improve as much as Mexico's leaders might have liked.

Some have argued that it is *the system itself* that is the real problem in Mexico. The relative stability of Mexico until recent times was based upon real reforms, particularly reforms in land ownership, that occurred as a result of the revolution, and that were considered during the period from 1934 to 1940 when Lázaro Cárdenas was president. The PRI, it has been argued, dominated the Mexican political arena for so long precisely because it embodied those reforms. As those reforms became inadequate in more recent years, problems of stability (and stagnation and corruption) resulted.[70] With the ouster of the PRI as the dominant power in Mexican politics, this may be an era in which some long-term assumptions and practices in Mexican politics are questioned and reassessed.

DISCUSSION QUESTIONS

1. How would you compare Mexico's political stability with the stability of other Latin American nations? What has helped Mexico to be as stable as it has been through its modern history?

2. How is Mexico similar to other federal political systems we have met in this book? How is it different? What are the major institutions that affect and reflect federalism in Mexico?

3. How does Mexico's presidency illustrate both the strengths and the weaknesses of presidential systems of government that we described earlier in the text? Is Mexico a typical presidential system? Does the Mexican president have any unusual presidential powers?

4. What is the relationship between the Chamber of Deputies and the Senate in Mexico? Which has more political power? What are the special roles of the Senate? What functions does it perform in the political system?

5. What happened to the Institutional Revolutionary Party? What does its future appear to be today? How would you characterize the party system in Mexico today?

6. What do you view as the key economic challenges to Mexico today? What economic crises has it managed to survive and work through in recent years? How has it made the progress that it has made? What does the future appear to be?

KEY TERMS

Calderón Hinojosa,
  Felipe 400
corporatism 394
Fox Quesada,
  Vincente 398
fraud in elections 404
hyperurbanization 406
migration from Mexico
  to the United States 405

North American
  Free Trade
  Agreement 407
partial proportional
  representation
  for Chamber of
  Deputies 402
presidential
  dictatorship 394

representative
  government 394
Salinas de Gortari,
  Carlos 392
stability 393
Zedillo Ponce de Leon,
  Ernesto 398

SUGGESTED READINGS

Caroline Beer, *Electoral Competition and Institutional Change in Mexico* (Notre Dame, IN: University of Notre Dame Press, 2003). The Mexican political system has done a remarkably effective job of responding to electoral demands of the public over time, for many years in what was essentially a one-party state, and then in a more competitive framework. This volume describes Mexican elections and how they have helped to shape Mexican democracy.

Matthew Cleary, *The Sources of Democratic Responsiveness in Mexico* (Notre Dame, IN: University of Notre Dame Press, 2010). Mexico is the most stable democracy in Latin America. Why? This volume talks about the integration of democracy with Mexican political culture, and describes the ways that the state has tried to respond to popular demands.

Burton Kirkwood, *The History of Mexico* (New York: Palgrave Macmillan, 2005). This is a very good source for the student interested in a general history of Mexico. It is comprehensive and analytical, and relates key issues in Mexican history to changes in Mexican political behavior.

Santiago Levy, *Good Intentions, Bad Outcomes: Social Policy, Informality, and Economic Growth in Mexico* (Washington, DC: Brookings Institution Press, 2008). This is a very good study of the Mexican public policy system. Mexico has faced some remarkable challenges in its history, and has been able to respond to social demands through a variety of institutional and behavioral channels.

Andrew Selee and Jacqueline Peschard, *Mexico's Democratic Challenges: Politics, Government, and Society* (Washington, DC: Woodrow Wilson Center Press, 2010). The world within which Mexican politics operates has changed over time, and so have the challenges to Mexican government. This book discusses many of the most important challenges to Mexican government and describes how the government has attempted to respond to them.

NOTES

1. L. Vincent Padgett, *The Mexican Political System* (Boston, MA: Houghton Mifflin Company, 1976), p. 10. A good historical treatment of the Mexican political heritage can be found in Elisa Servin and Leticia Reina, *Cycles of Conflict, Centuries of Change: Crisis, Reform, and Revolution in Mexico* (Durham, NC: Duke University Press, 2007).

2. There was very widespread coverage of these charges in the foreign press. On the 2006 election see "Mass Protest Over Mexican Election," July 9, 2006, on BBC.Com, at *http://news.bbc.co.uk/1/hi/world/americas/5161862.stm*; or James C. McKinley, Jr., "Throngs Call Loser Mexico's 'Legitimate' President," *New York Times* September 17, 2006, available at *http://select.nytimes.com/search/restricted/article?res=F20717F938550C748DDDA00894DE404482*.

3. See Tim Golden, "In Remote Mexican Village, Roots of Rebellion are Bared," *New York Times* January 17, 1994, p. A1. See Todd Eisenstadt, *Politics, Identity, and Mexico's Indigenous Rights Movements* (New York: Cambridge University Press, 2011).

4. Jorge Castaneda, "Mexico at the Brink," *Foreign Affairs* 64 (1985–1986): 287. See also Sidney Weintraub, *Unequal Partners: The United States and Mexico* (Pittsburgh, PA: University of Pittsburgh Press, 2010).

5. A good historical overview can be found in Kenneth Johnson, *Mexican Democracy: A Critical View* (New York: Praeger, 1984). Chapter Two is titled "The Aztec Legacy and Independence," and Chapter Three is titled "Emerging Nationhood and the Great Revolution." A very good general history is that of Burton Kirkwood, *The History of Mexico* (New York: Palgrave Macmillan, 2005).

6. A good discussion of the revolution can be found in Alicia Hernandez Chavez, *Mexico: A Brief History* (Berkeley, CA: University of California Press, 2006).

7. A good discussion of this use of the term *stability* can be found in Daniel Levy and Gabriel Szekely, *Mexico: Paradoxes of Stability and Change*, 2nd ed. (Boulder, CO: Westview, 1987); and in Larissa Lomnitz, Rodrigo Salazar Elena, and Ilya Adler, *Symbolism and Ritual in a One-Party Regime: Unveiling Mexico's Political Culture* (Tucson, AZ: University of Arizona Press, 2010). For more on this subject, see Ronald Schneider, *Latin American Political History: Patterns and Personalities* (Boulder, CO: Westview Press, 2007).

8. Daniel C. Levy, "The Political Consequences of Changing Socialization Patterns," in Roderic Camp, ed., *Mexico's Political Stability: The Next Five Years* (Boulder, CO: Westview Press, 1986), p. 19.

9. This theme is discussed in Joe Foweraker and Ann Craig, eds., *Popular Movements and Political Change in Mexico* (Boulder, CO: Lynne Rienner, 1990). See also Laura Randall, *Changing Structure of Mexico: Political, Social, and Economic Prospects* (Armonk, NY: M.E. Sharpe, 2006).

10. Much of the discussion in the few paragraphs that follow is derived from much more extensive discussion in "more extensive discussion in Juan Felipe Leal, "the Mexican State, 1915–1973: A Historical Interpretation," in Nora Hamilton and Himothy Harding, eds., *Modern Mexico: State, Economy, and Social Conflict* (Beverly Hills, CA: Sage Publications, 1986), pp. 29–32.

11. Barbara Stallings and Rogerio Studart, *Finance for Development: Latin America in Comparative Perspective* (Washington, DC: Brookings Institution Press, 2006). See also Roderic Camp, *Mexico's Military on the Democratic Stage* (Westport, CT: Praeger Publishers, 2005).

12. Leal, "The Mexican State," 30. See also Jorge Castaneda, *Perpetuating Power: How Mexican Presidents Were Chosen* (New York: New Press, 2000); and Nora Jaffary and Edward Osowski, *Mexican History: A Primary Source Reader* (Boulder, CO: Westview Press, 2010).

13. Bailey, *Governing Mexico*, p. 139. See also Howard J. Wiarda, *Authoritarianism and Corporatism in Latin America—Revisited* (Gainesville, FL: University Press of Florida, 2004).

14. See Francisco Zapata, "Mexican Labor in a Context of Political, Social, and Economic Change, 1982–2002," in Laura Randall, ed., *Changing Structure of Mexico: Political, Social, and Economic Prospects* (Armonk, NY: M.E. Sharpe, 2006).

15. See Edward Gibson, *Federalism and Democracy in Latin America* (Baltimore, MD: Johns Hopkins University Press, 2004).

16. Padgett, *The Mexican Political System*, p. 204. See also Andrew Selee and Jacqueline Peschard, *Mexico's Democratic Challenges: Politics, Government, and Society* (Washington, DC: Woodrow Wilson Center Press, 2010).

17. William Glade, "Distributional and Sectoral Problems in the New Economic Policy," in Roderic Camp, *Mexico's Political Stability: The Next Five Years* (Boulder, CO: Westview Press, 1986), p. 95. See also Alberto Diaz-Cayeros, José Antonio Gonzá, and Fernando Rojas, "Mexico's Decentralization at a Crossroads," in T. N. Srinivasan and Jessica Wallack, eds., *Federalism and Economic Reform: International Perspectives* (New York: Cambridge University Press, 2006).

18. Bailey, "Impact of Major Groups," p. 126.

19. Johnson, *Mexican Democracy*, p. 116. See also David Samuels and Matthew Shugart, *Presidents, Parties, and Prime Ministers: How the Separation of Powers Affects Party Organization and Behavior* (New York: Cambridge University Press, 2010).

20. The use of "he" here is intentional: The constitution requires that the individual chosen as President of Mexico must be male.

21. Recent works on the Mexican presidency include Scott Mainwaring and Matthew Shugart, *Presidentialism and Democracy in Latin America* (New York: Cambridge University Press, 1997).

22. Bailey, *Governing Mexico*, p. 32. Emphasis his.

23. Padgett, *The Mexican Political System*, p. 199.

24. Again, in addition to sources cited above, an example of articles covering the presidential and congressional elections would include Alan Riding, "When the Bubble Burst for the Mexican Rulers," *New York Times*, July 9, 1988, p. 5. A good general study is by Edgar Butler and Jorge Bustamante, eds., *Succesion Presidencial: The Nineteen Eighty-Eight Mexican Presidential Election* (Boulder, CO: Westview Press, 1990).

25. See Jorge I. Dominguez and Alejandro Poire, *Toward Mexico's Democratization: Parties, Campaigns, Elections, and Public Opinion* (New York: Routledge, 1999). See also "Country Profile: Mexico," Foreign and Commonwealth Office, *http://www.fco.gov.uk/servlet/Front?pagename=OpenMarket/Xcelerate/ShowPage&c=Page&cid=1007029394365&a=KCountryProfile&aid=1019744986727*.

26. Padgett, *The Mexican Political System*, pp. 188–189. See also Gretchen Helmke and Steven Levitsky, *Informal Institutions and Democracy: Lessons from Latin America* (Baltimore, MD: Johns Hopkins University Press, 2006).

27. Frank Brandenburg, *The Making of Modern Mexico* (Englewood Cliffs, NJ: Prentice Hall, 1964), pp. 145–150. See also Laura Randall, *Changing Structure of Mexico, op. cit.*

28. These events were covered in the Special "Timeline: Campaign and Candidates Timeline," *Financial Times Online*, *http://specials.ft.com/ln/specials/spc3e6.htm*.

29. Julia Preston, "The Mexico Election: The Overview; Challenger in Mexico Wins, Governing Party Concedes," *New York Times*, July 2, 2000, section A, page 1, column 5. See also "Fox Sworn In As President," *Facts On File* Accession No: 2000195230 (December 1, 2000).

30. See S. Lynne Walker, "Fox defends record, admits much work left," *San Diego Union-Tribune*, September 2, 2001, p. A-1.

31. On the 2000 election see Jorge Domínguez and Chappell Lawson, *Mexico's Pivotal Democratic Election: Candidates, Voters, and the Presidential Campaign of 2000* (Stanford, CA: Stanford University Press, 2004). The quote on the 2006 election is from the British Broadcasting Corporation, "Mexico Court Rejects Fraud Claim," August 29, 2006, available at *http://news.bbc.co.uk/2/hi/americas/5293796.stm*. See also Jaime Suchlicki, *Mexico: From Montezuma to the Rise of the PAN* (Washington, DC: Potomac Books, 2008); and Matthew Cleary, *The Sources of Democratic Responsiveness in Mexico* (Notre Dame, IN: University of Notre Dame Press, 2010).

32. Grindle, *Bureaucrats, Politicians, and Peasants*, p. 7. See Luis Carlos Ugalde, *The Mexican Congress: Old Player, New Power* (Washington, DC: CSIS Press, 2000).

33. Hellman, *Mexico in Crisis*, p. 127.

34. Inter-Parliamentary Union, "Mexico: Last Elections," *http://www.ipu.org/english/parline/reports/2212%5fe.htm*.

35. Under the system enacted in 1963, Deputies were chosen by a combination of winner-take-all and proportional representation. "Under this system, opposition parties were granted five seats in the Chamber of Deputies if they received at least 2.5 percent of the national vote and up to fifteen additional (twenty in all) deputies, one for each additional 0.5 percent of the national vote. In 1973 the threshold for representation in the Chamber was lowered from 2.5 to 1.5 percent and the maximum number of seats available to an opposition party under this system was increased to twenty-five. This greatly improved the opposition's opportunities to win seats in the Chamber but also decreased the PRI's need to allow the opposition to win some district elections as a means of indicating the competitiveness of the political and electoral systems." Klesner, "Changing Patterns," p. 99.

36. Roderic Camp, "Potential Strengths of the Political Opposition and What It Means to the PRI," in Roderic Camp, *Mexico's Political Stability: The Next Five Years* (Boulder, CO: Westview Press, 1986), p. 187. See also Caroline Beer, *Electoral Competition and Institutional Change in Mexico* (Notre Dame, IN: University of Notre Dame Press, 2003).

37. Bailey, *Governing Mexico*, p. 62. Discussion of this can be found in some detail in Bailey, *Governing Mexico*, pp. 83–88. See also Eduardo Torres Espinosa, *Bureaucracy and Politics in Mexico* (Brookfield, VT: Ashgate, 1999).

38. Merilee Serrill Grindle, *Bureaucrats, Politicians, and Peasants in Mexico: A Case Study in Public Policy* (Berkeley, CA: University of California Press, 1977), p. 3. See Robert Wilson and Marta Santos, *Governance in the Americas: Decentralization, Democracy, and Subnational Government in Brazil, Mexico, and the USA* (Notre Dame, IN: University of Notre Dame Press, 2008).

39. Bailey, *Governing Mexico*, p. 61.

40. Todd Eisenstadt, *Courting Democracy in Mexico: Party Strategies and Electoral Institutions* (New York: Cambridge University Press, 2004).

41. See Yemile Mizrahi, *From Martyrdom to Power: The Partido Acción Nacional in Mexico* (Notre Dame, IN: University of Notre Dame Press, 2003); and Andrew Selee and Jacqueline Peschard, *Mexico's Democratic Challenges: Politics, Government, and Society* (Washington, DC: Woodrow Wilson Center Press, 2010).

42. See Evelyn P. Stevens, "'The Opposition' in Mexico: Always a Bridesmaid, Never Yet the Bride," in Judith Gentleman, ed., *Mexican Politics in Transition* (Boulder, CO: Westview Press, 1987), pp. 217–226. See also Philip McMichael, ed., *Contesting Development: Critical Struggles for Social Change* (New York: Routledge, 2010).

43. Wayne A. Cornelius, "Political Liberalization in an Authoritarian Regime: Mexico, 1976–1985," in Judith Gentleman, ed., *Mexican Politics in Transition* (Boulder, CO: Westview Press, 1987), pp. 32–36. See also Patricia Huesca-Dorantes, *The Emergence of Multiparty Competition in Mexican Politics* (Burlington, VT: Ashgate, 2003).

44. When the party was first organized in 1929 its name was the National Revolutionary Party; in 1938 it became the Mexican Revolutionary Party. In 1946 the name was changed for the third, and last, time to the PRI. A good discussion of the development of the PRI can be found in Hellman, *Mexico in Crisis*, pp. 33–57, Chapter Two: "A Ruling Party is Formed." See also John Bailey, "What Explains the Decline of the PRI and Will It Continue?" in Roderic Camp, ed., *Mexico's Political Stability: The Next Five Years* (Boulder, CO: Westview Press, 1986), p. 159.

45. Bailey, "The PRI," pp. 163, 179 n. 1. On authoritarianism in Mexico, see Kevin Middlebrook, *Political Liberalization in an Authoritarian Regime* (San Diego, CA: Center for U.S.-Mexican Studies, 1985). See also George Grayson, *Mexico: Narco-Violence and a Failed State?* (New Brunswick, NJ: Transaction Publishers, 2010).

46. See the article published by the British Broadcasting Corporation, "Mexican Political Crisis Deepens," September 17, 2006, available at *http://news.bbc.co.uk/2/hi/americas/5353074.stm.*

47. Students interested in Marxism and Communism in Mexico should consult Barry Carr, *Marxism and Communism in Twentieth-Century Mexico* (University of Nebraska Press, 1992); or Susana Nuccetelli and Ofelia Schutte, *A Companion to Latin American Philosophy* (Malden, MA: Wiley-Blackwell, 2010).

48. See Barry Carr, "The PSUM: The Unification Process on the Mexican Left, 1981–1985," in Judith Gentleman, ed., *Mexican Politics in Transition* (Boulder, CO: Westview Press, 1987), pp. 281–304.

49. Klesner, "Changing Patterns," p. 101. See also Gavin O'Toole, *The Reinvention of Mexico: National Ideology in a Neoliberal Era* (Liverpool, UK: Liverpool University Press, 2010).

50. See Dale Store, "The PAN, the Private Sector, and the Future of the Mexican Opposition," in Judith Gentleman, ed., *Mexican Politics in Transition* (Boulder, CO: Westview Press, 1987), pp. 261–273.

51. Johnson, *Mexican Democracy*, p. 145. See also Camp, "Potential Strengths," p. 186.

52. A very good discussion of this liberalization can be found in Cornelius, "Political Liberalization," pp. 15–40. In this chapter Cornelius seeks to understand "the impulse toward liberalization in a 57-year-old hegemonic party regime, in which the ruling Institutional Revolutionary Party (PRI) has never lost—or been forced to surrender—a single nationally important office" (p. 15).

53. See Jorge Domínguez and Alejandro Poiré, *Toward Mexico's Democratization: Parties, Campaigns, Elections, and Public Opinion* (New York: Routledge, 1999); or Michael Ard, *An Eternal Struggle* (2003), *op cit.*

54. Bureau of Inter-American Affairs, U.S. Department of State, "Background Notes: Mexico, March 1998," *http://www.state.gov/www/background_notes/mexico_0398_bgn.html;* for the 2006 data see Inter-Parliamentary Union, "Mexico: Last Elections," *http://www.ipu.org/english/parline/reports/2212%5fe.htm.* On the 2009 election data, see Newsweek, "Mexico's Blast from the Past," *http://www.newsweek.com/2009/07/01/mexico-s-blast-from-the-past.html* (accessed May 2011).

55. Joseph Klesner, "Changing Patterns of Electoral Participation and Official Party Support in Mexico," in Judith Gentleman, ed., *Mexican Politics in Transition* (Boulder, CO: Westview Press, 1987), pp. 95, 98.

56. A good discussion of this problem can be found in Laura Randall, *Changing Structure of Mexico: Political, Social, and Economic Prospects* (Armonk, NY: M.E. Sharpe, 2006).

57. See James B. Pick, *Mexico Megacity* (Boulder, CO: Westview, 2000).

58. See *Globalis*, a database showing urban concentrations of national populations. *Globalis* uses data from the United Nations Population Division Estimates. See *http://globalis.gvu.unu.edu/indicator_detail.cfm?IndicatorID=30&Country=MX* (accessed May 2011).

59. Robert Long, "Urban Migration: The Dilemma of Mexico City," in Robert E. Long, ed., *Mexico* (New York: H. W. Wilson, 1986), p. 98. See also Daniel Hernandez, *Down and Delirious in Mexico City: The Aztec Metropolis in the Twenty-First Century* (New York: Scribner, 2011).

60. United States Department of State, "Consular Information Sheet: Mexico," *http://www.travel.state.gov/mexico.html*. On the 2009 data, see the World Bank, *World Development Report*, online format, "Population in the Largest City," *http://data.worldbank.org/indicator/EN.URB.LCTY.UR.ZS* (accessed May 2011).

61. Otto Friedrich, "A Proud Capital's Distress," in Robert E. Long, ed., *Mexico* (New York: H. W. Wilson, 1986), 100.

62. Tony Payan, *The Three U.S.-Mexico Border Wars: Drugs, Immigration, and Homeland Security* (Westport, CT: Praeger, 2006). By one estimate in 1980 more than 3 million Mexicans were in the United States illegally. Johnson, *Mexican Democracy*, 20.

63. Facts On File, "Mexico: President-elect Meets With U.S. Leaders," Accession No: 2000185020, Story Date: August 24, 2000. See Lionello F. Punzo and Martin Anyul, *Mexico Beyond NAFTA* (London, UK: Routledge, 2001); or J. Ernesto Lopez Cordova, *NAFTA and the Mexican Economy, UK: Analytical Issues and Lessons for the FTAA* (Washington, DC: Inter-American Development Bank, 2001).

64. Casteñada, "Mexico at the Brink," p. 287. See Francesco Duina, *The Social Construction of Free Trade: The European Union, NAFTA, and MERCOSUR* (Princeton, NJ: Princeton University Press, 2006).

65. World Bank, *World Development Report* 1993, p. 279.

66. See Andres Oppenheimer, *Bordering on Chaos: Guerrillas, Stockbrokers, Politicians, and Mexico's Road to Prosperity* (Boston, MA: Little, Brown, 1996).

67. See Facts on File, "Mexico: Early Repayment Set for U.S. Loan," Accession No: 1996064244, Story date June 18, 1996.

68. David Barkin, "Mexico's Albatross: The U.S. Economy," in Nora Hamilton and Timothy F. Harding, eds., *Modern Mexico: State, Economy, and Social Conflict* (Beverly Hills, CA: SAGE 1986), p. 107.

69. World Bank, *World Development Report 2011*, online format, found online at *http://data.worldbank.org/topic/poverty* (accessed May 2011).

70. This problem is discussed in Jaime E. Rodriguez, ed., *The Revolutionary Process in Mexico* (Berkeley, CA: University of California Press, 1990). See also Santiago Levy, *Good Intentions, Bad Outcomes: Social Policy, Informality, and Economic Growth in Mexico* (Washington, DC: Brookings Institution Press, 2008).

The Kenyan Political System

Presidents often play important roles in events that have symbolic importance. Here Kenya's
President Mwai Kibaki holds Kenya's new constitution after its formal unveiling in Nairobi, in 2010.

TONY KARUMBA/AFP/Getty Images/Newscom

Kenya has a history of being one of East Africa's most stable political units, even if it has had challenges with issues of corruption and economic development. Kenya has functioned as East Africa's financial and communications center, and while it has to deal with many of the same challenges as other developing nations in Africa, it has often been cited as the "major" political system of the region. As one author has noted,

> Until the 1980s Kenya was considered one of the continent's success stories, exemplifying stability, free-enterprise, and relatively benign leadership; a rare example of a state with a vibrant legislature, free press, an independent judiciary, and institutionalized grass-roots political life—despite a cultural heterogeneity and socio-economic problems that had brought instability elsewhere in Africa.[1]

The elections that took place in Kenya in December of 2007, however, led to violence, murder of hundreds, and a level of what was commonly interpreted as ethnic-based conflict that many found frightening. If this could happen in the most stable system in East Africa, what lessons were to be learned

KENYA

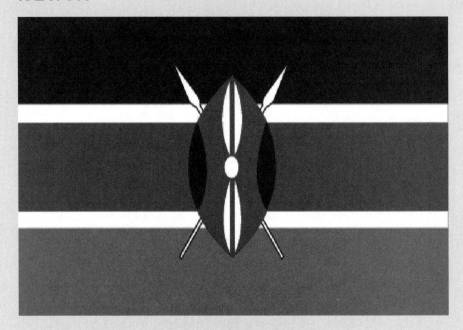

Total Area (rank)	580,367 sq km (48)
Population (rank)	41,070,934 (33)
Population Growth Rate (rank)	2.46% (29)
Urban Population	22%
Life Expectancy at Birth (total population) (rank)	59.48% (189)
Literacy	85.1%
Government Type	Republic
Legal System	Mixed: English common law, Islamic law, customary law
Head of Government	President Mwai Kibaki
Chief of State	President Mwai Kibaki and Prime Minister Raila Odinga
Gross Domestic Product (GDP)	$32.16 billion
GDP Per Capita (rank)	$1,600 (199)
GDP Real Growth Rate (rank)	5% (73)
Unemployment Rate (rank)	40% (185)

KENYA

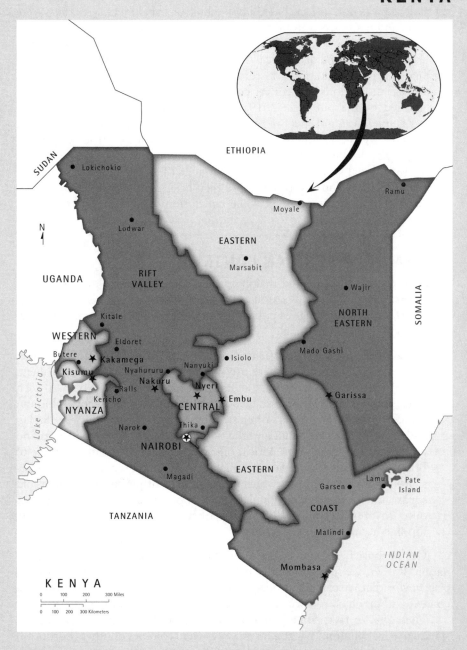

for other systems that were less stable and less secure? While some argued that the violence was not, in fact, based upon ethnic or tribal identity,[2] others were less sure, and many were afraid for the future of the nation.

In this chapter we will look at Kenya's status today, and how it came to be where it is in terms of political and social development. Kenya's political heritage and its constitutional history will be briefly examined to show why its political institutions are as they currently are. Because a new constitution was ratified by the public in 2010, much of what we will describe in this chapter is *intention*, not fact, and we will describe those plans, as well. Thus, this chapter will be an interesting (we hope!) combination of looking *back*, at history, and looking *forward*, to the future, to what will happen when the new constitutional system comes into effect in 2012. We will examine Kenya's political structures and institutions, and then briefly observe political participation in recent events to draw some conclusions about the nature of the Kenyan political culture.

KENYA IN AN AFRICAN CONTEXT

Africa is a vast territory, and making general observations about politics in such a varied region involves serious risks. With fifty-four independent states,[3] Africa has a staggering range of political institutions, political histories, political cultures, and political customs.

> To lump these states together and talk about "African politics" is somewhat misleading because there are important differences between them. There is, for example, a wide cultural gap between the North African states and the Black African states south of the Sahara. The geographic and demographic differences are often striking, as witnessed by the huge Sudan and Zaire on the one hand, and the tiny Rwanda, Burundi and Swaziland on the other; within West Africa, oil-rich Nigeria—four times the size of Britain and with a population in 1999 of some 124 million—contrasts sharply with the Gambia, which, with an area of just over ten thousand square kilometers and a population of approximately 1.3 million, was once (in pre-independence days) described as "an eel wriggling its way through a slab of French territory."[4]

Our purpose here is not to attempt a comprehensive "continental" examination. Rather, we seek to identify just a few of the major themes or patterns of behavior that we can see as being significant in Africa, which will provide a context within which to appreciate political developments in Kenya.

There *are*, in fact, some patterns that we can identify that *most* African states have in common.[5] Most African states were colonies of other (European) powers, and achieved independence from those colonial powers after 1960. Most states are still working to develop their own identities as nation-states. Most states are very poor, very rural, have significant public health problems (it has been estimated that over 14 percent of the adults of Zimbabwe have AIDS—the fifth-worst in the world), and are very vulnerable to the world economy. Most states have a very heterogeneous political culture, as a result of the number and variety of traditional tribal units within their borders.[6]

Contrary to what many think, elections and democratic politics *do* have a significant history in the African setting. "Elections have long been a conspicuous element of the political landscape of independent Africa ... Africans were elected to legislative councils in the 1920's in Ghana, Kenya, Nigeria, Sierra Leone, and Zambia."[7] In recent times, however, the "conventional wisdom" about the success and significance of elections in Africa has become more and more negative and pessimistic.

> Elections in much of contemporary Africa were widely regarded as irrelevant or a sham. There was growing evidence of elections which did not reflect democratic values; that those responsible followed neither the electoral procedures set out in the institutions bequeathed at independence nor other requirements of free and fair competition. Some concluded that the misuse and abuse of electoral institutions demonstrated that the process was ill-suited to Africa.[8]

One recent study of West African politics was subtitled "Seeking Unity in Diversity," [9] and this, in brief, tells the trials of most African nations. As noted above, with the exception of Liberia, *all of* the states of West Africa, and *most* of the states of the rest of Africa, were the creation of colonial powers that divided the continent up during the late nineteenth century.

The various **colonial powers** that ruled Africa into the twentieth century, including Italy, France, Germany, Portugal, and the United Kingdom, were concerned about the development of these nations as suppliers of goods and services; national integration was not a high priority on their political agendas. Thus, railroads and highways were designed to run from the hinterlands of the nations to the coast, so that raw materials could be shipped to the colonial power, but transportation *within* the African state, from one interior location to another interior location, might have remained very difficult.

In addition to a lack of development of those infrastructures that could have promoted a sense of national integration, the borders of the African states were, themselves, entirely artificial creations. The *primary* units of loyalty in Africa, tribal units, have never corresponded to what we today look upon as "national borders." British colonial officers may have decided to draw a national border between what today is Kenya and what today is Uganda, but as far as the people living in those regions were concerned, some of the soon-to-be-Kenyans had more in common with soon-to-be-Ugandans than they did with other soon-to-be-Kenyans. This made it very difficult to develop any sense of what it meant to be a "Kenyan" for much of the population.

Recent years have seen prolonged and bloody civil wars in many nations in Africa, most recently resulting in the independence of the new nation of South Sudan in July of 2011.[10] Where actual warfare hasn't broken out, we have seen essentially authoritarian governments that have been clear in their intention to remain in power, whatever the cost. The cost of these wars, of course, in addition to the thousands and thousands of lives that have been lost (the estimate for South Sudan was two million killed), has been a lack of economic and political development. It has been hard enough for developing nations to make progress in their economic development, even when they have been able to focus all of their resources and efforts on the process of development itself. When their resources and efforts have been diverted to fighting to remain in power, or to drive someone else out of power, the nations have lost momentum in the development process, and some are almost hopelessly behind in the quest for political stability and economic progress.

THE KENYAN POLITICAL HERITAGE

Britain established its presence in East Africa in the middle of the nineteenth century, and the **British East African Protectorate** dates to 1895. It is worth noting that initially, Britain was more interested in Uganda and Zanzibar than Kenya, because of their relation to the Nile River.

> To ensure its claims on Uganda and to ease communication with this interior region, as well as making certain any lingering elements of the slave trade were ended, Britain built the Uganda Railway, from the coastal city of Mombasa to Lake Victoria. Completed in 1901, it included, about halfway along, a railhead of workshops and offices that started as little more than a tented camp.... From these foundations the camp grew over the next three decades to become the city of Nairobi.[11]

In what was fairly typical British colonial practice, a small white minority became economically dominant in East Africa, farming and growing tea and coffee, and the native Kikuyu and other ethnic groups of the region (primarily the **Maasai** and **Kalenjin**) lost much of their land and standing.

Kenya officially became a British colony in 1920, but from then until independence in the early 1960s it was still run by and for British **expatriates**, British citizens who were residents of Kenya at the time.[12] Africans were not permitted to vote or run for office, and it wasn't until 1944 that even a few appointed (not elected) native representatives were allowed to sit in the legislature. Between 1951 and 1959, primarily 1951 to 1954, Kenya endured a continuing state of crisis as a result of the Mau Mau uprising against British colonialism.

The **Mau Mau** were a secret society, made up of ethnic **Kikuyu** who were unhappy with Kenya's colonial status, and were especially unhappy with the practice of white foreigners having control of much of Kenya's best land. (Indeed, **Jomo Kenyatta**, president of the Kenyan African National Union, was arrested in 1952 for Mau Mau activity, and sentenced to seven years hard labor for his activity.) Membership in the Mau Mau required the individual to take an oath to drive the white settlers out of Africa.[13] During the period of violence, over 70,000 suspected Mau Mau were arrested by the British, while over 13,000 were killed. Kenyatta was released from prison at age 71, in 1961, and was elected Kenya's first prime minister in 1963. It was not until 2003 that the Mau Mau movement was legalized in Kenya.[14]

BOX 16.1

Crises of Political Development

In 1963, a study of political modernization and political development started at the Center for Advanced Study in the Behavioral Studies at Palo Alto, California.[*] The study was based on the premise that political development involves a number of "crises," and *all* nations, modern or not, go through these crises.[†] Each of these "crises" will be briefly described here.

The Crisis of Identity

How do individuals describe themselves politically? One of the major hurdles faced by new nations is to help citizens develop a national identity. Failure to do so can result in national stress, and possibly civil war: The situation in Lebanon in which citizens identified themselves not so much "Lebanese" as Christians, Muslims, or Palestinians, led to a civil war there. This is not restricted to new nations: Civil war and genocide in what was Yugoslavia is an illustration of the quest by ethnic groups to develop their own national identities;[‡] similarly, many French-Canadians today identify themselves as "Québécois," not Canadians, and this continues to place stress on the Canadian political system.

The Crisis of Legitimacy

The concept of "legitimacy" suggests a sense on the part of the public that the government in power has a right to exist, or is acting "appropriately." People may disagree with specific governmental decisions without denying the legitimacy of the regime. When governments lose their legitimacy, they have increased difficulty in staying in power and may do so usually only with the coercive support of the military.

It is often difficult to define precisely when a loss of legitimacy becomes "critical." There will always be some people in any regime who do not feel that the regime is acting legitimately. Established regimes can tolerate some challenge; newer regimes can tolerate less, since they have less past legitimacy upon which to draw. At some point a loss of legitimacy may become *critical* and the system may suffer irreparable harm.

The Crisis of Penetration

Do the policy decisions of the government "trickle down" to all levels of society? Are there areas of the nation in which the laws and policy decisions of the regime simply do not apply? To the extent that a region may exist in which the laws of the regime are ignored, or to the extent that certain specific laws or administrative guidelines from the government are ignored throughout the nation, we can speak about problems of penetration. The crisis of penetration refers to the government's ability to follow through on, and to enforce, its

(*continued*)

(*continued*)

decisions. Governments that are not able to do this, that are not taken seriously by their publics, are less stable than others.

The Crisis of Participation

A system may suffer stress in both quantitative and qualitative dimensions of participation. Too little participation (e.g., an election in which only 15% of the population participated) may result in a lack of legitimacy; too much participation—perhaps too many demands made—may put too great a burden on the structures of the regime that are designed to respond to such communications. In addition, relatively few demands that are in themselves extreme may put stress on the system. Examples of a question that may create a dimension of crisis in a political regime, would be: (a) a racial majority demanding political opportunity in a regime that has been racially discriminatory, such as existed for many years in Rhodesia (now Zimbabwe); (b) a mass demonstration bringing hundreds of thousands of protesters together to criticize a regime, such as the Arab Spring demonstrations across the Middle East in 2011.

The Crisis of Distribution

One of the most visible problems of developing nations today is a *material* one: Food, medical supplies, housing, water, electricity, and so forth are either not being equitably distributed in a society, or, although equitably distributed, are not sufficient. New nations have an incredible set of demands made upon them, and among the most visible of these demands are those related to distributive goods. Long food lines in Ethiopia, which led to food riots, led to the eventual overthrow of Emperor Haile Selassie in 1974. A society in which a group feels that it is not receiving its "fair share" of the material benefits of government is a society ready for revolution.

These crises of political development show concerns confronting many developing nations today, not to mention established democracies, as well. These crises are exacerbated in the developing world by more acute problems, such as low levels of literacy, poor health care, high infant mortality, and an inability to control populations. As these challenges increase, new nations will experience great instability and turmoil.

---

* Among the many volumes published in the series (Princeton, NJ: Princeton University Press), were the following: Lucian Pye, ed., *Communications and Political Development* (1963); Joseph LaPalombara, ed., *Bureaucracy and Political Development* (1963); Robert E. Ward and Dankwart Rustow, eds., *Political Modernization in Japan and Turkey* (1964); James S. Coleman, ed., *Education and Political Development* (1965); Lucian Pye and Sidney Verba, eds., *Political Culture and Political Development* (1965); Joseph LaPalombara and Myron Weiner, eds., *Political Parties and Political Development* (1966); Leonard Binder et al., *Crises and Sequences in Political Development* (1971); and Charles Tilly, ed., *The Formation of National States in Western Europe* (1975).
† See especially Leonard Binder et al., *Crises and Sequences in Political Development.*
‡ See, for example, Sabrina Ramet, *The Three Yugoslavias: State-Building and Legitimation, 1918–2004* (Bloomington, IN: Indiana University Press, 2006).

When Kenya became independent in 1963, power was highly centralized, and politics was dominated by one party: the **Kenyan African National Union (KANU)**,[15] run by President Kenyatta. In 1978, when Kenyatta died, his vice president **Daniel arap Moi** became president. Moi was shortly thereafter elected president of KANU, and was its nominee for president at the next election. He was elected at that time, and in every succeeding presidential election until he finally stepped down from power in the election of 2002 when the current incumbent **Mwai Kibaki** was first elected president.[16]

Many argue that the dreams of Kenya's colonial leaders have not yet been achieved. There is no doubt about Kenya's independence; "what is debatable is whether the long-term goals of the nationalists, which included complete Africanization of the country's politics, economy and culture, have been realized."[17] The challenge is, as one student of Kenyan politics has observed, the process of "reconciling unity with self-determination."[18] That is, finding a balance between national unity on one hand and individual rights and liberties on the other.

THE KENYAN CONSTITUTIONAL SYSTEM

Kenya has had several different constitutions since its independence in 1963.[19] Like many/most members of the British Commonwealth—today referred to as The **Commonwealth**, not the *British* Commonwealth—Kenya's original independence constitution was negotiated with the colonial power over a several-year period of time at Lancaster House in London. Kenya's transition to independence under the British took place over a period of years, including several years of violence between the colonial government and the Mau Mau rebels who were seeking power. Its first constitution in 1963 was very much a British-style, "Westminster," constitution. Kenya had a parliamentary system of government with a head of state called the Queen, who was the same person as the Queen of England. When the Queen was not in Kenya—which was almost all of the time—the monarchy would be represented by a governor-general. The government had a two-chambered legislature, the National Assembly, with one chamber elected (The 117-member House of Representatives) and one appointed (the 41-member Senate, representing regional interests), and 7 regions, each with its own assembly (although Kenya remained unitary, not federal). The leader of the elected chamber of the legislature was to be the prime minister.

A year after independence, in 1964, the Kenyan constitution was changed to make Kenya a **republic** with a **presidential system**, cutting its ties to the British monarchy (although it remained a member of the Commonwealth).[20] The upper house was abolished, making the National Assembly a unicameral body. And, the old system of provinces was replaced by a new structure of regional government (although the regional governments were purely *administrative*, and Kenya never actually became *federal* in nature).

The 1964-model constitution was very centralized in terms of political power. It was typical in Kenya that most political institutions operated "at the pleasure" of the president, including parliament, courts, electoral commissions, and so on. This practice of presidential dominance was, some observers have noted, "a holdover from the colonial period," and simply became standard operating procedure in Kenyan politics.[21]

Kenya had a major constitutional change in 1982 when, following the wishes of President Moi,[22] it officially became a one-party state, and the Kenyan African National Union (KANU) legally took on constitutional status as a virtual branch of the government. Anyone wanting to run for office had to do so under the KANU banner, and within the KANU party organization. KANU's role in politics was solidified in the elections of 1983 and 1988 when the one-party nature of Kenyan politics was further entrenched, and the *party* came to be increasingly identified with the *state*.

Jennifer Widner has argued[23] that KANU was transformed from a loose-knit group of politicians into a "party-state" dominated by President Moi. Her thesis is that an increased importance of ethnicity moved President Moi to move to a single-party system, to jail opponents, and to put a priority on national solidarity rather than democracy. This lasted for several years, but ultimately domestic support for multipartyism developed, and that, combined with pressure from foreign aid donors in the West, pressed for a change back to a multiparty state format.

In 1991 a new constitutional structure was established with some serious amendments made to the 1982 constitution. Most important among the changes was that the one-party system of elections and government was repealed, and a multiparty system was established. Many different political parties participated in the elections of 1992, and the elections were essentially peaceful. Kenya was thereafter a multiparty state.

More recently, the demands of many increased that there be major constitutional change involving a diminution of presidential power. Many of the parties involved in the conversation suggested that political power had become *too* centralized in the hands of the president over the years, and that power "should be shifted from the executive branch to strengthen the judiciary and parliament."[24] The problem was that experts disagreed on how to actually make that shift happen, and the president of Kenya was certainly not in favor of a diminution of his power.

Kenya went through a period of serious constitutional self-evaluation and reflection between 2000 and 2004, although no significant changes were actually made to the constitution.[25] Following the 1997 elections, Parliament passed the Constitution of Kenya Review Act and called for a process of constitutional review, asking that comprehensive constitutional reforms be undertaken. Over the next five or so years, there were many prolonged conversations about changes that were needed in Kenyan society and politics, and the Constitution of Kenya Review Commission (CKRC) was established to prepare the way for a new constitution.[26] A draft of a new constitutional structure was completed in 2002, but in a referendum in 2005 that draft constitution was rejected by a majority of the voters, primarily because some ethnic groups felt that advantages were being given to other ethnic groups. Although constitutional change was stopped temporarily, the process through the first five years of the decade did show that (a) change was needed, and (b) there was substantial support for the idea of bringing about change, even if agreement had not been reached on exactly what that change should be.

Because the 2005 draft constitutional change was rejected, Kenya continued to be governed by the 1963 constitution, as amended in 1982. Following the 2007 elections, as we will further describe later, regional and ethnic tensions led to a political crisis for the nation when substantial political violence and killing across the nation threatened national unity in a way that had not happened since independence. This led to a temporary "power sharing" arrangement with a temporary appointment of a new prime minister to work with the president, and also to a national Committee of Experts being appointed to review issues of constitutional reform, and initially in November of 2009 with later drafts following, a new draft constitution was presented to the public.[27]

The 2009 draft constitution continued Kenya's presidential model of government, but established more opportunities to require the legislative branch to approve actions of the president; presidential power was slightly reduced in the new plan.[28] At the time of this writing (2011), the political system is still in the process of evolution and has yet to arrive at a permanent balance of power between the president and other political actors.

The new constitutional proposal also suggested bringing back a second house of the legislature, with its focus being *regions*. The proposal suggested that each county should elect one senator, and that the total number of elected and appointed senators would reach 60. The new plan further suggested that there should be some **devolution** of governmental power with some of the national legislative and administrative power devolving to county governmental structures, although the plan was very careful to make a distinction between this structure of *devolution* on one hand and a *federal* system on the other, which it was explicitly *not* advancing. (In a federal system the intermediate level of power has some *sovereign power* in some specific area(s), power that cannot be limited or taken away by the central government.)

This system specifically notes that the nation is to remain *unitary*, not *federal*, but that there will be some areas of authority that will be administered by the counties, specified in the Fourth Schedule of the constitution, and the central government is barred from interfering with those powers, unless Parliament deems such action necessary. The counties will oversee policy in the areas of agriculture, fisheries, county health, cultural activities, public entertainment, county transport, trade development, some education facilities, and implementation of specific national government policies on natural resources and environmental conservation.[29]

As we will note again below, on August 4, 2010, almost 70 percent of the Kenyan voters voted in favor of the new constitution,[30] perhaps partially in response to the violence following the December 2007 presidential election. It is certainly worth noting that *both* President Mwai Kibaki and Prime Minister **Raila Odinga** campaigned *in favor* of a new constitution (although it should be noted that President Kibaki is not eligible to run for re-election again, so a new constitution that would limit the president's power will not affect him).

The new constitution is still being constructed, as many of its key sections have yet to be enacted (such as the second chamber of the legislature). The new constitution includes provisions for multiparty elections, a strong system of entrenched freedoms and human rights, including freedom of expression, freedom of conscience and belief, equal opportunities for both genders, freedom of the media, and so on, a bicameral national legislature, a directly elected president with a cabinet that must be approved by the legislature, a developed system of courts, including a system of Islamic courts, and a system of regional government with some powers devolved from the center of politics.[31]

The new constitution is seen as a major improvement over its predecessor in a number of significant ways, highlighted in Table 16.1. Although the document was approved by an overwhelming majority of the public, and was supported by the two major contenders for the presidency in the 2007 election, it

---

TABLE 16.1

Constitutional Reforms of August 2010

- Executive authority resides with a president rather than being shared between the president and the prime minister, as was the case following the 2007 presidential election and the "grand compromise" that was achieved to resolve the conflict that followed that election.

- Although authority resides with the president, much of the president's power and patronage ability is limited, and requires confirmation by the National Assembly. The president's power to suspend or dissolve the National Assembly has been removed, as well.

- The power of parliament in relation to the president has been significantly increased. Included in its powers the parliament will now be able to impeach the president.

- The National Assembly will have at least forty-seven elected women, at least one from each county. The newly-elected Senate will have at least eighteen women members, 27 percent of the total membership.

- The new constitution created forty-seven elected county governments, and guarantees that funding for these governments will be provided by the national government. This guarantees some level of equality among Kenya's forty-two ethnic groups by encouraging the devolution of power from the center to the regions and guaranteeing some access to financial resources.

- The new constitution includes a list of political, economic, and social rights, with specific rights for women, marginalized groups, and people with disabilities.

Source: Joel D. Barkan and Makau Mutua, "Turning the Corner in Kenya," *Foreign Affairs* (August 10, 2010), http://www.foreignaffairs.com/articles/66510/joel-d-barkan-and-makau-mutua/turning-the-corner-in-kenya?page=show (accessed June 2011).

was not without opposition, which included some presidential aspirants who will likely run for office in 2012 and who were unhappy that it was endorsed by Odinga (who also likely will run for office in 2012; President Kibaki is not eligible to run for office again since he is currently in his second term), and also many Christian clergy who felt that the ban on abortions was not strong enough and who were also unhappy about the constitutional retention of the existence of Muslim Kadhis courts.[32]

REGIONALISM AND UNITARY GOVERNMENT IN KENYA

As has been noted, Kenya does not have a federal government, but instead has a unitary government with some regional characteristics based in counties, that periodically lead some Kenyans to speculate about federalism. There is even a word in Swahili—"majimbo"—for a federal-like power-sharing structure that is advocated by some, most notably current Prime Minister Raila Odinga. **Majimboism** has been in use in political vocabulary since the Lancaster House (London) Constitutional Conference in 1962, in fact. According to one source,

> Majimboism envisaged a system of government where executive, legislative and financial powers were shared between central and regional governments. The bulk of the power, however, still remained with the central government. The regional boundaries were loosely based on ethnic boundaries carved up by the British.
>
> The Majimbo issue had split the African leadership down the middle in the run-up to independence in 1963. To a large extent the system was predicated on the fear by the leaders of "smaller" ethnic groups that their communities would be dominated by the "larger" groups on national matters—economical or political.[33]

In the run up to independence in the early 1960s, much discussion was focused on the debate over centralized and decentralized power. As we noted earlier, one of the most common reasons for federal government is a large nation in which regional groups want to retain some control over issues that are regionally important, issues that they do not want determined by a single national government for all regional groups in the same way. This tendency is exacerbated in political settings in which *ethnic* identities are *regionally* concentrated. This was clearly the case in Kenya in its early years.

In the constitution being planned in 1962 and early 1963, "there were to be 6 Jimbos (regions) constituted along ethnic lines. Tribes with close similarities were put under one region; for instance, Coast and North Eastern provinces were put under one state as the two are predominantly Muslim while Kikuyus, Embu, Meru were put in Central State." [34]

Following the election of Jomo Kenyatta in 1963 when Kenya attained self-governing status, the federalism/majimboism debate was ended, and a unitary and much more centralized approach to power was adopted. Kenyatta saw majimboism as a threat to national unity, and wanted a unitary government structure.

In September of 1982, President Moi led the government to adopt a strategy that started to make the regional districts the focal point of planning and implementation of development initiatives. One of the objectives of the new regional focus was to make administration more efficient, but another key goal was political: Moi felt that by decentralizing administrative action he could work around the Kikuyu-dominated state that he had inherited from Kenyatta. This strategy gave him the opportunity to work with other regions of the nation that were dominated by other ethnic groups (including the Kalenjin, his ethnic group).[35]

The 2010 constitution includes a full chapter that focuses on the devolution of power to the counties, Chapter Eleven: "Devolved Government." In the constitution the argument is presented that "the objects of the devolution of government are" as follow:

(a) to promote democratic and accountable exercise of power;
(b) to foster national unity by recognising diversity;
(c) to give powers of self-governance to the people and enhance the participation of the people in the exercise of the powers of the State and in making decisions affecting them;
(d) to recognise the right of communities to manage their own affairs and to further their development;
(e) to protect and promote the interests and rights of minorities and marginalised communities;
(f) to promote social and economic development and the provision of proximate, easily accessible services throughout Kenya;
(g) to ensure equitable sharing of national and local resources throughout Kenya;
(h) to facilitate the decentralisation of State organs, their functions and services, from the capital of Kenya; and
(i) to enhance checks and balances and the separation of powers.[36]

Kenya today continues to be a unitary state, with sovereignty residing at the national capital, Nairobi. The nation is divided into administrative subdivisions, however, including 140 districts, joined to form 7 rural provinces. The Nairobi area has special status. Under the new constitution that was approved in a referendum on August 4, 2010, and is still in the process of being implemented, the primary administrative subdivisions will be forty-seven counties, each with an elected governor. These counties will be the basis of representation in the second chamber of the national legislature—also not yet in existence, but planned. It can be argued that once the second chamber actually comes into existence, Kenya will be ready to become even more federal than it is at the present time. Indeed, some other East African nations have wondered whether "Kenyan federalism" could work in their government as well as it does in Kenya![37]

ETHNIC AND TRIBAL TENSIONS IN KENYA

Kenya, as is the case for many nations in Africa, is an example of a political system whose *national* borders do not mirror traditional *tribal* and *ethnic* borders. That is, when the western colonial powers were drawing national boundaries, they were more concerned about geopolitical issues involving their neighbors than they were in drawing borders that made sense in terms of tribal and ethnic population distributions. Many of Kenya's tribal groups spread *across* Kenya's border, going into Ethiopia, Somalia, Tanzania, Sudan, or Uganda, for instance.

The **multiethnic makeup** of Kenya has periodically appeared to be significant when conflicts arise and ethnic groups start to feel vulnerable or are worried that "their" members are not getting the same resources as members of other ethnic groups. There are today nearly forty different ethnic groups in Kenya, made up of three distinct linguistic families, the Bantu (including the Luhya, Kikuyu, Kamba, and Mijikenda groups), the Nilotic (the Luo, the Kalenjin, and the Masai groups), and the Cushitic (the Oromo and the Somali groups). The major ethnic groups are indicated in Table 16.2.

Many observers have suggested that the violence that followed the 2007 presidential election, was based upon ethnic group loyalty. Other have suggested that this isn't true.

> Contrary to prevailing attitudes, Kenyans have not traditionally identified themselves by ethnic group and studies have shown they do not have significant feelings of ethnic injustice. In a 2003 Afrobarometer survey, 70 percent said they would choose to be Kenyan if faced with a choice between a national identity and their ethnic group (28 percent refused to identify themselves as anything but Kenyan). Analysts say much of the unrest that erupted after the December 2007 polls was just the latest display of politically organized violence. Political coalitions on both sides hired thugs to do their bidding, and ordinary Kenyans were caught in the cross fire, they say.[38]

▶ TABLE 16.2

Kenya's Major Ethnic Groups

Kikuyu	22 percent
Luhya	14 percent
Luo	13 percent
Kalenjin	12 percent
Kamba	11 percent
Kisii	6 percent
Meru	6 percent
Others	15 percent

Source: Library of Congress, *Country Profile: Kenya, June 2007,* http://lcweb2.loc.gov/frd/cs/profiles/Kenya .pdf (accessed July 2011).

Kenya's prime minister, Raila Odinga, has indicated that in his view the normal day-to-day operation of politics in Kenya is *not* primarily based upon ethnic identity. His argument has been that it has been *regionalism* that is the real source of tension, since some regions have access to many resources while other regions do not. The fact that regions are associated with ethnic groups—many of Kenya's forty-two tribal groups are concentrated in one region of the nation rather than spread out across the nation—may make it *seem* that ethnic identity is the source of conflict, but it is really regionalism that is the source of conflict, he says.[39]

Although it may be possible to suggest that much of Kenya's ethnic violence can be attributed to short-term political explanation, the fact is that today there are many significant economic inequalities between some ethnic groups, and long-standing bitter disputes over land, particularly in the Rift Valley.[40] These regional variations result in some ethnic groups having many more resources than other ethnic groups, as a result of where they are. This has, understandably, exacerbated interethnic group tensions.

EXECUTIVE STRUCTURES

As we noted earlier, ever since Kenya was granted independence in the early 1960s the Kenyan political system has been characterized by having a strong—we should say "dominant"—president. The reader will recall that originally Kenya constitutionally followed the British model, with a prime minister as the chief executive and the Queen serving as the monarch of Kenya (and a governor-general serving in the Queen's place when she wasn't in Kenya). Shortly after independence the British-model constitution was changed to a republican-style constitution with an elected president and no separate head of state, moving from a parliamentary system of government to a presidential system.

Ever since 1964, Kenyan politics has been steered by the president. Jomo Kenyatta served as president from 1964 through 1978. Kenyatta was a remarkable national leader; he had already served time in prison for his Mau Mau sympathies and been released at age seventy *before* he became president! When he died at age 86 in 1978 he was succeeded by Daniel arap Moi, who had been the vice president of Kenya. Kenyatta had been criticized by many in his later years in office as being autocratic; Moi started to receive that same evaluation shortly after taking office.[41]

We noted earlier that shortly after Moi took office, in 1982, the constitution of Kenya was amended to make Kenya a one-party state, helping to cement Moi's power both as president of KANU and as president of Kenya. Moi decreased the size of the military service in Kenya for a period of time and closed the universities to avoid structured opposition to his rule, and through the 1980s he continued to centralize power, despite the fact that he was receiving increased criticism from western nations who were becoming more and more critical of Moi, of corruption, and of Moi's pattern of rigid governance.

In 1991 Moi finally permitted an amendment to the constitution so that multiparty elections could take place again, and in 1992 in the first multiparty elections in twenty-six years, the "ethnically fractured opposition failed to dislodge Moi and KANU from power."[42] Moi stayed in power through the next five years, and in the 1997 elections he again won the presidency, despite charges of electoral fraud.

The 1997 election was Moi's final election, however, because the constitution prohibited him from running again in December of 2002. Despite the fact that Moi managed to get Uhuru Kenyatta, son of Kenya's first leader, chosen to be KANU's candidate for president, Moi wasn't successful in the influencing the election. Mwai Kibaki, who ran against Moi in 1992 and 1997 and once was his vice president, won the majority of votes in 2002. Kibaki was the candidate of the largest opposition group, the National Rainbow Coalition (NARC). Not only did Kibaki win, but the National Rainbow Coalition won a parliamentary majority in the National Assembly. "The election, although not free of vote-rigging, was the most credible since independence."[43]

Starting shortly after the 2002 election, as we noted earlier, there was popular support for a movement to modify—or replace—the constitution, on the grounds that the president had become too powerful and that a number of changes (which we discussed earlier) were needed in the constitutional structure of Kenya, including a bicameral legislature, and devolution of some powers to regional levels. In 2005 the National Rainbow Coalition split over the issue of constitutional reform, and a new opposition party was created, the Orange Democratic Movement (named after the oranges that had been the symbol of opposition to the proposed new constitution).

In the election of December 27, 2007, President Mwai Kibaki was re-elected with 46 percent of the vote. The leader of the Orange coalition Raila Odinga received 44 percent, and Kalonzo Musyoka, Kibaki's vice president, received 9 percent. As we noted earlier, the December 2007 election was dismissed by many as highly corrupt and rigged, and massive violence followed the election. A consequence of the disputed election—in which President Kibaki stayed in power—was the ultimate interim "power sharing" agreement in February of 2008 between President Kibaki and the Leader of the Opposition Raila Odinga to create a prime minister position that would be held by the leader of the opposition, Raila Odinga, and the eventual (2010/2011) approval of a new constitution.[44] (See Table 16.3 for details of the power-sharing arrangement.)

In the current **power-sharing system**, Kenya has a president who serves as head of state; the president *also* serves as head of government. Although there is a prime minister (Raila Odinga), the current constitution says the president remains both chief of state *and* head of government; the prime minister is "charged with coordinating government business." Under the power-sharing agreement of 2008 the president appoints cabinet members, with the agreement of the prime minister.

In presidential elections the president is elected by popular vote to a five-year term of office, and is eligible to hold a second term, but no more. (Thus, President Kibaki is not eligible to run for re-election again in 2012, since he

▶ **TABLE 16.3**

The February, 2008 Power-Sharing Agreement

- There will be a prime minister of the government of Kenya, with authority to coordinate and supervise the execution of the functions and affairs of the Government of Kenya.
- The prime minister will be an elected member of the National Assembly and the parliamentary leader of the largest party in the National Assembly, or of a coalition, if the largest party does not command a majority.
- Each member of the coalition shall nominate one person from the National Assembly to be appointed a deputy prime minister.
- The cabinet will consist of the president, the vice president, the prime minister, the two deputy prime ministers and the other ministers. The removal of any minister of the coalition will be subject to consultation and concurrence in writing by the leaders.
- The prime minister and deputy prime ministers can only be removed if the National Assembly passes a motion of no confidence with a majority vote.
- The composition of the coalition government will at all times take into account the principle of portfolio balance and will reflect their relative parliamentary strength.

Source: The Christian Science Monitor, "Text of Kenya Power-Sharing Deal," February 29, 2008, http://www.csmonitor.com/World/Africa/2008/0229/p25s01-woaf.html (accessed June 2011).

was first elected in 2002 and then re-elected in 2007). In addition to receiving the largest number of votes in the election, the president must also win 25 percent or more of the vote in at least five of Kenya's seven provinces.[45]

Discussion of the structure and the role of the new president of Kenya in the 2010 constitution is found in Chapter 9, Sections 129 through 150.[46]

LEGISLATIVE STRUCTURES

Prior to the August 2010 constitution, the unicameral National Assembly consisted of 210 members, elected to a term of 5 years from single-member constituencies, plus 12 members nominated by political parties on a proportional representation basis.[47] The current National Assembly was elected under the old constitution in 2007, and has a total of 224 members (210 elected members, twelve members appointed by the president, and two *ex officio* members, the attorney general and the speaker of the Assembly).

The first election for the National Assembly under the new constitution will be in 2012. At that time the people will elect a bicameral parliament consisting of a National Assembly with over 300 members, and a Senate with under 100 members; parliament members will serve five year terms. According to Section 90 of the new constitution, some elections will be held on the basis of single-member districts, and others will be "on the basis of proportional representation by the use of party lists." The bicameral legislature is designed to offer more opportunities for representation of the regions than had been the case in the unicameral legislature of the previous several decades.

There are several very interesting structures that are part of National Assembly in the new plan.[48] The vast majority (290) of Members of the National Assembly are to be elected from single-member districts. In addition to these members, forty-seven women (one from each county) are elected to represent the counties in the National Assembly. In addition to these members, twelve members are to be nominated by political parties, in proportion to their support in the 290 single-member district elections. The constitution also indicates that "not more than two-thirds of the members of elective public bodies shall be of the same gender," (Section 81, part 2) but it is not clear at this time how this measure will be interpreted and applied.

The new Senate is designed to represent the counties, and "serves to protect the interests of the counties and their governments"(Section 96 part 1). The total number of senators is as yet unclear; the constitution indicates that the new Senate will be made up of

(a) forty-seven members each elected by the registered voters of the counties, each county constituting a single member constituency; and
(b) sixteen women members who shall be nominated by political parties according to their proportion of members of the Senate elected under clause (a) in accordance with Article 90;
(c) two members, being one man and one woman, representing the youth; and
(d) two members, being one man and one woman, representing persons with disabilities.[49]

The scope of jurisdiction of the new Senate appears to be limited: The constitution says: "The Senate participates in the law-making function of Parliament by considering, debating and approving Bills concerning Counties"(Section 96 section 2). This would seem to suggest that the Senate would *not* play a role in legislation that did not directly affect the counties.

THE COURTS

The structure of courts is described in Chapter Ten of the August 2010 constitution. The constitution calls for a Supreme Court, a Court of Appeal and a High Court, and a structure of subordinate courts. These are common structures, and do not require more of our attention here.

The most interesting judicial structure to be described in the new constitution from the perspective of comparative political analysis is the section of Chapter Ten (Section 170) that refers to a **Kadhi court**—a court of the Muslim religion. This was a controversial part of the new constitution; many in Kenya felt that the time had come to stop entrenching a place for Islam in the Kenyan constitution. However, at the end of the day, more people felt that it was important to include the structure for those Kenyans of the Muslim religion.

The constitution indicates that the jurisdiction of the Kadhi Courts[50] "shall be limited to the determination of questions of Muslim law relating to personal status, marriage, divorce or inheritance in proceedings in which all the parties profess the Muslim religion and submit to the jurisdiction of the Kadhi courts" (Section 170, part 5).

Kadhi Courts are not new to Kenya.

> Kadhis courts were in existence along the East Coast of Africa long before the coming of the British colonialists in the 19th century. The Kenyan coastal strip was then part of the territories controlled by the Sultan of Zanzibar. In 1895, the Sultan of Zanzibar authorised the British to administer the coastal strip as a protectorate, rather than a colony as distinct from the mainland, subject to certain conditions including the British agreeing to respect the judicial system then in existence in the said protectorate. The British agreed to these conditions and throughout their administration of the coastal strip this judicial system, which included the Kadhis courts, continued to exist.[51]

The Kadhi courts are not mosques; they are courts that are established to deal with a very specialized type of conflict. These courts have continued to provide an important function in terms of resolving personal status conflict for approximately 10 percent of the Kenyan population; there are over four million Muslims in Kenya.

POLITICAL PARTIES AND ELECTIONS

Since independence in 1963, Kenya has had a great deal of experience with elections and political parties. For much of this history, even though Kenya was having elections, they took place in the context of *single-party* politics. As we have already noted, from 1982 through 1991 Kenya was constitutionally and legally a one-party system, and any political party activity that took place had to be activity of the Kenyan African National Union (KANU) party.

We should be careful to note here that although the system involved only a single political party, this did *not* mean that there was no competition within the political system. Kenya could be called a **competitive single-party** state. There were many elections that were strongly contested; the difference was that the competition took place *within* the KANU structure. This often meant that there were robust and strongly contested *primary* elections— contests to see who was going to be the candidate of the KANU party in a given election—and then once the candidate was chosen for the election the result would be certain.

Why do this? One answer is that it promotes national unity by keeping all politics within a single umbrella of KANU identity, so that any *conflict* that occurs does not occur with the context of national elections—there isn't any real opposition or conflict in the national elections, since there are only KANU candidates running for office—but the conflict that exists takes place within the party structure. This allows for a period of reconciliation and national unification in the final election after the contests in the primary election.

Thus, in a given election there might have been a KANU-A candidate and a KANU-B candidate seeking the formal KANU nomination to run for the National Assembly. There would be a campaign that took place, people would have a choice, and eventually they would vote and select one of the two candidates. At that point the successful candidate would have to go through *another* campaign period without a serious opponent, knowing that he (or she) would be successful.

There is a history of elections being sources of tension and conflict in Kenya. There is a reason for this:

> Experts say elections are dominated by a winner-take-all mentality due to the consolidation of power in the executive branch. Though Kenya has had multiparty elections since 1992, the opposition has little power in the government....
>
> Because elections are such high-stakes affairs, political candidates are accustomed to hiring groups of young, armed men to protect their interests (this practice is also common in Nigeria). Each poll since the introduction of multiparty elections—in 1992, 1997, and 2002—has been accompanied by low-level outbreaks of violence. Most experts trace this violence back to tactics that President Daniel arap Moi, who led the country from 1978 until 2002, used to divide the population and retain political power.[52]

We have already noted that Kenya has a large number of ethnic groups—over forty—with the Kikuyu being the largest with over 20 percent of the population. This could be inflamed by a political leader, like Moi, who knew how to play one group against another.

> When Moi, who is Kalenjin, faced the prospect of losing power to an opposition party that contained many Kikuyu, he started an anti-Kikuyu campaign and incited land clashes in the Rift Valley between Kalenjins and Kikuyus in 1992 and 1997. Major rights groups such as Human Rights Watch and Amnesty International have reported extensively on the state-sponsored nature of this violence.[53]

Multipartyism in Kenya has a long history. Immediately upon receiving independence in 1963 Kenya was a multiparty state, and it stayed that way until 1982, when under the leadership of President Moi it legally banned all parties except KANU. By 1990, however, even KANU officials were arguing that Kenya would be better served by having opposition political parties, despite the objections of many that multipartyism would generate ethnic tensions and threaten political stability.[54] At the end of the day, the principle of multipartyism won out, and on December 10, 1991, Kenya's parliament passed the constitutional amendment that ended KANU's legal monopoly on political power.[55]

The most recent parliamentary election took place in December of 2007.[56] It should be recalled that in November of 2005 a proposed revision of the constitution was rejected by a majority of the voters. Many of the changes in that proposed constitution were directed to limiting the president's powers. One of the leaders of the "no" campaign was Raila Odinga, the Minister for Roads, who was opposed to the new constitution on the grounds that it was unfair to his ethnic group—the Lua people—and unfairly favored other groups in the nation. Because of that opposition, Odinga left the KANU party and started his own party, the Orange Democratic Movement. In August of 2007, in anticipation of the December election, Vice President Kalonzo Musyoka broke away from the Orange Democratic Movement to form another opposition party, the Orange Democratic Movement–Kenya (ODM-K) party.

In September of 2007, President Kibaki announced that he would run for a second term, but would run as the head of a coalition called the Party of National Unity (PNU), which had strong support from the Kikuyu tribal group (making up about 22 percent of the national population). Mr. Odinga ran in opposition to President Kibaki; he was from the Luo tribal group (making up about 13 percent of the national population).

At the time of the December 2007 election there were a total of 117 political parties in Kenya, running over 2,500 candidates for all offices, national and regional. When the elections were completed, the Orange Democratic Movement of Mr. Odinga won ninety-nine seats in the parliamentary elections, becoming the largest party in the newly-elected National Assembly; its ally, the National Rainbow Coalition, took three. President Kibaki's Party of National Unity and its allies won seventy-eight seats. President Kibaki was able to improve his showing by making a deal with the Orange Democratic Movement–Kenya of his former vice president, Mr. Musyoka and adding 14 seats to his block, increasing its total to 92 out of the 207 seats endorsed by the Electoral Commission to date. Outside observers from the European Union and the East African Community, who were in Kenya to monitor whether the elections were conducted fairly, said that the elections were significantly flawed. In one precinct, for example, turnout for President Kibaki was 115 percent of the registered voters.[57]

> When the presidential votes were counted, the Electoral Commission announced that Mr. Kibaki had been re-elected as President with 4,584,721 votes, while Mr. Odinga took 4,352,993. Mr. Kibaki was immediately sworn in and called for national reconciliation. [58]

The issue of a flawed election was important for all Kenyans, of course, but it was especially important for the candidates who participated in the election.

> Mr. Odinga said the presidential elections had been rigged and demanded that fresh elections be held. Opposition supporters led street protests and violence rapidly spread across the country. More than 1,000 people were killed in post-election violence. On 13 January 2008, the police announced that the death toll due to post-election violence had reached 693. The United Nations estimated that some 250,000 people had fled their homes.[59]

As we have already noted, with strong efforts by the former United Nations Secretary-General Kofi Annan, both President Kibaki and Mr. Odinga met at the end of January to see if they could find a way to stop the violence. A month later, on February 28, 2008, they signed an agreement under which Mr. Kibaki would remain president but Mr. Odinga would become prime minister (a position that did not exist at that time, and that was subsequently created by the parliament) for the duration of the Parliament. (See Table 16.4 for the details of the 2007 election.)

TABLE 16.4

The Election of December 27, 2007 for the Kenyan National Assembly

	Seats won
Orange Democratic Movement Party of Kenya (ODM)	99
Party of National Unity (PNU)	43 *
Orange Democratic Movement-Kenya (ODM-K)	16 *
Kenyan African National Union (KANU)	14 *
SAFINA	5 *
National Rainbow Coalition-Kenya (NARC-K)	4 *
National Rainbow Coalition (NARC)	3
Forum for the Restoration of Democracy–People (FORD-P)	3 *
SISI KWA SISI Party of Kenya (SKSPK)	2 *
Democratic Party (DP)	2 *
Party of Independent Candidates of Kenya (PICK)	2
CHAMA CHA UMA (CCU)	2
New Forum for the Restoration of Democracy-Kenya (NFK)	2
Peoples Party of Kenya (PPK)	1
Kenya African Democratic Development Union (KADDU)	1
United Democratic Party of Kenya (UDM)	1
National Labour Party (NLP)	1
Kenya African Democratic Union ASILI (KADU-ASILI)	1
KENDA	1
Forum for the Restoration of Democracy-ASILI (FORD-A)	1 *
MAZINGIRA Greens Party of Kenya (MGPK)	1 *
Forum for the Restoration of Democracy-Kenya (FORD-K)	1 *
Peoples Democratic Party (PDP)	1
Total	207

Total Members
   210 directly elected
   12 appointed by the president
   2 *ex officio* (attorney general and speaker of National Assembly)
   Men: 203
   Women: 21 (9.38 percent)

Note: Parties marked with an asterisk (*) were part of the PNU-led Coalition at the first session of the new legislature in 2008.

   The new constitution, adopted in August 2010, provides for a bicameral parliament comprising an enlarged 350-member National Assembly and a new 68-member Senate, yet to be established. The elections to both chambers are expected by March 2013.

Source: Inter-Parliamentary Union, PARLINE "Kenya—National Assembly," http://www.ipu.org/parline-e/reports/2167_E.htm (accessed June 2011).

THE KENYAN SYSTEM IN PERSPECTIVE

We started this chapter by observing that Kenya has played a leadership role among African nations over the years. The developing nations of Africa, Asia, and Latin America have a particular set of challenges that do not face the developed nations of North America and Europe: Not only do they need to resolve all of the "usual" political structural challenges that face all other nations, but they also need to do so in a way that allows for the most effective (and, they might hope, fair) opportunities for their citizens from a social and development economics perspective. The challenges that the developed nations face in terms of providing their citizens with education, with needed welfare resources, with medical care, and so on, all exist in the developing nations, too, only the developing nations need to work on the challenges with fewer resources and less developed infrastructure.

Following the December 2007 election, with the horrible riots and murders that took place in January and February of 2008, a power-sharing agreement was eventually worked out between the two major competing groups. It did bring peace, but with the hindsight of over three years it did not bring effective government. According to the country's former anticorruption tsar, "The grand coalition's most notable achievement is to have remained intact.[60]

Kenya is a political system that is finding its way. It started as a Westminster Model parliamentary regime, moved to become a presidential republic, and has struggled since that time, three decades ago, to find a formula that would allow its government to operate effectively while at the same time not exacerbate tensions between and among its many ethnic groups. Kenyans hope that the newest constitutional plan that they approved in August of 2010, and that is still not yet fully in existence, will continue to make real progress in this regard. We will have to wait and see.

DISCUSSION QUESTIONS

1. What are the key challenges that African nations have had to face over the last several decades? How has Kenya worked to control these challenges? Why do you think Kenya may have been more successful in this challenge than other nations?
2. What were the major forces that directed Kenya in its pre-independence period? Was the transition to independence similar to transitions elsewhere? What were the issues that motivated Kenyans in their most recent constitutional changes? Have the changes been effective?
3. How would you compare Kenya's unitary government with other unitary governments we have seen, such as governments in Britain or France. We argued that *regionalism* was very important in Kenyan public administration. Why? How does regionalism affect the way Kenyan politics operate?
4. How important an issue is ethnicity in Kenya? Why? What are illustrations of times when ethnicity became a flash point for domestic political conflict?
5. What are the key characteristics of the Kenyan political executive? How has it changed over time? Are there changes that you can imagine that would make

it more responsive to the Kenyan political system? How well does the Kenyan legislature meet the needs of the public? Can you imagine changes that would be helpful in this regard?

6. What does the case of Kenya show for the argument in favor of one-party states? Was the fact that Kenya was for many years a one-party state helpful or significant in Kenya's political development? How would you characterize the state of political parties in Kenya today?

KEY TERMS

AIDS 420
British East African
   Protectorate 422
colonial powers 421
competitive single-party
   state 436
Commonwealth 425
devolution 427

expatriates 422
Kadhi court 435
Kalenjin 422
Kenyan African National
   Union (KANU) 425
Kenyatta, Jomo 422
Kibaki, Mwai 425
Kikuyu 422

Maasai 422
majimboism 429
Mau Mau 422
Moi, Daniel arap 425
multiethnic makeup 431
Odinga, Raila 427
power-sharing
   agreement 433

SUGGESTED READINGS

Daniel Branch, *Defeating Mau Mau, Creating Kenya: Counterinsurgency, Civil War, and Decolonization* (New York: Cambridge University Press, 2009). The challenge of the Mau Mau to the British colonial power was significant. This volume offers a very thorough and even-handed analysis of the conflict and the ensuing departure of the British from East Africa.

Mwangi Kagwanja and Roger Southall, *Kenya's Uncertain Democracy: The Electoral Crisis of 2008* (New York: Routledge, 2010). Although the focus of this book is relatively narrow—the election of 2008—it is extremely important for an understanding of Kenyan politics today. The 2008 election showed the worst of Kenyan politics, including corruption, tribalism, regionalism, and also showed a commitment to establish a political system that *worked.*

Robert Maxon, *East Africa: An Introductory History* (Morgantown, WV: West Virginia University Press, 2009). This is a very comprehensive and accessible single-volume history of East Africa, covering the key issues that a student needs to understand, including colonialism, tribalism, ethnic tension, resource development, and others.

Robert Maxon, *Kenya's Independence Constitution: Constitution-Making and End of Empire* (Madison, NJ: Fairleigh Dickinson University Press, 2011). The creation of a constitution is always a challenge for a new nation. Kenya's independence came following many years of tension and violence, and the British left East Africa with much hostility in the political arena. This book describes the years of tension that led to independence and the creation of the new constitution.

Makau Mutua, *Kenya's Quest for Democracy: Taming Leviathan* (Boulder, CO: Lynne Rienner, 2008). Kenya had many challenges to overcome to become a stable democratic government, and to a substantial degree it succeeded. The challenges of tribal identity, economic development, regionalism, and colonial traditions all had to be resolved. This book discusses many of these challenges.

NOTES

1. Samuel Decalo, *The Stable Minority: Civilian Rule in Africa: 1960–1990* (Gainesville, FL: Florida Academic Press, 1998), p. 175. A good general history is by Robert Maxon, *East Africa: An Introductory History* (Morgantown, WV: West Virginia University Press, 2009).
2. Stephanie Hanson, "Understanding Kenya's Politics." Council on Foreign Relations web page > Kenya > Understanding Kenya's Politics, *http://www.cfr.org/kenya/understanding-kenyas-politics/p15322* (accessed June 2011).
3. South Sudan became the fifty-fourth independent state of Africa in July 2011.
4. William Tordoff, *Government and Politics in Africa*, 4th ed. (Bloomington, IN: Indiana University Press, 2002), p. 1. See also Jeffrey Haynes, *Democracy in the Developing World: Africa, Asia, Latin America, and the Middle East* (Malden, MA: Blackwell, 2001); and John Mukum Mbaku and Pita Ogaba Agbese, *Ethnicity and Governance in the Third World* (Burlington, VT: Ashgate, 2001).
5. This paragraph is based upon a much longer section in Tordoff, *Government and Politics in Africa*, pp. 1–3. See also Kelechi Amihe Kalu and Peyi Soyinka-Airewele, eds., *Socio-Political Scaffolding and the Construction of Change: Constitutionalism and Democratic Governance in Africa* (Trenton, NJ: Africa World Press, 2009).
6. On AIDS in Zimbabwe, see the Central Intelligence Agency *World Factbook*, section on "People," *https://www.cia.gov/library/publications/the-world-factbook/geos/zi.html* (accessed July 2011). See also Michael O'Neill and Dennis Austin, *Democracy and Cultural Diversity* (New York: Oxford University Press, 2000), for an international perspective of these issues.
7. Fred Hayward, "Introduction," in Hayward, ed., *Elections in Independent Africa* (Boulder, CO: Westview Press, 1987), p. 1
8. Ibid. See also John Mukum Mbaku and Julius Omozuanvbo, eds., *Multiparty Democracy and Political Change: Constraints to Democratization in Africa* (Trenton, NJ: Africa World Press, 2006).
9. *Global Studies: Africa* (Guilford, CT: Dushkin Publishing, 1991), p. 17
10. See the coverage in the *New York Times*, "After Years of Struggle, South Sudan Becomes a New Nation," July 9, 2011, available at *http://www.nytimes.com/2011/07/10/world/africa/10sudan.html?_r=1&hp* (accessed July 2011).
11. Neal Sobania, *Culture and Customs of Kenya* (Westport, CT: Greenwood Press, 2003), pp. 18–19.
12. There is much written about the British colonial period in Kenya, and the attitudes of the colonial power. Wunyabario Maloba writes that "colonialism was a dictatorship. It was imposed by violence and maintained by violence," and adds that the system "was socially racist." See Wunyabario Maloba, "Decolonization: A Theoretical Perspective," in B.A. Ogot and W.R. Ochieng', eds., *Decolonization and Independence in Kenya, 1940–1993* (Athens, OH: Ohio University Press, 1995), p. 9. On British treatment of the native populations, see Martin Wiener, *An Empire on Trial: Race, Murder, and Justice Under British Rule, 1870–1935* (New York: Cambridge University Press, 2009).
13. See the About.com website, "About.com> African History > Timeline: Mau Mau Rebellion," *http://africanhistory.about.com/od/kenya/a/MauMauTimeline.htm* (accessed July, 2011). See also Daniel Branch, *Defeating Mau Mau, Creating Kenya: Counterinsurgency, Civil War, and Decolonization* (New York: Cambridge University Press, 2009); and S. M. Shamsul Alam, *Rethinking Mau Mau in Colonial Kenya* (New York: Palgrave Macmillan, 2007).

14. See the About.com website, "About.com> African History > Timeline: Mau Mau Rebellion," *http://africanhistory.about.com/od/kenya/a/MauMauTimeline.htm* (accessed July 2011).

15. A very comprehensive study of the Kenya African Union is the volume by John Spencer, *The Kenya African Union* (Boston, MA: Routledge, 1985).

16. See the About.com website, "About.com>African History>Kenyan Leaders Since Independence," *http://africanhistory.about.com/library/bl/bl-leaders-kenya.htm* (accessed July 2011). See the essay by Anne Nangulu-Ayuku, "Reflections on the Postcolonial State in Kenya," in Pita Ogaba Agbese and George Klay Kieh, eds., *Reconstituting the State of Africa* (New York: Palgrave Macmillan, 2007).

17. W. R. Ochieng' and E.S. Atieno-Odhiambo, "On Decolonization," in B.A. Ogot and W.R. Ochieng', *Decolonization and Independence in Kenya, 1940–1993* (Athens, OH: Ohio University Press, 1995), p. xiii.

18. Francis M. Deng, *Identity, Diversity, and Constitutionalism in Africa* (Washington, DC: United States Institute of Peace Press, 2008), p. 197. See also the collection of essays by a group of anonymous authors titled *Independent Kenya* (London, UK: Zed Press, 1982).

19. See the website *Constitutionnet> Constitutional History of Kenya, http://www. constitutionnet.org/country/constitutional-history-kenya* (accessed July 2011). A very good and comprehensive study is by Robert Maxon, *Kenya's Independence Constitution: Constitution-Making and End of Empire* (Madison, NJ: Fairleigh Dickinson University Press, 2011).

20. See William Ochieng, "Structural and Political Changes," in B. A. Ogot and W. R. Ochieng', eds., *Decolonization and Independence in Kenya, 1940–1993* (Athens, OH: Ohio University Press, 1995), pp. 91–100. See also Patrick Lumumba, *Kenya's Quest for a Constitution: The Postponed Promise* (Nairobi, Kenya, KE: Jomo Kenyatta Foundation, 2008).

21. Stephanie Hanson, "Understanding Kenya's Politics."

22. See David Throup and Charles Hornsby, *Multi-Party Politics in Kenya* (Athens, OH: Ohio University Press, 1998), esp. Chapter Three: "The Creation of the Moi State," pp. 26–50.

23. Jennifer Widner, *The Rise of a Party-State in Kenya: From "Harambee!" to "Nyayo!"* (Berkeley, CA: University of California Press, 1992), p. 37.

24. Stephanie Hanson, "Understanding Kenya's Politics."

25. The volume by Makau Mutua, *Kenya's Quest for Democracy: Taming Leviathan* (Boulder, CO: Lynne Rienner, 2008) is a good study of Kenya's attempts to establish a stable, effective government in the period after independence. Mutua focuses upon constitutional reform as the way to solve the problems of the KANU elite.

26. See the full text of the report of the *Constitution of Kenya Review Commission*, *http://www.ldphs.org.za/resources/local-government-database/by-country/kenya/ constitution/Ghai%20Draft.pdf* (accessed July 2011).

27. The official website of the Committee of Experts can be found at *http://www. coekenya.go.ke/*. The May 6, 2010 proposal presented by the COE to the public can be found on the web at *http://www.coekenya.go.ke/images/stories/Resources/the_ proposed_constitution_of_kenya.pdf* (accessed July 2011).

28. The full text of the new constitution can be found on the web page of the Parliament of The Republic of Kenya, *www.parliament.go.ke* (accessed July 2011). The section on the new presidency can be found in Chapter Nine, Sections 129–151.

29. See the Constitution of Kenya web page, "The County Governments in Kenya," *http:// softkenya.com/constitution/the-county-governments-in-kenya/* (accessed July 2011).

30. Joel D. Karkan and Makau Mutua, "Turning the Corner in Kenya," *Foreign Affairs* (August 10, 2010), *http://www.foreignaffairs.com/articles/66510/joel-d-barkan-and-makau-mutua/turning-the-corner-in-kenya?page=show* (accessed June 2011).

31. See "The Kenya Constitution, > Composition of the Constitution," Kenyainformationguide.com, at *http://www.kenya-information-guide.com/kenya-constitution.html* (accessed June 2011).

32. Joel D. Karkan and Makau Mutua, "Turning the Corner in Kenya," *Foreign Affairs* August 10, 2010, available at *http://www.foreignaffairs.com/articles/66510/joel-d-barkan-and-makau-mutua/turning-the-corner-in-kenya?page=show* (accessed June 2011).

33. Mahathir, "Federalism in Kenya Popularly Known as 'Majimbo,'" *Muthumbi*, *http://muthumbi.blogspot.com/2007/11/federalism-in-kenya-popularly-known-as.html* (accessed June 2011). See also Kunle Amuwo and Irene Omolola Adadevoh, eds., *Civil Society, Governance, and Regional Integration in Africa* (Nairobi, Kenya, KE: Development Policy Management Forum, 2009).

34. Mahathir. "Federalism in Kenya."

35. Tordoff, *Government and Politics in Africa*, p. 159.

36. The full text of the new constitution can be found on the web page of the Parliament of The Republic of Kenya, *www.parliament.go.ke* (accessed July 2011).

37. Michael Madill, "Why Federalism Can Work in Kenya But Fail in Uganda," *The (Uganda) Independent*, September 8, 2010, *http://www.independent.co.ug/index.php/column/opinion/86-opinion/3435-why-federalism-can-work-in-kenya-but-fail-in-uganda* (accessed June 2011).

38. Stephanie Hanson, "Prime Minister Says Kenyan Politics 'Are Not Ethnic.'" Council on Foreign Relations web page > Democracy and Human Rights > Prime Minister Says Kenyan Politics 'Are Not Ethnic.' *http://www.cfr.org/democracy-and-human-rights/prime-minister-says-kenyan-politics-not-ethnic/p.19586* (accessed June 2011). See also Robert Maxon, *East Africa: An Introductory History* (Morgantown, WV: West Virginia University Press, 2009); and Maurice Makoloo and Yash Ghai, *Kenya: Minorities, Indigenous Peoples and Ethnic Diversity* (London, UK: Minority Rights Group, 2005).

39. Stephanie Hanson, "Prime Minister Says Kenyan Politics 'Are Not Ethnic.'" See also Gabrielle Lynch, *I Say to You: Ethnic Politics and the Kalenjin in Kenya* (Chicago, IL: Univeristy of Chicago Press, 2011); and the essay by Peter Kagwanja "Courting Genocide: Populism, Ethno-Nationalism and the Informalisation of Violence in Kenya's 2008 Post-Election Crisis," in the very good collection of essays edited by Mwangi Kagwanja and Roger Southall, *Kenya's Uncertain Democracy: The Electoral Crisis of 2008* (New York: Routledge, 2010).

40. Stephanie Hanson, "Prime Minister Says Kenyan Politics 'Are Not Ethnic.'" An interesting collection is by Kimani Njogu, Kabiri Ngeta, and Mary Wanjau, eds., *Ethnic Diversity in Eastern Africa: Opportunities and Challenges* (Nairobi, Kenya, KE: Twaweza, 2010).

41. See B.A. Ogot, "The Politics of Populism," in B.A. Ogot and W.R. Ochieng', *Decolonization and Independence in Kenya, 1940–1993* (Athens, OH: Ohio University Press, 1995), pp. 187–213.

42. Library of Congress, *Country Profile: Kenya* (June, 2007), *http://lcweb2.loc.gov/frd/cs/profiles/Kenya.pdf* (accessed July 2011).

43. Library of Congress, *Country Profile: Kenya* (June, 2007), *http://lcweb2.loc.gov/frd/cs/profiles/Kenya.pdf* (accessed July 2011). See Hervé Maupeu, Musambayi Katumanga and W.V. Mitullah, eds., *The Moi Succession: The 2002 Elections in Kenya* (Nairobi, Kenya, KE: Transafrica Press, 2005).

44. Library of Congress, *Country Profile: Kenya* (June, 2007), *http://lcweb2.loc.gov/frd/ cs/profiles/Kenya.pdf* (accessed July 2011). See *The Report of the Commission of Inquiry into Post-Election Violence* (Nairobi, Kenya, KE: Government Printer, 2008).

45. Central Intelligence Agency, *The World Factbook>* Kenya > Government, *https://www.cia.gov/library/publications/the-world-factbook/geos/ke.html* (accessed July 2011).

46. The full text of the new constitution can be found on the web page of the Parliament of The Republic of Kenya, *www.parliament.go.ke* (accessed July 2011).

47. Central Intelligence Agency, *The World Factbook>* Kenya > Government, *https:// www.cia.gov/library/publications/the-world-factbook/geos/ke.html* (accessed July 2011). A very good chapter on the development of Kenya's legislature is by Joel Barkan and Fred Matiangi, "Kenya's Tortuous Path to Successful Legislative Development," in Joel Barkan, ed., *Legislative Power in Emerging African Democracies* (Boulder, CO: Lynne Rienner, 2009).

48. See Section 97 of the Constitution.

49. Constitution, Section 98.

50. This is sometimes referred to as The Kadhi's Courts.

51. "The Kadhis Courts," *Wajibu: A Journal of Social and Religious Concern*, no. 17, *http://africa.peacelink.org/wajibu/articles/art_2120.html* (accessed July 2011). On Muslim law in Africa see the chapter by Abdulkadir Hashim, "Coping with Conflicts: Colonial Policy Towards Muslim Personal Law in Kenya and Post-Colonial Court Practice," in the volume edited by Shamil Jeppie, Ebrahim Moosa, and Richard Roberts, *Muslim Family Law in Sub-Saharan Africa: Colonial Legacies and Post-Colonial Challenges* (Amsterdam, The Netherlands, NL: Amsterdam University Press, 2010).

52. Stephanie Hanson, "Prime Minister Says Kenyan Politics 'Are Not Ethnic.'" See also Godwin Murunga and Shadrack Wanjala Nasong'o, eds., *Kenya: The Struggle for Democracy* (New York: Zed Books, 2007).

53. Stephanie Hanson, "Prime Minister Says Kenyan Politics 'Are Not Ethnic.'"

54. For discussion of the argument that multipartyism should be delayed until after fundamental stability is achieved, see John W. Harbeston, "Rethinking Democratic Transitions: Lessons from Eastern and Southern Africa," in Richard Joseph, ed., *State, Conflict, and Democracy in Africa* (Boulder, CO: Lynne Rienner, 1999), p. 51: "Kenya thus provides one of the clearest examples in Africa of the precariousness of undertaking multiparty elections as the first step toward democracy before interparty agreement has been forged and the fundamental rules of the game reformed."

55. B.A. Ogot, "Transition from Single-Party to Multiparty Political System," in B.A. Ogot and W.R. Ochieng', eds., *Decolonization and Independence in Kenya, 1940–1993* (Athens, OH: Ohio University Press, 1995), pp. 239–261. See also Michael Chege, Gabriel Mukele, and Njeri Kabeberi, *The Electoral System and Multi-Partyism in Kenya* (Nairobi, Kenya, KE: African Research and Resource Forum, 2007).

56. The paragraphs on the 2007 election come from the Inter-Parliamentary Union, PARLINE "Kenya—National Assembly," *http://www.ipu.org/parline-e/ reports/2167_E.htm* (accessed July 2011). See Adrienne Lebas, *From Protest to Parties: Party-Building and Democratization in Africa* (New York: Oxford University Press, 2011).

57. The paragraphs on the 2007 election come from the Inter-Parliamentary Union, PARLINE "Kenya—National Assembly," *http://www.ipu.org/parline-e/ reports/2167_E.htm* (accessed July 2011). On the 2007 election, see Kimani Njogu, *Healing the Wound: Personal Narratives About the 2007 Post-Election Violence in*

Kenya (Nairobi, Kenya, KE: Twaweza Communications, 2007); and Mwangi Kagwanja and Roger Southall, eds., *Kenya's Uncertain Democracy: The Electoral Crisis of 2008* (London, UK: Routledge, 2010).

58. See BBC News, "Kibaki Named Victor in Kenyan Vote," December 30, 2007, *http:// news.bbc.co.uk/2/hi/africa/7164890.stm* (accessed July 2011). See also Michael Chege, "Kenya: Back from the Brink?" in Larry Diamond and Mark Plattner, eds., *Democratization in Africa: Progress and Retreat* (Baltimore, MD: Johns Hopkins University Press, 2010).

59. The paragraphs on the 2007 election come from the Inter-Parliamentary Union, PARLINE "Kenya—National Assembly," *http://www.ipu.org/parline-e/ reports/2167_E.htm* (accessed July 2011).

60. Karen Allen, "Has Kenya's Power-Sharing Worked?" *B.B.C. News*, March 3, 2009, available at *http://news.bbc.co.uk/2/hi/africa/7921007.stm* (accessed July 2011). See Nicholas Cheeseman and Daniel Branch, *Election Fever: Kenya's Crisis* (Abingdon, UK: Routledge, 2008).

GLOSSARY

absolute veto in the legislative process A case in which a legislative chamber's refusal to approve legislation results in failure of the legislation in question.

advantage groups Groups that come into existence because a number of individuals see something to be gained (either materially or psychologically) by doing so.

agenda-setting function Deciding what the political agenda is going to be.

AIDS Acquired Immune Deficiency Syndrome, one of Africa's widespread killer diseases, caused by the Human Immunodeficiency Virus (HIV), which is transmitted through bodily fluids and significantly reduces the body's ability to resist infections.

analytic systems Groups of objects that are connected with one another in an analytic way.

anarchism A belief that all forms of government interfere with individual rights and freedoms and should, therefore, be abolished.

area studies Involves a detailed examination of politics within a specific geographical setting.

Article 16 powers Refers to the French Constitution and the emergency powers that are at the disposal of the president.

backbencher The name derives from positions in the British House of Commons, in which seats are arranged in two sets of rows facing each other. Party leaders sit on the front benches of their respective sides; nonleaders, or followers, sit on the back benches— hence backbenchers are followers.

basic law An alternative structure to a constitution in postwar Germany.

bicameral legislature A legislature with two legislative houses, or chambers.

Blackstone, William The eighteenth-century scholar whose work on British law is seen as being authoritative.

Blair, Tony Labour prime minister of the United Kingdom from 1997 to 2007.

blocked vote Legislative possibility in France that requires the legislative chambers to vote on a bill in its original text, incorporating only those amendments proposed or accepted by the government.

Bolshevik Name derives from the *majority* faction ("Bolshevik" means "majority") of the Russian Social Democratic Party convention held in 1903, before the creation of the Union of Soviet Socialist Republics. The Bolsheviks were led by Vladimir Lenin.

British East African Protectorate In Kenya, it dates to 1895, also known as British East Africa; it was the name of territory in East Africa controlled by Britain. It remained a protectorate until 1920, when it became the Colony of Kenya.

British North America Act of 1867 The Act of the British Parliament that created the Dominion of Canada and served as Canada's Constitution until 1982.

Bundesrat The upper house of the bicameral German national legislature. Its members are chosen by members of the Länder governments.

Bundestag The lower house of the bicameral German national legislature.

Its members are chosen in two different electoral processes in democratic elections.

bureaucracy Administrative structure of government, including organizational perspective, focusing upon structures, organizational charts, lines of communication, hierarchical organization, its formal rules, and how it operates.

cabinet Body of advisors to the monarch, or head of state in a parliamentary system. The head of the cabinet is the prime minister, or premier. The name also applies to the small group working with the president in a presidential system.

Calderón Hinojosa, Felipe Current President of Mexico. Elected in December 2006 for a single six-year term through 2012.

Cameron, David Current Conservative prime minister of the United Kingdom since the 2010 election.

Canada Act, 1982 At the request of the Canadian Government, the British Parliament passed the Canada Act in 1982, renouncing the right to legislate on behalf of Canada in the future.

capitalism An economic system in which the major means of production are owned by individuals, not by the government of the state. The economic philosophy emphasizes private ownership and a market economy; that is, nonregulation of the marketplace by the government.

case study method Involves the intensive study of individual cases.

Central Committee of the Chinese Communist Party The Central Committee of the CCP is a body of about 200 individuals—most recently documented at 204 members—elected by the Party Congress, to act in the name of the Communist Party when the Congress is not in session.

centralized federalism Federal system in which the central government has

much more powers than the intermediate governments.

chancellor The title for the role of the chief executive in the German political system.

Charlottetown Agreement 1992 Canadian constitutional conference seeking to find a compromise modification of the Canadian constitution that would be acceptable to Québec and other provinces.

Chiang Kai-shek Chinese political and military leader. Chiang was an ally and successor of Sun Yat-sen. Led the Chinese Nationalists in the civil war against the Chinese Communist Party following World War II, ultimately retreating to Taiwan where he served as president of the Republic of China and Director of the Guomindang until his death in 1975.

chief executive Head of the executive branch of government; In parliamentary systems typically elected as a member of the legislature, just as all of the other members of the legislature are elected. Head of cabinet. In presidential systems the president serves as chief executive.

Chinese Communist Party (CCP) Ruling organization in China.

civil society Can be defined as the way that the population of a nation organizes into associations or organizations that are independent of formal institutions of the state, the way that people organize groups to define their interests.

coalition government A case in which two or more nonmajority parties pool their legislative seats to form a majority parliamentary bloc in the legislature.

cohabitation This refers to the French situation of having a president from one political party and a prime minister from another political party.

collective good Any good that, if it is available to one person, cannot feasibly be withheld from the others in that group.

colonial powers   In relation to Africa, refers to the nations that had a colonial relationship with an African territory, in which the (typically European) nation established and maintained colonies in African territory, exercised sovereignty over that territory, and ran the social, political, and economic institutions of that nation.

committee of the whole   A technical device used to establish a different set of procedural rules; a legislative body can "dissolve itself" into a committee of the whole.

common law system   Sometimes called "Anglo-American" law, and referred to as "judge-made law." This is not to suggest that today's laws in these political systems are not made by the legislatures of those systems or, conversely, that today's laws are made by judges in those systems. This type of law is more culturally sensitive and more flexible, relying more upon judicial interpretation rather than legislative design.

Commonwealth of Independent States   Emerged in December of 1991 to serve as a structure to replace the USSR.

Commonwealth of Nations   Nations that were part of the British Empire at some point in their history. Today the Commonwealth functions as a political "family" with no formal/constitutional linkages.

communes   Part of the Chinese Great Leap Forward (1958–1961). Communes were groups of about 5,000 families that would work together for greater efficiency than had been the case previously.

communism   A belief in government ownership of the major means of production, and of the general primacy of politics over economics, the government should actively regulate and control all sectors of the economy with little or no private property.

comparative method of inquiry   Two or more case studies put together, with a search for similarities and/or differences between the cases.

comparative politics   Involves a comparative study of politics—a search for similarities and differences between and among political phenomena.

competitive single-party system   In Kenya under one-party government from 1982 to 1991, there were competitive elections, but they took place as primary elections within the framework of the Kenyan African National Union (KANU) party.

concrete, or real system   A set of objects that we can actually see (or touch, or feel, or measure).

concurrent powers   In Germany the Länder may legislate in areas of concurrent power, defined as: "as long as, and to the extent that, the Federation does not exercise its right to legislate."

confederal system   A union of sovereign states that each retain their powers, but agree to coordinate their activities in certain respects.

Confucius   (Kung Fu-tzu, approximately 551–479 B.C.) Chinese philosopher.

conservative ideology   Position can be described as being most satisfied with the way society is operating, satisfied with the status quo.

constituency vote   Refers to the vote in Germany that focuses on candidates running for office from districts, not the "at large" candidates.

constitution   A written constitution is a document including a basic expression of the ideas and organization of a government that is formally presented in one document. Some constitutions may be unwritten, but still exist.

Constitution Act, 1982   The renamed Canadian constitution, formerly known as the British North America Act of 1867.

Constitutional Council The highest constitutional authority in France, with the function of ensuring that the principles and rules of the constitution are respected.

Constitutional Court of the Russian Federation Has been described as the first independent court to be established in Russia since the Bolshevik Revolution.

constitutional government Can be described as limited government, specifically a limitation on governmental power.

constitutions as "power maps" for political systems It is often constitutions that tell us about the environment within which governments operates, and describe how power is distributed among the actors.

cooperative federalism A relationship in German federalism in which both the central government and the Länder can share jurisdiction over and responsibility for policy issues.

corporatism A belief that advocates a close degree of cooperation and coordination between the government and labor and business groups in the formation of economic policy.

corporatism in Mexico Refers to the close—some say overly close—relations between private businesses in Mexico and government policy-making.

coup d'état Revolution from above. Sudden substitution of one ruling group or individual for another.

court Political structure that helps to interpret and apply law in the political system.

Cultural Revolution In China, collective purging of individuals who were seen as not "good" Communists, took place between 1966 and 1976.

de facto Existing in fact.

de Gaulle constitution The French Constitution of the Fifth Republic. Although it wasn't literally authored by Charles de Gaulle (substantial credit is given to Michel Debré), it was de Gaulle's views of needed structures and relationships that shaped the document.

de jure Existing in law.

decentralized federalism Federal system in which the intermediate governments have more power than the central government.

democratic centralism The theory in China that means that key decisions are made at the center, and then moved out to the more democratic bodies and structures to be ratified.

Deng Xiaoping In China, statesman and leader of the Communist Party of China. While Deng never held office as the head of state, head of government, or general secretary of the Communist Party of China, he served as the supreme leader of the People's Republic of China from 1978 to 1992. Best known as being a reformer who led China toward permitting a market economy to develop.

départements The second level of French government. Since France is unitary and not federal, the départements do not have the power of states, cantons, or Länder, but they are major administrative units of France.

devolution (Britain) Moving power from the political center (London) to regional administration (Cardiff, Wales, Edinburgh, Scotland, and Belfast, Northern Ireland).

devolution of power Political power flowing from the center to more distant areas of the nation.

devolution of the Soviet Union Process by which the (former) Union of Soviet Socialist Republics *devolved* into a number of independent republics.

direct popular election of the presidency in France In 1962 a referendum was held in France to have the presidency directly elected by the public rather than by an electoral college. This was seen as giving the presidency more legitimacy and more power.

dissolution, writ of Head of state may dissolve (fire) the legislature and call for new elections by issuing a writ of dissolution.

dissolve the legislature The act by which the head of state may fire the legislature and call for new elections by issuing a writ of dissolution.

divine law Guidelines that are based upon the religious or theological conceptual framework from which law is said to be derived.

divine right of kings theory Argues that the monarch derives his power directly from God, not from the people.

duality of executive leadership In Britain (and parliamentary governments generally) there are *two* executive roles (as contrasted with one in presidential systems); one is the chief executive role and the other is the head of state role.

ecological level of analysis Relates to a type of observation and measurement we are using and the types of conclusions that we can draw from those observations and measurements. Focus on groups, not individuals.

economic globalization A rising share of economic activity in the world seems to be taking place between people who live in different countries rather than in the same country.

emergency powers of the president Refers to Article 16 of the French Constitution and the powers that are at the disposal of the president.

empirical approach to inquiry Relies on measurement and observation.

England An administrative unit of the United Kingdom of Great Britain and Northern Ireland, part of the island of Great Britain along with Scotland and Wales.

expatriates Refers to individuals who temporarily or permanently live in a country other than the one in which they were born, or in which they have citizenship.

Could refer to British residents of Kenya, for example.

experimental method of inquiry This approach to inquiry involves manipulation of variables in order to observe the effect upon other variables.

external environment of foreign policy Includes a general consideration of the global environment, those factors that can influence a nation's foreign policy that come from *outside* of the government itself, including economics, other nation's actions, and so on.

extraterritorial rights Foreigners could operate under their own national legal systems while in China, and not have to operate under Chinese law.

falling The termination of a cabinet. A Government "falls" when either of two things happens: It loses on a question of confidence or a major piece of legislation leading the prime minister to resign, or the prime minister resigns for some other reason.

fascism A belief (that includes National Socialism) that usually is said to include seven components: irrationalism, social Darwinism, nationalism, glorification of the state, the leadership principle, racism (more important in national socialism than in fascism), and anticommunism.

federal system The existence of two levels of government above the local level, both enjoying sovereignty in certain areas.

feminism A system of beliefs that has emerged primarily in the West in opposition to oppression of women, and opposition to sexism in general. Has developed different schools including Liberal or Reform Feminism, Marxist Feminism, Socialist Feminism, and Radical Feminism.

Five Percent Clause The characteristic of the German ballot that indicates that parties can win seats from the proportional representation "second votes" only if they poll at least 5 percent of the second votes.

formulating options function Determining how policy options are to be decided.

Fox Quesada, Vincente President of Mexico from 2000 to 2006.

fraud in elections It is not uncommon in contested elections to have charges of electoral fraud be filed by the losing party against the winning party. In this volume we have discussed this both in the Mexican case and the Kenyan case.

frontbencher The name derives from positions in the British House of Commons, in which seats are arranged in two sets of rows facing each other. Party leaders sit on the front benches of their respective sides.

Gaullism A French movement of support for Charles de Gaulle that claimed to be an alternative to divisive political parties.

gender A significant political construct. Makes a difference in terms of an individual's political behavior whether the individual is a man or a woman in our society.

general secretary of the Party In China, formal leader of the Secretariat of the Central Committee of the Chinese Communist Party.

Gorbachev, Mikhail General Secretary of the Communist Party of the Soviet Union from 1985 to 1991, and the last head of state of the USSR, serving from 1988 until its end in 1991.

government bills Bills originating in the Government frontbench—where the members of the Cabinet sit—are called Government bills.

government by market Belief that the government uses state power to create a market that fulfills a public purpose.

government by network Belief that the government should stop trying to do everything itself and should fund other organizations that do the actual work the government wants.

government With a capital "G" has a specific meaning in this volume: the prime minister and the cabinet. With a lowercase "g" government refers to the general structures of the political system.

governor-general The constitutional acting head of state who takes the place of the British monarch when the monarch is not in the nation. The Queen of England, for instance, is also the Queen of Canada; when she is not in Canada, she is represented by the Governor General of Canada in all political processes.

Grand Coalition In Germany, the (conservative) CDU/CSU bloc formed a Grand Coalition with the (liberal) SPD, and Angela Merkel became Germany's first female Chancellor.

Great Britain The principal island of the United Kingdom; it includes England, Scotland, and Wales.

Great Leap Forward In China, the name given to a five-year plan announced in 1958 by Mao Zedong.

guerrilla warfare Focuses attention on government targets, usually military targets, rather than the often random civilian targets used by terrorists.

Guomindang (GMD) Chinese name of the Nationalist Party led by Sun Yat-sen.

Harper, Stephen Prime Minister of Canada, elected to a minority government in February 2006.

head of state One of two executive roles. Symbolizes the state and the dignity of the political regime.

Hu Jintao President of the People's Republic of China.

Hundred Flowers Movement In China, based upon a saying of Confucius, "Let a hundred flowers bloom, let a hundred schools of thought contend," referring to the idea that the free and open exchange of ideas would be supported by Mao.

hung parliament In Britain, describes a parliament in which there is no majority party, which requires either a coalition government to be created or a minority government to be formed, in which the Government does not *quite* have a majority but has close to a majority, which makes it possible to govern.

hyperurbanization The trend in Mexico, and elsewhere, of substantial populations moving from rural areas in a nation to the major cities in search of a better life, often creating substantial health and environmental problems.

ideology Ideas that relate to the social/political world, and provide a general guideline for action. Philosophies or values of political regimes.

immobilisme A situation in a political system in which each actor has enough power to block the other, but not enough to achieve its own objectives, which means that it is possible that nothing will be accomplished.

individual level of analysis Relates to a type of observation and measurement we are using and the types of conclusions that we can draw from those observations and measurements. Focus on individuals, not groups.

input–output theory Easton's analytic framework viewed the political system as a continuously operating mechanism, with "demands" and "supports" going in ("inputs"), and authoritative decisions and actions coming out ("outputs").

interest groups Collections of individuals who share common beliefs, attitudes, values, or concerns.

internal environment of foreign policy Composed of the domestic factors that can influence foreign policy.

international policy Three different realms of such policy are military policy, economic policy, and development/political policy.

jacquerie Revolution from below.

Jiang Zemin General Secretary of the Communist Party of China from 1989 to 2002.

joint committees Legislative committees made up of members from both houses in a bicameral legislature.

judicial precedent Courts referring to previous decisions when they make decisions. The process is referred to as *stare decisis* (to stand by things decided).

judicial review The process by which courts are in the position to rule upon the propriety or legality of action of the legislative and executive branches of government.

jurisdiction Determination of which court (or level of court) has authority to adjudicate a specific question.

justice A sense of fundamental fairness, and that all actors in a political system are treated in a similar manner. The idea that a legal system treats everyone equally expresses a notion of justice.

kadhi court In Kenya, a system of Muslim courts that deal with issues of personal status (sometimes referred to as Kadhi's Court).

Kalenjin In Kenya, an ethnic group of people in western Kenya and eastern Uganda, numbering nearly 4.4 million total.

Kenyan African National Union (KANU) A political party in Kenya that served as the basis of government for Kenya for forty years from the time of independence from Britain in 1962 to its electoral loss in 2002.

Kenyatta, Jomo Kenyan nationalist leader, served as the first prime minister of Kenya (1963–1964), then as president (1964–1978). He served as president of the Kenyan African National Union, the political movement that was associated with driving the British out of Kenya.

Kibaki, Mwai The third (and current) president of Kenya. Served as vice president for ten years, from 1978 to 1988, and as minister of health from 1988 to 1991. He served as an opposition member of Parliament from 1991 to 2002, when he was elected president. He was re-elected for a second (and constitutionally last) term of office in 2007.

Kikuyu In Kenya, the most populous ethnic group, making up about 5,300,000 people, about 23 percent of Kenya's population.

Länder Units of the national territory in Germany. The Länder are the equivalent of provinces in Canada or cantons in Switzerland or states in the United States.

Law Lords Members of the House of Lords who served as the high court for the United Kingdom.

legal culture Focuses upon the beliefs, attitudes, and values of society relative to the law and politics.

legislative supremacy The idea that the legislature "hires" the chief executive (although the head of state may "nominate" him or her) or invests him or her with power.

legislature One of the three "Lockean" political structures, the law-making body of the government that derives its name from "law" ("legis").

Lenin, Vladimir Creator of the Soviet Communist Party and leader of the 1917 October Revolution; founder of the Union of Soviet Socialist Republics. His interpretation of and contributions to classical Marxist theory produced a distinct body of political theory referred to as Leninism.

liberal ideology An ideological position that is more content with society than is the radical, but still believes that reform is possible, perhaps necessary. Liberalism includes a belief in human potential, in the ability of individuals to change institutions for the better, in human rationality, and in human equality.

life peerages Practice of the British House of Lords in which an individual would be appointed to the Lords and would keep that seat for the duration of his life.

linkage mechanisms Political structures that serve to connect the voice of the people to the political leaders of the regime.

local government The level of political structure that is closest to the people. Unitary political systems have local government and national government. Federal political systems have local government, intermediate government (states, cantons, provinces, or Länder), and national government.

Long March In China, a massive military retreat led by Mao Zedong in 1934 to avoid capture and defeat by the Nationalist Chinese (Guomindang) forces led by Chiang Kai-shek. Mao's forces walked over 8,000 miles in 370 days. The Long March marked the beginning of the ascent to power of Mao and a generation of Chinese Communist leaders.

lower house of a legislature Refers to that house in a bicameral system (most) directly elected by the people.

Maasai In Kenya, an ethnic group numbering over 800,000 in the 2009 census, located primarily in Kenya and northern Tanzania.

majimboism Regional administrative decentralization in Kenya.

majority Defined as one vote more than 50 percent of the total votes cast.

Mao Zedong Leader of Chinese Communist Party and chairman of the CCP from 1949 until his death in 1976. Creator and developer of Chinese Communist ideology.

Marxism A complex political philosophical framework describing the economic system and the inevitable conflict between the working class and the owners of the means of production. Suggested the inevitability of class conflict, and was adopted and modified by Lenin to create Soviet Communism.

Marxism-Leninism An ideological structure that was based upon the

Communist Manifesto (written in 1848) and subsequent writings of Karl Marx and Friedrich Engels.

Mau Mau A secret society of Kikuyu Kenyans who were seeking independence from British colonial power.

Medvedev, Dmitry Third, and current president of the Russian Federation, elected May 2008.

Meech Lake Accord The Meech Lake process (1987–1990) was an attempt to "bring Québec into the constitution" in Canada, allowing for Québec to participate in a sense of renewed federalism. Ultimately the Meech Lake Accord was not ratified.

menshevik Name derives from the *minority* faction (*menshevik* means "minority") of the Russian Social Democratic Party convention held in 1903, before the creation of the Union of Soviet Socialist Republics.

Merkel, Angela Chancellor of Germany since November 2005.

metropolitan France Refers to the twenty-two mainland administrative regions of France containing ninety-six départements. Metropolitan France does *not* include the overseas territories and possessions of France.

Middle Kingdom In China, can also be translated as "the center of civilization." Phrase that is often used in China as its traditional name.

migration of illegal immigrants from Mexico to the United States One of the key challenges to the Mexican government is the constant loss of population across its northern border with the United States, individuals moving north to find better jobs and a better standard of living.

military coup Sometimes called a "generals' coup," involves military leaders taking over a government because of their dissatisfaction with civilian control.

ministerial instability Refers to the pattern in France of regular cabinet turnover in the Fourth Republic, of cabinets coming into existence and not lasting very long.

minority government A parliamentary situation in which the prime minister does not control over 50 percent of the seats in the legislature.

Mitchell Agreement In Britain the agreement in 1998 (also known as the Good Friday Agreement), named after U.S. Senator George Mitchell, that much authority over policy in Northern Ireland would move from London to Belfast.

Moi, Daniel arap The second President of Kenya, serving from 1978 to 2002.

moral law Refers to precepts or guidelines that are based upon subjective values, beliefs, and attitudes, focusing upon behavior.

most different systems design Instead of looking for *differences* between two or more essentially *similar* nations, this focuses upon *similarities* between two or more essentially *different* nations.

most similar systems design Investigators take two systems that are essentially similar, and then study differences that exist between the two basically similar systems.

multiethnic makeup of Kenya With over forty tribal groups, many Kenyans have loyalty to groups other than the nation.

multinational corporations Business enterprises that operate in more than one nation. They can be very large, and can have significant economic (and political) influence upon the countries in which they operate.

multiple-member district (MMD) voting system In each electoral district voters cast ballots and a number of the top vote-getters are elected. The district has more than one representative.

Nanjing Massacre In China, also known as the Rape of Nanjing. In December of 1937, the Japanese attacked Nanjing and hundreds of thousands of Chinese civilians and disarmed soldiers were murdered, and 20,000–80,000 women were raped by soldiers of the Imperial Japanese Army. The International Military Tribunal of the Far East estimates more than 200,000 casualties in the incident; China's official estimate is about 300,000 casualties.

nation   Has been used in an anthropological way to denote a group of people with shared characteristics, perhaps a shared language, history, or culture.

National Party Congress   Chinese Communist Party organization of 4,000 to 5,000 members that formally elects the Communist leadership body, the Central Committee.

National People's Congress   In China, the legislative branch of the national government of the People's Republic of China. (Do not confuse with National Party Congress!)

nationalism   Includes identification with a national group and support for actions that will support and benefit the national group. This may or may not correspond to borders of a particular state.

nationalist movements   A special case of social movements, in which a group of individuals that is articulating a common set of beliefs (for example, that India should become independent of Britain) starts to act within the political system to influence political policy.

Nationalist Party   Group that established the Republic of China in 1912. Fought with Chinese Communist Party and eventually was driven off of mainland China to Taiwan.

nation-state   If a *nation* denotes a group of people with shared characteristics, perhaps a shared language, history, or culture, and a *state* is a political entity, created by men and women based upon accepted boundaries, a "nation-state" involves an instance in which

the "nation" and the "state" overlap, where the unit that is found on the map corresponds to a meaningful use of the term *nation*.

natural law   Refers to a body of precepts governing human behavior that is more basic than man-made law, and is based on fundamental principles of justice.

navette   The sending of a bill back and forth between the two chambers of the national legislature in France until they agree on a compromise version.

neocorporatism   Takes up where the theory of pluralism leaves off. It suggests that groups are highly significant for the political system.

no confidence vote   The legislature voting that it does not want to be led by a specific prime minister and cabinet: whenever the chief executive loses the confidence of the legislature, whenever the legislature passes a resolution of no confidence.

normative approach to inquiry   Focuses upon philosophies, or "shoulds."

North American Free Trade Agreement   Treaty between Mexico, the United States, and Canada, guaranteeing free trade among the three nations.

October Manifesto (1905)   Declaration by Russian Tsar Nicholas II as a response to the Russian Revolution of 1905. The Manifesto pledged to grant civil liberties to the people; grant power to the legislature, the Duma, and make other concessions to critics of the Tsar's rule.

Odinga, Raila   Current prime minister of Kenya, elected in 2007. He ran for office in 2007 against the incumbent Mwai Kibaki; Kibaki was declared the victor despite many charges of electoral irregularities and corruption. After a period of intense interethnic group violence, Odinga reached a power-sharing agreement with Mwai Kibaki, and it was agreed that Kibaki would serve as president and Odinga would take a newly-created position of prime minister for that term of office.

open elite The possibility for the masses to become part of the elite.

Opium War (1839–1842) In China, when Britain pressed Chinese authorities to make concessions that resulted in China suffering from foreign interference in its domestic policy.

palace coup Forces behind the coup are typically members of a royal family; one member of the royal family tries to push out those in office so that he or she can take power.

parliamentary executive More complex than its presidential alternative, if for no other reason than that it is a multiple executive.

parliamentary question time In Britain, twice a week the prime minister appears in the House of Commons to answer parliamentary questions, primarily from the members of the Opposition. This occurs daily in the Canadian parliamentary setting.

parliamentary sovereignty In Britain the principle that whatever Parliament does is constitutional and becomes part of constitutional law.

partial proportional representation for Chamber of Deputies Structure in the Mexican Chamber of Deputies by which only some of the members of the Chamber are elected from electoral districts, and others are chosen as a function of how many deputies each party won in the district-based races.

Party Congress See **National Party Congress**, the highest organ of Communist Party power in China today.

party discipline Relates to the cohesion of the body of party members within the legislature, the extent to which members of a single political party vote the same way and say the same things.

party government In Britain and many political systems, the process by which political parties are the basis of organization of electoral activity and subsequently the basis of organization of the political institutions of the government.

patriation In Canada, the process of the creation of the 1982 Canada Act passed by Britain, on the request of Canada, by which Canada assumed full constitutional responsibility for its own future.

People's Liberation Army In China, military organization of all land, sea, and air forces of the People's Republic of China.

peripheral federalism A "minimal" federal government, in which the rulers of the federation can make decisions in only a few restricted categories of action without obtaining the approval of the rulers of the constituent units.

plurality voting The process of voting in which the candidate who receives the most votes is declared the winner. "Most votes" here means that the person need not have a majority—more than 50 percent of the votes—but simply needs to have more than anyone else. In a contest with many candidates, this could result in a candidate being elected with considerably less than 50 percent of the votes cast.

plenum The major debating and speaking arena of the legislative house.

pluralism The idea that competing groups in society determine public policy through bargaining and compromise.

plurality In a legislature, having more votes than any other party, although it may be less than a majority. May apply to elections, too, in which a candidate can win an election with more votes than any other candidate, even if less than a majority.

Politburo of the Central Committee of the Communist Party of China The most important political group within the CCP is the Politburo, a group of the top political leaders in the nation. This group of 20 individuals is chosen by the Central Committee of the Communist Party.

Politburo Standing Committee A subgroup of the Politburo that is at the center of power in China today. Today this group has nine members.

political culture Set of concepts focusing upon the political environment in which political action takes place describing values, traditions, and customs.

political elite Those who have relatively high levels of interest in politics and relatively high levels of involvement in the political process.

political ethnocentrism The assumption that because political institutions or relationships work one way in stable Western democracies they must work the same way in all political systems. An assumption that because "we" believe things work in a certain way that everyone else believes the same thing.

political parties Organizations that are long-lived, that seek to influence political process, and that seek to control power (or at least participate in governance) in the polity. They tend to be more permanent and institutionalized than interest groups and are concerned with a larger number of issues.

political recruitment The process by which individuals move from the mass public to positions of significant political influence and participation.

political role A pattern of expected political behavior for individuals holding particular positions in a system.

political socialization The process by which the individual acquires attitudes, beliefs, and values relating to the political system.

politics The patterns of systematic interactions between and among individuals and groups in a community or society involving power, rule, or authority.

positive law Legislation that has three major identifiable characteristics: (1) It is man-made law, (2) it is designed to govern human behavior, and (3) it is enforceable by appropriate governmental action.

positive or constructive vote of no confidence In order to dismiss a Chancellor in Germany, not only does a majority of the Bundestag need to vote against the incumbent but it *also* must agree in the same vote on a successor.

power must be a check on power The idea that political power, in order to be safe, had to be divided; the principle of the separation of powers was important to government.

power-sharing agreement In Kenya, following the election of December 2007, President Kibaki and the Leader of the Opposition Odinga agreed to create a position of prime minister for Odinga and agreed that Kibaki and Odinga would share power.

premier One of the names for the chief executive role in a parliamentary system. In this volume we have also seen systems using the term "prime minister" and "chancellor".

presidential "dictatorship" A characterization of Mexican political leadership in which the president has the right to issue executive decrees that have the force of law; despite the notion of "separation of powers" the president is permitted to introduce proposals in the legislature on his own authority.

presidential executive See presidential model below. A version of political executive in which both the political role and the symbolic role of the executive are vested in the same individual.

presidential model Centralizes both political power and symbolic authority in one individual, the president.

pressure groups Narrower in scope than interest groups, usually related to a single issue; their goal is to influence public policy, not hold office.

private members' bills Bills originating from any member of parliament, either in the Government backbenches or the Opposition frontbenches or backbenches, who is *not* a member of the cabinet.

privatized industry When the government sells off government-owned industries to private ownership: for instance, overseeing the conversion of British Telecom from a government-run business to being a private corporation with stockholders.

Privy Council Antecedent of a parliamentary cabinet, group of advisers to the head of state.

proportional representation (PR) voting system Voters vote for the party they prefer, not for candidates. The proportion of votes that a party receives in the election determines the proportion of seats it will receive in the legislature.

Putin, Vladimir Second president of the Russian Federation (1999–2008) and current prime minister of Russia.

quasi-presidential or quasi-parliamentary executive The French model of executive that is a significant deviation from the British Westminster model executive.

Québec nationalism The notion in Québec that it is a nation within the Canadian federation, and that it has a right to political independence.

Queen The title of the current Head of State of the United Kingdom. The Queen of the UK is also Queen of Canada, Queen of Australia, and Queen of many other nations that still have constitutional ties with what was the British Empire. At the time that Queen Elizabeth became Queen, she was *also* Empress of India. India has since become a republic and has its own head of state.

Quiet Revolution The people of Québec made it clear that they would no longer accept a second-class citizenship and wanted significant changes in their society. These changes took place with remarkable speed, in the early 1960s.

radical ideology Generally, radicals are extremely dissatisfied with the way society (and politics) is organized and are impatient to undertake fundamental changes in society.

rational choice theory Individuals will participate when it is in their personal interest to do so, when their individual participation will make a difference in terms of benefits (e.g., public policies) to them; personalized interests will necessarily join those groups.

reactionary ideology Corresponds to that of the radical, only on the right end of the spectrum. The reactionary position proposes radical change backwards, that is, "retrogressive change," favoring "a policy that would return the society to a previous condition or even a former value system."

real system A set of objects that we can actually see (or touch, or feel, or measure).

recruitment The function of the political system that draws members of the society into politics.

Red Guard In China, Red Guards were a mass movement of civilians, mostly students and other young people, who were mobilized by Mao Zedong in 1966 and 1967, during the Cultural Revolution.

Red versus Expert debate In China, one of the most divisive issues in China in the early 1960s pitting party loyalists against reformers.

referendum The situation in which legislative issues are submitted to the public for a vote rather than being resolved in the legislature.

reform coup Political takeover is often made in the name of reform, and the seizure of power may be undertaken by a labor leader or someone holding political office.

regionalism in Canada   Canada is a very large nation, and there have traditionally been regional forces that have contributed to political tensions there.

representative government   One of the key precepts of democratic government. The idea that in order to be democratic, since it is no longer possible for every individual to actively participate in every decision that government makes, government should have elected representatives to make decisions.

Republic of China, 1949   The creation of an independent China on the island of Taiwan by the Nationalist Party led by Chiang Kai-shek when the Nationalist forces were driven off the mainland by the forces of Communist China, which established the People's Republic of China at the same time.

residual powers   The Länder in Germany are given residual powers in Article 70. This means that any powers not specifically given to the central government remain with the states.

responsible government   Refers to the Government's ability to deliver on its promises. Because of the existence of *party discipline*, parliamentary governments tend to be more responsible than presidential governments.

role   A pattern of expected behavior for individuals holding particular positions in a system.

Romano-Germanic approach to law
Sometimes referred to as "code" law, this approach developed from the basis of Roman law at the time of Justinian (A.D. 533). This type of law, as contrasted with common law, is based upon comprehensively written legislative statutes, often bound together as "codes."

royal assent   The traditional act by which the monarch in Britain approved legislation passed by Parliament. Today royal assent is given by a commission, not by the monarch.

royal pretense   The idea that the Queen is still the *real* ruler of Britain, rather than a recognition that the monarchy is now primarily of symbolic importance.

rubber stamp power   A situation in which a house of a legislature may have *formal* power in the legislative process, but in fact must go along with other chamber.

Salinas de Gortari, Carlos   President of Mexico from 1988 to 1994.

Sarkozy, Nicolas   President of France, elected May 2007.

scientific law   Refers to observations and measurements that have been empirically determined and that focus upon physical, biological, and chemical concepts, not social questions.

Section 91 of the Canada Act, 1867
Deals with powers of the national legislature.

Section 92 of the Canada Act, 1867
Deals with powers of the provinces.

select committees   Legislative committees that tend to be given specific scopes of inquiry, or special problems, to address, as well as specific durations.

separation of powers   In the eighteenth century the idea was widely shared that centralized power is dangerous, and that political power should be separated, so that power could be a check on power. This resulted in the idea of three "branches" of government, each with a "check" on the others.

similar in principle   Canadian constitutional clause that said that Canada's constitution was to be "similar in principle" to that of the United Kingdom. This was for many years the source of many Canadian civil liberties.

simple vote of no confidence in Germany   An expression by the Bundestag that it no longer supports the chancellor, but cannot agree on a successor. This does not result in the chancellor being dismissed.

single-member-district, plurality (SMD-P) voting system In this kind of system, the entire nation is divided into a number of electoral districts. Each district corresponds to one seat in the legislative chamber, and whichever candidate receives the most votes wins (even if less than a majority).

Sinification of Marxism In China the practice of rooting the abstract formulations of Marxism-Leninism in the specific reality of China; modifying Marxism to work in China.

social class Refers to some kind of ordering of groups in society, usually including such characteristics as income, education, occupation, values, expectations, and affects.

social movements Defined as broad groups of individuals who share an interest in a given social issue.

social policy Government policy in relation to income, housing, medical care, education, and the like.

socialism An ideology that developed out of the Industrial Revolution advocating governmental concern with individuals' quality of life, including education, medical care, and standard of living. May be found in democratic versions—as in Great Britain or Sweden—or in authoritarian versions—as in Nazi ("nazi" was short for National Socialist) Germany or fascist Italy.

sovereignty The power to make political decisions that are final without being responsible to a higher authority.

Soviet federalism The idea of "independent republics" coming together into a unified political system that was nominally federal, but really political power was highly centralized. Developed by Lenin and Stalin as a vehicle for keeping many of the "independent republics" within a single political unit, the USSR.

Special Administrative Regions in China (SARs) Hong Kong, which reverted from British control in 1997; and Macau, which reverted from Portuguese control in 1999.

special status Québec has argued that it is not a province like the other nine Canadian provinces, but is special. This relates to the binational theory of Canadian federalism that suggests that Canada is a union of two nations, one English (made up of nine provinces) and one French (made up of one province).

Speech from the Throne Speech the Queen delivers in Britain (and other heads of state deliver in their respective nations) in which she outlines plans for "her" government for the year. The important consideration to recall is that the speech is written by the prime minister and cabinet, not the monarch.

stability of Mexico Refers to the fact that Mexico has been the exception to Latin American political systems' pattern of political instability and frequent regime changes over the years.

Stalin, Joseph Premier of the Soviet Union from 1941 to 1953 and first general secretary of the Communist Party from 1922 to 1953.

Standing Committee of the National People's Congress In China, the leadership group of the 3,000 member National People's Congress. Consists of a chairman, 15 vice chairmen, a secretary general, and 153 members.

Standing Committee of the Politburo In China, senior leadership of the Politburo, about 20 members.

standing, or permanent, committees Legislative committees that are established at the opening of the legislative term and that last for the life of the legislature.

stare decisis ("to stand by things decided") The practice of courts referring to previous decisions when they make decisions.

state An explicitly political entity, created and alterable by men and women, based upon accepted boundaries.

state council In China, the equivalent of the Cabinet in parliamentary systems.

statistical method of inquiry Involves more sophisticated forms of measurement and observation using public opinion polls, survey research, and various other forms of quantitative measurement to help make analysis that is characteristic of the empirical approach even more accurate

structural-functional analysis This analysis focuses upon what Almond referred to as political "structures," by which he meant either political institutions or behavior, and political "functions," by which he means the consequences of the institutions or the behavior. This kind of analysis asks the basic question, "What structures perform what functions and under what conditions in a political system?"

succession of leadership The concept related to political leadership that there needs to be a known process by which one person follows another as a political leader. This topic was introduced in relation to Russian politics because there was a long pattern of unpredicted and irregular leadership changes caused by one person taking over the powers of government from another.

Sun Yat-sen Chinese revolutionary and political leader. Played a key role in the overthrow of the Qing Dynasty and the establishment of the Republic of China in 1912. Later cofounded the Guomindang (Chinese National People's Party) where he served as its first leader.

Supreme Leader Leader of the Chinese Communist Party.

Supreme People's Court In China, the highest judicial body in China.

suspensory veto in the legislative process A structure in which a legislative chamber's refusal to approve legislation from the other house can only slow the legislative process down, not block the legislation from coming into effect.

systems theory Easton's analytic framework viewed the political system as a continuously operating mechanism, with "demands" and "supports" going in ("inputs"), and authoritative decisions and actions coming out ("outputs").

terrorism Political behavior that uses violence, the threat of violence to coerce governments, authorities, or populations to act in a certain way.

Thatcherism The style of contemporary British politics that came to be known first as "conviction politics," and subsequently as "Thatcherism." Much of its focus was on economic policy, nationalizing formerly state-owned industries, and weakening the power of labor unions.

Tiananmen Square In 1989 a peaceful political demonstration for more reform in China was brutally suppressed by the government of the day.

Third Republic French constitutional regime from 1870 to 1940. Came into existence at the end of the Second French Empire in the Franco-Prussian War, and ended with the German occupation of France at the start of World War II.

Three Represents Theory of Chinese philosophy of Jiang Zemin, general secretary of the Communist Party of China from 1989 to 2002. This thought is a continuation and development of Marxism-Leninism, Mao Zedong Thought, and Deng Xiaoping Theory.

Tiananmen Square Massacre In China, critical demonstrations that took place in 1989 in Beijing in which hundreds of thousands of Chinese demonstrated in favor of economic and political reforms, and were attacked by the Chinese government.

tied foreign aid Foreign aid—whether loans or grants—that must be spent in the donor nation.

totalitarianism A system in which the government controls individual political behavior and political thought.

two-party-plus political system A system in which there are two dominant parties at the national level, plus a number of other parties operating at the intermediate level. Used in the context of a discussion of Canadian party politics here.

unicameral legislature A legislature with one legislative house or chamber.

Union of Soviet Socialist Republics Communist state that existed between 1922 and 1991, including Russia and fourteen other Soviet Republics, dominated by the Communist Party of the Soviet Union. Its capital was in Moscow.

unitary government A political system with only one level of government above the local level, as distinct from a *federal* government that has more than one level of government above the local level.

United Kingdom of Great Britain and Northern Ireland Political system made up of Northern Ireland and the political units of Great Britain, including England, Scotland, and Wales.

untied foreign aid Fiscal assistance that the recipient nation can spend anywhere.

unwritten British Constitution Customs, traditions, and pieces of legislation that have come into existence over the years that collected together make up the British Constitution.

unwritten constitution Collection of constitutional principles that are widely accepted in the regime that are not formally approved as law.

upper house of a legislature The house in a bicameral system farther from direct public control, although today many upper houses are elected directly by the public as well.

urban migration, in Mexico There is significant population movement from rural Mexico to the capital city, where almost one in four of all Mexicans live.

vote of confidence Vote by a majority of the legislature indicating its confidence in, or support for, the prime minister and his or her cabinet.

warlord Used in connection to a network of political leaders in China in the early years of the twentieth century who dominated politics in that era, using private armies of regionally powerful individuals.

Weimar Republic The parliamentary republic established in 1919 in Germany to replace the imperial government that had preceded it.

Wen Jiabao Current premier of the State Council of the People's Republic of China.

Westminster model of government Model of government in Britain and many other nations, generally considered to be composed of four parts. First, the chief executive is not the same as the head of state. Second, the executive powers of government are exercised by the chief executive and his or her cabinet, not the head of state. Third, the chief executive and the cabinet come from and are part of the legislature. Fourth, the chief executive and the cabinet are responsible to, and can be fired by, the legislature.

writ of dissolution Head of state may dissolve the legislature—fire the legislature—and call for new elections by issuing a writ of dissolution.

written constitution An expression of the ideas and organization of a government that is formally presented in one document.

Yeltsin, Boris First president of the Russian Federation, from 1991 to 1999.

Zedillo Ponce de Leon, Ernesto President of Mexico from 1994 to 2000.

INDEX